D1629474

COMPANION TO PSYCHIATRIC STUDIES

VOLUME II

COMPANION
TO PSYCHIATRIC STUDIES

VOLUME II

Editor: Alistair Forrest

CHURCHILL LIVINGSTONE   EDINBURGH AND LONDON 1973

Printed in Great Britain by Bell and Bain Ltd., Glasgow

CONTRIBUTORS TO VOLUME II

WENDY ACTON, M.B., *formerly Senior Registrar, Royal Edinburgh Hospital.*

J. W. AFFLECK, M.B., F.R.C.P. (Edinburgh and Glasgow), F.R.C.Psych.

G. W. ASHCROFT, M.B., F.R.C.P.E., M.R.C.Psych., *Department of Pharmacology.*

IVY BLACKBURN, M.A., Dip. Clin. Psych., Ph.D.

W. D. BOYD, M.B., F.R.C.P.E., M.R.C.Psych.

Professor G. M. CARSTAIRS, M.A., M.D., F.R.C.P.E., F.R.C.Psych.

A. J. COOPER, M.D., M.R.C.Psych., *formerly Lecturer, Department of Psychiatry, Royal Edinburgh Hospital.*

R. L. CUNDALL, M.Sc., M.B., M.R.C.Psych.

J. EVANS, B.Sc., M.B., M.R.C.P., M.R.C.Psych.

A. D. FORREST, M.D., M.R.C.P., F.R.C.P.E., M.R.C.Psych.

E. H. JELLINEK, M.A., D.M., F.R.C.P., F.R.C.P.E., *Medical Neurology.*

Professor A. K. M. MACRAE, M.B., F.R.C.P. (Edinburgh and Glasgow) F.R.C.Psych.

R. A. PARRY, M.B., M.R.C.P., M.R.C.Psych.

A. S. PRESLY, M.A., Ph.D., Dip. Psych., *Principal Clinical Psychologist, University of Dundee.*

E. B. RITSON, M.D., M.R.C.Psych.

ELIZABETH E. ROBERTSON, M.A., M.B., F.R.C.P.E., F.R.C.Psych.

J. R. SMYTHIES, M.A., M.Sc., M.D., M.R.C.P., F.R.C.Psych.

J. D. SUTHERLAND, C.B.E., B.Sc., M.Ed., Ph.D., M.B., F.R.C.P.E., F.R.S.Psych., F.R.S.E., F.B.P.S.

Professor H. J. WALTON, M.D., Ph.D., F.R.C.P.E., F.R.C.Psych.

SULA WOLFF, M.A., B.M., F.R.C.P., F.R.C.Psych.

A. K. ZEALLEY, M.B., CH.B., M.R.C.P.E., M.R.C.Psych.

CONTENTS

Volume II

Chapter I

PATHOLOGICAL FUNCTIONING OF THE PERSON: THE NEUROSES AND PSYCHOSOMATIC DISORDERS

J. D. Sutherland

INTRODUCTION

In Chapter X, Vol. I an outline was given of how the personality becomes structured into dynamic systems, each of which embodies a relationship-goal that has been fashioned from early conflicts. The incompatible goals of these systems are normally reconciled to a point where the ordinary person can feel a reasonable degree of unity in himself. Normality or maturity in adult personal functioning is then characterized by the free recognition and acceptance of the individuality and reality of others. There is a positive satisfaction from an investment in living, in close relationships within marriage and the family, in work and in leisure. Effective and satisfying functioning can be achieved in an infinite number of ways corresponding to the uniqueness of every individual who achieves this state. Normality does not imply a stereotype. We mean by it a capacity to achieve good relations with oneself in the business of living, to have the inner freedom to do what one aspires to in realistic terms and to be free of a sense of unfulfilled relationship needs.

Pathological functioning at the personal level occurs when the balance between conflicting need-systems and the central ego is tipped in favour of the former. The individual's behaviour then becomes too much influenced by these strong inner need-systems, or sub-selves, and symptoms, the compromise between the rival forces in the self, appear. The original aims of the repressed systems, with the anxiety and painful feeling that accompany their activity, are usually concealed in all kinds of ways, but their tendency to seek fulfilment remains. Two broad types of pathologically conflicted behaviour ensue. First, the individual feels more or less constantly engaged in inner conflict, in a battle with his symptoms, i.e. thoughts, acts or relationships he does not want in the main part of himself. Inner conflict may also be experienced as a struggle against inhibitions or forces blocking the achievement desired and so producing inaction or apathy. The second type of conflicted behaviour differs in that obvious conflicts are not experienced predominantly within the self. Instead, the individual presents as a more or less coherent person, but with an overall failure of development within himself or in adapting to others so that the discord is between him and others rather than inside himself. For instance, he may be too rigid, too ambitious with little or no sensitivity to the needs of others, or passively dependent and inadequate. Generalized distortions of the personality may range widely in the severity of their effects—from the character disorder of the eccentric to the obvious psychopathies. In the latter, the failure in development of the normal controlling roles of anxiety and guilt in social relations is such that destructive or inadequate behaviour may render the person unfit for the demands of everyday living.

Instead of conflict being manifested at the personal level, the tensions in sub-systems of the person may be discharged through disturbance of bodily function disorders. The nature of this process and the choice of a particular somatic function are as yet imperfectly understood. The result, however, may be very varied in the degree to which the somatic disturbance appears to be separated from personal conflicts.

The dynamic nature of conflicting systems, along with the central ego constantly carrying out its task of trying to seek compromise adaptation to inner requirements and the constraints of the environment, means that in appraising neurotic symptoms and difficulties we have to keep in mind the total inner and outer situation. The personality is a continuously active set of relationship systems interacting with the inner and outer worlds. The relative activity of inner forces may change because of alteration in the biological balance, e.g. in sexual drive, or from changes in the environment affording gratification to some needs or frustrating others. It is inherent in the person that he tries to master conflict. Spells of disturbance thus tend to be followed by some remission as the central ego achieves a new way of managing conflict either by some change inside the self or by some modification of the environment. When the individual experiences a sense of defeat in his attempts to maintain the organization of his central self, the range of 'positions' to which he may withdraw can be a wide one. He may regress to infantile helplessness; or his difficulties may be localized as in phobic anxieties or somatic disorder. One person may show different patterns of disorder at the same time or at different times and it is for this reason that the common diagnostic labels have only limited value in describing the neuroses. The task of diagnosis consists much more in constructing a picture of 'what this person is about', i.e. of what his needs, both conscious and repressed, are, of how he is dealing with these and what his resources are—his own inner strengths and the opportunities his environment can provide. Nevertheless, there are common patterns of pathological functioning which it is useful to identify. These patterns for the most part can be related to the main phases of development.

They represent the relationship tasks facing the child at successive critical stages and the typical ways of dealing with them. Each phase creates specific fantasy relationship systems appropriate to the stage of the maturational processes. Thus in the earliest phase, fantasies are 'oral' corresponding to the predominance of the intake of food in the experience of the infant. It is when the main conflicts are focussed on one developmental period that neurotic behaviour can acquire characteristic common features, e.g. in obsessional neurosis. A descriptive label then becomes more useful because it identifies the most prominent pathology. Nevertheless, it is not at all uncommon for the obsessional constellation of symptoms to fade and to be replaced by a more adapted spell or, conversely, by a regressive movement into depression. The fact, too, that conflicts mainly shaped at later phases often occur in personalities unduly affected by earlier failures leads to very mixed and changing manifestations because of the overlapping of aims belonging to several stages. At present we have no adequate means of assessing accurately the relative strength of pathological 'fixations', or developmental arrests, and consequently of their liability to 'take over'.

In the following sections some of the common patterns of neurotic behaviour corresponding to critical developmental stages are described. Our knowledge of the etiology of these phenomena is sketchy. A full consideration of what is involved in any one of these groupings can be obtained only from the extensive literature. What lies underneath a few of them is outlined to give a mode of approach to what is always unique to one individual and whose origins and nature have to be elucidated for each person.

SCHIZOID CONDITIONS

The first structuring of the person is the establishment of a trusting, secure central self through the loving care provided by the ordinary good mother. If painful experiences from frustration or deprivation are too intense and too recurrent, then a serious primary split occurs. The ego that develops becomes largely a conforming shell with most of the emotional security and liveliness of the 'true self' (see Winnicott, 1958) lost behind varying degrees of apathy and withdrawal. When deprived of the necessary input from the constant responsive presence of the mother, the intense experiences from appetitive satisfaction do not add strength nor integration to the central core of secure self-feeling. Subsequent emotional development stays detached from this core and though the person learns to function instrumentally, even on occasion with great distinction, the severe split in the self prevents him from enjoying his basic needs for others. This disastrous situation produces all those manifestations that are covered by the term schizoid.

Fairbairn (1952), who first described the full nature of the primary splitting of the ego in the schizoid patient, suggested that this failure in development is an underlying factor in most subsequent psychopathology of whatever form. It is only where interactional deprivation is unusually severe that the familiar schizoid personality evolves later. The markedly schizoid person, nevertheless, has reached a stage beyond that in which little or no integration persists either in the central ego or in the withdrawn self, a condition which underlies the schizophrenias. While the central ego can function well in certain areas, what is being organized has as a rule to be free from the anxiety-arousing transactions of personal relationships. Taking his main emotional needs into his inner world, the schizoid invests heavily in his fantasy life where he can imagine relationships in which he can compensate for his failure in making actual relationships. Thus a highly gifted young man of great promise in the field of electronics became progressively absorbed in pondering on how he could control others by super-machines. The schizoid person feels deep in himself that he is unloved and that his own capacity to love, what he wishes to give affectionately, is unwanted. It is this profound mistrust of the acceptability to others of his own love that drives him to create so many ways of cutting himself off from others. His distress stems from a feeling of futility, moving at times to hopelessness and despair. Adult living, to be fully satisfying, needs others and so he is recurrently driven to make approaches towards achieving relationships. The fear of rejection then turns him back to his inner world where he can gain some mastery over the dreaded dangers of being dependent by omnipotently controlling others in his fantasies. In short, his relationships remain patterned on the one hand by the infantile need to 'incorporate' an unconditionally loving mother figure, and on the other to avoid being vulnerable to, or controlled by, anyone. By using the word 'incorporate', we emphasize the need to meet the hungry empty feeling so characteristic of these conditions.

Schizoid conflicts emerge with great suffering in adolescence and early adulthood because of the increased need for closeness to others that sexual maturation engenders. Thus the youth becomes unable to work because of his thoughts racing from the pressure of unconscious fantasy systems. He becomes increasingly self-conscious and withdrawn, and he may try to relieve the constant tension by masturbation only to find this relief followed by guilt and self-reproach.

The rejection of his love has also created harsh rejecting parental images in the schizoid person. Paranoid suspicious attitudes may emerge when these persecuting internal figures are excessively developed, especially towards any expression of his needs. Despite their 'badness', he is deeply 'attached' to these figures, an attachment that may in part arise from the nature of the early interaction processes with phenomena possibly akin to those of 'imprinting'. There is also a need to cling to them because a bad, persecuting parent is better than no parent —a state of emptiness and abandonment which appears to conjure up intense anxiety. Should he identify with the threatening images, he then attacks his own needing-self with a resultant feeling of being useless, bad or inferior, at times to the point of suicide. If, however, he feels violently angry with parental or other authority figures for his frustrating incapacity, these hated images, or the bad self he wishes to be rid of, are projected onto someone in the outer world who then has to be attacked or destroyed—a common origin of sadistic outbursts.

The deep splits in the personality between the conscious ego and what are sensed as the vital parts of the self may produce the feeling of having lost his self, i.e. he feels depersonalized. On the other hand, if this dead feeling is projected, then external figures or things feel like dead automata, remote, or unreal.

Persistent infantile dependent needs illumine the resort to alcohol and drugs. These provide the comfortable, even blissful, state of having surmounted the inner emptiness and helplessness; and, unlike the capricious behaviour of external figures, drugs can satisfy the wish for omnipotent control.

Although the schizoid patient often has remarkable insight because of his preoccupation with his inner world, radical psychotherapy is difficult and prolonged. He has built up massive defences, a whole 'false self', against the humiliating feeling of being helpless and dependent in a world which did not let him experience the normal pleasure of working through these early phases, the 'fun' in being a baby with parents who enjoyed their child. To develop sufficient trust in an external therapist for the undoing of the original rejections and the profound despair associated with them demands a great deal of long term work in which the resources of both patient and therapist can be severely tested.

PSYCHOPATHY

Psychopathy is a term notoriously difficult to define, especially as it has been applied to a wide range of disorders. Here it is used for the aggressive psychopath. Briefly, the chief characteristics are aggressive antisocial behaviour, often delinquent, which is not accompanied by feelings of guilt. As the history of attempts to alter such behaviour show, its relative intractability is typical and this feature links its origins with the earliest phases of development. Compared with the severely schizoid person, the psychopath has not withdrawn his core self in an inner despairing flight, though he has not been matured by the experience of the 'depressive position', when the capacity for concern and guilt are evolved. The antisocial acts have a quality of taking what he feels he should be getting from the social environment. (see Winnicott, 1965) Again, it is the degree to which the origins of this relationship pattern have been split off that leaves it so unchanged by the usual learning. That the deprivation in early mothering plays an important part in these people receives support from the finding that serious breaks in this relationship, as by separation, are more common in psychopaths. (see Bowlby, 1944)

DEPRESSIVE REACTIONS

The phenomenology of depressive states in their full-blown form is discussed in Chapter IX, Vol. II. Here the main pattern is outlined because depression emerges transiently in so many people with psycho-neurotic disorders, and because of its close link with obsessional manifestations.

It was the study of 'Mourning and Melancholia' which first enabled Freud (1917) to see the role of 'internal objects', an advance that was brilliantly supported by the parallel work of his colleague Abraham (1911). When patients were depressed, especially after the loss of a close figure, it was observed that they frequently began to behave as though they had become the person they had lost. They had identified with the lost person by taking him into a part of themselves or 'incorporating' him. Their anger with this person was then apparent in the form of self-reproaches or other attacks on themselves.

The failure to achieve the stage of having angry destructive feelings to the frustrating mother, especially at weaning, accepted by her and then superseded by the experience of refinding her as 'good', creates an inner situation wherein this hate has to be kept out of the central ego system because of the intense guilt and anxiety it evokes. To hate what is loved and needed is felt as imcompatible with this good figure coming back. In addition, the lost object may be felt as reproachful for the aggression directed to it.

Milder forms of depression are not always accompanied by recognized guilt feelings. Instead there is a sense of not being relaxed or of being unable to enjoy oneself. The precipitating factor can be traced to the loss of a parent or spouse, or another person who has been important emotionally. Often, too, the loss is of some possession or activity such as a work role which has taken the place of a previously loved person. What then emerges on exploration of these feelings is the anger and resentment over certain attitudes of the lost person towards the individual, feelings that are repetitious in large measure of those to a parent in early years. Unlike the schizoid state, there is here a good quality associated with the lost object and the painful feeling stems from wanting to hurt this person who is otherwise loved.

Paradoxically, the precipitating factor for a depressive feeling can be a success in achievement as in a man getting a promotion at work or a woman having more children than her mother. Here the success is unconsciously linked with triumphing over the parents.

Obsessional Behaviour

In this affliction, people suffer from compelling thoughts, feeling or actions which are felt as alien yet over which they have little or no control. Compulsive behaviour derives from conflicts at the stage of toilet training and hence its close connection with excretory processes and products. Fairbairn (1952) pointed out that whereas in the oral or infantile dependence phase, or under the pressure of sexual drives, needs are for another person, faeces and urine cannot occupy such a status. Their importance accordingly seems to come from their symbolic value. It is at this stage that the first sense of power is felt in asserting a self who can separate from the previous close ties to the mother. When this process is not facilitated by the mother's pleasure in the inherent drive to independence, aggressive and defiant behaviour is released. Intense hate towards the mother is now mixed with the need for her and it is the persistence of this ambivalence that underlies the almost constant tendency to doubt and indecisiveness. The rage has to be repressed and its effects in the inner relationships undone. If in fantasy, the 'bad' mother has been reduced to faeces, then an immense effort has to be made by the central ego to counteract these aggressive impulses. All dirt has to be washed away and all messiness undone by compulsive tidiness. Dirt and disorder may express the hate but they then threaten the individual with dangerous persecution, a state which may become phobic in intensity, e.g. of being poisoned by the dirt or attacked by some article which has got out of place, i.e. out of control. The use of magical thinking in the form of superstitions and minor rituals is universal in childhood as a means of preventing such disasters and residual manifestations in the adult are normally confined to minor actions. In obsessional behaviour, the pressure from latent hostile feelings, and the retaliations or catastrophes associated with them, force the individual to act in terms of this primitive magic.

The fact that the central conflict is around love and hate for the mother makes for a close connection between obsessional behaviour and depression. When the obsessional behaviour fails to maintain its defensive function, intense anxiety, guilt and depression are common because of the damage that is feared to have occurred in fantasy. The patient may remain moving between these feelings and periods of freedom from them when he can recover his defensive behaviour. When his defences fail he may become quite severely depressed.

Milder obsessional behaviour can usually be relieved by analytical psychotherapy, i.e. within a relationship in which the patient can learn to experience his love and hate and what these are about. More severe conditions are difficult to alter because the ambivalence is here rooted in more primitive systems. As with the schizoid and severe depressive, the terrors of loss of the self and of his good objects make any radical change so frightening that the defences are clung to in desperation.

HYSTERIA

Hysteria is the classificatory term whose value has been most debated. Originally, it covered certain prominent tendencies in behaviour, particularjy to dissociation of functions and to the presenting of a front of indifference to the effects of the symptoms. As was mentioned in Chapter X, Vol. I, one manifestation, the 'conversion' of the conflicts into a functional paralysis, has become less common since its origins were widely published after the first world war.

Dissociation may be shown in personal functioning, e.g. in memory loss of variable extent or in strange feelings about the self as in depersonalization. Such symptomatic behaviour may be absent and, instead, the patient exhibits a more generalized character distortion with dramatized exhibitionistic behaviour, marked egocentricity, changeable moods and a high degree of suggestibility. The severe hysteric is so disturbed in many areas of living that many of these patients are now described as borderline psychotics since much of their behaviour can be close to schizophrenia at times.

Hysterics seek relationships actively, but primarily to have others fulfil the requirements of their dependent needs. There is a strikingly infantile quality of demandingness and thereby an inability to maintain relationships. They do not deny sexual behaviour although, paradoxically, they are often frigid in intercourse. Sexual behaviour for them is fused with the conflicts of the earliest relationships. The sexual partner stirs up all the longings for mother and so they 'oralize' genital behaviour. It is this unconscious wish to treat the penis as a breast that creates much of their frigidity, their common difficulties about swallowing, and also their liability to nausea and vomiting (Fairbairn, 1954). Their 'greedy', attention-seeking behaviour, so self-defeating because of its clamant intensity, reflects the deprivations in the early stages of the mother–infant relationship with prominent feelings of emptiness and futility.

Because of their ease in making superficial contacts with others and their tendency to idealize and please at the beginning of relationships, hysterics can give a deceptive impression about the seriousness of their psychopathology. They can be helped to improve their management of themselves yet, like the schizoid, radical treatment is a formidable undertaking. Just what makes for the hysteric's development in contrast with that of the schizoid is still speculative. There seems in their case to be an inconsistent pattern of early care, periods of rejection mixed with over-exciting attention rather than of more chronic coldness. With most schizoids, the lack of parental warmth seems to continue into later stages of development, whereas hysterics tend to have exciting encounters during the oedipal phase and later with one or both parents. Their attempts to re-establish exciting relationships, which are then doomed to disillusionmen with anger and withdrawal, are in marked contrast with the more inhibited, or even 'cold-fish', quality of the schizoid.

The student mentioned briefly in Chapter X, Vol. I, who was referred for examination failure, proved to have a markedly hysterical personality. She had long felt her mother to be an unreliable person emotionally, with the result she had a much closer relationship with her father. As an academic, he wanted her to share in his interests and her failures were a great disappointment to him. She had begun to be fairly promiscuous after starting at the university, with none of the men meaning much to her. In treatment (in a group) she became markedly demanding for sedatives and practical help. Even though the other members pressed on her the irrational forces in her behaviour, she persisted in her denials of their reality. The complex relationships with her father were also resisted though the nature of some of them were clear enough, e.g. keeping away from him and attacking him for frustrating her sexual fantasies in which the oral incorporative needs were manifest in her liking of being 'spoon-fed' by him and her tutors.

It will be noticed that the reference to the hysteric have implied that this disorder is mainly one of women. Dissociation symptoms and other hysterical character features occur in men, but the typical pronounced hysterical picture tends to arise more often in women. Cultural factors may contribute to this sex difference though there are undoubtedly other factors, expecially those arising from genital differences. It would appear that similar conflicts in the male to those leading to hysterical formations in women can be dealt with by different methods. For instance, much homosexual perversion behaviour in the male fulfils some of the needs exhibited by the female hysteric.

ANXIETY STATES

Anxiety states are the most common personal disturbance for which help is sought. As the response to feared dangers, whether from a sense of some harm going to be done to him, or by him, or from a vague feeling of impending threat, loss or of going mad, anxiety is a prominent feature in most behaviour disorders. The term anxiety neurosis or anxiety state is used for conditions in which the anxiety is by far the predominant symptom, either in the form of a more or less constant tension with corresponding bodily responses, or as attacks in which the person gets into panics or near panic states.

Anxiety states usually prove to have as their immediate determinants conflicts around sexual relationships. In young people, especially, investigation almost invariably reveals the now familiar oedipal problems. The young man unconsciously links his growing sexual drives with the forbidden sexual attraction to mother and hence a fear of attack from father or some powerful rival male; and correspondingly with the girl. These fantasies come nearer to expression in anxious dreams and nightmares, and the anxiety associated with them is a common source of sleep disturbance. Masturbation also derives its besetting sense of guilt from the fantasies of involvement with the parents.

The young man referred to in Chapter X, Vol. I, presented many of the oedipal factors in anxiety states. On investigation, it soon emerged that his fascination with what had gone on between his wife and her previous employer was closely related to preoccupations in childhood about his parents' sexual relations. In one nightmare which occurred when he was about five years old, a terrifying phallic object appeared at the end of his parents' bed. He became extremely hostile to his father and protective of his mother about this time and these attitudes persisted till adolescence when they began to change. His marriage evoked these old anxieties and after he experienced their origins, he gradually lost them.

Once the sufferer is able to relive these early experiences there tends to be a marked reduction in the anxiety. It is not uncommon, however, for oedipal problems to exist as an outer layer in the person covering other difficulties. In Chapter X, Vol. I, it was pointed out that conflicts of earlier stages fuse with those of later stages and the working through of oedipal problems may open up the way to deeper conflicts involving fundamental insecurities in self-feeling.

Phobias represent an acute localized anxiety response which may become crippling. The projection of frightening fantasy objects on to external figures and situations is a universal mechanism in development and one which persists in some measure in almost everyone. The intense phobic reaction, often emerging for the first time in early adulthood, reflects a severe degree of disturbance. The situation which becomes the phobic one arouses anxiety to the point of panic or terror. The helplessness points to the early stage of development involved and the disintegration feared has led some psychopathologists to the view that the disaster dreaded is a psychotic fragmentation of the ego. The danger sensed is intensely dreaded and its primitive origins are perhaps best appreciated when we note that many sufferers have to make major alterations in their whole way of life to try to avoid the anxieties. The fact that individuals with intense phobic reactions can be well organized in other parts of their lives is apt to lead to the underlying severity of the condition being minimized. Phobias may represent a serious psychological disorder at the very roots of the person.

DEVIANT SEXUALITY

As the study of personal development has proceeded, the role of sexuality has tended to be viewed differently. When psychoneurotic conditions are investigated, sexual conflicts are frequently the first to be uncovered. It was this finding that led Freud to give sexuality such a central place in the development of the person. The study of the earliest phases are now bringing us to view the anomalies in ego and self development as the primary factors. Thus it has already been indicated that what happens at the oedipal stage is heavily influenced by what has taken place in the person before that as well as by the experiences during the working though of the triangular sexual situation with the parents. If the child has a secure self, his genital sexuality will be assimilated as part of the self and eventually fused with affectionate relationships. If, however, sexuality is felt to be attacked or rejected by repressive parental attitudes, the child has to disown it as bad. What is done with it can then take innumerable outlets. It becomes caught up in a variety of fantasy systems and the resultant inner relationships create the future deviations.

Development, as has been so often emphasized, is hardly ever ideal and so most persons retain residues of their earlier stages. Kinsey startled Western societies by showing how widespread the potential for deviant sexuality is. In this whole area we are a long way from separating what are cultural products from what are effects that could follow from our sexual endowment.

The essential characteristics of deviant sexuality can be understood when we consider the kinds of sub-self systems that mediate it. If an exciting object has been created in the repressed needing-self systems, then it may be of either sex. Whatever the sex, it is typical of behaviour motivated by a sub-system, that it seeks another person merely to coerce him or her into the role of the inner object. Also, the sub-system of this kind is born out of frustration and so although an exciting relationship is sought, there is woven into the relationship a good deal of aggression towards the object. With these origins, it is only to be expected that the relationship, though providing intense excitement, is not a progressively enriching one to the person. The object, being in part fashioned from fantasy, which in turn has drawn upon masturbational experience, tends to be reduced from being a person to being a part of a person. The homosexual seeks a penis, a substitute for the failed relationship with the first significant figure. The Don Juan likewise has a profound failure in the development of his capacity to relate to others; his conquests are reassurances against doubts about his sexuality and his acceptability. The degrading of the object can be seen more strikingly in the fetishist wherein the partner's individuality ceases to have much importance; all she is needed for is to carry the fetishistic conditions. Similarly with sado-masochistic behaviour.

Homosexuality was at first thought by psychoanalysts to be caused by castration anxieties. The reality of a person with no penis was intolerable. Further work suggests that it represents a considerable fear and hatred of the heterosexual object stemming from the boy's experience of his mother as too hostile to his sexual impulses. Endless variations can occur in this situation. The man may remain to all outward appearances completely masculine and he may feel this way apart from his attitude to women. At the other end of a scale, he may identify with the woman he fears. Deprivations in early experiences are seen in the oral perversions of both sexes in which the genital is treated like a breast. Conflicts more influenced by later stages may create the desire in men to be anally raped by a man, and in women to be the partner in sado-masochistic relationships.

When perversions are well established in practice, it is difficult to alter them. They then become comparable with the addictions in that they provide a quality of excitement and omnipotent control that exercises a great attraction for the personality threatened with the dangers of infantile vulnerabilities. The frustrations the more sensitive pervert detects may lead him to treatment and particularly when he begins to experience in later life emptiness and often depression.

When Freud first uncovered the importance and variety of childhood sexual behaviour, and the active fantasy life it gave rise to, he conceived much neurotic behaviour as due to the struggle against the childhood sexual impulses. As he put it, neurosis was what people developed when they did not become perverts. Although an over simplification, there is no doubt that a great deal of neurotic anxiety arises from the threat of unconscious perverse fantasies, expecially the fear of homosexuality.

Unconscious fantasies also play a prominent role in psychosexual dysfunctions which lead to reactive distress. Impotence or premature emission may be linked with fears of the woman's body and there may be fantasies of the vagina as a retaliating biting mouth. The incapacity may also stem from an aggressive wish to frustrate. Frigidity likewise arises from fears of the penis as a destructive penetrator or from fantasies of the vagina stealing it; it, too, can be an expression of resentment against the penis and what it has come to symbolize.

The Psychosomatic Disorders

Several somatic disorders with insufficient organic causation have been recognized as linked with psychological factors and these conditions have become familiar as the psychosomatic disorders. Asthma, peptic ulcer, hypertension and ulcerative colitis are well known examples, and the connection with emotional disturbance is often made manifest when increased stress leads to exacerbation of the physical disorder. Just how stress affects somatic reactions is obscure. Psychoanalytic investigation of personality development has suggested for example that when a child is deprived of a normal mothering relationship, it develops an incorporative attitude of wanting to swallow the mother. This mode of response at the personal level was shown by Engel (1962) to be strikingly paralleled in the alimentary system. The infant Monica with a gastric fistula, once she had established a good close relationship with her doctor, produced the same gastric response when he appeared as occurred when she was going to be fed.

Many attempts have been made to discover whether specific conflicts are associated with certain diseases rather than others. The balance of the evidence is against such a correlation and it seems instead that it is the earliest stress feelings of infantile deprivation, i.e. of helplessness and inadequacy, that are the common precursors for most psychosomatic disorders. There is, however, a view amongst several observers that some conditions are more affected by repressed rage than by the repressed infantile needs. The choice of a particular organ or body system in a psychosomatic disorder may stem from the many variables which lead to the dominance of that function in the responses to the particular stress. Balint (1957) showed, too, that the attitudes of doctors as perceived by the patient is an influential factor in this connection.

Conditions in which the psychological factors would be expected to be marked are anorexia nervosa and obesity and they are. Over-eating is psychologically an addiction and its origins are akin to those of addiction, i.e. in infantile deprivation. Several detailed studies of anorexia nervosa patients have shown the influence of a range of fantasies in producing the aversion to eating. The conflicting impulses, however, are not far to seek. Thomae (1967), for instance, showed that the aversion was at times accompanied by secret stealing of food.

Endocrine functions are another group which expectedly show a high sensitivity to emotional stress. Amenorrhoea and dysmenorrhoea follow in many instances from conflicts over the feminine role, and hyperthyroidism has long been associated with anxiety.

Other symptoms have in varying measure been related to psychological tensions. Headache, the most common of all symptoms, is of psychological origin in the large bulk of cases according to Wolff (1960) one of the most distinguished investigators in this field. For him, stress disorders are fundamentally related to 'threats to the stability of the individual's human relations, especially during the dependent years, and threats that wipe out hope and faith in man are grave in their significance'. In understanding the stress disorders, as with the neuroses and character disorders, what is happening to the individual as a *person* is the central task for the psychiatrist.

REFERENCES

(see also Chapter X, Vol. I)

ABRAHAM, K. (1911) *Selected Papers*. London: Hogarth.

BALINT, M. (1957) *The Doctor, His Patient, and the Illness*. London: Pitman.

BOWLBY, J. (1944) Forty-four juvenile thieves: their characters and home-life. *International Journal of Psycho-Analysis*, **25**, 19.

ENGEL, G. L. (1962) *Psychological Development in Health and Disease*. London: Saunders & Co.

FAIRBAIRN, W. R. D. (1952) *Psychoanalytic Studies of the Personality*. London: Routledge.

FAIRBAIRN, W. R. D. (1954) Observations on the nature of hysterical states. *British Journal of Medical Psychology*, **27**.

FREUD, S. (1917) Mourning and Melancholia. *Standard Edition Sigmund Freud*. London: Hogarth.

THOMAE, H. (1967) *Anorexia Nervosa*. New York: International Universities Press.

WINNICOTT, D. W. (1958) *Collected Papers*. London: Tavistock.

WINNICOTT, D. W. (1965) *The Maturational Processes and the Facilitating Environment*. London: Hogarth.

WOLF, H. (1960) In *Stress and Psychiatric Disorder*, p. 18, Edited by J. M. Tanner, Oxford: Blackwell.

Chapter II

ABNORMAL PERSONALITY

H. J. Walton

INTRODUCTION

An important decision-making procedure in diagnosing each psychiatric patient is to discriminate between illness and abnormal personality. This is sometimes difficult: the illness, as in the case of florid psychosis, may be so gross as to submerge temporarily the underlying personality traits; the personality type cannot be designated with confidence while the cluster of symptoms usurps the overall diagnostic presentation.

Illness is a syndrome which disrupts the normal continuity of the personality; it consists of symptoms such as phobias, obsessions, altered states of awareness, etc., which are behavioural events different in quality from any presenting in health. There are no such qualitative aberrations when the personality is abnormal; instead, behaviour differs from the normal only quantitatively, the person showing too much or too little of an attribute present in everybody.

The diagnostic differentiation between psychiatric illness and abnormal personality is the more necessary because very often the two coexist. Indeed, clinical convention has it that hysterical psychoneurosis commonly supervenes in individuals with hysterical personality, obsessional neurosis in those with obsessional personality disorders, etc. This neat etomological concordance is by no means as usual as the textbooks give forth. In addition to their presentation with psychotic illnesses and psychoneuroses, people with abnormal personalities often appear clinically with psychosomatic disorders, such as peptic ulcer, ulcerative colitis, asthma, etc., and may be chronic hospital attenders or the subjects of polysurgery. Abnormal personalities may not enter the medical ambit at all, but be encountered in penal settings. Still others may continue unrecognized in the community and only escape anonymity when widespread screening of the population occurs, as in wartime when obligatory intake to the armed forces exposes all adults to clinical scrutiny.

NORMALITY

In ordinary parlance 'normal' often implies an *ideal* state, as when a patient in a general hospital indignantly dismisses a projected referral to a psychiatrist, and insists that he is 'perfectly' normal: this popular concept appears in the constitution of the World Health Organization (1947) which defines health as a state of complete mental and physical well-being.

There is a second sense in which the concept 'normal' is applied: the *pragmatic* norm. For working purposes, e.g. in an epidemiological investigation, an arbitary definition is adopted, such as that everybody who has not seen a psychiatrist is to be regarded as normal.

The third use of the concept, which is that employed here, is to hold that normal is the usual manifestation customarily encountered, and abnormal are those forms which are relative rarities. This *statistical* concept of normality requires the clinician to be aware of the range of ordinary behaviour, and to discriminate from it those forms of personality which are unusual in the society under consideration. A person may be excessively isolated socially, or conspicuously passive, or unduly hostile: he is then recognized by his fellows or by the clinician as a definitely unusual person, an abnormal personality. Whether the quantitative deviation should include the overendowed as well as the underendowed is a matter of continual debate: the great abnormals like Strindberg, van Gogh, Joan of Arc, Lawrence of Arabia, the gallery of conspicuously aberrant individuals whose remarkable achievements have enlarged their era's consciousness, regularly feature in considerations of psychopathy, often without appropriate attention to possible associated illness or deviation such as paranoid reaction, epilepsy, nutritional lack or concealed homosexuality. Moreover, the exceptional intelligence of the great abnormals is insufficiently recognized as an attribute needing emphasis. As Jaspers (1963) has pointed out, the pearl secreted by the oyster is not a direct equivalent of the contaminating irritant: a lowlier bivalve will not oblige with as estimable a product.

A normal person is thus one who is usual in the culture which produced him, while an abnormal person has traits which are quantitatively different from those customarily encountered.

PERSONALITY

Personality is a theoretical concept, with reference to a person's identity and his differences from other people. It signifies the sum total of a person's actions and reactions. It refers to his qualities as they are observed by other persons. Included are his noteworthy characteristics, his emotional expression, his social traits, his interests, his values and beliefs. Personality is regarded as evident in all the person does, and especially in his imaginative and creative activities: this fact has been made use of in introspectionist studies of personality such as Wundt (1903) pursued, and in projective tests which provoke responses on the basis of vague, unstructured or ambiguous stimuli, the Rorschach test, a famous if dubiously respectable example.

Personalities differ, and are relatively uniform over time. Some people are exceptionally consistent and dependable, while others are notably unstable, an observation which is the basis for a well-known test of 'neuroticism' (Eysenck and Eysenck, 1963), a factor that—in the view of some investigators—has to do with proneness to anxiety. Some authorities link the degree of instability with postulated somatic variations in such organic structures as the autonomic nervous system; others view the abnormality as psychogenic rather than inherited.

The most common view of the origin of personality is that two classes of determinants are operative, genetic-physiological and sociocultural. Personality is grounded in an individual's constitution. Current concepts of inheritance emphasize that only an aspect of a person's genetic endowment is active: the level of activity of genes is altered by the hormonal state, by diet and by emotional states. Variable gene activity, influenced by environmental factors, contributes to a view of personality development that from the start of life constitution is mutatively affected by experience, and that physiogenesis merges with the attributes of personality which are socially acquired. It is difficult to apportion the relative contribution of heredity and environment in the development of personality (Cattell, 1965). Individual traits are likely to be determined by multifactorial genetic influences. As expected, personality is more similar in monozygotic than in dizygotic twins (the respective correlations for extraversion were reported as .42 and −.17, and for neuroticism .38 and .11). Even when reared apart, the differing environments were reported to have had relatively small effect on personality in monozygotic twins (Shields, 1962). A very high concordance for homosexual tendencies was reported between monozygotic twins (Kallmann, 1952), but more recently discordant instances have been reported (Parker, 1964).

Chromosome studies, carried out recently in Edinburgh and Sheffield, have identified a number of men in special security institutions for mentally abnormal offenders who had abnormal sex chromosomes. Men of XYY constitutions were of particular interest: they were reported as excessively aggressive and of more than average height. (Usually they were also of low I.Q.) These findings have been interpreted as evidence that both the criminality and the tallness could be attributed to the extra Y chromosome, and the question arose whether XYY individuals were also not excessively represented in special security hospitals for offenders. The XYY syndrome was in fact subsequently identified more often than would be expected by chance in such state institutions. These criminal XYY men had normal intelligence and physical appearance; however, it is not known how many men with an extra Y chromosome are contained normally in society. It has yet to be convincingly shown as the mental and physical differences between these men and ordinary XY males are further studied, that an extra Y chromosome leads to greater proneness to delinquency.

Another approach to physiogenesis in abnormal personality has been by means of electro-encephalography. Abnormal E.E.G.'s have been found in aggressive sociopaths, in the form of low-frequency theta waves (Schwade and Geiger, 1956). Such anomalies are frequent in young children, giving rise to the suggestion that retarded maturation of the central nervous system is present in some cases of sociopathy. It has also been reported by Schacter and Latane (1964) that the learning of imprisoned subjects could be improved by administration of adrenalin, leading them to speculate that psychopathic reactions implicate an anomaly of the autonomic nervous system. Much of the research on the genetics and physiology of personality has been done on infra-human animals, and the findings cannot be generalized to complex personality. There is a great deal yet to be discovered about the metabolic and neurophysiological correlates of personality.

Much work has been done on the social and psychological determinants of personality. The 19th century psychologists concentrated on intrapersonal events, on what went on in people's minds: the concepts and entities they stressed were instincts, mental energies, perceptions, images and thoughts. Thus Freud was concerned with sexual and aggressive drives, with cathexis, with perceptual distortions, with phantasies and with symbolic substitutions. These were 'internal' phenomena.

With the development of behaviourism attention came to centre less upon postulated mental events and more upon observable behaviour. Thinking was studied in terms of how people process information about their environment, and how variations in the way people think were related to their general personality differences. Behaviour in social situations was investigated, and differences in interpersonal interactions were related to differences in the way people process information about others (cognitive style). From one aspect, when the person is viewed in his human environment, abnormal personality may be regarded as manifesting in disturbed relationships with other people.

PERSONALITY DEVELOPMENT

A person acquires his personality in the course of a maturational sequence extending over time, during which various processes are operative. Internalization implies that properties of an admired person get taken into the personality through identification; as is seen when a small boy adopts behaviour displayed by his father, when teenagers behave like a pop idol, or when trainees incorporate in their professional repetoire the technical and personal mannerisms of their professor. Piaget and Inhelder (1969) has named this process 'assimilation', the incorporating into the self of a representation from the environment, so that inner schemata are laid down.

Social learning of a more negative type also takes place. A reaction, such as anger at being frustrated, or sexual curiosity, may be suppressed by the force of parental displeasure, and lead the child to mask the impulse (repression) or even vow to be the contrary of what one actually is and to display the opposite behaviour (reaction formation). Piaget calls such changes in the individual 'accommodation', a permanent modification in the developing personality as a result of pressure from the environment.

Developmentally the personality passes through a sequence of stages from infancy to maturity, different systems predominating at the various phases. The most widely adopted account is that of Freud (1962), whose psychosexual theory of personality development postulates three crucial maturational phases: oral, anal and phallic. Abnormal personality, according to this systems concept, results when the individual has not negotiated the critical developmental steps. Instead 'fixation' has occurred at the point in the course towards maturation where the social climate was unfavourable. The child may not progress beyond a particular infantile phase or, if he does develop in psychosexual maturation, he will fall back under conditions of stress to show behaviour characteristic of the earlier arrest ('regression').

1. An *oral* personality has failed to master very early infantile impulses, and has tendencies to be passive, to cling to other people for support, and to be grasping and demanding; the oral residues persist as excessive mouth activities and an urge to greedily possess other people and things.

2. An *anal* personality has developmental residues relating to the stage of life when the child was being socialized in the parental family, and was required to accommodate to its hygienic rules and arrangements: in maturity he is excessively neat and tidy, suppresses emotion, and is pedantic, obstinate, stingy and punctual.

3. The *phallic* personality is viewed as having encountered a block to development at about five years of age when the child was in rivalry with the parent of the same sex for the affections of the other parent. A person impeded emotionally at this level has to repress sexual impulses and deny mature erotic needs, while simultaneously attracting others sexually. Such people have little capacity for intimacy and keep relationships superficial. Women of this type are usually frigid; men generally

have associations with many women but are unable to form an enduring relationship with anyone.

While the behaviour components of these different personality types are evident to clinicians, the theoretical explanation for their basis is excessively conjectural. This is not to say that a concept of personality must be derived solely from observable behaviour. To do so would not account for many of the phenomena which clinicians encounter: dreams, slips of the tongue, post-hypnotic behaviour, traumatic neuroses in wartime and civilian catastrophe, etc. Personality is a concept about another person's behaviour; it exists in the head of the observer. There is no objection to a construct of personality which takes account of data which are outside the person's awareness but accessible to the external observer. Only the behaviour of a person and the circumstances under which the behaviour occurs can be observed; the underlying structures have to be inferred, and personality description is thus inevitably a theoretical task.

The problem of inference is tackled in a different way by Erikson (1966). The system he devised to explain the observed stages in the development of personality does not concentrate as narrowly as the psychoanalytical model does on the sequence of changes during childhood. Erikson emphasizes also the adolescent's efforts to gain a personal identity in social life, and the additional tasks presenting later during adult life. He describes eight stages in an ordered sequence of psychosocial development with a specific nuclear conflict for each age, grounded in the then current interpersonal relationships. The solution of each developmental crisis is dependent on adequately solving earlier ones.

1. *Basic trust* is suggested as the initial component of a healthy personality to develop, about the first year of life; if the child's relation with the mother is not satisfactory, an impaired perspective is adopted, characterized in adulthood by basic mistrust.

2. About the second and third years of life the child has to cope with conflicts between co-operation and wilfulness, between self-expression on the one hand and its suppression on the other; the child will acquire a sense of *autonomy* if this developmental crisis is resolved successfully, whereas the personality features of shame and doubt will result if frustrations and parental overcontrol prevent self-reliance.

3. *Initiative* is added to the personality if the stage labelled by Freud as phallic is negotiated; if not, the trait of guilt is acquired instead.

4. The crisis which comes about when the child is called upon to collaborate with others and to learn in school, if successfully resolved, gives a sense of mastery which is expressed as *industry*; the negative outcome is a sense of inferiority.

5. *Identity*, implying confidence in one's ability to maintain inner

sameness in the face of a variety of social roles, is achieved in adolescence; if not the personality is characterized by identity diffusion, often demonstrated by inability to decide on a work future for oneself.

6. The first of the three stages of adulthood which Erikson differentiates is capacity for *intimacy* with others, in work, friendship and heterosexual mutuality; failure in this phase of maturation results in isolation.

7. The seventh phase of personality growth relates to the capacity for concern with establishing the next generation, *generativity*; the negative counterpart is interpersonal impoverishment and a sense of stagnation.

8. *Ego-integrity* implies acceptance of one's life and the people important in it as something that has to be, and recognition that one's life is one's own responsibility. Lack of such accrued ego integr ation is characterized by despair and disgust, with contempt for institutions and persons.

This widely-known schema of personality development is unacceptable to some clinicians, who object to the terminology which signifies a specifity not yet substantiated by adequate clinical investigation, and which carries value-judgements and idealistic inclinations which may not be of general applicability across cultures. Such critics may nevertheless admit the need for a schema of psychosocial development during the course of personal maturation.

Whitehorn (1952) has provided a developmental framework which is not as well-known as it deserves to be. He differentiates four levels, again relating each to the adult's behaviour in interpersonal relationships, focusing particularly on his degree of responsibility. The concepts are put forward to describe persons who are physically and chronologically grown up, but who have been impeded emotionally at an earlier phase of personality growth, or who have reverted during illness to attitudes characteristic of the earlier level.

1. The *infantile* person expects from others a limitless amount of service and consideration, without feeling reciprocal obligations. His main emotional need is for affection and attention.

2. The *childish* person, arrested at a later phase, requires thorough reliability in others, but formal effort only up to the 'excuse level' in himself. Alibis are a conspicuous feature in his behaviour; the 'good excuse' condones his failures of responsibility. Great circumstantiality in speech is characteristic. The main emotional need is for security. Praise or blame is the focus of attention. Obsessive scrupulosity may serve as the substitute for adequate performance.

3. The *early adolescent* person seeks as his main need to be assured about his personal significance. His behaviour is exhibitionistic and prestige-seeking. He strives to be accorded personal recognition and makes repeated demonstrations to gain such attention. Support outside

the family is sought, characteristically by idealistic hero-worship and in gangs. Badges and trophies are valued. A conception of group responsibility, which may be fanatical in intensity, develops, usually related to the gang or to one's buddy.

4. The *late adolescent* person is capable of loyalty to a cause and to personal groups. He is arrested in the stage of '-isms': romanticism, cynicism, idealism, etc., giving expression to some doctrinaire excess or other. Pseudo-sophistication and a 'line of talk' are characteristic; sex interest and courtships occur, but the focus is on conquest rather than mutual devotion.

These arrests are differentiated from the *mature person*, who is viewed as balanced in his perspective regarding himself, his work, and his standing with others. Instead of a stereotyped pattern, the person can manage a series of social roles, shifting from one to the other without constraint or anxiety.

THE MATURE PERSONALITY

Clinicians customarily view themselves as professionally equipped to identify and treat abnormality, and often disclaim that their responsibility is to identify on positive grounds that a person is healthy. This approach leads to a negative identification of normality; i.e. a person is considered mature if definite indices of arrest are lacking.

There have however been efforts, such as the description by Jahoda (1958), to categorize maturity on the basis of positive clinical evidence. The concept implies that a person has negotiated in succession each of the maturational phases, and demonstrates attributes which allow his personality to be declared normal.

Six attributes of personality maturity can be mentioned:

1. *Self-perception* is reasonably correct, the person's sense of identity being sufficiently congruent with his actual ability and performance.

2. *Adjustment* is present, the person showing the self-mastery and the environmental mastery to take things as they come and to make the best of them.

3. *Autonomy* operates, the person being able to function independently and to exercise self-determination.

4. *Reality-testing* is accurate, the person not perceiving his environment in a distorted way.

5. *Integration* implies a coherence of the personality, a relatedness of its separate systems, so that the person is aware of his various attributes and determining psychological processes.

6. *Self-actualization* occurs when the person gives expression to his abilities and needs, doing so in ways which are acceptable to the culture in which he lives; the concept relates to a person's achieve-

ments relative to his endowment, his motivations, and his associations with others in obtaining his public and intimate satisfactions.

Many of these concepts have cultural value connotations, have not yet been translated into operational terms, and are unsystematic. Many are inferences as yet ungrounded in tested observations. Concepts of normality are still in a pre-scientific stage; empirical indicators have yet to be devised for use in clinical research, and a generally accepted concept of the personality has still to be agreed upon. For the present, clinicians decide on a largely intuitive way whether a person is normal, their main emphasis being on detecting the presence of abnormality.

DIAGNOSTIC PROCEDURES

To make a personality diagnosis, the clinician systematically carries out two procedures:

AN HISTORICAL ACCOUNT OF THE PATIENT'S SOCIAL INTERACTIONS

The clinician obtains an account from the patient (or from an independent informant, usually a relative) about the patient's behaviour in personal relationships. The patient is helped to provide detailed descriptions, so that complete accounts of particular interactions become available: the dates when they occurred, the exact names of the chief protagonists, the specific events which took place, and the patient's behaviour and feelings in each episode.

After a series of interactions have been related, a picture begins to take shape of the patient's characteristic behaviours in certain social settings. Repeated patterns of association are the most informative, indicating habitual modes of interpersonal behaviour: e.g. A man describes a poor relationship with his wife who makes excessive demands on him, and then goes further to relate that at work his colleague imposes on him by requiring him to carry out menial chores (such as replacing files used by the colleague, a task which the patient accepts although it is in no way part of his legitimate responsibilities). The patient may then relate that his mother had deserted his father and the home for another man when he was eight, and that he never afterwards felt secure or confident. In his relationship with his paternal grandparents he exerted himself to please them but 'never felt I could do enough for them'. It is from such uniformity of behaviour in a series of different relationships that the clinician makes his initial inferences about the patient's patterns of behaviour in significant personal relationships.

THE PATIENT'S BEHAVIOUR IN THE CLINICAL SETTING

Throughout the clinical interview the psychiatrist studies how the patient relates to him while providing his autobiographical account about himself. The psychiatrist is of course a participant observer. He knows from experience what his habitual effect is on patients, and he observes whether the patient reacts to him in any unusual or striking manner. Technically he identifies with the patient, empathically striving to grasp as perceptively as he can the events the patient is describing. This procedure facilitates the patient's frank and self-revealing account of past and present interpersonal difficulties. Periodically the psychiatrist detaches himself somewhat, the better to objectify his perceptions, and at such times notes how the patient is behaving towards him. If in the context of the interview the patient's behaviour to the psychiatrist reflects behaviour already apparent from his self-descriptions, direct evidence is obtained to confirm the personality diagnosis which is emerging. The clinician has introduced himself as a measuring instrument, making himself available to the patient as a person with whom to interact there and then. The patient described above was submissive and ingratiating to the psychiatrist, as his account indicated he also was to his grandparents, his wife, and his colleague at work. Patients may make use of the interview to display stubbornness, overassertiveness, hostility, suspicion, etc., and in doing so provide corroboration of prominent traits already inferred by the psychiatrist from the patient's account of the difficulties in his chief personal relationships.

Personality Tests

The psychiatrist can himself select and administer personality tests, or enlist the aid of a clinical psychologist colleague for the purpose, to clarify further the patient's characteristic modes of behaviour. A large range of tests are available (see Chap. IX, Vol. I) to evaluate quantitatively the patient's attitudes, motivations or traits. Projective techniques provide relatively vague, ambiguous or unstructured stimuli. Other tests measure dimensions of personality, including such factors as neuroticism, extraversion, hostility, etc. Certain tests comprise a battery of scales, enabling a profile to be drawn of the patient's traits and attitudes in a range of psychological sectors (Cattell, 1956).

Clinical Presentation of Abnormal Personality

The abnormal personalities began to receive attention only late during the development of psychiatry as a medical discipline (Kavka, 1949); they have been recognized increasingly as the outpatient responsibilities of psychiatrists have extended, and as psychiatric units have developed in general hospitals.

In many instances the person suffering from abnormal personality does not come to direct attention, but is noticed from the repercussions of his social ineffectiveness, or from the effects on others of his difficulties in personal relationships. The initial presentation of the patient may be as a parent of a disturbed child (Wolff and Acton, 1968), or with a suicide attempt, or with alcoholism, or in the context of a marital problem.

The concurrence of psychiatric illness and abnormal personality has long been recognized (Henderson, 1939). An experimental study of psychiatric diagnosis (Shepherd *et al.*, 1968) showed that psychiatrists consider more than one diagnostic term necessary for adequate description of some cases, e.g. by adding a personality disorder to qualify the principal psychiatric diagnosis. The association between illness and personality emerges clearly when individuals are studied in a hospital context. Then it becomes essential to evaluate each patient first for the presence of illness, and second regarding the type of personality (Foulds, 1965). Often the two occur concurrently in the same person. In a general population a very marked association was found (Hare and Shaw, 1965) between abnormal personality and psychoneurotic illness.

The central feature of abnormal personality is some degree of persistent abnormality of character which is frequently, but not necessarily, antisocial in its manifestations. The abnormality varies considerably, ranging in character from schizoid people who are valuable if somewhat unstable members of the community, through cyclothymics who have useful lives between their phases of disturbance, to psychopaths who are socially destructive (Bullard, 1941).

The association between the different types of psychiatric illness and the various forms of abnormal personality is now recognized as a more complicated problem than the earlier statements of the position suggested. Little systematic research to explore the various relationships between form of illness and personality type has yet been carried out (Walton *et al.*, 1970).

Degrees of Abnormality

The person with a *mild* degree of abnormality (the character disorders) may subjectively identify impairment in his sense of well-being, or a block in the proper expression of his impulses, and if sophisticated may spontaneously seek psychotherapeutic help.

Abnormal personality of *moderate* degree (e.g. hysterical, schizoid, obsessional, etc.), is usually identified clinically, often when the affected person presents with accompanying physical, psychosomatic or psychiatric illness.

Severe abnormality of personality is found in those who harm society by aggressive acts or are a gross liability because of their fecklessness. In recent decades, to remove the stigma attaching to the label of psychopathy, the term 'sociopath' has been advocated to designate the

B

most gross forms (Partridge, 1930). This term replaced 'psychopathic personality' in the official U.S. nomenclature (American Psychiatric Association, 1952), but it in turn has lately been dropped in favour of the term 'antisocial personality' (American Psychiatric Association, 1968). Section V in the International Classification of Disease of the World Health Organization, which deals with personality disorders is to be reviewed in 1970 (Shepherd *et al.*, 1968). Psychopathic personality, not surprisingly, therefore, continues to be 'a notoriously unsatisfactory diagnostic category' (Lewis, 1953).

Types of Abnormal Personality

1. CHARACTER DISORDERS

The character is the acquired pattern of habits, attitudes and ideals which render a person's actions stable and predictable. When a patient has a character disorder, he often comes for help with relatively minor deviations of personality, which prevent him from achieving his potential, or interfere with his personal relations so that he does not gain satisfactions from them.

Two types of this mild variety of personality deviation can be distinguished:

(a) *Dependent type*

Such a person is compliant, and may at times give an impression of some helplessness. He clings to other more dominant people. He does not compete, but rather avoids situations in work or social life which call for assertion. If frustrated by the person on whom he is dependent, he can react with irritation, or with weeping which is close to an overt expression of reproach or anger, and indeed can become obstinate and obstructive when his wishes are not met.

As applies also in the case of the next type of deviation, the dependent personality shows such emotional decompensation only under conditions of stress.

(b) *Overassertive type*

This sort of deviant personality can be recognized from the tendency to officiousness and aggressiveness, evident at times of strain when the person reacts with undue anger. Otherwise he is domineering, and controls others by brow-beating them. Often notably successful in business or administration, the over-assertive personality achieves his ends by relative insensitivity about the susceptibilities of others. Driving, energetic and forthright, at times he misjudges social situations, and in the cold light of later reflection may be guilty and worried at harm he may have done to others. His triumphs and gains may be at the expense of trusting and friendly relationships with others, and medical help may be sought because of the absence of pleasant social responses or the lack of any real fellowship with family or friends.

2. PERSONALITY DISORDERS

The intermediate group of abnormal personalities, as already indicated, are those sufficiently deviant to be clearly identifiable by trained clinicians. Although some authorities describe more forms—Schneider in his famous book (1950) mentioned ten types—the following three types are most often encountered:

(a) *Obsessional Personality*

The obsessional person gives scant regard to the emotional aspects of a situation or an interaction. He is rigid rather than flexible, over-attentive to details rather than to the wider scope of an event or encounter, and prefers to have everything predictable and orderly. He often appears officious, sometimes so pedantically so that he can be comical, and excessively controls not only himself but attempts also to dominate others. He appears to behave in an excessively egotistical manner, and responds in an overriding way when involved in a venture calling for co-operation. He is over-careful, methodical, liking things cut-and-dried, concerned with neatness and orderliness. He can be very meticulous, punctual and over-organized, to the extent of becoming uncomfortable and even upset if his routines are disturbed by any unexpected development. He has a set of fixed standards and points of view, from which he can deviate only with great difficulty. He is uninfluenced, therefore, by the wishes, needs, opinions or views of other people.

The meticulousness and preservation of sameness extends to the person's mode of dress, which can be scrupulously neat. He can be overconscientious, paying greatly excessive attention to minutiae. He may work compulsively, and be unable to make use of opportunities for relaxation. Such a person, in consequence, can be of particular usefulness in a bureaucratic post calling for scrupulous concern with details. He may be highly obstinate when faced by any requirement that he should deviate from his straight and narrow path.

At times such a person appears to leave some loophole in the personality fabric, so that the conformity, inhibition and rigidity is waived in some context or other. The precise, neat youngster, who must have everything in place, may for example permit himself to have his clothes cupboard in disorder, or may periodically forget thrift to overspend in a foolish self-indulgence which rationally is at odds with his habitual miserliness.

The gross form of the disorder is easy to recognize. Less severe forms may be less obtrusive, and may only be particularly evident at times of pressure, as when an examination is looming for a youngster or when a houseproud woman has relatives coming to stay.

(b) *Schizoid Personality*

The schizoid person is essentially solitary. He is aloof in his loneliness, detached and distant from other people. He has few close relationships, and may be much more preoccupied with some impersonal activity in the realms of electronics, physics, mathematics or engineering. Often the engrossing venture is a personal fad or invention, which may be of negligible application in ordinary life, but may be pursued with a single-minded devotion inappropriate to a mere hobby or interest.

Cold, quiet and shy, the person's abnormality may already have been apparent early in childhood, from an inability or disinclination to mix, and a preference for solitary pursuits. The lack of friendships may have been upsetting to the parents; as the person grows up, he can himself be distressed by his incapacity for any intimacy in his associations with others.

The person may appear odd, eccentric, gawky, and in his awkward isolation may appear as a figure of fun. He may seem excessively secretive. Schizoid people are often solitary workers, who cannot function satisfactorily in a team. The common physical configuration is asthenic. Bookish, reserved, out of touch with others, relatively blind to social cues, their personal lives may appear barren. However, this remote exterior may belie the strong emotions which some schizoid people cannot express. Others find a vehicle for their private feelings, and may keep a diary, or indulge in daydreaming, or succeed in establishing some relationship in which the expression of affect is allowed.

The schizoid person is at times mistrustful, seeing slights where none are intended. He is rigid and brittle. He has little empathy with other people, and so remains unaware of their intentions, feeling and wishes. When he attempts to appraise others intuitively, he is often wildly wrong, thereby complicating his already attenuated relationships. He can be made profoundly uncomfortable when well-meaning but misguided mentors or therapists attempt to have him mix more, or become intimate with another person, perhaps another isolate as lacking in interpersonal skills as himself.

In clinical investigations carried out at Edinburgh, we have evidence for considering the core of this type of deviation to consist of social detachment and avoidance of close relationships, mistrustfulness, and consistency. We find unawareness of the psychological reactions of others, the opposite of Kretschmer's (1936) 'oversensitivity', more characteristic of individuals who group in this category: he viewed this deviation as predisposing to schizophrenia, and argued backwards from observations which derived from histories of psychotic patients. While the schizoid person may come to attention when his condition is complicated by psychosis, clinicians able to identify the type will also recognize it when the person seeks help in a social crisis, or because of psychosomatic illness (Ruesch, 1948), or on account of psychoneurotic disorder. Suspicion can become the prevailing response to others, the person believing that he is being exploited, misused or disparaged. Some clinicians would differentiate this development separately, diagnosing such a personality as paranoid.

(c) *Hysterical Personality*

People of this type can be identified on the basis of a constellation of behaviours: they seek to please and influence others; they crave attention; they are insincere; and they are given to excessive displays of emotion.

An hysterical person appears to be exploitative, with an eye always on the other person. She talks for effect, not to convey any honestly-felt intention. One feels her need for appreciation, and her readiness to express herself with that aim in view. She plays up in order to evoke a response, and that response is one which she has already 'decided' to elicit.

Psychiatrists probably over-diagnose this type in abnormal women, attaching the label very much less often to men (Walton and Presly, 1972). Hysterical personality disorder characteristically announces itself as lack of sincerity. The person is showy, histrionic in manner and dress, with a quality of spuriousness and exaggeration, even theatricality, in what they do. The exhibitionism appears intended to impress others, even to shock them. Speech is superficial, with plentiful hyperbole ('heavenly', 'ghastly'), which only heightens the effect of shallowness.

Hysterical personalities crave to appear, both to themselves and others, as more than they are, and to experience more than they are capable of (Jaspers, 1963). The personality comes to lack a central core, and consists of a series of masks or exteriorized presentations of self. The hysteric can be miserable when unnoticed, or when she considers that some prerogative of her own is being usurped or some acknowledgement which is hers by right is being given to another person.

Lying occurs, either to impress the other person, or in gross form without the hysteric being fully aware of the misrepresentations: she may be taken aback herself after the untruth, but to correct the error would be too threatening to her precarious self-esteem. *Pseudologia phantastica* is a term applied to cases of repetitive telling of major untruths. The hysterical type of personality disorder does not improve with adverse experience, and is also unfortunately resistant to therapeutic effort. However, these people can gain considerable support from

an ongoing clinical relationship, and can be helped to recover themselves from social misadventures. Women of this type suffer also from
sexual timidity and frigidity, the more distressing to them because their
frequently seductive manner and provocative dress invites advances
with which they cannot cope; hysterical men also have difficulty in
establishing a close relation with one woman, and may seek intimacy
in a series of attachments of short duration. The hysterical person
becomes wearisome, the more irritating because she usually shows
little consideration for others and small capacity for real affection.

3. SOCIOPATHY

In 1835 John Prichard described 'moral insanity', emphasizing
that in this condition there was no defect in intellect or reasoning, nor
any insane illusion or hallucination. The state consisted of 'a morbid
perversion of the natural feelings, affections, inclinations, temper,
habits, moral dispositions and natural impulses'.

The same characteristic is emphasized in contemporary descriptions
of the most pathological form of abnormal personality. The sociopath
has a serious defect of feeling. He cannot perceive adequately how his
impulses harm others, nor can he comprehend at all accurately the
feelings of other people. He is described as having a severely defective
conscience, and as being affectionless.

The sociopath cannot form satisfactory relationships, and major
failures repeatedly occur in his marriage, his work and his social life.
He is seen as loveless, indifferent and destructive. He comes into
conflict with the norms, customs and laws of his community, not learning
from his failures, however catastrophic; already present from an early
age, his social ineptitude is persistent, leading him chronically to be in
trouble. Many sociopaths are likeable and charming, and initially
mislead well-meaning people whom they subsequently disappoint and
mortify.

Impulsiveness is usually evident, the sociopath dismaying those
associated with him by uncontrolled, often destructive outbursts in the
absence of sufficient provocation. Such precipitate and deplorable
action has been spoken of as 'short circuit reactions', to indicate that
often the person is aware of the build-up to the outburst, and will often
admit that after the aggressive or destructive episode he feels calmer
and relieved of tension.

The sociopath does not show ability to modify destructive behaviour
reactions, or to learn from even drastic setbacks; he may be punished
repeatedly for the same unacceptable behaviour, and yet continue it; the
individual's antisocial patterns are often monotonously repetitive.
Kleptomania, gambling, or physical assaults may each be associated
with excitement which the sociopath seeks and indulges repeatedly;

the antisocial behaviour can be seriously destructive to others, as in cases of sadistic attacks on children or of pyromania.

The lack of regard for the possible consequences of his actions is also impressive, the sociopath appearing not to care about the outcome, and scant in his consideration even of persons on whom his welfare depends. He disregards his obligations to others: it is on this account that the Mental Health Act (England and Wales) of 1959 described the sociopath's conduct as 'seriously irresponsible'. The lack of concern can be so extreme that the callousness of the sociopath towards his victims is disturbing to the psychiatrist who, struck with the total absence of self-reproach, may from his own subjective response of recoil suddenly grasp the nature of the abnormality.

The sociopath is often described as conscienceless, but he is in fact capable of holding ethical views so insistently as to appear moralistic (Greenacre, 1945). However, it is other people who are required to meet standards and to observe ethics of which the patient absolves himself. It is therefore more accurate to describe the conscience as defective, extending to others but sparing only the sociopath himself. His own glaring shortcomings he passes over with rationalizations and apparently adequate excuses, appearing himself to consider his misdemeanours as reasonable and justified. The sociopath can thus condone his falling-short of his own severe moral principles, and can maintain without self-criticism his high expectations of others. Sexual deviations are common.

His social relationships are shallow and transient. He is not loyal to individuals or to groups. He has poor judgment of situations, and often lies his way out of complications. He is indifferent to the welfare of others. He requires immediate satisfactions, not being able to postpone gratifications; he seeks instant excitement or relief of discomfort, and may misuse drugs or alcohol so that secondary addictions are common.

Two types of sociopathy are distinguished:

(a) *Aggressive type*

The hostility displayed in attacks on other people, damage to property, thefts, fraud, swindling and deception may bring the sociopath to legal attention. The Mental Health Act (England and Wales) of 1959 makes provision for the transfer of individuals from the courts to hospital, provided two medical practitioners testify, in written or oral evidence, that an offender is suffering from a psychopathic disorder, of a nature and degree which renders him suitable to be detained in a hospital for treatment. The higher courts have power to restrict discharge from hospital, either without limit of time, or during a period specified in the order. In addition to this provision for the compulsory hospitalization of aggressive sociopaths, the Secretary of State can, on the basis of two medical reports, order transfer from prison to hospital of psychopaths meeting the requirements of the Act.

(b) *Passive type*

A person of this type is seriously inadequate and cannot adapt to social requirements; he is chronically inept, passive and dependent. Many are placid and responsive; others are cold, withdrawn and apathetic. They may exist as aimless drifters, to be found in places where hobos congregate. If supported within a family or protective environment such as a half-way house or hostel, such people may survive but are liable to develop drug addiction or alcoholism.

TREATMENT

I. PREVENTION

Proper parental care during childhood is necessary for personality development. If children are separated from their parents, care should be taken to provide adequate substitute parents. Institutions for children, such as orphanages and approved schools, should be humanized by subdivision into small sections, each with a housemother and father, permitting at least some identifications.

Delinquency in childhood and adolescence needs to be treated not merely punitively, but with regard to any social and emotional deprivation the child or youngster may have suffered. Recent research has reassuringly demonstrated the plasticity of the personality; some effects attributed to deprivation and considered irreversible may in fact have been reinforced by continuing adverse social circumstances.

2. NEUROLOGICAL FACTORS

Abnormal behaviour may be an expression of organic brain disorder. The cerebral impairment can have occurred during personality development; cases of personality disturbance consequent upon brain damage are instances of pseudo-psychopathy, as Schneider (1959) has pointed out. The behaviour is not expressive of any meaningful emotional content related to biographical events, but is a misdirected hyperkinetic activity, characterized rather by restlessness which is blind, a state which has been named 'organic drivenness' (Kahn and Cohn, 1943).

The brain disorder may be active when the patient presents, as with epileptic equivalents, or the behaviour change may be due to such damage as frontal lobe syndrome following head injury, or a post-encephalitic state. Necessary neurological examination should be done early in the course of investigation, should be comprehensive, and—if the indications exist—should be carried out definitively, so that an organic approach is not episodically resorted to in a series of after-thoughts which can be most disruptive of rational management.

3. PSYCHOGENIC FACTORS IN MANAGEMENT

Behaviour is a meaningful expression of the person's needs and feelings, and as such requires psychological exploration. When the clinician comes to consider the patient's personality abnormal, he then sets out to explore by clinical analysis the exact nature of the deviation, in terms of the difficulties the patient has with the people important to him.

Such knowledge is gained by talking to the person during the course of serial interviews. The interview will focus at times on 'genetic' events which occurred early during personality formation, and at times on 'dynamic' events which took place later during adult life and which are currently operative as a source of distress. The earlier disturbances during personality maturation and the presently-occurring miscarried relationships can only be explored with the co-operation of the patient.

The clinician's aim is to understand the meaning and the basis of the patient's recurrent interpersonal problems, and to identify with him ways in which to improve his present maladaptive relationships.

The clinician does not set out to supply the patient's unsatisfied needs (e.g. for a home in which to live, for companionship, for 'love', etc.): the patient may insistently expect such reality-based emotional supplies, but can be helped to grasp—in all but gross abnormality—that the clinician's intervention is a technical one, intended to make the patient himself more effective in his close personal and other social interactions.

4. INDIVIDUAL PSYCHOTHERAPY

The aims of dyadic interviewing are of course dependent on the treatment facilities available, the skills of the clinician, the available ego resources of the patient, and the realities of his social situation. Such 'situational variables' as a wretched marriage, a social network of delinquent companions, missed educational and training opportunities, past prison experiences, etc. need to be assessed and recognized for the limitations they impose, and the relative imperviousness to change of the moderately and severely abnormal have to be kept in mind.

The important *principles* of psychotherapy with cases of abnormal personality are:

1. *Flexibility of technique*, the clinician being prepared to space his interviews and interventions, so that they can be infrequent when the patient is adapting satisfactorily, but more regular when he is in more serious difficulty.

2. *Consistency* on the part of the clinician himself, to balance the extremes of distress or unreliability which the patient may experience.

3. *Stress reduction* in the course of each interview, the clinician helping to identify possibly alterable aspects of an apparently hopeless condition.

4. *Demonstration* by the clinician of his progressive understanding of the difficulties that befall the patient.

5. The clinician aims to help the patient to recognize when a *characteristic train of events* is beginning to build up which will lead to a setback.

6. The clinician needs to be *scrupulously honest* with the patient, not receiving information about him from third parties which he then fails to convey back to the patient.

7. *Avoidance of critical attitudes* by the clinician is necessary, but this does not imply sentimental permissiveness: the patient is defective in his reality sense, and often very poor at perceiving environmental cues. The clinician at such times functions as an auxiliary ego for the patient, which calls on him to set out all the facts, including painful ones.

5. SMALL GROUP PSYCHOTHERAPY

Of considerable current interest is the use of closed group psychotherapy to identify a person's problems in his personal relationships, to help him to see them also, and to provide ongoing opportunity for him to experiment socially with new behaviour patterns (Walton, 1971).

6. SOCIAL THERAPY

To treat the more serious personality disorders, inpatient treatment is required in a small inpatient unit providing milieu therapy. Both sexes are treated together, therapeutic community principles being used.

The hospital unit is best sited near a town, and the support of the adjacent community must be gained. Relatives must be involved. Regular staff meetings are required. Group methods are the main component of treatment (Walton, 1971).

These units should not be separate from psychiatric hospitals, for a number of reasons. The scientific study of sociopathy should proceed in the context of general psychiatry, and as already indicated abnormal personality is frequently complicated by psychiatric illness.

7. PRISON PROGRAMMES

Many sociopaths will continue to be managed in prisons and in special institutions for offenders, and the further development of rehabilitative programmes in such settings is an important aspect of forensic psychiatry. The use of parole and hostels, in conjunction with probation services, will replace some present regimes.

8. SOCIAL SERVICES

Abnormal personalities make relatively greater call on welfare and other community services. Social workers are aware that family disorganization, marital breakdown, child neglect or cruelty, repeated unemployment etc., complicate personality disorder. Psychiatrists and their team colleagues such as clinical psychologists and psychiatric nurses cannot abdicate their responsibility, but need to co-operate with social services in providing suitable care.

9. PROGRESS IN CLINICAL RESEARCH

Clearer grasp of the type of disorder will permit planning of more rational and effective programmes of management. Clinicians can with advantage differentiate psychiatric illness from abnormality of personality in all cases. It may also be possible in time to diagnose the latter with more precision.

The diagnostic scheme set out above is a *category* one (Walton and Presly, 1972). The personality of a patient is described by applying one diagnostic label, such as 'hysterical'. This is an approach which is clearly inadequate. It makes very considerable difference whether an hysterical personality is also dependent and passive on the one hand, or is assertive and energetic on the other. Our expectation is that in the future abnormal personality will not be categorized by means of a single diagnostic phrase, but will be conveyed by a profile (Presly and Walton, 1972). When such a dimensional scheme is used, each patient will be classified clinically according to his degree of deviation in a number of areas. Our research in Edinburgh indicates that deviation in each of the following dimensions should be evaluated and specified when providing a personality profile:

1. *Social deviance*: lack of regard for consequences of acts; inability to learn from experience; egocentricity; irresponsibility; impulsiveness; conscience-defect; superficiality in personal relationships; sexual provocativeness.

2. *Passivity*: timidity; meekness; self-punitiveness; indecisiveness; avoidance of competition; dependency; absence of officiousness; submissiveness.

3. *Hysterical*: ingratiation; need for attention; excessive emotional display; insincerity.

4. *Obsessional*: meticulousness; stubbornness; low suggestibility; over-independence; officiousness.

5. *Schizoid*: detachment; suspiciousness; avoidance of close relationships; stubbornness; insensitivity to feelings of others.

A profile of a patient may, for example, indicate peaks in the first, in the second and in the fifth dimensions, and describe him better than would the label 'sociopathic personality disorder, passive type'. A woman who would be labelled 'hysterical' can be described more informatively if a profile is provided which shows definite peaks in the first and second dimensions as well as in the third. Such an approach can be of still further value if a terminology is established which is clearly enough defined to be used reliably by different clinicians. The unreliability of category diagnostic systems at present in clinical use throws considerable doubt on the findings of investigations (Essen-Moller, 1956) purporting to establish the association of certain psychiatric illnesses with particular types of abnormal personality.

It can be argued that abnormal personality presents the major challenge before psychiatry at the present time, and its better understanding and more effective treatment will be of great and general benefit to society.

REFERENCES

American Psychiatric Association (1952) *Diagnostic and Statistical Manual, Mental Disorders*, 1st edn. Washington D.C.

American Psychiatric Association (1968) *Diagnostic and Statistical Manual of Mental Disorders*, 2nd edn. Washington D.C.

Bullard, D. M. (1941) Mood disorders and psychopathic personality. *Psychiatry*, **4,** 231.

Cattell, R. B. (1956) Validation and interpretation of the 16 P.F. *Journal of Clinical Psychology*, **12,** 205.

Cattell, R. B. (1965) Methodological and conceptual advances in the evaluation of heridity and environmental influences and their interaction. In *Methods and Goals in Human Behaviour Genetics*, pp. 95–130. Edited by S. G. Vanderberg. New York: Academic Press.

Erikson, E. (1966) Eight ages of man. *International Journal of Psychiatry*, **2,** 281.

Essen-Moller, E. (1956) Individual traits and morbidity in a Swedish rural population. *Acta psychiatrica et neurologica scandinavica*, Suppl. 100.

Eysenck, H. J. & Eysenck, S. B. G. (1963) *Eysenck Personality Inventory*. London: University of London Press.

Foulds, G. A. (1965) *Personality and Personal Illness*. London: Tavistock.

Freud, S. (1962) Introductory Lectures on Psychoanalysis. Lecture 21, pp. 320–338. Vol. 16 of *The Complete Works of Sigmund Freud*. London: Hogarth Press.

Greenacre, P. (1945) Conscience in the psychopath. *American Journal of Orthopsychiatry*, **15,** 495.

Hare, E. H. & Shaw, G. K. (1965) *Mental Health on a New Housing Estate*. London: Oxford University Press.

Henderson, D. K. (1939) *Psychopathic States*. New York: Norton.

Jahoda, M. (1958) *Current Conceptions of Positive Mental Health*. New York: Basic Books.

Jaspers, K. (1963) *General Psychopathology*. English translation by J. Hoenig and M. W. Hamilton. Manchester.

Kahn, E. & Cohn, L. C. (1943) Organic drivenness. *New England Journal of Medicine*, **210,** 748.

KALLMANN, F. J. (1952) Comparative twin studies on the genetic aspects of male homosexuality. *Journal of Nervous and Mental Diseases*, **115**, 283.

KAVKA, J. (1949) Pinel's conception of the psychopathic States. *Bulletin of the History of Medicine*, **23**, 461.

KRETSCHMER, E. (1936) *Physique and Character*. Second edn, revised London: Miller.

LEWIS, A. J. (1953) Health as a social concept. *British Journal of Sociology*, **4**, 109.

PARKER, N. (1964) Homosexuality in twins: a report on three discordant pairs. *British Journal of Psychiatry*, **110**, 489.

PARTRIDGE, G. E. (1930) Current conceptions of psychopathic personality. *American Journal of Psychiatry*, **10**, 53.

PIAGET, J. & INHELDER, J. (1969) *The Psychology of the Child*. London: Routledge and Kegan Paul.

PRESLY, A. S. & WALTON, H. J. (1972) Dimensions of abnormal personality. In press.

PRICHARD, J. G. (1835) *A Treatise on Insanity and Other Disorders Affecting the Mind*. London: Sherwood, Gilbert and Piper.

RUESCH, J. (1948) The infantile personality: the care problem of psychosomatic medicine. *Psychomatic Medicine*, **10**, 134.

SCHACTER, S. & LATANE, B. (1964) Crime, cognition and the antonomic nervous system. in *Nebraska Symposium on Motivation*. Edited by D. Levine. University of Nebraska Press.

SCHNEIDER, K. (1950) *Die Psychopathischen Personlichkeiten*, 9th edn. Vienna: Translated by M. W. Hamilton, 1958. London: Cassell.

SCHNEIDER, K. (1959) *Clinical Psychopathology*. Translated by M. W. Hamilton. London: Grune and Stratton.

SCHWADE, E. D. & GEIGER, S. G. (1956) Abnormal E. E. G. findings in severe behaviour disorders. *Diseases of the Nervous System*, **17**, 307.

SHEPHERD, M., BROOKE, E. M., COOPER, J. E. & LIN, T. (1968) An experimental approach to psychiatric diagnosis. *Acta psychiatrica et neurologica scandinavica*, Suppl. 201.

SHIELDS, J. (1962) *Monozygotic Twins Brought Up Apart and Brought Up Together. An Investigation into the Genetic and Environmental Causes of Variation in Personality*. London: Oxford University Press.

WALTON, H. J., FOULDS, G. A., LITTMANN, S. K. & PRESLY, A. S. (1970) Abnormal Personality. *British Journal of Psychiatry*, **116**, 497.

WALTON, H. J., Ed. (1971) *Small Group Psychotherapy*. Harmondsworth, Middlesex: Penguin Education.

WALTON, H. J. & PRESLY, A. S. (1972) A category system for diagnosis of abnormal personality. In press.

WHITEHORN, J. C. (1952) Basic psychiatry in medical practice *Journal of the American Medical Association*, **148**, 329.

WOLFF, S. & ACTON, W. P. (1968) Characteristics of parents of disturbed children. *British Journal of Psychiatry*, **114**, 593.

WUNDT, W. (1903) *Grundzuge der Physiologischen Psychologie*, 5th edn, Vol. 3. Leipzig: W. Engelmann.

Chapter III

PSYCHIATRIC ILLNESS IN CHILDHOOD

Sula Wolff

The Scope of Child Psychiatry

Two unique aspects of childhood dominate the practice of child psychiatry. Firstly, children are in varying stages of a developmental process which profoundly affects their physical, intellectual, emotional and social characteristics. Secondly, each child is dependent on adults: his parents, teachers and other people in the community, who have definite obligations towards him for providing care and education.

THE CHILD AS A DEVELOPING ORGANISM

Behaviour in childhood changes remarkably as a result of maturation. The diagnostic process must therefore operate with a variable yardstick adjusted to the child's developmental level. The significance of certain behaviour patterns changes with the age of the child. Sphincter control, for example, is achieved by most children between two and four years so that bed-wetting and soiling constitute deviant behaviour patterns only in older children. Similarly, most children speak their first words at around one year of age and begin to produce intelligible phrases at two. Absence of speech is a more ominous symptom in a three-year-old than in a younger child.

Other changes in behaviour, while not themselves direct manifestations of the developmental process, also and for a variety of reasons reflect the characteristic of individual stages of development. For example, specific fears and phobias occur most often in the animistic stage of cognitive development, between four and seven years of age, and delinquency during the stage of identity formation at adolescence. Developmental factors thus play an important part in determining the symptomatology of psychiatric disorders in childhood. In addition they impose some quite specific characteristics on the psychotherapeutic techniques to be used with children.

In his account of the first psychoanalytic treatment of a childhood phobia, Freud (1909) suggested that children would communicate their thoughts and feelings only to their parents and could best be treated by using the parents as therapists. The invention of play therapy by Melanie Klein (1963) enabled psychiatrists to overcome the constraints in verbal communication imposed on young children by their cognitive and linguistic immaturity. Quite apart from difficulties in communi-

38

cating with young children, Anna Freud (1946) has described other important differences between children and adults in psychotherapy. For the child, the doctor can never be an equal because he is grown up. He can exert control; he must assume responsibility for safety; and, because the child inevitably sees in him a role model, he cannot altogether escape the functions of an educator.

Because childhood is a period of rapid change in many aspects of physique and personality, it is also a time at which environmental influences exert enormous effect. This has given much hope to educators, welfare workers and psychiatrists that improved education, care and psychiatric treatment for children can have permanently beneficial effects in later life. B. S. Bloom (1964) has pointed out that certain human attributes develop most rapidly during specific, time limited periods of the life cycle while others are open to change throughout life. The characteristics whose development is subject to 'sensitive periods' tend, at the end of these periods, to be stable and irreversible. Examples are height and intelligence. Characteristics whose development is open to change throughout life are unstable. Bloom writes: 'Variations in the environment have greatest quantitative effect on a characteristic at its most rapid period of change and least effect on the characteristic during the least rapid periods of change'.

While Bloom presents much evidence from longitudinal studies of child development for the existence of sensitive periods in the development of intelligence, aptitudes and achievement, he stresses that as far as other aspects of personality are concerned, there is much theory but there are few facts. The evidence that exists points to the possibility of change persisting throughout life but diminishing with increasing age.

THE CHILD AS A DEPENDENT BEING

Parents and teachers in fulfilling their child rearing functions are constantly modifying the behaviour of children by setting goals, conveying expectations, encouraging, rewarding, disapproving, punishing, setting limits and especially, and often unselfconsciously, by acting as role models. When a child does not conform to the standards his parents or teachers have set for him, he is likely to be identified by them as deviant.

The identification of behaviour disturbance in children depends very much on the symptom tolerance of parents and teachers, and this is influenced by both cultural and personal factors.

When children suffer from depression, excessive anxiety or other neurotic disorders rather than difficult behaviour, they are dependent on adults to complain to doctors on their behalf. Children do not seek psychiatric referral themselves. Psychiatrists are always responsible to the child's parents as well as to the child himself.

Because of the child's lack of choice in parents and teachers and because of his constant exposure to the same home and school environment, environmental stresses, apart from accidents, death and illness, often spring from personality disorders of the parents and from adverse classroom experiences. Treatment of the child therefore also involves the modification of parental behaviour or of the school setting.

Parents and teachers are not the only adults with responsibilities for children. Deprived children are cared for by parent substitutes and may be the responsibility of community social workers. Delinquent children too are often in the charge of community social workers or of special schools. Child psychiatry is characteristically practised within a network of relationships between the psychiatrist and his team (of social worker and psychologist) and the child's parents, teachers, family doctor, substitute parents and other people who may have statutory obligations towards the child and his family.

THE BOUNDARIES OF THE FIELD

Child psychiatry is concerned with a group of disorders which are also often the concern of other medical and non-medical professionals. It is one of the unique aspects of his work that the child psychiatrist must collaborate with and advise the practitioners of many other disciplines.

It is often a matter of chance, of referral practice and of the known interests of paediatric specialists, whether children with developmental disorders (such as language disorders, enuresis or encopresis) are first seen by *paediatricians* or by psychiatrists. The same applies to children with anxiety states (manifesting for example as abdominal pain or sleep disturbance) and to children with behavioural or intellectual impairments due to cerebral dysfunction. Moreover chronic physical handicap and illness in childhood is often accompanied by reactive emotional disorders (Rutter *et al.*, 1970b). Finally, paediatric hospital practice and the organization of nursing care can have profound influences on the psychiatric sequelae of hospitalization. Prugh *et al.* (1953) for example showed that behaviour disorders most commonly follow a brief period in hospital when this occurs under the age of four, when operative procedures are involved and when the child already has impaired relationships with his family. In older children preparation for admission, free visiting and case assignment for nurses (where each nurse is responsible for the total care of a small number of children) rather than task assignment (where each nurse takes on specific nursing tasks and the children are cared for by a large number of different nurses throughout the day) can do much to prevent the occurrence of psychiatric disturbances both during and after a hospital admission.

The overlap between the areas of concern and practice of child psychiatry and paediatrics is considerable and there is much to support the customary arrangement in which the main base for child psychiatric services is within a children's hospital or paediatric centre.

Child psychiatrists also share much important ground with *general psychiatrists* because of the intimate association between psychiatric disorders in parents and children (Rutter, 1966; Wolff and Acton, 1968).

While the relationship between parental attitudes and child rearing practices on the one hand and childhood behaviour and behaviour disorders on the other is largely a reflection of social class differences in the behaviour and attitudes of parents and children, psychiatric disorders in parents are one of the most important causes of emotional disorders in childhood (Wolff, 1970). Personality disorders of parents, sociopathy in particular, are most strongly implicated, associated as they often are with family disorganization, separation experiences and domestic violence. The treatment of a majority of children with behaviour disorders also involves treatment of their parents. To help them to achieve a better personal adjustment, to improve their marital relationship or to influence their pathological reactions towards their children is often the child's psychiatrist's primary task. Many parents with florid psychiatric disorders are first identified as ill in the setting of a psychiatric service for children.

Psychiatric disorder in childhood, especially at adolescence, often manifests as delinquency. Increasing numbers of children and young persons who break the law are referred for diagnostic assessment and treatment to psychiatrists. Child and adolescent psychiatrists as well as *forensic psychiatrists* share in this work, depending on the age of the young person involved and on the nature of the local psychiatric services available. Delinquent children are also the concern of local authority *social workers* as are children deprived of family care. There is now considerable overlap between social workers in child psychiatry departments and community social workers in their responsibilities for deprived and delinquent children. The working relationships between the child psychiatric and community social work services are changing as a result of recent recommendations and legislation (Report of the committee on Local Authority and Allied Personal and Social Services, 1968; Social Work (Scotland) Act, 1969) and will no doubt become better defined in the near future.

Of great importance also is the borderland between child psychiatry and education. Teachers and local authority *educational psychologists* provide special diagnostic and remedial services for many children who are also psychiatrically disturbed. The incidence of reactive behaviour disorders in intellectually subnormal children and in children with learning disabilities is much higher than in the general population

(Rutter *et al.*, 1970*b*); emotionally disturbed, anxious children tend to do less well at school than well adjusted children of the same intellectual level; and a number of rare constitutional disorders, such as childhood autism and certain forms of brain damage, result both in cognitive and emotional handicaps.

It is the child psychiatrist's task to be available in a consultative capacity to all these different services and also to mobilize and co-ordinate the resources of these services for individual children in his care.

CLASSIFICATION OF PSYCHIATRIC DISORDERS IN CHILDHOOD

In 1967 the World Health Organization set up a seminar to evolve a classification of child psychiatric disorders which would be internationally acceptable and could be used without ambiguity. Rutter had pointed out in 1965 that any classification must be based on observable behaviour rather than inference and that it should if possible have etiological and prognostic relevance.

The classification of the psychoses, of the adult-type psychoneuroses and of the behavioural manifestations of cerebral dysfunction have not presented any insuperable difficulties. The great problem has been the classification of behaviour disorders, that is of those common conditions in childhood which tend to present to psychiatrists when they are severe and persistent.

The classical study by Hewitt and Jenkins (1946), in which a factor analysis was done of the behaviour disorders recorded in the case notes of 500 consecutive child guidance clinic attenders and the emerging clusters of symptoms were correlated with clusters of background factors, promised to provide a solution to the problem of the classification of childhood behaviour disorders. Hewitt and Jenkins isolated three symptom clusters: socialized delinquency (including stealing, gang activities, wandering and truanting); unsocialized aggression (comprising initiatory fighting, cruelty, defiance, inadequate guilt feelings); and over-inhibited behaviour. Children who exemplified each symptom pattern were found also to have characteristic situational patterns: a background of parental neglect and delinquency; of parental rejection; and of either exposure to chronic physical illness or family repression.

The best long-term follow-up of child guidance clinic attenders showed that children presenting initially with neurotic (i.e. over-inhibited) disorders were as well adjusted in adult life as control children not referred to a clinic, while delinquent children in later life had an excess of sociopathy, crime, alcoholism, mental hospital admission, poor work record and social decline (Robins, 1966). Hewitt and Jenkins' work together with Robins' follow-up study suggested that behaviour disorders could be classified satisfactorily into (1) Acting-out or conduct disorders (including both aggressive and delinquent behaviour); (2) Neurotic disorders; and (3) Mixed disorders.

Unfortunately, a replication of Hewitt and Jenkins' study, admittedly on a restricted sample of delinquent boys in a remand home failed to confirm the findings (Field, 1967). Moreover, a cluster analysis of behaviour systematically recorded (that is, not abstracted from clinical records) for 100 children with reactive disorders attending a psychiatric clinic, showed that five symptom clusters occurred: aggressive behaviour; anxiety symptoms; symptoms of depression; delinquency, negatively associated with manifestations of anxiety; and disorders of elimination (Wolff, 1971). Most children had symptoms in more than one cluster. Phenomenologically children's behaviour disorders do not fall neatly into conduct and neurotic disorders, most children having a mixed symptomatology. Nevertheless, Rutter has shown that the presence of delinquent or of aggressive behaviour, whether or not associated with neurotic symptoms is associated with other important factors (Rutter *et al.*, 1970b). Children who are aggressive or delinquent are more likely to be boys, to come from large families, to have a background of family disruption, and to be retarded in reading.

The contribution of the W.H.O. working party was to suggest a classification of psychiatric disorders in childhood along a number of independent axes (Rutter *et al.*, 1969): (1) the clinical psychiatric syndrome; (2) the child's level of intelligence; (3) the presence of organic factors; and (4) psychosocial associated or etiological factors. The fourth axis has so far been the most difficult one to define. This four-axial classification has the merit of including all important and often independently varying diagnostic aspects of a case without forcing the diagnostician into unrealistic categorizations.

The following classification of clinical syndromes is based on but not identical with provisional W.H.O. classification (Rutter *et al.*, 1969).

BEHAVIOUR DISORDERS

Neurotic disorders—consisting of clusters of symptoms among which the following predominate: manifestations of anxiety, specific fears, over-inhibited behaviour, over-dependency, excessive shyness, sleep disturbances, eating disorders, masturbation, tics and other habit disorders.

Conduct disorders—consisting of clusters of symptoms among which the following predominate: stealing, lying, truanting, wandering, aggressive behaviour, restlessness, destructiveness.

Mixed disorders. Many children with predominantly conduct disorders are also anxious; in a number of children stealing occurs as an isolated anti-social symptom in the setting of a neurotic disorder.

Enuresis and encopresis can be associated with any type of behaviour disorder and also occur as an isolated disorder (see below).

SPECIFIC DEVELOPMENTAL DISORDERS

Speech and language disorders—including dyslalia, dysphasia, specific developmental reading and writing difficulties (dyslexia, dysgraphia).

Stammering
other specific learning disorders
abormal clumsiness (developmental dyspraxia)
enuresis as an isolated disorder.
encopresis as an isolated disorder.

Many children with the above symptoms have a family history of similar conditions and no evidence of neurological impairment, while in others these symptoms are associated with definite or suggestive evidence of cerebral dysfunction.

PSYCHONEUROSES

anxiety neurosis
hysteria
obsessive–compulsive neurosis
phobic reaction
depression

PSYCHOSOMATIC DISORDERS

For example: asthma, ulcerative colitis.

PSYCHOSES

early childhood autism (this may or may not be associated with evidence of neurological impairment)
adult-type schizophrenia
manic-depressive psychosis

SPECIFIC BEHAVIOURAL SYNDROMES ASSOCIATED WITH NEUROLOGICAL IMPAIRMENT

hyperkinetic syndrome
other clinical syndromes

PERSONALITY DISORDERS

For example: schizoid, hypersensitive, hysterical, obsessional, or associated with severe, early maternal or social deprivation.

OTHER CLINICAL SYNDROMES

acute confusional state e.g. associated with meningitis or drug intoxication.
dementia associated with chronic, progressive neurological disorders
Anorexia Nervosa
Gilles de la Tourette's syndrome

History Taking and Examination

THE HISTORY

It is often helpful to give older children and adolescents an opportunity to express their view of the problems first and to see the parents
together with their child subsequently. Younger children are best
interviewed after the parents have discussed their difficulties fully in
the child's absence. As with adults, each diagnostic interview is aimed
to help members of the family to present their complaints in their own
way, to get relief from full disclosure of their anxieties and to take the
initiative in recounting their life experiences. At the same time a number
of specific areas of enquiry are covered systematically.

The presenting complaint

What is it about the child's behaviour that really concerns the
parents? When did it begin? Were there known precipitating events?
How do the parents themselves explain the behaviour complained of?
What are the main fears in relation to the sysmptoms?

The child's current behaviour

Enquiry is made into his eating, sleeping and elimination patterns;
his social behaviour in relation to parents, siblings, teachers and other
children; his prevailing mood, his fears and anxieties; his motor
behaviour and his capacity for sustained attention; his habits (e.g.
nail-biting, thumb-sucking, tics and masturbation); his attempts to
satisfy his sexual curiosity and how these were met; anti-social patterns
of conduct (e.g. stealing, lying, truanting, wandering); his educational
performance, and reactions to school (teachers, work and peers); his
out-of-school activities (e.g. club membership).

The family history

Here the aim is to make a personality assessment of each parent on
the basis of known facts about his or her life. This assessment is fundamental to an understanding of the parents' contribution to the child's
disturbance, their reactions to it, and their potential response to
treatment. For example, parents themselves deprived of normal family

life in early childhood may be limited in their capacities to be good parents. They have had no ordinary model of parenthood before them during crucial years of development. Other parents, whose relationships with their parents were conflict-laden and stressful, often continue to re-enact these early conflicts with their own children. The psychiatrist must ask about the age of the parents, their work and health histories, their own childhood family composition and relationships, how they feel about their childhood in retrospect, any particularly traumatic events that occurred in their lives and their marital relationship including their sexual adjustment. The enquiry extends to the other children in the family, their ages, health, personality, school and social adjustment. The family history should also reveal those rare illnesses, handicaps or personality traits among the child's relatives that may be genetically linked to his disorder.

The developmental history of the child

This should illuminate two aspects of the child's personality: his temperamental traits and his rate of intellectual development. Physical illnesses which may have interrupted or impaired this development are recorded here.

A full obstetric history is followed by a description of the child's first year: his personality traits and the management of feeding. Developmental milestones are noted, e.g. the age of first smiling, sitting without support, standing alone, walking unaided, speaking the first clear word, speaking in phrases, acquiring bladder and bowel control by day and night. Parental training methods and attitudes are recorded. A suspicion of general or selective mental retardation prompts a more detailed enquiry into the child's attainment of other social, self-care and scholastic skills (e.g. language skills, eating with utensils, undressing and dressing, play and educational activities).

Social development as a toddler and school child is the next focus of enquiry and includes the child's opportunities and capacities for play with other children, his reactions to nursery experiences and his adaptation to school.

Important events in the child's life

Serious illnesses, accidents, hospital admissions, illnesses of parents, separations from parents, changes in family composition, deaths of important people and pets, moves of house and school should be recorded in chronological order together with the child's and parent's reactions to these events. From this information we learn whether the child has ever been exposed to maternal or social deprivation, or to experiences arousing excessive anxiety. Both are of crucial importance for subsequent personality development and symptom formation.

The parents' treatment expectations

THE EXAMINATION

To be complete this should include a physical, psychological and psychiatric examination of the child and a psychiatric assessment of both parents.

In practice, many children referred to child psychiatrists will already have been examined physically by a paediatrician and children referred by school psychologists will already have been tested psychologically. Little is to be gained by the routine intelligence testing of children but psychologists, both clinical and educational (their functions in relation to children overlap widely), can contribute greatly to diagnosis and treatment when they are called upon to answer specific questions or to undertake specific remedial, educational or therapeutic tasks.

Psychological tests can provide information about the child's general level of intelligence, specific intellectual handicaps, educational attainments and the presence of organic neurological deficits. They can also define various personality traits and, in the case of projective tests, stimulate the child to reveal his feelings and preoccupations.

The psychiatric examination of the child must take place in a setting appropriate to his age and one which allows him to display a wide range of behaviour. In a child psychiatry department the interview room generally contains a sand tray with small toy animals, cars, soldiers, etc.; a sink and running water; a doll's house with family figures; and material for drawing, painting and modelling. The psychiatrist exerts himself to put the child at ease by being friendly, but relatively detached, interested but unintrusive, non-critical and gentle but ready to take over controls if the situation requires this. His only demands of the child are that he reveals his life experiences, his thoughts and feelings as frankly as possible.

The doctor encourages conversation sitting at a table with an older child, at a sand tray with pre-school children. Conflict-free areas are discussed first; topics known to be painful are explored later. Direct questions about such topics are best avoided. When a mother complains that her child steals, the doctor may, for example, broach the subject by saying to the child, 'Your mother is worried because you took some money from her purse. You must have been very worried about that too.' Such statements, which leave the child free to respond or not, are less threatening than questions.

During the interview the child is invited to play and his responses to a number of social demands are noted. He is asked to sit down and draw a picture and, if old enough, to produce a specimen of his handwriting.

Observations are recorded on the following aspects of his appearance and behaviour:

Physical development and appearance, including size, physical maturity, body build, dress and general social appeal.

Motor Behaviour. The child's general level of motility is observed. Is he over-active and restless or unusually restrained and immobile? If over-active, is this because of anxiety or exposure to unaccustomed toys, or is the hypermotility a sign of organic cerebral impairment? Anxiety may manifest as fidgetiness in an otherwise rather immobile child, or as restlessness in relation to particular, emotionally highly charged, topics arising in play or conversation.

Hyperkinesis associated with organic impairment on the other hand is less clearly related to the content of the interview, is associated with poor attention span and distractability, often also with implusiveness, lack of shyness and reserve and an all too bland acceptance of the visit to the psychiatrist.

Posture, gait, balance and skills at stair-climbing and kicking are observed as well as the child's handling of toys and crayons and his ability to take off and put on his outer clothes. An assessment is made of the child's laterality of his manipulative skills and co-ordination in relation to age. Tremors and clumsiness are noted, as are repetitive movements such as tics, or the much rarer stereotyped flapping and gesturing of autism.

Mood is assessed on the basis of the child's expression and behaviour and of what he says about his feelings. Is he a cheerful child or is he unhappy and depressed? If he is sad, is this related to coming to the clinic or is his prevailing mood one of depression? Does he cry when sad topics are discussed or does he control and hold back his unhappy feelings? Is his level of anxiety appropriate to the situation of the interview; is he tense and over-anxious or alternatively bland and unconcerned? Is he a frightened child, timid and shy or is he confident and self-assured? Is he sullen and angry or eager to be helped? Is he outgoing and communicative or inhibited and withdrawn? A sample of conversation in which the child himself describes how he feels is the best evidence for his mood at the time.

Form and level of speech. Articulation defects, speech hesitancies or stammering are recorded and also the child's vocabulary and sentence construction in relation to his age. Repetitions and unusual forms of speech are noted. Examples from what the child actually said should illustrate the descriptions.

The Form and Level of play and the use of drawing and writing materials. These provide indications of the child's level of general abilities, his manipulatory and visuo-motor skills, his confidence in the use of material and his ability to express himself in play.

Concentration, attention span and distractability. Anxiety can interfere with attention and concentration on set tasks. Organic brain damage characteristically results in heightened distractability; more rarely in perseveration and rigid adherence to self-imposed tasks from which the child cannot be diverted.

Over-all intelligence is estimated on the basis of motor and verbal skills, performance with pencils and crayons and the level of play.

Unusual modes of thinking or perception. Unusual phantasies, obsessional thoughts, panic attacks, body pains or other physical sensations are described. Hallucinations are very rare in childhood but can occur in acute toxic confusional states, in hysterical dissociative states and occasionally in psychoses associated with organic brain damage.

The content of the child's inner life, as revealed in his conversation and play. This includes his relationships with members of his family, other children, teachers: his interests and out of school activities; his fears and worries; his dreams; his hopes for the future.

Uncommunicative children can often be helped to reveal something about their inner lives by questions about their dreams, their 'earliest memories' and what they would choose if they had 'three magic wishes'.

The child's capacity to relate to the psychiatrist. This includes the child's difficulty or otherwise in separating from the parent, his attitudes to the doctor and the ease and fluency of his communications verbally and in play.

CLINICAL SYNDROMES, THEIR DIAGNOSIS AND TREATMENT

BEHAVIOUR DISORDERS

Prevalence and Sex incidence

Behaviour disorders are the commonest psychiatric disorders of childhood. Estimates of their prevalence depend in part on the symptom tolerance of observers. Early studies of the recognition of these disorders in school (Wickman, 1928) indicated that teachers fifty years ago evaluated aggressive, acting-out behaviour as of most serious significance and rated as psychiatrically disturbed those children who, on symptom check lists, had high scores for such behaviour. Child guidance clinic workers, in contrast, thought symptoms of anxiety and inhibition to be the most ominous and assigned overall ratings of serious psychiatric disturbance to children with these symptoms. Over the years the views of teachers and psychiatric clinic staff have become more alike. Teachers tend now to be as sensitive to neurotically disturbed children as to children with aggressive and delinquent behaviour while psychiatrists are more concerned about the future outlook for children with conduct disorders.

Nevertheless a recurrent finding of school surveys is that children are either identified as disturbed at school or by their parents at home but rarely, and only in the most severe cases, do they manifest their disturbances in both settings (Rutter et al., 1970b; Mitchell and Shepherd, 1966). The explanation is at least twofold. Firstly, some disorders by their very nature occur only at home (e.g. sleep disorders, jealousy of siblings, nocturnal enuresis) or at school (e.g. truanting, poor concentration on work, unpopularity with peers). Secondly, children are frequently under stress and hence prone to display symptoms in one setting and not in another: behaviour disorders are often situationally determined. For example, a child, happy and accepted within his own family may, if a backward learner, be under great stress at school, suffer loss of self-esteem and resort to day-dreaming, restless over-activity or even to stealing from classmates. On the other hand a depressed and irritable mother may be so roused to anger by her child's minor misdeeds that he responds by constantly testing out the limits of her tolerance, while at school the same child, if reasonably well endowed and given consistent approval and concern, may be perfectly well adjusted. In addition there are of course individual biases both of teachers and parents in their evaluation of children's behaviour. It is not surprising that descriptions of the same child by his teachers and parents often do not tally.

Any estimates of the prevalence of behaviour disorders in populations of school children must be based on information derived both from teachers and parents. This was in fact done in the recent Isle of Wight study (Rutter et al., 1970b) where the estimated prevalence of significant psychiatric disorder among 10- and 11-year-old school children was 6.8 per cent.

Boys are more often disturbed than girls and more frequently attend child guidance clinics (at a ratio of 2 to 2.5:1). In the pre-school age group as many girls as boys are identified as disturbed; during the primary school period behaviourally disturbed boys predominate and this is so also at adolescence if delinquency (very much more common in boys than girls) is included. Moreover boys tend to display aggressive, acting-out behaviour disorders while girls more often have neurotic disorders.

The excess of male children among those with behaviour disorders cannot be accounted for solely by the increased incidence of develop-mental and organic handicaps (reading retardation, for example, or sequelae of brain damage) known to predispose children to develop behaviour disorders. It is thought that socio-cultural factors also play a part. Boys, from an early age, are expected by their mothers and teachers to be more aggressive and assertive than girls and mothers are known to treat their boys differently from their girls even in infancy

(Caudill *et al.*, 1966). Moreover all children in their early years are largely reared by women: by their mothers and by female teachers in primary schools. Girls can use these as role models for social behaviour. Boys must aspire to become different. Their role models are more remote and this may explain why social adjustment is more difficult for them.

It is known that women teachers tend to evaluate both the school performance and behaviour of boys less positively than of girls even in the case of children of similar measured abilities and attainments (Douglas, 1964). Moreover, there is now some evidence that children's attainments and behaviour are significantly influenced by teachers' expectations. Rosenthal and Jacobson (1968) gave psychological tests to a group of culturally deprived school children and then deceived the teachers of a random sample of the children into believing them to be potential 'spurters'. After a year, retesting showed these children to have made significantly more intellectual gains than the rest. Moreover the teachers of children falsely identified as 'spurters' rated these children as emotionally better adjusted, happier, more curious, more interesting, more appealing and more affectionate. The self-fulfilling prophesy may well play a part in increasing the incidence of behaviour disorders among school boys whose female teachers tend to regard them as more difficult than girls.

Psychopathology

It is helpful to view behaviour disorders as persisting patterns of *maladaptive behaviour*. Child rearing practices vary enormously between cultures and sub-cultures and also from one family to the next. The behaviour of children varies too, and, on the whole, children respond to the training pressures and role models they encounter by adapting their behaviour accordingly. In a family where to take food without asking is called stealing, children learn to ask before approaching the biscuit tin. In other families children will help themselves when they are hungry. The behaviour of most children most of the time is adaptive and based on reality testing: on discovering how their parents and teachers are likely to respond to their own actions and modifying these in turn. Behaviour disorders are maladaptive in that they are often based on misperceptions and are not fully within the child's control. When an insecure four-year-old, for example, clings to her mother, refusing to let her leave the nursery class, a socially insecure mother, shamed by this public display of her apparent maternal incompetence, is likely to respond with disapproval. Such a mother will strenuously discourage clinging, pushing the child forward and shaming her by indicating she is no longer a baby. The more the mother pushes, how-ever, the more the child clings. The child's disturbed behaviour makes it difficult for the mother to respond with approval and confident support. Yet without these the child cannot conduct herself better. Her disturbed behaviour, arising from feelings of insecurity, evokes responses from others which make her feel even less secure. To this extent it is maladaptive.

Stealing often occurs in children who for a variety of reasons, such as the loss of a parent, feel themselves to be unworthy and unloved. They try exceptionally hard to present only nice aspects of themselves, for example to their step-parents, repressing—often quite consciously *suppressing*—their aggressive feelings because they fear further rejections. When they steal, they get precisely those responses: punishment and disapproval, which they most dreaded. Their denial of the thefts (the usual reaction of children who steal) despite abundant proof, serves only to mystify and enrage the distressed parents who now view the child as without guilt feelings, a potential delinquent. The more anxious the child and the lower his self-esteem, the more likely he is to steal; the more he steals, the more ostracized he becomes within his family and the greater his anxiety and loss of self-esteem. A mutually reinforcing pattern of behaviour has become established between child and parents which may not resolve without intervention.

Two main sets of environmental factors contribute to the etiology of behaviour disorders in childhood: (1) events arousing experiences of excessive *anxiety* and the coping mechanisms these evoke from the child. and (2) *social deprivations, maternal and cultural*. These can prevent children from acquiring basic social skills, for example, of verbal communication and emotional interaction with others. Such personality deficits constitute definite handicaps and, associated as they tend to be with severe lack of self-esteem, they often result in behaviour disorders.

Anxiety in childhood, as in adult life, can be *primary*, that is related to fears that basic needs will not be met (i.e. that vital supplies of food and nurture, necessary for survival, are threatened) or to fears about his own physical integrity. Separation anxiety and anxiety related to threats of being abandoned or 'sent away', are of this nature, as is castration anxiety. Anxiety can also be associated with *loss of self-esteem and feelings of shame*. This is a very common source of anxiety in childhood, springing, for example, from the child's perception of personal handicaps, physical or intellectual, and of socio-cultural disadvantages of the family or neighbourhood within which he lives, and from excessive dispproval on the part of others of the child's characteristics. Even such an apparently minor handicap as having an odd name can, in school children, contribute to reactive psychiatric disorders. Bagley and Evan-Wong (1970) found that surnames rated as odd were commoner in child guidance clinic attenders than in a control group of school children and also that the case histories of clinic attenders with odd names disclosed fewer other adverse causal factors than the histories of clinic attenders with unremarkable names.

Finally, anxiety, as in adult life, is very commonly associated with *guilt*, the child's impulses being at variance with the dictates of an over-strict conscience.

Children up to the age of seven or eight years are particularly prone to experience irrational anxieties of all three types because of their level of cognitive development (see Chapter IX, Vol. I). During Piaget's stage of pre-operational logic (from two to seven years) children's reasoning is magical, and their deductions are not based on observations. Children during this stage are insensitive to contradictions, believe what they are told unquestioningly, cannot conceive of chance events, tend to see themselves as the cause of whatever happens and behave according to an authoritarian standard of morality. When catastrophies, such as serious accidents and illnesses, or family disruption, happen to a child during this stage he is likely to argue that the event is a punishment for something he himself has done wrong. More common and less hazardous is a fear that activities on his part, which his parents have taught him are wrong, will be followed automatically by some dire consequence. Moreover, during this stage the child cannot differentiate between thoughts and the actions and things thought about. For him words and thoughts are as powerful as deeds and his own bad thoughts and impulses, as a consequence, often induce excessive guilt.

Like adults, children use psychological defence mechanisms to protect themselves against the disorganizing effect of overwhelming anxiety. In contrast to adults, however, *repression* of impulses and feelings in childhood may consist of quite conscious 'forgetting' and should then perhaps more correctly be called '*suppression*'. The commonest defence mechanisms in childhood are *regression*, the child reverting to behaviour characteristic of an earlier developmental level, e.g. bed-wetting, thumb-sucking, baby talk, in response to excessive anxiety; and *denial*, the child falsifying his experience for the sake of mental comfort. The child who steals, for example, denies this to himself and others; the child whose mother has recently died, behaves as if the event had not occurred. All known defence mechanisms can be seen in childhood. As in adults, repressed thoughts and impulses are not lost, but find expression indirectly in the form of symptoms that are now not fully within the individual's control. For example the child who because he was abandoned by his mother has excessive anxieties that he may not be acceptable to his new stepmother, may try to present only good aspects of himself to her. He inhibits all oppositional behaviour and never tests out in reality how she would react if he were ordinarily naughty. His repressed, or suppressed, impulses instead find expression in the form of impulsive stealing, which he cannot control, and his new mother now reacts as he had feared she might all along.

Excessive use of defence mechanisms to ward off anxiety results in inadequate reality testing and the development of symptoms. If severe and prolonged, the use of excessive defensive manoeuvres can also lead to distortions of personality development.

There is much evidence (summarized elsewhere: Chap. XIX, Vol. I) that *deprivation of continuous maternal care* between the ages of six months and two years of life can result in permanent personality deficits. During this period of life, the child's capacity for specific social attachments is greatest and it is at this time that the foundations of language and other social behaviour are acquired through imitation of close and familiar adults. Substitute care, unless it takes the form of continuous mothering has been shown to be much less effective in developing the child's linguistic and social skills. Children seriously deprived of continuous mothering during this sensitive period tend to remain in later life impaired in their capacity to form deep and lasting relationships with others and also in their intellectual development, especially in language. This can result in serious educational handicaps during the school years so that in addition to not having a family of his own, the maternally deprived child has to face the loss of self-esteem that results from educational failure.

Many children, although from united families and normally responsive emotionally, are handicapped at school because they are reared in *culturally deprived* families and neighbourhoods. The patterns of verbal communication are different in these families and the children, especially in large sibships where verbal contact with adults is limited, are retarted linguistically. Even if their overall intellectual potential is good, they tend to be poor readers and to function well below their potential at school.

Moreover, the patterns of child rearing in unskilled working class families differ from those of the middle classes (Sears, *et al.*, 1957; Newson and Newson, 1965 and 1968) and engender behavioural characteristics in children which their teachers often find unacceptable. The culturally deprived child from an unskilled working class background tends to be not only inarticulate, but dependent and lacking in self-reliance; impulsive, i.e. unable to postpone immediate gratifications for the sake of a more distant goal; and aggressive. Such characteristics adapt him well to his family and neighbourhood environment, aggressive and unpredictable as this often is. They serve him poorly at school, where the negative responses of his teachers tend merely to reinforce his sense of shame and his poor self-esteem. Massive defences of denial and projection are then used by the child, and often by his parents too, in the face of the anxieties engendered by his school failure. Aggressive behaviour disorders and delinquency are common consequences in educationally retarded, maternally and culturally deprived children, especially in boys.

On the whole it has not been possible so far to relate specific behaviour disorders to specific etiological factors, except that aggressive behaviour and conduct disorders are commoner in boys, in socially deprived children and in children who are also educationally retarded.

The determinants of symptom choice are multiple. The child's temperament plays a part; the timing of past traumatic events in relation to stages of emotional development at which the child may have been fixated is important; the socio-cultural environment contributes to the child's preferred modes of habitual behaviour; and his present developmental level influences his reactions to current stresses. Sleep disorders and specific fears, for example of the dark, of dogs, etc., are commonest during the genital stage of emotional development which coincides with the animistic stage of cognitive development between about three and seven years of life. In most cases the etiology of the disturbance has to be determined for each child on an individual basis. There are few useful, all-purpose generalizations.

SOME SPECIFIC SYNDROMES

Sleep Disturbances

These are neurotic disorders. They include the persistent *nightly screaming of infants*, the toddler's and young child's *anxious insistence on parental company at night*, the *night terrors and nightmares* of young children and the *sleepwalking* of the older child and adolescent. Children referred to a psychiatric department with major sleep disorders (night terrors, nightmares and sleep walking) were found to differ from a control group of other neurotic children in more often having highly anxious mothers with irrational sexual fears and in having themselves experienced more hospitalization and separation from parents. Symptom choice, however, was found to depend more on developmental and temperamental factors (Anthony, 1959).

Constitutionally sensitive babies wake easily in response to minor stimuli and can cause parents months of broken nights, fatigue and irritability. Anxious mothers, unsure of their own maternal qualities can become disheartened and depressed by what they perceive as their failure to comfort the child. Often they misinterpret their *infant's nightly screaming* as an accusation and react with feelings of hostility towards their child. These induce anxiety in the older infant and a symptom which usually disappears with age may persist, sometimes as a prelude to continued difficulties in the mother–child relationship.

In their second and third years of life children often suffer from separation anxieties when parted from their parents. In the fourth year fears of the dark are very common. Many young children are reluctant to face the night alone fearful, and envious of the company the parents provide for each other from which they are excluded. Their *insistence on parental company at night* can lead to a persistent pattern of maladaptive behaviour when the parents themselves are ambivalent in their sexual relationship. When the mother, for example, fearing another pregnancy seeks to avoid intercourse but is reluctant to face this, the child's nocturnal overtures are met with ambivalence. Unconsciously the mother welcomes the intrusion. She feels guilty however and expresses these feelings by reprimanding the child. Often he is crossly ordered back to his own bed, only to be admitted to the parental bed an hour or so later. Alternatively he may be admitted readily only to be shamed the next day for being a baby. The mother's anger has the effect of increasing the child's anxiety and her invariable surrender to his nocturnal demands reinforces the behaviour disorder.

In a *night terror* the child wakes terrified and screaming in a state of clouded consciousness, often unable to recognize his parents and familiar surroundings. Visual hallucinations are common. He cannot at the time recollect any dream and the following day he has no memory for the events of the night. Night terrors are commonest between four and seven years. *Nightmares*, commonest at between eight and ten years, consist of bad dreams which waken the child with feelings of great fear, but which are fully remembered at the time and often the next morning. When *sleepwalking*, the child, usually aged 11 to 14, calmly rises from his bed in a state of altered consciousness and walks about with no subsequent recollection of any dream content.

Unless reinforced by adverse parental reactions, sleep disorders tend to be outgrown. Sedation and/or tranquillization may work well in cutting short the nightly screaming of irritable infants. Medication is much less effective in counteracting the separation anxieties of older children nor is advice to parents to be more consistent in not yielding to their children's demands particularly successful. A psychotherapeutic approach focussed on the parents' own contribution to the symptom is indicated.

Eating disorders

Food fads, poor appetite in an otherwise healthy child, disobedience at table are not usually causes for psychiatric referral. Occasionally, however, an anxiously over-protective mother may become severely distressed by what she unrealistically perceives as her child's inadequate food intake. Eating may then become the focus of a prolonged and self-perpetuating struggle between mother and child, often on the basis of the mother's latent feelings of rejection towards the child.

Enuresis

Nocturnal enuresis is defined as the involuntary voiding of urine during sleep after the age of three to four years, in the absence of demonstrable organic pathology. It is very common. At the age of three years one child in five is wet more than once a week. The prevalence drops with age, at first rapidly then more slowly until at 14 years it amounts to one in 35. It is commoner in intellectually subnormal children and in boys. It persists longer in children from socio-economically deprived families. There is a strong familial tendency. In a minority of cases *diurnal enuresis* is an associated symptom.

Five per cent of children attending an enuretic clinic were found to have urinary infections (Shaffer *et al.*, 1968), more than would be expected in a normal population. Only microscopy and bacteriological examination of the urine could detect this. The majority of bed-wetters have never learnt to be dry. More rarely, enuresis starts during a time of stress after some years of continence.

Enuresis may be symptomatic of a developmental disorder, of a neurotic behaviour disorder or of a conduct disorder. When it occurs in children with intellectual or other developmental lags, or with a strong family history of enuresis and in the absence of other associated behaviour disorders, in a child who at interview is not found particularly anxious or disturbed, enuresis is best considered as a *developmental disorder*. On the other hand, the symptom itself can act as a stress, especially when parents are intolerant of it, so that even developmental enuresis is often associated with other behaviour disorders. Moreover, any child with a developmental predisposition is more likely to display the symptom if he has in addition been inadequately trained or if he has been exposed to anxiety-inducing life experiences.

For the purposes of classification, if enuresis is associated with other behaviour disorders, the child's disturbance is labelled either a neurotic or a conduct disorder according to the predominant symptomatology. This does not mean that developmental factors are not also involved.

When enuresis is part of a neurotic disorder the history often reveals a period of bladder control which has been interrupted by an anxiety-inducing event such as the arrival of a sibling, an admission to hospital, traumatic separation from a parent or educational failure at school. The symptom may then represent the indirect expression of feelings (such as hostility towards the new baby, frustration and rebellion in an unrewarding school setting, anger at an over-restrictive parent) which are too threatening for the child to show openly. The symptom represents a regression and at times the history reveals earlier traumatic experiences, associated with the stage of toilet training, thus pointing to a possible anal fixation. Usually parents, nurses and teachers recognize such a regression in behaviour as caused by anxiety and take steps to reassure the child. The symptom is then outgrown. When instead it evokes not understanding but hostility and reprimands on the part of others, the stage is set for a more protracted, mutually reinforcing,

c

pattern of maladaptive interaction between the child and his caretakers and the symptom persists.

Bed-wetting is extremely common in emotionally deprived children, especially in institutions. It is also commonly found in association with other *conduct disorders* in children from socially deprived families. How much the child's ability to control his discharge of urine voluntarily depends on consistent training is debatable. All children, including enuretics, know from their third or fourth years onwards what is expected of them in relation to their toilet functions. The difficulty enuretics have is that they cannot voluntarily control their micturition.

Of course, when enuresis is part of a wider disturbance, treatment concerns itself with the whole child and his life situation. On the other hand, the symptom itself often responds to medication and to rid a child, even a severely disturbed child, of an unpleasant and undignified symptom may contribute greatly to his overall improvement by increasing his self-esteem and enabling his parents or teachers to become less rejecting of him.

Imipramine is the drug of choice. It is given in doses of 25 to 50 mg at night. Because high relapse rates after discontinuing the drug are very common (Shaffer *et al.*, 1968), it should be continued, if successful, for many months. If, after two weeks, there is no improvement, it is worth increasing the dose. The effect is empirical and not related to the anti-depressant actions of Imipramine.

Drug treatment is much easier for families to manage than the behaviour therapy approach in which a conditioning apparatus is used which was devised by Mowrer (Lovibond, 1964). The apparatus consists of a urine sensitive pad placed under the child at night. When he urinates, the urine wets the pad and triggers a relay circuit with an electric bell. The noise inhibits urination and wakes the child. The theory is that repeated such experiences lead to avoidance learning. The unconditioned stimulus, the noise of the bell, causing sphincter contraction and relaxation of the detrusor, becomes associated in the child's mind with the increase in bladder tension (which led to voiding and the ringing of the bell). In time increased bladder tension becomes the conditioned stimulus and itself causes sphincter contraction and relaxation of the detrusor, thus leading to continence and avoidance of the noxious stimulus of the bell.

Unfortunately, although an initial improvement in the majority of children takes place after two to three weeks of consistent treatment (many families are worn out long before then!), relapses occur in about 50 per cent of cases and do not then respond as well to a second course of treatment (Lovibond, 1964).

Encopresis

Encopresis is defined as repeated, involuntary evacuation of faeces into the clothes or other receptacles not meant for the purpose, in the absence of physical disease. Often children not only soil but actively refuse to use the pot or toilet. When under excessive pressure from their parents, they may start to hide their soiled pants and deny the symptom.

The characteristics of encopretic children vary according to how they are identified. Bellman (1966) in an epidemiological study of all Stockholm school children aged seven years, found that soiling more than once a month occurred in 2.3 per cent of boys and in 0.7 per cent of girls. Half the soilers had acquired toilet control early in life to relapse later (discontinuous type) often in response to identifiable stresses such as starting school or a separation from parents. The rest had soiled since birth (continuous type). Associated other behaviour disorders were more common than in a control group of continent children. Over a third of soilers were also enuretic. Prolonged constipation occurred in eight per cent and a past history of anal fissure in nine per cent. The soilers were of normal intelligence. Two years later the symptom had cleared up in half the children without any treatment (Bellman, 1966).

In contrast, encopretic children referred to child psychiatrists are more often of the discontinuous than the continuous type and faecal retention with overflow is common. More encopretic children attending a psychiatric clinic have been found of low intelligence, and more have evidence of cerebral dysfunction or other associated developmental symptoms (for example a developmental language lag) than other psychiatric clinic attenders (Olatawura, 1969).

Encopretic children with organic lesions of the rectum, for example an anal fissure, are most likely to be referred to a paediatrician in the first place. Fissure in ano with painful defaecation may lead to voluntary retention in anxious children. Hard faeces accumulate in a rectum which becomes distended and watery stool leaks past this accumulation many times a day. This situation often persists long after the fissure has healed. In every case of encopresis constipation must be excluded, since unless it is treated by means of laxatives, suppositaries or rectal washouts (laxatives being given daily and gradually reduced in dose over many weeks) no hope of improvement exists.

The emotional sequelae of elimination disorders and their treatment in children between two and six years, in whom they are most common, derive from the specific anxieties of the anal and genital stages of development and from the child's animistic modes of thought at this time. The mothers of children with *persisting retention and overflow* are often found to set unrealistically high standards for their young children and it is no coincidence that 'jobbies' and duties' are common names for faeces. Retention with overflow can be acute in onset and very distressing, the child developing a phobia about defaecation, magically wishing his excretary products out of existence. He tends to react to all physical treatment as if it were punishment, a view often reinforced by the distraught mother's exhortations to the child to 'be good' and to 'stop crying' while the doctor examines him or the nurse administers the enema.

In older children, long-standing retention and overflow, perhaps without any past acute episode, is often preceded by a history of constipation since infancy and is in later life associated with a redundant loop of colon which can be demonstrated radiologically. Such a loop is usually regarded as of functional origin but as contributing in turn to the persistence of constipation. In such cases, very long-term regular use of laxatives is indicated.

In child psychiatric clinics most soilers do not have retention with overflow. They pass normally formed motions into their pants. Like enuresis, soiling can be primarily a *development disorder*, or, commonly, part of a *neurotic disorder* or, more rarely, of a *conduct disorder*. Developmental and other etiological factors are often associated. Most encopretic children are anxious children and many come from socially deprived families (Olatawura, 1969).

Treatment is often not immediately successful and the results of different treatment methods have not yet been evaluated. In a follow-up of hospital attenders Bellman found that, whatever the type of encopresis and whatever the treatment, the symptom had disappeared in all patients by the age of twenty and in almost all before sixteen (Bellman, 1966).

Habit disorders

Rocking, head-banging, thumb and finger-sucking and masturbation have been regularly observed in babies and young children and also in mentally retarded older children in institutions under conditions of sensory monotony. Blind children too sometimes engage in 'blindism', that is, rocking and repetitive, stereotyped finger movements (resembling the movements of autistic children) apparently in an attempt to relieve sensory monotony. Self-stimulation occurs in normal children when they are bored.

Rocking and *head-banging* are particularly common in normal children under three, occurring especially when the child is in his cot waiting to fall asleep. The symptoms can be very anxiety-inducing for parents; their etiology is ill understood; there is no specific treatment. The symptoms are quite common too in older retarded and autistic children.

Nail-biting and *nose-picking* are common tension habits which rarely cause much alarm to parents. *Thumb-sucking* too, tends to be accepted unless it acquires the characteristics of an obsessional symptom.

Masturbation, especially when engaged in often and openly or in public (for example, at school) can cause much concern to parents and teachers. It constitutes a neurotic disorder and a contributory factor is often the mother's or father's own anxiety in relation to sexual matters, deriving from their own early childhood experiences, and leading them to punish their child excessively for what at first were normal manifestations of sexual curiosity and exploration. Parental punishment tends to have precisely the reverse effect of what was intended, especially if it is accompanied by excessive interest on the part of the parent in the child's developing sexuality. The more guilty and anxious the child, the greater his need for self-gratifying, tension-reducing behaviour; the more he indulges his habit, the more the parents remonstrate and the greater his anxiety. What is usually a temporary and very common behaviour pattern of early childhood has become a neurotic symptom.

In persistent cases, especially when the symptom is confined to school or when psychological treatment has already helped child and parents towards greater tolerance of the child's sexual curiosity and interests, a behaviour therapy approach may succeed (Wagner, 1968).

Over-inhibited Behaviour and other Neurotic Disorders

It is important to distinguish children with neurotic inhibition from constitutionally shy and sensitive children and from children with schizoid personality disorders (p. 13). Constitutionally shy and sensitive children are emotionally responsive but uncomfortable with strangers in large groups especially in a novel situation. A close relative often has similar personality traits. The neurotically inhibited child, in contrast, is prevented by anxiety from making easy contact with others even with familiar people. The history reveals life stresses to which the child has reacted with repression of aggressive impulses becoming instead shy, withdrawn, tearful and at times depressed. The treatment approach is psychotherapeutic. When depression is a marked feature, the disorder may respond to anti-depressants either of the M.A.O.I. or the tricyclic group, in addition to other measures.

Aggressive Behaviour

Disobedience, temper tantrums, destructiveness, excessive fighting and *firesetting,* are common reasons for psychiatric referral in childhood. These symptoms occur more often in boys than in girls and indicate that something has gone wrong with the socializing process. Often parents themselves present a model of aggressive behaviour which the child adopts under stress. When the father is an excessive weekend drinker, for example, the child, witnessing repeated acts of violence between the parents, has to cope with recurrent and overwhelming feelings of anxiety. Under the age of seven or eight he tends to see himself as somehow responsible and he is likely to test out his own badness by behaving aggressively. When this happens, parents often react with excessive punitiveness because they see a part of themselves of which they are ashamed emerging in their child. This increases the child's anxiety and provokes him to further outbursts. Parents who are both hostile and repressive often have children who inhibit their aggressive impulses at home, project feelings aroused by parents and siblings on to teachers and peers, and act out aggressively at school.

Mothers themselves deprived of parental care and forced into too early an assumption of responsibility, often treat their children as much older than in fact they are. Such mothers expect impulse control from toddlers, not realizing that children under the age of three or four still require physical intervention and protective control from parents, rather than exhortations and explanations, to stop them from engaging in outrageous behaviour which, were it to occur, would frighten the child himself. Instead of exerting control on behalf of their children such mothers punish with increased severity when their children fail, as they cannot help doing at this early stage, to internalize their standards. The normal aggressiveness and impulsiveness of two to four-year-olds can rouse some mothers to a degree of violent anger that they fear they may seriously harm their children. Their anger and lack of protective care for the child arouses his anxiety and this often stimulates him to test out his mother with repeated acting-out behaviour. Her actual responses are never as bad as his fears of what she might do, so that when he has been punished he experiences temporary relief to be followed once more by mounting anxiety and repeated aggressive behaviour on his part.

Truanting and Wandering

This may occur in delinquent children but in older children these symptoms can also be manifestations of depression. The depressed child, characteristically, is a solitary wanderer, feels miserable as he walks about, sleeping rough and often not caring what happens to him. Adolescent girls may take inadequate care of themselves, having intercourse with chance acquaintances; boys may steal or engage in housebreaking.

The symptom of wandering occurs most often in emotionally deprived children and in children who feel rejected. Truanting is frequently directly related to school failure. Both symptoms require a careful assessment of the child and of his home and school environment. If they are not symptoms of an underlying depressive illness, they often respond to improvements in the child's life situation, such as moving him to a small remedial group at school where he can get not only more help with his work but more individual recognition and opportunities to display his assets rather than his shortcomings.

Stealing

Stealing is the commonest conduct disorder. It occurs in about five per cent of primary school children and, if it persists, it is generally regarded by both parents and teachers as of serious significance. Often the child is viewed as a potential criminal.

Stealing can be an expression of neurotic conflict in anxious children. Johnson and Szurek (1952) proposed a theory that stealing and other symptoms of delinquency, in otherwise well socialized children, may be an expression of the parent's own unconscious impulses. Parents themselves were often found to have suggested the behaviour by, for example, warning their child repeatedly to be honest or their adolescent daughter not to 'get into trouble' with boy friends. Such parents get vicarious satisfactions from their children's exploits which, to satisfy their own conscience, they then proceed to punish excessively. Johnson and Szurek suggested that by their inconsistent behaviour such parents transmit their own 'super-ego lacunae' to their children.

At the other end of the etiological spectrum are children whose persistent stealing is not an outcome of neurotic conflict and anxiety but a manifestation of serious personality disorder, the result of early maternal deprivation. Among 44 juvenile thieves studied by Bowlby some 25 years ago, were 14 'affectionless characters'. There were none among a control group of other child guidance clinic attenders. Seventeen of the thieves, among them 12 with 'affectionless characters', had suffered complete and prolonged separation from their mothers in their first five years of life compared with only two among the controls (Bowlby, 1946).

More common then either neurotic or affectionless thieves are children whose stealing is part of a more general conduct disorder and who, while not particularly dull, are under-achieving at school and live in urban deteriorating areas. It is sometimes argued that such children are not disturbed but merely identify with the standards prevailing in the culture in which they grow up. Yet only a minority of children, even in areas with high delinquency rates, are themselves delinquent and most delinquent children claim a moral code almost stricter than that of the adults who sit in judgement on them. The difficulty of delinquent children is not ignorance of what is right and wrong but failure to incorporate the accepted standards of society because of their parents' inconsistent child rearing methods.

Treatment of children with aggressive or conduct disorders, just as the treatment of children with other behaviour disorders, is determined less by the symptoms themselves than by the child's personality characteristics, his life experiences and his family and school environment.

When the child's symptoms are due to a recent stress, e.g. physical or psychiatric illness of a parent, unemployment, bereavement or

mounting debts threatening the disruption of a previously well functioning family, treatment aimed to help the family in this period of crisis
will also help the child, especially if the school staff can be mobilized
to offer special understanding and support to the child. In other cases,
the pressures on the child are of long standing and intimately related to
serious personality disorder in one or both parents or to educational
retardation. Some such parents respond well to prolonged psychiatric
and/or social work treatment. Meanwhile the child can benefit from
psychotherapy designed to provide him with an uncritical relationship
and with an alternative adult role model. When parental personality
disorders are so severe that no change is possible and when the result
is recurrent family disruptions and violence, the child needs a compensa-
tory environment as a supplement to or substitute for his own home: a
small day school for maladjusted children for example, in which he can
make a close and relatively enduring relationship with his teacher or a
residential school from which he returns home only in the holidays.
Remedial teaching and the restoration of the child's self-esteem in
the school setting, are important components of treatment.

It needs to be stressed that not all children with conduct disorders
are socially deprived. When the symptom is part of a neurotic disorder
it should respond to a psychotherapeutic approach.

SPECIFIC DEVELOPMENTAL DISORDERS

A relative lag in the developmental rate of one specific function is
the basis for a number of disorders of learning and behaviour. Specific
developmental language disorders (e.g. dyslalia, dysphasia, dyslexia)
are the commonest to come to psychiatric attention. The basis for
specific developmental disorders may be genetic, with a family history
of a similar or associated disability in a high proportion of affected
children. Alternatively they can be the expression of 'minimal cerebral
dysfunction' with other evidence of paranatal or early childhood
neurological damage and often with associated other symptoms
indicative of neurological impairment such as epilepsy, hyperkinesis or
mental retardation. Often the frustrations and loss of self-esteem
imposed on a child by the handicap, especially if its constitutional basis
is unrecognized, result in secondary behaviour disorders which blur
the clinical picture.

Specific language disorders

Ingram found that all developmental language disorders (developmental dysphasia, dyslexia and dysgraphia) may be associated in
individuals or families (Ingram, 1959). A simple delay in the acquisition
of speech, compared with a child's general social and motor development, is very common. Usually there is also an undue persistence of
infantile pronunciation especially of consonants (dyslalia) but in most

of these mild cases verbal comprehension is unimpaired. In later life there may be difficulties in reading or writing and intelligence testing may show a relative depression of the verbal as compared with other intelligence test scores. Most severe disorders take the form of serious reading and/or writing difficulties so that affected children require special allowances to be made for them and also special remedial teaching. Sometimes reading and writing skills remain impaired throughout life even in highly intelligent people. In other cases such skills are acquired towards the end of or even after the school years. Even more serious are those rare language delays affecting comprehension of the spoken word. Unlike other language disorders which predominate in boys severe dysphasia affecting receptive and expressive language occurs in boys and girls equally. It is also the only developmental language disorder frequently found to be associated with partial deafness, occasionally with schizoid personality traits and, very rarely indeed, with early childhood autism. The diagnostic problems presented by 'non-communicating children' are often formidable and their educational needs are as yet inadequately catered for (Mittler, 1970).

Stuttering

Abnormalities of the rhythm of speech with repetitions and hesitations at the beginning of words or syllables is common as a transient phenomenon between two and four years. Established stuttering however, in more severe cases accompanied by associated movements of respiratory muscles, shoulders and face, increases in frequency during the primary school years (McCulloch and Fawcett, 1964) and then declines. Four per cent of children have an episode of stuttering at some time in their lives, a quarter being transient stutterers between two and four years. Often there is a positive family history (Andrews and Harris, 1964).

Two types of stutterers are recognized: Firstly, children in whom the speech defect is associated with dullness, a poor social background and often a history of birth trauma: Secondly, children of average or superior intelligence from socially striving families with perfectionistic and over-anxious mothers. Johnson (1959) has advanced the theory that in this group of children, over-anxious mothers have reinforced what might have been a transient early childhood stutter by repeatedly drawing the child's attention to his difficulty and thereby impeding verbal fluency further.

While stuttering itself is not a sign of psychiatric disturbance, it is increased by anxiety and itself results in tension, shame and loss of self-esteem so that secondary, neurotic behaviour disorders may require treatment in their own right.

Stuttering is generally outgrown. In more severe and persisting cases speech therapists can help to teach the child means of overcoming the hesitancies (e.g. by giving equal weight to each syllable of a sentence) and by increasing his self-esteem.

Clumsiness and specific visuo-motor difficulties affecting for example a young child's level of self care, his skill at ball games, his writing skills, and even mental arithmetic, are other specific developmental disorders, whose presence is confirmed by neurological and psychological examinations.

Enuresis and encopresis, especially when monosymptomatic and when there is a positive family history or other evidence of cerebral dysfunction, and in the absence of identifiable life stresses, form a further group of developmental disorders.

PSYCHONEUROSES

Psychoneurotic illnesses begin to occur from the genital stage of emotional development (3 to 5 years) onwards. The forms of the illness are the same as in later life.

Obsessional psychoneurosis is quite rare. It can easily be missed because children under seven or eight years can usually not conceptualize and verbalize their experiences adequately. They cannot yet distinguish a thought from the object or action thought about. Obsessional thoughts and impulses are not regarded as ego-alien but as a bad part of the child himself and this experience for young children is totally bewildering and very distressing. The parents' complaint may be that the child is miserable, cries for no apparent reason and has become withdrawn. Children often reveal their preoccupations only in the consulting room, being so identified with their obsessions that they find it necessary to conceal the symptom just as delinquent children generally conceal their stealing.

There are as yet no studies of the natural history of obsessional neurosis in childhood. There are only follow-up studies of adult obsessionals whose symptoms may have begun in childhood.

Hysterical psychoneurosis. Conversion hysteria, such as hysterical disorders of gait or vision are quite rare in childhood and so are hysterical dissociative states. Older children are more often affected and the psychopathology and treatment are similar to those of the illness in adult life.

Anxiety states are common in childhood but they are often classified by child psychiatrists as 'neurotic behaviour disorders'. The common symptoms are feelings of anxiety, sleep disorders, specific fears (of the dark, of dogs, of thunderstorms), fidgetiness, restlessness, inability to concentrate, loss of appetite, shyness, social withdrawal, abdominal pain, vomiting and headaches.

An eight year old child, Susan, always resented the fact that she and her younger sister were treated as twins. They shared the same push chair and were dressed alike. She never felt she could protest because her sister was as tall as she, cleverer and preferred by the parents. In later childhood Susan's playmate was a boy cousin of exactly her own age, and once again they were looked upon as twins. This boy, of whom she was very fond, died of leukaemia. Shortly after his death Susan developed nightly attacks of panic, with palpitations, breathlessness and choking feelings, and the fear that 'a man' might enter her room and attack her sister and herself. She could be pacified only if her parents stayed by her side.

Her cousin's death revived in Susan death wishes towards her sister which were too frightening for her to face, associated as they were with fears of retribution. Her anxiety neurosis expressed her fear that something could happen to her sister as well as to herself and also, at last, permitted her to demand the comfort and affection from the parents that she craved. Susan's hostility to her sister became clear when she told of her greatest wish: an alsation dog, and went on to say how very frightened her sister had become of dogs ever since she sustained a severe dog bite. Although her symptoms helped her to function with only episodic distress, they were maladaptive because, as they persisted, the sleepless parents became not more loving, but ever more hostile to Susan.

Phobic states

The commonest childhood phobia is *school phobia*, also called *school refusal*. The child is reluctant to leave home for school in the morning in contrast to the truant who leaves home but does not arrive at school. Children with school refusal tend to be 'model' children, to have other neurotic symptoms (e.g. shyness, fears, physical symptoms, such as abdominal pain and vomiting), and to do well at school. They want to go to school but are prevented by irrational feelings of panic. The child is afraid to leave his mother in case some harm befalls her; often what he fears most is the potentially damaging effect on her of his own hostile impulses.

In many cases parents collude with their children's symptoms, reinforcing their separation anxiety by over-protective or even frankly hostile behaviour. Mothers of school refusers tend to be socially competent, over-protective women, often subject to depressive illnesses (Hersov, 1961 *a* and *b*).

A few affected children, usually boys, are dull or relatively immature, threatened by the prospect of having to cope with school failure in the face of older boys and male teachers. For such children temporary educational help and support in a smaller class with a graduated return into the larger school community may be all that is needed.

In other cases treatment requires a psychotherapeutic approach to the child and his parents plus an insistence that the requirements of society, that all children must go to school, will eventually be met. It is important, even in mild cases, to acknowledge the child's real anxieties and to help the parents towards a firm, non-hostile and optimistic approach to their child's difficulties. Young children may need to be taken to school by their parents and to be reassured that they will manage to get back to school, if not today then tomorrow. School teachers will need help in acknowledging the school refusal as an illness, in welcoming the child when he gets to school and in not reacting with hostility if his efforts fail.

In more severe cases, especially in older children and in children with psychiatrically disturbed parents who cannot react optimally to the school phobia, inpatient treatment is necessary. Some children need to be physically separated from their parents in order to disrupt their mutually reinforcing interactions. A minority of children with school phobia are resistant to treatment and require education in a residential school.

When school phobia occurs in the setting of a depressive illness or when there are anxiety symptoms over and above those related to the phobic situation itself, anti-depressants should be given since the result may be dramatic. Manifestly depressed children often respond to tricyclic anti-depressants, such as Imipramine or Trimipramine, predominantly anxious children to mono-amine oxidase inhibitors such as Phenelzine.

Depressive illness

The phenomenology of depressive illness in childhood is as yet imperfectly known. The observation has been made (Frommer, 1968) that a proportion of children with behaviour disorders respond to anti-depressant drugs. No study has yet shown how the symptoms of children who respond to anti-depressants differ from children who do not respond. In my own clinical practice anti-depressants have been very helpful to some school phobic children (see above), to children with unexplained irritability and physical complaints, and to solitary delinquents, especially when the presenting symptoms, the phobia, the aggressive behaviour, the solitary truanting, wandering or stealing, were accompanied by a change of mood, deterioration in peer relationships, sleep disturbances and no past history of behaviour disorders.

Manic-depressive illness in childhood hardly ever occurs before puberty (Anthony and Scott, 1960). The illness in childhood is but a very early manifestation of the adult affective illness.

PSYCHOSOMATIC DISORDERS

These are organic illnesses in whose etiology and course psychological factors play a more important role than they do in other physical diseases. Examples are asthma, the commonest psychosomatic illness in childhood, eczema, ulcerative colitis and peptic ulcer. These disorders are chronic and both recovery and relapse are often associated with emotional changes. However, clear-cut causal relationships between behaviour and disease have not been demonstrated and attempts to discover specific personality attributes or a particular psychopathology in affected patients have failed. Moreover, by no means all such patients have demonstrable psychological disorders. Asthmatic children in the community display only a small excess of behaviour disorders (Graham *et al.*, 1967).

One of the difficulties is to determine whether the emotional disturbances found in psychosomatic patients are primary or secondary to the physical illness.

Asthmatic children for example, are often in conflict over dependency needs. Their strivings for independence from parents are associated with great anxiety and this triggers off an asthmatic attack. Each attack enforces further dependency. While this provides the child with satisfaction derived from his ability to control the parent through illness, it also enforces further submission to adult control of his strivings for independence which then seem to be even more dangerous. A helpful etiological theory (French and Alexander, 1941) is that the emotional conflict over dependency becomes associated with the asthmatic attack because for physiological reasons bronchospasm is particularly common in the second and third years of life, precisely at the time when children begin to cope with the conflict between strivings for autonomy and separation anxiety. In some children if the experience of the conflict is repeatedly associated with asthma it becomes a conditional stimulus for an attack and can in future precipitate attacks in the absence of the physical causes originally responsible.

The need for psychiatric treatment depends not on the severity of the physical illness but on the psychiatric pathology, that is, the child's associated psychiatric symptoms and the adverse life circumstances to which he has been exposed. These are the focus of psychiatric treatment, the aim being to improve the child's life adjustment rather than to rid him of his psychosomatic illness. Such an indirect approach often helps to improve the physical condition too.

CHILDHOOD PSYCHOSES

Early Childhood Autism

The commonest psychosis in childhood is early childhood autism, first described by Kanner as 'early infantile autism' in 1943. The main symptoms he listed were 'an extreme autistic aloneness', an 'inability to relate themselves in the ordinary way to people and to situations', and 'an anxiously obsessive desire for the maintenance of sameness', limiting the variety of spontaneous activity and leading to attacks of rage or panic when external conditions were changed. Kanner also mentioned the children's failure to use language for the purpose of communication, some children having no speech at all, others using language abnormally. In addition he described the fascination for objects autistic children display, their high level of fine motor skills and their good cognitive potentialities at least in some areas of functioning which distinguish them from mentally defective children.

British psychiatrists tend to use the label 'early childhood autism' to include brain-damaged and also defective children provided they display certain crucial behavioural patterns.

These are firstly autism, that is impaired emotional contact with people. The most striking sign of this is gaze-avoidance, the child refusing to look other people normally in the eyes. Secondly, impaired language development, the child either losing what speech he had or never developing language at all, or alternatively speaking abnormally. The chief characteristic of the autistic child's speech is repetition of what he hears (echolalia) either immediate or delayed. The effect is of parroting with pronominal reversals, the child referring to himself as 'you' and to others as 'I'. One little boy for instance when he wanted an ice-cream would invariably say to his mother, 'You want some ice-cream, Thomas? Yes, you may'.

In addition to these two cardinal symptoms there is often much aimless, repetitive motor activity with pirouetting, jumping, flapping of hands, fine finger movements, manipulation, mouthing and staring at objects. There are obsessional patterns, the child insisting on certain rituals, for example on the way his food is served to him, or on certain objects: a favourite length of string or garment or food, refusing to accept alternatives. There may be panic and screaming attacks when obsessional patterns are interfered with, sometimes for no discernible reasons. There is selective attention to sensory stimuli, the child at one moment appearing insensitive to noise or pain, at another over-reacting to the same stimulus. There are usually some areas of intellectual functioning, often in the perception and matching of shapes, in which the child performs better than in others. Onset is either insidious from birth or follows a period of one or two years' normal development. Very rarely the illness begins after the third year of life.

The condition varies greatly in severity, some children being incapable of any social adaptation and spending their lives mute, engaged in a few patterns of aimless, repetitive activity. In others the illness is so mild that in later life the child is somewhat odd and eccentric but functioning well at school and at home.

Childhood, commoner in boys than girls, autism occurs in between 2 and 4 of 10,000 school children, being as common in Britain as blindness

(Lotter, 1966). Its etiology, when not associated with identifiable brain damage, is unknown. Because a number of parents of autistic children are themselves aloof and obsessional, it was at one time thought that autism was caused by insufficient maternal warmth and stimulation in infancy. However, children brought up in depriving institutions do not become autistic and it is extremely rare for parents to have more than one autistic child. Kanner states categorically that the condition is constitutionally determined, not 'man-made'. Nevertheless, the tendency for parents of autistic children to have schizoid personality traits has been noticed repeatedly and it is possible that a genetic factor is involved. At present there is no definite evidence for this. Certainly there is no genetic link between childhood autism and adult schizophrenia.

The prognosis is poor. Rutter (see Wing, 1966) found that only 14 per cent of children have a satisfactory school and social adjustment in adolescence. In 27 per cent recovery is 'fair'; but about 60 per cent have a poor outcome and often need long-term hospital care. The best indices of outcome are the presence of useful speech at 5 years (in which case half the children do well) and the level of tested I.Q. when the child is first seen.

No particular treatment approach has so far been proved to affect long-term outcome. Educationally, autistic children do best when they are given very active and consistent teaching, much of it in a one-to-one situation between teacher and child. In classes for the mentally handicapped the autistic child often wanders about aimless and uninvolved. He needs an adult to engage him actively in learning, always building on his particular interests and aptitudes.

Tranquillizers have a part to play in controlling attacks of panic, sleep disorders and ritualistic behaviour when these interfere with social adaptation.

In recent years consistent positive reinforcement of desirable behaviour has been used in special schools for autistic children and, via the parents, in socializing the children at home. Some success has also been achieved by these methods in increasing the child's spoken language.

Parents of autistic children, like parents of children with other types of handicaps, require long-term support in understanding and caring for their child and in coming to terms with his condition.

Adult-type Schizophrenia (Kolvin *et al.*, 1971) and, even more rarely *Manic-depressive psychosis* (see Chap. IX, Vol. II) can start at around puberty and occur very rarely indeed in younger children. The clinical picture, etiology and outcome resemble those of the adult psychoses.

PSYCHIATRIC SYNDROMES ASSOCIATED WITH NEUROLOGICAL IMPAIRMENT

An association between brain damage and childhood behaviour disorders has been found repeatedly. Pasamanick *et al.* (1956) found an excess of complications of pregnancy and delivery when he compared large numbers of child guidance clinic attenders with non-referred school children. He postulated a 'continuum of obstetric casualty' whereby paranatal injury could end in the death of the child, severe physical or mental handicap, or minor behaviour disorders.

In other studies, in which 'special risk' groups of children were examined, affected children had more behaviour disorders than controls. Drillien (1964), for example, showed premature babies, especially those weighing less than 1500 kg, to have a significantly higher incidence not only of physical and intellectual handicap in later life, but also of behaviour disorders as identified by teachers at school. The difference persisted even when social class factors were held constant. Rutter et al. (1970a) showed that among school children with neurological disease above the brain stem, five times as many were psychiatrically disturbed as among healthy controls.

Two arguments have been advanced. One is that minimal organic brain damage affects many children, especially those in poor socio-economic circumstances, and is a frequent if non-specific cause for later behaviour disorders (Stott, 1966). This postulate is almost certainly erroneous. In a recent study (Wolff, 1967) in which a hundred children attending a psychiatric clinic were compared with a hundred children in the community, no difference at all was found in the incidence of obstetric complications in the two groups when the three cases diagnosed as having a brain damage syndrome had been excluded from the clinic group. It is not surprising that, when special risk groups of children are examined, relationships between specific hazards and subsequent behaviour disturbances are found which disappear when they are looked for in a more general childhood population. This merely means that the hazardous events are rare and cannot account for the majority of behaviour disorders found in children.

The second argument concerns the specificity of the relationship between brain damage and behaviour. It is certainly a fact that the size and site of a known lesion do not determine the type and degree of behavioural difficulty. Some children with severe cerebral palsy have no psychiatric disorder; others with marked psychiatric impairments have only minimal signs of organic cerebral damage. What is less clearly established is whether brain damage is associated with any specific behavioural syndromes. In older children these are undoubtedly often masked by the development of secondary, reactive, behaviour disorders. Stealing, enuresis and soiling for example may occur in brain-damaged children, especially if their condition is not recognized and they are held responsible for their educational and social failures. Adverse parental responses and excessive pressures at school can impose intolerable stresses on a child.

The Hyperkinetic Syndrome

The main features are motor restlessness, impulsiveness and distractability which are noticed by parents usually at around three or four years of age when normal children begin to acquire impulse control. Affected children are abnormally responsive to all incoming stimuli which interfere with attention and goal-directed activity (Werry, 1968). Learning is severely impaired and this affects both school work and the acquisition of social skills and standards.

Other syndromes associated with cerebral dysfunction

Disturbance of attention and concentration can occur without marked over-activity. In such cases parents are usually most troubled by their child's failure of social learning. He has no sense of danger, wandering out of the house, climbing fearlessly, heedless of repeated parental warnings. He remains inaccessible to reason, unaware of the consequences of his action.

Many neurologically impaired children have general or specific intellectual difficulties with or without the disturbances of mobility, attention and concentration described above. Many brain-damaged children are also mentally handicapped; others of normal general intelligence are found on psychological testing to have specific disabilities giving rise to discrepancies between verbal and performance scores. These most commonly affect visuo-motor skills, the child having a depressed score on performance tests. Often there is a history of motor clumsiness substantiated by neurological examination. Occasionally specific language impairments are found and a history of relative delay in speech development supports the psychological test results.

Some brain-damaged children, especially when older, display not hyperkinesis but lethargy and sluggishness; a few are markedly rigid in their behaviour, unable to shift their mental set, with perseveration and even obsessional symptoms.

Occasionally autism is seen in children in the presence of a history of birth injury, early meningitis or other cerebral disease, an abnormal E.E.G. and/or neurological evidence of brain dysfunction.

Treatment

It is a fallacy to regard constitutionally determined behaviour disorders as necessarily having a worse prognosis than reactive disorders. If the child can be protected from adverse responses to his handicap, the natural history of the hyperkinetic syndrome is towards improvement with age. The same holds for the selective intellectual impairments found in brain-damaged children.

When teachers, parents and the child himself are made aware of his inherent handicap, his self-esteem is preserved and his motivation and co-operation in remedial education are increased. Moreover the school setting can be modified to suit his needs: a small classroom with a minimum of distracting stimuli.

Drugs are extremely helpful in controlling hyperkinesis and improving attention. Amphetamine and Amphetamine-like drugs such as Ritalin have a paradoxial effect and are useful when given in adequate doses (Sykes *et al.*, 1971). Chlorpromazine is generally effective if Ritalin fails. In the presence of epilepsy it may be necessary to combine Largactil with an anti-convulsant, or to use Diazepan or Haloperidol instead. Phenobarbitone has no place in the treatment of behaviour disorders of any kind. In brain damaged children in partic- ular, it may have a paradoxical effect, resulting in increased irrit- ability, lack of control, occasionally severe depression. This drug is indicated in children only for the treatment of epilepsy.

In children with behavioural or educational impairments, the cerebral insult usually took place in intra-uterine life, at birth or in the first two years of life. All psychiatrists need to be alert, however, to the fact that very rarely progressive, neurological disease (a tumour, for example, a lipoidosis or demyelinating disease) can present in childhood as an unexplained deterioration of behaviour or school performance.

PERSONALITY DISORDERS

Many children display characteristics of adult personality disorders, e.g. the passive compliance of the dependent personality; the theatrical shallowness of the hysterical personality; the punctuality, pedantry and parsimony of the obsessional personality; the aggressive impulsiveness of aggressive sociopathy. Clinicians hesitate however to use these diagnostic labels in childhood because they imply the presence of enduring abnormalities when in fact children have immense capacities for change.

Schizoid Personality

One type of personality deviance is, even in children, characterized by specific and enduring abnormalities and is frequently associated with adjustment difficulties. This is the schizoid personality. Affected children, usually boys, are sometimes labelled 'atypical' or 'borderline psychotic' because they resemble psychotic children without having the classical symptoms of psychosis (Weil, 1953).

Schizoid children generally come to medical attention during their school years because of educational failure and poor social relationships with other children and teachers. They are withdrawn, aloof, solitary, unable to make normal emotional contact with others. They tend not to share in the usual interests and pursuits of their age group but to be preoccupied with their own idiosyncratic ideas and activities. Their lack of interest and motivation and their absence of competitiveness lead to school failure in often highly intelligent children. Only in areas allied to their predominating interest do they excel: in electronics, for example, or politics. Affected children themselves feel different, astonishing others with their cool and objective self-appraisal. While extremely sensitive to the reactions of others to themselves, they tend to be insensitive, even callous, to the feelings and needs of other people. Rigidity is a further characteristic, schizoid children often insisting fanatically on getting their own way and refusing to conform to quite ordinary social demands. Opposition evokes temper outbursts, incomprehensible to parents and teachers who are at a loss to understand why the refusal of some apparently trivial wish had aroused so much feeling.

Some schizoid children are extremely quiet, secretive, even silent in certain situations, for example at achool. (Among children with the very rare syndrome of *elective mutism*, a number have schizoid personalities.) Others are superficially communicative but express themselves oddly and metaphorically. One fourteen-year-old always held his right arm flexed across his chest because 'I don't like to feel exposed'; another, asked whether he felt that he was 'getting somewhere' as a result of his interviews, said quite seriously 'I like travelling'.

Parents often describe personality difficulties beginning in the pre-school years. It is during the school years, however, when demands for gregariousness and conformity are greatest, that these children feel most unhappy and cope least well.

Often a parent or other close relative has a similar personality disturbance. One father said of his son: 'He demonstrates a number of things which are personality characteristics of my own, I'm afraid' and he went on to describe how a minor professional disagreement with a colleague led him to give up a remunerative occupation in order to devote five years to a research project designed to prove his point. This he was able to achieve. Of his son he said: 'His approach has been to bang his head against a brick wall. I've a sympathy for him, but his mother says she can't understand him'.

The first step in treatment is to recognize the condition and to help parents, teachers and the child himself to accept it. Once the diagnosis is made it becomes much easier for parents and teachers to respect the child's need for privacy, to educate him by building on his own interests and aptitudes, and to be more flexible and less hostile in demands for essential social behaviour.

The diagnosis of *sociopathic personality* is rarely made in childhood, although the malignant effects of early maternal and social deprivation are only too well known. Child psychiatrists prefer to label children with persistent aggressive or conduct disorders as having 'behaviour disorders', knowing that children have enormous potential for change and knowing too that to accept a gloomy prognosis (implied by the term sociopathy) may in fact contribute to a poor outcome. Although Robins (1966) showed that children with conduct disorders are more often sociopathic in later life than neurotic and normal children, by no means all children with conduct disorders have a poor outcome and we do not know how many seriously deprived children in fact have a normal personality adjustment in later life.

The Child Psychiatrist's Roles and Functions

THE TEAM APPROACH OF THE CHILD GUIDANCE CLINIC

The Child Guidance movement in Britain began on the American model in the nineteen twenties with the setting up of child guidance clinics. These were to meet the needs not only of parents worried about their children's deviant behaviour but of schools and juvenile courts. From the start clinics were staffed by a team of psychiatrist, who took overall clinical responsibility and usually treated the child, psychologist, responsible for the intellectual and educational assessment of the child and for contact with the school, and psychiatric social worker, responsible for treating the parents, for exploring possible social factors causing the child's disorder and for helping the family towards a better integration into their community. Clinics were established by voluntary agencies, by local authorities and by hospitals. With the birth of the National Health Service hospital based child psychiatry departments were fully integrated with other hospital services while many child guidance clinics became joint ventures of local authority health or education departments and the hospital service. In contrast with adult psychiatry the practice of child psychiatry was largely community based with close links with education and social work services, but often in relative isolation from hospital medicine.

A contributory factor to the isolation of child psychiatric services from hospital medicine is that, again in contrast to adult psychiatry, relatively few children require inpatient treatment. Because children are dependent on their parents for care and on their schools for education, most psychiatric treatment is confined to outpatient treatment of the child with attempts to modify parental attitudes and behaviour and to provide remedial education for the child where this is indicated.

Only when school attendance has broken down completely, when a state of intolerable mutual hostility exists between parents or teacher and the child, when a child wanders repeatedly or is otherwise out of control, when he has an incapacitating psychoneurotic or psychiatric illness, is inpatient psychiatric treatment essential.

In Britain children who require residential care or education do not live in hospitals but in foster homes, children's homes and special residential schools. While many children who have lost their parents or who have parents unable to provide adequate care for them, or who are themselves educationally or physically handicapped are also psychiatrically disturbed, they tend to be cared for in residential homes and schools visited by psychiatrists, rather than in hospital units.

The result of these developments is that hospitals, with the exception (at the time of writing) of mental subnormality hospitals, are not used to provide custodial care for children and this is all to the good. On the other hand there is at present a considerable shortage of psychiatric inpatient accommodation for children who need this and in many centres paediatric and psychiatric services for children are poorly integrated.

The psychiatrist in the child psychiatric clinic is called upon to provide a diagnostic service to general practitioners, paediatricians, the schools, the courts and the social work departments. He organizes long-term supportive treatment, medication and educational advice to families with handicapped children of all kinds: the physically, intellectually or educationally handicapped and the psychotic.

For children for whom the main treatment is psychotherapy, the classical team approach, whereby one therapist has primary responsibility towards the child and the other towards the parents, enables conflict between child and parents to be tolerated without breaches of confidence and trust between therapist and patient. In every case a decision needs to be made whether the main disturbance is within the child, within one or other parent, between the parents or between parents and child. Often a child is brought forward for treatment when the main disturbance lies elsewhere, when the mother, for example, has a depressive illness making her so irritable that her child responds with temper tantrums and disobedience, or when the marriage has been strained for years and the mother's frequent threats to leave the family are causing the children to respond with anxiety symptoms.

The team's decision that only the mother requires treatment, or that the couple should be taken on for marital therapy may come as a relief to parents who hesitated to ask for help for themselves. On the other hand some families may need much emotional support before they can locate the source of difficulty as elsewhere than in their child and the child himself may meanwhile need the opportunity for free expression of his thoughts and feelings to someone uninvolved with his parents.

The principles of psychotherapy with children are similar to those applying to adults except that the medium of communication is play as well as conversation. The therapist inevitably serves as an alternative role model for the child and he remains responsible for preserving safety (Wolff, 1969).

Increasingly, and especially in the case of older children, when a child's behaviour disorder reflects conflict between parents and children, techniques of family group therapy are used. Parents and all the children of the family meet as a group with one or two therapists at fortnightly or three weekly intervals. Children are often surprisingly well able to communicate both with each other and the parents in this setting. The technique has been well described by Skynner (1969).

THE CHILD PSYCHIATRIST IN THE HOSPITAL SETTING

The child psychiatrist in a hospital setting has three additional and quite specific tasks. Firstly, he provides a consultative service for children in the paediatric wards; secondly, he collaborates with paediatric and nursing colleagues in formulating hospital policies which may affect the social and emotional welfare of child patients in general; thirdly, he is responsible for establishing a therapeutic community in the inpatient unit for psychiatrically disturbed children. This involves collaborating with a wider team of colleagues which now includes nurses, teachers and occupational therapists.

THE CHILD PSYCHIATRIST IN THE COMMUNITY

A major responsibility of child psychiatrists is to provide a consultative service for other agencies concerned with education and child care.

This service takes three forms: Firstly, children are referred by the schools, the courts or the social work departments, like other children for diagnosis and treatment. Secondly teachers, social workers, educational psychologists, probation officers, etc. need the opportunity to discuss their problem cases and to have diagnostic help even if they themselves, and not the child psychiatric team, continue the treatment. Thirdly, every institution in which emotionally disturbed children are cared for (special residential schools for the maladjusted or the delinquent, children's homes, schools and homes for handicapped children) requires a child psychiatrist not only to offer the two kinds of services described above, but also, as a professional and relatively uninvolved outsider, to discuss with the staff of the institution as a group the difficulties they encounter in their day-to-day interactions with the children and their parents. Such regular group discussions led by a psychiatrist or a psychiatrically trained social worker, provide ongoing support for the staff of residential homes and schools for children and serve also as a valuable in-service training in the therapeutic care of disturbed children.

REFERENCES

ANDREWS, G. & HARRIS, M. (1964) *The Syndrome of Stuttering*. Clin. Dev. Med. no. 17. London: Spastics International Medical Publications in association with Heineman Medical Books.

ANTHONY, E. J. (1959) An Experimental approach to the psychopathology of childhood: sleep disturbances. *British Journal of Medical Psychology*, **33**, 19–37.

ANTHONY, E. J. & SCOTT, P. (1960) Manic-depressive psychosis in childhood. *Journal of Child Psychology and Psychiatry*, **1**, 53–72.

BAGLEY, C. & EVAN-WONG, L. (1970) Psychiatric disorder and adult and peer group rejection of the child's name. *Journal of Child Psychology and Psychiatry*, **11**, 19–27.

BELLMAN, M. (1966) Studies on encopresis. *Acta paediatrica neurologica scandinavica* suppl. no. 170.

BLOOM, B. S. (1964) *Stability and Change in Human Characteristics*, London: John Wiley and Sons.

BOWLBY, J. (1946) *Forty-four Juvenile Thieves*. London: Baillière, Tindall and Cox.

CAUDILL, W. & WEINSTEIN, H. (1966) Maternal Care and Infant Behaviour in Japanese and American Urban Middle Class Families. In *Yearbook of the International Sociological Association*. Edited by R. Koenig and R. Hill.

DOUGLAS, J. W. B. (1964) *The Home and the School*. London: McGibbon and Kee.

DRILLIEN, C. M. (1964) *The Growth and Development of the Prematurely Born Infant*. Edinburgh: Livingstone.

FIELD, E. (1967) *A Validation Study of Hewitt and Jenkins' Hypothesis*. Home Office Research Unit Report no. 10, H.M.S.O.

FRENCH, T. M. & ALEXANDER, F. (1941) Psychogenic Factors in Bronchial Asthma. *Psychosomatic Medicine Monographs*, **4**.

FREUD, A. (1946) *The Psycho-Analytical Treatment of Children*. London: Imago Publishing Company.

FREUD, S. (1909) Analysis of a Phobia in a Five-year-old Boy. In *Collected Papers*, Vol. 3. London: Hogarth Press.

FROMMER, E. A. (1968) Depressive Illness in Childhood. In *Recent Developments in Affective Disorders a Symposium*. Edited by A. Coppen and A. Walk, London: Headley Brothers.

GRAHAM, P. J., RUTTER, M. L., YULE, W. & PLESS, I. B. (1967) Childhood Asthma: a psychosomatic disorder? Some epidemiological considerations. *British Journal of Preventative and Social Medicine* **21**, 78–85.

HERSOV, L. A. (1961a) Persistent non-attendance at school. *Journal of Child Psychology and Psychiatry*, **1**, 130–136.

HERSOV, L. A. (1961b) Refusal to go to school. *Journal of Child Psychology and Psychiatry*, **1**, 137–145.

HEWITT, L. E. & JENKINS, R. L. (1946) *Fundamental Patterns of Maladjustment: the Dynamics of their origin*, Illinois: Michigan Child Guidance Institute.

INGRAM, T. T. S. (1959) Specific developmental disorders of speech in childhood. *Brain*, **82**, 450–467.

JOHNSON, A. M. & SZUREK, S. A. (1952) The genesis of antisocial acting out in children and adults, *Psychoanalytic Quarterly*, **21**, 323–343.

JOHNSON, W. (1959) *The Onset of Stuttering*, Minneapolis: University of Minnesota Press.

KANNER, L. (1943) Autistic disturbances of affective contact. *Nervous Child*, **2**, 217–250.

KLEIN, M. (1963) *The Psychoanalysis of Children*, London: Hogarth Press.

KOLVIN, I., OUNSTED, HUMPHREY, M. & McNAY, A. (1971) The phenomenology of childhood psychoses *British Journal of Psychiatry*, **118,** 385–395.

LOTTER, V. (1966) Epidemiology of autistic conditions in young children: I. prevalence, *Social Psychiatry*, **1,** 124–137.

LOVIBOND, S. H. (1964) *Conditioning and Enuresis*, Oxford: Pergamon Press.

McCULLOCH, J. W. & FAWCETT, P. G. (1964) Some factors affecting the prevalence of stammering. *British Journal of Preventive and Social Medicine*, **18,** 146–151.

MITTLER, P. J. (1970) Language Disorders. In *The Psychological Assessment of Mental and Physical Handicaps*, Edited by P. Mittler, London: Methuen and Co.

MITCHELL, S. & SHEPHERD, M. (1966) A comparative study of children's behaviour at home and at school. *British Journal of Educational Psychology*, **36,** 248–254.

NEWSON, J. & NEWSON, E. (1965) *Patterns of Infant Care in an Urban Community*, London: Penguin Books.

NEWSON, J. & NEWSON, E. (1968) *Four Years Old in an Urban Community*, London: Allen and Unwin.

OLATAWURA, M. (1969) *Encopresis: a Review of 32 Cases*, D.P.M. Dissertation, University of Edinburgh.

PASAMANICK, B., ROGERS, M. E. & LILIENFELD, A. M. (1956) Pregnancy experience and the development of behaviour disorders in children. *American Journal of Psychiatry*, **112,** 613–618.

PRUGH, D. G., STAUB, E. M., SANDS, H. H., KIRSCHBAUM, R. M. & LENIHAN, E. A. (1953) A study of emotional reactions of children and families to hospitalization and illness. *American Journal of Orthopsychiatry*, **23,** 70–106.

Report of the Committee on Local Authority and Allied Personal Social Services (1968), H.M.S.O.

ROBINS, L. N. (1966) *Deviant Children Grown Up*, Baltimore: Williams and Wilkins.

ROSENTHAL, R. & JACOBSON, L. F. (1968) Teacher expectations for the disadvantaged. *Scientific American*, **218,** 19–23.

RUTTER, M. (1965) Classification and categorization in child psychiatry. *Journal of Child Psychology and Psychiatry*, **6,** 71–83.

RUTTER, M. (1966) *Children of Sick Parents: an environmental and psychiatric study*, Maudsley Monogr. No. 16, Oxford University Press.

RUTTER, M., LEBOVICI, S., EISENBERG, L., SNEZNEVSKIJ, A. V., SADOUN, R., BROOKE, E. & LIN, TSUNG-YI (1969) A tri-axial classification of mental disorders in childhood. An international study. *Journal of Child Psychology and Psychiatry*, **10,** 41–61.

RUTTER, M., GRAHAM, P. & YULE, W., (1970a) *A Neuropsychiatric Study in Childhood*, Clin. Dev. Med. No. 35, Spastics International Medical Publications in assoc. with Heineman Medical Books.

RUTTER, M., TIZARD, J. & WHITMORE, K. (1970b) *Education, Health and Behaviour*. London: Longmans, Green.

SEARS, R. R., MACCOBY, E. E. & LEVIN, H. (1957) *Patterns of Child Rearing*, Illinois and New York: Row Peterson and Co.

SHAFFER, D., COSTELLO, A. J. & HILL, I. D. (1968) Control of enuresis with Imipramine. *Archives of Diseases in Childhood*, **43,** 665–671.

SKYNNER, A. C. R. (1969) A group-analytic approach to conjoint family therapy. *Journal of Child Psychology and Psychiatry*, **10,** 81–106.

Social Work (Scotland) Act (1969), H.M.S.O.

STOTT, D. H. (1966) *Studies of Troublesome Children*, London: Tavistock Publications.

SYKES, D. H., DOUGLAS, V. I., WEISS, G. & MINDE, K. K. (1971) Attention in hyperactive children and the effect of methylphenidate (Ritalin). *Journal of Child Psychology and Psychiatry*, **12,** 129–139.

WAGNER, M. K. (1968) A case of Public masturbation treated by operant conditioning. *Journal of Child Psychology and Psychiatry*, **9,** 61–65.

WEIL, A. P. (1953) Certain severe disturbances of ego development in childhood. *Psychoanalytic Study of the Child*, **8,** 271–287.

WERRY, J. S. (1968) Developmental hyperactivity. *Pediatric Clinics of North America*, **15,** 581–599.

WICKMAN, E. K. (1928) *Children's Behaviour and Teachers' Attitudes*, New York: The Commonwealth Fund.

WING, J. K. (1966) *Early Childhood Autism: Clinical, Educational and Social Aspects*, London: Pergamon Press.

WOLFF, S. (1967) The contribution of obstetric complications to the etiology of behaviour disorders in childhood. *Journal of Child Psychology and Psychiatry*, **8,** 57–66.

WOLFF, S. (1969) *Children Under Stress*, London: Allen Lane, the Penguin Press.

WOLFF, S. (1970) Behaviour and Pathology of parents of disturbed children. In *The Child in his Family*, Edited by E. J. Anthony and C. Koupernik, New York: John Wiley and Sons.

WOLFF, S. (1971) Dimensions and clusters of symptoms in disturbed children. *British Journal of Psychiatry*, **118,** 421–427.

WOLFF, S. & ACTON, W. P. (1968) Characteristics of parents of disturbed children. *British Journal of Psychiatry*, **114,** 593–601.

Chapter IV

PSYCHIATRIC PROBLEMS OF ADOLESCENTS

W. Acton and J. Evans

INTRODUCTION

Adolescence is a time of challenge; social and personal values are ruthlessly dissected and no system, authority or individual is spared the process. Psychiatry and the psychiatrist are by no means exempt. Many psychiatrists, having been exposed to adolescent patients, adopt self-defensive tactics and refer them 'elsewhere'. These phenomena may contribute to the fact that adolescents have for long been neglected Cinderellas amongst psychiatric patients. In fact, it was not until the late 1940's that the first units, specifically designated for the treatment of disturbed adolescents, were opened in this country, at the Maudsley and St. Ebba's hospitals.

In contrast, facilities for the guidance of disturbed children (presenting in the form of distressed parents, schools, society, etc.) were instigated in the 1920's. Children, of course, are much less threatening people than are adolescents.

In 1962, a North American survey showed that one quarter of all psychiatric referrals were teenagers (Rosen *et al.*, 1965). In this country, a Ministry of Health memorandum to Regional Hospital Boards in 1964 (H.M. (64) 4. Ref: F/C54/01) pointed out that there was at that time a total of 157 beds in the whole of Great Britain for the treatment of disturbed adolescents (approximately four per million population). It was recommended that all regions should aim for a minimum of '20 to 25 beds per million population for assessment and relatively short-term treatment, with additional provision for long stay treatment, at first on the scale of 25 beds per region'. Hence, the mushrooming of adolescent units all over the country which is currently apparent.

While it is clear that the adolescent population has been sadly neglected by psychiatrists until recent years, they have not been forgotten by local authority children's departments, education and penal authorities. Approved schools, Borstals, and young offenders institutions, while overcrowded, heavily outnumber psychiatric units for the age group and have catered for them when no one else did. The contributions of these other agencies should not be overlooked as they have a considerable body of knowledge and experience available for psychiatrists attempting to help this age group. Hopefully, with the implementation of the Seebohm Report and Social Work Act (Scotland)

and closer liaison between Social and Psychiatric Services, valuable pooling of knowledge and experience, together with increased inter-service respect, should occur.

Since adolescence is the period of the life cycle when the developing child begins, as a newly forming individual (as oppposed to member of the family, school, etc.) to integrate with society at large, the psychiatrists' contribution must always be considerably influenced by that of the Social Scientists. Similarly, since in Western culture adolescence is the period when educational achievement is at a premium, the psychiatrist needs constantly to draw upon the experience of educational psychologists.

None the less, psychiatrists as a group have a major contribution to make to the treatment of adolescents in distress, especially those with a special knowledge of child development, interaction processes and family and group dynamics.

Psycho-Social and Physiological Aspects of Puberty and Adolescence

In order to be in a position to make an evaluation of the psychiatric state of an adolescent, it is essential to have some understanding of the psychological processes occurring in this developmental phase. The problem of evaluation differs from that in adults since the adolescent is in a state of very active physiological and psychological growth, which can be seen as a prolonged series of 'crises' (Caplan, 1964), beginning with the onset of puberty and ending with the achievement of young adulthood.

The form of 'crisis' can be related to the phases of adolescence, and these may for simplicity be sub-divided into three major stages:

Puberty—which refers to children aged approximately 10 to 12 years, who are beginning to mature physiologically, but cognitively still operating in Piaget's phase of concrete operations; emotionally they are still very dependent on the family of origin and the social structure reinforces this dependence.

Early Adolescence—which describes children aged approximately 12 to 15 years, who show external signs of physical maturation and have moved cognitively into Piaget's phase of formal operations, becoming capable of abstract thinking; emotionally they are becoming less dependent on the family and have a need to separate themselves, but social pressures tend to maintain them in their former state of dependence.

Late Adolescence—which covers young people aged 15 to 18 who are more or less physically and cognitively mature, and who are in active process of emotionally separating themselves from their families and endeavour to achieve independent identities. Depending upon a number of factors such as culture and social class, social pressures may be assisting or retarding their emancipation, but, by and large, society permits them more freedom than the former group.

It will be clear that these definitions are operational and that individual children frequently demonstrate aspects of all three phases at one and the same time. However, the authors feel that the internal processes and external pressures upon the three groups are sufficiently different to merit the sub-grouping. The ages given are approximations and do not imply any fixed periods. In general, the broad term 'adolescence' will be used through most of the foregoing, breaking down into sub-groups only when this is necessary for emphasis. For the main part the reader is asked to use his own discretion in interpreting the term within its context.

In common with the child psychiatrist, the adolescent psychiatrist must invariably formulate his thoughts around the key conceptual framework of *maturation*. This entails a thorough knowledge of the maturational tasks of adolescence and an awareness that these changes and developments are inherently stressful. One therefore comes to think of the adolescent period as a time of 'normal crisis' in the life of the individual, so that some degree of disturbance, distress and symptom-formation is the norm rather than the exception (A. Freud, 1958; Shields, 1964). It follows automatically that one of the major diagnostic difficulties in adolescent psychiatry lies in the recognition of distress which is age-appropriate and inevitable, i.e. a healthy reaction, and that which is pathological.

The following outline of the maturational tasks of adolescence is derived mainly from Freudian concepts, modified by works such as Peter Blos, E. Erikson and J. Piaget (see Flavell, 1963).

PHYSIOLOGICAL ASPECTS

Broadly speaking, the physiological and anatomical changes in puberty are: (1) rapid growth of general physique so that the individual is larger and stronger; and (2) special development of the reproductive organs, with increased size of internal and external genitalia, the development of secondary sexual characteristics, and the new capacity for procreation. It is well known that there has been a marked trend towards a lowering of the median age of onset of puberty (Tanner, 1962) so that it now occurs some four years earlier than it did a century and a half ago. This in itself is producing special problems, since the biological phase of adolescence is becoming increasingly protracted, whilst social and educational provisions are not changing at an equal rate. Many girls of 11 or younger are now biologically capable of childbearing.

INTELLECTUAL ASPECTS

Cognitively, the changes of puberty and adolescence are the acquisition of the capacity for abstract thought and the concept of reciprocity (i.e. a shift in one parameter in a system will alter other parameters in the system, Inhelder and Piaget, 1958). Proceeding from this, one may assume that the adolescent is becoming intellectually capable of conceiving some of the complexities of how his behaviour affects others—and vice versa.

In the absence of evidence to suggest that cognitive development has accelerated at the same pace as physiological development, the question arises as to whether today's adolescents are intellectually less well equipped to deal with their biological development and its emotional concomitants than were their forebears. This question as yet remains unanswered but may legitimately be asked when considering the aetiology of the present apparent increase in adolescent disturbance, e.g. drug abuse.

SOCIAL ASPECTS

Erikson has clearly outlined the social tasks of adolescents—namely those of emancipation from the family of origin, achieving comfort with the sexual and working roles, and effectively identifying with the status, pleasures and responsibilities of an acceptable adult, rather than a child. Erikson's concept of 'identity' includes all the above areas and the value of his contribution to the understanding of the adolescent is that he has delineated the crisis of identity inevitable in the change of self-concept from child to adult in which a certain amount of confusion and uncertainty about 'who one is' is unaviodable. Identity, as defined by Rycroft (1968) is 'a sense of one's continuous being as an entity, distinguishable from all others' and it is eminently understandable that this sense should be shaken by the internal and external changes of puberty and adolescence. The concept of 'identity crisis' has been of immense value both in conceptualizing adolescent processes and in providing the basis for a language through which to usefully communicate with adolescent patients. A common situation which can be very confusing for parents, adolescent and psychiatrist alike is the adolescent tendency to 'role-play', in an attempt to find a comfortable self-concept. Experimentation is usually necessary before the adolescent finds a self-concept with which he can comfortably 'fit'; thus it is common for a boy to be dreamy, 'artistic' and altruistic for a week or two, and then dramatically to switch to a hardheaded, down to earth business-like approach. Likewise, a girl may dramatically shift her role from 'virginal purity' to 'scalp-collecting madam'. It is vital that the psychiatrist should realize that these roles may be fragile, poorly fitting but transient.

Social Pressures

The changing physical status of the adolescent and his increasing age bring new social pressures to bear upon him. These, of course, will be very different at different phases of adolescence; in the pubertal phase (roughly defined as age 10 to 12) he is simply expected to be a little more responsible and self-sufficient. In early adolescence (roughly 12 to 15), he is expected to apply himself to his studies, demonstrate some adult attitudes and begin to participate in adult activities. In late adolescence (roughly 15 to 18), he will begin to be treated as a man and be expected to behave as one—think about work, prepare for a profession, or look for a job, take the initiative in dating girls, etc. One feature of this inevitable trend, which may prove very disturbing to some adolescents, is that the way people behave towards them is quite incongruous with the way they feel about themselves, e.g. they may still feel very much like children and yet are expected to find and do a man's job. This is further complicated by the mood swings which are characteristic of this age group and by the role-playing described above; the complications lie in the interaction between the rapidly fluctuating adolescent and his more stable social environment. It is extremely difficult to keep up with, let alone accommodate, the youngster who is fluctuating between feeling like a child and an adult, an artist and a bricklayer. Consequently, the youngster is frequently confronted with gross discrepancies between his internal world and the external world's attitude to him, all of which exacerbates his identity confusion.

INTRA-PSYCHIC ASPECTS

To avoid confusion these will be dealt with in the three separate phases of adolescence.

Puberty. At the time of writing, most children under 12 are seen by child psychiatrists and the reader is referred to the section on child psychiatry. The present author's viewpoint has already been indicated in the definition of the phase.

Early Adolescence. The intra-psychic processes occurring in the early adolescent do not differ significantly in nature from those occurring in the late adolescent; the difference is more of a quantitive than a qualitative one and the main area of difference is in degree of detachment. The early adolescent is less emotionally and intellectually equipped to detach himself from his parents, though his need to do so may be equally great.

With this proviso, the processes which will be described as occurring in the late adolescent can equally be applied to early-adolescents.

Late Adolescence. The processes occurring within the adolescent can most easily be understood in terms of the maturational tasks which he must accomplish to achieve adult maturity. This latter state is defined by Erikson (1963) in 'Childhood and Society' as having the capacity to 'have mutuality of orgasm with a loved partner of the other sex with whom one is able, and willing, to share a mutual trust and with whom one is able and willing to regulate the cycles of (a) work, (b) procreation, (c) recreation, so as to secure to the offspring too, all the stages of a satisfactory development'. This is no mean feat! Ronald Fairbairn (1952) in 'Psychoanalytic Studies of the Personality' describes a position of 'mature dependence' as the end point of psycho-sexual maturation; he defines it thus: '. . . . a genital relationship involving evenly matched giving and taking between differentiated individuals who are mutually dependent and between whom there is no disparity of dependence'.

To these admittedly idealized goals of personality development must be added the exclusion clause that the loved partner cannot be a parent or member of the nuclear family. This clause is of vital importance to the understanding of adolescents, since the position from which he starts this uphill trek is one where his primary love objects must inevitably (provided one allows that the family may be a substitute family) belong to the excluded group (Freud, 1905). It is therefore necessary that the adolescent should:

1. Relinquish his primary loves upon whom he still to some extent dependent.

2. Tolerate the grief of this detachment and the fear of isolation.

3. Tolerate the grief he observes in his family as he detaches, and the fear that they will abandon him in retaliation.

4. Transfer his attachment needs with their forbidden erotic component, to a suitable member of the opposite sex, while at the same time continuing to care about his family.

5. Effectively differentiate between the forbidden nature of incestuous sexuality and the increasingly permissible fact (indeed expectation) of hetero-sexual experimentation.

The above can all be summarized in the phrase: 'the adolescent must decathexe the incestuous objects', but this phrase does little justice to the enormity of the task. Difficulties occur at all of these stages and clearly it is appropriate for an adolescent to have episodes of depression, to feel isolated, guilty, abandoned; it is appropriate that he may temporarily split off loving from erotic feelings and then feel ashamed of his sexuality; that he may feel angry with the parents 'who make him feel ashamed'.

In order that the adolescent may cope adequately with the threat of his incestuous drives, he must detach himself from his parents and become independent. Provided that the threat is not too intense he can do this gradually, allowing both himself and his parents to adjust to the new family situation. There are also, of course, positive drives towards self-sufficiency, irrespective of the incestuous threat; he wishes to become an adult and be permitted to taste formerly forbidden fruits; at the same time, he fears independence with its threat of isolation and failure. The whole area of independence/dependence is fraught with intense feelings and many family battles are fought on this field.

Adolescent rebellion serves many intra-psychic and intra-family needs, painful though it is for all concerned. The need of the youngster to separate from his primary love objects must inevitably be ambivalent—and yet it is essential for his psychic integrity. His newly acquired physical strength, verbal fluency and ability to reason, equip him with effective weapons of attack. The small child may be very angry with his parent but knows that the parent is stronger than he; this however is not the case for the adolescent who may well be physically stronger and verbally more aggressive than either parent. Hence, he can no longer rely on his parents to control his aggressive impulses and has to develop his own internal controls. This also can be an alarming situation, especially when the need to use aggression as effective self-assertion, in the cause of achieving separation and independence, is heightened, e.g. as in the case of the only son of a widowed mother who weeps whenever he goes out with a girl.

The search for an independent adult identity again comes into the picture and is weaved in among the struggles for control of aggressive and incestuous impulses and the need to separate from the family. In order to be a truly separate individual, it is necessary that the adolescent should question his parents' values and ultimately decide whether or not to adopt them as his own. His precarious sense of identity—leaving behind the well-known 'self' of childhood and moving into the unknown 'self' of adulthood—frequently leads him to fight furiously for whatever he has currently chosen as the basis of his independent identity—be it long hair, Communism or the legalization of Pot. The issue that is really being fought out (though very few adolescents can admit this) is a life and death struggle to exist as a separate individual—hence the 'heat'.

To summarize the essential areas of adolescent intrapsychic conflict, they are: the control of (1) sexuality and (2) aggression; (3) the need to separate from parents in order to become (4) independent and thus develop an adult (5) identity. It should be clear from the above that these areas are all inexorably inter-twined.

THE ADOLESCENT IN CONTEXT

Psychiatrists are increasingly coming to realize that people can not be assessed in isolation. Child and adolescent psychiatrists were driven to this conclusion earlier than those dealing with adults for the simple practical reasons that (1) children are unable to refer themselves for help (and even if they could their verbal fluency is generally inadequate to the psychiatrist's needs), and (2) adolescents are notoriously unwilling to admit that they are in trouble and accept help. These 'fortunate' coincidences have led child and adolescent psychiatrists to the view that the presenting (or more often in the case of adolescents—presented) patient is often the signal of family distress. In the case of school or institutional referrals, the child may be the symptom of distress in these settings.

Thus it is essential in the assessment of adolescent disurbance to view the adolescent within his immediate social context, and to obtain as much information as possible about his position in other areas of interaction, e.g. school, work, peer-group.

In the Family

As will be clear from the previous section, adolescence presents a crisis to the whole family. Not only does the young person have to detach and grieve, but his parents, the deserted love objects, have their own inevitable grief. Their ability or otherwise to cope with this family crisis (which can often precipitate a marital crisis because previous patterns of marital adjustment are no longer satisfactory) is crucial to the adequate resolution of healthy adolescent conflict. It must be understood that the child's adolescence produces disequilibrium in the whole family system of adjustment and any family member may be unable to readjust to the new situation, e.g. siblings, grandparents, etc. This in turn reflects back upon the adolescent.

To illustrate this, it is not uncommon for parents to refer an adolescent for unruly behaviour which the psychiatrist considers well within normal limits (bearing in mind the social status of the family). Further examination of the adolescent reveals no abnormality apart from excessive guilt and anxiety about his parents. Exploration with the parents in such cases frequently reveals a marriage which has provided insufficient satisfaction to one or both parents; equilibrium has been maintained however, by turning to the child for satisfaction. Thus, when the child attempts to become independent of the parents, the marital equilibrium is threatened with disturbance, and the parents not unnaturally attempt to maintain the status quo by infantalizing the adolescent. A somewhat unusual example of this was that of a 15 year old boy, an only son, referred on account of a lift-phobia. In a joint interview with his parents, it emerged that the family lived in a top storey flat which could only be reached or left by using the lift. Mother was an anxious frigid woman with a history of hospitalization for depressive illness; father was a detached isolated man with an unacknowledged but violent distaste for domesticity and feminine interests.

D

The story unfolded that the boy and his father together shared many masculine interests and pursuits, all of which totally excluded mother. Mother, though neurotic, had women friends among the neighbours. Father, without his son, was totally friendless and, in view of his disdain for feminity in general, could not share interests with his wife. Thus this boy's maturation presented an enormous threat to (a) his father's adjustment and (b) the marital partnership, since the couple were brought face to face with their dissatisfaction with each other. The 'lift-phobia' could thus be understood as the boy's unconscious attempt to protect his father and the parental marriage, and the threat which their vulnerability presented to his developing independence; by remaining unable to use the lift he was unable to leave his parent's home and was thus colluding with their need to infantilize him and maintain the status quo. He was also defending himself against his own internalized fear that becoming independent from his parents inevitably symbolized desertion and isolation.

Any deviation from the standard family structure in this culture, e.g. one-parent families, adoptive or foster parents or institutional care, will present special difficulties which must be examined in their own right.

In School

A youngster may have difficulties in school which may reflect problems in the school itself, in the home or in the child. The special difficulties of educationally sub-normal or exceptionally intelligent children are well-known.

Physical handicap, immaturity or hyper-maturity may all present problems, as may marked social class distinctions.

The educational achievement expected of adolescents differs markedly according to their intelligence, social class, the school itself and parental aspirations. Marked discrepancies between the adolescent's capacity and the achievement expected of him can lead to disturbance.

Work

At the time of writing, children can leave school at 15 and are expected to work. Thus it is not uncommon for a very immature 15 year old, looking outwardly like a 12 year old, to be placed in a man's job.

Some youngsters have work aspirations for themselves which bear no relation to their abilities and can become very depressed and despondent as a result of repeated failure. Likewise family aspirations may not match up to those of the adolescent, or his capacity.

On leaving school, many adolescents have little idea of what sort of career they wish to pursue. Hence it is not uncommon for a youngster to change jobs five or ten times in a year before settling into a work environment in which he can function adequately and comfortably.

While, in itself, this frequent change of jobs does not carry the same implications as it does for an adult, the psychiatrist must exercise caution in interpreting the phenomenon, since it may be associated with disturbance in many other life areas. Clearly the implications are quite different for a youngster whose father or mother changes jobs frequently than for one whose wage-earning parent is in regular employment.

Peer-Group Relationships

The nature of the adolescent's relationships with his peer-group is of paramount importance in assisting or retarding his separation from the family. If there is no satisfactory peer-group with whom to identify, or if the adolescent has physical or psychological difficulties within himself (or his family) which prevent him from approaching his peers, then the task of separation is doubly difficult. The isolated adolescent, for whatever reason, is always vulnerable, since there is no one to whom he may transfer his attachment needs from his parents. However, many adolescents go through transient periods of withdrawal from the peer-group, maintaining contact with only one or two close friends.

The state of unstable identity inherent in the adolescent process drives many youngsters to attach themselves firmly to the peer-group, with whom they identify (thus achieving a temporary form of identity). Thus the well-known phenomenon of teenage 'gangs' with the unshakeable loyalty of individuals to 'the gang'. The factors which determine the nature of the gang with which any individual youngster chooses to identify are numerous, but any attempt to modify the behaviour of an individual young person must take into account the nature and force of the gang. Gangs may be idealistic—devoted to helping the aged or infirm—or they may be 'delinquent', with all gradations in between. In the desperate struggle for an independent identity and separation from the parents, an adolescent may unconsciously choose to identify with a gang which, in his parents' eyes, are 'unsuitable' if not 'delinquent'. This is usually an indication that the family as a whole are unable to adapt to the crisis of adolescence.

Homosexual Relationships

'Bosom-friendships' with a member of the same sex are typical of adolescents, and may or may not be accompanied by active homosexual experimentation and mutual masturbation. The significance of this must be assessed within the total context of the adolescent's life situation and, in itself, must not be taken to indicate dawning homosexuality. Often, it is an attempt to deal with the 'loss' of the parent of the same sex, when the opposite sexed parent has been absent or only distantly attached to the youngster; thus older people such as school teachers or youth leaders are frequently invested with passionate feelings ('crushes').

Equally often, it is a temporary compromise solution for an adolescent who feels that he or she is unattractive to the opposite sex.

Hetero-sexual Relationships

Relationships with the opposite sex are a frequent source of anxiety and embarrassment to the developing youngster. This is understandable in the context of the maturational needs of the adolescent to find a suitable love object to whom he can transfer his intense love and need of his primary love-object, and who will accept his now potent sexuality. Set against this positive need to attach are all the adolescent's fears about his new body, his unstable identity and sexuality itself, which has not yet been freed from all the old taboos. Thus he has an intense wish for a love-object complicated by a profound fear that he will be found unacceptable.

Some adolescents deal with this conflict, using counterphobic defenses, by jumping in at the deep end and rapidly forming a lengthy series of short-lived heterosexual relationships, with or without active sexual experimentations. The value of this approach is that it allows the youngster to approach girls (or boys in the case of girls), 'have a look and then run for safety'. Gradually, as he or she discovers that the other sex is neither as dangerous nor as rejecting as he feared, he can allow himself to form deeper, more lasting relationships.

Others are frankly phobic about the opposite sex and either 'adore from a distance', or deny any hetero-sexual interest. Yet again, a sibling-like relationship may be made with deep affection but little conscious sexual attraction on either side; this allows the adolescents a safe base from which to tentatively investigate other members of the opposite sex.

Fantasy-life

Adolescents have a very rich fantasy life which allows them, under optimal circumstances, to be extremely creative. Their fantasies, however, are not easily revealed to others. The function of this active fantasy (day-dreaming) is to allow considerable experimentation to occur intra-psychically—so that the adolescent does not have to act out all his questions and wishes about himself and life. Active fantasy is of considerable positive value to the adolescent and should only be considered 'sinister' when it clearly and persistently interferes with his relationship to external objects, or day-to-day living.

Masturbation fantasies

The fantasies associated with masturbation are considered essential information in standard psychiatric history-taking, and indeed, if obtainable, can provide useful information about the direction of an adolescent's psychic functioning. However, in the author's experience, this material is not easily obtainable in a relatively brief assessment, and probing questioning can make the further progress of the interview difficult, and sometimes impossible. Indeed, if masturbation fantasies are readily revealed then this, in itself, may indicate that there is something far wrong with this youngster's sense of reality and appropriateness. Broadly speaking, the psychiatrist is advised to approach this area with extreme caution and to be fully prepared to leave it as ignorant as he was when he approached it. Information about how the adolescent is actually functioning, i.e. how he is making use of and/or controlling his fantasies, is of infinitely more value.

The presence or absence of active masturbation is a little more easy to elicit, provided the psychiatrist exercises demonstrable respect for the adolescent's privacy. The total absence of masturbation in boys usually indicates excessive conflict over sexuality; it does not have the same significance in girls, many of whom do not actively masturbate.

THE INCIDENCE OF PSYCHIATRIC DISORDER IN ADOLESCENTS

As will be clear from the above, attempts at estimating the incidence of psychiatric disorder in the adolescent population are fraught with the difficulties of differentiating 'healthy' disturbance from 'unhealthy'. Masterson (1967) has compared a large group of psychiatrically referred adolescents with a matched control group; his findings would suggest that the few epidemiological surveys which have been carried out, using psychiatric referral as the criterion of illness, have been accurately identifying unhealthy adolescents, i.e. psychiatric referral appears to be a reasonably reliable index of adolescent morbidity. However, no full scale epidemiological survey of the adolescent population has yet been reported and so one must assume that reported figures are marked under-estimates. In fact, following Masterson's suggestion, from his findings, that adolescent turmoil merely exacerbates and gives a characteristic flavour to pre-existing and continuing psychiatric disorder, one should perhaps include all young people on probation, in approved schools, Borstals etc., whether or not they have been referred for psychiatric assessment. However, this brings into question the whole area of overlap between psychiatric disorder and social malaise and so must remain an unanswered question.

Henderson *et al.*, (1967) investigated all adolescents (excluding the mentally retarded) who were referred for psychiatric opinion in Edinburgh in 1964 to 65. They found the annual referral rate to be 5.6 per thousand at risk, and it was notable that only 6 of their sample of 230 teenagers were referred from the Courts. This situation has already changed considerably and to some extent would appear to depend on the existence or otherwise of psychiatric facilities for adolescents. Another interesting feature of their study was that only half of their sample were referred by General Practitioners and this correlated with relative social affluence; the 30 per cent who were referred following attempts at self-poisoning or injury came from the lower social classes.

Kidd and Dixon (1968) conducted a similar study in Aberdeen in the same year, and arrived at a similar figure, i.e. the annual referral rate was 6.6 per thousand at risk. There were, however, interesting regional differences in that a far higher percentage of the Aberdeen sample were referred by the Courts (17 per cent) and there were considerably fewer referrals following attempted self-poisoning or injury (6 per cent of boys contrasted with 30 per cent in Edinburgh).

FACTORS PRE-DISPOSING TO BREAKDOWN AT ADOLESCENCE

PREVIOUS ADJUSTMENT

As would be expected, an import factor predisposing to breakdown at adolescence is the adequacy or otherwise of previous adjustment: 30 per cent of a consecutive sample of disturbed adolescents seen by the authors had had previous referrals to Child Guidance or Psychiatric Clinics. Severely phobic or obsessional children are particularly at risk, as are those with marked anti-social conduct disorders. A proportion of autistic children, on the other hand, appear to improve with increasing age (Rutter, 1966). The 'too good' childhood personality described so frequently by parents of adolescent schizophrenics leads one to the clinical impression that it is of some significance.

It is well known that unresolved conflicts of early childhood are reactivated at adolescence and analysts especially emphasize the recurrence of unresolved difficulties of the Oedipal phase of development. However, the adolescent task is of such proportion that it must call upon all areas of the personality for its mastery, so that failure at any previous stage of personality development will inevitably affect the outcome of the adolescent phase.

SEPARATION EXPERIENCES

The work of Bowlby, (1969) and others have illuminated the importance of separation experiences in childhood for later personality development. Adolescents who have been separated from their parents in early years are vulnerable, and the indications are that such children are most likely to later display character traits of over-dependency and compliance, depression or anti-social aggression. Any of these characteristics is likely to interfere with one or more aspects of the adolescent task. The most frequent clinical finding is that delinquent adolescents have suffered separation experiences in childhood and this is supported by many research studies, (e.g. Banks, 1965; Gregory, 1965).

Adopted children have by definition been separated from their natural parents. However, it is now well documented that the earlier a child is adopted the more successful is the outcome. Children adopted after 9 to 12 months of age are likely to be vulnerable in similar, though less severe ways, to any other 'separated' children. There are, however, few published reports of the psychiatric status of adopted adolescents (McWhinnie, 1967).

Adopted adolescents comprised 4 per cent of a consecutive sample of 239 youngsters seen by the authors and tended to display severe disturbance. A common factor appeared to be associated with parental difficulties in adapting to their child's independence and their inability to tolerate hostility from the adolescent. Confronted with the latter, adoptive parents tend to withdraw interest from the child and blame genetic endowment. Thus, the factor of adoption can be seen to add to parental difficulties in dealing with the crisis of adolescence, which would support the views of other workers in the field of adoption (Kellmer Pringle, 1967) that the success or failure of adoption is significantly related to the adjustment of the adoptive parents—in particular their ability to accept the need to adopt, for whatever reason —as well as to the age and previous experiences of the child.

It is not uncommon for adopted children to want, if not attempt, to seek out their natural mother at adolescence. This can be a very painful experience for loving adoptive parents, who now find themselves confronted with the search for the now idealized natural parent. However, just as it is easy for adoptive parents to 'blame' genetic endowment for their adolescent children's faults, so it is equally easy for adopted children, in attempting to detach from the parents who have reared them, to look for the 'ideal' parent who would magically solve their maturational suffering. Whether or not it is useful to assist adopted adolesents in the search for the natural parent, as some adoptive parents and Youth Workers do, is open to question. In an ideal world it should be possible *both* to introduce the young person to his natural parent *and* to help him see this search as an inappropriate solution to his real problem of separating from the parents who have reared him, and to whom he is attached.

PARENTAL AGE

Older parents have more difficulty in adapting to their child's adolescence than do younger ones, and this may explain why the parents of referred adolescents are often older than would be expected. This is relevant to the possible adoption factor, since it is not uncommon for couples to decide to adopt after many years of trying unsuccessfully to have children of their own.

One must also consider ante- and peri-natal factors and possible chromosomal aberrations, since it is known that the frequency of complications in all these areas is related to increasing maternal age; it may therefore be that a higher proportion of disturbed adolescent children of elderly parents suffer from a minimal degree of cerebral dysfunction.

CHRONIC ILLNESS, PHYSICAL DISABILITY OR ABNORMALITY

A child who is in any way disabled or abnormal is at risk of psychiatric complications at adolescence. This is understandable partly in terms of the increased identity conflict with which these adolescents have to struggle, their embarrassment at being 'different' from their fellows, and their special problems in education, finding employment and maintaining proximity with the peer-group. In addition, the prolonged enforced dependency of physically ill or disabled children gives the process of separating and becoming independent of the parents special and increased difficulties.

The outcome of the adolescent process for these children is particularly dependent on the capacity of the family to support the youngster, and themselves successfully adapt to the intra-familial changes.

Chronic illness in other family members produces its own problems in the family's adaptation to adolescence, e.g. the wife of a disabled man may be especially dependent on her eldest son or daughter as a bread winner, and may resist the developing independence of her child.

MINIMAL CEREBRAL DYSFUNCTION

The syndrome of minimal cerebral dysfunction is well known to all child and adolescent psychiatrists. The diagnosis is notoriously difficult to make except in the few clear-cut cases who have already been seen by paediatric neurologists and who show some definite neurological signs. Psychologists are frequently asked to test children or adolescents in order to determine whether or not cerebral functioning is impaired; Herbert (1964), in her comprehensive review paper on the subject has made it clear that psychologists are no more able to answer this question than are psychiatrists or neurologists.

Accepting that there are some adolescents who, for whatever reason (e.g. head injury, encephalitis, pre-natal factors etc.) have some impairment of cerebral functioning, it is clear that these young people may have special difficulties in mastering the adolescent process. A history of difficulty in the pre-natal, natal or post-natal period of disturbed adolescents is not uncommonly obtained from their mothers and leads the authors to support studies which suggest that this syndrome is related to adolescent difficulties more frequently than has been generally acknowledged (Hertzig and Birch, 1966; Conners, 1967). Graham and Rutter (1968) have attempted a controlled study with behaviour disordered school children, and found a history suggestive of organic brain dysfunction to be five times as common as in the general school child population.

FAMILY DISHARMONY OR DEVIANCE

Adolescents are especially vulnerable to social pressures and thus any deviation of their families from the cultural norm makes them more vulnerable than the general adolescent population. Gregory (1965) has shown that adolescent children of one-parent families are especially vulnerable to delinquency and academic failure in the absence of the parent of the same sex.

There is a wealth of literature on the significance of the 'broken home', whether by death, separation, or divorce, for psychiatric disturbance in later life, and there seems little doubt that this is an important pre-disposing factor. Banks (1965) in a study of delinquent boys in detention centres, found that whereas homes broken by death were three times as common as in the normal 15 year old population, those broken by separation or divorce were five times commoner. Thus it seems reasonable to conclude that children of stable marriages are better able to withstand parental loss than are children of disturbed marriages.

The families of disturbed adolescents almost invariably exhibit evidence of disturbance in themselves. The old 'hen or the egg: which comes first?' argument becomes irrelevant if one views adolescence as a family crisis, rather than one for the adolescent alone. All families must adapt their former adjustments to accommodate to this major change in one of their members and whether they do this successfully or not depends on innumerable factors, not least of which is the basis on which the previous adjustment was made. One is tempted to think simply in terms of the marital adjustment of the parents since, at the present time, it is unusual for the psychiatrist to see other members of the family. If one regards the family as a dynamic system, it is clearly irrational to confine one's thinking to the parents alone. However, at the time of writing, information regarding the influence of other family members is sparse and thus one is largely confined to equating 'the family' with 'the parents plus adolescent'. In the authors' sample, marital dysharmony had occurred in over 30 per cent of parents and was severe in 28 per cent. Separation had occurred in 19 per cent and 10 per cent were divorced.

Bearing in mind the fallacies inherent in this way of thinking, a number of parental patterns are seen with sufficient frequency to be regarded as significant. As mentioned in a number of examples above, marriages in which one or other parent uses the adolescent as a substitute for some aspect of their spouse, are vulnerable. Families in which communication patterns are indirect (Bateson, 1965) or the relationships 'skewed' (Lidz, 1964) are thought to be associated with schizophrenia in the offspring. Johnson and Szurek in 1952 described how parents may unconsciously encourage their children to act out their own anti-social impulses. The 'absent father' and families in which parental roles are reversed have all been incriminated, in adolescent disturbance. To date, there is no acceptable classification of family patterns and it is not therefore possible to correlate specific types of family structure with syndromes of adolescent disturbance.

MATERNAL ATITUDE TO PREGNANCY

Forssmann and Thuwe (1966) conducted a study in Scandinavia in which they showed a clear relationship between the attitude of a mother towards her pregnancy and the future mental health of the child. 'Unwanted' children showed a significantly higher incidence of delinquency, school failure and psychiatric ill-health in adolescence and young adulthood, than did a control group of 'wanted' children.

SOCIAL CLASS

There is no known social class bias in the incidence of adolescent disturbance but, as is indicated in the epidemiological studies, social class appears to influence the route by which adolescents reach the psychiatrist. This must, however, be considerably influenced by the type of facilities available, and areas with 'Walk-In' Counselling Services will see a different population from those where the only facilities are in the local Mental Hospital. At the present time, however, young people from the lower social classes are more likely to be referred either by the Court or following an attempt at self injury, while those from the middle and upper classes reach the psychiatrist via their parents and the General Practitioner.

While there have been studies suggesting that delinquency occurs equally in all social classes, the existence of delinquent sub-cultures is generally accepted. The implications of delinquent behaviour in youngsters from such a culture are very different from the same behaviour in those from middle-class homes; in the latter it is usually indicative of more serious psychiatric (as opposed to social) disturbance.

Examination of the Adolescent

With the rare exception of the self referred, intelligent and verbally fluent young person, examination of the average adolescent patient within a mental hospital setting is fraught with hazards. Likewise, examination in the setting of a remand home or prison in response to a request from the Court for a psychiatric report has its special difficulties, the only advantage in the second setting being that the examiner can at least be guaranteed a captive audience!

Adolescents almost universally assume that they must be insane if they are asked to see a psychiatrist; hence a good deal of energy is spent in their attempts to persuade the examiner to the contrary. The adolescent who is truly insane is often considerably easier to examine than his sane, though terrified, counterpart.

It follows automatically from the assuptions with which adolescents approach psychiatrists that they are usually unwilling to do so. Harassed, perspiring parents extracting an unwilling youth from a taxi at the door of the clinic are not an uncommon sight; neither is it unusual for a parent to arrive having 'lost' their offspring en route! The wise adolescent psychiatrist, having respect for his own health and time, will not invite an adolescent to come alone for a preliminary interview at the request of the family doctor; if he does, one of the following events may occur; (1) the patient will not come; (2) the patient will come and deny all knowledge of the problem for which he has been referred; he certainly does not stay out all night, neither have drugs ever touched his lips—he is a picture of righteous indignation, against which the psychiatrist has no defence; (3) he will come but remain mute throughout the interview; (4) there may be a productive interview.

These unhappy experiences should be avoided where possible and, since the parents are asking the psychiatrist to help them with their offspring, it is not unreasonable that the psychiatrist should ask them to help him, by at least bringing the patient.

This is only one reason, albeit an important one, why psychiatrists should always attempt to see an adolescent with his parents—at least initially. In the writers' experience, there are very few exceptions to this rule, provided it is applied with common-sense, (i.e. one does not expect parents to travel from Southampton to Edinburgh to interview a medical student complaining of pre-examination insomnia). Clearly, if a young person is living away from home, has achieved a reasonable amount of independence and is willing to come for help, then this is a very different situation and the conduct of the interview approximates more to that of an adult. These young adults are not the subjects of the present paper.

Where an adolescent lives in an institution, it is advisable, where possible, for the psychiatrist to interview him within the institution, so that he may have the opportunity to meet the surrogates or staff, and gain some acquaintance with the dynamic inter-personal forces operating in this particular setting. If a visit is not possible, then significant members of staff should be asked to accompany the young person to the Clinic.

The principal reason why every effort should be made to examine an adolescent within his immediate social environment is in order that the psychiatrist should have an opportunity to observe interactions. It is frequently argued that the presence of the psychiatrist (and psychiatric social worker, as is usually the case) inevitably alters the dynamics of the situation, and one will never see a representative sample of interaction between the family members; while this point is indisputable, it is equally applicable to individual interviews and observer bias can never be avoided in any psychiatric interview. However, in the writers' view, it is unquestionable that joint family interviews yield an enormous amount of information about the behaviour of the family, within a fixed setting (i.e. the consulting room), from which useful working hypotheses about family dynamics can be made.

It is also often said that conjoint family interviews can be harmful to the adolescent in that he may hear parental arguements or criticism of him. The writers operate from the stand-point that the joint interview is of little value if the family do not air the problems and grievances which are troubling them; one can be confident that it is highly unlikely that the adolescent will hear anything which he has not heard, or suspected, before. In fact, the writers' experience has been that the airing of family grievances and anxieties in the presence of a neutral observer (who is prepared, if necessary, to intervene in order to support the weakest member) can often be very helpful and tension-reducing.

As a general rule, therefore, the preliminary interview of a referred adolescent should be together with his parents (or surrogates), it being made clear that the psychiatrist sees the reason for the referral as a problem for the whole family, rather than for the adolescent alone. This approach gives one the combined advantages of (1) seeing the patient, (2) observing family interaction, (3) learning, at first hand and in the presence of the adolescent, the nature of the problem. Future interviews with the adolescent alone are not precluded and the writers have not found that these have been adversely affected by the initial joint family interview, especially if it can be arranged that the psychiatrist sees the adolescent alone immediately afterwards. The simplest practical arrangement is for psychiatrist and P.S.W. to interview the family jointly and then to divide up, P.S.W. to see the parents and psychiatrist to see the adolescent. Before the family leave the Clinic, the five should briefly come together again to discuss arrangements for future interviews; this provides the examiners with an opportunity to help the family to re-integrate as a unit.

SPECIAL TECHNIQUES IN INTERVIEWING ADOLESCENTS

As will already be clear, there are special difficulties in interviewing adolescents and these may require special techniques. The difficulties vary according to the stage of the adolescent process at which the referred young person is functioning, and with individual psychopathology. As a rule of thumb, younger adolescents require techniques resembling those used in interviewing children, and the older ones respond to an approach similar to that used with adults.

The adolescent's expectations of the psychiatrist have already been referred to and, by and large, it can be accepted that the psychiatrist will be seen as an authority figure threatening to reveal the young person's feared insanity, rather than as a potential helper. This is less marked during puberty and late adolescence, and maximal in early adolescence. The expectations with which young people approach psychiatrists are also determined by factors such as the place where they are seen, e.g. Remand Home, Borstal, and the reason for the referral; if the adolescent knows that the psychiatrist has to prepare a report for the Court, he often believes that his report will finally determine his destiny, i.e. he endows the examiner with all the power of the Court. In these circumstances, it should be made clear to him that the psychiatrist's power to influence the Court is limited, in the hope of diminishing this omnipotent transference situation. Nonetheless, youngsters interviewed in circumstances such as the above, can be expected to confabulate, 'forget' the circumstances surrounding their alleged offence or even to remain mute, refusing to say anything at all on the assumption that it may get them into even worse trouble. The psychiatrist who is aware of the power with which he may be endowed is in a much better position for coping with the adolescent's fears.

Negativism is a frequent attitude encountered in adolescents and can be responsible for mutism. Thus, a youngster who knows that he is in trouble with the law or his family, but who does not understand why, often defends himself against frightening fears of insanity and helplessness by assuming that he has been 'wronged'. The authors are familiar with a young sexual offender, who has been diagnosed as schizophrenic by three experienced adult psychiatrists on the basis of his mutism and flatness of affect; they had interviewed him in a closed Remand Unit where the boys spent a proportion of their time in solitary confinement. Discussion with the Remand Unit Officers revealed that the boy did not behave abnormally at communal meals or recreation times, and appeared able to mix adequately with his peer-group. When released from the Remand Unit into an open Adolescent Unit, the question of schizophrenia immediately became inappropriate and he was able to explain his mutism as an angry expression of hopelessness to the adults who had asked impossible (from his point of view) questions, and showed no understanding of his real confusion about his maturational difficulties.

Pubescent adolescents may have real difficulties in expressing themselves verbally and often find 'talking' much easier if they are concurrently engaged in some activity. The provision of materials for drawing and the willingness of the psychiatrist to participate in Winnicott's 'squiggles' can rapidly minimize these difficulties and make communication considerably easier.

Highly resistant adolescents may have to be 'seduced' into the psychiatric interview, by deliberately engineering the situation so that the interview removes the youngster from an even more intolerable situation. For example, prior discussion with the parents can give information about which school subjects the adolescent hates most actively; arranging the time of the interview to coincide with this subject may help to bring a resisting adolescent to the Clinic. The wise psychiatrist is advised to contact the school (preferably via the Clinic psychologist) before using this technique, as otherwise he may make an enemy of an institution which can prove to be an important therapeutic ally.

A basic attitude of respect for the young person as a developing adult goes a long way towards easing the problems of interviewing adolescents.

THE TRIPARTITE APPROACH

The 'holy trinity' of psychiatrist, P.S.W. and psychologist, which is the basic diagnostic and treatment team of Child Psychiatric Units, is equally necessary for adolescents. The work of the P.S.W. in clarifying parental difficulties in relation to the child, themselves and each other, and in contacting the relevant Community Agencies is indispensible; likewise, the psychologist's evaluation of the adolescent's cognitive functioning, knowledge of the local schools, places of further education, and conditions of employment, and liaison work with all these bodies, are equally invaluable tools in assessment and therapy. The value of projective testing has been much disputed but the writers have found information gained from the Rorschach, Object Relations Test and T.A.T., administered and interpreted by a competent psychologist, of value in assessing the nature and degree of disturbance, and suitability for psychotherapy. The behaviour and information given by an adolescent in the more structured test situation can usefully be compared with that in the less structured psychiatric interview.

The team approach has much of value to offer in the assessment of adolescent disturbance and can add an additional dimension, in the hands of experienced, insightful and mutually trusting workers, to the diagnosis of family dynamics. The behaviour of team members towards each other is to some extent influenced by their experience of the family and frank discussion between the team can often clarify some hitherto unexplained area of family interaction.

ASSESSMENT

Diagnostic assessment, if it is to be of any value in making decisions about further management, must be attempted on five levels; (1) phenomenological, (2) developmental, (3) level of functioning, (4) intra-personal, and (5) intra-familial, including a formulation of the predominant patterns of interaction in the family. The psychiatrist should beware of confusing the latter two aspects of the diagnostic formulation: both are essential and complementary, but he will be using different theoretical frameworks for each (with the additional complication of an often common language) and the inter-relation between individual and inter-personal theories is as yet ill-defined.

While it is well known that operational formulations of intra-personal and inter-personal dynamics are difficult and time-consuming, the difficulties of the accurate phemomenological diagnosis of adolescents are less appreciated. There are no psychiatric syndromes peculiar to adolescence but the way in which 'adult' syndromes present is considerably coloured by the maturational processes of adolescence. Masterson (1967) has emphasized the difficulties of accurate diagnosis during the adolescent period and has also put forward a convincing argument (based upon his careful reasearch study) for its importance. In contrast, other authorities argue that phenomenological diagnosis is of little value in decisions as to management and that it has a negative value in that it deflects the psychiatrist's attention from maturational processes and leads to an attitude of therapeutic nihilism. However, since one important function of diagnosis is prognosis, in the absence of controlled follow-up studies other than Masterson's, the psychiatrist must be cautious in his avoidance of the task of phenomenological diagnosis.

CLASSIFICATION AND SPECIFIC SYNDROMES

The classification of disorders of children and adolescents has attracted much recent attention, since the categories currently in use have been found to be of limited value, especially in prognosis. Hence a number of new systems of classification have recently been devised but are all subject to many of the same criticisms applied to the older systems in psychiatry. The writers adhere to a modified version of the system suggested by the Group for the Advancement of Psychiatry in 1966. This system takes account of developmental disorders in children and adolescents and has recently had support from other workers (Bemporad et al., 1970).

The popular terms 'adolescent crisis', 'adolescent turmoil', 'identity crisis', are of no diagnostic value whatsoever for they fail completely to discriminate between essentially 'healthy' and 'unhealthy' reactions. It would be equally meaningless to diagnose an adult as suffering from 'the adult crisis'.

Thus, while the vital concept of maturation can never be forgotten by the Adolescent Psychiatrist, it should not be used as an excuse for failure to diagnose pathology. Clearly, there is still much confusion in the inter-relationship between maturational processes and psychopathology, and it will be many years before the Adolescent Psychiatrist can confidently outline criteria of health or sickness in young people, without falling somewhere between these two stools.

DIAGNOSTIC CATEGORIES

(following a modified version of the G.A.P. classification)

Healthy Reactions

These can be defined as the transient reactions of adolescents to stresses which are either intra-psychic and developmental, or exogenous. Thus an adolescent grieving the loss of a loved person cannot be defined as 'sick'. Likewise, transient episodes of depression, euphoria, brief periods of depersonalization or derealization with occasional ideas of reference, can be related to maturational stresses and are not necessarily indices of serious disturbance.

In making this diagnosis, the psychiatrist must make a careful evaluation of the precise maturational stresses with which the adolescent is struggling, and relate this meaningfully to his evaluation of the mental state.

The most significant indicator of whether or not an adolescent is seriously disturbed is his level of day to day functioning, i.e. his relationship with the family and his peer-group; his attitude towards his developing sexuality and the degree of interest and experimentation with the opposite sex; his school or work performance. If an adolescent is functioning reasonably satisfactorily in most of these areas, the psychiatrist is justified in diagnosing an essentially healthy maturational reaction with some confidence, despite the presence of symptoms. In the assessment of an adolescent, an accurate knowledge of the adolescent's reality level of functioning is of infinitely more value in determining the degree of his disturbance than any detailed examination of his fantasies or 'worrying thoughts'.

Developmental Deviations

This diagnosis is applicable to a youngster who displays either a deviation in *time* of maturational patterns, i.e. precocity, delay or fixation at an earlier stage, or in a specific *area* of development, i.e. motor, sensory, speech, cognitive, social, sexual, affective or integrative.

Thus, an enuretic adolescent could be classified under this heading; likewise, a late adolescent with no drive to become independent and who is quite content to spend most of his time with his parents may be exhibiting maturational delay in the social and sexual areas of development. In such cases, the differential diagnosis between developmental deviation, reactive disorder, psychoneurosis and personality disorder can be difficult.

Mental subnormality can be seen as a specific maturational delay of the cognitive and social areas but is dealt with in a sepatate section. Nonetheless, the adolescent's level of intellectual development can affect the level of overall development appropriate to him, and should be taken into consideration in the diagnosis of maturational delay.

Psychoneurotic Disorders

Adolescents can present with all the neurotic patterns seen in adults, though the presentation is inevitably flavoured by the age-appropriate maturational processes. Frankly delinquent, anti-social behaviour, occurring in young people with no previous history of delinquency, can sometimes be the presenting symptom of neurotic conflict in adolescents, and it is important to differentiate 'neurotic delinquency' from anti-social character formation, since the treatment and prognosis for the disorders are quite different.

Hysterical dissociative states are not uncommonly seen in adolescents (particularly girls) but these are usually associated with more profound disorders of personality.

Anxiety states and depression are particularly common in adolescence when maturational stresses have reactivated previously unresolved conflicts or grief reactions.

Psychotic Disorders

Manic Depressive psychosis. This is rarely diagnosed in adolescence. There being no logical reason to suppose that the disorder does not have a prodromal phase, it can only be assumed that it is in fact either missed or misdiagnosed in adolescents, unless it presents in florid form. The reasons for this are two-fold: (1) most adolescents show pronounced mood-swings, though these are rarely other than transient, and (2) 'depression' and 'mania' in adolescents are well-known prodromal features of an incipient schizophrenic breakdown. Thus it may be that a number of youngsters diagnosed as schizophrenic may in fact be displaying the prodromal features of a manic depressive psychosis. To date, there is no reported long-term follow-up study of depressed or elated adolescents which could clarify this issue.

The difficulties of making this diagnosis can be illustrated by the following example: a 14 year old adolescent girl presented with typical features of an obsessive-compulsive psychoneurosis: her mother had suffered for many years from a severe obsessional illness. The girl was treated for two years with intensive psychotherapy, during which it became apparent that her neurotic symptoms fluctuated with her mood swings (as is well documented in adult obsessional patients). Six months after what had appeared to be a moderately successful termination of therapy, she was re-referred in a floridly hypomanic state. Treatment with phenothiazines was rapidly effective but soon afterwards she became profoundly depressed. She then proceeded to fluctuate for many months between hypomania and depression before stabilizing to a state approximating to that existing at the termination of psychotherapy. The question then remains of whether this girl was in fact suffering from an obsessional neurosis, complicated by pronounced adolescent lability of mood which was exacerbated by termination of therapy; or, were her obsessional symptoms in fact prodromal to an adult manic depressive disorder? A third possibility is that she was in fact exhibiting the prodromal phase of a schizophrenic illness which has yet to manifest itself.

Schizophrenia. It is well-known that the age of onset of the catatonic and hebephrenic forms of schizophrenia is during adolescence and early adulthood. It is equally well-known that the modes of presentation of an early schizophrenic illness are protean. An illustration of this is a 17 year old girl, presenting with all the classical features of a depressive illness precipitated by the breakdown of a love affair. When treated with a combination of tricyclic antidepressants and psychotherapy, she appeared to make a good recovery within a few months; however, before the termination of therapy was even completed, she presented as an emergency, with all the cardinal signs of catatonic schizophrenia which thereafter followed a relapsing and remitting course.

When the psychosis is full-blown, the diagnosis of adolescent schizophrenia does not differ from that in young adults; however, the psychiatrist must beware of placing too much emphasis on symptoms such as withdrawal, depersonalization, ideas of reference in adolescents, when these occur in relative isolation. As already stated, the degree of adolescent disturbance is most reliably assessed by his everyday level of functioning, and if this is reasonably adequate then one need not be unduly alarmed about him.

Personality Disorders

The accurate diagnosis of a specific personality disorder is notoriously difficult in adults, and even more so in adolescents, where the personality structure is still in a state of flux.

The type of personality disorder most commonly seen by adolescent psychiatrists is the impulsive, disorganized type, prone to react to frustration by 'acting out' in some form, i.e. young people who rapidly discharge tension in behaviour which is socially maladaptive or unacceptable and fall somewhere within the 'delinquent' group. While the 'tension-discharge' personality disorder is an easily recognizable entity, the psychiatrist should exercise caution in (a) the diagnosis and (b) its apparent equation with adult psychopathic states. The adolescent's developmental immaturity must be remembered, and his capacity to inhibit impulses must not be equated with that of an adult. As mentioned under 'psychoneuroses', an extremely inhibited, compliant adolescent may on occasion react to severe neurotic or maturational conflict with anti-social behaviour; to diagnose such an adolescent as having a 'tension-discharge' personality disorder would be quite erroneous. Anti-social or delinquent behaviour must therefore be viewed within the total context of the adolescent's life-history, current stresses and maturational state. When regarded in this light, delinquent behaviour can be seen to fall into two major categories: (1) reactive to maturational or neurotic conflict and (2) a lifelong pattern, or personality disorder. Inevitably, there is considerable overlap between the two categories but an attempt must be made to discern the predominant trend.

Alcoholism and Drug-Addiction

These disorders are classifiable under 'Personality Disorder' and patients suffering from them should primarily be assessed in a similar manner, with the same caution and reservations. The additional complication of their drug-dependence or addiction has the same implications as with adults.

The current social alarm about the use of drugs by an increasing number of pubescent children and the 'epidemic' of drug addiction amongst teenagers cannot be simply explained. Judging from published figures, the social alarm is reality-based and, as members of society, most psychiatrists share it. It is another question as to whether psychiatrists are the appropriate people to explain and deal with this social phenomenon, apart from making their skills available to those addicts who seek help. Nonetheless, all psychiatrists dealing with adolescents are obliged to discuss fully the implications of drug or alcohol usage with those youngsters who are tempted to dabble in the field.

If the psychiatrist has anything to offer in the disquieting area of juvenile addiction to alcohol and other drugs, it is most likely to be in the form of co-operating with social scientists in an attempt to understand why the adolescent phase of maturation is currently clashing with social mores to such an extent that our young people are (1) bent on self-destruction or (2) unable to tolerate the situation in which they find themselves, without distorting their perceptions.

Organic Brain Syndromes

The position of adolescents with a degree of cerebral impairment such as would be classified under 'minimal cerebral dysfunction' has already been referred to under factors predisposing to breakdown. These young people may present with difficulties of all types, e.g. neurotic, delinquent etc., which can be understood either in terms of the primary, (presumed) organic basis, or, more usefully as far as treatment is concerned, as the result of the prolonged psychosocial effects of their disability. Life-long restlessness, irritability, clumsiness, poor concentration etc., are all liable to produce difficulties in inter-personal relationships. As children, their difficulties may have gone unrecognized so that at adolescence they present with 'chips on their shoulders'; conversely, they may have been over-protected by anxious parents and thus have increased difficulty in separating and becoming independent.

Epileptic adolescents have similar difficulties and additional problems in finding employment. The differential diagnosis between hysteria and epilepsy arising de novo at adolescence can be difficult.

Dyslexic adolescents require special educational and vocational assistance, e.g. they may require a scribe for writing examinations.

Psychosomatic Disorders

Adolescents are prone to all the known psychosomatic disorders; those which affect their social adjustment, e.g. ulcerative colitis, eczema, can present special difficulties.

Adolescents with life-long psychosomatic illnesses are likely to have special difficulties in achieving independence, irrespective of the psychopathology of their illness. Diabetic adolescents may begin to show a psychosomatic picture by refusing insulin or ignoring diets, these having become symbolically equated with dependence on the parents.

Anorexia Nervosa frequently begins in adolescence and the interested reader is referred to Warren's (1968) paper on the subject.

Mental Retardation

The Adolescent Psychiatrist is most often approached by the parents of retarded young people on account of the adolescents' social incapacity and general developmental delay, e.g. they may persistently play with small children. Another reason for referral is when the parents have never been able to accept their child's handicap and have unrealistic aspirations for him; this in turn produces conflict and feelings of worthlessness (perhaps leading to self-defensive rebellious acts) on the part of the adolescent.

Retarded young people are especially vulnerable if they become attached to a delinquent sub-culture, as may be the case if they are rejected by their more advanced peer-group, and have not been introduced to the special social facilities available for them in many areas. In view of their poor intellectual endowment, they are the members of 'the gang' who are especially likely to be 'caught' when engaged in minor delinquent activities.

Parents are often alarmed by the sexual maturation of their retarded youngsters and the adolescent may perceive a general 'taboo' on sexuality which adds to his own maturational conflict.

Special Symptoms

Of the wide variety of special symptoms seen in adolescents, only some of the commonest will be discussed:

Pregnancy in Adolescence. It is questionable, in our present 'permissive' society, whether pregnancy in an adolescent girl can be regarded as symptomatic of underlying disturbance. Nonetheless, one is clinically impressed by the number of girls and boys who wish to have intercourse but are totally opposed to the use of contraceptives. One is thus led to suspect that some pregnant adolescents (and their boy friends) are having particular difficulty with some aspect of the adolescent process, and many authors have suggested this.

Whether or not the pregnancy can in part be accounted for by disturbance in the girl, it is fairly certain that she will be disturbed thereafter. Continuance of pregnancy must inevitably impede her educational and work prospects and she is plunged into an adult, maternal role for which she is not yet emotionally prepared. If she requests termination, and this can be arranged, the psychiatrist has an obligation to ensure that some professional helper remains in contact with her. The more disturbed the girl, the more likely she is to have repeated pregnancies.

Illegitimate pregnancy appears to run in families and adolescent girls who become pregnant tend, more frequently than would be expected by chance, to have themselves been conceived out of wedlock.

Sexual Deviations. The question of adolescent homosexual anxiety has already been mentioned and it is not usually difficult to discriminate between those youngsters who are using homosexuality as a transient defence against maturational stresses, and those in whom the disturbance is more profound and likely to be lasting. The latter may be distressed by their desires but show no positive interest in the opposite sex, in contrast to the former, who tend to be more anxious and to fluctuate between homo- and hetero-sexual pursuits.

Homosexual panic is not infrequent in adolescents and may indicate serious underlying pathology, e.g. schizophrenia.

Exhibitionism is a fairly frequent reason for referral (often from the Court) and occurs most commonly in boys with intense sexual inhibition and general feelings of inferiority and worthlessness.

Summary

In the foregoing section, the writers have not attempted to make a comprehensive description of psychiatric syndromes in adolescence. The most commonly seen syndromes have been described and the emphasis has been on aspects of syndromes which differ in presentation or implication from their adult equivalents. It is assumed that the reader is familiar with adult psychiatric disorders and, when considering the presentation of these in adolescence, will take due cognisance of the maturational processes occurring, and how these interrelate with syndrome-specific psychopathology.

Again, it must be said that adolescent disturbance can only be assessed within the total context of the life situation and no single symptom or syndrome (with the few obvious exceptions) should be regarded *in isolation* as indicative of serious disturbance.

Symptom patterns may fluctuate with great rapidity in disturbed adolescents but the overall picture remains constant over a longer period of time (Masterson, 1967).

TREATMENT APPROACHES

When considering treatment of a distressed adolescent, presented by his distressed family, the psychiatrist must ask himself four essential questions:

1. *Is treatment necessary*, or would intervention impede an essentially healthy developmental process by diminishing the adolescent's and family's confidence in their ability to cope with the crisis within themselves? Offering psychoanalysis to an essentially healthy adolescent who is simply asking for reassurance about his sadistic fantasies is likely to be damaging to him. Likewise, such an offer to their child, may disrupt a family who would have been able to cope with their difficulties, with a little professional reassurance that all was essentially well.

2. *Who should be treated*? Should it be the adolescent alone, his parents (either individually or jointly) or should the whole family be included? Parents who are overtly complaining that their 15 year old is not always home by 10 p.m. are almost certainly seeking help for themselves (although they may not recognize it) and are using the adolescent as an 'admission ticket'. In such circumstances it would clearly be detri-

mental to offer treatment to the adolescent; it may however be necessary to involve him in a rather prolonged 'assessment phase' until his parents are able to acknowledge their own wish for help, and during this phase the adolescent must be handled with considerable tact and respect.

3. *What is the optimum treatment for this particular family?*—Psychoanalysis for all, removal of the adolescent from home, antidepressants for mother, vocational guidance for the adolescent?—etc.

4. *What treatment is practicable*, bearing in mind the facilities and available agencies, the motivation of the family, forthcoming changes in their life-situation (e.g. the adolescent is about to leave school and embark on an apprenticeship) and the predicted side-effects of treatment on their lives (e.g. time off work or school; neglect of other children)?

Having answered these questions, the psychiatrist is left with a wide range of treatment approaches from which to choose:

1. Admission to an inpatient psychiatric unit for one or more family members (or the whole family).

2. Individual psychotherapy or psychoanalysis for the adolescent alone.

3. Individual psychotherapy for the adolescent and casework or psychotherapy for one or both parents.

4. Individual treatment for the parents alone.

5. Group therapy for the adolescent, with or without concurrent treatment for his parents (group, joint or individual).

6. Conjoint family therapy.

7. Multi-family group therapy.

8. Supportive therapy for one or more family members.

9. Remedial education for the adolescent.

10. Vocational guidance.

11. Drugs or physical treatment (rarely advisable with the exception of psychotic adolescents, or for the parents).

12. Behaviour therapy, e.g. aversion therapy for tics; the use of 'the buzzer' for enuresis.

13. Speech therapy for stammerers.

14. Residential schooling—maladjusted or otherwise.

15. Committal of the adolescent to the care of the local authority if he is outwith parental control and 'in need of care and protection'.

With the exceptions of the treatment approaches indicated for specific disorders, the indications for other treatment methods vary so widely that one must conclude that, in the present state of our knowledge, psychiatrists prescribe whatever form of treatment that (1) they believe to be most helpful and (2) they are most comfortable in providing. At best, indications for treatment can only be relative since available facilities vary so widely.

PSYCHOTHERAPY WITH ADOLESCENTS

Individual

Psychiatrists differ widely in the psychotherapeutic techniques they consider appropriate to adolescents (Holmes, 1964; James, 1964; Gladstone, 1964). The spectrum of views ranges from the use of classical psychoanalytic techniques to conscious collusion with the adolescent's pathology in order to establish a treatment alliance. This latter method has most often been advocated for use with delinquent teenagers (Schwartz, 1967).

In the authors' view psychotherapy with adolescents undoubtedly requires the development of special techniques in order to cater for maturational needs. The classical 'blank-screen' approach, which must inevitably heighten identity conflict, has been found to be too anxiety-provoking for many adolescents and may drive them out of therapy. Anxieties about body-image, dependency and sexuality frequently prevent the use of the couch, with its implications of passivity for the adolescent. A strictly passive, non-directive approach may imply a lack of interest to the adolescent, especially those who are experiencing difficulty with impulse control. Conversely, sympathetic involvement may be interpreted by the adolescent as threateningly 'incestuous', as evidence of weakness and manipulability in the therapist, or an attempt to infantilize him.

Most adolescents rapidly identify their therapists as powerful authority figures and limit-testing frequently occupies a substantial portion of therapeutic time. This, together with the apparent 'destructive hatred' to which the therapist is frequently subjected in the transference can sorely try the psychiatrist, who must be constantly and keenly aware of his counter-transference. The attempt to avoid adolescent criticism and self-aggrandizing (defensive) destructiveness has led many therapists to infantilize the patient, thus depriving themselves of their most valuable therapeutic ally—namely, the adolescent's forward drive towards maturation (Acton, 1970).

The authors have found two guiding principles helpful in therapeutic interactions with adolescents: (1) the need to set clearly-defined limits which are well within the therapist's level of tolerance. This is considered necessary because it provides reassurance for the adolescent that his aggressive and sexual drives will not get out of control and either damage or drive the therapist away; also because the therapist must inevitably withdraw interest and cease to provide objective care if his personal limits of tolerance are exceeded: (2) the use of confrontation techniques which both confirm the therapist's respect for the adolescent and provide evidence of his capacity to maintain control of the situation. The adolescent's tendency to project his relatively low anxiety tolerance, his fear of aggressive and sexual drives and their counterpart, the regressive drive towards childhood, his precarious sense of identity and frequent fears of desertion and isolation, must always determine the therapist's approach and comments.

Insight Therapy, with all the above reservations is the treatment of choice for adolescents suffering from psychoneurotic or reactive disorders. It must, however, be remembered that adolescents are supremely capable of using intellectual insight as a defence against emotional change.

Ego-Supportive Therapy and environmental manipulation is generally more useful with delinquent and brain-damaged adolescents.

Group Therapy

Group therapy has many advantages for adolescents in view of their tendency to 'gang formation' (Evans, 1965; Acton, 1970). Adolescents are less likely to be overwhelmed by 'authority-laden' or 'incestuous' transference situations when supported by their peers and outnumbering the adults present. Similarly, therapists are prevented from avoiding adolescent aggression by infantilization in the group setting. The inherent tendency of groups or gangs towards autonomy and self-sufficiency can be turned to therapeutic advantage and systems of values and internal controls develop, which reinforce and confirm the adolescents' drive towards independence.

Adolescent groups have their specific features which require the development of special techniques on the part of group therapists. As with individual therapy, the authors feel that emphasis is required on limit-setting and confrontation. Silence, acting-out and the projection of unacceptable aspects of the group on to vulnerable members are the most frequent problems encountered and require much activity on the part of the therapist for their successful management.

PROGNOSIS

The assumption that adolescents will 'grow out of it' without treatment has been shown to be erroneous by Masterson, (1967). The majority of Masterson's group of 72 disturbed adolescents continued to show both symptoms and impairment of functioning at five-year follow-up. One can conclude then that the current emphasis on facilities for the treatment of disturbed adolescents has been, and will continue to be, essential.

REFERENCES

ACTON, W. P. (1970) *Analytic Group Therapy with Delinquents*. Paper read at the Fifth Conference of the Association of Psychiatric Study of Adolescents, Edinburgh.

BANKS, C. (1965) Boys in Detention Centres. In *Studies in Psychology*, Edited by C. Banks and P. L. Broadhurst. London: University Press.

BATESON, C. (1965) Towards a Theory of Schizophrenia. In *Behavioural Science*, Vol. 1, 251–264.

BEMPORAD, J. R., PFEIFER, C. M. & BLOOM, W. (1970) Twelve Months Experience with the G.A.P. Classification of Childhood Disorders. *American Journal of Psychiatry*, **127**, 658.

BLOS, P. (1962) *On Adolescence*. New York: The Free Press and London: Collier-MacMillan Limited.

BOWLBY, J. (1969) *Attachment and Loss*. Vol. 1, London: Hogarth Press.

CAPLAN, G. (1964) *Principles of Preventive Psychiatry*. London: Tavistock Publications.

CONNERS, G. K. (1967) Syndrome of minimal cerebral dysfunction: psychological aspects. *Paediatric Clinics of North America*, **14**, 749.

ERIKSON, E. H. (1963) *Childhood and Society*, 2nd edn, New York: Norton.

EVANS, J. (1965) Inpatient analytic group therapy of neurotic and delinquent adolescents. *Psychotherapy and Psychosomatics*, **13**, 265–270.

FAIRBAIRN, W. R. D. (1952) *Psychoanalytic Studies of the Personality*. London: Tavistock Publications.

FLAVELL, J. H. (1963) *The Developmental Psychology of Jean Piaget*. Princeton: D. Van Nostrand Co. Inc.

FORSSMANN, H. & THUWE, I. (1966) One Hundred and Twenty Children Born After Application for Therapeutic Abortion Refused. *Acta pyschiatrica et neurologica scandinavica*, **42**, 71–88.

FREUD, A. (1958) Adolescence. *Psychoanalytic Study of the Child*. **13**, 255–278.

FREUD, S. (1905) Three essays on the theory of sexuality. In *Collected Works* (Standard edition) VII, London: Hogarth Press.

GLADSTONE, H. P. (1964) Psychotherapy with adolescents: Theme and variations. *Psychiatric Quarterly*, **38**, 304–309.

GRAHAM, P. & RUTTER, M. (1968) Organic brain Dysfunction and child psychiatric disorder. *British Medical Journal*, **iii**, 695–700.

GREGORY, I. (1965) Anterospective data following childhood loss of a parent. *Archives of General Psychiatry*, **13**, 99–109.

GROUP FOR THE ADVANCEMENT OF PSYCHIATRY (1966) *Psychopathological Disorders in Childhood: Theoretical Considerations and Proposed Classification*. Report No. 62.

HENDERSON, A. S., McCULLOCH, J. W. & PHILIP, A. E. (1967) Survey of mental illness in adolescence. *British Medical Journal* **1**, 83–84.

HERBERT, M. (1964) The concept and testing of brain damage in children: A review. *Journal of Child Psychology and Psychiatry*, **5**, 197–216.

HERTZIG, M. E. & BIRCH, H. G. (1966) Neurologic organization in Psychiatrically disturbed adolescent girls. *Archives of General Psychiatry*, **15**, 590–598.

HOLMES, D. J. (1964) *The Adolescent in Psychotherapy*. London: J. A. Churchill.

INHELDER, B. & PIAGET, J. (1958) *The Growth of Logical Thinking from Childhood to Adolescence*. Trans. Anne Parsons and Stanley Milgram. London: Routledge and Kegan Paul.

JAMES, M. (1964) Interpretation and management in the treatment of pre-adolescents. *International Journal of Psychoanalysis*, **45**, 499–511.

JOHNSON, A. M. & SZUREK, S. A. (1952) The genesis of anti-social acting out in children and adults. *Psychoanalytic Quarterly*, **21**, 323–328.

KELLMER PRINGLE, M. L. (1967) *Adoption—Facts and Fallacies*. London: Longmans.

KIDD, C. B. & DIXON, G. H. (1968) The incidence of psychiatric illness in Aberdeen teenagers. *Health Bulletin*, Vol. XXVI, **2**, 7–9.

LIDZ, T. (1964) *The Family and Human Adaptation*. London: Hogarth Press.

MASTERSON, J. F. (1967) *The Psychiatric Dilemma of Adolescence.* London: J. A. Churchill.

McWHINNIE, A. M. (1967) *Adopted Children: How They Grow Up.* London: Routledge and Kegan Paul.

ROSEN, B. M., BAHN, A. K., SHELLOW, R. & BOWER, E. M. (1965) Adolescent patients served in outpatient psychiatric clinics. *American Journal of Public Health*, **55**, 1563–1577.

RUTTER, M. (1966) Prognosis: Psychotic children in adolescence and early adult life. In *Early Childhood Autism*, Edited by J. K. Wing, London: Pergamon Press.

RYCROFT, C. (1968) *A Critical Dictionary of Psychoanalysis.* London: Nelson.

SCHWARTZ, L. J. (1967) Treatment of the adolescent psychopath—Theory and case report. *Psychotherapy Theory, Research and Practice.* Vol. **4**, 133–137.

SHIELDS, R. W. (1964) *Mutative Confusion at Adolescence.* Report of the twentieth child guidance inter-clinic conference.

TANNER, J. M. (1962) *Growth at Adolescence.* 2nd Edn, Oxford: Blackwell.

WARREN, W. (1968) A study of Anorexia Nervosa in young girls. *Journal of Child Psychology and Psychiatry and Allied Disciplines*, **9**, 27–40.

WINNICOTT, D. W. (1971) *Therapeutic Consultations in Child Psychiatry.* London: Hogarth Press.

Chapter V

ALCOHOLISM AND DRUG MISUSE

R. A. Parry

GENERAL PRINCIPLES

DEFINITIONS

For the limited purpose of this chapter, a *drug* is a substance which alters perception. It may become heightened, diminished or changed; and as a result, the user's appreciation of reality is modified. A drug is *misused* when, not being pharmacologically or physiologically necessary, it is used in the face of legal prohibition, or when, in the case of those substances not so proscribed, the amount used exceeds that generally regarded as socially acceptable.

Drug addiction was defined by the World Health Organization in the following terms in 1950: 'Addiction is a state of periodic or chronic intoxication detrimental to the individual and society produced by the repeated consumption of a drug (natural or synthetic). Its characteristics include an overpowering desire or need (compulsion) to continue taking the drug and to obtain it by any means; a tendency to increase the dose; a psychic (psychological) and sometimes a physical dependence on the effect of the drug'. This definition has stood the test of time, but has been modified periodically in an endeavour to eliminate the confusion occasioned by the use of such words as habituation, addiction, dependence and compulsion. However, many regard this distinction as having clinical validity.

In 1965, an Interdepartmental Committee chaired by Lord Brain defined a drug addict as: 'A person who not requiring the continued use of a drug for the relief of the symptoms of organic disease has acquired as a result of repeated administration an overpowering desire for its continuance and in whom withdrawal of the drug leads to definite symptoms of mental or physical distress or disorder'.

In this section the following, strictly clinical, approach will be made (Parry, 1971). An individual may be psychologically dependent on a substance or he may be addicted to it. *Psychological dependence* means that he is unable to live a normal life without the substance. For example, the heavy smoker will take a cigarette as a preliminary to every task he undertakes, however familiar. When the task is unfamiliar or creates undue anxiety, he is likely to take a larger quantity of the substance more frequently. When the stress passes, he reverts to his previous dose. In terms of this definition, tobacco is to be regarded as a drug of psychological dependence.

Addiction is a clearly defined clinical syndrome characterized by a diagnostic triad of psychological dependence, change in tolerance and a specific abstinence syndrome. Psychological dependence has already been described. *Change in Tolerance* (habituation) is usually in the direction of increase in tolerance, so that the addict may take a dose which would be many times that considered to be fatal in the non-addict. For example, the morphine addict may take a dose of 2 g—40 or 50 mg might be fatal to the non-addict. In the later stages of alcohol addiction, there is a paradoxical decrease in tolerance. The *abstinence syndrome* is a pathological systemic reaction, presumably of biochemical origin, which occurs when the substance is abruptly and completely withdrawn. In alcohol addiction, the abstinence syndrome is delirium tremens. For barbiturate addiction, an acute confusional state usually occurs. This is usually ushered in by epileptiform fits.

AVAILABILITY

The substance may not be legally available in the addict's country of residence (e.g. heroin in the United States). Supplies can therefore be obtained only by illegal means.

Most drugs to be considered are available only on the prescription of a doctor, dentist or veterinary surgeon. Their undesirable use may arise by injudicious prescription, as a result of self medication by persons to whom they are available (e.g. doctors and nurses), and by illegal manufacture or purchase.

Some substances are freely available, and addiction or dependence may occur without any illegal act (e.g. alcohol, heroin in Britain before 1919).

TYPES OF DRUG DEPENDENCE

Narcotics, the 'hard' drugs. These are predominantly powerful pain relieving substances such as opium, its derivatives and its synthetic analogues.

Hypnotics, sedatives and mild analgesics. The most important members of this group are the barbiturates and the non-barbituarate hypnotics.

Stimulants, especially amphetamine, its analogues and combinations. Cocaine falls within this group.

'Phantastica' or 'hallucinogens'. There are the drugs which are taken because of the changes in perception which they produce. They include cannabis, mescaline, L.S.D. and S.T.P.

Alcohol. This is the only substance to which addiction can occur without indulging in illicit activities, and the only substance which is subject to fiscal rather than legal controls.

AETIOLOGY

Addiction or dependence are nearly always secondary to a primary disease or to a social situation which facilitates the heavy use of the substance. The primary disease is usually a psychiatric one, although it is sometimes a physical one.

The primary conditions may be classified as follows:

The major psychoses. A small group of psychiatric patients find a substance such as alcohol which acts effectively as a tranquillizer or anti-depressant. Sometimes it also provides people who are isolated or withdrawn with the opportunity of mixing with other illegal users. The depressed patient may be relieved of the recrimination of his conscience, the schizophrenic of his persecutory delusions and hallucinations. The primary illness is often amenable to appropriate psychiatric treatment in these patients.

Severe personality disorders of the sociopathic type. Patients in this category readily become dependent or addicted, but they are totally unreliable, and although they may seem sincere in their intention to reform, their protestations are rapidly shown for the shallow insincerities that they are. The sociopath who becomes addicted readily changes his addiction from one substance to another, and represents an almost impossible therapeutic prospect.

Psychoneurosis. If psychoneurotic illnesses are considered to be compromise reactions arising from a conflict between instinctual drive and social controls, it can be readily understood that the symptoms are rapidly alleviated when one of the opposing forces is removed. For example, alcohol 'dissolves away' social prohibitions, and the neurotic personality is particularly liable to become addicted to it. Such patients may show release phenomena of markedly aggressive or promiscuous type following the consumption of a drug.

Physical illness. The primary illness tends to be a long continued, disabling, relatively non-killing disease, such as arthritis and bronchitis. Some of these patients use drugs to alleviate their physical discomforts, and in due course become addicted. The use of heavy doses of narcotics in terminal illnesses is one of the few instances of acceptable iatrogenic addiction.

Social and professional use. Alcoholism may occur in people for whom alcohol is relatively cheap (e.g. the very rich, the 'expense account men', people concerned with the manufacture and sale of alcohol, people who live in some wine producing countries). The risk of addiction following self medication by a doctor or nurse is well recognized and falls into this category, as may that following extensive and unnecessary prescription of barbiturates by doctors for their patients.

It may be noted here that some psychotic patients claim to be drug addicts. This is particularly likely to occur in those with depressive delusions and low self-esteem. They may ask for treatment of a disease which they regard as shameful but appropriate. The doctor may be tricked into undertaking the treatment of such patients, perceiving their depression as appropriate to their addiction.

TREATMENT

Withdrawal. It is nearly always necessary for the patient to be admitted to hospital for this purpose. Often, he will protest vigorously and with sincerity that he can manage alone, but he is seldom able to do so. Where applicable, appropriate prophylactic treatment for the abstinence syndrome is instituted: a tranquillizer and an anti-convulsant are usually included.

Treatment of the primary condition (see earlier section)

OUTCOME

The individual should never again use the substance, or any other substance to which dependence or addiction may occur. In exceptional circumstances (e.g. severe pain in a former morphine addict) the substance may be administered under medical supervision under strictly inpatient conditions. When the substance is one which is commonly used socially (e.g. alcohol), the patient is very likely to relapse. This is particularly so when the underlying condition is not amenable to treatment (e.g. sociopathy).

ALCOHOLISM

DEFINITION

Alcohol is used to help people enjoy the company of others. It promotes relaxation and good fellowship. It is part of a ritual which is concerned with pleasure, celebration, success and sometimes failure. Alcoholism grows insidiously out of social use when ordinary limits are exceeded and alcohol becomes an end in itself. It is a continuous process, not a single state, and terminates with serious addiction and the gross stigmata of chronic alcoholism—cirrhosis of the liver, peripheral neuritis, Korsakov's psychosis, Wernicke's encephalopathy, and so on. The road to this terminal state is well charted, and the features will be given later in this section.

It is not easy to give a brief definition which adequately describes the total picture, but the one most commonly accepted is that used by the World Health Organization (1952): 'Alcoholics are those excessive drinkers whose dependence on alcohol has attained such a degree that they show a noticeable mental disturbance or an interference with their mental and bodily health, their inter-personal relations and their smooth social and economic functioning, or who show the prodromal signs of such developments. They therefore require treatment'.

From the points of view of aetiology, diagnosis, treatment and prognosis, this definition may be modernized by rephrasing it as follows: Alcoholism is a disease of interpersonal relationships. One or more members of the relationship become excessively dependent on alcohol, to such a degree that noticeable mental disturbance develops. Their smooth social and economic functioning is impaired, leading to interference with their mental and bodily health. They therefore require treatment.

PREVALENCE

The true prevalence of alcoholism is unkown, although various ingenious attempts have been made to estimate it. The problem presents two major difficulties. The first is to formulate the disease in terms which can be translated into clear, epidemiological variables (Keller, 1960). The second arises out of the alcoholic's tendency to deny the illness on his own account and to produce impressive rationalizations which encourage others to deny it too (Parry, 1969).

The best known method of estimating the prevalence employs the Jellinek formula (Jolliffe and Jellinek, 1941), which endeavours to derive the number of alcoholics in a community from the number of deaths attributable to cirrhosis of the liver when the proportion of these which are due to alcoholism is known. It is necessary also to know the percentage of alcoholics who die from cirrhosis of the liver. Using this formula, it is estimated that there are about 11 alcoholics per 1000 of the adult population in the United Kingdom (W.H.O., 1951). This indirect method is based on assumptions which are not necessarily justified, and Jellinek himself suggested that the formula should be abandoned (Jellinek, 1959).

A careful study in Cambridgeshire (Moss and Davies, 1968) with the help of 13 social agencies disclosed a prevalence rate of 6.2 per 1000 males and 1.4 per 1000 females of the population aged 15 years and over.

Many alcoholics, however, avoid the organizations which might be able to help them. For example, the general practitioner knows only one in nine of his alcoholic patients as such (Parr, 1957).

These figures appear to be rising. There is a steady increase in the first admissions of patients with a diagnosis of alcoholism to psychiatric hospitals notably in Scotland, although this must be balanced against the greater readiness of patients to accept psychiatric treatment. If it is assumed that the number of alcoholics in a population is proportional to the amount of alcoholic beverages consumed, Customs and Excise figures indicate that this quantity has risen considerably of recent years (H.M. Customs and Excise, 1970). The amount of spirits consumed more than doubled between 1959 and 1969, and the amount of wine imported nearly doubled in the same period. About 25 per cent more beer was consumed in this time.

The conclusion is that the prevalence of alcoholism is about one per cent of the population, and is probably increasing.

PHARMACOLOGY OF ETHYL ALCOHOL

The pharmacological action of ethyl alcohol is three-fold: local, reflex and central. The local action is on the mouth and oesophagus and is usually perceived as pleasant; but not all people, and certainly not all alcoholics, enjoy the taste of alcohol. Shortly after drinking, the individual may experience reflex dilatation of the peripheral blood vessels, which is perceived as a warm glow, so pleasant at the end of a cold, winter's day. Alcohol is absorbed directly and rapidly from the stomach and small intestine into the blood stream, and thereupon exerts its central effects on all organs of the body, particularly the central nervous system.

It is for its effect on the central nervous system that alcohol is usually consumed. It causes suppression of cortical activity to a degree proportional to the level of alcohol in the blood. The first effect of alcohol is to impair the 'highest' functions of the brain—those concerned with the perception of a total situation and the choice of a socially appropriate response. These functions are those concerned with what is 'right' and what is 'wrong', what is 'good' and what is 'bad' what is 'correct' and what is 'incorrect'. 'Bad' behaviour is inhibited in favour of 'good' behaviour. These functions are subserved by the conscience, which has been humorously but accurately defined as 'that part of the personality which is soluble in alcohol'.

When the function of the conscience is 'dissolved away', the individual is to some extent relieved of those inhibitions which are concerned with the dictates of his culture; and his release may be experienced as stimulation. He feels more free and his inhibitions concerned with sexual and aggressive behaviour may be lifted. If the blood concentration rises, lower levels of brain activity are affected. At first, those functions concerned with muscular co-ordination are depressed, so that the individual's gait becomes unsteady, his speech becomes slurred and his visual skills impaired. With greater intoxication, he loses consciousness, lapsing into coma. Ultimately, those functions concerned with the maintenance of respiration are suppressed; and at this point, the individual is in danger of death.

Alcohol by its action on other organs complicates the total picture. By its direct action on the kidneys, it acts as a diuretic. Because of its high calorific value, it can act as a food substitute (the alcohol in a bottle of whisky will supply 5000 calories); but because of its poor vitamin content (especially of vitamin B12, riboflavin, thiamin, etc.)

E

it may lead to such deficiency disorders as Wernicke's Encephalopathy and cirrhosis of the liver.

AETIOLOGY OF ALCOHOLISM

Alcoholism spans the whole spectrum of psychiatric disorder, and a careful psychiatric examination as well as a careful physical one is required when the diagnosis is made. The following is a list of some of the more restricted aetiological factors:

Age and sex. Most investigators agree that alcoholism is more prevalent in men than in women. Moss and Davies (1968) found a ratio of four to one, whilst the rather higher figure of seven to one was found in a study of the clients of Alcoholism Information Centres (Edwards *et al.*, 1967). The age group most affected is 40 to 54. The mean age of the male alcoholics in Moss and Davies' study was 44.3. For women it was 47.0.

Marital status. Individuals without a marital partner show a higher incidence of alcoholism. This is strikingly shown by Moss and Davies (1968) for divorced people of both sexes and for unmarried women. In these groups, the prevalence of alcoholism was very much higher.

Socio-economic status. Alcoholism appears to be least common in the middle socio-economic groups (Moss and Davies, 1968) (Glatt, 1961).

Race and religion. There is a low prevalence of alcoholism in Jews and a high one in Roman Catholics (Bailey *et al.*, 1965; Mulford and Miller, 1960). The incidence is higher in negroes than in the white population of North America (Bailey *et al.*, 1965). Of the countries of Western Europe, France has the heaviest consumption of alcohol, with Italy next, finally the Scandinavian countries, and the Netherlands coming last. The United Kingdom lies in a midway position (W.H.O., 1969) with Scotland showing higher rates (H.M.S.O., 1965). Rather different criteria are used for the diagnosis of alcoholism in different countries, and the available comparative statistics are unsatisfactory. It may be inferred that the pattern of alcoholism will vary correspondingly.

Employment. People concerned in the manufacture, distribution and sale of alcoholic beverages and workers in ancillary trades are particularly at risk. Business executives with liberal expense accounts are at risk if much of their work is done in the hotel lounge.

Hereditary factors. It is usually assumed that alcoholic parents are more likely to breed alcoholic children. It was noted in one survey that the sons of alcoholics are twice as likely to become alcoholics themselves as the sons of non-alcoholics (McCord and McCord, 1960). A large number of alcoholics are however the children of teetotal parents, and preoccupation with extremes of behaviour is likely to be an important factor. Example plays a part, but there are probably genetic factors at work.

Urban-rural differences. There is evidence that the prevalence is higher in rural than in urban areas (Moss and Davies, 1968; Parr, 1957).

THE DEVELOPMENT OF ALCOHOLISM

Kessel and Walton (1969) describe three stages: the stage of excessive drinking, the stage of alcohol addiction, and the stage of chronic alcoholism.

The stage of *excessive drinking* begins when the patient's intake exceeds the normal range for his culture. He may find that neurotic symptoms are alleviated by a drink, and in consequence he spends more time in social drinking and drinks more than his companions. He makes excuses to obtain drink, but feels guilty about his increased intake. He finds that he is unable to work unless he first has a drink, and his unsatisfactory performance requires increasingly elaborate excuses. During this stage, his tolerance for alcohol increases, so that he requires to drink more to bring about the same effect.

The second stage of *alcohol addiction* is heralded by one or more of the following groups of symptoms:

The alcoholic amnesia. In the argot of the alcoholic, this is known as the 'blackout'. It is due to a failure of registration. Although not particularly drunk, the alcoholic fails to register what is going on around him, and in consequence, when he comes to review the events of the previous hours, he finds he has no memory of them. There may be appointments which he has forgotten, promises which he fails to keep. He may say and do things of which he has no memory. He is puzzled at first; and worrying that he may have behaved badly, may make surreptitious enquiries of his companions about his behaviour. However, his behaviour appears normal to those around him, and they reassure him. In this respect, the alcoholic amnesia must be differentiated from drinking to near unconsciousness, which may happen in a very heavy drinking spree by a social drinker.

Morning tremulousness (the 'shakes'). On wakening in the morning, the patient finds that he is unable to keep still. His hands tremble violently and often he has a sense of apprehension for no apparent reason. The symptoms are relieved by a drink. The morning tremor is a pre-delirious symptom and, if not checked, may proceed to delirium tremens.

Delirium tremens ('D.T.s'). This is a serious illness and is diagnostic of alcohol addiction, of which it represents the abstinence syndrome. It occurs when the addict is deprived of his supply, and may be the first objective manifestation of the disease. Often, there has been no suspicion of alcoholism. The patient may be admitted to a general hospital for a serious, acute condition such as myocardial infarction. Supplies of alcohol are of course stopped, since the addiction is unrecognized. Within two or three days, the patient becomes increasingly tremulous, and a spike of temperature heralds the onset of the delirium. This is characterized by an emotional state of fear or terror and is accompanied by vivid and frightening hallucinations—the pink elephant of the cartoonist is far removed from what actually happens; more often the patient sees insects, rats or Lilliputian figures. The patient's level of consciousness is impaired. He may be disorientated for time, place and person, and demand to leave the hospital. He is often very suggestible in respect of the terrifying aspect of his illness. This is a serious illness which may result in death or a dysmnesic syndrome (see Chap. XIII). Delirium tremens usually occurs within three or four days of the withdrawal of alcohol, but sometimes does not emerge until two weeks afterwards.

Change in tolerance. In the later stages of alcohol addiction, a paradoxical drop in tolerance is seen. The patient may hitherto have been able to drink a bottle of whisky without marked effect; but now he becomes intoxicated after a very small intake. Like delirium tremens, this is presumably due to a change in metabolism. The nature is not yet defined.

As addiction proceeds, the patient shows serious impairment of his efficiency at work. Sometimes he comes late, sometimes he comes drunk, and sometimes he does not come at all. His employers know him to be a good worker and give him many chances. He promises repeatedly to pull himself together, but eventually he is given a final last chance, and then loses his job.

The family is affected. The wife takes over its management, whilst he becomes less tolerant of her, and so their relationships start to deteriorate. Heavy drinking leads to a reduction in his sexual drive, together with an increase in libido; but he is an unwelcome and unsuccessful sexual partner, and begins to develop jealous misinterpretations of his wife's behaviour which sometimes attain delusional proportions. He may blame her for his loss of sexual activity and accuse her of taking a lover. His wife may leave him because of his drinking, and he will regard this as confirmation of his suspicions. Periodically he has episodes of terrible remorse, during which a serious suicidal attempt may be made. One survey showed that 39 per cent of males who made a suicidal attempt were alcoholics (Kessel, 1965). The figure for women was 8 per cent. The parallel between alcoholism and suicide has been observed over the course of many years, and Menninger has described alcoholism as chronic suicide (Menninger, 1938).

As a result of these factors, the alcoholic becomes increasingly isolated. Sometimes in order to counteract his isolation he has periods of extravagance and over-generosity. When these fail to bring him the comfort he expects, he resorts to self pity, and uses the situation as an excuse for further drinking.

The stage of *chronic alcoholism* is one of progressive detrioration, with continuous drinking, serious physical and mental symptoms, malnutrition, and sometimes the use of cheap wine and methylated spirit. The patient has reached the 'bottom of the barrel' and he may seek help only at this point.

TYPES OF DRINKING PATTERN

Two types of drinking pattern are commonly seen—the 'loss of control' type and the 'inability to abstain' type (Jellinek's gamma and delta types respectively (1960)). The *loss of control* type (the 'compulsive' or 'uncontrolled' alcoholic) is unable to stop once he begins to drink, and he may pass through gross intoxication to unconsciousness. A favourite quotation from Alcoholics Anonymous which applies to this type is 'One is too many, twenty is not enough'. Patients who show this drinking pattern may remain abstinent for long periods.

The patient who is *unable to abstain* drinks steadily over long periods and maintains a fairly constant level of blood alcohol. He is never completely free from alcohol, although he may never become drunk. Walton has produced evidence that the personality structures of the patients who show these drinking patterns is distinctive (Walton, 1968). A third type of drinking pattern, rarely seen, is Jellinek's *epsilon* type, or '*dipsomania*'. In this, the patient is able to control his drinking for long periods, but there are bouts of loss of control when his drinking pattern takes the gamma form.

Jellinek describes two further types of alcoholism—the alpha and beta. The alpha type is alcohol dependent. He suffers periodically from emotional distress which is alleviated by alcohol, but he is able to maintain control and, if necessary, to abstain. He drinks very large quantities and in due course his physical and mental health may be affected. The beta type is seen particularly in wine drinking countries and is characterized by inability to abstain and progressive physical complications. Abstinence symptoms are prominent if supplies are cut off.

PSYCHIATRIC COMPLICATIONS OF ALCOHOLISM

1. Delirium tremens (see p. 123–124)
2. Korsakov's psychosis (Chapter XIII, Vol. II)
3. Wernicke's encephalopathy (Chapter XIII, Vol. II)

Alcoholic hallucinosis:

This is an uncommon condition and is characterized by the development of (usually) auditory hallucinations when alcohol is withdrawn. There are no other symptoms, and the hallucinations subside spontaneously, sometimes within a few weeks but sometimes after a very much longer period. It rarely continues for more than twelve months. It responds to an appropriate dose of a tranquillizer. Differential diagnosis is from other causes of hallucinations.

TREATMENT OF ALCOHOLISM

There is no cure for alcoholism *per se*, and the aim of treatment is to help the patient to become totally abstinent. Treatment therefore resolves itself into three stages (Parry, 1970): acknowledgement of the illness, withdrawal of alcohol and maintenance of abstinence.

Acknowledgement of the Illness

This is the biggest hurdle for the patient to overcome, since it means that he must face his denial. The psychological meaning of denial is demonstrated very clearly in alcoholism when the patient has been totally unable to perceive what is so obvious to everyone else—that his drinking is ruining himself, his family, and everything that is important to him. Direct confrontation is dismissed as biassed persecution, and the patient will seek every opportunity to avoid the acknowledgement of confirmatory evidence. Some patients are able to acknowledge the extent of their illness only when they have reached the 'bottom of the barrel'; but others who are less vulnerable and less defended may be helped at a much earlier stage. Many patients who apparently acknowledge their alcoholism show their true attitude by putting the need for total abstinence to the test very shortly after or sometimes even during the period that they are under medical supervision. When this happens, it is clear that denial has not been overcome.

There may be some uncertainty about the need for total abstinence even amongst the patient's medical advisers. When not experienced in the disease, they may tell their patient that it is all right for him to have one drink, provided that he does not let it get out of control. Unfortunately, alcoholics are almost never able to fulfil this condition. Evidence of the possibility of reversion to a normal drinking pattern by alcoholics (Davies, 1962; Kendell, 1965) is seized on with avidity. However, the evidence for such 'cures' must be examined very carefully. The original diagnosis must be differentiated from bout drinking and from a primary disorder of mania or hypomania, which may be characterized by excessive drinking. Further, the reliability of subsequent statements that the patient is drinking with control needs careful examination. There is no doubt that the only possible and acceptable medical advice is that the patient should stop drinking completely for the rest of his life.

Withdrawal of alcohol ('drying out', 'detoxification').

Unless domestic conditions are unusually propitious and efficient nursing can be guaranteed, alcohol is best withdrawn under inpatient conditions. There is no reason why it should not be withdrawn completely and immediately, provided that adequate precautions are instituted to combat the possible development of delirium tremens. Commonly, the patient is given a tranquillizer such as chlorpromazine, 100 mg four times daily, and an anticonvulsant such as phenobarbitone, 60 mg four times daily. Some clinicians use chlormethiazole ('Heminevrin') in divided dosage descending from 4000 mg daily to 1000 mg daily. If the patient is seriously ill, the anticipated development of delirium tremens may be prevented by betamethasone, 0.5 mg twice daily for two days, then once daily for two days. In an emergency, an intravenous injection of 100 mg of hydrocortisone sodium succinate may be used. The patient who develops delirium tremens whilst seriously ill with another condition, for example, myocardial infarction, may be treated with alcohol in the form and quantity to which he is accustomed. His alcoholism can be dealt with when he has recovered from the acute illness.

Whilst alcohol is being withdrawn, the opportunity should be taken to make a detailed physical examination and to attend to any organic condition which requires treatment. The patient is likely to require sedation for a few nights, but dependence on sedation is rapidly acquired, and it should be withdrawn as soon as possible.

In this period, it is useful to provide vitamin supplements either orally or intravenously. The aim should be to have the patient off all drugs within a week to ten days.

Maintenance of Abstinence

This may be achieved by medical or non-medical means.

Medical sources. When the primary disorder is amenable to medical treatment, this will be provided if it is available. Many psychiatrists consider that group psychotherapy offers the best prospects for suitable patients (Walton, 1961). This may be started during the patient's inpatient treatment and continued when he becomes an outpatient.

He may be encouraged to take such substances as disulfiram ('Antabuse') or citrated calcium carbimide ('Abstem') which impair the metabolism of alcohol. If drink is taken whilst these drugs are being used, metabolism ceases at the stage at which acetaldehyde is formed, and the patient suffers from acetaldehyde accumulation. As a result, there is vasodilation with flushing of the cutaneous vessels, suffusion of the conjunctivae, throbbing headache, and in addition, nausea, vomiting and muscle cramps. There is a fall in blood pressure and some fatalities have been reported as a consequence. These facts should be explained to the patient, and he should be given a card to carry naming the drug that he is taking and warning that in the event of an accident, alcohol must not be given. If it is given inadvertently, an intravenous injection of 500 mg of ascorbic acid will facilitate the oxidation of acetaldehyde.

In some centres, it is the practice to give the patient a small 'test dose' of alcohol in the form to which he is accustomed, to demonstrate the unpleasant consequences of these substances. Elsewhere, the patient is merely warned, and the possible effects left to his imagination.

The use of these drugs is greatly reassuring to the patient's family, who can be certain that he is not drinking provided that they have seen him swallow the tablet. Since often he takes the substance for the sake of his family, he should take it in full view of them. They should never be prescribed without his full consent, and he should be told that if he proposes to start drinking again, he should allow an interval of three days, to allow the drug to be completely eliminated.

In some centres, metronidazole is used as an anti-alcohol drug, and some people believe that it has the effect of diminishing craving.

In some centres, *aversion therapy* is employed; but this is a purely symptomatic treatment, and does not avoid the need for supportive psychotherapy. The patient is given a full physical examination, and thereafter for several days he is given only water and alcohol in the form and quantity to which he is accustomed. Prior to each alcoholic drink, he is given an injection of apomorphine or emetine, so that he vomits shortly after the drink is given. In this way, a conditioned response is established (Lemere and Voegtlin, 1950). The response should be reinforced periodically. The treatment is drastic and unpleasant; but in some hands, it is undoubtedly highly effective. There is as yet no clear indication as to which type of patient will respond to this approach.

Non-medical treatment. The most important source of non-medical treatment of alcoholism is through *Alcoholics Anonymous*. This was introduced in the United States in 1935 by two alcoholics, Bill W and Dr Bob. It pursues a course of extensive self examination amongst one's peers based on the 'Twelve Steps'. These begin with an admission that 'We were powerless over alcohol' and conclude with a determination to 'Carry this message to alcoholics and to practice these principles in all our affairs'. 'Alcoholics Anonymous' is open to everyone who has a drinking problem, and the principle of anonymity is adhered to punctiliously. Practitioners can be assured that their patients will receive great assistance from members of 'Alcoholics Anonymous' and that if the patient himself is prepared to submit to the ideals of the organization, his future will be very hopeful. Some patients, having tried the organization, are highly critical of it; but on the whole, their criticisms represent denials of their own positions, and an indication of the inadequacy of their motivation. 'Alcoholics Anonymous' makes few claims for itself; but the external observer cannot but be impressed by their sincerity, their compassion and their effectiveness. 'Alanon' and 'Alateen' are sister organizations devoted to helping the families and children of alcoholics. They too have considerable measures of success.

In recent years, a number of *Alcoholism Information Centres* have been established in the United Kingdom (see Chap. V, Vol. I). These are generally staffed by abstinent alcoholics, and provide information and counselling not only to the alcoholic himself, but also to his family, his friends and to all interested organizations.

The Family of the Alcoholic

If alcoholism is seen as a disease of inter-personal relationships, then it is obvious that the family must be intimately involved in the treatment. The problems faced by the alcoholic's family are vividly described by Kessel and Walton (1969); and their problems, their difficulties, and also the contribution made to the patient's illness should be examined, together with the problems of the patient himself. This may be achieved in the form of joint interviews or joint psycho-therapeutic groups. Group therapy for the wives of alcoholics is part of our practice in Edinburgh.

Outcome

This depends on the ability with which the patient can be rein-tegrated into the society from which he has excluded himself (Walton *et al.*, 1966; Ritson and Hassall, 1970). The patients who have a warm, supportive, family relationship, a job, and friends who understand their illness do well. So do those of the older age groups with a long history of alcohol misuse and no more than moderate abnormality of personality. Psychopathic or isolated patients, patients without a marital partner and patients with grave personality disorders do badly.

DRUG MISUSE

THE NARCOTICS: THE 'HARD' DRUGS

These include opium, its derivatives such as morphine and heroin and its synthetic analogues such as pethidine and methadone.

The poppy has been cultivated for its opium for more than 4000 years, and has been used from the time of the Babylonian empires. Originally, it was smoked or taken by mouth; but with the invention of the hypodermic needle in 1853, it was hoped that since the alimentary tract was avoided, addiction would be overcome. Unfortunately, a speedier route of administration was provided instead. In 1896, heroin (diacetyl morphine) was introduced. This was regarded as non-addictive until 1915. Subsequently, other 'non addictive' narcotics, particularly pethidine and methadone, were introduced. It appears that all powerful pain killing substances carry with them the likelihood that they are potentially addictive.

Opium and its derivatives were freely available in Great Britain until 1920, when the Dangerous Drugs Act came into force. Some preparations of opium are still freely available ('chlorodyne' contains 1.5 mg per ml of anhydrous morphine). Kolb's classic study of addiction (1925) indicated that addiction was not necessarily accompanied by social, moral or intellectual deterioration. Eighty-six per cent of Kolb's cases showed seriously abnormal personality prior to the development of addiction.

The misuse of heroin ('H', 'horse', etc.) has increased dramatically in recent years. The number of known addicts has risen from 57 in 1954 to 2,240 in 1968 (Spear, 1969). During the same period, the number of methadone addicts has also risen considerably, but there has been only slow increase in the number of known addicts to other 'hard' drugs.

The great increase in addiction to heroin is due to the popularity of its use amongst people under the age of 35 (Spear, 1969). Older users tend to be individuals who use the drug in the course of their professions—medicine, dentistry and veterinary surgery.

Clinical features of Heroin Addiction

The heroin addict who seeks treatment is a frightened man. He willingly provides the diagnosis himself, and gives detailed information about the dose he has been taking and the frequency of administration. He pleads urgently for reassurance that he will not be denied supplies. He is rather dirty and untidy and is usually poorly nourished. There may be scars of infected injection sites on the arms, legs or lower abdomen. The restlessness, anxiety and depression are rapidly relieved by an injection, and are followed by a sense of drowsy euphoria.

For the opiates, the abstinence syndrome is unpleasant, prolonged and sometimes dangerous. Within a few hours, the patient becomes restless and irritable and shows such physical manifestations as lachrymation, rhinorrhoea and heavy perspiration. There are paroxysms of extreme yawning, which may be so violent as to lead to dislocation of the jaw. Within 48 to 72 hours, the symptoms rise to their peak, and the restlessness is such that the patient may pace the ward like a caged animal. He develops painful cramps in the legs and back, together with vomiting, diarrhoea, loss of appetite and extreme weakness. Blood pressure, pulse and respiration rates increase, and hyperglycaemia develops. These symptoms decline in severity over the next five to seven days, but the patient remains weak, anxious, restless and depressed. His appetite continues poor and he has difficulty with sleeping. He may not revert to moderate health for two to three months. The abstinence syndrome may be precipitated in the addict who is taking an opiate by the subcutaneous injection of the morphine antagonist nalorphine, and this is sometimes used as a diagnostic test.

Treatment of Narcotic Addiction

The patient is admitted to hospital and the opiate is withdrawn immediately. Methadone is substituted, and a dose of 10 to 15 mg is given by mouth at the frequency that is required to control the symptoms of withdrawal. When the dose of methadone has been stabilized, it too is gradually withdrawn. A tranquilliser is usually required at this stage—chlordiazepoxide or diazepam may be sufficient. Maintenance therapy has probably only a limited place in treatment. Further details of services for addicts are given in Chap. V, Vol. I.

The Hypnotics and Sedatives

These comprise the barbiturates and the non-barbiturate hypnotics ('sleepers', 'goof balls', 'yellow terrors', etc.)

An enormous quantity of hypnotics are prescribed by doctors for their patients, and dependence on the barbiturates or one of the non-barbiturate hypnotics is commonplace. In 1968, 25 million prescriptions were issued for barbiturates and 5.5 million prescriptions for non-barbiturate hypnotics. Dunlop estimates 'that every tenth night's sleep in the United Kingdom is hypnotic-induced' (Dunlop, 1970). There can be no doubt that a much greater quantity of hypnotics is prescribed than is necessary, and the medical profession must bear full responsibility for this regrettable state of affairs. Prevention of such gross dependence is of first importance, and the use of sleeping tablets should be restricted to patients who are acutely ill, or who are suffering from severe acute anxiety. The doctor who prescribes hypnotics should assume the responsibility of ensuring that they are withdrawn as soon as is possible.

A few persons are truly addicted; and for these, barbiturates have a stimulating rather than a sedating effect. The abstinence syndrome is usually ushered in by a series of epileptic fits and followed by an acute confusional state characterized by anxiety, tremulousness, disorientation, and (usually) visual hallucination (Isbell et al., 1950; James, 1963).

Management of Barbiturate Dependence

Withdrawal of barbiturates can be achieved simply and rapidly for most patients with the aid of the simple techniques of supportive psychotherapy—explanation, reassurance and support.

Two promises may be made to the patient before withdrawal is undertaken. The first is that within a week or ten days, he will be sleeping as well without the hypnotic as he was with it. The second is that within two to three weeks, he will be sleeping better without it. When he does sleep, the patient will dream rather more vividly than usual, although it need not be anticipated that these dreams will be unpleasant. It must be conceded that the first night or two are likely to be restless.

If the patient is taking more than 600 mg nightly, the dose of hypnotic must first be reduced, and this will mean that the withdrawal period is prolonged. In patients taking 600 mg or less, the drug can be withdrawn immediately.

During the withdrawal period, the sleeping time will be limited to a specified part of the day—perhaps 11 p.m. at night to 7 a.m. the next morning. The patient may sleep poorly for the first few days, so withdrawal should be undertaken at a time when he is relatively free of domestic and business responsibilities. A long weekend is ideal. He may not take a sleeping tablet at any time during the period of withdrawal, and he may regard his periods of wakefulness as a 'physiological' sleeping tablet.

He should make himself as comfortable as possible in bed, and need not try to 'make' himself go off to sleep. If he finds himself becoming drowsy, he may turn off the light to see what happens. If he does not sleep, he should read or listen to the radio. Before trying to settle down again, he should empty his bladder.

He should set his alarm clock for the agreed wakening time and should get up when it rings, even though he may then find himself dozing. He may not have an afternoon nap. He should follow the same routine on the second and subsequent nights. Within two or three days, his 'physiological' sleeping tablet will begin to work.

This simple regime works very effectively with most patients; and provided the patient is reasonably motivated to discontinue the use of hypnotics, he will succeed. It is not worth while employing the procedure in patients who are unwilling to give up their hypnotic. They are more likely to turn their energies to proving the doctor's prophecies incorrect.

The Stimulants

This group includes particularly amphetamine, its derivatives and its combinations. These have various nick-names, the most common of which are 'purple hearts' (amphetamine combined with amylobarbitone), 'black bombers' (laevo- and dextro-amphetamine bonded to an ion exchange resin), 'French blues', 'dex', 'bennie', 'pep pills'. About three to four million prescriptions are issued for amphetamine under the National Health Service every year (Dunlop, 1970) and so here too, the medical profession carries a heavy burden of responsibility.

The *amphetamines* were introduced in the 1930s for the treatment of depression. Their stimulating effect and their alleged action in reducing the appetite made them appear ideal substances for the treatment of obesity. However, the British Medical Association Working Party (1968) considered that they had very limited use in modern therapeutics, and that they should be used for conditions for which no reasonable alternative exists. The Working Party considered that they should be avoided in the treatment of obesity and depression. The only condition in which they were likely to be of value was in narcolepsy and in certain other rare forms of epilepsy.

If amphetamine is used over a prolonged period, a paranoid psychosis indistinguishable from paranoid schizophrenia may develop (Connell, 1958). People may use methyl-amphetamine intravenously for its speedy effect. Amphetamines may be detected in the urine of misusers by a fairly simple laboratory test (Beckett and Rowland, 1965).

Dependence on *cocaine* ('coke', 'snow', 'C') is relatively uncommon and occurs mainly in heroin addicts who take it in combination with heroin ('H and C'). Cocaine may be taken by injection or in the form of snuff. It produces a sense of elation, apparent precision of thought, and freedom from fatigue. Cocoa leaves, from which cocaine is obtained, have been chewed by the Incas of South America since the 11th century as part of their religious rites.

Some users of cocaine develop a psychotic illness characterized by a paranoid delusional state which is sometimes prolonged. Tactile hallucinations may be experienced, taking the form of a sensation like small animals crawling below the skin—formication.

The stimulant drugs are popular amongst drug misusers for the excitement and elation which they may cause. There are few or no abstinence phenomena, and these drugs should therefore be regarded as drugs of psychological dependence. They may be withdrawn totally and immediately without any ill effect.

The 'Phantastica'—the 'Hallucinogens'

These include the 'psychedelic' or psychoto-mimetic drugs. Examples are cannabis, mescaline and lysergic acid diethylamide (L.S.D.).

Cannabis. This is available in several forms—hashish, hemp, marihuana, bhang, ganja, charas. It may be mixed with cigarette tobacco to make reefers, and enjoys such nick-names as 'pot', 'weed', 'tea' and 'grass'.

The illegal use of cannabis has grown to very large proportions indeed in recent years, particularly amongst younger people. Convictions for the use of cannabis rose from 554 in 1964 to 4,683 in 1969 (Advisory Committee on Drug Dependence, 1968) and this is likely to represent only a fraction of the actual use. Users of cannabis protest vigorously and vehemently against what they see as persecution by society; and it is certainly not easy to make a strong medical case against the use of cannabis.

The Effects of Cannabis. The active principle in all forms is delta-tetrahydrocannabinol (D.H.C.). It is most commonly mixed with tobacco and smoked, but it may also be taken by mouth, by injection or as snuff.

It is easier to describe the physical effects of cannabis than the psychological ones. The physical effects include reddening of the conjunctivae and injection of the pharynx, sometimes causing a slight tightness in the chest and a mild cough. The blood pressure and pulse rate tend to rise. The effect on blood sugar and appetite varies.

The psychological effect of cannabis varies with the expectation and degree of sophistication of the user, as well as with the strength of the preparation used. It is said that the individual experiences a rather drowsy sense of euphoria in which considerations of time and space are forgotten. At first, the subject is rather more talkative and experiences a floating sensation which is called 'being high'. In due course, this proceeds into a state of 'delicious lassitude'. Psychologically, perception is altered both qualitatively and quantitatively. Perceptions tend to be heightened—colours appear brighter, hearing is more acute, perfumes are more exciting, tastes are more pungent, touch is more exhilerating. Qualitatively, perceptions are confused, so that for example *sounds* may be *seen* and *colours* may be *heard*. The beat of the drum may be accompanied by an array of coloured lights. This phenomenon is called synaesthesia.

It is said that aggression is reduced. The action of cannabis as an aphrodisiac probably depends on the expectation of the user. The use of cannabis is often accompanied by a complex ritual, not only in ancient religions, but in modern ones too. The sense of rhythm is said to be heightened, and users claim the ability to communicate with each other in a new and significant way. The following description of the 'psychedelic experience' (Guardian, 1969) attempts to put into words an experience which is essentially non-verbal and uncommunicable:

'How strange—I remember thinking—it is exactly as people tell you it will be, and yet until it has happened to you, you cannot have the faintest idea what they mean. Just as in making love or giving birth for the first time, you enter a new world of experience which, no matter how many times you may have heard it described, still comes as a revelation to you personally.

I felt utterly relaxed—rather sleepy in fact—and quite serene and composed. I could feel the texture and weight of the settee with startling clarity; could measure the precise curve of the cushion under my elbows, and the exact depth to which they sank into it. The radiator behind and to one side of me felt hotter to my left shoulder than to my right: a measurable difference in temperature, though I had never noticed it before. The texture of corduroy was microscopically detailed, each ridge of the material distinct and separate.

Time crawled. The music went on and on. I tried to smoke an ordinary cigarette but it tasted dry and boring and I soon stubbed it out. The cat jumped onto my lap and I stroked her, enjoying the sleek, glossy softness of her fur and the subtle curves and hollows of her body. Obviously I was stroking beautifully, for she purred like mad.

The room was full of delicate vibrations of light, which shimmered through the air. My mind too seeemed twanging with these vibrations, and my skin. They were palpable, rhythmic waves . . . I had taken my shoes off by now and the dense, opulent pile of the carpet felt even better to the soles of my feet than had the corduroy of the settee to my elbows—though still not as luxuriant as the cat. My senses were alight with more complexity and beauty of feeling than I had ever assimilated before. It was totally new and unimaginable. No words could have prepared me to expect this.

After a couple of hours (or so my watch recorded: it felt infinitely more) I went to bed and slept deeply and refreshingly, without dreaming. Next morning I woke with ease, earlier than usual, but full of energy and very clear-headed.

My description cannot convey the sensations I had when high; the word 'high' itself comes nearest, though I never felt disembodied or as though I were literally floating. I have simply set down with total honesty and as much clarity as I can bring to such a non-verbal experience, what happened and how it felt.'

The Wootton Committee (1968) concluded that the use of cannabis was a relatively innocent activity. It concluded that whilst legal sanctions against its use should be continued, they might be considerably softened.

d-Lysergic Acid Diethylamide-25 (*L.S.D.*). This was developed in 1938, and its effects on man were first described by Hofman (1959) after he had unwittingly ingested a small quantity. L.S.D. changes perception; but this change is usually very much more prolonged and dramatic than is the case with cannabis, and is accompanied by the abreaction of strong emotion, either in the direction of elation or despair. The user may experience great lucidity of thought and feel himself able to perceive highly complex relationships. He may experience fear or total panic with complete loss of emotional control, or at the other extreme an ecstatic, transcendental experience—a sense of cosmic oneness with the universe. It is for these profound experiences that it is used illegally, often by highly sophisticated though often rather unstable people who seek a 'trip' on 'acid', 'sugar' or 'zen'.

L.S.D. has three particular interests for the psychiatrist. The first is that its effects are produced by the oral administration of very small quantities—30 micrograms may be effective. Could L.S.D. be related to the substance postulated by Hoffer *et al.* (1954) as being the toxic metabolite which is responsible for schizophrenia? The second interest is in the use of L.S.D. in drug abreaction (Sandison and Whitelaw, 1957). The third interest lies in the illegal use already described. The individual enjoying a good 'trip' may indulge in dangerous activities— he may try to fly—whilst one suffering the effects of a bad 'trip' may be brought to a state of suicidal despair. The psychotomimetic effect of L.S.D. may usually be terminated by the administration of an adequate dose of chlorpromazine.

After the adminstration of L.S.D., an intractable schizophrenic psychosis has been precipitated in some people, although the potentiality was probably always there. There have been reports of chromosomal damage following its use (Neilsen *et al.*, 1968; B.M.J., 1967) and also reports of intrauterine damage to the foetus. These reports have been criticized, and the question remains open.

REFERENCES

ADVISORY COMMITTEE ON DRUG DEPENDENCE (The Wootton Committee) (1968) London: H.M.S.O.

BAILEY, M. B., HABERMAN, P. W. & ALKSNE, H. J. (1965) Epidemiology of alcoholism in an urban residential area. *Quarterly Journal of Studies on Alcohol*, 26, p. 19.

BECKETT, H. H. & ROWLAND, M. (1965) Determination and identification of amphetamine in urine. *Journal of Pharmacy and Pharmacology*, **17**, 59.

BRITISH MEDICAL ASSOCIATION (1968) Report of the Working Party on Amphetamine Preparations. London: B.M.A.

BRITISH MEDICAL JOURNAL (1967) L.S.D. and Chromosomes. *Leading article.* **ii**, 124.

CONNELL, P. H. (1958) *Amphetamine Psychosis.* (Maudesley Monograph No. 5). Institute of Psychiatry, London: Chapman.

DAVIES, D. L. (1962) Normal drinking in recovered alcoholics. *Quarterly Journal of Studies on Alcohol*, **23**, 324.

DUNLOP, D. (1970) Use and abuse of psychotropic drugs. *Proceedings of the Royal Society of Medicine*, **63**, 12.

EDWARDS, G., KELLOGG-FISHER, M., HAWKER, A., HENSMAN, C. & POSTOYAN, S. (1967) Clients of Alcoholism Information Centres. *British Medical Journal*, **4**, 346.

GLATT, M. M. (1961) Drinking habits of English (Middle class) alcoholics. *Acta Psychiatrica Scandinavica*, **37**, 88–143.

GUARDIAN (1969) 3 Dec.

H.M. CUSTOMS & EXCISE (1970) Report for the year. London: H.M.S.O.

H.M.S.O. (1965) *Alcoholics—Health Services for their Treatment and Rehabilitation.* Report of the Subcommittee of the Standing Medical Advisory Committee., pp. 8–11.

HOFFER, A., OSMOND, H. & SMYTHIES, J. R. (1954) Schizophrenia: a new approach Result of a year's research. *Journal of Mental Science*, **100**, 29.

HOFMAN, A. (1959) Psychotomimetic drugs. *Acta Physiologica et Pharmacologica. Nederland*, **8**, 240.

INTERDEPARTMENTAL COMMITTEE ON DRUG ADDICTION (1965) Second Report. *Drug Addiction.* London: H.M.S.O.

ISBELL, H., ALTSCHUL, S., KORNETSKY, C. H., EISENMAN, A. J., FLANARY, H. G. & FRASER, H. F. (1950) Chronic barbiturate intoxication: an experimental study. *Archives of Neurology and Psychiatry (Chicago)* **64**, 1.

JAMES, I. P. (1963) Drug withdrawal psychoses. *American Journal of Psychiatry*, **119**, 880.

JELLINEK, E. M. (1959) Estimating prevalence of alcoholism; modified values in the Jellinek formula and an alternative approach. *Quarterly Journal of Studies on Alcohol*, **20**, 261.

JELLINEK, E. M. (1960) *The Disease Concept of Alcoholism*. New Brunswick; Hillhouse Press.

JOLLIFFE, N. & JELLINEK, E. M. (1941) Vitamin deficiencies and liver cirrhosis in alcoholsm: Pt. VII. Cirrhosis of the Liver. *Quarterly Journal of Studies on Alcohol*, **2**, 544–583.

KELLER, M. (1960) Definition of alcoholism. *Quarterly Journal of Studies on Alcohol*, **21**, 125.

KENDELL, R. G. (1965) Normal drinking by former alcohol addicts. *Quarterly Journal of Studies on Alcohol*, **26**, 247.

KESSEL, N. (1965) Self poisoning. *British Medical Journal*, **ii**, 1265–1336.

KESSEL, N. & WALTON, H. J. (1969) *Alcoholism*. Penguin Books.

KOLB, L. (1925) Pleasure and Deterioration from Neurotic Addiction. *Mental Hygiene*, **9**, 699.

LEMERE, F. & VOEGTLIN, W. L. (1950) An evaluation of the aversion treatment of alcoholism. *Quarterly Journal of Studies on Alcohol*, **8**, 261.

McCORD, W. & McCORD, J. (1960) *Origins of Alcoholism*. London: Tavistock.

MENNINGER, K. (1938) *Man Against Himself*. New York: Harcourt Brace.

MOSS, M. C. & DAVIES, E. BERESFORD (1968) *A Survey of Alcoholism in an English County*. London: Geigy.

MULFORD, H. A. & MILLER, D. E. (1960) Drinking in Iowa; extent of drinking and selected socio-cultural categories. *Quarterly Journal of Studies on Alcohol*, **21**, 26.

NIELSEN, J., FRIEDRICH, J., JACOBSEN, E. & TSUBOI, T. (1968) Lysergide and chromosome abnormalities. *British Medical Journal*, **ii**, 801.

PARR, D. (1957). Alcoholism in general practice. *British Journal of Addiction to Alcohol*, **54**, 25.

PARRY, R. A. (1969) I Cannot Possibly be an Alcoholic. *Journal of Alcoholism*, (2), p. 162.

PARRY, R. A. (1970) Management of alcoholism in general practice. *Journal of the Royal College of General Practitioners*, **20**, 224.

PARRY, R. A. (1971) Alcoholism. *Scottish Medical Journal*, **16**, 357.

RITSON, E. B. & HASSALL, C. (1970) *The Management of Alcoholism*. Edinburgh: Livingstone.

SANDISON, R. A. & WHITELAW, J. D. (1957) Further studies in the therapeutic value of L.S.D. in mental illness. *Journal of Mental Science*, **103**, 332.

SPEAR, H. B. (1969) The growth of heroin addiction in the U.K. *British Journal of Addiction to Alcohol*, **64**, 245.

WALTON, H. J. (1961) Group methods in the psychiatric treatment of alcoholism. *American Journal of Psychiatry*, **118**, 410.

WALTON, H. J., RITSON, E. B. & KENNEDY, R. I. (1966) Response of alcoholics to clinic treatment. *British Medical Journal*, **ii**, 1171.

WALTON, H. J. (1968) Personality as a determinant of the form of alcoholism. *British Journal of Psychiatry*, **114**, 761.

W.H.O. Expert Committee on Drugs Liable to Produce Addiction. Report on the 2nd Session (1950) *W.H.O. Technical Report Series* 21.

W.H.O. Expert Committee on Mental Health (1951) Report on the First Session of the Alcoholism Subcommittee. *W.H.O. Technical Report Series* 42, Annex 2.

W.H.O. Expert Committee on Mental Health (1952) Alcohol Subcommittee Second Report. *W.H.O. Technical Report Series* 48.

W.H.O. Expert Committee on Drug Dependence (1969) *W.H.O. Technical Report Series* 407.

Chapter VI

GROUP PSYCHOTHERAPY

H. J. Walton

INTRODUCTION

Techniques for treating psychiatric patients together with other patients have developed since the beginning of the century. When J. H. Pratt (1907), the Boston physician, first brought together his patients with tuberculosis, his intention was to form a class for instruction in personal hygiene. The increase in morale of his patients showed that unexpected therapeutic benefits resulted from the group interactions.

A similar, relatively unsophisticated use of groups for therapeutic purposes has been highly successful with other categories of patients whose personal habits initiate and sustain illness. Alcoholism has been treated often with spectacular success by Alcoholics Anonymous, and the obese have also responded to group approaches directed by laymen. Other applications of group methods have culminated in diverse techniques that include psychodrama, in which the patient enacts his central life conflicts together with other participants (Moreno, 1945). Methods for treating the family as an entity have been devised (Ackerman, 1958). Wards and even whole hospitals can be administered by group methods to bring about a therapeutic community (Jones, 1953).

DEFINITION OF GROUP PSYCHOTHERAPY

This form of treatment calls for the same small group of patients to meet together regularly with a trained conductor, to achieve sympton relief and personality change.

Therapy groups constitute a distinct modality of psychiatric treatment. A different mode of operation on the part of the clinician is called for than in two-person psychotherapy. The terminology used to describe group processes is also unlike that which applies in dyadic psychotherapy; the effects of the forms of treatment differ in many respects. Individual psychotherapy may more effectively unravel the biographical origins of psychoneurotic illness, whilst greater improvement in socialization may result from group therapy (Lewin, 1947).

Inexperienced group conductors sometimes err by attempting to employ psychoanalytic methods in groups, or to conceptualize group processes by using constructs which have been developed in individual psychotherapy. However, it is self-evident that the processes found in a group interaction will vary from those occuring when only a pair of individuals interact. A reason for developing expertise in group psychotherapy is that it offers a treatment potential which does not merely duplicate the effects of dyadic psychotherapy.

This differentiation will become evident if attention is paid to the communication network. In two-person psychotherapy the interaction is between the patient and clinician; in groups, however, equally significant communication occurs among the members of the group themselves. Because a therapy group meets repeatedly over months, or years, a highly complex store of communication is developed. Over time the gradual evolution takes place of a new and complicated social structure, to which all the members of the group have contributed. Inevitably, this complex interpersonal organization becomes strained by problems, the more so because the members of the group are psychiatrically ill or otherwise socially maladapted. As the group members themselves progressively recognize, clarify and solve the group's problems, their own maladaptive behaviour patterns undergo change.

Such change cannot be assumed as inevitably an improvement. Groups can be dysfunctional. The therapeutic potential of the group is only mobilized when pathological behaviour is systematically identified and neutralized. Essentially, such corrective action stems from healthy behaviour on the part of certain of the group members. It follows, therefore, that the conductor is called upon to identify personality assets present in at least some group members at difficult phases of the group's life, and he facilitates the constructive contributions of these members in times of group need.

This is one of the processes that plays no part in dyadic psychotherapy. Other group phenomena with which the group conductor is concerned are the climate of the group, its values, the sequence of changes in the status of members at different epochs in the group's career, and the cohesiveness of the group. The last process refers to the sense of identity and the degree of investment of group members, as evidenced by the regularity of their attendance, the interest they take in the sessions, and the extent of their participation. The conductor's main responsibility is to intervene in a session when the discussion makes this necesssary, and to monitor and influence the group processes. In dyadic psychotherapy the clinician's interpretations are aimed at clarifying psychopathology of an individual patient. In groups, however, the conductor comments on phenomena which are of relevance to a number of group members simultaneously. It is relatively rare in group psychotherapy that the conductor has to focus on one of the members, and to make individual interpretations of relevance only to the patient concerned.

Closed Groups

The therapeutic group is described as 'closed' when all members start treatment at the same time, and then continue as group members until the group terminates. In other words, although patients improve at different rates, they all leave treatment simultaneously. Some members, of course, do not keep to this undertaking and leave before the termination date. Such loss of a member occurs particularly in groups with low cohesiveness. A new member can then be introduced as a replacement. In advance of his arrival, the old members are given the opportunity to discuss his advent, and to consider in detail the effects of his inclusion once he has joined.

A closed group is the preferred approach. Group therapists, particularly those working in private practice, are sometimes compelled to have a 'closed-open' group. Patients are allowed to depart as they improve, and new patients are then introduced as replacements. The group may thus continue in existence over a considerable period of time, but with constantly changing membership.

In addition to keeping his group as 'closed' as possible, the group conductor will want to restrict as much as possible the interference of other, perhaps competing, forms of treatment. Individual psychotherapy is not usually feasible concurrently with group psychotherapy (although one form of treatment may with advantage precede the other), and when drug treatment has to be used in addition it is as well to make it the responsibility of another psychiatrist than the group conductor.

COMPOSITION

Experience suggests that eight is the optimal number of patients in a closed therapeutic group. The conductor may be the sole clinician. When two clinicians combine, the participating colleague is a considerable asset. The second clinician may be an observer, who is minimally active and reserves his comments for individual discussion with the conductor subsequent to the sessions. Another arrangement, increasingly used, is for two clinicians together to act as co-therapists, usually designating to themselves in advance of a particular session which one will take the main responsibility. The advantage of the co-therapist arrangement is that the sessions can continue to take place when one of the clinicians has to be away on vacation or for some other unavoidable professional or personal reason. It is essential that inexperienced group conductors should ensure that they receive supervision (see below), enabling them to discuss their groups' sessions with an experienced colleague, preferably each week (MacLennan, 1966).

ADMINISTRATION OF SESSIONS

The group meets each week, for a session lasting one and a half hours. The session should take place each week at the same time and on the same day.

Group members will want to know when they start treatment, how long the group will remain in being. A suitable answer is that the effects of treatment will begin to be evident after six months, and definite improvement can be expected after one year. Members themselves take part in deciding how long treatment will continue.

As many chairs should be set out as there are group members (including the conductor and the observer). The seats are arranged in a circle so that all participants are readily visible. When a member is absent his empty chair is left in the circle. Although members tend to develop a pattern regarding their seating, the group conductor will often find that members vary their positions according to current group pressures. The conductor does not usually take notes during a session, but afterwards; for training or research purposes an audiotape recording of selected sessions is useful.

Another responsibility of the conductor is to keep an attendance register. The symbol often used to indicate when a member attends is P; A indicates that the patient is absent; O signifies that he is absent by arrangement; late arrival can be recorded by using the symbol L (Walton, 1971, p. 23).

The group, stimulated by the conductor if necessary, will of course explore the reasons any member has for turning up late to a session. If attention is not paid to late-coming, important information may be lost, and an irresponsible attitude regarding attendance can develop among group members.

Absence from a session is still more disruptive. The absent member misses out on the information which is conveyed during that session, and is often not able to follow the subsequent session accurately. He may, in addition, have absented himself because of an important event in his personal life, or because of tension within the group itself, frequently in his relation to another member. For these reasons a member who has been absent is always asked when he returns to account for his non-attendance. The conductor in addition ensures that a letter is written to a non-attender immediately after the session at which he was not present, to maintain contact and to draw attention to the effect his absence had on the group.

SELECTION OF PATIENTS

The conductor (with his co-therapist if possible) selects the patients he wishes to include in his group. If inexperienced, he does so in full consultation with his supervisor. Because people of different age-groups have varying preoccupations and conflicts, the group should be relatively homogenous in respect of age. Both sexes should be equally represented. The intelligence level of all the members should be roughly equal, although this is not a pressing requirement. Experience indicates that patients with a variety of types of illness and personality disorder should be brought together (Foulkes, 1964). A group consisting of patients with similar disorders, such as young mothers troubled by hostile impulses to their children, or homosexuals, or shoplifters, is desireable only when a primary aim is to conduct research into the psychodynamics of a particular disorder.

It is rarely wise to accept for inclusion patients referred by other psychiatrists whom the conductor has not previously seen and evaluated. Such personal screening is essential, not only to ensure that the patient will fit in well with the other members selected, but also to provide necessary information about the nature of the group, its duration, and the expectations the patient will be required to meet. Patients drop out from therapeutic groups more often than they do from individual psychotherapy (Frank, 1961), therefore all precautionary steps should be taken to reduce the likelihood of such loss through inadequate clarification of the patient's expectation.

Not all patients are suited for group psychotherapy. Those who are very tense at the prospect of entering a group often stop attending, or gain confidence to persist only if the conductor provides them warm initial support. Individual interviews between group sessions may be called for as well, to deal with any reservation or alarm which insecure members cannot deal with adequately in sessions. Certain patients may require a period of individual psychotherapy to prepare them for group participation: this may be so especially with individuals who have never had a trusting relationship with another person, such as those from broken parental homes who experienced much personal insecurity. Markedly hostile patients may not be able to associate constructively with others, and on this account fail to evolve supportive bonds with the other group members; grossly paranoid patients tend to leave because they may so mistake group comments or incidents that they find the group atmosphere intolerable.

While it is not usual to treat psychotic patients with explorative psychotherapy, patients with schizophrenic illness have often responded well in group therapy. A mildly psychotic patient in a therapeutic group often confers positive benefit, in that he contributes experiences or preoccupations which non-psychotic patients find too alarming or bizarre to initiate in the discussion themselves.

A selection principle often followed is that no patient should be a conspicuous isolate, for example by being the only Jew, the only black person, the only woman, etc.

THE TASK OF THE GROUP MEMBER

The patient in a therapeutic group has as his main responsibility the task of self-revelation. His purpose is to disclose the major difficulties he has with other people, and his chief forms of misuse of self. It follows that he is making proper use of the session when he conveys the thoughts that preoccupy him, no matter how anomalous, and the most pressing conflicts of the moment.

The collectivity of members engages during each session in free-floating discussion. Not all patients talk an equal amount. Indeed, those verbally active at one phase of the group's life, may be less prominent in subsequent stages. It is not to be supposed that silent members do not benefit, although of course they are not contributing optimally to the processes of the group when withholding their individual contribution.

At first, attempting to make the conductor the major participant, group members will address most of their remarks directly to him, and will be puzzled or angry when he does not respond as authoritatively as they expect. However, by not complying in these expectations, the conductor will rapidly establish that all members of the group are potentially therapeutic, and that the bonds between group members themselves will be the channel which may promote personality change as effectively as the link between members and the conductor. Unlike individual psychotherapy, detailed reminiscences of childhood experiences are much less valuable than exploration of current events (the 'here-and-now'), both in the group session and in the patient's private life.

When the conductor requires to see a group patient for an individual interview, he exerts himself to report back at the next session of the group what transpired during the interview. On all group members he places three obligations. The first is that when two members happen to meet outside a session, they should report back at the next session what transpired between them. Second, each member is required to inform the group about any important change which takes place in his life, such as a change in his job, the termination of a personal relationship, some other shift in his behaviour with a significant person, etc. The third obligation of the group members has already been emphasized: to disclose thoughts and experiences as fully and as frankly as possible.

The patient's right to be a group member stems from his psychiatric disorder or social maladjustment. There is thus in the group no stigma attaching to personal difficulties, and indeed the research potential of therapeutic groups derives from the frankness with which members reveal their preoccupations and conflicts.

THE CONDUCTOR'S ROLE

The progress of the therapeutic group depends primarily on the conductor. Through his action the group members were selected and the group brought into being. The effectiveness of his attention to group processes will determine the extent of the group's cohesiveness (whether members are retained or some lost through drop-out), and the extent to which the group functions to the benefit rather than to the detriment of members.

The conductor helps patients to discuss their difficulties at a pace which neither leads to disorganization nor generates disabling anxiety. Some anxiety, distress, fear and anger is inevitable. Therapeutic groups are a setting for considerable emotion; this heightened affect needs to be sufficiently localized to the period of the session for members to cope with their everyday responsibilities. One member may evoke much feeling in other group members. When an individual member is under very serious attack from the group, he is in danger of leaving, therefore the conductor often intervenes protectively if excessive hostility is being conveyed. Such singling out of one member as an objectionable or destructive person is known as 'scape-goating', and is a resistance to acknowledge similar propensities in oneself.

One of the conductor's main tasks is to help the group perceive that the attitudes or difficulties disclosed by one member may, in fact, be common to a number of them. Objection to a homosexual disclosure, for example, may be the prelude to admissions about similar experiences; the same applies to broaching of sex with siblings. In addition to generalizing the incidents contributed by individual members to see how applicable they are to others also, the conductor minimizes time-wasting through concentration on trivialities; he encourages members to explore latent phenomena which they may be too anxious or ashamed to admit.

The conductor aims to be minimally active, while not in any way avoiding his task of managing and monitoring the group forces (Whitaker and Lieberman, 1964). For example, he commences his non-directive role by not introducing members to one another at the first session; instead he courteously enables them to arrive at the procedure they wish to adopt for becoming acquainted. The conductor does not set out to teach patients psychological theory, nor to give them clinical information. Because it is necessary for pathology to become manifest before it can be treated, he permits the expression in the group of illness behaviour to the extent that the patient can himself tolerate, and the group contain.

The conductor declines the invitations of group members to turn him into their leader. In avoiding the role of authority the conductor fosters the independence of group members and minimises dependency attitudes. In fact, it is when a group resists engaging in therapeutic work that dependence of members becomes most prominent; then efforts are redoubled to have the conductor exercise himself to 'cure' the members; other prominent forms of resistance are withdrawal or aggressiveness, and the formation by two of the group's members of a partnership, such 'pairing' designed to seal off the couple from optimal interaction with other group members (Bion, 1961). Such a development when inexpertly handled can go to lengths of an engagement or even a marriage, or a couple may depart from the group. Often the other group members condone such a partnership between two of their number, and they actively oppose the efforts of the conductor to clarify why the partnership represents an escape from therapy.

The conductor's direction is needed to some extent in the early stages of the group (McPherson and Walton, 1965). Then members look to him for indications about the procedures they should adopt, and the sort of activity likely to prove most effective. In time the members look progressively less to the conductor for indications as to how they should proceed, and the extent and pace of self-disclosure which should be adopted.

In the last stage of treatment the conductor helps the group to set the date for termination, and helps them work towards disbanding. The conductor again enables members to see what is common in apparently individual experiences, and to detect the concealed implications of each individual experience once its collective implications have been exposed.

The emotional level at which group members relate to one another varies during the course of treatment, and is more intensive when progress is being made. Relationships among group members are often strongly emotional and reflect directly the habitual responses adopted in customary social interactions. These often become evident to other members before they are perceived clearly by the patient himself. Once he has been helped by his fellows to grasp how he acts and reacts socially, they can go further and help him to make the necessary modifications in his social conduct. The group sessions also provide the patient with an opportunity to replace maladaptive behaviour by different patterns of conduct; he will already have practised the new interactions with group members before putting them into effect with associates outside the group.

CONSTRICTING AND FACILITATING GROUP ATMOSPHERES

A therapeutic group is a change system. Patients alter their behaviour because properties of therapeutic groups facilitate personality change.

In any session the prevalent atmosphere may either prmote communication or impede it. The group atmosphere is *constricting* when the overall emotional state is one of distrust and fear. Then only a narrow range of topics arise for discussion, and members have obvious difficulty in expressing themselves freely.

In contrast, the group atmosphere becomes a *facilitating* one when feeling can be freely expressed, and a wide range of matters are raised for discussion. The conductor will be concerned at the times when communication is blocked, meagre or trivial, and will exert himself to alter the group atmosphere to become more facilitative. At times his efforts will miscarry, and patients will fail to co-operate with him in restoring the climate of the group to a therapeutic one. On occasion his attempts to help may actually serve to raise the anxiety level of the group. He will be greatly assisted when he detects readiness in one of the group members to respond to an intervention on the part of the conductor. In general, the conductor only succeeds in making the group facilitative when he can call on corrective activity in one or other patient with which to counteract restrictive forces.

SUPERVISION

Often the conductor will not succeed in comprehending why phases of the group's career prove anti-therapeutic, unless he receives external help. This may be provided by his co-therapist, but more often by the supervisor. Of particular value is an arrangement whereby the conductors of a number of therapeutic groups are supervised together (Stein, 1963). In addition to reporting their own sessions, conductors have the advantage in a supervisory seminar of hearing the reports of their fellow trainees. Most of the discussion will take place among the trainees themselves and the supervisor will tend to intervene and make comments only when he considers the supervision group needs his help. The similarity between the supervisory session and what happens in therapeutic groups is obvious. A group conductor may fail to recognize or decipher symbolic or fantasy material in his therapeutic group, and perceive such material only when his co-trainees or the supervisor draw his attention to it. For example, a conductor did not know what to make of extended discussion in his group about motor accidents. The symbolic meaning of this topic was brought to his attention in a supervision seminar when it was suggested to the conductor, on the basis of other material presented, that his group members were pre-occupied with latent fantasies about parental intercourse. The conductor made an intervention to this effect in the next session of his group; a facilitative atmosphere immediately resulted, several patients actively discussing their early awareness about their parents' sexual relationships.

The conductor does not disclose his own life circumstances in his therapeutic group, but on occasion he may elect to do so in his supervision seminar, especially when he is experiencing difficulty in managing his group, or it is in protracted conflict regarding one of the patient members. A supervision seminar can thus help the conductor achieve some personality change himself. Moreover, the conductor of a therapeutic group shares in the processes affecting the patients and may himself derive not only psychological insight, but also subjective benefit.

THERAPEUTIC INGREDIENTS OF GROUPS

The first beneficial aspect of a therapeutic group is that patients can disclose their private pre-occupations and discover that they are not alone in their misfortune. Very considerable relief is often obtained, early in the group's career, when patients who previously regarded themselves as singular, and therefore stigmatized, discover that other group members have or had very similar troubles.

The second mutative element in therapeutic groups derives from the group's capacity to bring about modification of attitudes. The sessions are a setting in which the patient can express his beliefs. He may find that these beliefs are quite idiosyncratic, not shared by other members. The patient may for example have an ingrained belief, a notion derived from parents during growing-up, that it is wrong to experiment sexually. The contrary views of other group members permit him to re-evaluate his belief system, and they then help him with their ongoing appraisal to make the necessary modifications which he may contemplate.

In this way, a patient can considerably alter the 'assumptive world' derived in the parental family, according to which the patient has attempted to conduct his adult life.

A third basis for personality change, related to the above, has to do with the *idealized self* (Horney, 1951), according to which many patients attempt to pattern their lives. A patient may set himself impossibly high standards, which he believes are in accordance with parental wishes. He may never permit himself to react with anger, for instance, even if misused by others. When he finds that the group members view his perfection as idiosyncratic, or even ridiculous, the patient can embark on a gradual replacement of his idealized self by a set of standards which accord with the actual demands of his adult personality.

Finally, a crucial mechanism for personality change that a therapeutic group offers, derives from the setting it provides for the expression of behaviour which the patient previously forbad himself. The patient may not have permitted himself certain actions or reactions because of an unreasoning terror of possible consequences. He may have placed a taboo, for example, on sexual advances, considering as dishonourable any approach to a 'respectable' woman which could be construed as erotic. Often such non-permissible behaviour has been repudiated by the patient because he dreads that, should he step out of character, some disastrous consequence will follow (Ezriel, 1950).

With the encouragement of group members, however, and in a facilitative atmosphere, he will be more prepared to risk new behaviour. Once this is seen to be unattended by the dreaded consequences, the patient can go further and transfer the altered reaction into his life outside the group. In this way habitual patterns of behaviour, which may have been grossly ineffective socially, can be replaced by more adaptive behaviour. Patients can be helped to become less timid, they can be helped to restrain impulses which may have been socially damaging, they can be made more companionable and less solitary, they can be helped to remedy traits of officiousness, and dependent patients can be helped to be less reliant on others.

RESEARCH

A considerable number of objective investigations of group therapy have been carried out. Therapeutic groups provide a productive setting for the exploration of personality (Gottschalk and Auerbach, 1966).

Therapeutic groups also permit the study of face-to-face social interactions. The phases through which groups pass can be charted (Tuckman, 1965). The evidence suggests that a group passes first through a 'forming' stage, then through a stage of conflict ('storming'), then through a co-operative phase ('norming'), and finally to a stage of solving problems ('performing' stage).

The general dimensions of interaction among group members have been studied (McPherson and Walton, 1970). The participation of each group member can be categorized along three dimensions: (1) a patient is either relatively dominant or submissive; (2) he may be emotionally sensitive to others, on the one hand, or emotionally insensitive; (3) in treatment he may operate effectively, or in contrast may provide ineffective group membership.

Much active research is currently aimed to establish the effectiveness of group psychotherapy, the parameters to be included in carrying out such research receiving much attention at present (Kiesler, 1966). Outcome with treatment can be studied in terms of the patient's improved social effectiveness, his greater subjective well-being, and his increased self-awareness (Kelman and Parloff, 1957).

The effectiveness of group therapists has been investigated, these studies revealing how considerably therapists vary in their competence. It is well that group therapists should not only seek to improve their clinical ability, but also that they should acquaint themselves with the relevant research literature. Much waits to be discovered about group therapy, therefore associated ongoing research whenever possible should be a concomitant of therapy. The variables which need to be studied in such operational research have been extensively documented (Chassan, 1967; Fiske *et al.*, 1970; Walton and McPherson, 1968).

APPLICATION OF GROUP METHODS IN WARD ADMINISTRATION

A psychiatric hospital or ward is a small society. The term 'therapeutic community' implies that the hospital setting can be structured to provide planned social interactions which foster social learning, thus preparing the patient for improved adjustment in his social relationships outside the hospital. *Milieu therapy* occurs when use is made of the potential in patients to help each other, with the assistance of the staff.

The main technique employed for enabling the patient to play an active treatment role in relation to other patients is through the *daily ward meeting*. Such mutual help by patients is only possible when they obtain the participation of the psychiatrists, nurses, clinical psychologists and social workers, who form the ward team. Under these conditions patients can take over a considerable amount of responsibility, and participate in the decisions regarding the programme for each day, and the planning of the ward arrangements. When patients share responsibility with the staff, dependency and low self-esteem are counteracted.

In the daily ward meeting an examination is undertaken of the current problems and the behaviour of each of the patients. Patients and staff together attempt to understand the incidents of each day, and particularly the major crises which are inevitable, and potentially highly therapeutic, in a psychiatric ward. The events that take place in these meetings have much in common with the processes in small group treatment (see also Chap. XVI).

Each daily ward meeting should be immediately followed by a *staff review session*. Through mutuality of interaction the staff members give consideration to the information obtained during the preceding meeting with the patients. Staff members should be readily accessible, fully 'visible' to their colleagues. Skilled leadership is called for, together with a willingness on the part of each staff member to have his performance scrutinized. Multiple leadership is sought, and not authoritative control by the most prominent staff member.

The staff review meeting, in addition to its therapeutic importance, is a valuable teaching experience, in which new members of staff can develop their treatment skills. Sensitivity training groups for staff members can be used in addition (Wolff, 1964).

When all members of staff recognize their contribution to the overall therapeutic atmosphere, the patients in the ward are more likely to benefit from social learning. This can occur whenever a patient is motivated to express emotions. Times of crises can be utilized to help patients gain greater understanding about their behaviour. Five requirements are needed for such learning to take place (Jones and Polak, 1968):

1. *Face-to-face confrontation*

This requires that all the important protagonists in any ward crisis should be brought together as soon as possible after the disruptive event. Each participant then gives his account of the incident. The staff member present in the confrontation facilitates discussion so that each patient can gain greater awareness of the part he played.

2. *Timing*

Social learning is less likely to take place if the confrontation is deferred until emotions are no longer aroused. Provision must be allowed for the paricipants to express their feelings with the least possible delay.

3. *Skilled leadership*

The third requirement makes it possible without rancour or threat of retaliation for all patients concerned to convey fully and frankly how they may have contributed to the occurrence of the ward crisis.

4. *Open communication*

This implies that freedom of expression becomes a chief principle of ward conduct, with a readiness on the part of the staff to listen to all points of view.

5. *An Appropriate level of feeling*

Adequate emotional expression is of great importance, significant changes of behaviour occurring most readily when feelings are roused.

It is not possible for a staff member to make adequate use of the ward atmosphere unless he is knowledgable about group dynamics. He also needs to be in sufficient possession of relevant facts. One of the main reasons for failure of milieu therapy is that psychiatrists are often not trained to convey the material of their individual interviews to the ward team. With appropriate explanation, patients readily understand that when their disclosures and self-discoveries during individual sessions are communicated to the ward team, they can then proceed in the daily ward meeting to elaborate and build on the progress they achieved in their dyadic interviews.

REFERENCES

ACKERMAN, N. S. (1958) *Psychodynamics of Family Life*. New York: Basic Books.

BION, W. R. (1961) *Experiences in Groups*. London: Tavistock Publications.

CHASSAN, J. B. (1967) *Research Design in Clinical Psychology and Psychiatry*. New York: Appleton-Century-Crofts.

EZRIEL, H. (1950) A psychoanalytic approach to group treatment. *British Journal of Medical Psychology*, **23**, 59.

FISKE, D. W., LUBORSKY, L. & PARLOFF, M. B. (1970) Planning of research on effectiveness of psychotherapy. *American Psychologist*, **25**, 727.

FOULKES, S. H. (1964) *Therapeutic Group Analysis*. London: George Allen and Unwin.

FRANK, J. (1961) *Persuasion and Healing*. London: Oxford University Press.

GOTTSCHALK, L. A. & AUERBACH, A. H. (1966) *Methods of Research in Psychotherapy*. New York: Appleton-Century-Crofts.

HORNEY, K. (1951) *Neurosis and Human Growth*. London: Routledge and Kegan Paul.

JONES, M. (1953) *The Therapeutic Community*. New York: Basic Books.

JONES, M. & POLAK, P. (1968) Crisis and confrontation. *British Journal of Psychiatry*, **114**, 169.

KELMAN, H. C. & PARLOFF, M. B. (1957) Intercorrelations among three criteria of improvement in group therapy. *Journal of Abnormal and Social Psychology*, **54**, 281.

KIESLER, D. J. (1966) Some myths of psychotherapy research and the search for a paradigm. *Psychological Bulletin*, **65**, 110.

LEWIN, K. (1947) Group Decision and Social Change. In *Readings in Social Psychology*. Edited by T. M. Newcomb and E. L. Hartley. New York: Henry Holt and Co.

MACLENNAN, B. W. (1966) Group supervision as a method of training group psychotherapists. In *International Handbook of Group Psychotherapy*. pp. 529–538. Edited by J. L. Moreno, New York: Philosophical Library.

McPHERSON, F. M. & WALTON, H. J. (1965) Changes in communications of patients treated in a closed therapeutic group. *Selected Lectures, Sixth International Congress of Psychotherapy*, p. 91, Basel: Kager.

McPHERSON, F. M. & WALTON, H. J. (1970) Dimensions of Psychotherapy group interaction: an analysis of clinicians' constructs. *British Journal of Medical Psychology*, **43**, 281.

MORENO, J. L. (Ed.) (1945) *Group Psychotherapy*. New York: Beacon.

PRATT, J. H. (1907) The class method of treating consumption in the homes of the poor. *Journal of the American Medical Association*, **49**, 755.

STEIN, A. (1963) The training of the group psychotherapist. In *Group Psychotherapy and Group Function*. pp. 558–576. Edited by M. Rosenbaum and M. Berger, New York: Basic Books.

TUCKMAN, B. W. (1965) Developmental sequence in small groups. *Psychological Bulletin*, **63**, 384.

WALTON, H. J. & McPHERSON, F. M. (1968) Phenomena in a closed psychotherapeutic group. *British Journal of Medical Psychology*, **41**, 319.

WALTON, H. J. (Ed.) (1971) *Small Group Psychotherapy*. Harmondsworth: Penguin Books Ltd.

WHITAKER, D. STOCK, & LIEBERMAN, M. A. (1964) *Psychotherapy through the Group Process*. London: Prentice-Hall International.

WOLFF, S. (1964) Group discussions with nurses in a hospital for alcoholics. *International Journal of Nursing Studies*, **1**, 131.

Chapter VII

SEXUAL BEHAVIOUR AND DEVIANT SEXUALITY

G. M. Carstairs

In recent years not only physicians and psychiatrists but also medical students themselves have complained of the lack of teaching about human sexual behaviour in their undergraduate courses. Curiously enough, in this respect medicine has lagged behind public opinion. During the past fifty years there have been marked changes in social attitudes concerning sexual matters, changes which were heralded in literature and the arts. Immediately after the first World War the influence of writers such as D. H. Lawrence, Aldous Huxley and the Freudian psychologists broke down the unhealthy Victorian taboos which had prevented frank discussion of sex. Since the second World War this process has been carried still further, and in the wake of this freedom of expression quite fundamental rules of conduct have been challenged and re-examined. Formerly, sexual morality was governed by religious decrees but with the decline in religious belief there has been a tendency to apply humanistic principles in drawing up new codes of socially approved behaviour. According to these principles, behaviour is disapproved not because it violates sacred precepts but only when it causes other people to suffer distress or unhappiness. This revision of social values has been reflected in progressive changes in popular attitudes concerning birth control, pre-marital sex, medical termination of pregnancy, and the treatment of homosexuals and other sexual deviants.

Nowadays, we like to believe that our thinking about sex is less clouded by emotional prejudices than used to be the case; but rational opinions on this, as on any matter, have to be based on objective, factual knowledge. Here we have to admit that in the field of sexual behaviour, although there is an enormous volume of historical, didactic and popular literature, from the ancient Kama-Sutra of Vatsyayana to the latest treatises on how to ensure sexual satisfaction in marriage, the advent of scientifically valid information is still both very recent, and incomplete. Here, Havelock Ellis (1936) undoubtedly paved the way, at least for the English-speaking world, with his monographs on the psychology of sex, which first appeared in successive volumes between 1897 and 1910. Much of his material was anecdotal rather than strictly scientific, but it did offer a descriptive account of the physiology of sexual activity in men and women and indicated certain important differences in the subjective accompaniments of these experiences in either sex. Havelock Ellis showed that sexual behaviour could be dispassionately studied and analysed: he taught how to distinguish between the stages of tumescence, orgasm and detumescence, and drew upon clinical experience to show how men and women of his period tended to regard their sexual life. He pointed out the considerable range of variation in sexual behaviour, both within and between different cultures, and argued in favour of a more humane approach towards sexual deviants: in his view, which after half a century is now coming to be generally accepted, peculiar forms of sexual gratification should be tolerated unless they are demonstrably harmful either to the individual or to other people.

Subsequent advances in knowledge have come from the two complementary disciplines of comparative zoology and social science. Zoologists have long been concerned with animals' reproductive behaviour, as the expression of an important instinctive drive. Anthropologists, too, found that sexual behaviour and the social institutions associated with it played a key role in the functioning of primitive societies. At first, this subject was tackled somewhat nervously; Henri Junod (1927) who contributed a masterly account of the life and customs of the Tonga tribe in South Africa was typical of ethnographers of his age in cloaking his careful descriptions of their sexual behaviour in the decent obscurity of Latin. Malinowski (1929) in his classic work *The Sexual Life of Savages* was the first anthropologist to give his subject the attention it deserved. It was Margaret Mead (1935, 1949), however, who drew upon field observations in seven primitive societies to show the extent to which human concepts of masculinity and femininity, and the roles deemed appropriate for either sex can be determined by cultural traditions. Each society has its own definition of 'natural' male and female conduct; and while none can ignore the primary sexual characteristics, or the woman's function of childbearing, nearly every other attribute that we assume to be sex-related is contradicted in one society or another. Margaret Mead advanced the theory that the insistent emphasis on male superiority found in so many cultures is not due to biological factors such as their greater physical strength and aggressiveness but represents an over-compensation for their inability to bear children. As she puts it 'The recurrent problem of civilization is to redefine the male role satisfactorily enough . . . so that the male may in the course of his life reach a solid sense of irreversible achievement. In the case of women, it is only necessary that they be permitted to fulfil their biological role, to attain this sense of irreversible achievement.' (Mead, 1949, p. 160).

It is no longer possible to subscribe to the naive view that sex 'comes naturally' in primitive societies. Many ethnographers have shown that the conventions and taboos surrounding sexual behaviour in a jungle

F

tribe can be just as complex and restrictive as in the court of Queen
Victoria. Margaret Mead described remarkable differences in sexual
experience in different tribes of New Guinea: among the Arapesh, the
men feel threatened by women's sexual demands, but in fact most
Arapesh women never experienced orgasm; among the Manus, neither
men nor women found sex pleasurable, whereas among the Mundugu-
mor it was taken for granted that both men and women derive the
same kind of satisfaction from physical love-making. Among all the
peoples she studied, Dr Mead found that Samoans had the sunniest and
easiest approach to sex. This could partly be explained by a social
organization which minimized the tensions which tend to arise between
parents and adolescent children in isolated nuclear families, and partly
by the young people's freedom to practise courtship and love-making
before marriage. Mead advanced a further generalization that the
societies which encourage relatively prolonged love-play before sexual
intercourse takes place are those in which women are least likely to
complain of failure to achieve orgasm.

The first major contribution of biological research to this field came
with the publication of the Kinsey reports (1948, 1953) on sexual
behaviour in the human male and female. Until this time, all generalizations about such behaviour had been based upon individual experiences
or upon studies of extremely small and biased examples (e.g., on groups
of college students, of psychiatrists' clients, or delinquents). Kinsey's
samples (5300 white males and 5900 white females) were the largest
yet reported, but it is important to remember that they were composed
for the most part of volunteer subjects, and thus cannot be regarded
as representative of the population as a whole. With this reservation
in mind, Kinsey's findings still gave the best information yet available
about the frequency of different types of sexual behaviour. For example
93 per cent of male subjects reported that they had masturbated, almost
invariably beginning during adolescence. Masturbation was less
common among women (28 per cent by age 20, 62 per cent by age 45)
both in incidence and in frequency, whereas sexual excitement during
'heavy petting' was experienced equally often by either sex; it was noticed
that women who had masturbated, and those who had experienced
'heavy petting' were more likely than their fellows to enjoy physically
satisfactory sex relations in marriage.

Kinsey confirmed that homosexual experiences are much commoner
in men than in women but one of his most surprising findings was that
no less than 37 per cent of the male respondents reported at least one
homosexual experience leading to orgasm: among men still unmarried
at the age of 35, almost exactly 50 per cent reported such experiences.
Kinsey devised a seven-point heterosexual-homosexual rating scale:
applying this scale he found that eight per cent of men showed exclusively

homosexual interests and behaviour for at least three years of their active sex lives; four per cent did so throughout their lives. The incidence of homosexual activity in women was about one-third that in men; where it occurred, it was less prolonged and more often confined to a single partner or two, whereas male homosexuals tended to have numerous partners. Kinsey showed that male sexual activity increases very rapidly with the onset of puberty, reaching its peak in late adolescence and begins its long decline during the twenties, but that women tended to show a more gradual increase in sex activity, reaching their peak between the mid-twenties and the thirties, and sustaining a high level of sexual activity well into middle life.

In contrast to what was generally believed, Kinsey claimed to have demonstrated an essential similarity in the physiology of male and female orgasm. Here he may have been misled by the technique of his inquiry, in which he personally interviewed more than half of the respondents; his own pre-formed opinions may have involuntarily influenced some of their replies. In 1966, however, the remarkable Masters-Johnson study presented data on physiological changes during orgasm, based on over 10,000 observations, and was able to confirm and to elaborate much of the descriptive accounts given by Havelock Ellis and by Kinsey, while also contributing some new knowledge: for example, they found that orgasm in women is accompanied by a series of three to as many as fifteen localized contractions of the engorged outer third of the vagina. The psychological intensity of the orgasm is directly related to the number of vaginal spasms. Both men and women show a rapid detumescence after orgasm, but whereas in the male this process of resolution must proceed until the pre-excitation level is reached before sexual arousal can be repeated, the female need retreat only a little way, to the condition of partial arousal which these authors term 'pre-orgasmic plateau' before becoming capable of repeated orgasms if further tactile stimulation is given.

Both of the above studies claimed to be strictly objective, Kinsey's being concerned with categorizing and counting sexual 'outlets', and the Masters-Johnson one being essentially limited to measurements of pulse rate, blood pressure, local engorgement and dilatation of tissues, and muscular contractions during sexual excitation. Nevertheless, many of Kinsey's questions and some of those studied by Masters and Johnson required the respondents to report upon their feelings. For example, Kinsey showed clear differences between men's relatively greater capacity to be sexually aroused by erotic pictures, by the sight of a naked female or even by the thought of making love; in contrast, women tended to be aroused only by the physical stimulation of being touched, caressed and embraced. Girls and women were much less inclined than boys to discuss frankly sexual matters among themselves, although they freely discussed their romantic attachments. Both men and women appear to show a diminished sensibility to pain and other environmental stimuli during the peak of sexual excitement; but the human female, in common with the female of several other mammalian species, is more easily distracted than the male during the early stages of such excitement.

Many critics have complained of the fact that the Kinsey study, with its statistical analyses of 'sexual outlets' appeared to reduce human behaviour to the level of the barnyard. Kinsey himself described his work as: 'a study of all aspects of human sexual behaviour, and not a study of its biologic aspects, or of its psychologic aspects, or of its sociologic aspects, as separate entities', but in spite of this intention it is evident that his primarily zoological training—his previous research had been on the taxonomy of insect behaviour—meant that the physiological aspects of human sexual behaviour were much more thoroughly investigated than the social or the psychological. Admittedly, this research did document the male's greater responsiveness to sexual imagery and fantasy and the female's bias towards the romantic accompaniments of sex. The influence of social factors was shown in the different behaviour of highly educated and less educated persons, and of those with and without strong religious affiliations: but little or no attempt was made to elicit the subjective aspects of sexual experience. It is important to appreciate that an accompaniment of the male's more active, aggressive sexual role is the sense of heightened self-esteem which comes when he has successfully played his part—and also the nagging fear that he may *not* perform well enough. Every young man's Achilles' heel is the anxiety that he may not prove manly enough. On the other hand, young women are conditioned to be receptive, loving and dependent: *their* greatest anxiety is lest their lover should prove inconstant, and reject them. If young people's sex education is to be thorough, they should learn to appreciate these emotional nuances, as well as the physiology of sexual responsiveness in themselves and in their partners (Masters and Johnson, 1970).

Shortly after the appearance of the first Kinsey volume, two 'behavioural scientists' at Yale University, Ford and Beach (1951) published a book entitled *Patterns of Sexual Behaviour*. In this work they brought together the latest knowledge about the sexual life of animals (particularly primates) as studied in laboratories, in zoos and in the wild, and the reports about patterns of human sexual behaviour contained in some 64 detailed ethnographic field reports. Their interest lay in indicating the similarities, as well as the differences between human sexual behaviour and that of the most closely related animal species. One finding to which they drew attention was that sexual behaviour, in the higher primates, calls for the mastery of somewhat complex skills, especially on the part of the male, and that these skills are acquired by young monkeys' observations, imitation and practice. When either a male or a female chimpanzee is reared to the age of sexual maturity in isolation from their kind, and so deprived of this learning experience, and then is confronted with a mature partner they are manifestly sexually aroused, but do not know how to copulate. Interestingly enough, in experiments where two equally untutored apes have been confronted with each other, the female appears to learn her role more quickly, and acts as mentor to the fumbling male (Ford and Beach, 1951, p. 194).

In their review of the anthropological literature, these authors found that in almost all primitive societies small children have ample opportunities to learn about physical love-making, and often rehearse it in play without arousing the disapproval of their elders. In contrast, most Western societies have tended, until quite recently, to make a mystery of sex and to discourage childish curiosity about the subject. Since we know that feelings of apprehension and guilt can very readily disrupt human sexual behaviour, this conspiracy of concealment seems calculated to have made it more difficult for young people in the West to enjoy that 'sunny and easy' approach to making love which Margaret Mead found characteristic of young Samoans.

During the last two decades, as has happened many times before in our social history, there have been repeated public expressions of concern (voiced most emphatically by the middle-aged and the elderly) about the laxity of sexual morals shown by young people today. Previous outcries of this kind have of necessity consisted of expressions of individual opinion, supported by anecdotal evidence; but in 1965 there was published a well-documented factual study of the sexual life of British boys and girls between the ages of 15 and 19 (Schofield, 1965). Unlike the Kinsey surveys, this research was based on true random samples of the general population, stratified for age, social class and area of residence. Preliminary studies had shown the stages which most young people go through with remarkable uniformity before their first experience of intercourse. These are: kissing, 'deep kissing', fondling the breasts over clothes, fondling the unclothed breasts and finally genital apposition without actual penetration. Schofield showed that in the early 1960's at least 11 per cent of 16 year old boys and 30 per cent of 18 year olds had already experienced sexual intercourse; for girls of the same ages the percentages were 6 and 16 respectively.

In contrast to Kinsey's findings in the U.S.A., children from lower social class backgrounds did not show a higher incidence of sexual experience. Schofield inquired into attitudes and values, and found these often contradictory: for example, a majority of youngsters, especially among the sexually experienced, were in favour of premarital sexual experience, and yet there was still a tendency to believe that a girl (though not necessarily the boy) should be a virgin at the time of her marriage. The young people's knowledge about pregnancy, contraception and venereal disease proved extremely incomplete, and this was equally true for those who already claimed to 'know all about it'. Most of this inadequate knowledge was learned from classmates. With the exception of middle-class mothers, in relation to their daughters, most parents still seemed to shrink from discussing sexual matters with their children. The commonest source of the first accurate information about sex which these young people reported was sex instruction in school: but interestingly enough this was least likely to be given in private schools attended by boys from better-off families.

If we turn from the study of normal sexual behaviour to that of sexual deviation, the first question to ask is, which departures from the normal pattern of sexual satisfaction are most commonly found in our society? This cannot be stated with precision, because epidemiological studies of their incidence have not been carried out; but one can at least distinguish conditions which are very commonly encountered from those which are less common, and others which are quite infrequent. In the first category come failures to achieve sexual satisfaction: premature ejaculation, impotence and frigidity. Women's failure to achieve orgasm has been so common, in our recent history, that it was seldom the subject of complaint; it is a sign of a more natural acceptance of sex that women are increasingly coming to expect that the experience should be pleasureable for themselves as well as for their husbands. Kinsey found that total failure to achieve orgasm during married life was commoner in women of lower educational background.

Another frequent cause of distress is masturbation, or rather, the guilt occasioned by masturbation in young people of both sexes who have been told that it is sinful and destructive to their health.

The element which all of these conditions have in common is *anxiety*, which may be prompted by fears of which the subject is quite aware; but in many cases the anxieties are irrational, and are the expression of unconscious conflicts, carried over from experiences in childhood. In either case, a doctor can best help these patients by giving them an opportunity to discuss these (for them) highly emotional topics with a sympathetic, understanding and non-condemning listener. This presupposes that the doctor is indeed not 'shocked' by what he hears, and this in turn requires that he has come to terms with his own sexual impulses. Patients often beg for reassurance, but it is important not to be in too great a hurry to give such reassurance: the first essential is to help the patient to unburden himself or herself of their inmost fears. It is the relief of this unburdening to a listener who takes it calmly, rather than the assurance to a masturbating boy that he will not go mad, or to a frigid girl that she is not abnormally constructed, which represents the first step towards improvement. Many of these disturbances are relatively minor, the result of faulty learning, and can be overcome with simple supportive psychotherapy of this 'unburdening' variety. Many others are due to the failure of one partner in a marriage to recognize, and meet, the emotional needs of his or her spouse; and in such cases the spouse may have to be also involved, if treatment is to be effective. Sometimes, however, impotence and frigidity prove to be symptoms of more profound neurotic disturbance, and when this becomes apparent a more prolonged type of psychotherapy, aiming at modification of the personality, may have to be recommended. In suitable cases, treatment on behaviour therapy principles can be effective (see Chapter XVIII).

One ought perhaps to add to the above category of common sexual disturbances certain other forms of behaviour which have tended to attract less attention because they have been in accord with prevailing social attitudes, such as the total repudiation of sex, and the tendency to brand it as an evil element in human nature. This tendency is rare, but not unknown in primitive societies, but it has been relatively common in the moral and religious teachings of highly developed societies. Many religions, including Christianity and Hinduism, have regarded sex as inimical to spiritual advancement. It is noteworthy that this tends to be associated with a degrading of the female sex, as the source of temptation. In our society some individuals who have been denied sexual fulfilment either through external circumstances or because of personal inhibitions have shown warped personality development as a result: this becomes evident in their violent emotional reactions to the manifestations of sexuality in others. It is these sexually thwarted people who denounce the immorality of the younger generation most vehemently, and who demand severe punishment for all sorts of sexual offenders; but since they are usually quite unaware of the source of their own emotional perturbation, they seldom seek help for themselves.

In the second category, of relatively less frequent sexual disorders, are several conditions which not only may distress the patients but also may bring them into conflict with the law. Here we are dealing with *sexual deviation*, which can take so many forms that it is not easily defined. As Peter Scott (1964), an experienced forensic psychiatrist, has pointed out, such a definition should include: sexual activity or fantasy, directed towards orgasm, other than genital intercourse with a willing partner of opposite sex and of similar sexual maturity, persistently recurrent, and contrary to the generally accepted norm of sexual behaviour in the community. The commonest forms of deviant sexuality which are encountered clinically are prostitution, homosexuality and exhibitionism. The latter phenomenon is found only in men: it consists in exposing the genitalia to women, or more commonly to immature girls. These patients obtain sexual gratification from the girls' alarm at this sudden confrontation; they very seldom actually molest their victims. Prostitution and homosexuality, on the other hand, occur in both men and women, although prostitution is predominantly female, and homosexuality predominantly a male activity: the extent to which these activities have been regarded as deviant, in the sense of violating the community's accepted norms of behaviour has varied widely in different societies, and in our own society at different times. For example, in 1957 the Wolfenden Committee's recommendation that homosexual activity conducted in private between consenting adults should no longer be treated as a criminal offence was considered unacceptable to public opinion, but only ten years later an Act embodying this principle was endorsed by both Houses of Parliament.

Prostitutes seldom consult a psychiatrist about their sexual behaviour, and for many this behaviour simply represents a means of livelihood into which they have been led partly by circumstances and partly by choice. On the other hand there are many young girls who exhibit promiscuous behaviour as a more or less conscious rebellion against their emotionally deprived home life. Promiscuity and gestures of attempted suicide are girls' most frequent ways of acting out their familial revolt, just as delinquency is the preferred outlet for adolescent boys. In both the principal disturbance is likely to be found in their family relationships but in some cases these may be aggravated by anxieties and neurotic conflicts which can be helped by individual psychotherapy.

Homosexuals too may be relatively content with their lot. If Kinsey's estimate that four per cent of males have an exclusively homosexual orientation is not wildly inaccurate (and we have no better estimate to act upon) the vast majority of such men must have come to terms with their peculiarity. Most homosexuals who seek help are either anxious young men, seeking reassurance as to whether they are really homosexual or not, or else are men who seek medical protection against being treated as criminals.

It should be remembered that individuals who have exclusively homosexual interests (i.e., who would be rated six on the Kinsey scale) represent only a minority of homosexuals: the majority of those who have had some homosexual experience fall into categories three, four or five of the scale. This is reflected in the fact that one-quarter of all the homosexual offenders brought to court in Britain in recent years have been married men. The potentiality for homosexual behaviour appears to be almost universal among adolescent and young adult males: there are in fact a number of societies in which all the young men are expected to take part in such activities during the early stages of their development.

Turning to the less common forms of deviation, one may encounter cases of paedophilia, sado-masochism, voyeurism, fetishism or transvestism all of which are found much more often in men than in women. Paedophilia is a condition in which a man can only be sexually aroused by a sexually immature child. This is the case with a few homosexuals (whose behaviour, incidentally, is bitterly condemned by the rest of the homosexual community) but it may also be shown by men with exclusively heterosexual inclinations. Such behaviour naturally excites violent emotions in the public as a whole, and especially the parents of the children whom they seduce or exploit: and yet these men are usually gentle and timid rather than violent and lustful. The fact that they respond only to immature partners is due to their unconscious fear of adult women, combined with a profound insecurity in their own sex role. So far from wanting to frighten their victims, they often show a desperate, and hopeless, longing to be loved, as Nabokov has shown so clearly in his tragi-comic novel *Lolita*.

Fetishism is a condition in which sexual satisfaction is derived not from intercourse itself, but from some object (usually an article of clothing, a woman's shoe, or a rubber mackintosh) which comes to dominate the patient's sexual fantasy. Here we can see the mental mechanisms of *displacement* and *fixation* in operation.

It should be noted that an element of fetishism enters into normal male sexual arousal. As Kinsey showed, men are particularly liable to be stimulated by cues which are only indirectly associated with sexuality, response to which is an example of conditioning. Every society has exploited this male propensity by developing conventions of feminine dress, adornment and display which are sexually stimulating only to those who have acquired the appropriate conditioned responses: for example, in our own society in earlier times the sight of a lady's ankle could be highly provocative, while in still earlier times (and once again in contemporary America) an accentuation of the bust was the customary method of heightening her desirability. The difference is, of course, that whereas in normal sexuality these eye-catching features are only signposts on the way towards sexual consummation, the fetishist remains preoccupied with one element among these accessories of courtship. As in a severe obsessive-compulsive neurosis the patient usually recognizes the absurdity of his preoccupation and struggles against it, but it proves too strong for him to resist.

Transvestism is a variant of fetishism, in which the patient derives sexual gratification from dressing himself in women's clothes. Some transvestites are passive homosexuals, who take pleasure in identifying themselves with the female role, but others may be actively heterosexual—quite a number, indeed, are married men who may have taken pains to conceal from their wives this behaviour, of which they are quite ashamed. Here again, the obsessive-compulsive element is quite apparent.

While transvestites obtain a recurrent excitement and gratification from temporarily mimicking the female role, trans-sexualists display an unshakable conviction that they really belong to the opposite sex. Quite often this faulty gender identification stems from childhood, although the patient may, during late adolescence, make conscious efforts to behave like his or her sex-mates, and may even marry. Randell (1970) who has made a special study of these conditions, reports that in terms of the Kinsey scale, nearly two-thirds of a large series of transvestites showed more heterosexual than homosexual traits; surprisingly, among trans-sexuals the proportion with predominantly heterosexual drive was even higher. The great majority of these patients do not ask to be relieved of their peculiarity, but rather to be helped to enjoy it more freely. In some cases surgical intervention to facilitate the adoption of a change of sex has been followed by marked improvement in the patient's social adjustment and peace of mind. Where the symptom distresses the patient, and there is motivation for change, aversion therapy offers some hope of cure, but it is more likely to effect change in transvestites than in trans-sexuals (Gelder and Marks, 1969).

In sado-masochism, sexual gratification occurs only when the patient either inflicts pain upon his partner (sadism) or is hurt by her (masochism). A common variant of this is flagellation, in which the subject or his partner has to be whipped; another is to require that he or she be tightly bound. There are, in fact, a wide variety of bizarre performances in which the partner (or the patient himself) instead of being physically hurt has to be degraded or humiliated. These rituals contain elements of fetishism and are also clearly obsessive-compulsive, in that the patient is often ashamed of them and struggles against the urge to repeat them, but in vain. When described literally these practices often seem pointless and disgusting: they can be understood only as the acting-out of unconscious fantasies which have come to take the place of normal sexual satisfaction. Nor should it be forgotten that here, too, we have only an exaggeration of and arrest at one element which enters into normal sexuality. The infliction of a little pain, in love-bites and squeezing is a very common accompaniment of love-making: and one need only recall the enormous popularity of the novelist Ian Fleming's character James Bond to realise how widespread is the relish for the combination of sado-masochism with erotic fantasies.

One other form of deviant sexuality which occasionally comes to the doctor's attention is voyeurism, in which the patient obtains excitement by peeping at women who are undressing, or spying on couples who are making love. This behaviour, like exhibitionism, may be shown by previously highly respectable men who are undergoing a period of depression or emotional strain in later middle age: it may also be the only sexual activity of severely emotionally handicapped younger men, who are too lacking in self-confidence to venture into female company, and become caught up in this furtive vicarious sex life. In milder degree, almost every man will confess to pleasure in looking at the unclothed female form, a trait which is exploited to the full by the advertising media.

The question now arises, why *do* some people find it impossible to enjoy mutually gratifying sexual relations with a mature partner of the opposite sex?

The most general explanation is that all these deviations, the so-called sexual perversions, represent *failures to learn appropriate sexual responses* and these failures in turn are believed to be due to fear; that is, to unconscious fears which are carried over from traumatic experiences in early childhood. Patients who exhibit any of these different forms of sexual deviation (and many patients will exhibit more than one) have this in common, that they have failed to achieve sexual maturity, which has been well defined by Storr (1964) as the ability to form a stable relationship with the opposite sex which is both physically and emotionally satisfying, and in which sexual intercourse forms the main, though not the only, mode of expression of love. Failure to achieve sexual maturity is associated with a failure to form relationships with other people on equal terms.

The commonest cause of arrested sexual maturation is fear, or rather neurotic anxiety. Both fear and anxiety are normal responses to the presence, or threat, of physical danger; but neurotic anxiety occurs in response to fantasied fears, which may develop when there has been a faulty relationship with either or both parents during the patient's early years. Ordinarily, after the period of infancy and complete dependence on the mother, every child passes through a phase of possessive love for the parent of the opposite sex, which is relinquished more or less reluctantly during the latency period which precedes the onset of puberty. In a well-integrated family, this development is made easier because the child turns to the parent of the same sex as the 'role model' for his or her adult behaviour. The early history of sexual deviants, however, very often reveals that their parents were on bad terms with each other, and that they were either quite unhelpful to the growing child, or turned to him for their own emotional gratification. In the case of the male homosexual there has often been an excess of physical and emotional dependence upon his mother, while his father remained aloof and unimpressive: such men have never been able to disengage their emotional tie with the mother, and to them every heterosexual encounter has the unconscious threatening overtones of an incestuous relationship. Very commonly, therefore, relations with mature women are feared because of unconscious fantasies equating them with the mother; in some cases, however, the hidden nightmare contains a dreaded father figure who prohibits any heterosexual activity: but in every such case the common element is unconscious anxiety.

The achievement of emotional and of sexual maturity is not a once-for-all affair. All of us are capable of regressing to childish attitudes at times—for example when we are sick, or confronted with severe setbacks, disappointments or bereavements. Under stress, people may 'unlearn' their adult attributes, and may then revert to behaviour which they had long abandoned except in fantasy. It is not uncommon for middle-aged men in such a period of stress, to give way to earlier, half-forgotten urges; and even much younger men may find themselves faltering, and turning to homosexual activities when confronted for the first time with adult responsibilities. These are instances of regression, and on the whole they have a better prognosis, whatever the form of sexual deviation, than those cases which have always remained fixated at an infantile level of sexual response.

Since it is assumed that faulty learning during infancy, resulting from distorted relationships with the parents or other emotionally significant figures, is the main cause of failure to achieve sexual maturity, the logical way to treat such cases would be to try to undo this faulty learning by means of psychotherapy. It has to be admitted, however, that many of these cases, especially those in which fixation, rather than regression, appears to be the main feature, have proved extremely difficult to treat. Some, in fact, do not really want to be treated, but are content to plan their lives in such a way that their peculiarity can be kept a secret; they remain somewhat limited, but functioning members of society. Some others are not so fortunate. They may be so driven by the intensity of their deviant sexual urges that they become unable to conceal their activities, and run the risk of public censure, or criminal proceedings. Where there is a compulsive element in their behaviour, these patients may become intensely agitated, self-reproachful, and understandably fearful of bringing public disgrace upon themselves and their families.

Even where a cure cannot be effected, these patients can generally be helped to adapt more successfully to their peculiarity and to prevent its getting them into trouble. Group psychotherapy has proved especially helpful here, because many sexual deviants are socially isolated, and reproach themselves bitterly for behaviour of which they are ashamed, but which they are unable to control. In group sessions they realize that other people have to contend with similar problems, and this fortifies their self-respect.

There remain some patients, however, in all of the above categories (but especially among homosexuals and exhibitionists) whose sexual drive is so imperative that they keep repeating their deviant behaviour even though this is likely to lead to their arrest and punishment. Such patients may need, and beg for, measures which will help them to control these unwelcome urges. It has been found that a course of oestrogens (e.g., Stilboesterol 5 mg daily until mammary enlargement begins to be apparent, and 1 mg per day thereafter) will damp down the sexual drive, and this can give symptomatic relief to such patients while an attempt is made through psychotherapy either to let them develop other, more socially acceptable forms of sexual satisfaction, or else to ease the emotional crisis which has caused their heightened sex activity.

In recent years a number of homosexuals and fetishists have been treated by aversive conditioning, a form of behaviour therapy designed to link the deviant practice, or the fetish object, with subjective sensations of nausea and disgust. This is a very arduous treatment, which requires a high level of motivation on the part of the patient if it is to be carried through successfully, but in suitable cases it has been shown that deviations of quite long standing can be unlearned by this means (Marks et al., 1970; Marks, 1968; Oswald, 1962). This therapy has been especially successful in patients with considerable personality assets, who were able to advance in social and sexual maturation once they were able to by-pass the deviant form of gratification at which their sexual development had become arrested. Many deviants, however, have rather little ego-strength on which to build—they are, in fact, severely handicapped personalities. With these patients, one's aim must be to help them find social satisfactions which will make their lives more rewarding, and to support them psychotherapeutically and if necessary with the aid of drugs. With advancing years, as Kinsey showed, the sexual drive tends to decline, so time is on the side of therapy. However, as has been indicated throughout this chapter, these disorder are indicative not merely of sexual dysfunction but also of thwarted, limited and often unhappy individuals whose personalities, as much as their sex lives, are in need of help.

REFERENCES

ELLIS, Havelock (1936) *Studies in the psychology of sex* (6 vols.). New York: Random House (One volume edition, 1936—reprinted 1960).

FORD, C. S. & BEACH, F. A. (1951) *Patterns of Sexual Behaviour.* New York: Harper.

GELDER, M. G. & MARKS, I. M. (1969) Aversion treatment in transvestism and trans-sexualism. In *Trans-sexualism and Sex Reassignment.* Edited by R. Green, Baltimore: Johns Hopkins Press.

JUNOD, H. (1912) *The Life of a South African Tribe.* Published by David Nutt, London: (MacMillan in 1927).

KINSEY, A. C., POMEROY, W. B. & MARTIN, C. E. (1948) *Sexual Behaviour in the Human Male.* Philadelphia and London: W. B. Saunders Co.

KINSEY, A. C., POMEROY, W. B., MARTIN, C. E. & GEBHARD, P. M. (1953) *Sexual Behaviour in the Human Female*. Philadelphia and London: W. B. Saunders Co.

MALINOWSKI, B. (1929) *The Sexual Life of Savages*. London: Kegan Paul.

MARKS, I. M. (1968) Aversion Therapy. *British Journal of Medical Psychology*, **41**, 47.

MARKS, I. M., GELDER, M. & BANCROFT, J. (1970) Sexual deviants two years after electric aversion. *British Journal of Psychology*, **117**, 173.

MASTERS, W. H. & JOHNSON, V. (1966) *Human Sexual Response*. New York: Little, Brown and Co.

MASTERS, W. H. & JOHNSON, V. (1970) *Human Sexual Inadequacy*. New York: Little, Brown and Co.

MEAD, M. (1935) *Sex and Temperament in three Primitive Societies*. New York: Wm. Morrow.

MEAD, M. (1949) *Male and Female*. New York: Morrow. London: Gollancz.

OSWALD, I. (1962) Induction of Illusory and Hallucinatory Voices with considerations of Behaviour Therapy. *Journal of Mental Science*, **108**, 196–212.

RANDELL, J. (1970) Transvestism and Trans-sexualism. *British Journal of Hospital Medicine*, **3**, 211.

SCHOFIELD, M. (1965) *The Sexual Behaviour of Young People*. London: Longmans Green.

SCOTT, P. D. (1964) Definition. Classification, Prognosis and Treatment. In *Pathology and Treatment of Sexual Deviation*. p. 88. Edited by I. Rosen, London and New York: Oxford University Press.

STORR, A. (1964) *Sexual Deviation*. Harmondsworth: Penguin Books.

Chapter VIII

PRACTICAL TREATMENT METHODS FOR SEXUAL INADEQUACY

A. J. Cooper

INTRODUCTION

Male sexual inadequacy may be manifested clinically in three main ways: *Impotence*—which is the persistent inability to develop or sustain an erection sufficient to conclude coitus to orgasm and ejaculation; *Impotentia ejaculandi*—which is the persistent absence of orgasm and ejaculation during coitus (which may be greatly prolonged) despite the presence of normal desire and erection, and *Premature ejaculation*—which is the persistent occurrence of ejaculation and orgasm before or immediately following penetration, in practice usually within one minute, which occurs against volition, and before the male wishes. These conditions are not mutually exclusive; they may occur in the same subject at different times according to circumstances. However, in any individual there is a distinct tendency for one or other to dominate the clinical picture.

One of the shortest and yet at the same time comprehensive definitions of 'frigidity' is that of Kleegman (1959), a gynaecologist, who states:

'Frigidity in the female is the inability to have complete sexual response to orgasm in coitus. Absolute frigidity is the lack of any satisfying emotional response. Some frigid women are entirely passive without negative reaction and others react with active rejection or even revulsion. Relative frigidity is the ability to respond to a variable degree with inability to achieve orgasm. Frigidity may be primary or secondary'.

It should be emphasized that the term frigidity refers solely to diminished or absent physical and/or emotional responsivity *during* coitus; it carries no implication of personality such as 'coldness, passivity, aloofness, etc.'. Indeed, Malleson (1942) has drawn attention to the fact that many (sexually) 'frigid' women have warm, engaging personalities; she and others (Masters and Johnson, 1966) have suggested that the term 'frigidity' be dropped from the English language to be replaced by 'lacking in orgasmic capacity', 'altered (reduced) responsivity', or some such non-denigratory designation. Although there is some merit in this suggestion, for the present the better known term 'frigidity' as defined above will be retained.

Vaginismus is a spontaneous 'protective' muscular spasm of some, or all of the voluntary and/or involuntary muscles comprising the perineum, which occurs during attempted penetration. In severe cases there may be lordosis of the lumbar spine, adduction of the thighs, and opisthotonos; it may be impossible to insert even the tip of a little finger. The condition is one cause of dyspareunia and is the commonest factor in non consummation; it may often, but not always be associated with frigidity.

Impotence and frigidity which are essentially counterpart conditions (there is no female equivalent to premature ejaculation which presents for treatment), may be 'constitutional', 'organic' or 'psychogenic'. 'Constitutionally' determined sexual inadequacy is characteristically associated with persisting evidence of low sexual drive and responsiveness, dating from puberty which may be late (Cooper, 1967): indeed some cases, profoundly indifferent sexually, will neither have masturbated nor sought out any other type of sexual outlet during their entire lives. There is no organic lesion nor causal psychopathology in these cases. 'Constitutional factors' which have been neglected by most authorities seem to be of somewhat greater significance in impotence than frigidity. Strictly speaking, 'constitutional inadequacy' although statistically unusual cannot be seen as pathologic in the sense that 'organic' or 'psychogenic' can. It merely represents one extreme of normal biologic variation, the other pole of this continuum being occupied by exceptionally high outlet subjects, over 30 per week (Kinsey et al., 1948, 1953). This distinction, however, is largely academic since 'constitutional inadequacy' can cause much sexual unhappiness, especially if the respective needs of the partners are greatly discrepant.

Unless coexisting 'constitutional factors' are dominant, or the condition is congenital, 'organic inadequacy' will have developed from prior competency in association with an organic lesion; it tends to be constant and persists unchanged, irrespective of the nature and intensity of any sexual stimulation which might be provided. 'Organic disorders' which probably account for less than five per cent of cases may follow any debilitating disease, be associated with metabolic disorders, disorders of the central nervous system, cardiovascular disease, following some drugs, and with endocrinopathies, etc. (Cooper, 1969c).

In contrast to 'organic impairment', 'psychogenic' is selective and transient occurring in certain situations and at certain times but not others (Cooper et al., 1970b). 'Psychogenic factors' are usually stated to be dominant in the majority of cases (Stafford-Clark, 1954; Simpson, 1950; Allen, 1970). Since aetiologic overlap may occur it is comparatively unusual to see these conditions in pure culture. It is however generally possible to judge whether a disorder is 'predominantly constitutional', or 'predominantly organic' or 'predominantly psychogenic'; this is a prerequisite of optimum therapy. 'Organic disorders' can only be relieved if the underlying pathology can be compensated for or removed by, for instance, excision of a temporal lobe tumour

(Johnson, 1965*a*) or androgen substitution therapy in traumatic or 'medical' castration, etc. (Simpson, 1950). 'Constitutional disorders' which are usually attributed to a complex genetic basis (although the ineradicable effects of early experience probably also play a part (Johnson, 1965*b*; Tanner, 1964)) are often unrewarding to treat if the aim is potency, indeed they may be immutable to presently available methods. However much can be done psychotherapeutically, helping the subject and/or his partner to accept and adapt to his/her inadequacy. Especially important in this respect may be initial clarification as to the nature of the condition and later discussions and decisions relating to artificial insemination and/or adoption, etc.

The treatment of predominantly 'psychogenic disorders' which forms the rest of this section, aims to remove or modify psychological factors which may prevent an individual (male or female) from performing and/or responding to his/her capacity. It should be emphasized that without the active and willing cooperation of both sexual partners, significant and permanent change is unlikely.

A vital preliminary to treatment is a detailed psychosexual history taken from both sexual partners. Ideally this should be taken first individually then jointly. All aspects of sexual development and experiences should be covered. Topics are best dealt with chronologically, as follows:

1. First awareness of sex and sexuality.
2. Puberty data, e.g. menarche in females, initial ejaculation in males, other secondary sexual characteristics in both etc.
3. Masturbation history, including frequencies, attitudes and fantasies etc.
4. Menstrual history in females, including attitudes, fantasies etc.
5. Types and extent of premarital sexual experience including extent of sexual education, etc.
6. Marital sexual history especially honeymoon experiences, pregnancies in females, pattern of activities up till initial failure.
7. Precise circumstances, and type of initial failure.
8. Sexual history subsequent to failure, up to present, including alternative sexual outlets, etc.
9. 'Non-sexual' psychiatric data.

One or more joint interview(s) are invaluable for the purposes of corroboration and also to ascertain the tenor of the interpersonal relationship between the partners and the likelihood of good treatment cooperation.

During the initial diagnostic interview, to minimize tension and blocking, it is often advisable to begin with more remote aspects of the sexual history such as 'age of puberty', 'source of sexual education', 'adolescent sexual outlets' etc. and gradually lead up to topics likely to be more disturbing to the patient. Although the interview should convey a non-judgmental and sympathetic attitude, questions should be put in a matter-of-fact manner without hesitancy or apology. Euphemisms should be avoided. Enquiries should be framed in such terms as to place the burden of denial on the patient. For instance when enquiring about masturbation the following sort of phraseology may be used: 'Masturbation is an extremely common practice both when adolescent and also in marriage. It is a normal way of relieving sexual tension and is indulged by practically all men and women at some time or other. At what age did you start?' *This* introduction logically extends into questions relating to frequencies, techniques, accompanying fantasies, etc. Sometimes arising out of educational or social factors, to avoid misunderstanding or ambiguity, it may become necessary to use the vernacular.

It is perhaps worth mentioning that in the author's experience female patients are generally less embarrassed and more candidly forthcoming than males who more often seem to feel 'threatened' by the interview situation. The point to be made is that sexually disordered females do not require 'special handling'.

As already indicated, impotence and frigidity are in all essentials counterparts; with few exceptions the same treatment principles apply for both. To avoid needless repetition the treatment of impotence will be detailed, unless specified otherwise this may be taken to apply equally to frigidity. The treatment of premature ejaculation and vaginismus are described separately.

TREATMENT OF IMPOTENCE

The following four treatment principles are combined in permutation considered optimum to the needs of the individual patient.

PROGRESSIVE MUSCULAR RELAXATION

This manoeuvre is of the most use in males who experience high levels of somatic anxiety in the sexual situation; however, on the assumption that some degree of anxiety, even if not obvious, is present in most cases of impotence it's inclusion generally is recommended.

The rationale for deep muscular relaxation in impotence (particularly anxiety type) is based on the following over-simplified psychosomatic model. In the male satisfactory copulation depends upon the maintenance of 'equilibrium' between the sympathetic and parasympathetic components of the autonomic nervous system. Physiologically, penile erection may be seen as a predominantly 'parasympathetic response' and ejaculation as a 'sympathetic' one. Unpleasant psychological states such as anxiety, anger, etc. may be associated with an increase in sympathetic tone which may disrupt sexual performance, causing either a failure of erection or premature ejaculation, or both. Treatment aims to suppress the sympathetic dominance by increasing parasympathetic activity (employing deep muscular relaxation). This is the principle of reciprocal inhibition. The phenomena originally recognized by Sherrington (1947) was later modified by Wolpe (1958) into a treatment for certain kinds of neuroses.

Initial instruction in progressive relaxation is best given in the clinic.

To ensure optimum conditions, instruction is given with the patient either lying on a couch or sitting in an easy chair, according to his preference. The subject is instructed to close his eyes, and to concentrate on his toes. It is suggested that they are becoming heavy, loose and relaxed. This and similar suggestions are monotonously intoned until it is thought that muscular relaxation is proceeding. Suggestions are made in turn for other parts of the patient's body. (For therapeutic purposes the body may be arbitrarily divided into toes, calves, thighs, fingers, arms, shoulders, eyes, neck, head and chest). This procedure should be continued until complete muscular relaxation is obtained, as determined by slow steady pulse and slow regular respiration, and by the patient indicating that subjectively he feels calm and tranquil.

Initial training sessions should last about 30 minutes: in addition the patient may with benefit practise on his bed at home for 30 minutes a day until he becomes proficient at induci ʒ physical and mental relaxation. The next step is for him to contin ɔ to practise progressive muscular relaxation in bed whilst his partner stimulates him sexually (see optimum sexual stimulation). The patient should be advised to delay attempting sexual intercourse until (1) he is able to sustain a strong erection for several minutes and feels sufficiently relaxed and confident to stand a good chance of succeeding, and (2) his partner is also roused.

PROVISION OF OPTIMUM SEXUAL STIMULATION

Optimum sexual stimulation is that combination of psychological and physical stimuli which allow a male to respond to his sexual capacity. It can only be provided if: (1) the male is in an emotionally receptive state of mind and wishes to respond, and (2) the female sexual partner is willing and able to cooperate fully in providing the type and intensity of stimulation required.

Many males, who emotionally desire it, are unable to engage in certain types of sexual practices or experimentation because of a fear that they might be rebuffed as perverted; they are often concomitantly unable to discuss these matters with their partner. An important part of therapy is to promote frank communication between the sexual partners and to help them to gain insight into each other's sexual attitudes, preferences, inhibitions, etc. Hopefully, this might encourage the couple to experiment sexually and to mutually improve the variety and intensity of their stimulative exchanges.

However, insight—that is—intellectual awareness that one is not sexually depraved and that one's fantasies and unfulfilled sexual desires may, in fact, be enjoyed by numerous other perfectly normal individuals, may make it no easier to throw off restraint and inhibition developed and consolidated over many years.

In its actual implementation, a slow progression, but *always* within the limit of emotional tolerance, is advocated. For example, an inhibited couple should be advised to communicate verbally to each other their stimulative requirements, degree of arousal, satiation, etc. and to experiment in such a fashion as to become a little more unrestrained and adventuresome each time as long as this is compatible with 'emotional comfort'.

An important prerequisite is that they should only engage in new practices, etc. when both are fully roused. In order to reinforce each new unrestrained pattern of sexual stimulation, it is important that a degree of satisfaction results each time. Therefore, if a situation arises when any type of sexual experimentation evokes anxiety, the couple should discontinue it and revert to a familiar and predictably pleasurable activity. The objective is to arrive at the point, by mutually acceptable experimentation and communication, where both partners have discovered the means of producing maximum arousal in the other without anxiety or shame. Although in the first instance, the female is advised to take a greater initiative in sexual activity, it is incumbent upon the male to respond reciprocally once roused; as confidence grows, he is likely to assume the dominant role.

An example of the sort of 'new type of sexual activities suggested' and agreed to by both partners in sequential order of implementation might be: encouragement to linger over precoital sex-play in order to maximize the possibility of full arousal; encouragement of the female to handle the male's penis (as directed by him) sufficiently to induce and maintain a strong erection; encouragement to experiment and adopt different coital positions and techniques; encouragement of the female to provide mouth-genital stimulation, etc. Also the deliberate use of fantasy during coital attempts may prove stimulatory in some cases.

In all these situations, verbal and 'physical' feedback from the male to the female as to his level of arousal, stimulative instructions and especially reciprocal caresses are mandatory. Simultaneously, he should indicate his appreciation for her selfless cooperation by appropriate verbalization; this is a useful moral-booster and reinforcement to continue with her role in therapy. Sometimes changing the hour of love-making from evening or night-time to early morning may be helpful, especially if the male customarily experiences erection on awakening. It is interesting that in an impotent subject these erections may be the strongest he ever has. Similarly, if during the night he awakens with a strong erection, usually from a sexual dream, providing good cooperation is possible from his partner (some people are of course irritable at having their sleep interrupted) she should be awakened for a coital attempt.

Regarding the frequency of 'therapeutic sessions', whenever strong sexual feelings are in evidence and the circumstances allow it, a coital attempt is in order. If however 'emotional desire' remains at a low level or is absent altogether, a not uncommon eventuality, regular weekly sessions of sexual activity should be scheduled. These offer the best chance of rekindling desire which is the necessary precursor to physical arousal.

SEX EDUCATION

If indicated, appropriate sex education should be given to both partners, jointly, who should be encouraged to ask any questions they choose. For example, it may be necessary to provide information on coital techniques, female sex anatomy, physiology and psychology, and to rectify false impressions resulting from misinformation derived during adolescence or later. A frequently encountered problem in this area (particularly in our culture) concerns ideas that certain sexual practices are abnormal or perverted and therefore, taboo. It should be stressed to both that any type of stimulation which is mutually pleasurable and acceptable is perfectly 'normal' and can be indulged without fear or guilt.

PSYCHOTHERAPY

The role of psychotherapy is to create, as far as possible, the conditions in which the practical components of therapy can be carried through. Psychotherapy is thus superficial; emphasis should be on explanation, education and encouragement. Interpretations are kept to a minimum. Transference situations which are unnecessary are not encouraged. If they do develop, unless the patient prevents it, they are best circumvented. In some cases, however, a more analytical approach may be forced on the therapist; this usually hinders or postpones the optimal implementation of the practical part of therapy.

TREATMENT OF PREMATURE EJACULATION

As in the case of impotence, training in deep muscular relaxation, appropriate sexual education and psychotherapy may be necessary. However the most important component of treatment for this condition is Seman's (1956) manoeuvre. This consists of provision by the female partner of extravaginal manual stimulation of the penis, which should be carried out in a relentless, but undemanding manner to the male's directive, when he is fully roused sexually, but non-anxious. This should be interrupted when the male indicates to his partner that orgasm is imminent. When the feeling has faded away stimulation should be recommenced, until once again the sensation premonitory to ejaculation is reached; again it is discontinued until the feeling dissipates. Ejaculation may thus be delayed for a considerable time. Once mastered, this procedure can be transferred to actual coitus; eventually, some measure of ejaculative retardation is possible in most cases.

Recently, arising out of clinical observations that certain mono-amine-oxidase inhibitor and phenothiazine drugs may delay or inhibit ejaculation as a side effect (Sandison *et al.*, 1960; Freyhan, 1961; Haider, 1966), some workers have used these substances specially for this purpose in premature ejaculation. Although the results have often been unpredictable and variable, some impressive successes have been claimed. Thus Santanelli, (1960): 38 out of 40 cases (iproniazid), Bennet (1961): six out of six cases (isocarboxazid) and Mellgren (1967): 29 out of 40 cases (thioridazine).

In some chronic recalcitrant cases and particularly those who show marked somatic anxiety, as an adjunct to the practical regime it may thus be worth while prescribing oral thioridazine (50 to 75 mg) to be taken 30 minutes or so before coitus.

TREATMENT OF VAGINISMUS

This consists of teaching the patient deep muscular relaxation (see p. 170) together with gradual vaginal dilation using glass or plastic dilators of progressively increasing size whilst fully relaxed. If during this a spasm occurs the dilator is retained in the vagina and the patient is encouraged to relax until it passes off, this can often be facilitated by deep abdominal breathing.

At the end of the training sessions the patient is encouraged to examine herself manually and then to pass the dilator, thereby to gain anatomical knowledge and confidence regarding the dimensional adequacy of her vagina. In some very severe cases initial relaxation and dilation may be made easier by the use of intravenous Sodium Amytal (Cooper, 1964) or Brietal (Brady, 1966). Appropriate psychotherapy consisting of (1) education and (2) encouragement to air her sexual fantasies and fears is usually necessary.

Alternatively hierarchical desensitization to visual imagery may be employed (Wolpe, 1958; Lazarus, 1963). However in the author's view this may be technically more difficult and less effective than the method described above.

The role of the male partner in the management of vaginismus may be decisive: he should be instructed to rouse his partner fully, with appropriate fore play and try to ignore any protest of discomfort from her, since with continuous adequate stimulation as sexual tension mounted she would become relatively insensitive to pain, which would tend to dissolve. He should also be advised if a vaginal spasm occurred during penile penetration not to withdraw, but to remain *in situ* until the spasm and associated pain waned, then he should complete insertion in a leisurely but relentless fashion.

In some cases 'unconscious collusion' between the partners may hamper a full therapeutic response. This most often takes the form of a 'gentle, submissive and sympathetic' male partner, over-responsive to his spouse's cues of pain, and not being able to proceed to full penetration fearing he might damage her physically and/or mentally. (Cooper, 1969*b*; Friedman, 1962; Malleson, 1942). This impasse may be overcome by repeating the 'dilator procedure' in his presence and/or encouraging him to pass them himself. Sometimes, however, the male may himself have problems of potency which are unrelated to his wife's condition; these require treatment in their own right.

Vaginismus and frigidity which may coexist in the same individual (successful treatment of one may reveal the other (Cooper, 1969*a*)) are usually aetiologically discrete (Malleson, 1942; Friedman, 1962); vaginismus has much the better prognosis.

Before embarking on a specific treatment program for sexual inadequacy, the therapist and patient should agree mutually on its duration—in most cases this should not exceed 20 fortnightly sessions (see below).

PROGNOSTIC POINTERS IN SEXUAL INADEQUACY

In both impotence and frigidity, even chronic and recalcitrant cases (Cooper, 1970*a*; Lazarus, 1963), the nature of the treatment response in the first few sessions may offer a guide as to the ultimate outcome. Early improvement generally augurs a completely satisfactory outcome, usually within 10 sessions or so. If, however, there has been no change in the condition by this time, thereafter even prolonged therapy over months or years is unlikely to be successful. Indeed, Masters and Johnson (1970) in their controversial, continuous two-week, eight hour a day therapeutic programs for (male and female) sexual inadequacy, have shown that maximum improvement occurs well within this period. They believe that unless change occurs during this time it is unlikely thereafter. Recognition of this fact could perhaps save both patient and physician time and money; it is doubtful whether there is any justification for prolonging treatment beyond one year.

The type of disorder and its developmental characteristics are importantly related to the outcome of treatment: premature ejaculators fall into two main sub-categories: (1) those in whom the response has been the habitual one since adolescence, and (2) those in whom the precipitancy has developed *de novo* from previous competency. Impotence can also be sub-divided into acute onset and insidious onset types: the main feature of the former condition is that it develops suddenly most often in young, normally sexed and responsive but naive and inexperienced subjects, frequently as an acute response to anxiety or other psychophysical stress. On the other hand, insidious onset impotence is often associated with a progressive and relentless decline of sexual interests, activities and performance over months or years; although anxiety may be prominent, it frequently appears to be the consequence of the impotence rather than its cause (Cooper, 1969c). These men often seem unable to respond with an erection adequate for coitus, to a type and intensity of sexual stimuli that formerly had been effective. This decline, which in some cases apparently begins in the late 20's or early 30's is probably due to a combination of biological factors and psychological fatigue. This latter phenomena recognized by Kinsey and his coworkers (1948, 1953) is most likely due to repetition of the same sort of sexual stimulation and activities with the same partner over many years. In these patients, measures to induce a resurgence of a 'flagging sex drive' by innovations like novel techniques, new types of stimulation, etc. are important constituents of any therapy.

The best treatment response may be expected in acute onset impotence and the premature ejaculation, arising *de novo*. In these patients, failure to show improvement within five to ten sessions usually indicates complications, such as a personality disorder, or severe neurotic diathesis in one, other, or both partners. These may have to be modified before practical therapy can be instituted with any expectation of significant success.

Impotentia ejaculandi and insidious onset impotence probably have a similar, but less favourable prognosis than the acute onset disorders. However, some improvement, or even complete restoration of potency can be expected in most patients; even if comparatively short-lived. It is perhaps feasible that the provision of sex clinics, where middle-aged couples could obtain appropriate prophylactic information and/or advice, might postpone or even prevent the disorders of potency which seem prevalent in this group.

In the writer's experience, habitual premature ejaculation, probably determined largely by constitutional factors, generally has an unfavourable outcome.

In frigidity the best treatment response may be expected in females with partial and/or intermittent frigidity especially if of acute onset or related to a specific psychophysiological event, such as pregnancy (Cooper, 1970a). Not surprisingly, complete and/or persistent unresponsiveness, particularly if coitus is actively disliked, has a worse outcome.

Also relevant as a prognostic pointer is the time of onset—'late onset' disorders developing from previous sexual potency or responsiveness are associated with a better outcome than disorders which persist from the first coital attempt—'early onset' disorders. Thus both males and females experienced in premarital (teenage) coitus, and/or other sexual activities such as masturbation, which was emotionally and physically satisfying more often respond better to treatment if at a later date they develop problems of sexual inadequacy. The common denominator in both these situations seems to be the prior habit established either premaritally during the late teens (or in the first few years of marriage) of responding successfully to orgasm during coitus, or other activity. Successful repetition of a pleasurable act produces a behavioural response which is difficult to eradicate completely.

The duration of the disorder influences the treatment response in both male and female sufferers; the longer the inadequacy has persisted, the more difficult change becomes. This seems to be bound up with motivation for therapy which is inversely related to the duration of the dysfunction. Those with prolonged histories of inadequacy tend, over the years, to adapt to it; in many cases it has ceased to be of importance to them. These subjects who prefer to retain the sexual status quo are generally loth to embark on a treatment course perhaps involving sexual communication and experimentation which at best is emotionally neutral, or as is more often the case, distasteful to them. On the other hand inadequacy of short duration is often seen in individuals in whom acceptable substitutes for coitus have not yet evolved. There is likely to be greater optimism in these people who may feel that sex is still important and potentially pleasurable for them.

Although not an absolute barrier to a successful outcome, increasing age, especially in the male, with its concomitant decline in virility augurs a poorer prognosis. The female's decline in responsivity, although tending to commence later, generally parallels the male; unlike the male, however, she may retain or show a remarkable resurgence of libido and orgasmic capacity even after many years of inactivity (Kinsey et al., 1953).

There are many arguments concerning the genesis, nature and even the definition of sex drive in the male. It seems that the total number and consistency of sexual outlets to orgasm and ejaculation within a given time and the capacity to engage in repeated intercourses within a single limited period of sexual activity probably reflect sexual strength. In the female objective appraisal is more difficult; however, the degree of interest in sexual matters and/or activities and the frequency and intensity of spontaneous and/or evoked sexual arousal and desire for sexual outlets, probably reflect the strength of sex drive. In both male and female, strength of sex-drive is remarkably constant, high drive and low drive subjects alike tending to remain so throughout life.

Direction of sex-drive which refers to the nature of the preferred sexual object (viz. heterosexual, autosexual, bestiosexual, etc.) is largely self explanatory and is a less controversial entity. Surprisingly, perhaps, sexual strength *per se* is not the vital prognostic pointer that might be imagined. Providing there is a basic interest in heterosexual activities and therapy is optimum, high drive subjects do no better than low outlet ones.

The direction of sex drive is much more significant; the outcome of treatment is likely to be unfavourable unless the preferred sexual outlet is heterosexual coitus. Thus, homosexuality and, to a less extent, autoeroticism (viz. subjects who prefer and practise self masturbation) are poor prognostic indicators. The occasional exception to this generalization is the subject who has a very powerful bi- or polysexually oriented drive; providing heterosexual coitus represents one of the preferred outlets. Sexual inversion is of course much rarer in females than males.

The personality of the male and/or his female sexual partner may have a decisive influence on the therapeutic response. Patients and/or their female spouses, with a personality disorder do much worse than subjects with integrated personalities. In such cases, the inadequacy may merely be symptomatic of a generalized incapacity to develop and sustain empathic and affectionate relationships with others. Improvement may depend to a large extent upon improving the underlying personality defect. It is generally agreed that disordered personality, especially hostile, hysterical or psychopathic types, are notoriously difficult to modify whatever type of therapy is used, even if prolonged over many years. In fact some authorities believe that severe abnormality may change only as a consequence of maturation and that such people may remain disturbed until middle age or beyond (Craft, 1966). If this is so then the time factor in therapy may be crucial, especially for the potency disordered male; less so for the frigid female; by the time such individuals have become stable and capable of sustaining affectionate relationships with others they may, because of the natural decline, with age, of sexual responsiveness (Kinsey *et al.*, 1948, 1953; Masters and Johnson, 1966) be no longer 'physiologically' able to respond fully to sexual stimuli; even if they wished, this would limit the efficacy of *any* treatment unless the personality abnormality could be modified within an individual's active sexual life.

An evaluation of the current status of the marriage, as well as the feelings of both spouses, may provide helpful prognostic information. There is no doubt that an emotionally satisfactory marriage, based on mutual feelings of affection augurs well for recovery. This, not surprisingly, is due to the fact that both partners are more likely to cooperate maximally in therapy.

Since the degree of motivation for cure must influence the outcome, an attempt to assess this should be made. Generally, patients strongly motivated for change will: (1) have referred themselves, (2) want an improvement in sexual capacity for its own sake and not to placate a frustrated spouse, or to improve interpersonal relationships, or even to become pregnant etc. and (3) attend regularly for treatment. Poor or suspect motivation is suggested if the patient's (1) referral is instigated by others, (2) has other than a primary sexual reason for seeking help and (3) consistently fails to keep treatment appointments.

It is perhaps relevant at this point to comment on what is probably the most exciting and most discussed treatment for sexual inadequacy: that of Masters and Johnson (1970) (respectively, a gynaecologist and a sociologist) who followed up their cases for five years. They claim lasting relief for 50 per cent of males who had been impotent since adolescence and 80 per cent in those who became impotent later; for premature ejaculators they claim a 100 per cent cure rate. In females 80 per cent were recovered. It is worth speculating on possible reasons for their high success rate. Masters' and Johnson's treatment which consists of an intensive 14 day exposure of the patient and his spouse to male and female co-therapists, first one, then the other, then both together, is based on their research findings (Masters and Johnson, 1966); even more important is that therapy is applied under as near optimum conditions as is likely to be attained in a Western culture— thus, both partners, must be prepared to devote two weeks full time to rectifying or modifying inhibitory patterns of behaviour and/or improving stimulative techniques based on frank discussions with each other and the therapists. Another prerequisite is that both should see the problem as mutual and have a sincere desire arising out of affection to improve their marriage. In short, patients are only taken on for therapy if genuinely motivated and are willing and able to work hard to improve their situation. In addition, Masters' and Johnson's method of accepting patients only from bona-fide professional sources coupled with their own careful pre-treatment screening is designed to eliminate those with serious coexisting psychiatric problems.

Masters' and Johnson's treatment results are doubly remarkable since one of their requirements for acceptance was a previous unsuccessful therapeutic venture, of at least six months (in most cases this had been psychotherapy of some sort or other). In accounting for this success their very stringent 'motivational' and 'cooperational' requirements from both sexual partners would seem crucial; in essence they treat a group highly selected with 'tools and in surroundings' maximally conducive to a favourable outcome. Shainess (1968) commenting on their work, succinctly points this out; she reminds us that in psychiatric practice, because of the very nature of the patients (who are often personality disordered, etc.), these 'pre-treatment requirements' can rarely be met; a melancholy fact of which many psychiatrists are only too aware. However, these qualifications not withstanding, a review of the available literature suggests that superficial practically oriented therapy is more often effective and quicker than other measures, especially 'depth psychotherapies' (Cooper, 1970c). It would seem reasonable, therefore, that any patient considered 'treatable' should have superficial therapy for six months or so; failure to respond by this time might be one indication for a different and perhaps mainly psychotherapeutic approach.

In summary, an admittedly oversimplified profile is drawn of the sexually inadequate subject who predictably is a good responder to the sort of superficial, practically oriented therapy described. He/she is likely to have referred him/herself, or it will have been a mutual decision following frank discussion between both partners. He/she will be married and 30 years of age or under. He/she will have developed acute onset impotence, premature ejaculation, vaginismus or frigidity in response to anxiety or other psychophysical stress, such as recent marriage, disappointments, physical illness, pregnancy, etc. He/she will have a positive emotional interest in sex generally and heterosexual activities in particular; his/her potential to respond sexually may be evidenced by his/her continuing to masturbate successfully to orgasm and ejaculation, although the preferred outlet will be heterosexual coitus. He/she will have a good and affectionate relationship with his/her spouse, who is willing to cooperate fully in helping him/her overcome his/her problem. Both will have pleasant personalities and be able to communicate frankly with each other; they will attend treatment sessions together and regularly.

On the other hand, the poor responder is likely to be at least 40 years old with an insidious onset disorder of impotence, absent ejaculation or chronic frigidity. His/her attendance instigated by others, usually the spouse, will be for non-sexual reasons. The marital relationship will be generally hostile and affectionless; one or other, or both will have personality disorders; there will be considerable problems of communication. He/she will be erratic in attendance for therapy.

PROPHYLAXIS

It is generally agreed by the most experienced practitioners that in Western Civilization (psychogenic) sexual inadequacy is most often due to 'inhibition' the consequence of negative conditioning, religious, social etc., throughout early life and adolescence (Gutheil, 1959; Masters and Johnson, 1970; Tuthill, 1955; English and Pearson, 1945; Kinsey *et al.*, 1948, 1953, etc). Walker and Strauss (1948) comprehensively and poetically summarize the position. In concluding I quote at length from their textbook:

'There is a disposition on the part of some married couples to feel that while certain methods of lovemaking are right and proper, others are illegitimate and degrading . . . It is chiefly because the British (and presumably the Americans) pay great respect to convention that their method of lovemaking rarely departs from a certain accepted model. But love has not always been so conventional. In the Khama Sutra, we read of at least seven different ways of kissing; eight varieties of touch, eight playful bites, four methods of stroking the body with the hands and eight sounds that may be emited whilst doing so. For the India of Khama Sutra, sexual congress was looked upon not merely as a conjugal duty or as the necessary preliminary to the obtaining of children, but as an activity from which both partners could derive pleasure and experience amongst the richest with which life could provide them. And in writing his great work on love, the author was in no way pandering to the sensuousness of youth. On the contrary, there is every reason to believe that when he penned it, he was himself living the life of a religious recluse in Benares. In undertaking this work at such a time, he must of necessity have felt that in sexual love there was no element that need be in enmity with or in any way contradict the highest spiritual aspirations of mankind.'

For the future the best insurance against 'sexual inadequacy' is, in a single word, 'education'. There are signs that this is already underway.

REFERENCES

ALLEN, C. (1970) *A Texbook of Psychosexual Disorders*, 2nd ed., London: Oxford University Press.

BENNET, D. (1961) Treatment of ejaculatio praecox with monoamine oxidase inhibitors. *Lancet*, **ii**, 130.

BRADY, J. P. (1966) Brietal relaxation treatment of frigidity. *Behaviour Research and Therapy*, **4**, 71–77.

CUOPER, A. J. (1964) Behaviour therapy in the treatment of bronchial asthma. *Behaviour Research and Therapy*, **1**, 351–356.

COOPER, A. J. (1967) Unpublished M.D. Thesis. University of Bristol.

COOPER, A. J. (1969a) A clinical study of 'coital anxiety'. *Journal of Psychosomatic Research*, **13**, 143–147.

COOPER, A. J. (1969b) An innovation in the 'behavioural' treatment of a case of non-consummation due to vaginismus. *British Journal of Psychiatry*, **115**, 721–722.

COOPER, A. J. (1969c) Factors in male sexual inadequacy: a review. *Journal of Nervous and Mental Disorders*, **149**, 337–259.

COOPER, A. J. (1970a) Frigidity: Treatment and Short-Term Prognosis. *Journal of Psychosomatic Research*, **14**, 133–147.

COOPER, A. J., ISMAIL, A. A. A., SMITH, C. S. & LORAINE, J. A. (1970b) Androgen function in 'psychogenic' and 'constitutional' types of impotence. *British Medical Journal*, **ii**, 17–20.

COOPER, A. J. (1970c) Treatment of male potency disorders: The present status. *Psychosomatics*, **12**, 235–239.

CRAFT, M. (1966) In *Psychopathic Disorders*, Chap. 12, pp. 216–218. Edited by M. Craft, Oxford: Pergamon Press.

ENGLISH, O. S. & PEARSON, G. H. (1945) *Emotional Problems of Living: Avoiding the Neurotic Partner*. New York: Norton.

FREYHAN, F. A. (1961) Loss of ejaculation during Melleril treatment. *American Journal of Psychiatry*, **118**, 171–172.

FRIEDMAN, L. J. (1962) *Virgin Wives*. London: Tavistock.

GUTHEIL, E. H. (1959) Sexual dysfunction in men: In *American Handbook of Psychiatry*, Vol. 1, pp. 708–728. Edited by S. Arieti, New York: Basic Books.

HAIDER, I. (1966) Thioridazine and sexual dysfunctions. *International Journal of Neuropsychiatry*, **2**, 255–257.

JOHNSON, J. (1965a) Sexual impotence and the limbic system. *British Journal of Psychiatry*, **111**, 300–303.

JOHNSON, J. (1965b) Prognosis of disorders of sexual potency in the male. *Journal of Psychosomatic Research*, **9**, 195–200.

KINSEY, A. C., POMEROY, W. B. & MARTIN, C. F. (1948) *Sexual Behaviour in the Human Male*. Philadelphia: Saunders.

KINSEY, A. C., POMEROY, W. B. & MARTIN, C. F. (1953) *Sexual Behaviour in the Human Female*. Philadelphia: Saunders.

KLEEGMAN, S. J. (1959) Frigidity in woman. *Quarterly Review of Surgery, Gynaecology and Obstetrics*, **16**, 243–248.

LAZARUS, A. A. (1963) The treatment of chronic frigidity by systematic desensitization. *Journal of Nervous and Mental Disorders*, **136**, 272–278

MALLESON, J. (1942) Vaginismus: Its management and psychogenesis. *British Medical Journal*, **ii**, 213–216.

MASTERS, W. H. & JOHNSON, V. E. (1966) *Human Sexual Response*. Boston: Little Brown.

MASTERS, W. H. & JOHNSON, V. E. (1970) *Human Sexual Inadequacy*. Boston: Little Brown.

MELLGREN, A. (1967) Treatment of ejaculatio praecox with thioridazine. *Psychotherapy and Psychomsomatics*, **15**, 454–460.

SANDISON, R. A., WHITELAW, E. & CURRIE, J. D. C. (1960) Clinical trials with Melleril in the treatment of schizophrenia. *Journal of Mental Science*, **106**, 732–741.

SANTANELLI, R. (1960) *Le Sindromi Depressive*. Turin:

SEMAN, J. H. (1956) Premature ejaculation: A new approach. *Journal of Urology*, **49**, 533–537.

SHERRINGTON, C. S. (1947) *The Integrative Action of the Nervous System*. Cambridge: Cambridge University Press.

SHAINESS, N. (1968) The therapy of frigidity: In *Current Psychiatric Therapies*, **8**, pp. 70–79. New York: Grure and Stratton.

SIMPSON, L. B. (1950) Impotence. *British Medical Journal*, **i**, 692–697.

STAFFORD-CLARK, D. (1954) The aetiology and treatment of impotence. *Practitioner*, **172**, 397–404.

TANNER, J. M. (1964) *Human Biology: An Introduction to Human Evaluation*, Oxford: Clarendon Press.

TUTHILL, J. F. (1955) Impotence. *Lancet*, **i**, 124–128.

WALKER, K. & STRAUSS, E. B. (1948) *Sexual Disorders in the Male*. Baltimore: Williams and Wilkins.

WOLPE, J. (1958) *Psychotherapy by Reciprocal Inhibition*. Stanford: Stanford University Press.

Chapter IX

AFFECTIVE DISORDERS
G. W. Ashcroft, I. M. Blackburn and R. L. Cundall

INTRODUCTION

The term 'affective disorders' is a controversial one as D. Hill (1968) points out: 'The solution proposed long ago to group all illnesses in which alteration of mood is the major symptom under the general heading of 'affective disorders' whitewashes the problem but in fact solves nothing'. Recent pre-occupation with the classification of this group of illnesses, whilst obviously a proper field for the exercise of psychiatric intellect and providing a testing ground for rising contestants in the academic ranks, has so far failed to provide the basis for a logical and practical approach to diagnosis and treatment. Each psychiatrist faced with a patient with an affective illness will seek a theoretical system relating to aetiology, phenomenology and treatment which carries a maximum of internal consistency and provides him with a reasonable working basis for management of the illness. In this chapter we shall attempt to review information on some of the different aspects of this problem.

MOOD AS A NORMAL PHENOMENON

In considering the affective disorders we shall be looking at those disorders involving the happiness–unhappiness mood continuum. Whilst the term might logically be extended to include other affective states (e.g. anxiety, anger) conventionally these are excluded and dealt with separately or considered only in as far as they complicate the picture of depression or elation.

The range of mood subjective responses along the happiness/unhappiness continuum is described by the use of adjectives varying, for example, from elation on the one hand to despair on the other. Mood is a complex background state of the organism, the subjective feeling state being accompanied by changes in cognition with appropriate colouring of the thought content, in motor behaviour, in autonomic reactivity and in the state of arousal. Description of mood state will hence involve a complex statement of behaviour, feeling, bodily state, thought content and a description of these components will also form the basis of the description of an affective disorder. Moreover, the description will not be complete unless the environmental situation to which the response is geared is specified and the effect of the altered mood state on the subsequent behaviour of the individual and his environment is outlined.

In addition to the changes in mood linked to environmental factors there is evidence in normal individuals of slow shifts in mood lasting hours or days at a time, apparently unrelated to immediate situational factors. Physiological events such as menstruation and the puerperium are often associated with shifts in mood.

Separation anxiety

In young animals separation from the mother is followed by a characteristic pattern of searching behaviour accompanied by apparent distress. Similar behaviour is shown by young children when separated from their mother.

This type of behaviour with stereotyped searching, agitation and obvious unhappiness has been designated as separation anxiety although it seems more appropriate to consider it as the prototype of the depressive rather than the fear response. Situational depressive reactions in the adult often occur in response to situations involving separation or loss.

Bereavement and Grief

In the adult bereavement represents the commonest cause of a 'normal' severe and prolonged depression of mood. Classical studies have been carried out by Lindemann (1944) and by Parkes (1964).

Normal grief has a maximal intensity, lasting six to ten weeks and resolving by the end of a six month period. Marris (1958), however, in a study of 72 widows found that only 14 had fully recovered from bereavement after 2 years.

Whilst the manifestations of the grief reaction vary greatly in severity, and in the pattern shown in a given individual, a general picture can be outlined.

Ruminations about the deceased. These are particularly prominent in the first month after bereavement when they often occupy the whole of waking thought.

Disturbances of perception. Whilst the bereaved individual is often reluctant to talk about these in case they are considered as evidence that he is mentally ill, a wide range of perceptual disturbances are common in the early stages of a grief reaction. Illusions, misidentifications, hallucinations and feelings of the 'presence' of the dead person are all common. Characteristically, the bereaved individual entering the empty house will briefly have an image of the dead relative and a strong feeling of the 'presence' of the relative. In some instances, the relative's voice is heard, usually calling out a simple, well-known greeting or the bereaved subject's name. Whilst the visual and auditory imagery is extremely vivid, the subject is aware that it is not real and hence the phenomenon is best classed as a pseudo-hallucination. A variant of the phenomenon is to be found in the frequent occurrence of misidentification when the bereaved subject will catch a glimpse of a face in a crowd or of a retreating figure and for that moment will be convinced that he has seen the dead relative.

Whilst these manifestations of grief might be alarming and disturbing, in fact, some bereaved subjects report that they find some comfort in the continuing 'presence' and may seek to prolong the experience by seeking help from spiritualist sects.

Depression and agitation. The mood of the bereaved individual characteristically shows the two components of depression and agitation. Whilst the depression in the early stages is unremitting there are in addition waves of accentuated distress and agitation.

Somatic symptoms. The presence of changes in autonomic activity is easily recognized: the pale skin, constipation and indigestion of the grief-stricken subject. Headaches and dyspnoea or choking sensations, 'choked with grief', are also common as is a sensation of physical weakness and exhaustion. Morbidity and mortality have been shown to rise in the close relatives following bereavement so that it seems possible that the somatic changes provoked by bereavement may provoke or accentuate structural change in some systems.

Behavioural Changes

Restlessness. Aimless activity and social withdrawal occur. These changes are usually seen in association with a subjective feeling of tension and agitation. The behaviour is often stereotyped with pacing, hand-wringing, etc., and in some societies formalized grief rituals seem to be based on this type of behaviour, encouraging its free and exaggerated expression.

Searching behaviour, as in separation anxiety in the infant and in other animal species, co-ordinated overactivity in the form of searching behaviour occurs. The bereaved subject will wander about the house in a restless fashion, searching for a trace of the dead person or will find himself returning to the places they had visited together. This may be associated with an inability to accept the death and with the perceptual manifestations described above.

Tendency to cling to possessions of the deceased, such as clothes, pipes, tobacco. The term 'mummification' has been used for this phenomenon. In extreme form it may result in the preservation of areas of the house for years in exactly the state in which they were left by the deceased.

Hostility. Often this is at first generalized and associated with social withdrawal. In many individuals it then changes and is projected against those individuals who have failed in their attempts to save

G

or comfort the deceased, e.g. doctors, clergy. This extrapunitive hostility is often associated with guilt feelings where the circumstances of the death are the subject of constant rumination in which the subject blames himself for failing to prevent actions leading to death or in failing to summon appropriate help early enough. Retardation and suppression of drive and exploration are seen. Whilst these features represent the most characteristic presentations of grief, other patterns are also observed.

A frequent variant is an initial state of *frozen emotion* during which the individual may appear composed and efficient and carry out all the practical tasks of arranging burial and supporting other members of the family. Subjectively, the report is of an absence of feeling—a paralysis of feeling. This state may last for a varying time, then merges into the more characteristic bereavement reaction.

There are, of course, also *cultural variations* in the expression of grief varying from encouragement of the behavioural manifestation in the form of wakes or rituals to the attempted control and suppression of all external behavioural signs. Evidence does not seem to be available on the relative effects of the different cultural systems on the resolution of the grief reaction.

The intensity of the reaction is related to the strength of the emotional bonds between deceased and bereaved.

Grief is maximal amongst young adults and is at its most intense in a parent mourning for a full-grown child. Next comes the grief of a husband or wife for a spouse.

As might be expected, the suddeness of the bereavement is also an important factor in the severity of the reaction. Sudden, accidental death in the young, leaving no period for adjustment prior to bereavement, is particularly likely to provoke a severe reaction.

Atypical (Complicated) Grief Reactions. Grief reactions may be altered from the normal either because they are excessively prolonged or are atypical in form.

Parkes (1965) noted that his patients with complicated grief reactions showed:

> Persistent difficulty in accepting the loss, sometimes denying it altogether.
> Marked ideas of guilt and self-blame.
> Intense hostility.
> Hypochondriacal symptoms—sometimes mimicking the last illness of the deceased.

A considerable space in this chapter has been devoted to the normal phenomena of separation anxiety and grief. Frequently the physician will be called in to see patients who are suffering during an episode of this type and, unless he is aware of the range of normal response, he may too readily make a diagnosis of depressive illness and resort to antidepressant drugs. He should be aware of the type of situations which are likely to precipitate this type of reaction in the adult, e.g. bereavement, separation, broken engagement, moving house, children leaving home, retirement and other life situations involving loss. Vulnerability to such situations will vary considerably and the previous life history may suggest the patterns of predisposition. The personality traits of dependency show a close relationship to a general vulnerability to such reactions.

The management of these depressive reactions is dealt with under the later section on treatment of affective disorders.

CLASSIFICATION OF AFFECTIVE DISORDERS

THE CLINICAL APPROACH

The disease concept. We have already touched on the problems of classification in relation to depression when we discussed the problem of distinguishing 'normal' mood changes from 'pathological' reactions. This distinction is the basis of the *disease concept* of affective illness and of most of the clinical classification systems. These systems assume that the clinicians can decide whether or not a depressive reaction is pathological. The criteria were defined succinctly by Mapother (1926) who pointed out that the essence of an attack of depression (illness) 'is the clinical fact that the emotions for the time have lost enduring relation to current experience and whatever their origin and intensity, they have achieved a sort of autonomy'.

The disease concept has been applied to depression since the dawn of Western Medicine. Taken from a consideration of physical medicine 'a disease' has a defined aetiology and pathology, a characteristic clinical picture and clinical course, and may respond to a specific method of treatment. At best, depressive attacks can never be said to satisfy all these criteria, e.g. aetiology and pathology are as yet a subject of debate. The claims for a 'disease' designation must rest (as often in the past in clinical medicine) on the presence of a characteristic clinical picture and course and the response to physical therapies.

In many situations, whilst we may recognize components of an affective reaction, we do not have definite evidence of a specific disease process. At this level, the term 'depression' may be used in a variety of ways; to describe the single symptom of lowered mood or to describe a recognizable syndrome or group of symptoms without going on to specify recognition of a disease process.

One might set out the process of clinical classification in the following stages:

Stage 1 Definition of symptoms.

Stage 2 Definition of syndromes.

The process by which it is recognized that certain symptoms tend to group together and recur in association with each other.

Stage 3 Definition of aetiological, pathological factors and clinical course.

In addition, information on personality structure, situational precipitants and genetic background are gathered.

An attempt to recognize 'specific disease' entities involves the combination of information from Stages 2 and 3. The nature of 'pathological' versus 'normal' reaction must be defined. The physiological and psychological processes in the normal reaction will need elucidation and the way in which these processes are distorted in a pathological reaction must be specified. The attempt to develop such a clinical approach to the diagnosis and treatment of 'affective' illness is to be found throughout the history of psychiatry.

CLINICAL SYNDROMES OF ENDOGENOUS OR PSYCHOTIC *v* REACTIVE OR NEUROTIC DEPRESSION

Two apparently conflicting views were represented in the debate between 1920 and the late 1950's.

'Separatists' in the Kraepelinian tradition (Kraepelin, 1921) drew a sharp distinction between the two types of depression, whilst gradualists in the Meyerian (Meyer, 1922) tradition upheld a more unitary view.

Mapother (1926) in a lecture to the British Medical Association was the first to challenge the predominant separatist view of the day and would not recognize any clinical distinction between neurotic and psychotic depression. Ross (1926) took the opposite view acknowledging the prognostic and therapeutic importance of the differentiation and listed the differences between the two groups; the psychotic blamed himself whereas the neurotic blamed others, they differed in personality, the psychotic being a hard worker, the neurotic not, and they differed in their reaction to the environment in that the psychoneurotic could improve greatly with re-orientation whereas psychotherapy could achieve little with the manic-depressive.

Gillespie (1926, 1930) entered the debate with a report on a detailed study of 25 cases. He claimed to differentiate three groups: *Group I* (14 cases), distinguished by its responsiveness to external factors, very often mixed with anxiety, showing lack of concentration but not retardation, and causally related to conscious factors. *Group II* (7 cases): a group of autonomous depressions in whom the affective variation was spontaneous and not related to external stimuli. A family history of psychoses was common in this group. *Group III* (4 cases), distinguished chiefly by hypochondriacal preoccupations and an involutional stamp. He concluded that no one sign could serve as diagnostic but that 'reactivity' of mood was an important sign.

Lewis contributed three important papers to the controversy. The first (1934) was a clinical survey of depressive states in a detailed analysis of 61 cases, then came a prognostic study on the same material (1936), and finally a summary of his views in 1938. He failed to substantiate the differential clinical criteria put forward by Ross and Gillespie, and concluded that it was impossible to place the majority of cases in either group and that the term 'reactive depression' and the grouping it denotes should be abandoned. He was particularly impressed by the fact that the more closely and longer a patient was studied, the more difficult it became to make clear-cut, qualitative distinctions. In his prognostic study he concluded 'it proved extraordinarily difficult to classify the patients in order of favourable results, or of direction of attack'.

With the advent of E.C.T. and the antidepressant drugs, attempts were made to examine the responses to treatment of different syndromes, e.g. Sargant and Slater (1946): 'some neurotic types of depression may be aggravated by very few convulsions'. Sands (1947) considered that it was the patients with psychotic depression who gained from E.C.T. Garmany (1958) however, following the traditional classification into reactive, endogenous and involutional depression, concluded, 'The distinction between these three forms of depression and particularly between the reactive and endogenous variations, is an unreal one. Constitutional pre-disposition and the incidence of stress factors appear to be much the same in these groups. The distinction traditionally made appears to be a distinction between those depressions which show more reactivity, are less severe, and infrequently require E.C.T. and those depressions sharing the reverse features. It is believed that this resolves itself into a distinction between mild and severe depression'.

If one is to attempt to summarize the position at the end of this period one might argue that if strict criteria were applied to define two different depressive syndromes then a proportion of depressed patients could be fitted into each group, and that the grouping showed some practical use in that it had predictive value with regard to response to treatment. A large number of depressed patients, however, did not fit readily into either group and the problem of classifying these remained. Interpretation of this situation varied from those who felt that the groups endogenous/psychotic and reactive/neurotic represent *separate* clinical entities to those who considered that they represent the extreme ends of a continuum of depression.

Statistical approach—an examination of the continuum or dimensional model

Advances in statistical techniques and in computer science in the 1950's provided the impetus for further studies of classification. Basically, the techniques have consisted of gathering standardised clinical information in depressed patients by clinical interview or questionnaire, and then of processing this information by one of a number of multivariate statistical techniques, the most popular being factor analysis.

These seek to condense the information by looking for the minimum number of parameters or dimensions which can be used to define the depressed patient and by examining the ways in which the depressed patients differ along these dimensions. Each patient, therefore, contributes to the classification process in as far as he can be given a numerical rating for a given dimension.

Eysenck (1970) in an article on *The Classification of Depressive Illness* puts forward a critical assessment of factor analytic studies in depression. Eysenck sees the problem of the nature and classification of depression as twofold:

1. Is there one kind of depression differing in severity, chronicity, etc. or are there two quite different types of depression: unitary v/s binary hypothesis or quantitative v/s qualitative difference?

2. Are psychiatric diagnoses categorical disease entities or points of intersection on a dimensional model?

Let us briefly consider the studies carried out by Hamilton and White (1959), Roth and the Newcastle group and by Kendell (1968).

Hamilton and White factor-analysed a correlation matrix derived from 17 symptoms on 3 or 5 point scales in 64 consecutive male patients presenting with depression. A first factor was identified as representing retarded depression comprising depressed mood, guilt, retardation, loss of insight, suicide and loss of interest; Factor II with agitated depression; Factor IV with psychopathic depression; while Factor III was mainly related to outcome of treatment. They also claimed that the first factor was a measure of endogenous depression and the distribution of scores on Factor I showed a double 'hump' suggesting that the endogenous depressives were qualitatively different from the reactive depressives.

The Newcastle group, of Roth and his colleagues has produced a series of papers providing evidence for a differentiation between endogenous and neurotic or reactive depression. Kiloh and Garside (1963), in a study on 143 patients, extracted two factors, one general factor indicating the extent to which depressive illness was defined by the sum of the clinical features and a second bipolar factor differentiating between neurotic and endogenous depression. Carney, Roth and Garside (1965) using a principle component factor analysis obtained similar results. Kay *et al.* (1969) in a 5 to 7 year follow-up study suggested the term 'retarded depression' could replace 'endogenous depression'.

Kendell (1968) in the 'Classification of Depressive Illnesses' reported a retrospective study of 1080 patients diagnosed as neurotic, psychotic or involutional depressives on the Maudsley Item Sheet completed by Registrars. He used a series of multivariate analytic techniques to find out whether psychotic and neurotic depressions can be differentiated. The techniques used were a discriminant function analysis, a canonical variate analysis, and a factor analysis. Though neurotic depressives were differentiated from psychotic depressives and involutional depressives, when the scores of individual patients were plotted, Kendell obtained unimodal distributions.

Finally, Kendell applied the criterion analysis technique developed by Eysenck. His conclusions were that high correlations gave evidence that the constitutional basis of psychotic depression is also present in weaker form in neurotic depressives and conversely that the constitutional basis of neurotic depression is also present in some degree in psychotic depressives.

A study of re-admission patients showed that individual diagnostic scores often changed from a positive to a negative score or vice versa, i.e. from psychotic to neurotic or from neurotic to psychotic, suggesting quantitative rather than qualitative differences.

Kendell found that the diagnostic index score was linearly related to important parameters like outcome of treatment and choice of treatment, and concluded that the index score is a more useful item of information than the psychotic/neurotic diagnostic dichotomy.

Eysenck (1970) in his critique of these statistical studies accepts that there are two types of depression. He suggests that these are, however, best defined by their placement on a two-dimensional system using two separate and independent continua, neuroticism and psychoticism.

It seems possible that the limits of the statistical method as applied to the problem of defining types of depression may have been reached and that it may be more useful now to consider other ways of approaching the classification problem. The problem can be compared with the attempts to classify and describe personality, where the description can be made at several different levels, viz. habitual response level, trait level or personality type. These might be compared in depression to symptom, syndrome and type (or disease).

Different Approaches

In some recent studies there has been a return to the syndrome level of description with an examination as to how these syndromes vary and co-vary in groups of depressives.

The most important of these studies is that of **Grinker** *et al.* (1961):

'The Phenomena of the Depressions'. The authors set out to answer three questions empirically:

1. On what basis may one say that a person is depressed?
2. What are the characteristics that seem significantly related to depression or the depressive process?
3. Why did this person become depressed at this particular time? After a pilot study, a 'feelings and concerns' and 'current behaviour' trait lists were established and patients rated by resident psychiatrists, a head nurse and a member of the research team. Factor-analysis revealed five factors describing the feelings and concerns of the patients.

I. A factor describing characteristics of hopelessness, helplessness, failure, sadness, unworthiness, guilt and internal suffering. There is no appeal to the outside world, no conviction that receiving anything from the environment would change how the patients feel. There is a self-concept of 'badness'.

II. A factor describing characteristics of concern over material loss and an inner conviction that this feeling state and the illness would be changed if only the outside world would provide something.

III. A factor describing characteristics of guilt over wrong-doing by the patient and wishes to make restitution.

IV. A factor describing the characteristics of 'free anxiety'.

V. A factor describing characteristics of envy, loneliness, martyred affliction, secondary gain.

Clinical interpretation of these factors suggested the hypothesis that Factor I is the essence of depression and its strength indicates the depth of the affective disturbance. The anxiety Factor IV seemed to be an indicator of activity in the process and perhaps a signal of increasing or decreasing affective arousal, while the three remaining factors indicate varying attempts of defence and resolution of the process.

The control groups seemed to indicate that the diagnosis of the depressive syndrome is contingent not only on the depressed affect but also on the presence of anxiety. In fact, it was found that in the presence of minimum sadness, anxiety is enough to weigh heavily for the diagnosis of depression.

Thus, though at no stage did Grinker *et al.* mention the dichotomy of neurotic-reactive versus psychotic-endogenous depression, their Factor I seems very akin to the traditional endogenous pattern. Other factors more traditionally neurotic, such as Factor II and V, did not differentiate the depressive group from control groups.

Friedman *et al.* (1963) rated 170 psychotic depressed patients on a structured rating scale of symptoms, traits and themes. Factor analysis yielded the striking result of four quite distinct clinical syndrome pictures:

1. The retarded, withdrawn, apathetic depressives.
2. Classic mood or affective depression with guilt, loss of self-esteem,

doubting and psychological internalising tendencies.

3. A primarily 'biological' form of reaction with marked loss of appetite, sleep disturbance, constipation and lesser degrees of agitation, loss of satisfaction and work inhibition.

4. An agitated, clinging, demanding, hypochondriacal type.

Another approach is the use of information other than psychic symptoms, e.g. physiological correlates or an emphasis on a characteristic clinical course, e.g. the absence or presence of mania.

Pollitt (1965), dissatisfied with current classifications, especially their shortcomings in naming 'the single solitary attack in which the patient presents with depression for the first time', suggests that 'we can at least separate reactions showing somatic symptoms based on disturbed physiology from those in which such changes are absent'. The somatic symptoms characteristic of some depressions, but 'not seen collectively in any other illness' are: diurnal mood swing, early morning wakening, loss of weight, constipation, loss of appetite, inability to weep, dry mouth, decreased sex drive, impotence, menstrual changes, diminished pulse rate, lowered blood pressure, lowered body temperature, loss of facial flush, cold extremities. These symptoms usually respond to treatment and disappear with no trace of disturbed physiology. Pollitt calls these symptoms the 'depressive functional shift' and attributes them to the hypothalamus, which has been said to be responsible for homeostasis, the regulation of certain biological rhythms, metabolism and the autonomic nervous system. Pollitt also quotes evidence suggesting that the mediation of emotional expression is a function of the hypothalamus.

He divides depression into two main types:

Type S = physiological or *somatic*.

Type J = does not include physiological changes and is fully understandable and *justifiable* in terms of the patient's predicaments. This diagnosis should be made only after excluding all the features of the depressive functional shift.

This method of classification may sound easier and more straightforward than it really is and probably re-states the classical dichotomy of psychotic versus neurotic depression with more explicit hypothetical constructs about the physiology of psychotic depression.

Many authors, probably starting with Kraepelin's work, seem to use 'manic-depressive illness' as synonymous with 'endogenous' or 'psychotic' depression, i.e. to cover patterns of illness with both manic and depressive phases as well as those with one or more depressive phases only.

Leonhard (1959) classified the endogenous psychoses into bipolar (manic-depressive) and unipolar (recurrent depressive) psychoses. Polarity is thus the decisive factor in differential diagnosis: bipolar psychosis is characterized by the occurrence of both manic and depressive episodes, unipolar psychosis by the occurrence of depressive episodes only. Leonhard demonstrated differences in heredity, personality traits and symptom patterns between these two groups. Other authors have shown an interest in Leonhard's classification, especially on the Continent: Astrup *et al.* (1959), Lundquist (1965).

Perris and his colleagues (1966) made a systematic study of homogeneous groups of bipolar and unipolar depressives and succeeded in presenting very convincing evidence of important differences between them. The recurrent depressives (unipolars) had had at least three episodes of depression with free intervals in between. The minimum requirement for the diagnosis of psychotic depression was 'globability of depressive pattern and impaired reality confrontation severe enough to warrant hospital admission'. The manic-depressives (bipolars) had 'suffered from both manic (or hypomanic) and depressive phases, irrespective of whether they were treated in hospital for both manic and depressive phases, or exclusively for one of them . . . . Short euphoria in direct connection with treatment has not been taken into account'. The differences found were in: genetic factors, childhood environment and precipitating factors, male celibacy rate, personality traits, flicker threshold, sedation threshold, response to therapy, treatment time, relapse rate, mortality rate.

Perris concluded from his evidence that the differences in test results between the bipolar and the unipolar groups could be perhaps accounted for by personality differences. Testing personality after remission he found the bipolars to be more cyclothymic and extraverted ('substable' in the terminology he adopts from Sjöbring (1958)) and the unipolars more introverted, 'psychoasthenic' or 'subvalid' (again in Sjöbring's terminology). Thus, the bipolars (extraverted group) have a lower flicker threshold during remission, relapse more often, respond more quickly to treatment, have a higher mortality rate than the unipolars (introverted group). 'Without additional information, bipolar and unipolar depressive psychoses could be regarded as expressions of the same illness with different colouring due to the pathoplastic influence of personality'. However, he finds the evidence from genetic studies, that the 'heredity is different between the two groups and, besides, specific within each group', a strong argument in favour of two separate disease entities.

Angst (1966) and more recently Winokur *et al.* (1969) have given some support to Perris's thesis. More work should be done on homogeneous groups such as those Perris studied. But in the meantime, it seems most unwise on the basis of present findings to combine unipolar and bipolar depressive psychoses in one group as so many studies seem to have done in the past.

Such work does not join the mainstream of the controversy over reactive versus endogenous, which we have discussed above, but throws light on the importance of detailed studies on a well selected group in such a field as the classification of depression.

SYMPTOMS OF DEPRESSION

The descriptions of depressive illness by the 19th century psychiatrists have never been bettered and form the basis of subsequent text book descriptions. Students should read these accounts for themselves, e.g. Kraepelin, 1921. We shall start this chapter with two brief descriptive outlines, the first by Clouston (1904) followed by Beck (1967).

Clouston (1904) listed the symptoms as follows:

Early psychic symptoms: 'loss of sense of wellbeing, of conscious enjoyment of everything, of volitional power, of spontaneity; paralysis of feeling'. Later psychic symptoms: 'delusions, loss of self control, intense mental pain, emotional depression, physical neuralgia, restlessness, excitement, suicidal or homicidal feelings and acts'.

Bodily symptoms: headaches, neuralgias, sleeplessness, falling off in flesh and colour, costiveness, indigestion, paralysis of appetite, facial and eye expressions, attitudes, gestures and postures, skin dry, sinking and pain in epigastrium'.

Beck (1967) from a survey of the literature conveniently categorised the symptoms of depression:

1. A specific alteration in mood–sadness, loneliness, apathy.

2. A negative self-concept associated with self-reproaches and self-blame.

3. Regressive and self-punitive wishes, desire to escape.

4. Changes in activity level, retardation or agitation.

5. Vegetative changes—anorexia, insomnia, loss of libido.

We can now take each of Beck's symptom categories in turn and examine them in more detail. Whilst such a descriptive categorisation is useful it should be realized that symptoms must often be considered in more than one category.

Mood

Characteristically the mood in depressive illness is unhappy or sad. Most patients describe this feeling state and show behavioural change in the form of facial expression, posture, consistent with the professed mood.

An important feature of the mood state is the degree of *reactivity* shown. Thus a mildly depressed patient may retain the capacity to show an improvement in mood state in congenial company or when pressures of work or domestic worries are temporarily lifted. In more severe states of depression this reactivity is lost. The patient may describe a *'loss'* or *'paralysis' of feeling* often experienced particularly in relation to those she normally loves e.g. 'I can feel no love for my husband nor my children.' Severe guilt feelings may be experienced as a result of this failure to feel for or with others. This symptom is often reported in puerperal depressive illness where it may be associated with a state of *perplexity*, the environment seeming strange and the inappropriateness of the lack of affective response bewildering both patient and observers.

Another characteristic of the mood response which is seen in some patients is a *diurnal variation* in mood state. In depressive illness of moderate severity the distress is often greatest in the mornings and is associated with a *sleep disturbance*. Patients wake in the early hours of the morning and for a period of minutes may feel reasonably well then, as one patient put it, 'the depression descends like a black cloud'. The mood may start to improve as the day goes on and there may be a period of relative relief towards evening.

Thought content is in general consistent with mood—and is occupied by morbid thoughts. The future is a void that holds no interest nor involvement for the patient.

In the presence of these characteristic mood changes, depressive illness is easily recognized but less commonly the mood state shows variations which may confuse the diagnosis. Most of these variations are concerned with the presence of discrepancies between observed and reported feeling state or with other components of the mood responses.

'Smiling depression' is a term used to describe patients who present at interview with a denial of depressed mood and maintain a smiling exterior. The smile however lacks warmth and spontaneity. Referral for medical advice is usually at the instigation of a close relative who has noticed a change in the patient's behaviour, e.g. falling off in efficiency at work, slowing down in thought and movement, withdrawal from social contact.

Depressive illness without subjective mood change. This apparent contradiction in terms describes the situation in which a patient presents with a gross change in activity level in the form of retardation of both motor movements and thought processes but denies any change in feeling state. A history of previous depressive attacks may provide a clue to diagnosis and this will be confirmed by a response to antidepressant treatment.

Depression in patients of hysterical personality. Patients are encountered who complain of a severe depression in mood, often presenting this in dramatic fashion but who on close observation appear to retain their reactivity of mood, show a normal motility and exhibit none of the other signs or symptoms of depressive illness. These patients show personality characteristics of the hysteroid type and experience characteristic difficulties in communicating the direction and extent of their emotions to others. The overall clinical picture must be used to assess the absence or presence of a depressive illness. In general the response to tricyclic antidepressants or E.C.T. is poor in this group and management is of a general supportive type with occasional use of monoamine oxidase inhibitors.

Other affective changes associated with depression

Anxiety. The relationship between *anxiety* and depression is often difficult to disentangle. Thus patients who present initially with an anxiety state commonly develop symptoms of depression as the condition progresses. On the other hand patients with a primary depressive illness often present with episodes of anxiety amounting to panic. The distinction between these states of primary and secondary anxiety is not purely academic for whilst anxiety symptoms complicating a depressive illness may respond to antidepressant drug therapy a primary anxiety state will not. The distinction is a clinical one based on the overall picture, the premorbid personality, the presence of situational factors precipitating anxiety, the apparently endogenous nature of the anxiety in some patients, all these features being given weight in arriving at the diagnosis. The predominance of anxiety in the clinical picture of some affective syndromes has led several authors, Roth (1959), Kessell (1968) to define a separate affective syndrome with a specific response to therapy (See Phobic-anxiety-depersonalization syndrome, page 209).

When *depersonalization* is seen in depressed patients it is associated with a high level of anxiety and probably represents a mechanism for terminating an unbearable state of anxiety. Such depersonalization should not be confused with the nihilistic or bodily delusions encountered in depression for whilst both these phenomena represent a change in body image their psychopathological basis is different.

Agitation

This symptom, common in depressive illness, is easy to confuse with anxiety and its definition presents problems. It is largely independent of environmental precipitants and the main component is one of excitement or restlessness which has both motor and psychic components. Mentally there is a turmoil of thoughts, a continuous presence of distressing preoccupations. Thoughts circle on certain topics, 'I am lost', 'What is to become of me', 'I shall never rest again'. The responses are stereotyped and original or exploratory thinking is inhibited so that whilst there is often a pressure of thought, thinking is non-progressive. This process is both distressing and exhausting for the patient. The motor component shows a comparable shift towards stereotypy with a pressure to restless activity similar to that seen in the psychic sphere. The patient paces restlessly, wrings her hands, picks at her skin, screws up her handkerchief or the bed clothes. There is no peace, mental or physical.

Response to drugs is to the phenothiazines rather than to the minor tranquillizers, a further distinction from anxiety. (Thus the agitation seen in depressive illness seems to be a state of excitement with much in common with the excited states of delusional mania or with the drug induced state of delirium).

Negative self-concept

The patient with a mild degree of depression notices a falling off in self-confidence and assertiveness which is most noticeable in social situations where the patient compares himself unfavourably with others. He tends to avoid company and in particular situations which involve conflict or confrontation. At interview he avoids direct eye contact and in general presents an *unfavourable self-image*.

In more severe depression the image of self becomes progressively more disturbed with the patient seeing himself as 'the lowest of the low, to be despised by everyone'. This negative attitude may also make him mistakenly assess his relations to others 'I have let my family down, they would be better off without me'. Thus *guilt feelings* become a part of the clinical picture and in the severely depressed patient these may assume *delusional* intensity 'I have brought disaster to my family, we are financially ruined. The police are coming to take me, I deserve to pay for my errors, I deserve to die'.

Delusions occurring in depressive illness have been grouped as delusions of guilt or sin, disease and poverty. Thus in addition to the delusions described above the patient may believe himself to be incurably ill or to be penniless when he is in possession of both health and wealth. Paradoxically in extreme cases the delusions may be seen to include a grandiose component e.g. the patient sees himself as the wickedest man alive, responsible for all the sins of the world or as the very devil himself.

Hallucinations. Other psychotic symptoms are also encountered in severe depressive illness e.g. hallucinations and ideas of reference. Hallucinations when present usually take the form of accusatory voices. Visual hallucinations are uncommon but in severe depression may consist of scenes of violence or death e.g. a patient reported seeing a coffin waiting for her body.

Somatic delusions (see discussion, pages 200–201.) In typical cases of depressive illness the content of the delusions and hallucinations is understandable if one accepts the basic assumptions that the patient has done wrong, is evil, dirty or an unsavoury character. However, other patients present with paranoid states in which the affective component is less typically depressive.

Paranoid ideation in depressive illness appears as an alternative to ideas of self-depreciation and guilt. In mild cases this may take the form of increasing irritability with a tendency to blame others for the alleged misfortune. In severe cases delusions of paranoid type may be present e.g. the patient may allege his house is bugged and that the police and his neighbours are seeking evidence against him. Such symptoms are particularly frequent in the middle aged and elderly. Response to anti-depressant therapy suggests that such illnesses have a closer affinity with the affective rather than the schizophrenic disorders.

Other psychic symptoms in depressive illness

Florid *hysterical symptoms* may be precipitated by the development of a depressive illness e.g. fugue states, hysterical paralysis and, particularly in the middle aged and elderly, depressive illness should be considered whenever such symptoms appear.

Obsessional symptoms also may appear during a depressive illness and may add to the distress of the patient. A common example is the develop-ment of an obsessional fear of harming others often referred to the patient's own children.

Regressive and self-punitive wishes

The depressive position is a dependent one and as such the depressed patient may appear inadequate, dependent, indecisive. There is a danger that the physician will judge pre-morbid personality on the basis of behaviour during the illness. Both physician and patient's family may find the demands for support and reassurance wearing and at times irritating and these attitudes even if transient may react on the patient to intensify his feelings of inadequacy.

The depressed patient tends to withdraw from contact with others and to show *regressive trends* in behaviour. The withdrawal may lead to the patient retiring to his bed, rejecting attempts to approach him, becoming irritable when disturbed. This withdrawal combined with the retardation which is a feature of depression may in the severe case lead to the development of depressive stupor.

The desire to escape from his intolerable suffering together with his feelings of guilt and worthlessness may lead the patient to conclude that his only remaining course of action is to take his own life.

Suicide. Suicidal wishes are thus a common symptom of depression and enquiry regarding these should form part of the examination of any patient. Questions such as 'Have you ever felt that life may not be worth living?' are usually sufficient to elicit the appropriate response. The patient may be relieved to share his suicidal preoccupation with someone, whilst on other occasions the manner in which a negative answer is given, e.g. 'I may have thought this occasionally but, of course, could never kill myself' may convey to the examiner the fact that the patient has such thoughts although he is afraid to reveal them openly. The assessment of the seriousness of the wish of suicide represents a complex clinical judgement requiring considerable experience and rules or guidelines are difficult to put down. From time to time all of us are shocked by our failure to predict a suicidal attempt. Certain general facts have been established: thus suicidal thoughts and risk of suicide are most prevalent in the early hours. Men are more likely to conceal their suicidal thoughts than women and are more likely to succeed than women. Social isolation, widowhood, lack of support from family or social group, co-existing alcohol abuse are all bad prognostic signs. (Sainsbury, 1968).

Motor activity in depression

The motor features of agitation have already been described and retardation has been mentioned.

Retardation implies the inhibition of constructive activity both motor and mental. It shows in the appearance of the patient when he enters the room as a lack of spontaneity in movement, a lack of emotional expression of the face and the severly retarded patient may be mistakenly suspected of suffering from Parkinsonism. Retardation also affects the thought processes, originality fails and the initiation of a simple act requires intense concentration.

Severe retarded states may progress to depressive stupor, motor movement being slowed to the state of immobility and muteness. The patient is still aware of his surroundings and, as mentioned above, whilst constructive thought is inhibited he may be flooded by stereotyped depressing thoughts.

It should be pointed out that retardation and agitation are not mutually exclusive phenomena but that both may be present in a single patient.

Physical symptoms and depression

Complaints of physical symptoms are common in depression. For the most part these can be seen as secondary to the autonomic disturbances of the depressive syndrome or to the associated anxiety. Examples include dry mouth, constipation, headache, muscle pains.

However other somatic symptoms are encountered in depressive illness which are more specifically related to the syndrome e.g. acute facial pain may occur in depressed patient and may be the main presenting feature and may not be recognized as a depressive variant for some time.

Hypochondriasis and depression. Kreitman (1965) and his colleagues studied a group of hypochondriacal patients in general hospital and concluded that a high proportion of these could be considered to be suffering from a depressive illness.

Somatic delusions. In severe depression somatic delusions are encountered e.g. bizarre hypochondriacal delusions, where the patient may state that his bowels are blocked or eaten away and nihilistic delusions where he denies his own presence or alleges the absence of his brain.

The account given above of the symptoms of depression is based on the classical accounts of the last century which have stood the test of repeated critical re-examination by generations of clinicians. Several attempts have been made recently to examine the relevance of these accounts to present practice. Beck examined the presence of selected symptoms in a group of hospitalized patients without psychiatric illness, and groups with mild, moderate and severe depression. The results of this study are shown in the following tables.

Table 9.1

EMOTIONAL MANIFESTATIONS: FREQUENCY AMONG DEPRESSED AND NONDEPRESSED PATIENTS

	Depth of depression			
	None (%) (n = 224)	Mild (%) (n = 288)	Moderate (%) (n = 377)	Severe (%) (n = 86)
Dejected mood	23	50	75	88
Self-dislike	37	64	81	86
Loss of gratification	35	65	86	92
Loss of attachments	16	37	60	64
Crying spells	29	44	63	83
Loss of mirth response	8	29	41	52

n = No. of patients

Table 9.2
COGNITIVE AND MOTIVATIONAL MANIFESTATIONS: FREQUENCY AMONG
DEPRESSED AND NONDEPRESSED PATIENTS

| | *Depth of depression* | | | |
| | None (%) (n = 224) | Mild (%) (n = 288) | Moderate (%) (n = 377) | Severe (%) (n = 86) |
Manifestation				
Low self-evaluation	38	60	78	81
Negative expectation	22	55	72	87
Self-blame and self-criticism	43	67	80	80
Indecisiveness	23	48	67	76
Distorted self-image	12	33	50	66
Loss of motivation	33	65	83	86
Suicidal wishes	12	31	53	74

n = No. of patients.

Table 9.3
VEGETATIVE AND PHYSICAL MANIFESTATIONS: INCIDENCE AMONG
DEPRESSED AND NONDEPRESSED PATIENTS

| | *Degree of depression* | | | |
| | None (%) (n = 224) | Mild (%) (n = 288) | Moderate (%) (n = 377) | Severe (%) (n = 86) |
Manifestation				
Loss of appetite	21	40	54	72
Sleep disturbance	40	60	76	87
Loss of libido	27	38	58	61
Fatigability	40	62	80	78

n = No. of patients.
From Beck (1967).

SYMPTOMS OF MANIA

Again the classical accounts of manic illness are to be found in the writings of 19th century psychiatrists e.g. Kraepelin (1921). Until recently the study of the phenomenology of mania had received little systematic attention but Winokur *et al.* (1969) have now published a detailed study of the presenting symptoms and it is on this account that this section will be based.

In general terms the illness ranges from mild hypomanic reactions to states of uncontrolled manic excitement. For descriptive purposes Kraepelin (1921) divided the illness into four subtypes (a) hypomania (b) mania (c) delusional mania (d) delirious mania, the terms being largely self explanatory. We should like to suggest the following arbitrary staging of the illness according to severity which may facilitate description.

Stage 1

Patient experiences a feeling of well-being, an increase in energy. He relishes a challenge and takes on new problems. Judgement is retained and as yet distractibility does not seriously interfere with completion of the task in hand.

Stage 2

Overactivity is accentuated and increased assertiveness and combativeness lead to conflict with others in the environment. He becomes aggressive or irritable when challenged, judgement is suspect and distractibility interferes with task completion. Others at home and at work tend to suffer.

Stage 3

Patient's manner is intolerable and overbearing. He is obviously sick. Judgement is seriously impaired, behavioural restraints are absent and he may run into serious conflicts with family, workmates or with the police.

Stage 4

Normal activities are now impossible. The patient is distractible, overactive and thought disordered.

Stage 5

Psychotic symptoms now dominate the clinical picture.

Winokur and his colleagues (1969) list the early signs and symptoms of mania observed prior to hospitalization: an extravagant and grandiose self image, insomnia, overtalkativeness and physical overactivity.

Admission to hospital is often against the will of the patient who shows little insight into his condition, admission being precipitated by the fact that those in his immediate environment cannot tolerate his behaviour any longer. The manic patient on arrival at the hospital is recognisable by the contrast between his apparent buoyant good health and the exhausted, anxious appearance of his accompanying relatives.

SYMPTOMS AND SIGNS OBSERVED IN HOSPITAL (based on Winokur, 1969)

The percentage of manic patients in Winokur's series showing each symptom is shown in brackets.

Mood change

(a) Elevated mood varying from cheerfulness to exaltation (98 per cent)
(b) Hostility (83 per cent)
(c) Irritability and distractibility (85 per cent)
(d) Transient depression (68 per cent). This lability of mood was seen more frequently in females than in males.

Thus there may be fleeting episodes of morbid preoccupation accompanied by weeping and all the signs of a transient depressive reaction.
(e) Diurnal variation of mood (67 per cent). Whilst the pattern varied between patients, some being worse in the morning others in the evening, it was constant for a given individual.

Motor activity

(f) Overactivity—this symptom was present in almost every case varying from a mild accentuation of the normal pattern of activity to a constant, wild overactivity leading to exhaustion and threatening life.
(g) Posturing and stereotyped movements (7 per cent).

Thought processes

(h) Pressure of talk (99 per cent). This symptom can be seen as a psychic equivalent to the motor symptom of overactivity.
(i) Flight of ideas (93 per cent). When present in mild degree, this is evident as a frequent switching of subject by a process of logical association which can be readily followed by the observer. Punning and rhyming may be present. In severe cases it may be extremely difficult to follow the associations which determine the frequent changes in direction of thought and in such cases the thought disturbance may be difficult to distinguish from shizophrenic disorder. Both these symptoms have their parallel in the written word, the written output of the manic patient often being voluminous and showing typical flight of ideas.

Psychotic symptoms

(j) Ideas of reference and passivity feelings (27 per cent).
(k) Delusions (48 per cent). In many patients these could be understood as stemming from the grandiose self-image. Many have a religious content, e.g. the patient believes himself a prophet or even Christ. Delusions are often of a changing, evanescent nature.
(l) Hallucinations—auditory (21 per cent), visual (9 per cent). Again, they are usually grandiose and consistent with the disturbed mood, e.g. the patient receives messages from God or has visions of God or the Devil.

As in depression, the point is made that when delusions and hallucinations occur they are consistent with a diagnosis of affective illness, when they can be understood on the basis of a primary disorder of *mood*. We must, however, consider whether the insistence on an elevation of mood is essential to the diagnosis of mania. Cases of mania undoubtedly occur during which the patient is certainly not happy. He is highly 'aroused' but the predominant mood is anger or anxiety and in such cases, paranoid delusions may predominate making the diagnosis difficult.

Behavioural disinhibition

(m) Increased sexuality (68 per cent). This was usually observed as an increased sexual content of the conversation or in socially accepted outlets such as increased sexual demands within marriage. The increased libido was expressed in a socially unacceptable fashion as hetero or homosexual promiscuity in only 11 per cent of cases.

(n) Increased alcohol intake. (o) Insight was impaired in 63 per cent although in half of these there was considerable variability with insight present for at least part of the time.

REGRESSION OF SYMPTOMS OF MANIA DURING TREATMENT IN HOSPITAL

Winokur and his colleagues (1969) report that the symptoms of a severe attack of mania disappear in a predictable sequence:

(a) Delusions and hallucinations when present disappear first within 7 and 10 days of admission.

(b) Decrease in the manic thought disturbance then follows in the following order (i) flight of ideas; (ii) pressure of talk; (iii) distractibility.

(c) Irritability was the last symptom to disappear.

Relationship of depressive and manic episodes

In Winokur's study (1969) approximately half of the reported manic episodes were preceded by a depressive episode of longer than one month's duration.

Mixed manic depressive episodes

Patients may occasionally show a mixture of manic and depressive features. As a rule, such episodes resemble mania as regards hyperactivity and pressure of speech. Thought content tends to be predominantly depressive and there may be present an assortment of bizarre, morbid delusions. The bizarre nature of such reactions frequently leads to an erroneous diagnosis of schizophrenia.

DEPRESSIVE SYNDROMES

The grouping together of symptoms into different syndromes has already been discussed at some length in the section on classification and endogenous (psychotic) *v* reactive (neurotic) and unipolar *v* bipolar subdivisions will receive no further attention at this stage. Classifications which depend on certain outstanding features, e.g. retardation, agitation, have also been discussed and will receive further attention in the treatment section in as far as they indicate selective response to certain therapies.

We are still left with certain syndromes which although they embrace only a relatively small number of depressed patients are important either because there is evidence that they respond to specific therapies or because they show features which are of theroretical interest in the consideration of affective illness in general.

AGITATED DEPRESSION

Whilst most patients with severe agitated depression respond to the conventional antidepressant therapies there is also evidence that many patients respond better to the combination of antidepressants and phenothiazines (i.e. thioridazine).

PUERPERAL PSYCHOSIS

There is no very good reason for regarding a *puerperal psychosis* as being distinct from a psychosis occurring outside the puerperium. However, it is customary to regard a psychosis as puerperal if it occurs during the first year post-partum, though some would limit this to three or six months.

The *incidence* of puerperal psychosis is usually taken as 2 to 3 per 1000 pregnancies. Engelhard (1912), restricting the puerperal period to the first three months after delivery, found an incidence of 1.4 per 1000 pregnancies. Tod (1964) found post-partum depression in 2.9 per cent of pregnancies. Jansson (1964) included both psychosis and neurosis in his figure of 6.8 per 1000. Nilsson and Almgren (1970) found that 19 per cent of the 165 women in their study had significant psychiatric symptoms during the first six months post-partum.

The *aetiological relationship of childbirth* to puerperal psychosis is still obscure in spite of attempts to invoke organic (endocrine or biochemical changes) and psychological causes (attitudes to childbirth, stress of delivery, etc.). It does seem that primiparae (especially those over 30 years of age) and the unmarried are more prone, as are those with unwanted pregnancies and with pre-morbid personality disorders (particularly with respect to neurotic reactions). The pregnancies tend to be shorter and stormier, but there is no clear relationship to obstetric complications. The similarity to 'post-operative psychosis' has been noted by Stengel *et al.* (1958).

Many of the *clinical features* of puerperal psychosis are characteristic, though there is some overlap between the affective and schizophrenic types. The onset, typically on the third or fourth day after delivery, is heralded by clouding of consciousness with perplexity, delusions and hallucinations. Sleep disturbance is an early symptom, often with vivid nightmares. The patient may become agitated, incoherent and confused; stupor may follow, alternating with lucid intervals. As clouding lessens, more clearly depressive or schizophrenic features emerge. The depression, if present, is severe with paranoid, hypo-chondriacal, and nihilistic ideas. The presence of auditory hallucina-tions, thought disorder and volitional disturbance at this stage is of more ominous portent. If a neurotic picture emerges, it may take the form of an anxiety, phobic, or depressive state.

The *treatment* of choice in puerperal psychosis is E.C.T. with the addition of phenothiazines where indicated; and, almost invariably, the patient requires admission to hospital. In neurosis, tranquillisers and antidepressants are of value. In all cases, the patient and her family will require supportive psychotherapy.

Two classical studies will be described. The first is that of Protheroe (1969) who made a *retrospective study* of patients admitted to St. Nicholas Hospital with puerperal psychosis. A case-note analysis of 134 cases and follow-up of 114 cases revealed the following diagnostic categories: affective (68 per cent of patients), schizophrenic (27 per cent) and 'organic' (4.5 per cent). The outcome was good for 86 per cent of the affectives but poor for two-thirds of the schizophrenics. A previous non-puerperal psychosis was reported in 11 affectives (none in schizo-phrenics), and 49 patients had a further psychotic illness (9 puerperal, 35 non-puerperal, and 5 both). Protheroe also carried out a genetic study of 98 patients and found that morbidity risks were similar to the figures obtained for non-puerperal psychosis; from which it could be concluded that there is no specific genetic pre-disposition to puerperal psychosis.

Nilsson and Almgren (1970) made a *prospective study* of 165 women attending a pre-natal clinic in Lund. Psychiatric interviews were carried out in early pregnancy, on the second and third day post-partum, and six months post-partum; together with the application of various tests and questionnaires (650 variables were measured). They discovered 'pronounced psychiatric symptoms' before (in 14.5 per cent of women), during (17 per cent) and after pregnancy (19 per cent). Although specific diagnoses were not reported, this study is of particular interest because of the assessment of 'neurotic' features.

The psychiatrist is often faced with the problem of *counselling*. It can be stated with some confidence that the immediate prognosis in puerperal psychosis is good, except for a minority of cases in which chronic schizo-phrenia develops. The chance of a further puerperal psychosis is about 1 in 5. The chance of developing a puerperal psychosis for a woman who had previously had a non-puerperal psychosis is about 1 in 10.

INVOLUTIONAL MELANCHOLIA

A controversy exists as to whether 'involutional melancholia' can be regarded as a distinct disease entity with its own natural history, symptomatology and prognosis or whether it should be regarded simply as a variety of psychotic depression, the term 'involutional' being a temporal description.

The classical picture conveyed by those using the term is this: a major depressive illness occurring for the first time in the involutional age: 40 to 55 for women, 50 to 65 for men. It is more common in women than in men and the most prominent features are: motor agitation and restlessness, anxiety and apprehension, hypochondriasis sometimes with bizarre somatic delusions, occasional paranoid ideas, nihilistic delusions and feelings of unreality. The pre-morbid personality is often described as rigid, overconscientious and restricted. The untreated course of the illness is felt to be long, but response to E.C.T. is excellent.

Aetiological factors have been felt to be mostly endocrinological and psychological, heredity being perhaps less important than in manic-depressive illness (Hopkinson, 1964).

Lewis (1934) in his review of melancholia pointed out that symptoms of agitation and hypochondriasis were found in the younger age groups as well as in involutional patients.

Tait, et al. (1957) have provided a good review of the concept of involutional melancholia and present a clinical study of 54 women aged 40 to 55 who were first admissions to a mental hospital. Twenty-nine of these were considered to suffer from endogenous depressive psychotic illness, 20 from neurotic illness, a further 5 from late schizophrenia. The last were excluded and comparisons made between the psychotically depressed group and the miscellaneous non-psychotic group. The symptoms that differentiated the two groups significantly were limited to the constellation of pure depression and secondary psychotic manifestations. The authors conclude: 'We found that the 29 depressives among our 54 patients showed effectively only the primary signs of a psychotic depression and rarely any of the stigmata which are or were ordinarily regarded as peculiarly typical of involutional melancholia'. They suggest, in their discussion, that the availability of effective treatment may be stopping the traditional involutional symptomatology from appearing.

Rosenthal (1968), in perhaps the latest review of the syndrome, commenting on the rarity of typical involutional melancholia in current hospital patients, makes the same point as Tait et al. He also suggests that the fact that patients come earlier for treatment now than previously, stops them from developing the florid symptoms of the old text books. Another point is dilution: with the greater number of younger and neurotic patients treated in hospital, the proportion of psychotic involutional melancholics has dwindled markedly. He says: 'involutional melancholia as classically described may perhaps represent a moulding of secondary symptoms such as severe agitation, marked hypochondriasis and paranoia onto the basic autonomous depressive picture. The particular form of these secondary symptoms may be related to ageing or may be influenced by pre-morbid character or by chronicity. In any case the full differentiation of symptoms is discouraged in modern hospitals with the early use of effective therapy'.

Post (1962), in a consecutive series of 100 patients over the age of 60 with affective syndromes, did not find the 'pre-involutional psychosis personality' nor typical involutional symptoms to be more common in patients whose first illness developed after the age of 60. Kay, Roth and Hopkins (1955) compared 175 admissions over the age of 60 who had had previous depressive illnesses with 89 first admissions, and found no significant differences in symptoms or outcome between the two groups.

Other evidence militating against the concept of involutional melancholia as a distinct disease entity has come from genetic studies (see p. 214).

(see p. 214)

PHOBIC-ANXIETY DEPERSONALIZATION SYNDROME

This syndrome, which shows features of both anxiety and depression was described by Roth (1959).

The majority of the sufferers are female and in the age group 20 to 40. There is a history of diffuse anxiety progressing to a crippling restriction of activities. This may begin with an inability to enter crowded places such as shops, and panic attacks may occur in such situations. Fainting attacks may occur and are followed by an increase in severity of symptoms.

Symptoms of depersonalization and derealization may be associated with the panic attacks. At times these phenomena are accompanied by groups of symptoms reminiscent of temporal lobe epilepsy with distorted perception of time and space, and olfactory hallucinations.

The patient usually reports that she can perform many otherwise impossible journeys if accompanied by a spouse or parent.

Depressive symptoms (e.g. weight loss and anorexia) are constant components of this syndrome.

Treatment by antidepressant drugs is usually effective but E.C.T. may tend to make the condition worse.

RATING SCALES AND MEASUREMENT

The assessment of the present clinical state and subsequent symptomatic changes and improvement is of great importance in the whole of psychiatry and particularly so in the affective illnesses.

Here, only a few of the most widely used techniques for rating depression will be mentioned. Several good reviews of rating scales are already in existence, e.g. Lorr (1954), Aitken and Zealley (1970). Rating scales can be described as either self-rating or observer-rating scales.

SELF-RATING

The best known self-rating scale of depression is probably that of Beck and his colleagues: Beck's Depression Inventory (B.D.I.) (Beck *et al.*, 1961; Beck, 1967).

It consists of 21 categories of symptoms and attitudes. Each category describes a specific manifestation of depression in a graded series of four to five self-evaluative statements. Numerical values of 0 to 3 are given to each statement reflecting neutrality to maximum severity. Sometimes two statements appear at the same level of severity and are then labelled a and b, e.g. 2a, 2b, have the same severity value. The examiner reads the statements in each category while the patient follows from his own answer sheet and he is asked to circle the number of the statement which best describes him at the moment, right now. His score is the total score obtained by summing up the scores of the individual symptom categories. The Inventory has been shown to be reliable, consistent and valid in several studies in America, as well as in France and in Britain. (Beck, *opus cit.*, pp. 189–207) Delay *et al.* (1963), Metcalfe and Goldman (1965).

Other popular self-rating scales are Zung's self-rating depressive scale (Zung, 1965), and Lubin's adjective check-lists (Lubin, 1965), but they have not been widely used in this country.

OBSERVER-RATING

The most widely used observer-rating scale is that of Hamilton (1960, 1967).

It is not a diagnostic scale in that it is to be used only on patients already diagnosed as depressed. Its use is to quantify the results of an interview to facilitate the assessment of such factors as depth of depression and response to treatment.

It consists of 17 variables rated on a 5-point (0-absent, 1-mild, 2 and 3-moderate, 4-severe) or 3-point scale (0-absent, 1-slight or doubtful, 2-clearly present). Symptoms which are difficult to quantify are rated on the 3-point scale, e.g. insomnia, agitation. Also included on the rating scale are four additional variables which are rated separately because, as in the case of depersonalization, paranoid symptoms, obsessional symptoms, they occur very rarely, or as in the case of diurnal variation, it is deemed to characterize type of depression rather than intensity of depression. Hamilton (1960) recommends that two raters should independently score a patient at the same interview, for training purposes and to calculate inter-rater reliability. He quotes a correlation coefficient of 0.90 for two raters' summed ratings of 70 patients.

The obvious difficulty with a rating scale like Hamilton's is that its efficiency depends to such a large extent on the skill of the interviewer, his commitment, interest and bias. The ubiquitous 'halo effect', for example, must be guarded against consciously and constantly, if one is to avoid rating a patient high or low on several variables because he is rated as such on one key variable. Similarly, if the rater is biased towards the belief that certain variables go together and not with others, his ratings may be less than objective.

Hamilton (1967) factor-analysed the ratings of 152 men and 120 women separately and found similar factors in both groups, with minor differences in the order of symptoms as determined by the saturations. The first factor was a general factor of depressive illness, the second factor was a bipolar factor contrasting agitation and anxiety, with retardation and loss of insight. Factors 3 and 4 were less clear-cut, though they seemed to be related to 'instability of personality, and social history'. Hamilton found a correlation of 0.93 between a total score on the 17 variables of the rating scale and a first factor score and is satisfied that 'the scale thus fulfils its purpose of providing a simple way of assessing the severity of a patient's condition quantitatively, and of showing changes in that condition.'

OTHER RATING METHODS

Shapiro (1961) has developed a personal questionnaire technique suitable for measuring changes in individual patients. It is essentially a card-sorting technique tailor-made for each patient and, though easy to perform, takes an extremely long time to construct. It is not, therefore, a suitable technique for large follow-ups or drug trials, but ideal for detailed individual studies.

Recently Aitken and his colleagues (1969, 1970) have suggested that visual analogue scales should be very suitable for the rating of mood change: 'As moods vary in continuous fashion, it seems logical to present the patient with a kind of symbol which will avoid the need for him to rate in categories'. The authors use a 10 cm line with the ends defined as extremes of the mood under consideration and the patient marks with a cross the point which characterises how he feels. Measurement is in terms of cms. Aitken, et al., provide graphs showing the sensitivity and apparent validity of this type of self-rating. When used in a drug trial by Kellner and Sheffield (1968), it showed highly significant differences between diazepam and placebo.

The ease and simplicity of this technique militate in its favour, but its comparative value has not yet been established.

AETIOLOGY OF AFFECTIVE DISORDERS: HEREDITY

It is generally accepted that heredity plays an important part in the aetiology of affective disorders. Affective illness can be traced through several generations of many families and the greater the degree of consanguinity the greater the chance of developing the illness. Most family studies report a morbidity risk (that is the percentage of relatives who would develop an affective illness if they passed through the age of risk, usually 15 to 60 years) for parents, siblings and children of manic depressives of between 10 and 15 per cent. This incidence is well above the usual population figures of 0.6 to 1.6 per cent.

EARLY STUDIES

In 1936 Slater proposed that manic depressive psychosis was transmitted by a single autosomal dominant gene with reduced penetrance. The gene was believed to be autosomal because fathers of affected sons could have the illness and dominant because the illness often occurred in successive generations; it was of incomplete penetrance because not all patients had ill parents, less than 50 per cent of siblings were affected and not all monozygotic twins were concordant.

Probably the most efficient method for calculating the importance of heredity is by comparison of the concordance rates for monozygotic (M.Z.) and dizygotic (D.Z.) twins. Kallmann (1954) claimed a concordance for M.Z. twins of 100 per cent but somewhat lower figures were obtained by other workers (da Fonseca, 1959; Rosanoff et al. 1935; Slater 1953). The concordance for manic-depressive psychosis in seven twin studies, reviewed by Price (1968), was 68 per cent for M.Z. pairs (N = 97) and 23 per cent for D.Z. pairs (N = 119).

BIPOLAR AND UNIPOLAR FORMS OF MANIC DEPRESSIVE PSYCHOSIS

In the studies so far described it was assumed that manic depressive psychosis was a single disease entity as proposed by Kraepelin (1921). It is now believed that there are at least two distinct forms of the illness; these were described by Leonhard (1959) as bipolar (episodes of mania and depression) and unipolar (depressions only). Leonhard et al. (1962) found that bipolar patients tended to have bipolar relatives and unipolar patients, unipolar relatives. This work received strong support from Sweden where Perris (1966) conducted a careful family study. He found that among 138 bipolar (manic depressive) probands there was bipolar heredity in 16 per cent of cases (but unipolar heredity in only 0.8 per cent of cases) and among unipolar (recurrent depressive) probands there was unipolar heredity in 11 per cent of cases but bipolar heredity in only 0.5 per cent of cases. Perris, like Leonhard, found that the morbidity risk in first degree relatives was greater for bipolar than for unipolar patients.

Angst (Angst and Perris, 1968) also found a higher familial incidence in the bipolar patient and, like Perris, he showed that bipolar illness was extremely rare in the families of unipolar patients. However, he found a much lower frequency (3.7 per cent) of bipolar illness in the families of bipolar probands than did Perris (11 per cent) and a higher frequency (11 per cent) of unipolar illness than did Perris (only 0.5 per cent). These discrepancies can be explained by differences in definition and diagnosis: e.g., Perris required at least three episodes of depression in his unipolar patients.

A STUDY OF MANIA

That the presence of mania should have such a marked effect on the inheritance of affective illness is not a new finding. Clouston (1904) believed that heredity was strongest in those exhibiting undue mental exaltation and excitement (Price, 1968).

Winokur et al. (1969) carried out a detailed clinical and genetic investigation of 61 patients admitted to hospital at the Washington University School of Medicine, St. Louis, with a clear diagnosis of mania at the time of admission. The family study included personal interviews of all first degree relatives and it was found that a large proportion of these relatives suffered from a primary affective disorder. However, many of these had suffered from depression only and had never experienced a manic attack (this heterogeneity would support the findings of Angst rather than those of Perris.) Winokur and his coworkers were able to calculate morbidity risks for the first degree relatives of 56 manic probands (information being available on all their parents and siblings) and found that, of the 25 male manic probands none at all had a father who was ill with affective disorder but 63 per cent of their mothers had suffered from an affective disorder. Of 31 female manic probands, 23 per cent had ill fathers and 50 per cent had ill mothers. Female manic probands tended to have more ill sisters (46 per cent) than ill brothers (23 per cent). For the whole group of manic probands (61) 34 per cent of the parents and 35 per cent of the siblings (19 per cent of males, 50 per cent of females at risk) had affective disorders.

SEX-LINKAGE

It has often been noted that manic depressive illness appears to occur more frequently in females. Sex-linked inheritance was proposed by Rosanoff (1931), and Burch (1964) thought that two dominant genes might be involved, one X-linked and the other autosomal. On the basis of their study of 61 manic probands, Winokur and Tanna (1969) concluded that an X-linked dominant gene might be a major aetiological factor. This mode of inheritance is supported by the absence of father-son transmission and the fact that twice as many female as male relatives were affected.

If penetrance were complete, then affected males would always have an affected mother. In their study 63 per cent had affected mothers and penetrance was therefore assumed to be incomplete.

In previous studies (for example that of Winokur and Pitts, 1965) it was found that both parents could transmit the disorder equally to their children and it is only in the recent study of manic probands that father-son transmission was found to be absent.

AGE OF ONSET OF ILLNESS.

The earlier the onset of an affective illness the stronger appears to be the genetic loading. Schulz (1951) reported that the illness was quite as common in the parents of patients with an early onset. Hopkinson (1964) found that there was a lower family incidence when depressions began after the age of 50.

The relatives of patients with involutional melancholia tend to have affective illnesses which are indistinguishable from the other affective disorders but the morbidity risk in parents and siblings is lower (Stenstedt, 1959). Kallman (1954) found a lower concordance in M.Z. twins. However, although the age dimension is an important variable, there is no evidence for a clear dichotomy (Price, 1968).

PRE-MORBID PERSONALITY

In their study of mania Winokur et al. (1969) found that of 61 manic probands and their 17 bipolar relatives, 62 (80 per cent) could be regarded as having cyclothymic or hypomanic personalities. The same personality features were discovered in 12 (29 per cent) of the 34 relatives who suffered from unipolar depression and in 36 (31 per cent) of the 116 relatives who had no affective disorder (86) or who had other psychiatric problems (30).

Perris (1966) reported significant differences in personality between bipolar manic depressives, who tended to be active and sociable types, and unipolar depressives who were more likely to be insecure, obsessional and sensitive personalities (using the concepts of Sjöbring). As might be expected the presence of precipitating factors is associated with a low family risk (Forrest et al., 1965).

ALCOHOLISM, GAMBLING AND SUICIDE

The frequent occurrence of alcoholism in families of patients with affective disorders, raises the possibility that a gene for affective illness might be expressed as alcoholism in some family members especially in males. Winokur and Pitts (1965) found that alcoholism was five times more common in the parents of a group of 366 'affectively disordered' patients than in a group of 250 stratified controls from a general hospital.

There are many similarities between alcoholism and compulsive gambling of which Winokur and his colleagues (1969) found a high incidence among the male relatives of three female manic patients; there were five compulsive gamblers, none of whom showed any sign of affective disorder.

Leonhard et al. (1962) found that bipolar patients had a considerably higher incidence of suicide in their family members than did the patients with unipolar psychoses. Perris (1966) found that female bipolar patients seem more likely to attempt suicide than do any other group.

THE SEARCH FOR A GENETIC MARKER

If it were possible to find a clear association between manic depressive illness and a known genetic trait, such as blood group, then it would establish a genetic factor in the illness and clarify the mode of trans-mission. Linkage occurs if two genes, each responsible for a separate trait, are on the same chromosome and close enough together; in any single family the characteristics of both genes would be found together in 50 per cent of the individuals in that family. Linkage occurs for only a few generations of a family until the association disappears through crossing over of chromosomes and it appears but briefly in a population (Winokur et al., 1969).

Parker et al. (1961) and Masters (1967) found an increased associ-ation between type 'O' blood group and manic depressive psychosis, using published figures as a controlled group, but Tanna and Winokur (1968), who used siblings as a control, were unable to confirm these findings. In a subsequent work, Winokur and Tanna (1969) investigated several blood systems in a limited number of families and found some suggestion of linkage between manic depressive disease and the Xg blood system locus (which appears on the X chromosome).

An association between colour blindness and affective disorder was found by Reich et al. (1969) in two families which, between them, had 11 people suffering from affective disorders who were all colour blind or carriers of the colour blindness gene which is an X-linked recessive. The authors therefore suggested that an X-linked dominant gene for manic-depressive (bipolar) illness would be located in the same place on the short arm of the X chromosome as the gene for colour blindness.

AETIOLOGY OF AFFECTIVE DISORDERS:
BIOCHEMISTRY

INTRODUCTION

The idea that manic-depressive psychosis might be caused by some biochemical lesion is not of recent origin. Kraepelin (1921) believed that a pathological disease process would one day be discovered and he cited a number of biochemical studies in support of his view. That there should be a 'physical' basis is suggested from various features of the illness: depressive illness in particular is often accompanied by marked somatic changes (in weight, sleep, sexual function, and so on), is hereditary, and is dramatically relieved by drugs and electroconvulsive therapy. Pollitt (1965) suggested that these somatic changes might be the result of a disturbance, or 'functional shift', in the hypothalamus which is responsible for autonomic regulation and perhaps also for emotional expression.

Many approaches have been made to this subject which has been reviewed by, among others, McFarland and Goldstein (1939), Coppen (1967) and Gibbons (1968). In the following selective account, attention will be drawn to the major findings in the areas of endocrine function, electrolytes and cerebral amines, to some possible biochemical interactions, to the problems of study in human subjects, to some ideas for future research, and to the biochemical effects of lithium.

ENDOCRINE FUNCTION

Significant changes in mood are often seen in disorders of endocrine function, especially in Cushing's Syndrome, Addison's disease, myxoedema, and thyrotoxicosis; and following medication with glucocorticoids. Mood changes are also common in the premenstrual, post-partum and involutional periods. Of course, a wide variety of psychological disturbances are seen in association with endocrinological changes and during hormone treatment, but the mood changes and other clinical features are often identical to those seen in classical mania and depression. Particular interest has been shown in the activity of the hypothalamic-pituitary-adrenal system, in disorders of thyroid function, and in the metabolism of cyclic AMP.

The Adrenal Cortex

The activity of the adrenal cortex is regulated by the release of adrenocorticotrophic hormone (ACTH) from the anterior pituitary gland, which is itself believed to be under the influence of the hypothalamus. This system is activated by psychological stress or emotional arousal and it would be surprising if disturbed psychiatric patients did not show some evidence of increased adrenocortical activity.

Attempts have been made to determine such changes, particularly in depressive illness, by the measurement of plasma cortisol levels, the urinary excretion of 17-hydroxycorticosteroids (17-OHCS) and 17-ketogenic steroids (17-KCS), the secretion rate of cortisol (by isotope dilution techniques), and by the methopyrapone and dexamethasone suppression tests. There are many methodological problems, not the least of which is the diurnal variation of cortisol secretion which occurs in normal subjects.

For example, Gibbons and McHugh (1962) found that the mean plasma cortisol level was significantly increased (20.8 micrograms per 100 ml) in a series of 18 depressed patients compared to the mean level after recovery (10.8), although 5 patients did not show any marked changes in their levels during recovery.

Carroll et al. (1968) used the midnight dexamethasone suppression test and found that the plasma 11-hydroxycorticosteroid (11-OHCS) level did not undergo its normal reduction in 14 out of 27 patients with severe depression. Resistance to dexamethasone suppression correlated with the clinical rating of severity of depression and recovery was associated with the return of normal responsiveness to dexamethasone. The reason for this failure of 'feedback' control in the pituitary-adrenal axis is unknown.

Coppen, et al. (1971) were unable to show any significant differences in C.S.F. cortisol concentration between controls, depressives or manics.

Most investigations have reported an increase in adrenocortical activity in at least a proportion of patients although, as Sachar et al. (1970) have pointed out, the literature is quite inconsistent, with many reports suggesting elevated corticosteroid levels and others normal or even reduced levels, with variable correlation between these levels and severity of illness. Perhaps the most illuminating report in this field is that by Sachar et al. (1970) who found that cortisol production (measured by isotope dilution) was elevated in patients who showed the greatest amount of emotional arousal and psychotic disintegration. Apathetic depressed patients, on the other hand, showed little or no change in cortisol production.

Thus, any group of patients, collected together with the general qualification of 'depressed', would be likely to show variable degrees of cortisol production and this may account for the wide differences between reports in the literature. The possible influence of changes in adrenocortical function on electrolyte and amine metabolism will be considered later.

The Thyroid Gland

As far as the thyroid gland is concerned, such measures as protein-bound iodine (PBI), basal metabolic rate (BMR) and radioactive iodine (I^{131}) uptake have all given values within the normal range (for

H

example: Gibbons *et al.*, 1960). Although a slight increase in thyroid activity may occur in depressive illness, it seems unlikely that this has much aetiological significance.

CYCLIC AMP

Adenosine $3^1 5^1$ cyclic monophosphate (cyclic AMP) was first identified by E. W. Sutherland as a factor required for the activation of liver phosphorylase. Cyclic AMP is formed by the conversion of adenosinetriphosphate (ATP) by adenyl cyclase and is inactivated by phosphodiesterase to form 5-AMP. It is now believed (Sutherland, 1970) that cyclic AMP is an extremely important intracellular agent which is activated by hormones, within the target cell, and triggers a sequence of events which lead to the physiological response associated with the hormone. This role as a 'second messenger' or, as Sutherland puts it, 'a master molecule of metabolic control and regulation' has been investigated in a wide variety of metabolic processes.

Cyclic AMP may be involved in central synaptic neurotransmission and has, therefore, attracted the interest of research workers in psychiatry. It has been claimed that urinary excretion of cyclic AMP is increased during mania and decreased in depression (Abdullah and Hamadah, 1970). Paul *et al.* (1971) confirmed these findings in their earlier work but later found that the increased excretion of cyclic AMP only occurred on the day of a 'rapid switch' from depression to mania. Ramsden (1970) has shown that antidepressant drugs have an inhibitory action on phosphodiesterase and could therefore cause an increased concentration of cyclic AMP in the body.

However, Brown *et al.* (1972) examined two short-cycle bipolar manic-depressive patients and one manic patient; they found no correlation between the patients' mood and their urinary excretion of cyclic AMP. It has been suggested that the changes previously reported may only reflect bodily activity (Eccleston *et al.*, 1970).

ELECTROLYTES

Electrolytes are of fundamental importance in cell function. The resting and action potentials of nerve and muscle cells are dependent on the different concentrations of sodium, potassium and other ions which are maintained inside the cell with respect to the extracellular fluid. Investigation of electrolyte changes in psychiatric patients have varied in complexity from estimations of plasma and urinary concentrations to whole-body studies using isotope dilution techniques. Early work on electrolytes in affective disorders has been reviewed by Gibbons (1963) and Coppen (1967); generally speaking, simple studies of plasma, urinary and C.S.F. electrolytes have failed to show any significant abnormality in depression or mania.

With the use of radioisotopes of sodium it is possible to measure, by the dilution principle, a considerable fraction of total body sodium. This fraction is called the total exchangeable sodium, and is the amount of sodium in the body with which the isotope mixes in a defined period of time. The non-exchangeable sodium is mostly in bone and is metabolically inactive. Gibbons (1960) found a 10 per cent increase in exchangeable Na in depression but this was not confirmed by Coppen and Shaw (1963).

Coppen and his colleagues have also used tritiated water and radioactive bromide to measure intra- and extra-cellular water at the same time as total exchangeable Na. By measuring the plasma concentration of Na, they were thereby able to calculate the total amount of Na in the extracellular compartment. Subtraction of this figure from the total exchangeable Na gave the 'residual sodium', i.e. the sodium outside the extracellular space, consisting mainly of intracellular Na and a small amount of exchangeable Na in bone. In a series of experiments (reviewed by Coppen, 1967) they found that 'residual Na' was increased by nearly 50 per cent in depression and returned to normal on recovery; and a much larger increase, almost 200 per cent, was found in mania. Total body potassium (K) and intracellular K were low and did not change with clinical recovery. More recently, Baer et al. (1969), using Na^{22}, found sodium retention during severe depression, and this was correlated with increased urinary excretion of 17-hydroxycorticosteroids (17 OHCS). Platman et al. (1970), however, found no significant change in total body K in mania or depression.

Coppen (1960) claimed that the rate of transfer of Na^{24} from blood to C.S.F. was lower in patients with a depressive illness than in schizophrenic patients and that the rate of transfer returned to normal with clinical recovery. Fotherby et al. (1963) were able to confirm these findings (but only in severely depressed patients) but Carroll et al. (1969) were not.

Another approach to the study of sodium transport was that of Glen et al. (1968) who used microelectrodes to measure Na and bicarbonate ions in saliva. They found that depressed patients appeared to have diminished rates of ionic transport across the salivary duct walls.

In summary, therefore, there is some evidence of an increase in intracellular Na concentrations in depression and mania. It may be suggested that there is some deficiency in the mechanism by which Na is transported across the cell membrane so that intracellular Na and water are increased while intracellular K is decreased. These changes are of considerable interest in view of the importance of Na ions in membrane transport (for example, of amino acids) and energy metabolism (ATPase activity).

Attention has also turned to changes in calcium and magnesium metabolism. Early reports of changes in plasma Ca and Mg in depressive illness have not been confirmed (Frizel *et al.*, 1969). Research into these ions is continuing because of increasing knowledge about the role of Mg and Ca in ATPase activity, and nerve excitability, respectively.

CEREBRAL AMINES

The 'amine hypothesis' may be stated simply as follows: it is suggested that certain neuronal systems in brain have important functions in relation to the control of mood and that the cerebral amines serve as transmitters (or as modulators of transmission) within these systems. Alterations in functional activity might be caused by changes in synthesis, storage, release or inactivation of amines; by changes in environmental stimuli; or by changes in receptor sensitivity. Research into this field was stimulated by the discovery that certain drugs, which would alter mood in man, caused changes in amine metabolism. The subject has been comprehensively reviewed by Dewhurst (1969).

Reserpine, a drug which can induce depression and sedation, produces a marked decrease in brain concentrations of 5-HT (Pletscher *et al.*, 1956) and noradrenaline (Holzbauer and Vogt, 1956). Alpha-methyl-dopa, which causes depression in man, brings about only a transient decrease in 5-HT but a profound and long-lasting fall in noradrenaline concentrations of animal brain (Bunney and Davis, 1965). The tricyclic antidepressant drug imipramine was shown by Axelrod (1966) to inhibit the uptake of noradrenaline into sympathetic nerve endings.

Another approach to the investigation of amine metabolism is by the measurement of metabolites in cerebrospinal fluid (C.S.F.). Ashcroft and Sharman (1960) reported that the concentration of 5-hydroxyindoles (for practical purposes, 5-HIAA) was lower in the lumbar C.S.F. of a group of depressed patients than in C.S.F. obtained from patients undergoing encephalography. It was then discovered that levels of 5-HIAA were equally low in groups of depressed and schizophrenic patients (Fotherby *et al.*, 1963; Ashcroft *et al.*, 1966) and in depressed and manic patients (Dencker *et al.*, 1966; Coppen *et al.*, 1972).

Ashcroft and Sharman (1960) also showed that levels of 5-HIAA were much higher in ventricular than in lumbar C.S.F.; it is now known from animal experiments (reviewed by Ashcroft, 1969) that in the interpretation of changes in the concentrations of amine metabolites in lumbar C.S.F. in man two major sources of variation should be considered: firstly, a change in the cerebral metabolism of the parent amine and, secondly, a change in the efficiency of the transport of metabolites (into or out of C.S.F.) or in the mixing of C.S.F. Dencker and coworkers (1966) also measured C.S.F. levels of HVA (dopamine metabolite) in some of their patients and found that these were normal, when 5-HIAA levels were low; therefore, as any disorder of transport might reasonably be expected to affect both acids, this finding would suggest that there is some alteration in the release or metabolism of 5-HT in depression.

There is now some evidence that the principal metabolite of noradrenaline in brain is 3-methoxy-4-hydroxy-phenylethyleneglycol (MHPG). Maas et al. (1968) have reported decreased levels of MHPG in the urine of depressed patients in whom other noradrenaline metabolite levels were normal. Wilk et al. (1972) studied MHPG levels in cerebrospinal fluid (C.S.F.) and found normal levels in 5 depressed patients but raised levels in 3 out of 6 manic patients. Two agitated schizo-affective patients had normal levels. These results are consistent with the theory that only the manic phase of manic-depressive illness is associated with abnormal brain noradrenaline levels.

The technique of tryptophan loading has been used both experimentally and therapeutically in an attempt to 'stimulate' 5-HT metabolism. It has been shown that the level of 5-HT in rat brain rises rapidly after an oral dose of tryptophan and is followed by a rise in brain 5-HIAA (Ashcroft et al., 1965). It has been claimed that the combined administration of tryptophan with a monoamine oxidase inhibitor is an effective treatment for depression (Coppen et al., 1963).

However, claims that tryptophan is as effective as electroconvulsive therapy (E.C.T.) in the treatment of depression (Coppen et al., 1967) have not so far been substantiated (Carroll and Dodge, 1971). Attempts to treat patients with dopa, with or without an inhibitor of monoamine oxidase, have usually been unsuccessful (Schildkraut and Kety, 1967).

Some of the evidence in support of the 'amine hypothesis' has been reviewed and it will be noted that much of the evidence is from animal experiments; however, by analogy, it can be argued that affective illnesses and their relief by drugs may be due to changes in monoamine concentrations in the brain. The little evidence available in man is in keeping with this theory (Gibbons, 1968).

BIOCHEMICAL INTERACTIONS

The cerebral amines are continuously being synthesised, released and metabolized under the regulatory influence of various factors. The synthesis of 5-hydroxytryptamine (5-HT) takes place as follows: tryptophan is converted by tryptophan hydroxylase to 5-hydroxytryptophan which is decarboxylated in the presence of pyridoxal phosphate to 5-HT.

Tryptophan Pyrrolase

Tryptophan also undergoes oxidation to kynurenine which is metabolised to a series of products (xanthurenic acid, etc.) and to nicotinic acid; this oxidation of tryptophan is catalysed by tryptophan pyrrolase, an enzyme whose activity in liver is increased by the administration of adrenal corticosteroids, oestrogens and tryptophan; pyridoxal phosphate is required as co-factor. The kynurenine products are excreted in the urine and provide an index of pyrrolase activity.

It has been suggested (Lapin and Oxenkrug, 1969; Curzon, 1969) that in depressive illness the production of tryptophan pyrrolase is stimulated by raised blood corticosteroid levels. This increase in pyrrolase activity causes a shunt of tryptophan metabolism away from 5-HT synthesis, and along the kynurenine pathway. Curzon and Green (1968) gave intraperitoneal injections of hydrocortisone to rats and found a reduction in brain 5-HT and 5-HIAA (the acid metabolite of 5-HT) which corresponded with an increase in tryptophan pyrrolase activity and was blocked by allopurinol (which inhibits pyrrolase). These changes were also produced in rats by immobilisation stress (Curzon, 1969).

Lapin and Oxenkrug (1969) also suggested that the decrease in brain 5-HT levels would lead to weakening of the inhibitory processes on the amygdaloid complex, activation of which in man causes an increase in plasma 17-OHCS levels. However, agents such as p-chlorophenylalanine (PCPA) which deplete the brain of 5-HT, do not cause activation of the adrenal cortex (Nistico et al., 1969). Therefore, it is suggested that in depression there is primary activation of the adrenal cortex, which causes a secondary reduction in brain 5-HT.

Curzon and Bridges (1970) gave oral loads of tryptophan to female depressed patients and controls. They found that the patients excreted greater amounts of certain kynurenine products.

Oral Contraceptives

The association between oral contraceptives and depression (Dennis and Jeffery, 1968) has led to the suggestion that oestrogen-progestogen mixtures cause a functional deficiency of pyridoxine (co-enzyme required for 5-HT production.) Rose (1966) found that oestrogens caused an increase in the urinary excretion of kynurenine products after tryptophan loading. Three of the patients were also given pyridoxine which appeared to restore the tryptophan metabolism to normal. Rose and Braidman (1970) also found that women on oral contraceptives (oestrogen-progestogen mixture) excreted increased amounts of xanthurenic acid, etc., after tryptophan load. There is some evidence (Winston, 1969) that pyridoxine-replacement therapy can alleviate the depression associated with oral contraceptives.

Catecholamines

It has been shown that the metabolism of the catecholamines is also under the influence of hormonal factors. The rate-limiting enzyme in the biosynthesis of the catecholamines (dopamine, noradrenaline and adrenaline) is tyrosine hydroxylase (Udenfriend, 1968) which catalyses the conversion of tyrosine to dopa. However, tyrosine also undergoes transamination in liver by the enzyme tyrosine transaminase. The activity of this enzyme is increased by adrenal steroids, insulin, glucagon and tyrosine, and decreased by injections of hypophyseal somatotrophin. Thyroxine and ACTH slow down the turnover of noradrenaline in rat heart; and the retention of noradrenaline in the sympathetic neurone is influenced by sodium and sodium-retaining hormones (Axelrod, 1968).

There is also evidence of interaction between the catecholamine and indoleamine pathways. For example, dopa and 5-HTP compete for the same decarboxylase: large doses of dopa cause a decrease in brain 5-HT levels (Garattini and Valzelli, 1965). Noradrenaline inhibits tryptophan hydroxylase and might regulate 5-HT synthesis, while 5-HTP inhibits tyrosine hydroxylase, causing a reduced synthesis of noradrenaline (Zhelyaskov et al., 1968).

Practical Problems in Human Studies

In all studies of biochemical changes in human subjects there is the major problem of ensuring controlled conditions with respect to diet, exercise, temperature and so on, as well as the collection and preservation of samples. The study of amine metabolism in humans is particularly limited by problems of access to nervous tissue, and evidence is therefore sought by the analysis of body fluids (blood, urine and C.S.F.). In the study of amines there are problems associated with the measurement of minute amounts of amine salts which are unstable in solution, being rapidly destroyed by changes in temperature and pH. It is also doubtful to what extent changes in cerebral metabolism are reflected by the constituents of urine and peripheral blood; for example, whilst VMA is the major metabolite of noradrenaline outside brain, it is likely that 3-methoxy-4-hydroxyphenylglycol (MHPG) is the major metabolite within brain (Schanberg et al., 1968). Similarly, although the major metabolite of 5-HT in the brain is 5-HIAA, it is believed that urinary 5-HIAA reflects mainly peripheral metabolism (Gibbons, 1968).

Diurnal Variation

It is becoming clear that many constituents of the blood and urine are prone to diurnal and other (e.g. hebdomadal) variations. Particular attention has been given to such changes in the levels of amino acids, hormones (such as cortisol), glucose, uric acid, and various electrolytes.

For example, the concentration of tyrosine in human plasma has been shown to vary in diurnal fashion, and this fluctuation does not appear to result simply from the ingestion of protein or from exercise. Daily rhythmic changes have been shown in tyrosine transaminase activity (in rat liver) and in tyrosine hydroxylase activity (in rat pineal gland) (Wurtman *et al.*, 1967).

Observations have been made on the diurnal rhythms of water and electrolyte excretion in 79 psychiatric patients (Elithorn *et al.*, 1966). Thirty-six patients with endogenous depression showed an average reduction in amplitude in their rhythms of water and electrolyte excretion, the effect being most pronounced with sodium and chloride, in comparison with 43 control patients with neuroses and personality disorders. However, it was shown that in both groups the amplitude of the diurnal variations decreased with age and part of the difference between the groups could be related to age differences.

Perhaps the most dramatic study in this field, and one which illustrates the difficulties, is that described by Jenner *et al.* (1968) who studied the effect of an altered time regime on biological rhythms in a patient with a 48-hour 'periodic psychosis'. By subjecting the patient (and one of the authors as a control) to an artificial environment in which day and night together were 22 hours, they showed that the 48-hour rhythm was changed to a 44-hour rhythm and that the biochemical changes (excretion of electrolytes, adrenal steroids, etc.) adjusted to this environmentally regulated rhythm. The subjects were isolated for a period of 11 days.

FUTURE RESEARCH TOPICS

It is particularly important that recent advances in the diagnosis of affective disorders should be applied to biochemical studies. For example, the concepts of unipolar and bipolar illness, formulated by Leonhard, have found general acceptance in psychiatry yet reports are still being published of biochemical studies on patients with 'depression'. However, recent work in the M.R.C. Brain Metabolism Unit in Edinburgh has shown that significant differences in C.S.F. levels of 5-HIAA exist between unipolar and bipolar patients.

Advances in technical methods are stimulating research into studies of cell metabolism (e.g. nucleic acids) and membrane transport (e.g. ATPase activity) while animal studies are clarifying the problems of the blood-brain barrier (by perfusion techniques) and the role of the monoamines in cerebral neurotransmission. In the face of such elegant experimental work, it is all too easy to lose sight of the need for rigid control of experimental conditions in human studies. It is becoming clear that such variables as age and sex have considerable bearing on the biochemical changes reported in psychiatric illness. For example, it has been shown that brain monoamine oxidase activity increases with age (Robinson, *et al.*, 1972) and that tryptophan metabolism is influenced by high oestrogen levels (Rose, 1966). Dilman (1971) has argued that, with age, the hypothalamus becomes increasingly insensitive to physiological feedback control; the effects on neuroendocrine mechanisms, and the possible relationship to the affective disturbances of later life, are obviously in need of further clarification. Indeed, the whole subject of physiological control mechanisms is as yet imperfectly understood and it is likely that further advances will be made in, for example, the relationship between monoamines and the pituitary-adrenal axis.

To end this review on a cautionary note, it should not be forgotten that changes in, for example, amine and amino acid metabolism have been discovered in a variety of medical conditions. Thus, abnormalities of 5-HT (serotonin) metabolism have been reported in schizophrenia, migraine, Mongolism and rheumatoid arthritis, as well as in depression and mania!

LITHIUM

Lithium carbonate is now well established as a prophylactic agent in affective disorders especially in bipolar (manic-depressive) illness, and in the treatment of acute mania (see section on Treatment). The mode of action of lithium is still unknown in spite of a vast amount of research into its pharmacological effects (reviewed by Schou, 1957 and 1968; and by Pearson and Jenner, 1971).

Electrolytes

Lithium is related chemically to sodium and potassium and is believed to interfere with biological systems which depend on these ions. Lithium can substitute for Na in the production of an action potential but eventually accumulates in the cell membrane and inhibits the transport of Na ions.

Lithium interferes with sodium balance in the body and causes a sodium diuresis; it is believed that lithium may alter a central mechanism which controls aldosterone release (Aronoff et al., 1971).

There is also a similarity between lithium ion and magnesium ion (Schou, 1957) which is concerned in such processes as protein synthesis and active transport.

Effect on Amine Metabolism

It has been shown that lithium interferes with the turnover of noradrenaline in rat brain. Intracisternal injections of tritiated noradrenaline were given before and after lithium administration, and the levels of noradrenaline and its metabolites determined in brain after varying periods. Lithium produced a shift of noradrenaline metabolism from O-methylation to intraneuronal deamination, with signs of increased turnover of noradrenaline, which suggested that lithium might decrease levels of noradrenaline at the receptor sites (Schanberg *et al.*, 1967).

Corrodi *et al.* (1967) found that lithium, when combined with an inhibitor of tyrosine hydroxylase, produced a fall in brain noradrenaline which was significantly more rapid than that produced by inhibitor alone. Lithium did not alter the levels of dopamine or 5-HT in the brain, either alone or in the presence of enzyme inhibitors. However, Perez-Cruet *et al.* (1971) have studied the effects of chronic administration of lithium on the metabolism of 5-HT in rat brain. They found that lithium appeared to increase the synthesis rate of 5-HT (by 60 to 80 per cent) and also increased the concentration of tryptophan in the brain (by 60 per cent).

AETIOLOGY OF AFFECTIVE DISORDERS:
EARLY PARENT-CHILD RELATIONSHIPS

Melanie Klein (1934) extended psycho-analytic speculations to the infant's first year of life. She believed that the infant was not merely narcissistically orientated but was object-orientated right from the start of the extra-uterine life. Thus the mother-child relation in the first year of life is all important. This first year of life contains the fixation points to which the individual will regress later under stress and strain. These fixation points Klein calls the 'paranoid' and the 'depressive position'. The paranoid position develops first, as defence against pain, in the form of projection, then comes the depressive position at about the time of weaning, around the first half-year of life. The child can only see the mother as all 'good' i.e. gratifying, or all 'bad' i.e. depriving. The internalized 'good' object makes the child feel good himself, but the internalized 'bad' object makes the child feel bad himself and hateful. In this inner conflict characteristic of the depressive position, Klein sees the first guilt feelings arise. The need of the mother for survival and the guilty anxiety prompt the child into repair actions, the magic of self-punishment, such as crying spells and the rage directed against the child's own body. When repair succeeds and the guilty anxieties are surmounted this leads to a more integrated ego and more realistic object relations. But an excess of the depressive anxieties without successful experiences of repair leads to a fixation to the depressive position. The adult regresses to this position whenever excessive stress overtakes the integration of his ego. The manic reaction is an attempt at integration and repair by the denial of the frustrating, depriving aspect of objects.

Spitz (1946) in his well known paper 'anaclitic depression' describes a 'striking syndrome' which affected 19 out of 123 unrelated infants in a nursery: 'In the second half of the first year, a few of these infants developed a weepy behaviour that was in marked contrast to their previously happy and outgoing behaviour. After a time this weepiness gave way to withdrawal. The children in question would lie in their cots with averted faces, refusing to take part in the life of their surroundings'. In addition to weepiness and withdrawal these infants showed retardation of development, slow reactions, retardation of movement, sometimes stupor, a fall in their developmental quotient, loss of appetite, loss of weight, insomnia. Spitz comments that the physiognomic expression 'would in an adult be described as depression'. The better the relationship between mother and child was before separation, the worse the depression would be.

The precipitating factor, therefore, seems to be the loss of the love object, as described in classical psychoanalytic theory by Abraham (1911) and Freud (1917). Spitz also thinks that he has provided clinical evidence for Fenichel's (1945) assertion that: 'Actually traumatic experiences in the nursing period can be found more often in subsequent manic-depressive patients than in schizophrenics'.

Bowlby (1951, 1953), following up Spitz's lead, put forward the influential thesis of maternal deprivation: 'What is believed to be essential for mental health is that the infant and young child should experience a warm, intimate, and continuous relationship with his mother (or permanent mother substitute) in which both find satisfaction and enjoyment'. Bowlby regards complete separation from the mother as the worst type of deprivation and institutional care as the most common example of it. He considers the effects of complete deprivation to be severe and long-lasting 'leading to anxiety, excessive need for love, powerful feelings of revenge and, arising from these last, guilt and depression'. The extreme example is the 'affectionless' character who cannot accept or reciprocate love and who very often develops anti-social behaviour.

Many authors have put forward evidence contradictory to Bowlby's e.g. Orlansky (1949) who found that events of childhood or later life could counteract and change 'the character structure tentatively formed during infancy'. The work from the Iowa Child Development Centre (Skeels *et al.*, 1948) and a great deal of work published since, (e.g. Clarke and Clarke, 1954), have shown that backwardness associated with deprivation need not be permanent and irreversible.

Bowlby's work has been widely criticized, chiefly by O'Connor (1956) and Wooton (1959), but it has stimulated a lot of research in the effect of early environment in mental illness.

Recently *Granville-Grossman* (1968) has reviewed the relevant literature for the affective illnesses. The difficulty in comparing studies is that 'parental deprivation' has been used rather loosely to mean childhood bereavement as well as separation from parents for some other reason, and defective relationship with parents. The term has also usually been taken to mean maternal deprivation, even though some authors have stressed the importance of paternal deprivation.

Without going into more detailed appraisal of the parental deprivation thesis in relation to affective illness (for extended discussion see Granville-Grossman, 1968; and Munro, 1965), a few of the main studies and their results will be mentioned here.

Brown (1961) comparing depressives with general practice patients and with control figures from the 1921 census, found a significantly higher incidence of childhood bereavement in depressive patients.

Forrest et al. (1965), using medical ward patients as controls, found significantly less childhood bereavement among their manic-depressives (bipolar depressions) than in their patients with depressive reaction. Perris (1966), on the other hand, did not find childhood bereavement a discriminating factor between his bipolar and unipolar recurrent depressives. Stenstedt (1952) found that dissolution of the home or serious parental friction may increase the risk that siblings of manic-depressives will themselves develop the illness.

Beck et al. (1963) rating their depressed patients as 'high-depressed' and 'low-depressed' on a depression inventory, found that prevalence of orphanhood before 16 years correlates significantly with severity of depression.

Dennehy (1966), using the 1921 census figures as control, found a significantly higher incidence of childhood bereavement in depressives.

On the other hand Oltman *et al.* (1952) found little difference in the degree of parental deprivation between manic-depressives and normals.

Munro (1965), using a selected group of 153 cases of primary depression and 163 medical out-patients as controls, found that depressives as a whole show no greater liability to have lost a parent by death before their 16th birthday. However, he found that severe depressives report a highly significant excess of disturbed relationships with both mother and father during childhood.

Gregory (1959) found no significant difference in the incidence of orphanhood between depressives and the expected figures for the general population. He also (Gregory 1962) found no difference in early bereavement among the diagnostic categories, one of which was affective psychosis.

Pitts et al. (1965) found no significant difference in the incidence of childhood bereavement between a group of manic-depressives and general hospital controls.

These studies have, as seen, failed to show a consistent association between early bereavement and subsequent development of affective disorder.

Cohen et al. (1954) published an influential psychodynamic study of the family background of manic-depressives, based on intensive psychoanalytic psychotherapy of 12 patients. They state 'our purpose is to delineate as far as possible the experiences with significant people which made it necessary for the prospective manic-depressive to develop the particular patterns of interaction which comprise his character and his illness'. They found a typical parent-child relationship and typical family-community relationship which influenced the character structure of the child and the way he interacted with other people in later life.

The child who is later to develop manic-depressive psychosis is very often selected as the special standard-bearer of the family, because of various reasons, such as high abilities, rank in family, etc.

The authors say: 'These early experiences probably lay the ground-work for the manic-depressive's later ambivalence'. Because of his special position in the family, the manic-depressive guards his position jealously and is envied by the other siblings and one or both parents. As he grows up he guards himself against others by underselling himself or by being extremely helpful to others. As an adult, during the periods free from illness, he seems well-adjusted and friendly.

Cohen et al., go on to give examples of how these people can be helped in psychotherapy. Most of their insight comes from transference and counter-transference situations according to psychoanalytic tradition.

The concepts put forward by Cohen and her group were followed up and a special questionnaire was devised based on previous findings. Cohen's colleagues satisfied themselves of its reliability by inter-rater and test-retest methods and studied a group of 17 schizophrenics, 27 manic-depressives, and her original group of 12 manic-depressives. They found no major differences between the two manic-depressive groups, but highly significant differences between the manic-depressive and schizophrenic patients: e.g. the manic-depressive's family had made a bigger effort to rise in social status and the patient was dealt with as an instrument for achieving social prestige.

Such studies are most promising in their therapeutic and psycho-dynamic implications, and should stimulate more family studies in affective illness. Many of the family patterns depicted here as significant tend to be typical of middle-class and upper middle-class families. More research is needed to clarify the importance of early upbringing in the development of affective illness.

AETIOLOGY OF AFFECTIVE DISORDERS:

PERSONALITY STUDIES

Psychotic depressives have often been said to have a 'good' or 'adequate' pre-morbid personality, though it is never too clear what it is 'good' or 'adequate' for. Presumably it is for living in general, or it may be good and adequate because it conforms with the clinician's values. In contrast neurotic depressives have been said to have hysterical, obsessional or inadequate personalities.

Many authors have supported *Kraepelin's* (1921) opinion that cyclothymic or cycloid personality is predominant in manic-depressives, e.g. Mayer-Gross (1954), Henderson and Gillespie (1956). Astrup *et al.* (1959) also found a preponderance of cycloid personalities among manic-depressives, whereas reactive psychoses had a preponderance of 'sensitive' personalities. *Leonhard et al.* (1962) found a cyclothymic temperament in his manic-depressives (bipolar) and a sub-depressive temperament in his recurrent depressives (unipolar).

Kraines (1957) however, found manic-depressive illness 'extremely common in persons who present a premorbid picture of good adjustment, extravert characteristics, and high basic levels of energy'.

On the whole, however, there have been very few systematic personality studies in affective illness. Most have been clinical, with vague, undefined criteria, and therefore not easily repeatable. Worse still, most authors have not differentiated among different types of affective illness (with the notable exception of Leonhard) and finally, very often statements have been made on the basis of assessments of patients when they are ill and therefore likely to give a distorted view of themselves. The effect of illness, the fact of being in hospital, etc., are bound to influence the way a person sees himself, reports himself, or is seen by others. Several authors have recently drawn attention to this important methodological point, notably Astrup *et al.* (1959), Perris (1966), Metcalfe (1968).

Some systematic and relatively objective studies of personality in affective illness have, however, appeared recently and these will be reviewed here.

Joseph Becker (1960) attempted to verify Cohen *et al's.* formulation of the manic-depressive character (see above) within the framework of McClelland's experimentally derived concepts of achievement (McClelland *et al.*, 1953). McClelland and his colleagues have identified two relatively independent types of achievement orientation: need achievement is said to characterise people whose concern is to live up to an internalized standard of excellence, whereas value achievement is characterized by people who value achievement for achievement's sake as a response to excessive parental stress or achievement striving. Becker studied 24 recovered manic-depressives (bipolars) and 30 non-psychiatric controls, keeping nationality, age range and minimum level of education constant. He administered a rating scale to check the reliability of the clinical judgement of remission and a series of eight other standard experimental tasks: a need achievement measure, a verbal level test, four attitude scales and two performance tasks. His results showed that the scores of the manic-depressives on the value achievement scale were significantly higher than those of the controls, indicating that the manic-depressives placed a 'strong, positive, conscious valuation on achievement'. Manic-depressives scored significantly higher on a scale measuring rigidly conventional authoritarian attitudes, conformity, intolerance of ambiguity and social imperceptiveness. Manic-depressives scored significantly higher on a scale (F scale) measuring submission to authority, emphasis on discipline and rigidly defined roles for family members. Their scores did not differ from the controls on the need achievement task or the two performance tasks.

Thus Becker's empirical findings seem to support Cohen's aetiological formulations. The fact that McClelland's concepts of value and need achievers are not well-known in the psychiatric literature must diminish the appeal of this work.

Using a different approach, *Perris* (1966) also made a systematic personality study. He compared two well defined groups of recovered depressives, bipolars and unipolars, using a multi-dimensional approach, that of the Swedish psychiatrist Sjöbring's (1958). Nyman (1956) and Coppen (1966) have presented Sjöbring's work in English. In summary Sjöbring speaks of four dimensions of personality:

1. Capacity or intelligence.
2. Validity: effective energy. The sub-valid person is bound to stability, routine, easily tired, cautious, tense, meticulous.
3. Stability: similar to introversion-extraversion. The sub-stable person is naïve, interested in his fellow-men, frank, open, weakly integrated.
4. Solidity: related to maturity. The sub-solid person is impulsive, weak, changeable.

Nyman and Marke (1962) have formed a 60-item inventory to measure three of these dimensions, leaving out capacity (see Coppen, 1966, for English translation).

Perris hypothesized that the two recovered depressive groups would score differently, that the manic-depressives would score as sub-stable which is equivalent to what other authors have called, cycloid, cyclothymic, warm, sociable, and that the recurrent depressives would score as sub-valid, which is equivalent to insecure, obsessional, sensitive, as called by other authors.

His hypotheses were borne out at high statistical levels of significance. Perris's work shows the dangers of making statements about depressives in general, without taking into consideration such important subclassifications as bipolar and unipolar, which his own work, as well as Leonhard's have shown to be a valid diagnostic differentiation.

Metcalfe (1968) gave support to Perris's findings using the Maudsley Personality Inventory (M.P.I.) to compare recovered depressed women with 'normal' women and other groups of patients. She reports that even though the neurotic score of recovered depressives does not differ from the norm for normals, when the individual questions are examined, it transpires that the women recovered from depression score higher on four questions and lower on four others, than 'normal' women. The same applies when the recovered depressives are compared with other groups of patients. The positive answers to the first set she interpreted as indicating 'a tense, worrying attitude to life', the negative answers to the second set she interpreted as indicating 'a denial of fantasy and imagination, and a rigid, limited, habit-bound personality'. This description closely resembles Perris's description of the sub-valid personality of the recurrent depressive.

A study by *Coppen and Metcalfe* (1965) using the Maudsley Personality Inventory (M.P.I.) in a follow-up of severely depressed patients showed startling effects of illness on personality. Thirty-nine patients were tested just after admission and again after treatment when considered recovered. The drop in average N score (neuroticism) was dramatic and significant and was parallelled by a significant rise in E score (extraversion). Ten patients were followed up a few months after discharge and the changes accompanying improvement were found to have been maintained and even increased.

Mayo (1967) in a similar study, but using different measures, namely the Hostility and Direction of Hostility Questionnaire, H.D.H.Q. (Foulds, 1965) found important psychological changes associated with improvement in depression. Testing 24 depressed in-patients at admission and when clinically improved, he found a significant drop in the mean level of general punitiveness and also in mean level of intropunitiveness, i.e. of hostility directed towards the self in self-criticism and guilt. Hostility directed towards others, extrapunitiveness, expressed as acting out hostility, criticism of others and projected delusional hostility, did not show any significant change with improvement, although they all showed a drop.

Foulds (1965) using the Hysteroid-Obsessoid Questionnaire (H.O.Q.), a personality questionnaire, to compare psychotically depressed and neurotically depressed women, found the psychotics to be more obsessoid. However, with improvement there was a significant change in that the recovered psychotics tended to score more than the neurotics, i.e. as more hysteroid. The mean neurotic score had scarcely changed. This is in strong agreement with Metcalfe's study reported above, which is not surprising since the reported correlation between the H.O.Q. and the M.P.I. is high. In addition to becoming more hysteroid, his improved psychotics also became more extrapunitive, less self-critical and less delusionally guilty. The improved neurotics showed changes in the same direction, but to a smaller extent. Foulds comments that psychosis disrupts personality to a greater extent than neurosis and inevitably makes accurate self-report more difficult.

Eysenck and Eysenck (1964) also reported an objective systematic personality study of depressives. They found that psychotic depressives have a higher mean N (neurotic) score than schizophrenics, their scores being nearer to the neurotic mean than the normal mean. They noted, however, that this may be due to 'the diagnostic failure to distinguish properly between endogenous and reactive depression'. According to Eysenck's theory depressives are dysthymics and are therefore expected to have low E (extraversion) scores. Eysenck and Claridge (1962) found some evidence for this.

The importance and interest of such objective personality studies is that they are repeatable, public and, above all, can provide independent variables for other studies, such as outcome of illness, biochemical factors, type of illness and symptoms pattern.

MANAGEMENT OF AFFECTIVE ILLNESS

The individual therapies used in the management of affective illness, e.g. antidepressant drugs, tranquillizers, E.C.T., prefrontal leucotomy, psychotherapy are described in detail in other chapters (see Chaps. I, VI and XV, Vol. II). We shall thus confine ourselves in this chapter to a discussion of the general principles of management and of the use of specific therapies under particular circumstances and in the individual syndromes.

MANAGEMENT OF DEPRESSION

This starts with a full assessment of the patient leading to as complete as possible a formulation of the case. Such a formulation will include a diagnosis and the following features should be defined: (1) is the depression out of proportion to the environmental precipitants for this particular patient? To make this assessment it will be necessary to arrive at an overall judgement on the personality of the patient, in particular, the traits of dependency, the presence of cyclothymic features. (2) The intensity of precipitating stimuli is also assessed, together with specific vulnerabilities of a given individual, e.g. to separation, to personal loss.

If the complaint of depression is assessed in this way in many patients we will conclude that the presenting distress is commensurate with the situation in which they find themselves, e.g. a bereavement reaction, response to moving house, to loss of a job etc. They may still present for help but there can be no rational reason to assume that drugs, e.g. tricyclic antidepressants, will have any specific role in their management. Drugs in such cases should be confined to the use of minor tranquillisers and sedatives to tide the person over the period of distress. The main part of therapy in such patients is a form of support which may be particularly effective in reactions many of which are variations of separation anxiety.

Dangers in such management are to be found in the encouragement of excessive dependency which may include the prolongation of the administration of tranquillizers and sedatives beyond the period of usefulness. Recognition of the predisposing personality features, realistic setting of limits for support and mobilization of support systems with the patient's environment, which may involve joint interviews with spouse and the involvement of the social services, all contribute.

DEPRESSIVE ILLNESS

This diagnosis makes the assumption that the reaction is out of proportion to the stimulus and that the function of brain systems concerned with the mediation of mood response is disturbed.

In assessing the response to drugs and E.C.T. it should be remembered that the affective illnesses normally run a remitting course in the absence of treatment. Thus response to treatment must be shown either to produce a relief of symptoms, to produce earlier remission, or to be effective in preventing relapse if its use is to be justified.

Comparative studies of tricyclics, E.C.T. and monoamine oxidase inhibitors with placebo have been reported, e.g. the M.R.C. trial of antidepressants, and on the whole have confirmed the value of E.C.T. and tricyclics. Such trials are becoming progressively more difficult to carry out on hospitalized patients as the widespread use of the drugs in general practice means that only patients selected by their failure to respond now reach a psychiatrist. More important perhaps now is the adequate study of the response of carefully selected subgroups or syndromes and it is on such groups that we shall concentrate in this brief survey.

RESPONSE TO TRICYCLIC DRUGS

The study of Kiloh and Garside (1963) suggests that response to tricyclics is correlated with the presence or absence of certain symptoms; thus a 'retarded' group shows an excellent response and the presence of many precipitating factors is a bad prognostic sign. Clinicians' impressions suggest that response to tricyclic agents may be preceeded by a brief period of increased agitation. A recent study by Aitken and Zealley (1970) using the analogue scale to assess mood indicates that the patient may feel subjectively worse before he feels better, a finding which may be explained by the initial increase in agitation.

RESPONSE TO E.C.T.

Marked anxiety as part of a reactive depressive illness may indicate the likelihood of a poor response to E.C.T. and such patients may become more anxious during such therapy.

Severe depressive illnesses may require treatment in hospital, the decision to admit being a question of clinical judgement paying due regard to all aspects of the patient and his illness. Whilst E.C.T. can be given on an outpatient basis, the treatment can be disrupting for both patient and family, and in general is probably better given in hospital.

PSYCHOTHERAPY OF DEPRESSION

The depressed patient is dependent, incapable of making or maintaining social contacts. He is susceptible to further defeats even in minor matters. He has a disastrous self-image. Much of the literature on the psychotherapy of depression is hardly relevant to the treatment of the acute attack; rather it describes attempts to change attitudes and life style in patients susceptible to recurrent depressive attacks.

In the management of acute attacks prolonged exploratory psychotherapy is both impracticable and unnecessary. We must remember that this is a self-remitting disorder. The aims of therapy in combination with physical methods of treatment are in the early stages to protect the patient and accept his dependency. The therapist can then use his position to attempt to counter the patient's negative self-image. The effect of reassurance and explanation is transient but relieves distress. Severely depressed patients lack the ability to explore in thought and action, they are trapped by a round of depressive ruminations and cannot be roused from these by exhortation or social contact.

As the patient improves he once again begins to explore the possibility of recovery. At this stage he will benefit from increased opportunity for social contact in an accepting environment. His hidden hostility may become more obvious at this stage, either directed against self in the nature of increased suicidal risk, or against others in the form of irritability and outbursts of transient aggression provoked by minor incidents.

The aim of therapy is to encourage an increase in activities whilst attempting to ensure that the patient does not take on more than he can cope with.

Most patients benefit from a simple explanation of their illness and the relatives may also appreciate such an explanation. Time spent with relatives may be extremely valuable as many may have temporarily exceeded their tolerance for the patient's behaviour and may find an understanding physician very helpful in relieving them of guilt feelings and in restoring a more positive attitude to the patient.

MONOAMINE OXIDASE INHIBITORS

Clinical Studies

It seems generally agreed that in classical depressive syndromes, tricyclic antidepressants and E.C.T. are superior in efficacy to the monoamine oxidase inhibitors. Further interest has recently been aroused by the claims that the M.A.O.I.'s combined with tryptophan may be effective in those depressive states normally treated with E.C.T. or tricyclic agents.

Atypical depression

In 1959, West and Dally described a group of patients with atypical depression responding to M.A.O.I.'s. These patients are characterized by the presence of symptoms of depression together with hysterical and phobic anxiety symptoms. Clinically, the group seem similar to the patients suffering from the phobic anxiety depersonalization syndrome described by Roth.

Kelly, *et al.*, (1970) reported a retrospective study of 246 patients with phobic anxiety treated with monoamine oxidase inhibitors. Improvement rates of approximately 90 per cent were reported at one year, compared with 60 per cent in patients treated by behaviour therapy.

M.A.O.I's and Tryptophan

Coppen *et al.* (1963) carried out a controlled trial comparing the antidepressant activity of a monoamine oxidase inhibitor given alone with that of a M.A.O.I. combined with tryptophan and claimed that the combination was more effective. (For further discussion of M.A.O.I. drugs see Chap. XV, vol. II.)

TREATMENT OF HYPOMANIA

Severe mania demands treatment in hospital as the patient's environment cannot contain or tolerate his behaviour. Admission in these circumstances is often by compulsory order.

Initial treatment in such patients must be energetic. Drug treatment is based on the administration of major tranquillizers of the phenothiazine and butyrophenone series in large doses.

Tranquillizers

Chlorpromazine in divided oral dosage of 400 mg to 1200 mg per day is required. Haloperidol may be given in a dose of 9 to 24 mg per day or the two drugs may be combined. Interestingly extrapyramidal side effects are rare during the acute phase of mania and general tolerance of the drugs is high, although regular monitoring of blood pressure is advisable as large doses of phenothiazines may provoke hypotension. The restlessness of akathisia can be mistaken for an increase in motor activity of mania, a useful differentiating feature being that whilst the patients complain bitterly of the motor restlessness of akathisia they rarely complain of the overactivity of mania.

Use of E.C.T.

Particular difficulty may be experienced in treating mania when it is accompanied by florid psychotic symptomatology. In such cases the patient may reject treatment in violent fashion. In the author's experience such psychotic reactions respond dramatically to E.C.T., as a rule only a small number of treatments being required. The other aspects of the acute manic reaction often continue unchecked but the patient is now more capable of co-operating in therapy and the drugs soon begin to take effect.

Other Drugs

Lithium carbonate has been used in the treatment of acute mania (see p. 238).

Ward Management of the Manic Patient

Confinement of the manic patient in a locked ward may occasionally be required but it is surprising how many severely disturbed patients can be managed in a general admission ward if the nurse–patient ratio is high enough to allow special attention to the patient over the initial period of maximal disturbance. The main principle of management practised instinctively by the good psychiatric nurse is the avoidance of direct confrontation which invariably provokes aggression and increased disturbance. The patient is easily distracted and welcomes physical activity and advantage is taken of these two features to divert him from conflict with other patients. He will respect a straightforward approach and react against management by subterfuge and pretence.

Management of Hypomania in Outpatients

Here the basis of management is a close follow-up with the use of phenothiazines, butyrophenones and, in patients with recurrent illness, lithium carbonate. Relatives will need to be supported and signs that their tolerance is being exceeded are usually an indication for further intervention, either hospitalisation or increase in drug dosage.

LITHIUM

Lithium is a monovalent metal ion which, administered as a variety of salts, has had a strange and stormy part to play in the history of therapeutics. Lithium was discovered in 1818 by Arfwedson following the analysis of the mineral petalite. For 80 years or so, lithium salts were used in the treatment of gout and diabetes but were ousted when more potent compounds became available. In the 1950's lithium was employed as a salt substitute in the U.S.A. in patients with cardiac failure on a salt-restricted diet. The effects were disastrous, several deaths occurring from encephalopathy and renal failure.

In psychiatry, lithium bromide was in use as a sedative around the turn of the century. The sedative effect was ascribed to the bromide ion but it is possible that the lithium ion also contributed to this effect in some patients. In 1949, Cade in Australia reported the use of lithium salts in the management of mania. With the introduction of reserpine and chlorpromazine in the mid 1950's, lithium seemed likely to be eclipsed in the treatment of mania. However, the drug found a Scandinavian champion, M. Schou, who proclaimed its value in the treatment of mania in 1957 and then, and perhaps more significantly yet more controversially, in 1968 in the prophylaxis of manic and depressive attacks. His claims made for the drug are striking: 'specific action in both mania and depression . . . action in mania without sedation . . . not action against manifest depression . . . in normal individuals results in only slight muscular tiredness'. (Schou, 1967).

Many reports followed suggesting the value of lithium both as a therapeutic and prophylactic agent.

In Britain we were shaken from our complacent acceptance of the drug when Blackwell and Shepherd (1968) entered the lists with a tilt at the new therapy suggesting that the evidence in support of the efficacy of the new drug in prophylaxis might not be soundly based. A healthy debate has developed and several controlled therapeutic trials have now been reported which appear to support a prophylactic action; the subject is by no means closed.

Lithium in Mania

Maggs 1963, published a double-blind cross-over trial comparing lithium carbonate with placebo in the treatment of 28 manic patients. Nine patients did not finish the trial, five of these because the acuteness of the symptomatology necessitated recourse to other drugs, two because of toxic reactions and two left hospital against advice.

The results in the remaining patients showed that lithium carbonate was superior to placebo in the management of mania, improvement occurring within two weeks of starting the drug.

The main disadvantage of the use of lithium salts alone in mania is that they do not act quickly enough to control excitement in severely disturbed patients. There is no clinical reason why lithium salts should not be combined with haloperidol or a phenothiazine or even E.C.T. in severely disturbed patients. Obviously, further trials studying such drug combinations are required.

In the management of mania with lithium carbonate precautions must be taken to exclude patients with a high risk of toxicity, e.g. those with cardiac or renal disease. The drug is then introduced at a high dose level, 500 mg three times daily. If possible, serum or plasma lithium levels are monitored at least weekly and the dose reduced when plasma levels rise to above 1.5 mEq per litre or when signs of toxicity supervene. This reduction is usually possible after a week and as symptoms recede then the dose is adjusted to a maintenance dose to maintain blood levels at 0.8 to 1.2 mEq per litre.

It is essential in the manic patient to ensure maintenance of adequate fluid and salt intake during lithium therapy.

The advantage of the drug in mania is that at least in some patients it appears to control the condition without the excessive sedation seen with the major tranquillisers.

Lithium in the prophylaxis of affective disorders

The major discussion as to the evidence for and against the value of lithium in prophylaxis has been debated at length and in the papers by Blackwell and Shepherd (1968) and Baastrup et al. (1970). In this section we shall concern ourselves with certain secondary considerations which follow once a decision to accept the value of lithium has been made.

Selection of patients. Most clinicians believe that a clear history of bipolar affective illness provides the best indication for the prophylactic use of lithium although they might accept that some patients with recurrent attacks of depression (unipolar) might also benefit.

A recent trial by Coppen *et al.*, has cast some doubt on this differential efficacy in patients with bipolar and unipolar disorders. In a multi-centre trial, 65 patients with recurrent affective illnesses were treated with lithium or placebo over periods of up to 112 weeks. Other drugs for treatment of mania or depression were prescribed as required. Eighty-six per cent of the patients on lithium were rated as showing little or no affective symptoms whereas only 8 per cent of the placebo groups showed such a response. No E.C.T. was given to the lithium group whilst 43 per cent of the placebo group required E.C.T. Lithium was at least as effective in preventing recurrences of unipolar illness as it was in bipolar cases.

The clinical impression that the main value of the drug is to be found in recurrent bipolar cases may be due to the fact that these patients are particularly likely to present with frequently relapsing illness as demonstrated by Angst et al. (1969). They studied 979 patients with relapsing affective illness followed through 2216 relapses; 'Bipolar manic-depressive, cyclothymic disorders initially have on average a two year cycle calculated from the beginning of one illness to the start of the next. Every subsequent cycle tends to be shorter than the previous one by 20 per cent. Recurrent depressions on the other hand have an initial cycle of seven years, the interval decreasing by 10 per cent with each relapse'.

Relapses on lithium. In an interesting article Aronoff and Epstein (1970) discuss relapses on lithium. They report the occurrence of treatment failures at times of a crisis reaction to stressful events, the relapse being associated with a rise in urinary 17-hydroxycorticosteroid excretion.

Therapeutic regime, toxicity and control of therapy

Preliminary clinical screening should detect patients with renal and cardiac disease who may be particularly vulnerable to toxic reactions on lithium.

In general, the aim of therapy is to maintain the maximum blood levels of lithium consistent with the absence of signs of toxicity. This means in most patients maintaining serum or plasma lithium levels between 0.8 and 1.2 mEq per litre. In our experience these blood levels are reached on doses of lithium carbonate varying between 500 and 1750 mg per day.

Symptoms and signs of toxicity

These have been conveniently listed by Melia (1970):
Diabetes insipidus-like symptoms: Polydipsia, Polyuria;
Nervous system: finger tremor; myoclonic twitching; localized dysthaesias; slurred speech; ataxia;
Gastro-intestinal system: nausea; vomiting; diarrhoea;
Miscellaneous: weight change, headaches, giddiness and palpitations.

Lithium therapy may give rise to goitre and thyroid dysfunction. Treatment with thyroxine is effective; lithium need not necessarily be discontinued, but usually is.

Severe toxicity is rare, usually being encountered at serum levels greater than 2.5 mEq per litre, but should be suspected when any of the following occur: drowsiness, steadily increasing to confusion and coma, with severe myoclonic jerks and epileptic attacks heralding the development of an encephalopathy. Renal damage may also be produced, as a condition resembling diabetes insipidus.

Treatment of mild toxicity is by simple withdrawal of the drug. Severe toxicity is best treated in a special poisons unit. In the presence of adequate renal function the basis of treatment is forced diuresis which must often be maintained for several days. Haemodialysis and peritoneal dialysis have been used with success.

Factors influencing serum lithium levels

Sedvall *et al.* (1970) examined the factors influencing serum levels of lithium in subjects receiving fixed regular doses of the drug. Serum levels were significantly correlated with renal lithium clearance. Steady state serum levels showed a highly significant correlation with the product of lithium clearance and body weight. Creatinine clearance showed no correlation with lithium clearance.

In our experience lithium clearance also declines with age so that we would be influenced by age and size in judging a starting dose which might vary from 250 mg per day in an elderly, frail, woman to 1000 mg in a large, young, healthy male.

REFERENCES

ABDULLAH, Y. H. & HAMADAH, K. (1970) 3-5-cyclic adenosine monophosphate in depression and mania. *Lancet*, **1**, 378–81.

ABRAHAM, K. (1911) Notes on the psychoanalytic investigation and treatment of manic-depressive insanity and allied conditions. In *Selected Paper on Psychoanalysis* New York: Basic Books, 1960.

AITKEN, R. C. B. (1969) Measurement of feelings using visual analogue scales. *Proceedings of the Royal Society of Medicine*, **62**, 989–993.

AITKEN, C. & ZEALLEY, A. K. (1970) Measurement of Moods. *British Journal of Hospital Medicine*, **3**, 215–224.

ANGST, J. (1966) Zur Aetiologie und Nosologie endogener depressiver psychosen. *Monographien aus dem Gesamtgebiet der Neurologie u. Psychiatrie*, Heft, **112**, Berlin.

ANGST, J. & PERRIS, C. (1968) Zur Nosologie endogener depressionen. Vergleich der Ergebnisse zweier untersuchungen. *Archiv für Psychiatrie und Nervenkrankheiten*, **210**, 373–86.

ANGST, J., DITTRICH, A. & GROF, P. (1969) Paper read at the Annual Meeting of the Royal Medico-Psychological Association, Plymouth, July, 1968. *Lancet*, 709–710.

ARONOFF, M. S. & EPSTEIN, R. S. (1970) Factors associated with poor response to lithium carbonate—A clinical study. *American Journal of Psychiatry*, **127:4**, 472.

ARONOFF, M. S., EVANS, R. G. & DURRELL, J. (1971) Effect of lithium salts on electrolyte metabolism. *Journal of Psychiatric Research*, **8**, 139–159.

ASHCROFT, G. W. (1969) Amine metabolism in brain. *Proceedings of the Royal Society of Medicine*, **62**, 1099–1101.

ASHCROFT, G. W. & SHARMAN, D. F. (1960) 5-Hydroxyindoles in human cerebrospinal fluids. *Nature (Lond.)*, **186**, 1050.

ASHCROFT, G. W., CRAWFORD, T. B. B., ECCLESTON, D., SHARMAN, D. F., McDOUGALL, E. J., STANTON, J. B. & BINNS, J. K. (1966) 5-hydroxyindole compounds in the cerebrospinal fluid of patients with psychiatric or neurological diseases. *Lancet*, **ii**, 1049–52.

ASHCROFT, G. W., ECCLESTON, D. & CRAWFORD, T. B. B. (1965) 5-hydroxyindole metabolism in rat brain: a study of intermediate metabolism using a technique of tryptophan loading. *Journal of Neurochemistry*, **12**, 483.

ASTRUP, C., FOSSUM, A. & HOLMBOE, R. (1959) Follow-up study of 270 patients with acute affective psychosis. *Acta Psychiatrica et neurologica scandinavica*, Suppl., **135**, 34.

AXELROD, J. (1966) Methylation reactions in the formation and metabolism of catecholamines and biogenic amines. *Pharmacological Review*, **18**, 95–113.

AXELROD, J. (1968) Hormones and electrolytes in the regulation of catecholamine synthesis. In *Adrenergic Neurotransmission*. Edited by G. W. Wolstenholme and M. O'Connor. London: Churchill.

BAASTRUP, P. C., POULSEN, J. C., SCHOU, M., THOMSEN, K. & AMDISEN, A. (1970) Prophylactic lithium; double-blind discontinuation in manic-depressive and recurrent depressive disorders. *Lancet*, **2**, 326.

BAER, L., DURRELL, J., BUNNEY, W. G., LEVY, B. S. & CARDON, P. V. (1969) Na^{22} retention and 17OHCS excretion in affective disorders: a preliminary report. *Journal of Psychiatric Research*, **6**, 289–98.

BECK, A. T., WARD, C. H., MENDELSON, U., MOCK, J. & ERBOUGH, J. (1961) An inventory for measuring depression. *Archives of General Psychiatry*, **4**, 561–571.

BECK, A. T., SETHI, B. B. & TUTHILL, R. W. (1963) Childhood bereavement and adult depression. *Archives of General Psychiatry*, **9**, 295–302.

BECK, A. T. (1967) Depression: Clinical, Experimental and Theoretical Aspects. London: Staples Press.

BECKER, J. (1960) Achievement related characteristics of manic-depressives. *Journal of Abnormal and Social Psychology* **60**, 334–339.

BLACKWELL, B. & SHEPHERD, M. (1968) Prophylactic lithium: another therapeutic myth? *Lancet*, **i**, 968.

BOWLBY, J. (1951) *Maternal care and mental health*. W.H.O. Publication.

BOWLBY, J. (1953) *Child care and the growth of love*. Penguin Books.

BROWN, F. (1961) Depressions and childhood bereavement. *Journal of Mental Science*, **107**, 754–777.

BROWN, B. L., SALWAY, J. G., ALBANO, J. D. M., HULLIN, R. P. & EKINS, R. P. (1972) Urinary excretion of cyclic AMP and manic-depressive psychosis. *British Journal of Psychiatry*, **120**, 405–8.

BUNNEY, W. E. and DAVIS, J. M. (1965) Norepinephrine in depressive reactions. *Archives of General Psychiatry*, **13**, 483.

BURCH, P. A. J. (1964) Manic-depressive psychosis; some new aetiological considerations. *British Journal of Psychiatry*, **110**, 808–817.

CADE, J. F. J. (1949) Lithium salts in the treatment of psychotic excitement. *Medical Journal of Australia*, **36**, 349–352.

CARNEY, M. W. P., ROTH, M. & GARSIDE, R. F. (1965) Diagnosis of depressive syndromes and prediction of E.C.T. response. *British Journal of Psychiatry*, **111**, 659–674.

CARROLL, B. J. & DODGE, J. (1971) L-tryptophan as an anti-depressant. *Lancet*, **i**, 915.

CARROLL, B. J., MARTIN, F. I. R. & DAVIES, B. (1968) Resistance to suppression by dexamethasone of plasma 11-OHCS levels in severe depressive illness. *British Medical Journal*, **3**, 285–7.

CARROLL, B. J., STEVEN, L., POPE, R. A. & DAVIES, B. (1969) Sodium transfer from plasma to C.S.F. in severe depressive illness. *Archives of General Psychiatry*, **21**, 77.

CLARKE, A. D. B. & CLARKE, A. (1954) Cognitive changes in the feeble-minded. *British Journal of Psychology*, **45**, 173–179.

CLOUSTON, T. S. (1904) Mental Diseases. 6th Edition. London: J. & A. Churchill.

COHEN, M. B., BAKER, G., COHEN, R. A. *et al.* (1954) An intensive study of 12 cases of manic depressive psychosis. *Psychiatry*, **17**, 103–137.

COPPEN, A. (1960) Abnormality of the blood-C.S.F. barrier of patients suffering from a depressive illness. *Journal of Neurology, Neurosurgery and Psychiatry*, **23**, 156.

COPPEN, A. (1966) The Marke-Nyman Temperament Scale. An English Translation. *British Journal of Medical Psychology*, **39**, 55–59.

COPPEN, A. (1967) The Biochemistry of affective disorders. *British Journal of Psychiatry*, **113**, 1237–64.

COPPEN, A., BROOKSBANK, B. W. L., NOGUERA, R. & WILSON, D. A. (1971) Cortisol in the cerebrospinal fluid of patients suffering from affective disorders. *Journal of Neurology, Neurosurgery and Psychiatry*, **34**, 432–5.

COPPEN, A. & METCALFE, M. (1965) Effect of a depressive illness on M.P.I. scores. *British Journal of Psychiatry*, **111**, 239.

COPPEN, A., NOGUERA, R., BAILEY. J., BURNS, B. H., SWANI, M. S., HARE, E. H., GARDNER, R. & MAGGS, R. (1971) Prophylactic lithium in affective disorders. *Lancet*, **ii**, 275–9.

COPPEN, A. & SHAW, D. M. (1963) Mineral metabolism and melancholia. *British Medical Journal*, **2**, 1439.

COPPEN, A., SHAW, D. M. & FARRELL, J. P. (1963) Potentiation of the antidepressive effect of monoamine oxidase inhibitor by tryptophan. *Lancet*, **i**, 79.

COPPEN, A., SHAW, D. M., HERZBERG, B. & MAGGS, R. (1967) Tryptophan in the treatment of depression. *Lancet*, **ii**, 1178–80.

CORRODI, H., FUXE, K., HÖKFELT, T. & SCHOU, M. (1967) The effect of lithium on cerebral monoamine neurons. *Psychopharmacologia (Berl.)* **11**, 345–53.

CURZON, G. (1969) Metabolic changes in depression. *Lancet*, **i**, 257.

CURZON, G. & BRIDGES, P. K. (1970) Tryptophan metabolism in depression. *Journal of Neurology, Neurosurgery and Psychiatry*, **33**, 698–704.

CURZON, G. & GREEN, A. R. (1968) In Curzon, 1969.

DELAY, J., PICHOT, P., LEMPERIERE, T. & MILANSE, R. (1963) La Nosologie des Etats Depressifs: rapports entre l'étologie et la sémiologie. Resultats du Questionnaire de Beck. *Encéphale*, **52**, 497–505.

DENCKER, S. J., MALM, M., ROOS, B. E. & WERDINIUS, B. (1966) Acid monoamine metabolites of C.S.F. in mental depression and mania. *Journal of Neurochemistry*, **13**, 1545.

DENNEHY, E. (1966) Childhood bereavement and psychiatric illness. *British Journal of Psychiatry*, **112**, 1049.

DENNIS, K. J. & JEFFREY, J. d'A. (1968) Oral contraceptives and depression. *Lancet*, **ii**, 454.

DEWHURST, W. G. (1969) Amines and abnormal mood. *Proceedings of the Royal Society of Medicine*, **62**, 1102–7.

DILMAN, V. M. (1971) Age-associated elevation of hypothalamic threshold to feedback control and its role in development, ageing and disease. *Lancet*, **i**, 1211–19.

ECCLESTON, D., LOOSE, R., PULLAR, I. A. & SUGDEN, R. F. (1970) Exercise and urinary excretion of cyclic AMP. *Lancet*, **i**, 612–3.

ELITHORN, A., BRIDGES, P. K., LOBBAN, M. C. & TREDRE, B. E. (1966) Observations on some diurnal rhythms in depressive illness. *British Medical Journal*, **2**, 1620–33.

ENGELHARD, J. L. B. (1912) On puerperal psychoses and the influence of the gestation period on psychiatric and neurological disease already in existence. *Zeitschrift für Geburtshilfe und Gynäkologie*, **70**, 727.

EYSENCK, H. J. & CLARIDGE, G. S. (1962) The position of hysterics and dysthymics in a two-dimensional framework of personality description. *Journal of Abnormal and Social Psychology*, **64**, 46–55.

EYSENCK, H. J. & EYSENCK, S. B. G. (1964) *Manual of the Eysenck Personality Inventory.* Univ. London Press.

EYSENCK, H. J. (1970) The classification of depressive illness. *British Journal of Psychiatry*, **117**, 241–250.

FENICHEL, O. (1945) *Psychoanalytic theory of Neurosis*. New York: W. W. Morton and Co. Inc.

DA FONSECA, A. F. (1959) *Analise Heredo-Clinica das Perturbacoes Affectivas*. Faculdada de Medicina, Oporto.

FORREST, A. D., FRASER, R. H. & PRIEST, R. G. (1965) Environmental factors in depressive illness. *British Journal of Psychiatry*, **111**, 243–253.

FOTHERBY, K., ASHCROFT, G. W., AFFLECK, J. W. & FORREST, A. D. (1963) Studies on sodium transfer and 5-hydroxyindoles in depressive illness. *Journal of Neurology, Neurosurgery and Psychiatry*, **26**, 71–3.

FOULDS, G. A., (1965) *Personality and Personal Illness*. London: Tavistock Publ.

FREUD, S., (1917) Mourning and Melancholia. In *Collected Papers* London: Hogarth Press.

FRIEDMAN, A. S., COWITZ, B., COHEN, H. W. & BRANIC, K. S. (1963) Syndrome and themes of psychotic depression. A factor analysis. *Archives of General Psychiatry*, **9**, 504–509.

FRIZEL, D., COPPEN, A. & MARKS, V. (1969) Plasma magnesium and calcium in depression. *British Journal of Psychiatry*, **115**, 1375–7.

GARATTINI, S. & VALZELLI, L. (1965) *Serotonin*, Amsterdam: Elsevier.

GARMANY, G. (1958) Depressive states: their aetiology and treatment. *British Medical Journal*, **2**, 341–346.

GIBBONS, J. L. (1960) Total body sodium and potassium in depressive illness. *Clinical Science*, **19**, 133.

GIBBONS, J. L. (1963) Electrolytes and depressive illness. *Postgraduate Medical Journal*, **39**, 19.

GIBBONS, J. L. (1968) Biochemistry of depressive illness. In *Recent developments in affective disorders*. pp. 55–64. Edited by A. Coppen and A. Walk, R.M.P.A. Publ.

GIBBONS, J. L. & McHUGH, P. (1962) Plasma cortisol in depressive illness. *Journal of Psychiatric Research*, **1**, 162.

GIBBONS, J. L., MAXWELL, H. & WILCOX, D. (1960) An endocrine study of depressive illness. *Journal of Psychosomatic Research*, **5**, 32.

GILLESPIE, R. D. (1926) Discussion. *British Medical Journal*, **2**, 872.

GILLESPIE, R. D. (1930) The clinical differentiation of types of depression. *Medical World*, **32**.

GLEN, A. I. M., ONGLEY, G. C. & ROBINSON, K. (1968) Diminished membrane transport in manic-depressive psychosis and recurrent depression. *Lancet*, **ii**, 241.

GRANVILLE-GROSSMAN, K. L. (1968) The early environment in affective disorder. In *Recent developments in affective disorders*. Edited by A. Coppen and A. Walk, R.M.P.A. Publ.

GREGORY, I. (1959) An analysis of family data on 1000 patients admitted to a Canadian Mental Hospital. *Acta Genetica (Basel)* **9**, 54–96.

GREGORY, I. (1962) Selected personal and family data on 400 psychiatric inpatients. *American Journal of Psychiatry*, **119**, 379–403.

GRINKER, R. R., MILLER, J., SABSHIN, M., NUNN, R. & NUNNALLY, J. J. (1961) The phenomena of the depressions. New York: Paul B. Hucker Ltd.

HAMILTON, M. & WHITE, J. M. (1959) Clinical syndromes in depressive states. *Journal of Mental Science*, **105**, 985–998.

HAMILTON, M. (1960) A Rating scale for depression. *Journal of Neurology, Neurosurgery and Psychiatry*, **23**, 56–62.

HAMILTON, M. (1967) Development of a rating scale for primary depressive illness. *British Journal of Social and Clinical Psychology*, **6**, 278–296.

HENDERSON, D. & GILLESPIE, R. D. (1956) *A textbook of Psychiatry for students and practitioners.* London: Oxford. Univ. Press.

HILL, D. (1968) Depression: Disease, reaction or posture. *American Journal of Psychiatry,* **125,** 37–49.

HOLZBAUER, M. & VOGT, M. (1956) Depression by reserpine of the noradrenaline concentration in the hypothalamus of the rat. *Journal of Neurochemistry,* **1,** 8–11.

HOPKINSON, G. (1964) A genetic study of affective illness in patients over 50. *British Journal of Psychiatry,* **110,** 244–54.

JANSSON, B. (1964) Psychic insufficiencies associated with childbearing. *Acta Psychologica Scandinavica,* **39,** Suppl. 172.

JENNER, F. A., GOODWIN, J. C., SHERIDAN, M., TAUBER, I. J. & LOBBAN, M. C. (1968) The effect of an altered time regime on biological rhythms in a 48-hour periodic psychosis. *British Journal of Psychiatry,* **114,** 215–24.

KALLMAN, F. J. (1954) Genetic principles in manic-depressive psychosis. In *Depression.* Edited by P. H. Hoch and J. Zubin, New York: Grume and Stratton.

KAY, D. W. K., GARSIDE, R. T., BEAMISH, P. & ROY, J. R. (1969) Endogenous and neurotic syndromes of depression. A factor analytic study of 104 cases. Clinical Features. *British Journal of Psychiatry,* **115,** 377–388.

KAY, D. W. K., ROTH, M. & HOPKINS, B. (1955) Affective disorders in the senium (1) Their association with organic cerebral degeneration. *Journal of Mental Science,* 101–316.

KELLNER, R. & SHEFFIELD, B. F. (1968) The use of self-rating scales in a single patient. Multiple cross-over trial. *British Journal of Psychiatry,* **114,** 193–196.

KELLY, D., GUIRGUIS, W., FROMMER, E., MITCHELL-HEGGS, N. & SARGANT, W. (1970) Treatment of phobic states with antidepressants. A Retrospective Study of 246 patients. *British Journal of Psychiatry,* **116,** 387.

KENDELL, R. E. (1968) *The classification of depressive illnesses.* Maudsley Monogr. No 18, London.

KESSELL, A. (1968) The borderlands of the depressive states. *British Journal of Psychiatry,* **114,** 1135.

KILOH, L. G. & GARSIDE, R. F. (1963) The independence of neurotic depression and endogenous depression. *British Journal of Psychiatry,* **109,** 451–463.

KLEIN, M. (1934) *Contributions to psychoanalysis.* pp. 282–310. London: Hogarth Press. 1948.

KRAEPELIN, E. (1921) *Manic-depressive insanity and paranoia.* 8th edn. Transl. by Mary Barclay, Edinburgh: Livingstone.

KRAINES, S. H. (1957) *Mental depressives and their treatment.* New York: MacMillan.

KREITMAN, N., SAINSBURY, P., PEARCE, K. & COSTA, A. W. D. (1965) Hypochondriasis and depression in out-patients at a General Hospital. *British Journal of Psychiatry,* **111,** 607.

LAPIN, I. P. & OXENKRUG, G. F. (1969) Intensification of the central serotonergic processes as a possible determinant of the thymoleptic effect, *Lancet,* **i,** 132.

LEONHARD, K., KORFF, I. & SCHULZ, H. (1962) Die Temperamente in den Familien der monopolaren und bipolaren phasischen Psychosen. *Psychiatria et neurologia (Basel),* **143,** 416–434.

LEONHARD, K. (1959) Abteilung der endogenen psychosen. Berlin, 2nd ed.

LEWIS, A. (1934) Melancholia: A clinical survey of depressive states. *Journal of Mental Science,* **80,** 277–378.

LEWIS, A. (1936) Melancholia: A prognostic study. *Journal of Mental Science,* **82,** 488–558.

LEWIS, A. (1938)   States of Depression. Their clinical and aetiological differentiations. *British Medical Journal*, **2,** 875–878.

LINDEMANN, E. (1944)   Symptomatology and management of acute grief. *American Journal of Psychiatry*, **101,** 141.

LORR, M. (1954)   Rating Scales. *Psychological Bulletin*, **51,** 119.

LUBIN, B. (1965)   Adjective check-lists for measurements of depression. *Archives of General Psychiatry*, **12,** 57–62.

LUNDQUIST, G. (1965)   Olika typen au psykisk depression. *Svenska Läkartidningen*, **62,** 1991–1994.

MAAS, J. W., FAWCETT, J. & DEKIRMENJIAN, H. (1968)   3-methoxy-4-hydroxy-phenylglycol (MHPG) excreted in depressive states. *Archives of General Psychiatry*, **19,** 129–134.

MAGGS, R. (1963)   Treatment of manic illness with lithium carbonate. *British Journal of Psychiatry*, **109,** 56.

MAPOTHER, E. (1926)   Manic-depressive psychosis. *British Medical Journal*, **2,** 872–876.

McCLELLAND, D. C., ATKINSON, J. W., CLARK, R. A. & LOWELL, E. L. (1953)   The achievement motive. New York: Appleton Century Crofts.

McFARLAND, R. A. & GOLDSTEIN, H. (1939)   The biochemistry of manic-depressive psychosis: a review. *American Journal of Psychiatry*, **98,** 21–58.

MARRIS, P. (1958)   *Widows and their families*, London: Routledge and Kegan Paul Ltd.

MASTERS, A. B. (1967)   The distribution of blood groups in psychiatric illness. *British Journal of Psychiatry*, **113,** 1309.

MAYER-GROSS, W. (1954)   The diagnosis of depression. *British Medical Journal*, **2,** 948–950.

MAYO, P. R. (1967)   Some psychological changes associated with improvement in depression. *British Journal of Social and Clinical Psychiatry*, **6,** 63–68.

MELIA, P. I. (1970)   Prophylactic lithium in recurrent affective disorders: A four-year study. *Journal of the Irish Medical Association*, **33,** no. 400, 353–357.

METCALFE, M. (1968)   The personality of depressive patients. In *Recent Developments in Affective Disorders*. Edited by A. Coppen and A. Walk, R.M.P.A. Publ.

METCALFE, M. & GOLDMAN, E. (1965)   Validation of an inventory for measuring depression. *British Journal of Psychiatry*, **111,** 240–242.

MEYER, A. (1922)   Inter-relations of the Domain of Neuropsychiatry. *Archives of Neurology and Psychiatry*, **15.**

MUNRO, A. (1965)   Childhood parent loss in a psychiatrically normal population. *British Journal of Preventive and Social Medicine*, **19,** 69–79.

NISTICO, G., SCAPAGNINI, U. & PREZIOSI, P. (1969)   Metabolic changes in depression. *Lancet*, **ii,** 159.

NILSSON, Å. & ALMGREN, P.-E. (1970)   Para-natal emotional adjustment. A prospective investigation of 165 women. *Acta psychologica Scandinavica*, **46,** Suppl. 220.

NYMAN, G. E. (1956)   Variations in personality. *Acta Psychiatrica*, Suppl., 107.

NYMAN, G. E. & MARKE, S. (1962)   Sjöbring's Differentiella Psykologi (with an English summary) Lund: Gleerups.

O'CONNOR, N. (1956)   The evidence for the permanently disturbing effects of mother-child separation. *Acta Psychologica*, **12,** 174–191.

ORLANSKY, H. (1949)   Infant care and personality. *Psychological Bulletin*, **46,** 1–48.

OLTMAN, J. E., McGARRY & FRIEDMAN, M. D. (1952)   Parental deprivation and the broken home in dementia praecox and other mental disorders. *American Journal of Psychiatry*, **108,** 658–694.

PARKER, J. B., MEILE, A. & SPIELBERGER, C. D. (1961) Frequency of blood types in a homogenous group of manic-depressive patients. *Journal of Mental Science*, **107**, 936.

PARKES, C. M. (1964) Recent bereavement as a cause of mental illness. *British Journal of Psychiatry*, **110**, 195–204.

PARKES, C. M. (1965) Bereavement of mental illness, Parts I and II, *British Journal of Medical Psychology*, **38**, 1.

PAUL, M. I., CRAMER, H. & BUNNEY, W. E. (1971) Urinary adenosine $3^1 5^1$-monophosphate in the switch process from depression to mania. *Science*, **171**, 300–3.

PEARSON, I. B. & JENNER, F. A. (1971) Lithium in psychiatry. *Nature*, **232**, 532–3.

PEREZ-CRUET, J., TAGLIAMONTE, A., TAGLIAMONTE, P. & GESSA, G. L. (1971) Stimulation of serotonin synthesis by lithium. *Journal of Pharmacology and experimental Therapeutics*, **178**, 325–30.

PERRIS, C. (1966) A study of bipolar/manic-depressive and unipolar/recurrent depressive psychosis. *Acta Psychiatrica Scandinavica* Suppl., **194**, 42.

PITTS, F. N., MEYER, J., BROOKS, M. & WINOKUR, G. (1965) Adult psychiatric illness assessed for childhood parental loss and psychiatric illness in family members. *American Journal of Psychiatry*, **121**, 1.

PLATMAN, S. R., FIEVE, R. R. & PIERSON, R. N. (Jr.) (1970) Effect of mood and lithium carbonate on total body potassium. *Archives of General Psychiatry*, **22**, 297–300.

PLETSCHER, A., SHORE, P. A. & BRODIE, B. B. (1956) Seratonin as a mediator of reserpine action in brain. *Journal of Pharmacology*, **116**, 84–89.

POLLITT, J. D., (1965) Suggestions for a physiological classification of depression. *British Journal of Psychiatry*, **111**, 489.

POST, F. (1962) *The significance of affective symptoms in old age*. Maudsley Monograph, 10, London: Oxford Univ. Press.

PRICE, J. (1968) The genetics of depressive behaviour. In *Recent Developments in Affective Illness*. Edited by A. Coppen and A. Walk, R.M.P.A. Publ., Kent: Headley Bros.

PROTHEROE, C. (1969) Puerperal psychoses: a long-term study 1927–1961. *British Journal of Psychiatry*, **115**, 9–30.

RAMSDEN, E. N. (1970) Cyclic AMP in depression and mania. *Lancet*, **ii**, 108.

REICH, T., CLAYTON, P. & WINOKUR, G. (1969) Family history studies: V. The genetics of mania. *American Journal of Psychiatry*, **125**, 1358.

ROBINSON, D. S., DAVIS, J. M., NILES, A., COLBURN, R. W., DAVIS, J. N., BOURNE, H. R., BUNNEY, W. E., SHAW, D. M. & COPPEN, A. J. (1972) Ageing, monoamines and monoamine oxidase levels. *Lancet*, **i**, 290–1.

ROSANOFF, A. J. (1931) Sex-linked inheritance in mental deficiency. *American Journal of Psychiatry*, **2**, 289–297.

ROSANOFF, A. J., HANDY, L. M. & PLESSET, I. R. (1935) The aetiology of manic-depressive syndromes with special reference to their occurrence in twins. *American Journal of Psychiatry*, **91**, 725–762.

ROSE, D. P., (1966) The influence of oestrogens on tryptophan metabolism in man. *Clinical Science*, **31**, 265–72.

ROSE, D. P. & BRAIDMAN, I. P. (1970) Oral contraceptives, depression and amino acid metabolism. *Lancet*, **i**, 1118.

ROSENTHAL, S. H. (1968) The involutional depressive syndrome. *American Journal of Psychiatry*, **124**, Suppl. 21–35.

ROSS, T. A. (1926) Discussion on manic-depressive psychosis. *British Medical Journal*, **2**, 877–878.

ROTH, M. (1959) The phobic anxiety-depersonalisation syndrome. *Proceedings of the Royal Society of Medicine*, **52,** 587.

SACHAR, E. J., HELLMAN, L., FUKUSHIMA, D. K. & GALLAGHER, T. F. (1970) Cortisol production in depressive illness. *Archives of General Psychiatry*, **23,** 289–298.

SAINSBURY, P. (1968) Suicide and depression. In *Recent Developments in Affective Disorders*. Symposium. Edited by A. Coppen and A. Walk. Brit. J. Psychiat. Special Pub. No. 2.

SANDS, D. E. (1947): Paper read to the International Conference of Physicians, London. (Quoted by Partridge, M., (1949) Some reflections on the nature of affective disorders arising from the results of prefrontal leucotomy. *Journal of Mental Science*, **95,** 795–825).

SARGANT, W. W. & SLATER, E. (1946) *Physical Methods of Treatment in Psychiatry*. Edinburgh: Livingstone.

SCHANBERG, S. M., SCHILDKRAUT, S. J., BREESE, G. R. & KOPIN, I. J. (1968) Metabolism of noradrenaline-H^3 in rat brain. Identification of conjugated 3-methoxy-4-hydroxyphenylglycol as the major metabolite. *Biochemical Pharmacology*, **17,** 247.

SCHANBERG, S. M., SCHILDKRAUT, S. J. & KOPIN, I. J. (1967) The effects of psychoactive drugs on norepinephrine-^{3}H metabolism in brain. *Biochemical Pharmacology*, **16,** 393–9.

SCHILDKRAUT, S. J. & KETY, S. S. (1967) Biogenic amines and emotion. *Science*, **156,** 21.

SCHOU, M. (1957) Biology and pharacology of the lithium ion. *Pharmacological Review*, **9,** 17–58.

SCHOU, M. (1967) Lithium, sodium and manic-depressive psychosis. Molecular basis of some aspects of mental activity. Edited by Walaas, Pub. Academic Press, 457.

SCHOU, M. (1968) Lithium in psychiatric therapy and prophylaxis. *Journal of Psychiatric Research*, **6,** 67–95.

SCHULZ, B. (1951) *Archiv für Psychiatrie und Nervenkrankheiten*. Berlin, **186,** 560.

SEDVALL, G., PETTERSSON, V. & FYRO, B. (1970) Individual differences in serum levels of lithium in human subjects receiving fixed doses of lithium carbonate. Relation to renal lithium clearance and body weight. *Pharmacologia Clinica*, **2,** 231.

SHAPIRO, M. B. (1961) A method of measuring psychological changes specific to the individual psychiatric patient. *British Journal of Medical Psychology*, **34,** 151–155.

SJÖBRING, H. (1958) *Strukturoch utreckling*. Lund: Gleerups,

SKEELS, H. M., UPDEGRALF, R., WELLMAN, B. L. & WILLIAMS, H. M. (1938) Studies in child welfare. Iowa Child Development Centre.

SKEELS, H. M. & HARMS, I. (1948) Children with inferior social histories: their mental development in adoptive homes. *Journal of Genetic Psychology*, **72,** 283–294.

SLATER, E. T. O. (1936) The inheritance of manic-depressive insanity. *Proceedings of the Royal Society of Medicine*, **29,** 39–58.

SLATER, E. T. O. (1953) Psychotic and neurotic illnesses in twins. M.R.C. Special Report Series, No. 278, London: H.M.S.O.

SPITZ, R. A. (1946) Anaclitic depression. In *The psychoanalytic study of the child*. Vol. 2. New York: Inter. Univ. Press.

STENGEL, E., ZEITLYN, B. B. & RAYNER, E. H. (1958) Post-operative psychoses. *Journal of Mental Science*, **104,** 389–402.

STENSTEDT, A. (1952) A study of manic-depressive psychosis, clinical, social and genetic investigations. *Acta Psychiatrica Scandinavica*, Suppl. 7.

STENSTEDT, A. (1959) Involutional melancholia. An etiologic, clinical and social study of endogenous depression in later life, with special reference to genetic factors. *Acta psychiatrica et neurologica Scandinavica*, **34**, Suppl. 127.

SUTHERLAND, E. W. (1970) On the biological role of the cyclic AMP. *Journal of the American Medical Association*, **214**, 1281–8.

TAIT, A. C., HARPER, J. & McCLATCHEY, W. T. (1957) Initial psychiatric illness in involutional women. *Journal of Mental Science*, **103**, 132–145.

TANNA, V. L. & WINOKUR, G. (1968) A study of association of linkage of ABO blood types and primary affective disorder. *British Journal of Psychiatry*, **114**, 1175.

TOD, E. D. M. (1964) Puerperal depression: A prospective epidemiological study. *Lancet*, **ii**, 1264.

UDENFRIEND, S. (1968) Physiological regulation of noradrenaline biosynthesis. In *Adrenergic Neurotransmission*. Edited by G. W. Wolstenholme and M. O'Connor, London: Churchill.

WEST, E. & DALLY, P. J. (1959) Effects of Iproniazid in depressive syndromes. *British Medical Journal*, **i**, 1491.

WILK, S., SHOPSIN, B., GERSHON, S. & SUHL, M. (1972) Cerebrospinal fluid levels of MHPG in affective disorders. *Nature*, **235**, 440–1.

WINOKUR, G., CLAYTON, P., REICH, T. (1969) Manic-depressive illness. St. Louis: C. V. Mosby Co.

WINOKUR, G. & PITTS, F. N. (Jr) (1965) A family history study of prevalences, sex differences, and possible genetic factors. *Journal of Psychiatric Research*, **3**, 113.

WINOKUR, G. & TANNA, V. (1969) Possible role of X-linked dominant factor in manic depressive disease. *Diseases of the Nervous System*. **30**, 89.

WINSTON, F. (1969) Oral contraceptives and depression. *Lancet*, **ii**, 377.

WOOTTON, B. (1959) Social science and social pathology. London.

WURTMAN, R. J., CHOU, C. & ROSE, C. M. (1967) Daily rhythm in tyrosine concentration in human plasma: persistence on low protein diets. Science, **158**, 660.

ZHELYASKOV, D. K., LEVITT, M. & UDENFRIEND, S. (1968) Tryptophan derivatives as inhibitors of tyrosine hydroxylase *in vivo* and *in vitro*. *Molecular Pharmacology*, **4**, 445.

ZUNG, W. W. K. (1965) A self rating depression scale. *Archives of General Psychiatry*, **12**, 63–70.

J

Chapter X

SCHIZOPHRENIA

J. R. Smythies

DEFINITION AND CLASSIFICATION

Nowhere is the difficulty of defining and classifying a disease solely on the basis of symptoms better exemplified than in the case of schizophrenia. This is generally recognized as a disease presenting with fairly characteristic disorders of perception, thinking, ideation, emotional reactions, volition and behaviour, but the limits of the process have remained decidedly fuzzy. There is a group of patients whom most psychiatrists in any one country would agree are schizophrenics. There are other groups variously labelled as 'atypical', 'pseudoneurotic' or 'schizophrenic reaction types', whom some psychiatrists would regard as suffering from types of schizophrenia and others as suffering from different disorders. When psychiatrists in one country are compared with psychiatrists in other countries, even greater disparities are found. For example, in a recent study using videotaped interviews, it was found that the same patients were regularly diagnosed as 'schizophrenic' by American psychiatrists and as 'affective disorders' by British psychiatrists. Many patients diagnosed as 'schizophrenic' by American psychiatrists would be classed as personality disorders by British psychiatrists. Thus schizophrenia not only shades off into a vague hinterland of 'atypical schizophrenias' in one direction, but it also merges imperceptibly with manic-depressive psychosis and with schizoid personality in other directions. However, this state of affairs is inevitable, given that nothing is known about the aetiology of the condition. The history of medicine has made it plain that all classifications based merely on symptoms are discarded as soon as systems based on aetiology become available. Therefore schemes of classification based on symptoms, or on patterns of behaviour, should be regarded as temporary expedients. Nevertheless it is empirically useful to make certain clinical distinctions based on different patterns of symptoms and behaviour in different cases. For the pattern of symptoms is often more important than the occurrence of any particular symptom in the clinical assessment of the case. Certain symptoms are practically pathogonomic of schizophrenia—such as the characteristic thought disorder—but these do not necessarily have to be present in order to make the diagnosis. Other symptoms, such as hallucinations, are commonly seen in schizophrenia, as well as in other psychiatric conditions.

Symptoms

Perception

In the past attention has been paid in this field principally to the hallucinations characteristic of psychosis, reflecting the commonly-held belief that seeing things that are not there is the first sign of insanity. However, the changes in perception, particularly in acute and florid cases, are more extensive and subtle than this. All manner of perceptual distortions and illusions may be found. Colours may become more intense, and various illusions of shape, size, position and movement may occur, as so vividly presented in 'The Cabinet of Dr Caligari'. More complex illusions involve the alteration of perceived objects—for example the faces of people around may change to those of pigs and other animals. Complex distortions of perception may occur in other sensory modalities. Finally, not only the more mechanical aspects of perception but the meaning and significance of objects may become distorted. Normally neutral objects may take on qualities of menace and horror, or of divine beauty and import. Very similar changes may be experienced by normal people under the influence of drugs like LSD and mescaline.

Experimental investigations of these perceptual changes include the finding by Weckowicz and Blewett (1959) that perceptual constancy and depth perception is often diminished so that schizophrenics tend to see the world as flat—in two dimensions much like the world depicted by fourteenth century artists. The hallucinations themselves may be in any sensory modality. In acute attacks visual, somatic, auditory and olfactory hallucinations may occur but in chronic cases auditory hallucinations are the rule. Their content often carries bizarre, fantastic, religious or sexual themes. The 'voices' are usually abusive, threatening or malignant and are classically described as talking about the patient who is addressed in the third person, whereas the 'voices' of severe depressive illness commonly talk to the patient in the second person. The somatic hallucinations are particularly distressing. All manner of weird, unpleasant and frequently indescribable bodily sensations may be experienced. These are a fertile basis of secondary delusion formation. Strange tinglings, vibrations and creeping sensations in the skin tend to lead to ideas of being played upon by rays manipulated by malignant neighbours. Dragging and gnawing sensations in the viscera may lead to ideas of being devoured by rats or to strange transmutations of the guts into lead pipe. These experiences may be more readily understood by the psychiatrist if he has experienced similar sensations under LSD or some similar drug. The experience of feeling one's head turning into a sheet of glass has to be experienced to be fully understood.

Our normal perception of the world around us, that we take so much for granted, depends on the precise functioning of complex inter-related cerebral activities. Disruptions of this system by the schizo-phrenic process leads to widespread disorders in all facets of perception.

Thinking

Many, but not all, schizophrenics show abnormalities in speech and language. In the past clinicians were content to describe these changes and wrote accounts familiar to all of a general woolliness of concepts, thought block, neologisms, a fracturing of grammar and syntax and the replacement of logical speech by speech based on chance associations, punning, rhyming and various symbolical associations—as in the prose of Finnegan's Wake—ending up in a jumbled word salad. It was widely considered that schizophrenics suffered from a defect of 'abstract' thinking. However, recently more attention has been paid to trying to determine why schizophrenics think and speak in this way. Cameron (1944) put forward the idea that the basic fault was 'over-inclusive thinking'. That is that schizophrenics are unable to conserve conceptual boundaries so that ideas remote from the central concept become incorporated into it. Payne and Hewlett (1960) devised psychological methods to test this hypothesis and they showed that approximately one-half of the schizophrenics showed over-inclusive thinking whereas the thought processes of the other half showed abnormal retardation. However, later studies by McGhie and his colleagues (1964) showed that hypomanic and obsessional patients gave higher over-inclusive scores than did schizophrenics and Hawks (1964) was unable to replicate Payne's results. Gathercole (1965) suggested that Payne's tests measured fluency of association rather than over-inclusive think-ing.

At about this time Bannister (1960, 1962) devised further tests for schizophrenic thought disorder based on Kelly's Repertory Grid Technique. This measures the degree of substantial correlation between concepts and Bannister was able to show that this test successfully discriminated between thought-disordered schizophrenics, other psychi-atric patients and normal controls. This work led him to make sugges-tions as to the optimum type of environment for patients with thought disorder (Bannister and Salmon, 1967). Recently it has been suggested (Payne, 1961) that some aspects of schizophrenic thought disorder are secondary to a primary defect of attention. Weckowicz and Blewlett (1959) suggested that 'The abnormalities of thinking and perception in schizophrenic patients could be described as an inability to attend selectively or to select relevant information . . .' Venables (1963) and Venables and Wing (1962) on the basis of their studies conclude that '. . . a broadened level of attention which causes the patient to be overloaded by sensory impressions from the environment.' was responsible for the condition. McGhie (1967) has carried out extensive investigations to test the effect of distracting stimuli on the performance of motor tasks by schizophrenic patients. He found that hebephrenic, but not paranoid, cases '. . . are distinguished by their inability to screen out irrelevant extraneous information and that this failure of the filtering mechanism is particularly evident where the situation demanded the rapid processing and short term shortage of information.' A second apparent abnormality in schizophrenics is an inability to '. . . utilize the transitional bonds between words which normally facilitate our perception of the passage as an organized whole. By processing speech in single words rather than in phrase units, they require to make decisions about what is being said at the rate of three to four per second . . .' whereas such decisions can normally only be taken with comfort at a rate of one per second.

Following up the impression of many psychiatrists that 'nuclear' schizophrenia is more akin in many of its manifestations to an organic dementia than to a functional illness, McGhie (1967) repeated his distraction tests and found a clear correspondence between the hebephrenic and cases of arteriosclerotic dementia. Other workers have pointed out similarities between the thinking of brain damaged cases and nuclear schizophrenics (Feinberg and Mercer, 1960; Weckowicz, 1960). McGhie has linked his findings to Broadbent's (1958) model of the brain's mechanisms for processing information. Basically he suggests that there is a single decision making channel of limited capacity in the brain. This is normally protected by a filtering mechanism which passes on only a small proportion of the sensory inflow—i.e. that part which is relevant. This mechanism may break down in schizophrenia, and so the decision making channel is bombarded with a 'booming, buzzing confusion' with which it is unable to cope. This formulation has led to practical proposals as to how the environment in which schizophrenics live should be structured.

Other factors also appear to be involved in schizophrenic thought disorder. Forrest et al. (1969) have studied the symbol referent connections in schizophrenia. They note that such speech is characterized (1) by its wandering quality—open-ended questions result in a free-associative monologue and (2) the personalized use of symbols so that the usual symbol-referent tie is distorted. They conclude, on the basis of a paired question test, that the disturbed speech of adult schizophrenics appears to be related to being reared in families in which communication was often devious and contradictory. Furthermore this type of speech could have a defensive property in that it enables patients who have been subject to years of double bind—in which every possible response is 'wrong' and therefore liable to be punished—effectively to disguise the meaning of what they are saying.

Ideation

Delusions are common in all types of schizophrenia and have been classified into 'primary', which arise in the patient's mind apparently *de nove*, and 'secondary' which are partially understandable reactions to the disorder of perception experienced by the patient. Common themes are religious, persecutory, jealousy, sexual, magical and grandiose, all coloured by the usual schizophrenic attributes of 'bizarre' and 'weird'. The content also depends to a considerable degree on cultural factors. The shift from X-ray to atomic machines as the origins of the malign influences is well known. Klaf and Hamilton (1961) compared the delusions of 200 patients admitted to Bethlem between the years 1853 to 1862 and another 200 in the years 1950 to 1960. The latter exhibited only one third the rate of religious delusions but twice the rate of sexual delusions when compared with the former.

Other common delusions are (1) *passivity feelings*—the belief that the patient is being controlled or influenced by others often by magical or telepathic means; (2) *ideas of reference*—the belief that events which really have nothing to do with the patient, nevertheless refer to him in some obscure and sinister way; (3) *ideas of thought control and thought insertion*—in which malignant persons are putting thoughts in and out of the patient's mind.

Emotional reactions

Episodes of elation and depression are common in certain cases of schizophrenia—particularly so in acute cases—but the most typical emotional change is 'flattening of effect'. This affects mainly the more civilized, higher emotions and the more primitive emotional responses such as rage, fear, hilarity and eroticism may remain intact longer. In early cases rapid fluctuations of mood may occur and sudden bursts of elation, ecstasy, panic and despair may overwhelm the patient and render normal behaviour impossible. A further change typical of schizophrenia is *incongruity of affect* in which inappropriate emotions are evoked by particular experiences. This erosion of warm human feelings and sympathy results in the marked inability of these patients to form or maintain normal human contacts and relationships. This is often described by the psychiatrist in terms of a 'glass wall' shutting the patient off from the world and exemplifying the feeling of chilly distance imparted by the patient.

Volition

This varies from indecisiveness and the inability to follow a planned course of action—or even any action at all—to a stubborn negativism in which the patient refuses to comply with any requests. Furthermore the patient often feels as though his actions were being controlled by some external agency. As one said 'It's peculiar, it's just as if I was being steered around, by whom or what I don't know.' These feelings may be at the root of many of the delusions of control and influence. The basic fault may be that certain subconscious mechanisms in the brain, that normally act in subserviance to the main central decision making channel (conscious mechanism) may break away from this and start to control the behaviour emitted. The conscious channel then transmutes this into control by external agencies.

Behaviour

Normal people take the order and form of their everyday world of consciousness very much for granted and do not normally pause to consider on just how complex and vulnerable a mechanism all this depends. Under the dualistic theories that still dominate our everyday thinking, disorders of the brain are equated with obvious conditions like epileptic fits, strokes and dementia. But the more subtle disorders of the brain, in which the very texture of reality becomes warped and changed, are explained in dualistic terms as disorders of the 'psyche'. However, it now seems clear that an explanation for all forms of psychological disturbance can be given, if still only in outline, in terms of the disturbances of brain function underlying them. This formulation does not require us to take any definite position in the argument over the nature of the brain-mind relationship. A monistic *causal* theory is quite compatible with a dualistic *epistemological* theory of mind-brain relationships. That is to say it is only necessary to assert that the events in consciousness as experienced by the subject (or Ego) are wholly determined causally by events in the brain. This leaves it quite open whether the events in consciousness are identical to certain brain events (as in the theory of psychoneural identity) or whether they are separate events linked causally (as in the theory of psychoneural interaction). Many psychiatrists have a distaste for theories that explain their patient's behaviour in terms of brain mechanisms, as they feel that this makes them into mechanical puppets bereft of human dignity and worth. However, this is to confuse a causal scientific explanation with a philosophical theory. The nature of the scientific process makes it inevitable that explanations of psychiatric disorder will come to be given in terms of brain mechanisms rather than in the psychodynamic terms that Freud himself recognized as merely stop-gap endeavours to be replaced when our knowledge of brain function was sufficiently far advanced.

Thus the disruption of the activity of the brain that is the physical basis of schizophrenia renders normal behaviour very difficult for the patient. Firstly the abnormal perceptions, thoughts and feelings that arise like luxuriant and gaudy weeds in his mind, distract his attention from any islands of normal function that remain, and in themselves present a new reality with which the patient has to come to terms. It is possible that in certain cultures, in which much time and attention is devoted to developing methods of dealing with such phenomena, which are interpreted as irruptions from the supernatural world, well trained subjects could cope with such experiences without becoming socially deviant. But our own culture provides us with no rules and no techniques for dealing with schizophrenic experiences, since the standard cultural response is to hold that these experiences are unreal, an attitude totally at variance with the nature of the subjective experience. Anyone who has experienced a 'bad trip' under LSD can readily understand what it means to say that the Ego has been submerged in the uprush of alien perceptions, thoughts and feelings. Thus behaviour may be disrupted, not only because the Ego is distracted or misled by its abnormal sensations and emotions and by the spanners thrown into the thinking machinery, but because it is completely knocked out of action and behaviour comes to be directed by unconscious elements. From our point of view the behaviour of a schizophrenic patient may be irrational, unpredictable or meaningless, but from his point of view may be the only thing he can do in response to intolerable torments or to the transmutation of subjective reality, or even because it is no longer himself that is responding.

Schneider (1939) distinguished a set of 'first rank' symptoms whose significance is that 'When any of these modes of experience is undeniably present, and no basic somatic illness can be found, we may make the decisive clinical diagnosis of schizophrenia'. The symptoms are as follows: 'audible thoughts, voices heard arguing, voices heard commenting on one's actions; the experience of influences playing on the body (somatic passivity experiences); thought withdrawal and other interferences with thoughts; diffusion of thought, delusional perception, and all feelings, impulses (drives) and volitional acts that are experienced by the patient as the work or influence of others'.

Mellor (1970) has conducted a study of 166 patients admitted to a psychiatric hospital over a period of 8 months diagnosed as suffering from schizophrenia. Of these 119 had first rank symptoms. The rest were mainly chronic schizophrenic defect states and some had clear evidence of having had first rank symptoms in the past. No significant correlations were found between these symptoms and the major subcategories of schizophrenia. The symptoms commonly occurred in clusters rather than singly.

AETIOLOGY

For many years a fierce debate has raged as to whether schizophrenia is 'really' a genetically transmitted biochemical disorder of the brain or whether its causes lie in psychological factors such as traumatic early experiences, faulty patterns of child rearing or pathological family environments. More recently people have tended to abandon either of these extreme positions and to think that the disease is most likely to represent the result of complex interactions between different genotypes and particular environments. The sophistication of modern genetics has rendered most of the previous polemeics otiose. The turning point in this debate was reached in 1968 with the publication of 'The Transmission of Schizophrenia', edited by David Rosenthal and Seymour Kety. This carried the transactions of a conference that had been held the previous year in Puerto Rico at which the principle proponents of the two schools were able to meet and for the first time general agreement was reached between them.

GENETIC STUDIES

Here two particular lines of research have been followed. The first is to study the incidence of schizophrenia in the families of patients and in particular identical twins. The second is to study the children of a schizophrenic mother, who were permanently removed from their biological mothers within a few weeks of birth and brought up in foster homes. It has of course long been known that schizophrenia tends to run in families and that the incidence follows the closeness of the relationship reaching a maximum concordance rate of 30 to 40 per cent (according to the latest studies) in identical twins and a rate of some 40 to 50 per cent in the children of two schizophrenic parents. But these figures do not in themselves establish the genetic theory as the same results would be expected if schizophrenia was based mainly on abnormal learned patterns of reaction transmitted by schizophrenogenic parents. To complicate matters further, psychiatric symptoms or psychological aberrations in the parents of schizophrenics could be the result of years of painful experiences, secondary guilt etc., generated by trying to cope with a child with developing schizophrenia.

Most workers today support a polygenic mode of inheritance rather than a simple Mendelian mode of transmission. Modern concepts of genetics see not the disease itself as being inherited, but rather a set of weak enzymes. In schizophrenia we can suggest that these may not be able to cope with their metabolic load if this load becomes excessive following exposure to stress or certain negative emotional experiences—if that enzyme of enzymes are concerned in the metabolic reactions subserving these psychological functions. Modern genetics has shown that each gene has many different effects and that most traits are under the control of many genes. For example, the direct effects of the ABO genes are manifest only following a blood transfusion, but they have small indirect effects on the incidence of duodenal ulcer, stomach cancer and other diseases. This formulation allows for the possibility that there are subtypes of schizophrenia in which one or other particular gene is of particular importance. Each gene certainly codes for one enzyme. But a process such as 'thinking' or 'the selection of the sensory input for relevant items of information,' may depend on the precise action of a most complex electro-chemical mechanism in which very many enzymes play a vital role, such that a failure of any one of them results in disruption of the entire mechanism and the production of schizophrenic symptoms.

But modern genetic studies do not simply measure incidence rates and some of the detail of recent studies is important, Gottesman (1968) and Kringlen (1968) find that hebephrenic and catatonic types show fairly high degrees of specificity—that is in concordant twins, hebephrenic cases nearly always have hebephrenic twins and the same holds for catatonic cases. Atypical (schizo-affective) cases do not show high degrees of hereditability—that is the co-twins are usually normal. They also studied the effect of the severity of illness. They found that the more severe the schizophrenia, the greater was the concordance rate. This is in line with the polygenic theory which suggests that severity is associated with a larger number of abnormal genes. Gottesman concludes 'As with pyloric stenosis, diabetes mellitus and clubfoot, incidences in relatives far below those found for characters inherited in a Mendelian fashion are sufficient to support a polygenic theory'. Kringlen also supports this theory. 'A polygenic inheritance can make intelligible the great variety of clinical pictures found in the families of schizophrenics and the fact that a number of patients with so-called 'forme frustes' are larger than the number of manifest schizophrenics.' Shields implicates '. . . a wide spectrum of genes varying in specificity and shading off into the genetic background as a whole'.

ADOPTIVE STUDIES

Our most reliable evidence as to the relative roles of nature and nurture in schizophrenia comes from two studies of adopted children carried out by Heston and by Kety and his colleagues. Heston and Denny (1968) studied the subsequent life history of 47 children born to undoubted schizophrenic mothers between the years 1915 and 1945 in an Oregon State Psychiatric Hospital and removed from their mothers by the age of two weeks. No history of psychiatric abnormality was noted in the fathers. About one half of these children were reared in foundling homes with subsequent adoption in most cases. The rest were reared in foster families usually composed of paternal relatives. A matched control group of 50 children was selected from the inmates of the same foundling homes with non-psychotic mothers. These were also divided subsequently in almost equal proportions between child care institutions and foster families.

Each of these children was submitted to an extensive follow up procedure. The subjects, their friends, relatives and employers were contacted. Extensive searches were made up of newspaper files, court records, various social service agencies, the records of all the psychiatric hospitals on the West Coast, etc. Each subject was interviewed and given psychological tests including the Menninger Mental Health Sickness Rating Scale (MHSRS). Table 1 gives the results.

TABLE 10.1

The data from Heston's Study

Category	Control	Experi-mental	p	Institu-tional	Family
Number	50	47		47	50
MHSRS mean score	80.1	65.2	0.0006	73	72.5
Schizophrenic	0	5	0.024	3	2
Mental defect	0	4	0.052	2	2
Sociopathic personality	2	9	0.017	5	6
Neurotic personality disorder	7	13	0.052	9	11
Period of more than 1 year spent in a penal or psychiatric institution	2	11	0.006	8	5
Total years incarcerated	15	112	0.054	79	48
Schizophrenic mother	all	0	—	25	22

The diagnosis of schizophrenia applied was conservative. Three behavioural traits were found almost exclusively in the experimental group. These were: (1) significant musical ability (7); (2) expression of unusually strong religious feelings (6); and (3) problem drinking (8). Eight of the nine sociopaths found in the experimental group conformed to a similar type. They lived alone in the decaying centres of large cities and were distinguished by antisocial behaviour of an impulsive and illogical nature. They all had extensive police records. No such subjects were found in the control group.

In order to ascertain the effect of institutional versus family care the data was redivided between the two groups. Table 1 shows that there was no significant difference between them.

Thus this study, which was the first follow up of foundling home children into adulthood to use a control group, disclosed no significant effect of institutional care on adult psychosocial adjustment. Nor did it point to any significant deleterious effect on the children of schizophrenic mothers on being reared in families consisting of their paternal relatives. Other variables investigated such as social class or type of placement were shown not to be operative. This study provides strong evidence for the hypothesis that schizophrenia is mainly subject to genetic transmission. The presence of an excess number of schizoid psychopaths in the experimental group also supports the polygenic theory. The increased incidence of mental defect is also of interest and merits further study.

The study carried out by Kety and his colleagues involved an intensive investigation carried out in Denmark which is uniquely qualified for such studies by the presence of three registers—the adoption register, the Folkeregister and the Psychiatric Register of the Institute of Human Genetics. Between them these contain data on all adoptions, all nervous and mental illness and all movements of the population since before 1920. Rosenthal *et al.* (1968) first reported a replication of Heston's study. They found an increased incidence of schizophrenia and border-line schizophrenia in the biological children of the schizophrenic mothers, but no increase in psychopathic personalities. Table 2

TABLE 10.2

Data from the Danish study

Number	Index	Control
	69	86
Hospitalized Schizophrenics	1	1
Non-hospitalized Schizophrenics	2	0
Borderline Schizophrenics	6	1
Schizoid Personalities	3	4

gives their principal results. The authors suggest that whether a subject with a basic 'schizoid' personality becomes a frank sociopath or not is determined by environmental factors—which are arguably more noxious in the United States than in Denmark. Kety *et al.* (1968) then compared the biological and adoptive parents of adopted schizophrenics and controls using material from the same Danish study. Between the years 1924 and 1947 there were 5483 adoptions in Copenhagen by people who were not biologically related to the child adopted. Of these 507 adoptees became psychiatrically ill and amongst these there were 33 schizophrenics, subdivided into chronic, borderline and acute schizophrenic reactions. Nineteen of these formed a subgroup of subjects removed from their families within one month of birth. An equal number of matched controls were taken. The results showed that there was a statistically significant excess of schizophrenia and related disorders (8.7 per cent) in the biological relatives of schizophrenics as compared with controls (1.9 per cent), but this was true only for the chronic (6/16) and borderline (5/10) cases and not for acute schizophrenic reactions (0/7). Thus this data supports the hypothesis that acute schizophrenic reactions and schizophrenia are different entities, but that borderline schizophrenia is a milder form of true schizophrenia. There was also an increased incidence of psychopaths in the biological relatives of schizophrenics. In contrast the adoptive parents showed no significant increase of psychiatric abnormality and what there was, was distributed randomly between the families of index cases and controls. These findings were also replicated in the sub-sample of 19 index (and 20 control) cases separated from their biological families within one month of birth.

Thus there is now overwhelming irrefutable evidence that a genetic causation is operative in schizophrenia and all those attending the conference agreed with this conclusion. The balance of the evidence favours a polygenic mode of inheritance. So what can we now say about possible psychogenic factors in causation?

The Family Environment Approach

For as long as it has been the common opinion that madness runs in families so it has also been believed that people can be driven mad by circumstances. Each culture has its own concept of what it takes to drive a person out of his mind, and themes on this basis are common in plays and novels. But our problem is to see what psychological factors are responsible in fact rather than in fiction for the development of madness, in this case schizophrenia. This enquiry can proceed only by the ordinary process of forming hypotheses and testing them by controlled experiments.

The orthodox psychoanalytical account might be condensed into the general statement that the psychosis develops owing to fixation of the libido on the Ego. This hypothesis may well represent a valuable insight into some aspects of schizophrenia, but there is little experimental evidence in its support and the concepts it contains can now be expressed in other and perhaps more easily testable terms.

In the last few years there has been a very considerable development of work in the field of familial factors in schizophrenia. The people mainly concerned have been Gregory Bateson, Theodore Lidz and Lyman Wynne. Each has founded a 'school' particularly fruitful in the generation of imaginative hypothesis some of which have been amenable to experimental test. There has also been a large volume of speculation in this field and the development of complex theoretical positions on the basis of uncontrolled clinical hunches. Many books and papers have appeared making a large number of positive statements of alleged 'fact' concerning the psychosocial factors in schizophrenia for which there is no real evidence. What is more disturbing is the fact that many of these authors do not feel that any controlled trials are necessary.

Since there is no substitute for controlled trial and sceptical evaluation of any new (or old) theory, treatment or psychosocial preventive programme, work of this kind can only be misleading, confusing and destructive to the development of a proper scientific psychiatry.

The three promising approaches are considered below.

1. *The Bateson Model*

Gregory Bateson is an anthropologist and his hypothesis about the aetiology of schizophrenia springs from a general model for human behaviour. The mainsprings of his approach derive from Russell's theory of paradox and from communication theory. Russell's theory points out that such paradoxes as the Cretan who says 'All Cretans are liars' (to which one may ask 'True or False?' with no hope of getting a 'rational' answer) depend on the illegitimate blending of statements at different logical levels. This solution ties closely in with the fact, which an anthropologist would be particularly liable to notice, that much human communication is conducted by non-verbal methods. This gives rise to the possibility that one person communicating with another may *say* one thing, yet may communicate something quite different by any of the non-verbal means of communication open to him (e.g. gesture, facial expression, tone of voice, etc.). The second message may even contradict the first, thus giving rise to a paradoxical situation for the recipient, particularly if the messages are connected with instructions how to act, what to believe, etc. Sometimes the 'emotional' contradiction can remain purely verbal, e.g. 'trust me or I'll go away'. Against this theoretical background Bateson observed the nature of schizophrenic communication and deduced the nature of the family environment that might lead to this form of faulty communication. For, clinically speaking, faulty communication is of the essence of schizophrenia and it is quite reasonable to suppose that these faulty patterns are learnt when the mode of communication is being imprinted in early childhood.

Bateson was thus led to formulate his famous hypothesis of the 'double-bind'. This holds that one factor in the development of schizophrenia is exposure, during childhood, to excessive 'double-bind' communication from the parents. Rational thinking and conduct depend on the learned capacity to distinguish clear meaning in situations, to filter out the important and relevant facts from the 'booming and buzzing' confusion of the world and to think, speak and act coherently with respect thereto. The ability to do this, the theory suggests, is not innate but is learned from the way in which our parents order their existence. If the parental world itself is highly confused, full of uncertain and shifting meanings and if the double-bind method of communication is extensively used, the child never learns to order its world and schizophrenia results. More specifically the 'double-bind' refers to instructions given to the child where 'do A' is said and 'don't do A' is simultaneously communicated by non-verbal means originating from dynamically ambivalent feelings on the part of the parent. The child is caught in a hopeless position for he cannot leave the situation and for whatever he does he will be punished. His only method of dealing with the situation is to do nothing (which may lead to simple schizophrenia) or to behave in a completely ambiguous manner. In particular all meaning in his replies must be disguised so that he cannot be held responsible for any of his actions—because any action for which he can be held to be responsible may be punished. Thus the characteristic disorders of thinking, emotion and behaviour of the schizophrenic derive partly by learning from his chaotic environment (logic must be learned) and partly as a defence against the impossible demands that the double-bind places upon him.

This theory and its later elaborations has caught the imagination of many psychiatrists. It has taught us to pay much more attention to the form of communication between parents and children. But, whereas such factors may well modulate the mode of development of a schizophrenic illness, or perhaps make manifest a latent schizophrenia, there is as yet no evidence that the double-bind can act as a necessary or sufficient cause of the illness. The rather limited statement of the theory in the form of the 'double-bind' has been recently developed into a much more extensive theory of paradoxical communication, which has seen its most sophisticated development in the form of systems theory. This has an extensive mathematical basis that includes the theory of games. However, this is too technical a subject for further development here and the interested reader is directed to the writings of Jackson (1965), Haley (1963) and Watzlawick (1963).

2. *The Lidz Approach*

This derived originally from applying orthodox psychoanalytical concepts to the family group structure (Lidz *et al.*, 1963). The Bateson school concentrates on relations between parent and child; the Lidz group on triadic relations between the parents themselves and the child. They view the entire family as pathological and the 'schizophrenic' member as just one selected to play a particular role. Particular emphasis is placed on the age–sex structure of the family. If these are blurred, the children in the family develop distortions in their identity development and this may predispose towards schizophrenia. Important concepts in their theory are 'skew' and 'schism'. A normal family depends on having two adequate parental figures. If one is defective in this role (e.g. schizoid, withdrawn, weak, inadequate, etc.) and the other is dominant, demanding, possessive, a skew is set up. The set of interpersonal relationships that normally develop between the parents, and the different set that normally develops between the parents, and the different set that normally develops between each parent and the children, become confused in such situations. This leads to faulty personality development in the children who are confronted not only by unsatisfactory parental models but also with a disturbed model of interpersonal behaviour. 'Schism' refers to interpersonal relationships of cold hatred, with either conflict or neutral withdrawal, a kind of 'emotional divorce' which leads to equally harmful consequences, though these are somewhat different from the 'skew' pattern.

A large number of studies of families using these concepts have been carried out but the majority of these have lacked any controls or were not carried out using proper double-bind methodology or both. It is clear that in so complex and difficult a field only the most vigorously controlled studies will carry any weight. Another factor is emphasized in a paper by Sanua (1963). He points out that most previous studies of schizophrenic families lacked any control for socio-cultural factors. One investigation reported excessive attachment between mother and child in schizophrenic families; another overt or subtle rejection; another open hostility. A closer look at these three studies reveals that the patients in the first group were mostly lower class Jewish and Italian; the second were upper class white protestants and the third was exclusively Negro. The differences clearly colour the findings. Sanua concludes: 'These enquiries do not clarify whether the existence of such distorted family relationships could be considered etiological of schizophrenia. Furthermore, there is little or no discussion of the possible presence of similar distortions in other deviant families since no controls, normal or abnormal, have ever been used'.

Kohn and Klausen (1956) studied the attitude towards their parents of schizophrenics and matched normal controls. They found that schizophrenics tended to see their mothers as strong authority figures and their fathers as very weak. However, they emphasized the importance of controlling for social class by showing that normals of low social class tended to see their mothers as dominant whereas normals of high social class saw their fathers as dominant. They also noted that this pattern of relative mother dominance was in no way specific for schizophrenia and had been reported for conditions as disparate as manic-depressive psychosis, ulcers, anorexia nervosa, juvenile delinquency and drug addiction.

3. *Wynne and Singer's approach*

The third major approach in this field was developed by Wynne and Singer. This is based on modern sociological theory and has been distinguished by the careful controls and adequate research design used by the investigators. Their main work has been presented in four papers in the *Archives of General Psychiatry* (Wynne and Singer, 1963*a*, *b*; Singer and Wynne, 1963, 1965). They start with a criticism of previous work in this field pointing out the deficiencies that we have referred to: the lack of proper blind controls; the failure to differentiate between the clinical grades of schizophrenia and to pay sufficient attention to cultural and social class variables. The schizophrenics often came from lower social classes and different ethnic groups than did the normal 'controls'. Neither had there been enough longitudinal studies and the supposition had usually been made that the faulty pattern was the cause of the illness when it might have been the result. Wynne and Singer studied family interaction patterns by means of taped interviews and a battery of psychological tests. They compared families with schizophrenic members with carefully matched families containing members with severe neurosis.

The hypothesis that they set out to test was that 'the types of thought disorder are functions of the mode of family transactions' and particularly of the styles of focusing attention and communication. 'The over-all transactional disorder in a family's communication sequences may be comparable stylistically to that found in the vagueness or fragmentation of a severely impaired schizophrenic'. In their classification of the forms of schizophrenic thought disorder they recognize three types: A (amorphous), F (fragmented) and M (mixed). The A group are characterized by the amorphous and undirected forms of communication with blocked or impaired use of language, vague and unstructured interpersonal relations and blunted affective expression without nuances. The F group have a different disorder and show actual fragmentation of their thinking.

In their main experimental group they took 35 families of young adult patients. The patients and their families were tested with Rorschach, T.A.T. and other tests, soley to provide samples of speech and 'test-taking behaviour'. The protocols were rated blind after all personal references had been rigorously deleted by another investigator. From the tests on the family the diagnosis of the patient was predicted. There were three diagnoses: schizophrenia (20), borderline (9) and non-schizophrenics (6 hospitalized neurotics). They recognized four types of thought disorder—A, F, M, and normal: and 5 degrees of Ego disorganization. The first task was to predict the diagnosis of the children from an examination of the protocols obtained from the parents. The results are shown in Table 3.

The attempt was then made to predict the type of thought disorder that would be present in the patient from an examination of the protocols obtained from the parents. The results were similarly successful as were the efforts to predict the degree of Ego disorganization. Lastly,

TABLE 10.3

Derived from Wynne and Singer (1963)

Diagnosis predicted from tests on the family	Clinical diagnosis independently rated		
	S	borderline S	non-S
S	17	1	1
Borderline S	2	7	1
Non-S	1	1	4
P < 0.001			

they attempted the ambitious task of placing blind each patient with his or her own family. The families were arranged in eleven matched sets for age, sex, social class and culture. The task was to match (blind) each patient's protocols with the protocols from the parents. The basis for this matching was as follows:

(a) family patterns for dealing with attention and meaning,
(b) erratic and inappropriate kinds of interpersonal closeness and distance,
(c) underlying feeling of pervasive emptiness, pointlessness and meaningless of life,
(d) a family psychological structure confusingly organized around the denial or reinterpretation of the reality of major anxiety provoking feelings and events. There were two sets of two families, six sets of three families, one of four and two of five families. The number of sets perfectly matched was scored (e.g. all four children in the set containing four families placed in their correct family). Table 4 gives the result. They make the point that matching must be done on the *form* of thinking, communication and Ego functioning; matching on the *contents* of the protocols was quite unsuccessful.

TABLE 10.4

Derived from Wynne and Singer (1963)

No. of families in each set	No. of sets	No. of sets perfectly matched	
2	2	2/2	
3	6	4/6	
4	1	1/1	
5	2	1/2	$p = 0.000002$

Wynne and Singer drew the following conclusions from their data: 'The individual's biological capacity for focusing attention and for perceiving, thinking and communicating and his characteristic vulnerability and predispositions, and his over-all affective and cognitive styles are based in part on genetic mechanisms which are then epigenetically elaborated. The inborn capacities are continually shaped and modified by interchange with the environment during development. The interchange of transactions at each developmental phase build upon the outcome of earlier transactions. This means that constitutional and experiential influences recombine in each developmental phase to create new biologic and behavioural potentialities which then help determine the next phase. If the transactions at any given developmental phase are distorted or omitted, all the subsequent developmental phases will be altered because they build upon a different substrate'.

Thus, to summarize, Wynne and Singer have demonstrated on the basis of carefully controlled investigations that the families of schizophrenics tend to have forms of organization of thought and communication similar to the disorders of these modalities found in the patients. The similarity is such that the details of the patient's illness can be successfully predicted from a knowledge of the former and schizophrenics can be placed 'blind' in their own families. They conclude that we are dealing with an interaction between genetic factors predisposing to these types of disorder and learning phenomena exacerbating these predispositions. The preschizophrenic child is thus doubly unfortunate as he is born with a nervous system geared to certain unsatisfactory modes of operation and he is reared in an environment where the context of references of communication are constantly and vaguely shifted, the areas to which attention is directed are not crisp and clear-cut but are ill-defined and amorphous and fragmented over such a large series of items that meaning cannot properly be integrated. This environment results in the faulty logical programming of an already faulty computor so as to bring out all the inherent weaknesses of the latter and to accelerate breakdown.

The inference that these studies offer support for the psychogenic mode of inheritance was criticized at the Puerto Rico conference and again by Slater and Roth (1969; p. 267). In the Lidz study the diagnostic basis has been questioned. As Slater and Roth say 'One of the weaknesses of this study is that it is by no means clear that anyone, either of the parents or of the probands themselves, would be diagnosed as schizophrenic by any European psychiatrist.' Other criticisms were levelled at the small number of cases, possible observer bias, the retrospective nature of much of the studies, the possible effect of the children on the parents, and the genetic origins of the abnormality in the parents. The last two considerations also apply to Wynne and Singer's work. Indeed Wynne himself says (1968; p. 195) 'Dr Singer . . . has also matched a relatively small number of 'well' siblings with their families . . . This matching seems to be equally possible for the families of non-schizophrenics and for the families of schizophrenics, again suggesting that principles of family relationships and organization are involved rather than anything idiosyncratic for schizophrenia as a disease entity'.

The most cogent evidence for the environmental theory comes from studies of monozygotic twins discordant for schizophrenia. Pollin et al. (1966) studied 11 such pairs intensively. The zygosity was confirmed by serological methods. A panel of five psychiatrists divided the index cases into two groups (1) certainly schizophrenic (n = 6) and (2) 'borderline' schizophrenic (n = 5). The co-twins had never been hospitalized for any psychiatric disorder but some had 'subclinical neurosis'.

The following findings emerged. (1) The index twins were smaller at birth and in 8 out of 11 cases were the second born. (2) In group 1, 5 out of 6 had been fed first and their survival had been regarded as dubious. In group 2, 4 out of 5 had been fed first but their survival had not been regarded as dubious. (3) In both groups there was a greater incidence in the index twin of stressful events (physical trauma, more frequent and more severe illnesses, multiple fractures, more feeding problems, cyanosis at birth, etc.). (4) The index twin had been the more anxious and emotionally unstable. In 9 out of 11 cases the co-twin was psychologically dominant. The authors suggested that one factor in such cases may be intrauterine damage or defective nourishment. Kringlen (1968) confirmed in his studies that the more introverted, dependent, submissive, obsessive twin usually is the one to become ill but he did not confirm the correlation with physical illness and the other physical factors listed by Pollin et al.

Other Factors

Claims have been made from time to time that various social stresses can lead to the development of a schizophrenic illness. For example it is certainly true that schizophrenia becomes more prevalent as one goes down the social scale (see e.g. Hollingshead and Redlich, 1957; Strole et al., 1962). However, there is no significant deviance from expectation in the social class of the parents of schizophrenics (Goldberg and Morrison, 1963; Dunham, 1965). This lends support to the hypothesis that the excess number of schizophrenics in social class 5 is due to the fact that they have drifted down the social scale by virtue of their illness—which is the so-called 'drift' hypothesis. Likewise the findings that there are more schizophrenics amongst some migrant populations than amongst the static population from whence the migrants came are as likely to be due to a selection process than to the alleged stresses of being a migrant. The unstable and pre-psychotic may well tend to migrate more often than the stable and settled. Hare (1967) has pointed out that since most of these epidemiological studies have been based on mental hospital admissions, the emigré psychotic may be admitted to hospital more frequently because he is tolerated less well in the community, or because migrants more readily attract the diagnosis of schizophrenia, or because migrant families are less able to cope with a sick member. Many such alleged epidemiologically revealed factors may be due to local variations in hospital admission policy and rates.

Some supporters of the 'psychogenic' theory have attempted to explain the greater incidence in monozygotic twins on the basis that such a twinship leads to more stress of a schizophrenogenic kind, or of a malignant psychodynamic nature. But this explanation is unlikely to be correct because schizophrenia is no more prevalent in twins of either kind. Others have been inclined to attribute higher concordance rates in monozygotic twins to the psychological process of identification, which might be expected to operate strongly in identical twins. However, it is arguable that the process of identification could work in either direction—that is a potentially schizophrenic twin could be kept well by identifying with his normal brother.

Although the evidence for the role of environmental factors in the basic aetiology of schizophrenia is debatable, studies carried out in Britain (Brown et al., 1958, 1962, 1966; Esterson et al., 1962; Renton et al., 1963) and in America, Freeman and Simmons (1963) have shown very clearly that environmental factors significantly influence the course of the illness. It has long been known that to be engaged in work within his capacity helps the schizophrenic to sustain a remission of his illness. Brown and his colleagues showed that relapse is less likely to happen if the patient lives in a setting where there is a low level of emotional involvement (the demands of married life are particularly taxing for the schizophrenic); Freeman and Simmons, studying those patients who succeeded in remaining out of hospital, found that their role-performance was best in settings where a high level of performance was expected of them. Laing and his colleagues showed that schizophrenics' relapse rates are significantly lower when both they and their families enjoy continuous support from the same treatment team, a finding which was confirmed by Renton et al. These studies show very clearly that environmental factors can influence a schizophrenic patient's illness for the worse, or for the better; and they lend plausibility to the argument that such factors may modulate, in some degree, the first appearance of the condition.

Thus, if we survey the evidence as a whole, we can conclude that the presence of genetic factors in schizophrenia has been established and that a polygenic mode of inheritance seems to fit the data best. The case for the alleged psychogenic factors is much weaker. The strongest evidence for comes from the study of discordant monozygotic twins;

the strongest evidence against comes from the studies of adopted children. In any case we can certainly support Brown's plea (1967): 'We do not have the knowledge to justify confident assertions about aetiology; and when these are made publicly and suggest that the family is directly responsible for bringing about the disorder, they may cause additional suffering to those who have already borne a great deal'.

However, one must distinguish between classical schizophrenia, which does not appear to have a significant environmental aetiology, and acute schizophreniform psychoses, that do. These are not linked genetically to schizophrenia, do not commonly lead to a chronic deterioration and may well represent a response in certain individuals to intolerable stress. This stress may well be of a subtle interpersonal and intrafamilial kind, as much as the intolerable stress of battle that leads to such breakdowns in time of war.

Biological Factors in the Aetiology of Schizophrenia

In spite of the strenuous efforts of many clinicians, biochemists, pharmacologists, endocrinologists, etc., over the last 50 years we still know nothing about the alleged biochemical or other biological lesion in schizophrenia. A large number of 'positive' results have been claimed, which have invariably turned out to be based on artifact, inadequate methodology or the influence of uncontrolled variables. At one time or another factors such as taraxein, the 'pink spot', adenochrome, the 'mauve spot', too much wheat, an imbalance of vitamin intake, auto-immunity, toxic indoles, etc. etc., have enjoyed a brief fame and notoriety, only to sink back into obscurity in a few months, adding to the general gloom and pessimism surrounding this subject in the minds of most medical scientists. I will not attempt to cover this ground since to do so would merely be to make the case once again for viable research designs and adequate controls. But I will describe the few clues that we have, faint as though these may be, that seem to merit following up. Only two empirical findings about the biology of schizophrenia, have ever widely been confirmed—the first is that schizophrenics are unusually resistant to histamine and the second is that in some cases methionine, in quite moderate doses, produces an acute psychosis.

HISTAMINE AND SCHIZOPHRENIA

Lucy in 1954 first showed that schizophrenics have an abnormally high level of tolerance to the systemic effects of injected histamine. Other workers have found that chronic schizophrenics produce an abnormally small wheal when histamine is injected intradermally (Ermala and Autio, 1951; Weckowicz and Hall, 1958; Freedman *et al.*,

1956; Simpson and Kline, 1961; Le Blanc, 1961). Jodrey and Smith (1959) were unable to confirm these results. Freedman *et al.* (1956) compared the reaction of the skin in schizophrenic patients to tuberculin and to histamine. The patients reacted normally to the former but persistently showed reduced reactions to the latter. Simpson and Kline (1961) showed that the abnormality is specific for chronic schizophrenia and is not found in acute cases nor in other psychiatric disorders. Le Blanc (1961) found that the skin of schizophrenic patients contains fewer mast cells than normal. The wheal produced by histamine return to normal following a therapeutic response to phenothiazines. Lovett-Doust *et al.* (1956) and Stern *et al.* (1957), report that schizophrenics have raised blood histamine levels but the methods in use at that time were not specific for histamine and this work needs repeating. Pfeiffer *et al.* (1969) report that schizophrenics can be divided into those with abnormally low and those with abnormally high blood histamine levels.

There is thus good evidence that chronic schizophrenics are more resistant to histamine than normals but the meaning of this remains obscure.

METHIONINE AND SCHIZOPHRENIA

In 1961 Kety and his co-workers (Pollin *et al.*, 1961) reported perhaps the most significant fact known about schizophrenia to date. They were interested in testing the 'abnormal brain amine' hypothesis and so wished to determine the effect of raising the levels of various amines in the brain. As the amines themselves do not cross the blood-brain barrier, they gave the parent aminoacid, which will, plus an MAOI prevent further breakdown of the amine produced in the brain by decarboxylation of the aminoacid. Out of the dozen or so compounds they tested only two had any effect. Tryptophane produced an intoxication like alcohol and methionine, in some cases produced an acute psychotic reaction. The chronic schizophrenic cases developed on acute psychosis with hallucinations, increased anxiety and thought disorder and behavioural disturbances. The other patients showed no effect. During the period following withdrawal of the methionine and replacement of phenothiazine therapy some patients showed a clinical amelioration over their previous state. This effect has been confirmed by Brune and Himwich (1962a); Alexander *et al.* (1963); and Park *et al.* (1965). Antun *et al.* (1971) found that methionine itself (in a dose of only 10 g a day which is 3 times the normal intake) produced the same effect, so the MAOI is not necessary. Brune and Himwich (1962a) found that betaine (another methyl donor chemically unrelated to methionine), and Spaide *et al.*, (1966) reported that cysteine will also induce the same symptoms. There has been some debate whether the psychosis produced is a 'schizophrenic' or an acute 'toxic' psychosis. However, this point is hardly relevant. Clinical observation suggests that some cases show a typical acute schizophrenic psychosis and others a more 'toxic' picture with some disorientation and clouding of consciousness. The differentiation between the two types of psychosis under these circumstances is difficult and perhaps unreal. What is important is that methionine in some cases induces an acute psychosis and in other cases has no effect at all. Nor are there any reports that methionine can have this effect in normal people. So this seems a worthwhile point of departure for further research. What one would like to know is what effect methionine has on the biochemical mechanisms in the brain, and which of these, in the methionine responders, is affected by the aminoacid. There would seem to be a number of possible mechanisms by which methionine could produce this effect.

Methionine is the principle donor of methyl groups in the transmethylation mechanisms in the body. Most hallucinogenic drugs of the LSD type are methylated derivatives of the central neurotransmitters and these drugs can induce in normal people an acute schizophreniform psychosis (the 'bad trip'). Thus it is possible that some cases of schizophrenia are associated with the production in the body of an endogenous toxic agent of this kind (for example some derivative of dimethyltryptamine). In which case giving excess methionine might be expected to increase the production of these abnormally methylated products and the psychosis would develop. Israelstam et al. (1970) report that schizophrenics metabolize methionine differently from normals. They gave subjects methionine with a radioactive label on the labile methyl group and measured the amount of radioactive carbon dioxide given off. The excretion was slower in the case of the schizophrenics indicating an overactive methylating pool. Heath et al. (1966) have investigated the effects of methionine sulphoximine (MSO) in schizophrenics. This is an antimetabolite of methionine that causes a toxic psychosis in normal people if given in a dose of over 200 mg per day, with E.E.G. signs of an organic reaction. The effects can be prevented by feeding a large excess of methionine. Heath fed MSO to ten schizophrenics and nine control subjects. All the controls reacted with acute psychoses characterized by thought disorder, disturbances of association and affect, paranoid symptoms, auditory hallucinations and catatonia. None of the schizophrenics showed any of these symptoms and indeed some appeared to show an alleviation of their condition. However, it was noted that MSO produced some memory impairment. The E.E.G. in the control cases was abnormal with slow waves but in the schizophrenic cases it was normal. The authors suggest that schizophrenics have an overactive methylating enzyme (or an underactive demethylating enzyme) and thus MSO has on them a normalizing effect. Thus either too much or too little transmethylation would appear to lead to psychotic symptoms in different subjects.

However, one cannot assume that these effects of methionine have anything to do with transmethylation, for methionine is closely concerned in other reactions. The clinical effects observed could be due to one of the following: (1) An excessive intake of aminoacid upsets the entire aminoacid balance and methionine is particularly effective in this. (2) Sprince (1967) has found that methionine (or some of its metabolites) exert an inhibitory effect at some point in the tryptophane → kynurenine → N-methyl nicotinamide pathway. If rats are fed on a diet containing excess methionine, homocysteine or cysteine, the urinary excretion of N-methyl nicotinamide fell sharply and that of indoleacetic acid—the end product of the alternative metabolic pathway of tryptophane via tryptamine—rises. This change was particularly well marked when the diet contained an excess of methionine.

An attempt to test this hypothesis was made by Berlet et al. (1965) who fed schizophrenics a diet low in tryptophane and methionine. However, no clinical benefit resulted and the urine levels of indoleacetic acid and 5-hydroxyindoleacetic acid paradoxically rose. The authors concluded that if insufficient of these aminoacids are fed, the result is an increased breakdown of tissue and thus the level of the aminoacids at active sites is maintained. Brune and Himwich (1962b) report increased levels of tryptamine excretion in schizophrenics. Antun et al. (1971) did not detect any increase in the excretion of VMA or HMPG in the urine of schizophrenics fed on excess methionine. Likewise metanephrine excretion in schizophrenia is normal (La Brosse et al., 1963). Himwich and his coworkers (Tanimukai et al., 1970) have detected dimethyltryptamine in schizophrenic urine. Thus abnormally methylated derivatives of tryptamine may be concerned in schizophrenia, and these in any case are much more potent hallucinogens than the derivatives of the catecholamines such as mescaline. Alternatively the schizophrenic may be reacting abnormally to some normal metabolite of this type.

Thus the 'aberrant methylation' hypothesis remains a valid guide for further research and suggests a number of investigations that need to be carried out. The mode of action of methionine on the brain needs to be further explored in animal experiments. The effect of MSO on schizophrenics needs to be confirmed as this may offer a means of treatment. Another investigation that may yield interesting results would be to measure the capacity of schizophrenics to demethylate small amounts of various methylated derivatives of tryptamine and amphetamine.

OTHER STUDIES

1. *Carbohydrate metabolism*

Normal human serum stimulates the uptake of glucose by rat diaphragm. Walaas *et al.* (1954) showed that serum from schizophrenics has a lesser stimulating effect. These authors demonstrated in 1964 that the prealbumin fraction of schizophrenic serum has an inhibitory effect on various metabolic pathways of the cell. This effect disappeared when the patients were treated with chlorpromazine. Furthermore the fluorescent intensity of the prealbumin fraction from the schizophrenics was ten times less than normal (at 340 nm). Walaas *et al.* (1965) suggested that this was due to the presence of an abnormal probably small molecule bound to the protein. Frohman has recently reported that his globulin fraction (see the next section) from schizophrenics is different from this same fraction from normals in that the protein contains a quantity of alpha-helical conformation whereas the same fraction from normals does not. As the two fractions have identical aminoacid sequences, this again suggests that the abnormality is caused by a small attached molecule. Buhler and Ihler (1963) noted that schizophrenic plasma reduced the rate of oxidation of C^{14} labelled glucose by chicken erythrocytes below the figure for the same cells bathed in normal serum.

2. *Aldolase and Creatine Fructokinase*

Meltzer (1968) reported that the blood levels of aldolase and creatine fructokinase are raised in certain cases of acute schizophrenia and in other psychoses, including that produced by LSD. In one patient with a cyclical illness the blood level started to rise some 1 to 2 days before the onset of the psychotic symptoms. However, we have been unable to confirm this claim in 12 acute schizophrenics (Harding 1971) but we did find that the levels were greatly increased in one case whose acute psychotic episode had been precipitated by d-LSD.

3. *Schizophrenic sweat substance*

It has long been known to doctors and nursing staff in charge of wards with chronic schizophrenics that such patients often have a peculiar musky smell (see e.g. Slater and Roth, 1969, p. 287). After ten years of effort Smith *et al.* (1969) finally isolated the agent responsible which is *trans*-3-methyl-2-hexenoic acid (Fig. 1a). This was found in 7 out of 7 schizophrenics studied and 0 out of 10 controls. Tests were then done to determine its origin. It did not appear to originate from any bacterial population peculiar to schizophrenic skin, although this was not established for certain. This compound is quite unlike any other chemical compound previously implicated in schizophrenia and the only chemicals listed in the Merck Index that it resembles are the hormones used by bees to control ovarian growth in bee larvae. Queen substance (Fig. 1b) inhibits ovarian growth and gives rise to workers, and Royal Jelly promotes ovarian growth and Queens result (Fig. 1c). This may be no more than a coincidence but there remains a faint but intriguing possibility that such compounds may play some role in human physiology. Certainly the endocrine development of many schizophrenics is distorted.

$$CH_3 \quad H \qquad\qquad H \quad H \qquad\qquad H \quad H$$
$$C_3H_7 \qquad COOH \quad CH_3CO(CH_2)_5 \qquad COOH \quad HO(CH_2)_7 \qquad COOH$$
$$\text{(a)} \qquad\qquad\qquad \text{(b)} \qquad\qquad\qquad \text{(c)}$$

Fig. 1

4. *The Mechanism of action of hallucinogens*

It is generally agreed that there are some notable similarities between the 'bad trip' psychoses that can be induced by drugs such as d-LSD and certain types of acute schizophrenic breakdown (Smythies, 1970). There are of course differences between the acute LSD psychosis and chronic schizophrenia but there are also similarities between chronic LSD users (acid heads) and chronic schizophrenics (see Smythies, 1970, p. 109). In any event if we knew how drugs like LSD act we should know at least the biochemical mechanism underlying one type of psychosis, which might suggest clues as to what to look for in the metabolism of schizophrenics. A recent Work Session at the Neurosciences Research Program was devoted to this problem and the report is published in the NRP Bulletin (Smythies, 1970). There is now extensive evidence that drugs like LSD have an important action on the serotonin-containing neurones in the brain, but there is still argument as to whether the effect is mainly an inhibition or excitation of the $_5HT$ receptor (Bradley, 1970; Fuxe *et al.*, 1970; Aghajanian, 1970). The serotonin containing neurones in the brain have their cell bodies concentrated in the raphe nuclei in the brain stem. Their axons are distributed widely to other neurons all over the brain. There is evidence that this system is closely concerned with sleep, with mood and with filtering the incoming sensory inflow for its information content. Thus these neurones may form part of the meta-organizational system of the brain that controls the flow of information around the complex computing circuitry. Unitary metabolic disturbances in such a system would be expected to have widespread deleterious effects on many of the functions mediated by the brain. The meta-organizational (MO) system of a computer organizes the flow of information in the computor. If this is a very large and complex one with many specified subunits, it would be enormously wasteful in power and energy to leave this all switched on all the time. Thus an MO system is needed to decide which components have to be switched on (arousal) and in which order and what elements in the sensory inflow must be directed where. The MO system may also be responsible for processing, organizing and subdividing the sensory inflow into manageable packets. A disorder in such a system would be expected to lead to just the sort of symptoms that we see in schizophrenia: the confused thinking, the peculiar disorder in processing the sensory input described above (p. 252), the divorce between the different functions of the brain leading to symptoms such as 'incongruity of affect' and the general divorce between the previously well integrated functions of the brain. Thus in this view schizophrenia is the result of a disorder of the meta-organizational system of the brain, which in turn is due to a metabolic disorder in the transmitter system used in the MO system, namely serotonin.

TYPES OF SCHIZOPHRENIA

No subdivision of types of schizophrenia can hope to produce a nice clear-cut scheme and many schizophrenics end up labelled as 'mixed' or 'atypical' no matter what scheme is used. The symptoms occur in diffuse and changing patterns. Within these limits it is possible to distinguish certain broad categories which have an empirical usefulness.

SIMPLE SCHIZOPHRENIA

This is distinguished by the absence of any 'positive' symptoms of the disease. It commonly starts in adolescence by a gradual withdrawal from company, day-dreaming and the development of an inert and indifferent attitude towards the world together with a flat affect. The patient ceases his studies and ordinary pursuits and shows a severe lack of initiative and drive. The only complaints may be vague hypochondriacal ones and the patient does not regard himself as ill nor his circumstances in any way unusual. If unsupported by his family, such patients slide down the social scale and commonly become tramps, prostitutes, petty thieves, etc. Symptoms such as thought disorder, delusions and hallucinations do not always develop and if they do they only appear after many years.

HEBEPHRENIA

This represents the 'core' as it were of malignant schizophrenia and it is characterized by the predominance of primary first rank symptoms and in particular thought disorder. The onset is usually insidious and difficulties in concentration and in dealing efficiently with events are commonly the first signs. This leads to unexpected failure of exams, a decline in performance at work, etc. The worry in the patient's mind that something is wrong is transmitted into hypochondriacal ideas and frequent visits to the family physician. The disorder progresses steadily. The loss of clear thinking leads to a dreamy state in which effective action in a complex world becomes impossible. The emotional tone becomes flattened and blunted and the mood is marked by silly giggling or a bland fatuity. All the first rank symptoms may be found in various combinations but hallucinations are not so prominent as they are in the catatonic form of the illness.

The onset may be disguised and the patient may present as a depressive reaction, or with a marked depersonalization and derealization, or with obsessional symptoms, before the typical symptoms of schizophrenia make their appearance.

CATATONIA

With the advent of modern physical methods of treatment, the classical picture of catatonia is rarely seen today. In the past the chronic wards of mental hospitals contained many catatonics with their prolonged periods of immobility and 'waxy flexibility' interspersed with sudden and unpredictable outbursts of wild violence. Subjects who have experienced catatonia and waxy flexibility under the influence of hallucinogenic drugs have attributed the condition to a disorder of proprioceptive feed back from the limbs. An arm placed, for example, over the head, feels perfectly comfortable as though freed from the effects of gravity and so it is kept there as comfortably as anywhere else. Such an explanation may also apply to the typical catatonic posturing in which the head may be kept a few inches off the pillow for hours or the patient will sit or stand in strange positions without apparent discomfort or fatigue. Other postural stereotypes may have some symbolic or religious significance. Other characteristic symptoms include negativism or its converse—automatic obedience, echolalia and echopraxia, grimacing—especially the classical pout or schnauzkrampf—and tics, and strange dissociated fragments of behaviour patterns. Highly stereotyped behaviour in animals may be induced by drugs that activate the dopamine system.

The periods of immobility may alternate with periods of hyperkinesia—of restless agitated behaviour—or with outbursts of aggression and excitement marked by facial expressions of horror or rage, or with no facial expression at all. In hyperacute cases these symptoms can lead to death from exhaustion. These catatonic symptoms may be accompanied by florid hallucinations, bizarre delusions, emotional storms of ecstasy, rage or horror and thought disorder of various kinds.

PARANOID SCHIZOPHRENIA

This is generally regarded as the most 'genuine' of the subdivisions of schizophrenia. 'Simple' schizophrenics may slowly develop in later years into typical catatonics or hebephrenics. Catatonic and hebephrenic symptoms frequently occur together or may alternate during the course of an illness. The paranoid form tends to run true. The onset is usually later than in the other forms and it commonly starts when the patient is middle-aged or elderly. The salient features are primary delusions and hallucinations with secondary delusional development. Disturbances of affect, thinking and volition are minimal and the deterioration of the personality so characteristic of other forms of schizophrenia may not occur. These features may be due in part to the fact that the late onset protects the more stabilized personality of later years. The delusions are characterized by their approach to a possible position, by their logical nature and cultural normality as opposed to the bizarre and culturally foreign nature of the beliefs held by other types of schizophrenics. Moreover the previous personality in about one half of the cases is normal (Miller, 1941). The common delusion is that of persecution by neighbours, workmates or by some agency such as the police, Communists or Freemasons. Strong affects may accompany these unpleasant convictions together with associated hallucinations and some degree of thought disorder. The intrusion of the delusional system into the life of the patient may vary from an encapsulated delusional system that may be nursed in secret for many years to a state of paraphrenia phantastica in which the entire past life of the patient is reconstructed in the light of the delusional system that itself fills most of the present thought. Likewise paranoid schizophrenia shades off nosologically into ill-defined regions of 'paraphrenia' and 'pure paranoia' as the accessory symptoms fall away leaving the paranoid delusions of persecution, jealousy or grandeur in pure culture. In other directions paranoid schizophrenia shades off into various types of paranoid personality, of a legion of cranks and eccentrics and fanatics with systems of over-valued ideas. Some 40 per cent of late paraphrenics suffer from deafness which leads to social isolation. In others brain damage or alcoholism may be found.

ATYPICAL FORMS

Schizo-affective Psychosis

In many cases features of manic-depressive psychosis and schizophrenia may be mixed. This has variously been regarded as a genuine concatenation of the two diseases, as a specific 'schizo-affective' psychosis, or merely as a variant of the kaleidoscopic picture of schizophrenia in which depressive or manic reactions happen to be marked. The third seems to fit most of the cases encountered in clinical practice.

2. *Pseudoneurotic schizophrenia*

This is a disease largely confined to North America and the label is used to describe confused adolescents with marked neurotic features who lack the crispness of thought and behaviour demanded by the North American culture. Slater and Roth (1969) regard such cases as instances of anxiety neurosis with features of depersonalization, or more rarely as cases of a primary depressive syndrome. There is no evidence that this is a form of schizophrenia. It is certainly the case that some cases of schizophrenia present with ill-defined neurotic complaints, but these soon give way to an unmistakeable schizophrenic illness.

3. *Schizophrenia in people of low intelligence*

The disease in such patients often takes peculiar forms. It is marked by childish and silly conduct together with a poverty of ideational content and primitive and monotonous delusions and hallucinations.

4. *Schizophrenic psychosis with clouding of consciousness*

In the majority of schizophrenic psychoses consciousness remains clear in contradistinction to the confusion and disorientation typical of delirium and other toxic psychoses. However, in some cases of schizophrenia, consciousness appears to be clouded, as in the subacute delirious phase of acute catatonia or the 'oneiroid' state in which the patient becomes totally immersed in an hallucinatory world and loses all touch with his surroundings. But it seems unlikely that these represent genuine subdivisions of schizophrenia.

5. *Acute schizophreniform reactions*

Evidence has been reviewed earlier that this condition is genetically distinct from true schizophrenia. Some people subjected to unbearable physical or emotional stress break down with an acute psychosis with many symptoms akin to those found in true schizophrenia. These include panic, hallucinations, delusions, depersonalization and derealization catatonia and thought disorder. However, blunting of affect and first rank symptoms, and the typical 'schizophrenic feel' are always lacking. A study of 61 such cases has been presented by Labhardt (1967). These breakdowns tend to occur in sensitive, overconscientious people rather than in withdrawn schizoid personalities. The condition usually clears up rapidly with treatment, or even without it, but these people may suffer from subsequent psychiatric illnesses of various types.

DIAGNOSTIC POINTS

The diagnosis of schizophrenia cannot be made on any one single symptom or sign. The entire clinical picture must be reviewed and assessed against the present and past circumstances of the patient and his cultural background. Few psychiatrists would disagree about the diagnosis of classical and advanced cases but the difficulty arises in early and atypical cases. Now that powerful chemotherapeutic weapons against schizophrenia exist, diagnosis is no longer an academic exercise as it was to some extent in the days when nothing could be done.

Features pointing to a positive diagnosis of schizophrenia are (1) the typical thought disorder which can now be sought for by the psychological tests described above; (2) other examples of Schneider's first rank symptoms together with emotional blunting, disturbances of volition, the absence of any insight and the classical 'splitting' between one psychological function and the others. In considering the diagnosis attention should always be paid to the possibility of organic factors. It is nowadays common knowledge that chronic amphetamine abuse and temporal lobe epilepsy (as well as other types of epilepsy) can induce a paranoid psychosis clinically indistinguishable from schizophrenia. Likewise the abuse of hallucinogenic drugs such as LSD, DOM etc., can induce acute schizophreniform psychoses in certain individuals. Many general medical conditions, in particular vitamin deficiencies, endocrine disorders and various toxic states can induce acute, subacute or chronic schizophreniform psychoses which must be distinguished from 'ideopathic' schizophrenia. Similar psychoses may occur in cases of cerebral tumour and other organic brain diseases, post-traumatic states, alcoholism and syphilis.

Schizophrenia must also be distinguished from schizoid personality disorders and schizoid sociopaths which is not always easy as the conditions merge imperceptibly. Such cases are often forme frustes of schizophrenia and as we saw are found more frequently in the families of schizophrenics than in normal families.

In spite of years of effort no biological test for the presence of schizophrenia has been developed. However, it should be possible to obtain useful information by performing a few simple tests such as the intradermal injection of histamine, tryptamine levels in urine and testing for the presence of trans-3-methyl-2-hexenoic acid in the sweat. An extensive survey along these lines may enable us to subdivide cases on a biological basis which may lead to improved therapy and prognostic formulations, as well as to providing a means of monitoring the progress of the condition.

COURSE AND PROGNOSIS

Advances in treatment have radically changed the gloomy prognosis attached to schizophrenia twenty years ago. However, this change is more manifest in some types than in others. Some cases may recover completely from an acute attack. In other cases improvement is contingent on the continued administration of medication. Many cases improve sufficiently to be discharged from hospital but a relapse soon occurs—which is usually due to the failure to take the tablets. The patient has to be re-admitted and again responds to treatment only to relapse again following discharge for the same reason. This process leads to what has been called the 'revolving door' policy. It may be much reduced by taking energetic measures to see that the patient continues to take his medication. In this the long acting phenothiazines such as Fluphenazine Enanthate and Fluphenazine Decanoate which only have to be injected once per 2 to 4 weeks, have proven very useful. In other cases the patient may be discharged home but residual symptoms remain and cause a great deal of distress to the family. Other cases may experience symptomatic relief but never recover sufficiently to leave hospital. The benefit of the drugs becomes clear if for any reason they are stopped. In a few cases medication is without effect and the steady schizophrenic deterioration continues.

If patients do recover from the psychosis, their personalities may remain damaged with a lessened capacity for work and enjoyment, for making warm human relationships and for taking effective action in the world. Wing et al. (1964) followed up 113 patients, diagnosed as schizophrenic, for five years. At the end of this time 49 per cent of cases were well and able to support themselves; 7 per cent showed minor symptoms but were still working; 16 per cent were unemployed but still without major symptoms; 17 per cent were or had been severely disturbed at some time during the last six months of the follow up period and 11 per cent had remained in hospital during the whole of this period.

Factors indicating a good prognosis also point to an expectation that the patient should respond well to drug therapy. Favourable factors include—a good previous personality, an acute onset, the presence of obvious precipitating stresses, a paranoid or catatonic clinical picture, the admixture of strong affective components and a well preserved affective response. Poor prognostic factors include—an onset before 20 years of age, a schizoid previous personality, and insiduous onset, a simple or hebephrenic clinical picture, early signs of flattening of affect and a family history of deteriorating schizophrenia. The body build has not been found to be a reliable guide.

TREATMENT

There is now abundant evidence from well controlled trials (see e.g. Goldberg et al., 1965) that the phenothiazines and the butyrophenones exert a specific therapeutic effect in schizophrenia and that the term

K

'tranquillizer' is a misnomer. However, the term 'neuroleptic' which is widely used on the Continent is no better as it rests on the mistaken belief that these drugs exert their effect in psychosis by virtue of their capacity to induce Parkinsonian symptoms. The drugs are most effective in cases with marked positive symptoms—hallucinations, agitation, excitement, catatonia, hostility etc.—and they are less effective in cases marked by negative symptoms such as apathy, hebephrenic symptoms and flattening of affect. The response will usually occur, if it is going to, within a few days. In acute cases of catatonic excitement the drug should be combined with E.C.T. and the first dose may be given by the intramuscular route (100 mg chlorpromazine). If depressive features are marked, the addition of a tricyclic antidepressant may be called for.

There are a large number of different effective phenothiazines and butyrophenones available and they differ mainly in the dose required and their side effects. There is little evidence that different drugs exert any specific efforts or are particularly indicated in any subdivisions of schizophrenia.

Phenothiazines

Chlorpromazine is still widely used although it is more toxic than the more recently introduced drugs. It forms a subgroup with thioridazine (Melleril). These two drugs commonly induce drowsiness, but less commonly, Parkinsonian symptoms. The second main group—which includes drugs like trifluoperazine (Stelazine), fluphenazine (Moditen) and perphenazine (Fentazine)—less commonly induce drowsiness but more commonly Parkinsonian symptoms.

These drugs produce a large number of side effects which are described in Chapter XV, Vol. II.

Atropine-like symptoms

Atropine-like symptoms are common in all these drugs and result in a dry mouth, constipation and blurred vision—particularly when reading small print.

The Butyrophenones

The first butyrophenone to be introduced into clinical psychiatry was haloperidol, and double-blind controlled trials (see review by Goldstein et al., 1968) have established it as an effective drug in the treatment of schizophrenia. In acute cases it may be administered by intramuscular or intravenous injection. In most cases an anti-Parkinson drug will be needed as well. Newer drugs of the same family include fluperidol and pimozide. The latter appears particularly promising as it can be given in a dose of only one (5 mg) tablet a day and the reported side effects are minimal. In general the side effects of the butyro-phenones are similar to those of the piperazine class of phenothiazines.

THE MECHANISM OF ACTION OF ANTI-SCHIZOPHRENIC DRUGS

An important clue to the nature of the biochemical lesion of schizo-phrenia would be obtained if we knew how the drugs effective in treating the condition worked. The difficulty here is that the phenothiazines have a very wide range of biological activities and it is difficult to know which of these is relevant to their action in schizophrenia. Amongst their most potent effects is their inhibition of adrenergic mechanisms. Furthermore, some of the more potent and newer butyrophenones have been shown to be specific blockers of dopamine receptors in the brain (Fuxe et al., 1970). Since it appears that schizophrenia may be associated with blockade of the serotonin mechanisms and over activity of the adrenergic (and particularly the dopamine) systems in the brain, the things to aim for in designing new therapeutic drugs, are the depression of central adrenergic function and the relief of the blockade of the serotonin system. The phenothiazines also inhibit the enzyme N-methyl transferase—that can turn tryptamine into the potent hallucinogen dimethyltryptamine, and so this action may be relevant to the relief of the serotonin blockade. In this department we are attempting to develop new drugs based on a new model of the serotonin receptor (Smythies, 1973) that may prevent the binding of possible endogenous toxins like dimethyltryptamine to the receptor.

SCHEDULES OF DRUG ADMINISTRATION

If the patient does not respond to the first drug exhibited within six weeks, this should be replaced by another since there are wide and as yet unpredictable variations in patient response to various phenothia-zines and butyrophenones. In some cases doses as high as 800 mg a day of chlorpromazine (or the equivalent dose of related drugs) are required. Nowhere is the disturbance of the metabolism of schizophrenics seen more clearly than in their capacity to absorb without apparent effect, doses of these drugs that would render a normal person almost comatose.

When the acute phase of the illness has been brought under control by means of a phenothiazine or butyrophenone, the next problem that arises is that of maintenance therapy. There is no doubt that many patients relapse because they fail to take their drugs at some time after leaving hospital. One possibility is to give a single dose at night (i.e. chlorpromazine, 200 mg) as long-term maintenance; another technique is to transfer to a depot phenothiazine starting with a small dose while the patient is still controlled with chlorpromazine. The fluphenazine decanoate has much less side effects than the enanthate and a 12.5 mg dose often lasts a female patient for 21 days, while males may need the full 25 mg. It is usual to give two injections while the patient is still under hospital observation; oral anti-Parkinsonian drugs (i.e. orphenadrine) are given for four to five days after each injection. After the patient is discharged further injections may be given at home by a member of the Community Nursing Service or at the hospital at a specific follow-up clinic. Where the diagnosis of schizophrenia is certain, medication should be continued for one to two years depending on clinical progress.

Individual psychotherapy and group therapy are of value but need to be continued for fairly long periods. Work with the families has proved to be of considerable benefit, allowing them to develop a different outlook to the patient and his illness. The value of rehabilitation need hardly be stressed; further details on hospital rehabilitation are to be found in Chapter XVII, Vol. II. Quite apart from the question of how long medication is continued, there is the question of how long should follow-up contact be maintained. Present evidence suggests that several years follow-up may have some preventative benefit.

REFERENCES

AGHAJANIAN, G. (1970) The effects of LSD on raphe nuclei neurons. In *The Mode of Action of Psychotomimetic Drugs, Neurosciences Research Program Bulletin*, **8**, 40–54.

ALEXANDER, F., CURTIS, G. C., SPRINCE, H. & CROSLEY, A. P. Jr. (1963) L-methionine and L-tryptophane feedings in non-psychotic and schizophrenic patients with and without tranylcypromine. *Journal of Nervous and Mental Disorders*, **137**, 135–142.

ANTUN, F. T., BURNETT, G. B., COOPER, A. J., DALY, R. J., SMYTHIES J. R. & ZEALLEY, A. K. (1971) The effects of L-methionine (without MAOI) in schizophrenia. *Journal of Psychiatric Research*, **8**, 63–71.

BANNISTER, D. (1960) Conceptual Studies in thought-disordered schizophrenics. *Journal of Mental Science*, **106**, 1230–1249.

BANNISTER, D. (1962) The nature and measurement of schizophrenic thought disorder. *Journal of Mental Science*, **108**, 825–842.

BANNISTER, D. & SALMON, P. (1967) Word context test as a measure of conceptualization in schizophrenia. Quoted by A. McGhie *loc cit*.

BERLET, H. H., MATSUMOTO, K., PSCHEIDT, G. R., SPAIDE, J., BULL, C. & HIMWICH, H. E. (1965) Biochemical correlates of behaviour in schizophrenic patients. *Archives of General Psychiatry*, **13**, 521–531.

BRADLEY, P. B. (1970) Electrophysiology of Psychotomimetic drugs. In *The Mode of Action of Psychotomimetic Drugs, Neurosciences Research Program Bulletin*, **8**, 55–65.

BROADBENT, D. E. (1958) *Perception and Communication*. New York: Pergamon.

BROWN, G. W., (1967) The family of the schizophrenic patient. In *Recent Developments in Schizophrenia, Brit. J. Psychiat.*, Special Publication No. 1. 43–60. (Edited by A. Coppen and A. Walk.)

BROWN, G. W., BONE, M., DALISON, B. & WING, J. K. (1966) Schizophrenia and Social Care. *Maudsley Monograph No.* 17, O.U.P.

BROWN, G. W., CARSTAIRS, G. M. & TOPPING, G., (1958) Post-hospital adjustment of chronic mental patients. *Lancet* **ii,** 685.

BROWN, G. W., MONCK, E. M., CARSTAIRS, G. M. & WING, J. K. (1962) Influence of family life on the course of schizophrenic illness. *British Journal of Preventive and Social Medicine,* **16,** 55–68.

BRUNE, G. G. & HIMWICH, J. E., (1962a) Effects of methionine loading on the behaviour of schizophrenic patients. *Journal of Nervous and Mental Disorders,* **134,** 447–450.

BRUNE, G. G. & HIMWICH, H. E., (1962b) Indole metabolites in schizophrenic patients: Urinary excretion. *Archives of General Psychiatry,* **6,** 324–328.

BUHLER, D. R. & IHLER, G. S. (1963) Effect of plasma from normal and schizophrenic subjects on the oxidation of labeled glucose by chicken erythrocytes. *Journal of Laboratory and Clinical Medicine,* **62,** 306–18.

CAMERON, N., (1944) In Experimental analysis of schizophrenic thinking. In *Language and Thought in Schizophrenia,* University of California Press, (Kasanin, ed.).

DUNHAM, H. W. (1965) *Community and Schizophrenia,* Detroit, Wayne State University Press.

ERMALA, P. & AUTIO, L. (1951) On intradermal histamine tests in schizophrenia. *Acta Psychiatrica Scandinavica, Suppl.* **60,** 136–144.

ESTERSON, A., COOPER, D. G. & LAING, R. J. (1962) Results of family-oriented therapy with hospitalized schizophrenics. *British Medical Journal,* **ii,** 1462.

FEINBERG, I. & MERCER, M. (1960) Studies of thought disorder in schizophrenia. *Archives of General Psychiatry,* **2,** 504–511.

FORREST, A. D., HAY, A. J. & KUSHNER, A. W. (1969) Studies in speech disorder in schizophrenia. *British Journal of Psychiatry,* **115,** 833–841.

FREEDMAN, D. X., REDLICH, F. D. & IGERSCHEINER, W. (1956) Psychosis and allergy: experimental approach. *American Journal of Psychiatry,* **112,** 873–877.

FREEMAN, H. & SIMMONS, O. (1963) *The Mental Patient comes Home.* New York: Wylie & Son.

FUXE, K., HÖKFELDT, T. & UNGERSTEDT, U. (1970) Morphological and functional aspects of central monoamine neurons. *International Review of Neurobiology,* **13,** 73–126.

GATHERCOLE, C. E. (1965) A note on some tests of overinclusive thinking. *British Journal of Medical Psychology,* **38,** 59–62.

GOLDBERG, E. M. & MORRISON, S. L. (1963) Schizophrenia and social class. *British Journal of Psychiatry,* **109,** 785–802.

GOLDBERG, S. C., KLERMAN, G. L. & COLE, J. O. (1965) Changes in schizophrenic psychopathology and ward behaviour as a function of phenothiazine treatment. *British Journal of Psychiatry,* **111,** 120–133.

GOLDSTEIN, B. J., CLYDE, D. J. & CALDWELL, J. M. (1968) Clinical efficacy of the butyrophenones as antipsychotic drugs. In *Psychopharmacology,* pp. 1085–1091. Edited by D. H. Etron, Washington U.S.P.H.S. Publication No. 1836.

GOTTESMAN, I. I. (1968) Severity/concordance and diagnostic refinement in the Maudsley-Bethlem schizophrenic twin study. In *The Transmission of Schizophrenia,* pp. 37–48. Edited by D. Rosenthal and S. S. Kety, London: Pergamon.

HALEY, J. (1963) *Strategies of psychotherapy,* New York: Grune.

HARDING, T. E. (1971) D.P.M. Dissertation, University of Edinburgh.

HARE, E. H. (1967) The epidemiology of schizophrenia. In *Recent Developments in Schizophrenia, British Journal of Psychiatry, Special Publication No. 1,* 9–24. Edited by A. Coppen and A. Walk.

HAWKS, D. V. (1964) The clinical usefulness of some tests of over-inclusive thinking in psychiatric patients. *British Journal of Social and Clinical Psychology*, **3**, 186–190.

HEATH, R. G., NESSELHOF, W. Jr. & TIMMONS, E. (1966) D. L-methionine-d,-1-sulphoximine effects in schizophrenic patients. *Archives of General Psychiatry*, **14**, 213–217.

HESTON, L. L. & DENNY, D. (1968) Interactions between early life experience and biological factors in schizophrenia. In *The Transmission of Schizophrenia*, pp. 363–376. Edited by D. Rosenthal and S. S. Kety, London: Pergamon.

HOLLINGSHEAD, A. B. & REDLICH, R. C. (1957) *Social Class and Mental Illness*, New York: Wiley.

ISRAELSTAM, D. M., SARGENT, T., FINLEY, N. N., WINCHELL, H. S., FISH, M. B., MOTTO, J., POLLYCOVE, M. & JOHNSON, A. (1970) Abnormal methionine metabolism in schizophrenic and depressive states: a preliminary report. *Journal of Psychiatric Research*, **7**, 185–190.

JACKSON, D. (1965) Family rules. *Archives of General Psychiatry*, **12**, 589–594.

JODREY, L. H. & SMITH, J. A. (1959) Releasable histamine levels and histamine tolerance in tissues of 291 psychotic patients. *American Journal of Psychiatry*, **115**, 801–807.

KETY, S. S., ROSENTHAL, D., WENDER, P. H. & SHULSINGER, F. (1968) The types and prevalence of mental illness in the biological and adoptive families of adopted schizophrenics. In *The Transmission of Schizophrenia*, pp. 345–362. Edited by D. Rosenthal and S. S. Kety, London: Pergamon.

KLAF, F. S. & HAMILTON, J. G. (1961) Schizophrenia—a hundred years ago and today. *Journal of Mental Science*, **107**, 819–827.

KOHN, M. L. & KLAUSEN, J. A. (1956) Parental authority behaviour and schizophrenia. *American Journal of Orthopsychiatry*, **26**, 297–313.

KRINGLEN, E. (1968) An epidemiological-clinical twin study on schizophrenia. In *The Transmission of Schizophrenia*, pp. 49–63. Edited by D. Rosenthal and S. S. Kety, London: Pergamon.

LA BROSSE, E. H., MANN, J. D. & KETY, S. S. (1963) The physiological and psychological effects of intravenously administered epinephrine and its metabolism in normal and schizophrenic men III. Metabolism of 7-H^3-epinephrine as determined in studies on blood urine. *Journal of Psychiatric Research*, 68–75.

LABHARDT, F. (1967) *Die Schizophrenieähnlichen Emotionspsychose*, Berlin: Springer.

LE BLANC, J. (1961) Response to histamine in mental patients before and after tranquillizer therapy. *Biochemical Pharmacology*, **8**, 152.

LIDZ, T., WILD, C., SCHAFER, S., ROSMAN, B. & FLECK, S. (1963) Thought disorders in the parents of schizophrenic patients: a study utilizing the object sorting test. *Journal of Psychiatric Research*, **1**, 193–200.

LOVETT-DOUST, J. W., HUDSON, H. & SALNA, M. E. (1956) Blood histamine and tissue-cell anoxia in mental disease. *Nature*, **178**, 492–493.

McGHIE, A. (1967) Studies of cognitive disorder in schizophrenia. In *Recent Developments in Schizophrenia, British Journal of Psychiatry, Special Publication No. 1*, pp. 69–78. Edited by A. Coppen and A. Walk.

McGHIE, A. & LAWSON, J. S. (1964) Disturbances in selective attention in schizophrenia. *Proceedings of the Royal Society of Medicine*, **57**, 419–422.

MELLOR, C. S. (1970) First rank symptoms of schizophrenia. *British Journal of Psychiatry*, **117**, 15–24.

MELTZER, H. (1968) Creatine kinase and aldolase in serum: abnormality common to acute psychoses. *Science*, **159**, 1386.

MILLER, C. W. (1941) The paranoid syndrome. *Archives of Neurology and Psychiatry* **45,** 953–963.

PARK, L. C., BALDESSARINI, R. J. & KETY, S. S. (1965) Methionine effects in chronic schizophrenia. *Archives of General Psychiatry,* **12,** 346–351.

PAYNE, R. W. (1961) Cognitive abnormalities. In *Handbook of Abnormal Psychology*. Edited by H. J. Eysenck, New York: Basic Books Inc.

PAYNE, R. W. & HEWLETT, J. H. G. (1960) Thought disorder in psychotic patients. In *Experiments in Personality*. Vol. II. Edited by H. J. Eysenck, London: Routledge and Kegan Paul.

PFEIFFER, C. C., ILLIEV, V., GOLDSTEIN, L. & JENNEY, E. H. (1969) Serum poly-amine levels in schizophrenia and other objective criteria of clinical status. In *Schizophrenia, Current Concepts and Research*, pp. 557–563. Edited by D. V. Siva Sankar, New York: PJD Publications.

POLLIN, W., CARDON, P. V. Jr. & KETY, S. S. (1961). Effect of aminoacid feedings in schizophrenic patients treated with inproniazid. *Science,* **133,** 104–105.

POLLIN, W., STABENAU, J. R., MOSHER, L. & TUPIN, J. (1966) Life-history differences in identical twins discordant for schizophrenia. *American Journal of Orthopsychiatry,* **36,** 492.

RENTON, C. A., AFFLECK, J. W., CARSTAIRS, G. M. & FORREST, A. D. (1963) A follow-up study of schizophrenic subjects in Edinburgh. *Acta psychiatrica Scandinavica,* **39,** 548.

ROSENTHAL, D., WENDER, P. H., KETY, S. S., SHULSINGER, G., WELNER, J. & ØSTERGAARD, L. (1968) Schizophrenics' offspring reared in adoptive homes. In *The Transmission of Schizophrenia*, pp. 377–391. Edited by D. Rosenthal and S. S. Kety, London: Pergamon.

SANUA, V. D. (1963) The socio-cultural aspects of schizophrenia: a comparison of protestant and Jewish schizophrenics. *International Journal of Social Psychiatry,* **9,** 27–36.

SCHNEIDER, K. (1939) *Clinical Psychopathology*. New York: Grune and Stratton.

SIMPSON, G. M. & KLINE, N. S. (1961) Histamine wheal formation and mental illness. *Journal of Nervous and Mental Diseases,* **133,** 19–24.

SINGER, W. T. & WYNNE, L. C. (1963) Differentiation characteristics of parents of childhood schizophrenics, childhood neurotics and young adult schizo-phrenics. *American Journal of Psychiatry,* **120,** 234–243.

SINGER, W. T. & WYNNE, L. C. (1965) Thought disorder and family relations of schizophrenics. III. Methodology using projective techniques. *Archives of General Psychiatry,* **12,** 187–212.

SLATER, E. & ROTH, M. (1969) *Clinical Psychiatry*. London: Balliere, Tindall and Cassell.

SMITH, K., THOMPSON, G. F. & KOSTER, H. D. (1969) Sweat in schizophrenic patients. Identification of the odorous substance. *Science,* **166,** 398–9.

SMYTHIES, J. R. (1970) (Ed.) *Neurosciences Research Program Bulletin*, 8, see comments by Dr. F. Ervin on page 109.

SMYTHIES, J. R. (1973) *The Molecular Structure of Receptor Mechanisms*. New York: Academic Press.

SPAIDE, J., TANIMUKAI, H., GUNTER, R. & HIMWICH, H. E. (1966) Schizophrenic behaviour and urinary tryptophan metabolites associated with cystein given with and without a monoamine oxidase inhibiter (tranylcypromine). *Life Sciences,* **6,** 551–560.

SPRINCE, H. (1967) Metabolic inter-relationships of tryptophan and methionine in relation to mental illness. In *Amines and Schizophrenia*. Edited by H. E. Himwich, S. S. Kety and J. R. Smythies, Oxford: Pergamon.

STERN, P., HUKOVIC, S., MADJEREK, Z. & KAVAVAIC, S. (1957) Histamingshalt im Blute von Schizophreniken. *Archives internationales de pharmacodynamie*, **109**, 294–299.

STROLE, L., HANGER, T. S., MICHAEL, S. T., OPLER, M. K. & RENNIE, T. A. C. (1962) *Mental Health in the Metropolis, The Midtown Manhattan Study*. Vol. I. New York: McGraw-Hill.

TANIMUKAI, H., GINTHER, R., SPAIDE, J., BUENO, J. R. & HIMWICH, H. E. (1970) Detection in psychotomimetic N,N-dimethylated indoleamines in the urine of four schizophrenic patients. *British Journal of Psychiatry*, **117**, 421–430.

VENABLES, P. H. (1963) Selectivity of attention, withdrawal and cortical activation. *Archives of General Psychiatry*, **9**, 74–78.

VENABLES, P. H. & WING, J. K. (1962) Level of arousal and the subclassification of schizophrenia. *Archives of General Psychiatry*, **7**, 114–119.

WALAAS, O., LINGJAERDE, O., LÖKEN, F. & JUNDERADT, E. (1954) The effect of sera from schizophrenic patients on glucose utilization of the isolated rat diaphragm. *Scandinavian Journal of Clinical and Laboratory Investigation*, **6**, 245–249.

WALAAS, O., WALAAS, E., SÖVIK, O., ALERTSEN, A. R. & LINGJAERDE, O. (1965) Metabolic effects on the isolated rat diaphragm of serum prealbumin fraction from schizophrenic and other psychotic patients. *Confinia Neurologica*, **25**, 175–182.

WATZLAWICK, P. (1963) A review of the double-bind theory. *Family Process*, **2**, 132–153.

WECKOWICZ, T. E. (1960) Perception of hidden figures by schizophrenic patients. *Archives of General Psychiatry*, **2**, 521–527.

WECKOWICZ, T. E. & HALL, R. (1958) Skin histamine reaction in schizophrenic and non-schizophrenic mental patient. *Journal of Nervous and Mental Diseases*, **126**, 413–470.

WECKOWICZ, T. E. & BLEWETT, E. (1959) Size constancy and abstract thinking in schizophrenic patients. *Journal of Mental Science*, **105**, 909–934.

WING, J. K., MONCK, E., BROWN, G. W. & CARSTAIRS, G. M. (1964) Morbidity in the community of schizophrenic patients discharged from London mental hospital in 1959. *British Journal of Psychiatry*, **110**, 10–21.

WYNNE, L. (1968) Methodological and conceptual issues in the study of schizo-phrenia and their families. In *The Transmission of Schizophrenia*. p. 195. Edited by D. Rosenthal and S. S. Kety, London: Pergamon.

WYNNE, L. C. & SINGER, W. T. (1963a) Thought disorder and family relations of schizophrenics. *Archives of General Psychiatry*, **9**, 191–198.

WYNNE, L. C. & SINGER, W. T. (1963b) Thought disorder and family relations of schizophrenics. II. A classification of forms of thinking. *Archives of General Psychiatry*, **9**, 199–206.

Chapter XI

EPILEPSY

E. H. Jellinek

Epilepsy defies easy definition or classification, and its pathogenesis is usually obscure. At least, management is straightforward, even though often only partially successful.

Hughlings Jackson spoke of the 'paroxysmalness' of epilepsy as its most striking characteristic, but this does not allow for the build-up experienced by some patents, and which may be seen in the electroencephalogram (E.E.G.). Perhaps we may define epilepsy as intermittent or continuous disorders of awareness, or consciousness (other than natural sleep), or of more limited cerebral functions, associated with changes in the electrical activity of the brain. Everybody is potentially epileptic, and there is endless variation in frequency and severity of fits among sufferers.

CLASSIFICATION

Earlier neurologists differentiated major fits, with falls, and loss of consciousness, and minor fits, with brief loss of awareness: or constitutional and symptomatic epilepsy, according to the absence or presence of brain disease. Electroencephalography has increased the complexity of the classifications of fits, and elaborate schemes have been proposed (Gastaut, 1969; Masland, 1969). Various focal cortical epilepsies, arising from tumours etc., had long been identified (Jackson and Beevor, 1890); the appearance of bilateral synchronous spikes over both cerebral hemispheres in the E.E.G. led to the concept of centrencephalic epilepsy, that is, fits arising from deep mid-line structures, presumably the reticular formation in the brain stem. (Penfield and Jasper, 1954).

These three modes of differentiation, viz: nosographic, aetiological, and anatomical, are all of course valid, but the old nosographic custom probably allows best for the overlapping of aetiological and anatomical factors in any one patient. Indeed, the aetiology of epilepsy, and of any one fit, is usually multifarious, and attacks originating in various parts of the brain often arise in one subject.

AETIOLOGY

Genetic predisposition to epilepsy has long been assumed, but is clear cut in only a minority of patients, (Pratt, 1967). It is common to be told of some cousin or other relative with fits, when one enquires about the family, but then epilepsy is a fairly common condition, with a prevelance of about 0.5 per cent. It is generally held that in most people with epilepsy the risk of affected offspring is increased about ten fold, from about one in two hundred to one in twenty. Genetic factors may play a part even in some of the symptomatic epilepsies such as infantile febrile convulsions (Ounsted *et al.*, 1966).

The lessening propensity to fits with increasing age is reflected in the diminishing disorder of electrical activity shown in the normal E.E.G. of childhood and adolescence, (Pond, 1963), but further increasing years usually lead to fewer fits, also in the later onset epilepsies.

The majority of all fits probably occur in infancy with feverish ailments ('teething convulsions'), and variations in body temperature may on occasion provoke fits at any age. The same applies to biochemical disorders of all sorts, and especially anoxia. The possibility of a vicious circle arises here, as major convulsions themselves cause anoxia, and anoxic brain lesions may subsequently lead to more fits.

Lowering of the epileptic threshold is produced most readily by hyperventilation, which results in hypocapnia. This may be done on the instruction of the physician, to bring out latent epileptic changes during an E.E.G. recording, or deliberately, by an hysteric.

Overhydration and fluid retention have a similar effect, and the latter process often seems responsible for the triggering of fits in the premenstruum.

Various drugs and alcohol may have a comparable action, but there is great idiosyncrasy, and an empirical approach to each patient is always preferable to some blind prohibitory rule. Sudden withdrawal of drugs and alcohol following a long period of intoxication often causes a catastrophic lowering of the epileptic threshold.

Most systemic diseases may provoke an exacerbation of epilepsy, especially in childhood; this is commonly mediated by some biochemical or metabolic abnormality, or by a change in body temperature.

The normal changes in the electrical activity of the brain on going to sleep, during sleep, and on waking up, are more physiological factors in the provocation of fits, and may lead to hypnagogic, sleep, or hypnapompic fits.

Psychic changes may bring about a drastic change in the fit threshold, either way. A purposeful, useful, and happy way of life often reduces the severity of epilepsy, whereas frustration, tension and depression lead to the reverse.

Diseases of the meninges and brain are, of course, generally more conducive to epilepsy than systemic diseases, but to a varying degree.

Meningitis frequently presents with a fit in childhood, but much less commonly in adult life. Bacterial infections of the meninges, especially by pneumococci, are worse in this respect than viral infections. Inflammation of the brain itself (encephalitis and abscesses) are particularly liable to lead to fits, at some point, and this is correlated with severe electrical abnormalities in the E.E.G. in these two conditions.

Primary and secondary brain tumours often lead to fits, but the attacks exhibit usually some focal features: meningiomata seem particularly liable to cause epilepsy.

Cerebrovascular disease and primary degenerative diseases of the brain (presenile dementia) produce epilepsy far less frequently than the pathologies mentioned above. Demyelinating disease is a rare cause of epilepsy, but when it occurs the attacks are often bizarre, and tend to go into prolonged remissions spontaneously (Ashworth and Emery, 1963).

Blunt cerebral trauma does not commonly cause epilepsy although there are occasions when a mild concussive injury may lead to an immediate fit, without later attacks. The situation is quite different in open head injuries, particularly when there has been some bleeding, or laceration of the cortex by depressed fractures (Jennett, 1969). The significance of birth trauma remains debatable, although damage to the mesial part of the temporal lobes has been attributed to this factor in some patients with temporal lobe fits (Falconer et al., 1964).

Indeed, there is an interesting variation in the liability to epilepsy with lesions of different parts of the brain. Apart from being apparently more prone to damage from anoxia, contrecoup and other injuries, the temporal lobes may themselves represent the most epileptic area of the brain (Ounsted et al., 1966). Frontal and parietal lobes seem less common sites of focal epilepsy, and the occipital lobes least so.

We do not, of course, know why any one fit starts when it does start, or why it finishes when it ends. While the E.E.G. tracing usually shows an increasing build-up of abnormal potentials before the onset of a convulsion, sometimes attacks seem to start without any heralding build-up, particularly petit mal attacks, and occasionally there is a diminution of electrical activity before the onset of a fit, as reflected in the E.E.G. tracing.

'Reflex epilepsy' was described at the end of the last century by Hughlings Jackson, and Gowers, (1901, 1907) amongst others. They pointed out the various actions and stimuli which could provoke a fit, usually the same kind of action in the same patient. Numerous different kinds of stimuli have been described (Symonds, 1959); simple flickering lights, or a change from light to darkness, or a highly complex visual stimulus such as reading (reading epilepsy), auditory stimulation (musicogenic epilepsy), certain visceral functions, especially micturition, and rarely eating; certain movements; or certain somatic sensory stimuli (one patient with an astrocytoma could be made to have a major convulsion when the plantar response was elicited in the opposite foot).

Even less is known of the neurochemical or biochemical factors which cause the end of any one convulsion. The basic action of the anticonvulsant drugs has not yet been elucidated (Woodbury, 1969); it may be that gamma-amino-butyric acid (GABA) has a role to play in the inhibiting of epileptic discharges (Symonds, 1959): we do not know why some patients have single fits, and some go on to serial fits, or to status epilepticus. The usual anoxia at the end of a major convulsion almost certainly does not cause the end of the fit, as anoxia by itself is a potent cause of convulsions. A theory of neuronal exhaustion following a period of hypersynchronous discharges was proposed almost a century ago by Hughlings Jackson.

NOSOGRAPHY OF EPILEPSY

Classical petit mal is essentially a disorder of childhood, though it may occasionally persist into adult life (Gibberd, 1966). The child is usually unaware of the disturbance, and it consists of an absence lasting from a few seconds to a minute or two. At the end of this the child continues to do what he left off before. To the observer it may be indistinguishable from inattention, and the hapless child may continue to be chastised for a long time before the true nature of the absences is diagnosed. The attacks may be brought on by overbreathing. Usually there is some slight motor accompaniment, in that the eye lids flicker, or there may be a jerk of the hands. Recovery from each petit mal is instantaneous. During the attacks the E.E.G. shows bilateral synchronous three cycle per second spike and wave discharges which distinguishes classical petit mal from similar minor attacks associated with temporal lobe spike discharges, and requiring quite different drug treatment. Occasionally classical petit mal discharges persist for longer, and may be atypical. Drop attacks occur accompanied by the E.E.G. of petit mal (Lennox, 1951). Brief petit mal discharges in the E.E.G. may have no overt clinical manifestation, although higher intellectual functions are impaired to a minor extent. If the attacks are very frequent, or continuous, the condition may lead to a prolonged confusional state know as petit mal status epilepticus (Goldensohn and Gold, 1960; Bohm, 1969).

Major attacks, or grand mal, usually occur without any warning, but there may be some particular aura, especially when there is a focal abnormality in the brain (see below). The patient suddenly loses consciousness with a powerful tonic contraction of the whole musculature. A forced indrawing or expulsion of air will constitute the epileptic cry at this point. During the brief tonic state the eyes are usually open and staring. The patient's colour becomes progressively more blue until after a varying period, lasting from seconds to perhaps a minute or so, the tonic phase is broken by a series of clonic convulsions. Often the eyes move with the clonic limb jerks. The clonic phase is usually brief, but may continue for a long time, and the appearance of the patient throughout a major convulsion can be extremely frightening to the onlooker. If the patient was erect at the onset then he will experience a heavy fall, and may injure himself; the tongue or lips are often bitten during the tonic phase, and the bladder usually empties. The period of asphyxia is followed by violent heavy breathing. Sometimes there is an abrupt recovery of consciousness, but more commonly a period of coma, which gradually merges into what looks like natural sleep, and may go on for many minutes, or even hours, if the patient is not roused.

The severity and duration of the convulsive phase bears some relationship to the period of post-ictal unconsciousness, and, in turn, to a varying period of confusion, on recovering consciousness. The patient is often not aware of the fact that he has had a fit, but may complain of aching muscles, some injury, or a headache.

Epileptics frequently experience a series of major fits, that is, two or three or more attacks in a row with, however, recovery of consciousness in between: 'serial epilepsy', and not a cause for alarm. Where one attack goes on to another without recovery of consciousness the condition then becomes one of status epilepticus in which the depth of coma between attacks becomes progressively greater, and life is in peril.

The focal epilepsies were described in the last century by Hughlings Jackson in his meticulous studies of the attacks suffered by patients with different kinds of focal brain lesions. Jackson's deductions about the mode of spread of the electrical activity (Walshe, 1943) have been vindicated by modern electrophysiological studies (Symonds, 1959). The most vivid example are focal fits starting in the motor cortex, with usually clonic twitching of the thumb, or the corner of the mouth, which goes on to spread, until it involves the whole of one side of the body before becoming generalized. Hughlings Jackson described comparable fits starting in the sensory cortex, when the patient would usually describe an indefinable sensation, sometimes like pins and needles, sometimes like a hot or cold feeling, which spreads in a similar fashion over his anatomy. The Jacksonian 'march' may become arrested at any point in its progress, spontaneously, or by some wilful action of the patient.

Fits with an aura of a gustatory or olfactory hallucination have been known to arise from lesions of the uncus (on the medial surface of the temporal lobe) since the last century (Jackson and Beevor, 1890) but electroencephalography has led to the recognition of a whole variety of auras indicative of a temporal lobe origin of fits, perhaps in as many as one third of all epileptics. Williams (1956) has tabulated the varieties of experiences in temporal lobe epilepsy. The commonest is an unpleasant hot sensation rising up from the epigastrium into the throat, and associated with a feeling of unreasoning fear and apprehension. Exceptionally, there may be a feeling of pleasure. Patients complain of a sensation of vertigo, with or without disorders of memory. Usually these consist of a feeling of familiarity (déjà vu), or unfamiliarity (jamais vu). The dream-like quality of this state was noted by Hughlings Jackson. Often there is some associated purposive or semipurposive motor activity, which may rarely lead to irrational actions of an aggressive type. The patient may describe a state of depersonalization. Distortions of space and time may also be complained of, but these are perhaps more a feature of epileptic discharges in the parietal lobe. The occurrence of some of the above symptoms will, of course, present considerable diagnostic difficulties if they are not followed by a major convulsion.

Epilepsies originating in the parietal lobes (other than in the post central gyrus) are particularly liable to have an aura of disordered concepts of space, with disorientation, or macropsia or micropsia (Critchley, 1953), or a lateralized visual hallucination.

Fits starting in the frontal lobes may begin with incontinence of urine or adversion, that is, a turning of the eyes, or eyes and head, to one or other side.

Focal occipital epilepsies are unusual, even after trauma to the occipital lobes, and may be heralded by a visual aura.

Most of the focal seizures either stop, without going on to a generalized convulsion, or proceed to do so, but on rare occasions the focal part of the seizure may persist, with continuing clonic twitching of part of the body, or a continuing sensory hallucination referred to some part of the body (epilepsia partialis continua).

Single powerful contractions of groups of muscles (myoclonus) may occur in patients who manifest other aspects of epileptic disease, and may be associated with isolated spike discharges in the E.E.G. As in chorea, these movements will interfere with skilled motor actions; myoclonus may mount in frequency before a major convulsion (Halliday, 1966).

Drop attacks may occur in epileptics who have other kinds of fits, but usually occur isolated, and may not be epileptic at all, e.g. when they are symptoms of transient ischaemia, although some general inhibitory epileptic discharge has been postulated as an explanation.

Many patients describe varying psychic symptoms before they have a fit, often going on for days, or even weeks. They describe feelings of tension or depression which may be relieved by the occurrence of the fit. Post-ictal confusional states are rather commoner, and may very rarely be associated with violent purposive or semipurposive behaviour.

The epileptic nature of such states may be particularly difficult to recognize where the actual fit was not observed, or where the epileptic activity of the brain does not amount to an actual convulsion, as with some of the temporal lobe disorders (temporal lobe fugues).

DIAGNOSIS

In the majority of patients the physician does not have the opportunity of observing an attack, and the patient is usually unaware of what happens during an attack, so a reliable eye witness account is mandatory. The primary objective consists in separating the functional from the organic attacks. In the former the patient does not hurt himself, and there is usually no incontinence. Bizarre behaviour during an attack is suggestive, but not conclusive, of an hysterical basis. The return to normal consciousness tends to be more abrupt in hysterical attacks, but this also happens in petit mal.

There are, of course, numerous non-epileptic causes for losses of consciousness and awareness, and the differentiation of these from epilepsy may present considerable difficulties. Syncopal attacks have a fairly typical and prolonged aura of faintness, and are usually associated with a more profound loss of colour than truly epileptic attacks, and hardly ever occur recumbent. Disorders of cardiac rhythm (Stokes-Adams attacks) usually occur without provocation, as does epilepsy. In other cardiac dysrhythmias the patient is usually aware of changes in pulse rate just before the onset of his attack. Transient cerebral ischaemic attacks may occur without any obvious cause for diminished cerebral blood flow, i.e. small emboli or vasospasm may come without a reason, but there is usually a setting of cardiovascular disease. Migraine sufferers will almost invariably complain of more severe headache, but complaints of headaches are also voiced by epileptics, and there is probably a group of patients who suffer from a combination of the two disorders, that is severe migraine with abnormalities of the E.E.G. and losses of consciousness.

A variety of disorders are associated with sleep, in particular narco-lepsy, with or without cataplexy (Symonds, 1954); and sleep paralysis (Levin, 1933). Somnambulism is more liable to occur in hysterics than in epileptics, but enuresis is often caused by nocturnal epileptic discharges.

Clinical examination during an attack is rarely feasible but may show extensor plantar responses. Where the underlying disorder is maximal in one or other cerebral hemisphere there may be a period of hemiparesis or aphasia following the attack (Todd's paralysis). Usually clinical examination between the attacks is entirely negative; the finding of any abnormal neurological signs should of course alert the clinician to the possibility of an underlying lesion. A suggestible hysteric may oblige by putting on an attack during the examination, but this does not necessarily mean that some of her attacks may not have an epileptic basis.

INVESTIGATIONS

Electroencephalography is essential in the examination of all patients suspected of suffering from epilepsy although its value is often limited (Matthews, 1964). The E.E.G. is really helpful only when it is positive, that is when it shows actual epileptic discharges. A normal E.E.G. between attacks is compatible with a diagnosis of epilepsy, although it is highly unlikely to occur in a person with frequent and disabling attacks, e.g. in some hysterics who are seemingly incapacitated by attacks.

The interpretation of the E.E.G. abnormalities in children, and to a lesser extent in adults calls for considerable expertise (Kiloh and Osselton, 1961; Pond, 1963).

If there is any suspicion of underlying cerebral ischaemia appropriate cardiovascular investigations must, of course, be carried out, in particular an electrocardiogram.

Once it has been decided that a patient suffers from epilepsy one must then delimit the extent of further investigations. If the patient is believed to suffer from idiopathic epilepsy, with perhaps a positive family history, and the attacks are well controlled, then further investigations are almost certainly unnecessary. However, focal fits, or a changing clinical or E.E.G. pattern, or uncontrollability of fits calls for further investigations, as indeed does epilepsy starting after the age of thirty (late onset epilepsy).

X-rays of skull and chest should be carried out in these patients, as well as in children with poorly controlled fits, and may be an indication for special E.E.G. studies, beyond the usual hyperventilation and photic stimulations, viz. sphenoidal E.E.G's, where there is a suspicion of temporal lobe epilepsy.

Recent years have seen the development of two methods of investigation which are completely free from hazard, namely echoencephalography and cerebral radioisotope scanning. The combination of these two procedures will indicate the majority of progressive brain lesions amenable to worthwhile surgery. In a small proportion it may be necessary to proceed to contrast radiography of the brain, that is angiography and pneumoencephalography.

Lumbar puncture is, of course, essential where there is a suspicion of an underlying inflammatory lesion of the meninges and brain, but should not be used as a routine investigation where there is a strong suspicion of an intracranial space occupying lesion, as it may provoke a fatal pressure cone.

Investigations will be pursued more actively whenever there is a suspicion of underlying organic disease. The presence of abnormal physical signs is, of course, a strong pointer, as indeed is failure to control the attacks symptomatically.

By and large, a focal epileptic aura, or a focal onset of the convulsions, means focal brain disease, but temporal lobe attacks, even uncinate fits, often prove an exception to this rule, and may occur in a setting of idiopathic epilepsy, probably the result of anoxic damage during convulsions (Ounsted *et al.*, 1966).

TREATMENT AND MANAGEMENT

There is no first aid treatment for a major convulsion other than the common sense measure of doing what one can to prevent asphyxia, e.g. not to allow a patient to lie face down in a puddle etc. The attempt to force any spoon or spatula into the mouth of a patient with a major fit only results in further trauma, but some patients may learn to put a gag into their mouth at the onset of a major convulsion to prevent tongue biting, or to reduce the amount of asphyxia.

Attacks can be prevented to some extent, or reduced in number, by avoiding provocative factors, such as drugs or drinks in certain cases, but most provocative factors, are, of course, unavoidable, such as the usual mental stresses of life, minor ailments, menses etc. However, an indirect mode of treatment is sometimes possible by the use of psychotropic drugs on the one hand, and hormones or diuretic treatment on the other, for menstrual epilepsy.

It may not be necessary to institute regular anticonvulsant medication in an adult who has only had a single fit, unless it happens in the setting of an epileptic family, or with a particularly epileptic E.E.G. Otherwise the usual practice is to start anticonvulsant medication only after a second fit, and to continue it for at least a year or two after the last attack, or longer, depending on the length of the history etc.

A wide choice of anticonvulsant medications is available at the present (Laurence, 1966). Certain rules should be observed in the treatment of epileptics. The physician should confine himself to drugs that he knows well, at least to start with. He should build-up the dosage gradually to an adequate dosage, or until there are clear-cut side effects, before changing to another drug. It is inadvisable to make any sudden changes, as the withdrawal of an anticonvulsant drug in an abrupt fashion can in itself provoke an exacerbation of epilepsy. The times of treatment should be chosen realistically, and frequent ingestion of pills avoided as far as possible. Equally there is no point in treating patients with anticonvulsants in the morning if attacks have all occurred at night during sleep. Conversely it is unnecessary to give anti-petit mal drugs in the evening.

The three drugs which are the most popular in the treatment of major epilepsy are Phenobarbitone, Primidone, and Phenytoin.

Phenobarbitone has been in use since the 1920's, and its side effects are well known, even though its exact anticonvulsant action remains unknown (Woodbury, 1969). It is customary to start with a dosage of 30 mg twice daily, and to work up to as much as 100 mg two or three times a day. When the attacks occur mainly in the early hours of the morning it may be advisable to give the drug as a long acting preparation (spansule 100 mg) on retiring to bed at night. The soporific effect of the drug persists in some patients, but the majority of epileptics come to tolerate the drug quite well, even in large dosage. Depression may be an intolerable accompaniment of phenobarbitone treatment.

Primidone (Mysoline) has proved extremely useful since its introduction in the 1950's particularly in the treatment of temporal lobe epilepsy. The usual dosage is 250 mg two or three times a day, working up to 500 mg three times a day. The main undesirable side effect is unsteadiness, which usually comes on when treatment is started, but remits, provided the dosage is built up gradually.

Phenytoin is sometimes used as the first drug of choice. Like Primidone it may cause unsteadiness, which really can be quite disabling in some patients, (acute trunk ataxia).

Treatment should start with 50 mg twice a day, and worked up if necessary to 200 or even 300 mg two or three times a day, in very refractory cases.

Phenobarbitone, Primidone and Phenytoin may be used in conjunction.

Ethosuximide (Zarontin) is the treatment of choice for petit mal. The drug often shows little effect on the frequency of attacks until the dosage has been pushed up to quite a large quantity, e.g. 250 mg five or six times a day.

It must be accepted that attacks in some patients simply are not completely controllable, and the optimum amount of control is usually achieved by the above mentioned drugs in adequate dosage, if necessary in combination. It is unusual to achieve better control by using some of the less popular drugs, but these may need to be tried.

Sulthiame (Ospolot) seems to have a different mode of action, and may be used in a dose of 200 mg three times a day.

Acetazolamide (Diamox) 250 mg two or three times a day, is a useful adjuvant when there may be some fluid retention, as in premenstrual fits.

Chlordiazepoxide (Librium) 10 mg two or three times a day, or *Diazepam* (Valium) 2 to 5 mg three times a day, are helpful drugs in cases where it is not quite clear whether attacks are primarily emotional, or epilepsy triggered by emotional factors, as both drugs have a tranquillizing and a mild anticonvulsant effect.

Children tend to tolerate anticonvulsant drugs to a remarkable extent, and may as a rule be given half the adult dosage, if over the age of four or five, but textbooks of paediatrics should be consulted, especially in the treatment of smaller children.

There are two unusual conditions in children which require forms of treatment normally contra-indicated in the adult. Some epileptic children suffer from an associated hyperkinetic state (Ounsted *et al.*, 1966) which responds, paradoxically, to treatment with Amphetamine (2.5 to 5 mg two or three times a day). The other is the condition of hypsarrhythmia in small infants which consists of ceaseless 'salaam' attacks, with a progressive mental deterioration and gross abnormalities of the E.E.G.; some of these seem to respond to treatment with corticotrophin and corticosteroids (Bower and Jeavons, 1961).

It should be remembered that fevers tend to lower the epileptic threshold, and that anticonvulsant treatment should be stepped up if necessary, or recommenced, in predisposed patients during days of fever.

Status epilepticus is a major medical emergency, as it may prove fatal if treated in a dilatory fashion, or produce more epileptogenic foci, by anoxic brain damage. There are three major lines of treatment. The best tried mode of treatment is intramuscular injection of *Paraldehyde*. An adult should be given 10 ml, and this may need to be repeated two, or even three times if the fits continue, after intervals of about fifteen minutes. Paraldehyde can only be given by a glass syringe, as plastic syringes, such as are in use at the time of writing, are attacked by Paraldehyde. Paraldehyde is offensive stuff to handle, and may cause sterile abscesses, but is safe, in that it does not depress respiration. The prolonged use of paraldehyde is said to cause toxic damage to the heart and liver etc.

Diazepam (Valium) has been used progressively in recent years in the treatment of status epilepticus, and is given by intravenous infusion (Nicol *et al.*, 1969) in a dose of 5 to 20 mg, with a maximum of 200 mg in twenty-four hours (Parsonage and Norris, 1967).

The third method is an intravenous infusion of Pentothal in small dosage (Brown and Horton, 1967).

If any real difficulty is experienced in controlling status epilepticus, without depressing respiration, then an anaesthetist should be consulted, as the patient may require prolonged intubation, general anaesthesia, and muscle relaxation.

Petit mal status is not life threatening, and responds usually to the passage of time and large doses of anti-petit mal drugs. Epilepsia partialis continua responds up to a point to an increase in ordinary anticonvulsant medication (e.g. to large doses of Phenytoin, up to 900 mg daily), but it is often a manifestation of some serious underlying brain disease, such as an astrocytoma.

All the drugs used in the treatment of epilepsy have undesirable side effects, whenever a large dosage is used for a long time. Mention was made of unsteadiness, which may rarely be totally disabling, in the case of Phenytoin; a commoner side effect of Phenytoin treatment is gum hypertrophy. All drugs may cause mental slowing, and interfere with higher mental functions. These are intoxications which do not seem to lead to permanent dementia.

Prolonged anticonvulsant medication can cause Vitamin B.12 and folic acid deficiencies, with the result of a blood dyscrasis, or even more rarely neuropathy. There is some doubt about the harmful effect of folate deficiency on the electrical activity of the brain (Wells, 1969).

The neurosurgical treatment of focal epilepsy in patients who do not harbour a tumour has been advanced largely by Wilder Penfield and his school. It has achieved worthwhile results in up to three quarters of selected series (Penfield and Paine, 1955), but its applicability in the epileptic population as a whole is rather limited. Considerable successes have been claimed for hemispherectomy in badly damaged children who are totally crippled by continuous epileptic discharges arising mainly in one atrophic hemisphere. Even the more limited excision of cortical scars in adults does, of course, leave a scar in turn, which may prove epileptogenic.

At the present time surgical treatment should probably be considered only in cases in whom medical treatment has failed, and in whom there is little or no major psychological disturbance. The electrical activity of the brain should be resonably normal, apart from the areas to be excised. Also, the part to be excised should be of dubious value to the patient, i.e. any operation on the major hemisphere is much more liable to lead to unsupportable defects.

The bulk of this work has been done in the temporal lobe epilepsies (Falconer et al., 1964; Green, 1967) where it has been found that the resection must be limited, especially in the dominant hemisphere. Bilateral temporal lobectomy causes a disastrous memory disturbance, and should never be contemplated.

Long Term Management

The prognosis in any one patient usually clarifies after a year or two of observation. It should by then have been possible to achieve optimal results of drug treatment, and by and large the epileptic tendency lessens with increasing years. Thus petit mal will stop in three quarters of patients by the age of thirty (Gibberd, 1966). The patient should, of course, be encouraged to live as full a life as he can, within the limits of his disability. Certain sports and occupations must be prohibited permanently, and he should be advised against too solitary an existence, e.g. bathing or swimming unattended.

Usually the pattern of the attacks does not alter, and most patients achieve some kind of modus vivendi, but allowance must always be made for the mental strain of having to live with a liability to sudden losses of consciousness.

The psychic aspects of epilepsy range from minor agoraphobic symptoms to the psychoses, and physicians vary in their attribution of the latter to epileptic predisposing factors. While the majority of epileptic patients convey an impression of mental normality, it is a common experience of neurologists to find sufferers from temporal lobe attacks particularly awkward, and time-consuming, in keeping with the old-fashioned shunning reaction of the lay public towards epileptics in general. In a survey of unselected epileptics culled from various general medical practices, Pond and Bidwell (1959) found an incidence of psychic difficulties among no less that 50 per cent of temporal lobe epileptics, as opposed to 29 per cent of ordinary epileptics. Sexual disorders of varying severity occur mainly with temporal lobe epilepsy (Taylor, 1969).

Mood disorders are encountered very commonly, especially during the pre-ictal phase, and may be relieved by the convulsion.

Aggressive psychopathic behaviour is only very rarely caused directly by epileptic discharges, but the criminal psychopathic population shows a much higher incidence of E.E.G. abnormalities, suggestive of delayed cerebral maturation, than other comparable prison inmates (Hill, 1963).

The transient psychic disturbance of some temporal lobe attacks has been compared to the more permanent mental state of schizophrenia, and a connection with the development of a psychotic illness has been postulated (Slater and Beard, 1963; Slater and Moran, 1969; Flor-Henry, 1969).

Be that as it may, there seems little reason for withholding customary psychotropic medication in epileptics with such disorders. The theoretical risk of aggravation of fits by Phenothiazines etc. is rarely borne out in practice.

The appearance of progressive mental deterioration in an epileptic presents a considerable problem of diagnosis (Pond, 1961). There are two kinds of pseudodementia: the electrical activity in the brain may remain so disordered, despite seemingly adequate anticonvulsant medication, that higher mental functions become difficult but they may yet return to normal, with lessening epileptic activity in the E.E.G. A commoner cause of pseudodementia is just drug intoxication. A true dementing process may be associated with continuing repeated major convulsions, probably due to repeated anoxia, but there is no clear correlation here. Some patients may remain bright and efficient despite persistent frequent major attacks, with marked anoxia.

Anoxic damage to the temporal lobe in ordinary centrencephalic major convulsions has been adduced as the explanation for the features of temporal lobe epilepsy found in association with centrencephalic epilepsy (Falconer *et al.*, 1964). The hippocampus is certainly a site of predilection for anoxic brain damage from all causes.

Very rarely uncontrollable epilepsy and progressive dementia are both the expression of some underlying progressive brain disorder, inflammatory, degenerative, or neoplastic, e.g. in tuberous sclerosis.

The majority of the epileptic population will remain well controlled, with only very rare convulsions, but may seek medical advice on problems of employment, marriage, and the driving of motor vehicles.

As regards the former, epileptics should be advised to seek the fullest and most satisfactory employment within their reach, as this will in turn lessen their epilepsy. They should be advised against seeking employment in public services where discovery of their epilepsy will lead to dismissal, and they are usually well advised to inform their prospective employer of their liability to fits, although this is sometimes better left until after a suitable relationship has been established. They should not work at height, or with major moving machinery, or in any capacity where a sudden attack could cause them, or any one else, a major risk of injury. Persons with severe and uncontrollable epilepsy should ideally be placed in a sheltered environment with, if at all possible, some regular occupation, such as gardening.

The majority of the population do not, of course, seek medical advice before contemplating marriage, and one often finds that the medical services may have led unwittingly to the meeting and mating of unsuitable individuals. Two epileptics should preferably not marry, but when there is only one epileptic parent procreation is usually not contraindicated, as an increased genetic risk from one in two hundred to one in twenty is generally considered acceptable (Hill and Parr, 1963). Exceptional families with a high incidence of epilepsy must be advised differently, should they seek eugenic advice.

Anticonvulsant medication for epilepsy may diminish potency. Epileptic mothers do not usually run into major trouble during pregnancy, delivery, and the puerperium, although there may be some transient exacerbation. Folic acid (5 mg thrice daily) should probably be given prophylactically during pregnancy alongside the anticonvulsants. A fit during, or just after, labour may arouse a false suspicion of eclampsia.

All epileptic attacks, whether major or minor, which occur during the waking hours are, of course, a potential major hazard in motorists.

However, a proportion of epileptics persist in the habit of driving cars despite this.

No epileptic should ever be allowed to drive a public service vehicle, but the attitude to the issuing of driving licences for private vehicles has recently been relaxed in the United Kingdom.

The Vehicle and Driving Licences Act, 1969, regulation 22, states that 'an applicant for a licence suffering from epilepsy shall satisfy the condition that (a) he shall have been free from any epileptic attack whilst awake for at least three years from the date when the licence is to have effect. (b) In the case of an applicant who has had such attacks whilst asleep during that period, he shall have been the subject to such attacks since before the beginning of that period, (c) the driving of a vehicle by him in pursuance of the licence is not likely to be a source of danger to the public'.

This new regulation no longer seems to debar epileptics who have remained completely controlled by anticonvulsant medication for three years or more, nor does it debar epileptics with attacks during sleep only. However, this pattern, of nocturnal fits only, must have been established for a period of at least three years.

It is perhaps appropriate to conclude this chapter in a psychiatric text by recording three patients whose epilepsy improved beyond recognition; the first made a satisfactory marriage, the second obtained a satisfactory job, and the third had a craniotomy at which it was planned to remove an epileptogenic focus, but the areas of abnormal brain was found too extensive for removal, and nothing was done to the brain by the surgeon.

Optimum management of epilepsy must be holistic, and should always extend beyond the routine prescription of anticonvulsant drugs.

REFERENCES

ASHWORTH, B. & EMERY, V. (1963) Cerebral dysrhythmia in disseminated sclerosis. *Brain*, **86**, 173.

BOHM, M. (1969) Status epilepticus petit mal. *Electroencephalography and Clinical Neurophysiology*, **26**, 229.

BOWER, B. D. & JEAVONS, P. M. (1961) The effect of corticotrophin and prednisolone in infantile spasms with mental retardation. *Archives of Diseases in Childhood*, **36**, 23.

BROWN, A. S. & HORTON, J. M. (1967) Status epilepticus treated by intravenous infusions of thiopentone sodium. *British Medical Journal*, **1**, 27.

CRITCHLEY, M. (1953) *The Parietal Lobes*. London: Arnold.

FALCONER, M., SERAFETINIDES, E. A. & CORSELLIS, J. A. N. (1964). Etiology and pathogenesis of temporal lobe epilepsy. *Archives of Neurology* (*Chicago*), **10**, 233.

FLOR-HENRY, P. (1969) Psychosis and temporal lobe epilepsy. *Epilepsia*, **10**, 363.

GASTAUT, H. (1969) Clinical and electroencephalographic classification of epileptic seizures. *Epilepsia* (Supplement), **10**, 2–13.

GIBBERD, F. B. (1966) The prognosis of petit mal. *Brain*, **89,** 531.

GOLDENSOHN, E. S. & GOLD, A. P. (1960) Prolonged behavioural disturbances as ictal phenomena. *Neurology (Minneapolis)*, **10,** 1.

GOWERS, W. R. (1901) *Epilepsy and Other Chronic Convulsive Diseases: Their Causes, Symptoms and Treatment.* 2nd Edn., London: Constable.

GOWERS, W. R. (1907) *The Borderland of Epilepsy.* London: Churchill.

GREEN, J. R. (1967) Temporal lobectomy with special reference to selection of patients. *Journal of Neurosurgery*, **26,** 584.

HALLIDAY, A. M. (1966) The clinical incidence of myoclonus. In *Modern Trends in Neurology*, p. 69, edited by D. Williams, 4th Edn., London: Butterworth.

HILL, D. (1963) The E.E.G. in psychiatry, In *Electroencephalography*, p. 368. Edited by D. Hill and G. Parr. London: Macdonald.

JACKSON, J. H. & BEEVOR, C. E. (1890) Tumour of temporo-sphenoidal lobe bearing on the localization of smell and on the interpretation of a particular variety of epilepsy. *Brain*, **12,** 346.

JENNETT, W. B. (1969) Early traumatic epilepsy. *Lancet*, **i,** 1023.

KILOH, L. G. & OSSELTON, J. A. (1961) *Clinical Electroencephalography.* London: Butterworth.

LAURENCE, D. R. (1966) *Clinical Pharmacology.* 3rd Edn. London: Churchill.

LENNOX, W. G. (1951) Juvenile petit mal (drop attacks). *Neurology, (Minneapolis)*, **1,** 357.

LEVIN, M. (1933) The pathogenesis of narcolepsy (sleep paralysis). *Journal of Neurology and Psychopathology*, **14,** 1.

MASLAND, R. L. (1969) Comments on the classification of epilepsy. *Epilepsia* (Supplement), **10,** 22–28.

MATTHEWS, W. B. (1964) The use and abuse of electroencephalography. *British Medical Journal*, **ii,** 85.

NICOL, C. F., TUTTON, J. C. & SMITH, B. H. (1969) Parenteral diazepam in status epilepticus. *Neurology (Minneapolis)*, **14,** 332.

OUNSTED, C., LINDSAY, J. & NORMAN, R. (1966) *Biological Factors In Temporal Lobe Epilepsy.* London: Heinemann.

PARSONAGE, M. J. & NORRIS, J. W. (1967) Use of diazepam in treatment of severe convulsive status epilepticus. *British Medical Journal*, **ii,** 85.

PENFIELD, W. & JASPER, H. (1954) *Epilepsy and the Functional Anatomy of the Human Brain.* Boston: Little, Brown.

PENFIELD, W. & PAINE, K. (1955) Results of surgical therapy in focal seizures. *Canadian Medical Association Journal*, **73,** 515.

POND, D. A. (1961) Psychiatric aspects of epileptic and brain damaged children. *British Medical Journal*, **ii,** 1377, 1454.

POND, D. A. (1963) The development of normal rhythms. The E.E.G. in paediatrics. In *Electroencephalography*, pp. 193 and 207, edited by D. Hill and G. Parr, London: Macdonald.

POND, D. A. & BIDWELL, B. H. (1959) A survey of epilepsy in fourteen general practices. Social and psychological aspects. *Epilepsia*, **1,** 285.

PRATT, R. T. C. (1967) *The Genetics of Neurological Disorders.* London: Oxford University Press.

SLATER, E. & BEARD, A. W. (1963) The schizophrenia-like psychoses of epilepsy: psychiatric aspects. *British Journal of Psychiatry*, **109,** 95–150.

SLATER, E. & MORAN, P. A. P. (1969) The schizophrenia-like psychoses of epilepsy: relation between ages at onset. *British Journal of Psychiatry*, **115,** 599.

SYMONDS, C. P. (1954) Cataplexy and other related forms of seizures. *Canadian Medical Association Journal*, **70,** 621.

SYMONDS, C. P. (1959) Excitation and inhibition in epilepsy. *Brain*, **82,** 133.

TAYLOR, D. C. (1969) Sexual behaviour and temporal lobe epilepsy. *Archives of Neurology (Chicago)*, **21,** 510.

WALSHE, F. M. R. (1943) On the mode of representation of movements in the motor cortex, with special reference to 'convulsions beginning unilaterally' (Jackson). *Brain*, **66,** 104.

WELLS, D. G. (1969) Anticonvulsant theory, folic acid deficiency and neuropsychiatric disorders. *British Medical Journal*, **ii,** 636.

WILLIAMS, D. (1956) The structure of emotions reflected in epileptic experiences. *Brain*, **79,** 29.

WOODBURY, D. M. (1969) Mechanisms of action of anticonvulsants. In *Basic Mechanisms of the Epilepsies*. Edited by A. H. Jasper *et al.*, Boston: Little, Brown; London: Churchill.

Chapter XII

PARANOID STATES AND PARANOID PSYCHOSES
A. D. Forrest

INTRODUCTION

Paranoid states have at many stages in the history of psychiatry been considered to be disorders of the intellect but Griesinger (1845) thought the cognitive defect to be secondary to the affective disturbance which is so often present.

Kahlbaum (1874) introduced the term paranoia but this concept of delusions arising independently of any disorder of affect has gained little acceptance amongst psychiatrists in Britain.

Kraepelin (1919) separated paranoia, paraphrenia and paranoid schizophrenia. Paranoia he considered to be characterized by prolonged course, fixed delusions and unfavourable outcome.

Bleuler (1912) was critical of Kraepelin's nosology and emphasized the cognitive defect underlying paranoid symptomatology.

The most famous paranoid patient was Daniel Paul Schreber, Presiding Judge of the Appeal Court in Dresden. His autobiography formed the basis for a psychoanalytic study by Freud (1911) and confirmed or developed his view that repressed homosexuality was the dynamic force underlying the paranoid projection.

It should be noted that there is a semantic difference in the usage of the term paranoid by British and Continental Psychiatrists. British psychiatrists use the word to refer to delusions of persecution while Continental writers use the term to refer to delusions of influence, arising from external sources and either benign or noxious in quality.

In this country Batchelor (1969) produced an excellent account of paranoid reactions, while Lewis (1971) has published a scholarly account of the development of the concept. It is interesting that Mayer-Gross *et al.* (1955) discuss paranoid reactions in three different sections of their textbook: under personality disorders, symptomatic psychoses and schizophrenia. Shepherd (1961) has provided a most detailed guide to the symptom of morbid jealousy.

AETIOLOGY

There seems little doubt that, as in other areas of psychiatry, age is a powerful variable when considering causal factors. Thus in young adults personality factors are of dominant importance. Kurt Schneider (1923) described the 'sensitive personality' who is liable to find meanings and coincidences which are not observed by his peers. Likewise drug intoxications, expecially L.S.D. and amphetamines, are factors to be considered in early adult life.

In the fourth and fifth decades alcoholic addiction in males and affective disturbances in females are common underlying factors. In older patients organic brain disease, depression and social isolation are common factors. Kay and Roth (1961) have drawn attention to the importance of deafness in patients in this older age group. Cognitive defects in older patients quite clearly underly some paranoid developments: the old lady hides her purse so that it will not get stolen, forgets where she put it and becomes convinced it has been stolen; the old gentleman who has workmen repairing the roof finds a ladder against the wall of the house and insists on phoning the police as he presumes burglars are about to break and enter. The general topic of persecutory states in the elderly is discussed by Post (1966).

CLASSIFICATION

It seems easiest to classify these paranoid states into paranoid personality disorders, paranoid states and paranoid psychoses.

PARANOID PERSONALITIES

These are people who, because of genetic factors or intrafamilial pressures, have always been 'abnormal' in Schneider's statistical sense. They have always been suspicious and sensitive and this may indeed have been part of the family culture.

Faced with the demands of adult life in the fields of work and sexuality they tend to develop persecutory ideas which may become very fixed.

Case (1), female, single, then aged 65. An only child she spent many years of her childhood in bed because of some alleged kidney disorder. In early adult life she became very attached to a homeopathic practitioner and developed many and various symptoms. Around 44 years she became convinced that her mother had killed her father and had tried to kill her. For several years she had psycho-analytic psychotherapy. In 1960 aged 53 she made an assault on her mother and was admitted to hospital under certificates. She improved with phenothiazines and was discharged in 1962 to live in 'digs'. She attended the clinic subsequently, focussing either on hypochondriacal complaints or on her belief that her mother was a homicidal megolomaniac and should be locked away. After her mother's death in 1968 she improved but became slightly grandiose. She now maintains that she has achieved a self analysis, something her medical advisers could never do.

Case (*2*) male, married, aged 39 years. This man had delusions of jealousy regarding his wife with most complex investigatory rituals. He scrutinized all the towels in the house and all the used tissues in the waste-paper baskets for signs of seminal staining and vaginal discharge. He also became convinced that his wife was masturbating with a face cloth and in evidence described the peculiar shape of the fabric when he examined it on return from work. For many years this man was greatly improved (at least in the opinion of his wife) with phenothiazine medication before he stopped attending the Clinic.

PARANOID STATES

These merge imperceptibly into the personality disorder group and in fact it is likely that the majority of patients in this group have an underlying personality problem. Usually however this has not been recognized until the onset of the illness. Again the symptoms are persecutory as a rule though there are complex variations on this theme. For example, some patients who consult the psychiatrist with a view to getting a recommendation for plastic surgery have basically a paranoid mechanism underlying their symptomatology. One woman who came to the clinic some years ago wanted an operation on her nose. She said it was red and stuck out. Underlying this was a complex of ideas of reference. A less common variant is the patient who complains of buzzing in the ears for which the E.N.T. Surgeon can find no cause. A Ph.D. student who had this complaint used a transistor radio to mask the sound and the irritation it caused. Basically he was a very introverted, sensitive and suspicious man and over several interviews it emerged that he really believed he had a simple mechanical problem in the ear and the reason that the doctors would not help him was somehow connected with a decision by higher medical authorities that he must not be allowed to complete his research. Why this was so was never divulged; he refused further treatment.

Usually, however, the presentation is sexual jealousy in men and persecution by the neighbours in women.

Case (*5*): male, married, aged 47 years. By trade he was a Fairground Operator, that is he had a 'merry-go-round' and travelled around Scotland doing business at the seasonal fairs. He had married a girl from Glasgow who came from a commercial background whereas all his people had been, as he said, in 'the entertainments business'. He was seen in 1969 and he said that in 1957 he had been at a dance with his wife. There was a good deal of drinking going on and at one point he got separated from her and later found her talking to 'Carlos'. This man was known to him as a 'lady-killer' and later in the evening he overheard a man say 'Carlos is doing well tonight'. He and his wife had a row when they got back to their caravan but he did not show signs of paranoid illness until two years later when he became convinced she was having an affaire with 'Carlos'. He received a course of E.C.T. and apparently remained well until 1964 when these same ideas returned. His wife, who came with him, said she was seriously thinking of leaving him. However, after five E.C.T. he was back to normal and has not attended the Clinic since then.

Paranoid states in women (at least in Scotland) usually refer to the neighbours. One spinster of 50 years was convinced that the neighbours, who all took it in turn to clean the common stair, brushed the dust under her door. Another married woman of 42 years was convinced that the neighbours in the flat above tormented her on purpose by keeping on the wireless until the early hours. She persuaded her husband to get another house only to find that there was a man upstairs who played the bagpipes at all hours of the night. It appears that this was indeed so, though the husband said the piper stopped about midnight. Although this lady was better with drug therapy, she persuaded her husband to move yet again, this time to England.

Occasionally the psychiatrist comes across such a bizarre delusion that the possibility of schizophrenia is raised. Such was a single lady of 50 years who believed she had a fish, probably a sturgeon, lodged in her gullet. She believed this animal had been inserted into her oesophagus some 15 years earlier by a Russian E.N.T. specialist whom she had consulted in Moscow. In fact the bizarre quality of delusions is a very unreliable guide to diagnosis which rests more securely on the total symptom pattern, the age of the patient and the course of the illness. In fact this lady between episodes (precipitated by stopping her medication) worked efficiently in a Department of the Civil Service.

PARANOID PSYCHOSES

In distinction to the preceding categories of personality disorder and paranoid states, paranoid psychoses are illnesses with a recognizable onset and hopefully a recognizable ending. There are so many possible aetiological factors that it is necessary to group them into quite broad categories:

1. intoxications: amphetamines, L.S.D., alcoholic addiction
2. endocrine disorders: thyrotoxicosis, myxoedema, Cushings Syndrome
3. post-operative and puerperal paranoid psychoses
4. paranoid psychoses in old people with organic impairment
5. paranoid psychoses in old people with deafness
6. affective illnesses with prominent paranoid features
7. paranoid illnesses without any affective component.

One distinguishing feature of paranoid psychoses is that the patient often experiences abusive or threatening auditory hallucinations alongside the delusions of persecution. Also in the toxic, endocrine, post-operative and puerperal groups, there may in addition be some degree of alteration or clouding of consciousness.

Intoxications

Amphetamine psychoses have been fully described by Connell (1958). The symptoms are predominantly paranoid in quality with associated abusive hallucinations and marked restlessness. L.S.D. can cause a paranoid psychosis ('bad trip') but auditory hallucinations are usually absent whereas some degree of thought disorder is often evident. Passivity feelings can also occur after L.S.D. Whereas most patients who have had bad reactions to L.S.D. remit within a matter of days or weeks, there are some subjects who develop a paranoid illness after L.S.D. which takes much longer to clear up.

Alcoholic Delirium has been described elsewhere (Chap V, Vol II) but Alcoholic Hallucinosis requires mention. This is perhaps not a common presentation but the pattern of symptoms is sufficiently florid that one recalls individual patients years afterward. The voices are abusive and are associated with the development of paranoid delusions. The affect is anxious or excited rather than depressed. Sometimes these illnesses persist for several months unless treatment is initiated early and continued vigorously.

It is sometimes questioned whether paranoid patients are really dangerous; Batchelor (1969) points out that this is one group of patients from whom unprovoked, unexpected and really violent assaults can be expected.

Case (8): male, 51 years, single, living in a Model Lodging House and working on a Construction Site as a labourer. One previous admission to hospital with delusions and abusive hallucinations. He had been drinking heavily every night for several weeks and had come to believe that some of the other residents were going to 'do him in'. Sometimes he heard voices whispering about him especially at night. This particular night he thought he heard the man in the next cubicle say 'we'll wait till later and then fix him'. The patient broke into the next cubicle and stabbed the man to death.

Endocrine Disorders

Psychiatric syndromes associated with endocrine disorders are described in Chap XIII, Vol II. Both in myxoedema and in thyrotoxicosis one sees patients with an atypical paranoid-depressive illness which is sometimes difficult to diagnose and often provides difficulties in management.

Case (9): female, 26 years, married; this wife of a country G.P. had become very disillusioned with her life and very hostile to her husband.

She felt he went out on calls really to get away from her and sometimes was abusive to patients when they phoned the house. At interview she was tense, irritable, very cross with her husband, sleeping badly. She had lost about 5 kilos in weight but she had a *very* good appetite. This factor led to the correct diagnosis and appropriate (and effective) treatment.

Cushings Syndrome can lead to a paranoid presentation (Chap XIII, Vol II).

Post-Operative and Puerperal Psychoses

Acute confusional states are described in Chap XIII, Vol II, and the affective illnesses that may occur in the puerperium are described in Chap IX, Vol II. There are, however, paranoid psychoses which erupt in the post-operative period where the alteration in the level of consciousness is minimal though still probably an important causal factor leading to cognitive difficulties. It does seem that certain operative areas are more prone to this complication, i.e. liver, gall-bladder, heart, kidneys, bladder and cataract operations. Perhaps there is always some cerebral insult whether from anoxia, hypotension or metabolic factor. Certainly acute paranoid reactions are seen after open-heart surgery, cholecystectomy and prostatectomy and at the time of interview there is often no convincing evidence of impaired cerebral function. Fortunately these conditions respond to appropriate medication.

Puerperal psychoses are sometimes essentially paranoid in character. Once again metabolic, anoxic or endocrine factors may be operative. One patient, an older woman, had worked as a trained nurse for many years before her marriage. In the first few days after the birth of her first child she became quite distressed and developed the conviction that the nurses were putting drugs in her food.

Paranoid Psychoses in Old People

This matter is fully described in Chap XIV, Vol II; but the importance of isolation, deafness and organic intellectual impairment all leading to cognitive defects so that cues are misinterpreted needs to be emphasized. It is difficult for the young psychiatrist in full possession of all his faculties to realize how easily misinterpretations can occur when cognitive skills are impaired and consensual validation (i.e. the opportunity to discuss the matter with someone else) is not possible. Imagine a letter from the Inspector of Taxes delivered to the wrong address but the right name (though wrong initial). The old man broods about it, opens it and finds there is a claim for unpaid tax. Alone and with some impairment of his critical faculties one can speculate on the plots which he could imagine. An added complication in old people living alone and who begin to harbour paranoid delusions in that they further isolate themselves and also tend to neglect their diet. This is clearly an area where preventitive psychiatry should be able to operate with some effect (see Chap VI, Vol I).

Affective Illnesses with a Paranoid Component

Lewis (1934) in his impressive survey of depressive states noted how many women aged 40 to 50 years had marked paranoid symptomatology. It seems that many middle aged women with paranoid features are liable to be labelled as paranoid schizophrenics and recent work in Edinburgh tends to confirm this view (Forrest and Hay, 1972). There can be little doubt that the majority of paranoid patients admitted to hospital in the fifth decade are women and that many of them have an affective (i.e. depressive) component. There are others without any affective component who have delusions similar to those described in the paranoid states but also experience abusive or threatening hallucinations. Some of these latter illnesses are very persistent unless treatment is instituted early and continued for many months or even years.

Case (*11*): female, 47, married; always perhaps a little suspicious of her neighbours but apparently content with her life with her husband and son until 10 years ago, when she began to think the house opposite was a brothel run by the Chief Constable. She became convinced that the food in the house was being poisoned and took all her meat and butter away with her (in a shopping-bag) when she went out. Admitted on a compulsory basis she improved rapidly with E.C.T. and trifluoperazine 5 mg t.d.s. After discharge she remained well for about a year and then had to be readmitted with the same symptoms. This pattern was repeated three times until two years ago when she was started on fluphenazine decanoate. She has attended monthly since then for her injection and keeps well.

TREATMENT

This can best be discussed by grouping (1) the intoxications and the endocrine disorders, (2), the post-operative, puerperal and paranoid psychoses of middle age (3) the paranoid illnesses of old people and (4) the paranoid states and personalities.

INTOXICATIONS AND ENDOCRINE DISORDERS

Treatment of the underlying condition is often imperative. Thus alcoholic hallucinosis requires abstinence and parenteral vitamin B complex. Thyrotoxicosis and myxoedema necessitate the appropriate treatment with carbimazole or L-thyroxine. In addition most of these patients need treatment with chlorpromazine 50 to 100 mg t.d.s.

Some patients with paranoid psychoses complicating thyroid dysfunction also need a short course of E.C.T. L.S.D. and amphetamine psychoses usually remit quickly and do not need long-term drug therapy but subjects with alcoholic hallucinosis may need chlorpromazine over several months.

2. POST-OPERATIVE, PUERPERAL AND PARANOID PSYCHOSES OF MIDDLE AGE.

Post-operative paranoid psychoses usually remit over a matter of weeks with chlorpromazine (or thioridazine in cases with hepatic disorder) 50 to 100 mg t.d.s. Puerperal paranoid psychoses often need a course of E.C.T. along with chlorpromazine. These patients need to be followed up for at least six months.

Paranoid psychoses in middle life are either associated with depression of affect or arise *de novo*. In both cases a course of E.C.T. along with trifluoperazine 5 to 10 mg t.d.s. is effective. For the paranoid psychoses without an affective component long term medication using parenteral fluphenazine decanoate is indicated (see Chap XV, Vol II).

3. PARANOID ILLNESSES OF OLD AGE

The treatment of these patients has been discussed in Chap XIV, Vol II. It should be noted however that old people do not tolerate the hypotensive effects of chlorpromazine and reliance on perphenazine 2 to 4 mg t.d.s. or trifluoperazine 2 to 5 mg t.d.s. may seem justifiable. E.C.T. is much less often required in old people than it is in the middle age group.

4. PARANOID PERSONALITIES AND PARANOID STATES

It is sometimes suggested that these patients should benefit from psychotherapy. This is likely to fail however because their paranoid explanatory model has been the best they can achieve; naturally they are reluctant to see it overthrown. On the other hand we think regular discussions with the psychiatrist are in some curious way valuable. Sometimes the patient comes really to abuse the psychiatrist for not *acting* on the patient's delusions. Some patients value practical discussion of how they can best live their lives in spite of their delusions. We think it is important neither to agree with a delusion nor yet seek argument in an attempt to overthrow it. Sometimes one can say 'Yes, I see how it must have seemed to you but personally I would put a different interpretation on it'. Both paranoid personalities and paranoid states can benefit from drugs (i.e. chlorpromazine 25 mg mane and 50 mg nocte or trifluoperazine 2 to 5 mg t.d.s.) but seldom will they agree to take them and, if they do, it is seldom for long.

Group therapy should be considered for some paranoid personalities;

L

theoretically they should benefit from the consensual validation (or negation) of their ideas and the socialization process (see Chap VI, Vol II).

PROGNOSIS

The intoxications and endocrine based paranoid psychoses usually remit within a matter of weeks. Relapses in patients with myxoedema unfortunately are not uncommon. The postoperative and puerperal paranoid psychoses generally respond to adequate treatment; peurperal patients need a six month follow-up programme. The risk of subsequent illness after another pregnancy is very hard to estimate; advice must be tempered by knowledge of the patients present circumstances and the patients and spouses feelings on the matter. Certainly a delay of two to three years before another pregnancy is commenced would seem to be appropriate advice.

The affective paranoid patients in middle age respond well to treatment but should continue maintenance trifluoperazine for six months. The paranoid psychoses without affective component almost always relapse unless phenothiazines are continued for several years. Paranoid illnesses in old age usually respond quickly to treatment in hospital but on return home the prognosis will depend on (1) what social measures can be taken to help the patient—i.e. Day-Patient attendance, Social Clubs, etc. and (2) whether they can be persuaded to continue taking their medication.

REFERENCES

BATCHELOR, I. R. C. (1969) Paranoid Reaction-types. In Henderson and Gillespie's *Textbook of Psychiatry*, pp. 307–320. Revised by I. R. C. Batchelor; London: O.U.P.

BLEULER, E. (1912) *Affectivity, Suggestibility and Paranoia*. New York: State Hospital Bulletin.

CONNELL, P. H. (1958) *Amphetamine Psychosis*. London: Maudsley Monograph.

FORREST, A. D. & HAY, J. (1972) Schizophrenia and paranoid psychoses: an attempt at diagnostic clarification. *British Journal of Medical Psychology*, in press.

FREUD, S. (1911) Psycho-analytic notes upon an autobiographic account of a case of paranoia (demential paranoides). In *Collected Papers* Vol. III, London: Hogarth Press.

GRIESINGER, W. (1845) *Pathologie and Therapie der Psychischen Krankheiten*. (Translated by C. C. Robertson, London: New Sydenham Society Publications, No. 33, 1862).

KAHLBAUM, K. (1874) Klinische Abhandlungen uber psychische Krankheiten. Ht. I. Die Katatonie, Berlin: Hirschwald.

KAY, D. W. K. & ROTH, M. (1961) Environmental and hereditary factors in the schizophrenias of old age ('late paraphrenia') and their bearing on the general problem of causation in schizophrenia. *Journal of Mental Science*, **107**, 649–686.

KRAEPELIN, E. (1919)   *Dementia Praecox and Paraphrenia* (translated by R. M. Barclay) Edinburgh.

LEWIS, A. J. (1934)   Melancholia: a clinical survey of depressive states. *Journal of Mental Science*, **80,** 277–294.

LEWIS, A. J. (1971)   Paranoia and paranoid: a historical perspective. *Psychological Medicine*, **1,** 2–12.

MAYER-GROSS, W., SLATER, E. & ROTH, M. (1955)   '*Clinical Psychiatry*' London: Cassall.

POST, F. (1966)   *Persistent Persecutory States of the Elderly.* Oxford: Pergamon Press.

SHEPHERD, M. (1961)   Morbid Jealousy: some clinical and social aspects of a psychiatric symptom. *Journal of Mental Science*, **107,** 687–753.

SCHNEIDER, K. (1923)   Psychopathic Personalities 9th Edn. (1950) Vienna. Translated by M. W. Hamilton, 1958. London: Cassell.

Chapter XIII

ORGANIC DISORDERS
E. E. Robertson

INTRODUCTION

There are certain characteristic psychological symptoms and symptom-complexes, the presence of which provide irrefutable evidence of a disturbance in brain functioning. The physical conditions which conduce to such brain disturbance and so lead to the appearance of the characteristic psychological features are designated in psychiatric classification, organic disorders. Organic disorders and their causes are numerous (see Table 1). Damage to the brain occurs as a direct consequence of head injury, cerebral degenerative disease or tumour but

TABLE I

Some Organic Disorders

INTOXICATIONS	Alcohol, barbiturates, bromide: amphetamine: cannabis: hallucinogens—mescaline and lysergic acid diethylamide (L.S.D.): the 'hard drugs'—morphine, heroin and cocaine.
INFECTIONS	(*a*) *Cerebral*—meningitis: viral encephalitis: syphilis: trypanosomiasis: typhus fever: malaria.
	(*b*) *Systemic*—septicaemia (streptococcal or staphylococcal): typhoid fever (bronchopneumonia and milder infections in children and the aged).
HYPOXIA	Carbon monoxide poisoning.
METABOLIC DISORDERS	Electrolyte disturbance: vitamin B group deficiencies: porphyria: liver and renal diseases: spontaneous hypoglycaemia.
ENDOCRINE DISEASE	Thyrotoxicosis: myxoedema, Cushing's syndrome.
CEREBRAL TUMOUR	(*a*) Primary
	(*b*) Metastatic
TRAUMA	Head injuries: traumatic encephalopathy (the 'punch drunk' syndrome): subdural haematoma.
VASCULAR DISEASE	Cerebral arteriosclerosis: sub-arachnoid haemorrhage.
DEGENERATIVE CONDITIONS	(*a*) Huntington's chorea
	(*b*) Presenile dementias: Alzheimer's disease: Pick's disease: Jakob Creutzfeld disease: Spongiform encephalopathy:
	(*c*) Senile cerebral atrophy.

disease in other organs can indirectly affect brain functioning which can also be disturbed by a variety of extraneous factors in the form of intoxications, infections and deficiencies. Identification of the cause of an organic disorder is not difficult if (1) the physical appearance of the patient is distinctive as in myxoedema and Huntington's Chorea, (2) the history provides relevant information, e.g. known addiction to alcohol or a recent head injury, (3) focal neurological signs indicating a cerebral lesion are elicited or (4) systemic disease known to affect brain functioning is present. In some cases, however, diagnosis is achieved only after prolonged observation of the patient, repeated physical and mental examinations, exhaustive laboratory tests, electroencephalo-graphic and radiological investigation supplemented in some instances by the exploratory techniques of the neurosurgeon.

An elementary rule for the recognition of organic mental syndromes is to look for (1) memory defects and intellectual impairment and/or (2) clouding of consciousness which are absent in the functional psychoses. This rule requires minor modification. Severe personality change observed in bilateral frontal lobe lesions, in some cases of multiple sclerosis and as a sequel to encephalitis lethargica (where it is restricted to children and adolescents) may be unaccompanied by intellectual impairment but such personality change nonetheless represents an organic disorder. Clouding of consciousness of whatever degree denotes an acute and usually temporary brain disturbance but mild clouding of a subtly different order can occur in affective disorders and schizophrenia and give rise to initial difficulty in diagnosis.

PRELIMINARY MENTAL EXAMINATION IN CASES OF SUSPECTED ORGANIC DISORDER

The presence of intellectual defects or mild clouding of consciousness usually becomes apparent at initial interview if the examiner takes a careful history and does not allow himself to be influenced by pre-conceived ideas on diagnosis—a common fault. Errors and inconsis-tencies in the patient's statements may be the first clue and should be a signal to the examiner to direct the conversation to obtaining the family history and a detailed account of the personal history, since this shows up a failure to remember exact dates and also discrepancies in the chronological sequence of events. If such are detected, questioning should be quickly switched to simple formal tests for patients suffering from organic disorder become easily fatigued and bored and constantly require new stimuli. These tests must needs be familiar, easily and quickly administered, require no special equipment and indeed no scoring, since they may have to be given in many different circum-stances. (Allison (1962) gives a good account of these and similar simple tests which he found of value in distinguishing focal from diffuse cerebral lesions). Memory is tested by asking the names of famous persons, the dates of well-known historical events and current newspaper headlines. That special aspect of memory which relates to the retention of immediate impressions is tested by giving the patient a name and address and a colour to memorize and asking him to repeat these after an interval of five minutes. Competence in calculation is assessed by the serial subtraction of 7 from 100 ($100 - 7 = 93$; $93 - 7 = 86$, etc.). This is more revealing than financial calculations which carry the familiarity of daily practice. Orientation in time is demonstrated by the accurate naming of the present day, month and year and the approximate hour of day. Spatial orientation has many facets, and unless there is clear evidence of specific spatial defects it is usual at this stage to assess only topographical memory—by asking the patient to name the place of examination, to describe its position in relation to local landmarks, and to enumerate the streets through which he passed on his journey. Constructional ability is tested by the reproduction or construction of designs using matches or pencil and paper. During this questioning the examiner looks for evidence of difficulty in word finding (dysphasia), e.g. hesitations, groping for the appropriate word and *circumlocution* or *periphrasia* (which terms are applied to the patient's substitute definitions, often inadequate, of the forgotten word, e.g. fountain pen—'you write with it'). Simple tests for dysphasia require the patient (1) to name some dozen objects from the commonplace to the, for him, unfamiliar, e.g. stethoscope, while he handles each object in turn and (2) to enumerate as many components of certain categories, e.g. flowers, animals, etc., as he can remember. Dysphasia must be confirmed or eliminated early in the interview since it denotes not only defects in verbal expression but decreased understanding of the spoken word and therefore nullifies the conclusions drawn from oral tests. Ideally, reading and writing should also be tested if dysphasia is suspected. The first part of the interview which should not take more than 45 minutes, is now terminated. The nearest relative or friend accompanying the patient is then interrogated (or arrangements are made to see this key person if the patient arrives alone). *Interrogate* is the operative word for the maximum amount of information must be extracted. That sympathy and tact are the hallmarks of a good interviewer needs no stressing, but the same degree of patience and sensitivity is not required in this interview as in the former, for relatives are eager to give information. The family and personal history is gone over again and omissions in the patient's statements noted. Special attention is paid to information relating to the patient's previous personality, intelligence rating and employment record so that comparison can be made between his present and former level of functioning. Thereafter a record is obtained of the *first* and subsequent departures from normal with their respective dates. These deviations may relate to the patient's behaviour, emotional outlook, his intellectual or practical performance: generally all four are affected in organic disorder. Questions should be pressed to elicit the common-place and trivial, the housewife's errors in cooking, the technician's faulty measurements, the business man's over-expensive buying, for these details represent the patient's response to his life situation ('the test of life'). Frequently it is not so much the mistake as the patient's reaction to it which is significant, for instance it is merely unusual for a careful driver to be involved in a traffic accident but it is ominous if he shows no subsequent concern.

The information thus acquired (which should be taken down verba-tim and later classified) varies in volume and quality in direct ratio to the intelligence and interest of the witness, but it is generally more accurate than that supplied by a patient suffering from an organic disorder. Furthermore it frequently opens up entirely new perspectives, and seldom fails to give clues to the aetiology, which can be followed up at a later stage.

Thereafter the patient is seen again, on this occasion for a shorter and more casual-seeming conversation to allay anxiety. Memory can now be tested more discreetly and effectively by questioning the patient on details of his history as obtained from his relatives, and this method, unlike general knowledge tests, is not dependent on previous educational standards. New information from the same source is lightly touched on and the patient's reaction noted. Meanwhile the examiner, in this as in the first interview, is constantly on the alert for certain known abnor-malities of conversation and behaviour which are near specific evidence of organic mental disorder, viz.,

1. *Catastrophic reaction*—this occurs as a response to failure in a test situation. Suddenly, without warning, the patient becomes pale and tremulous, then tearful and distressed or—more rarely—sullen and aggressive. This is a signal to discontinue questioning for a period.

2. *Perseveration*—this is illustrated by the patient who responds correctly to a stimulus but continues to make the same response after the stimulus is withdrawn and another introduced (Allison). Perseveration can affect all forms of response—single movements, co-ordinated actions and even tactile sensations but it is seen at its most obvious in speech and communication. The patient repeats his reply to the preceding question when another question is put to him, or on a higher level shows an inability to relinquish the train of thought initiated by the earlier question.

Clonic perseveration. This term is applied to a performance, which once initiated, is continued indefinitely—e.g. a patient requested to draw a circle, continues drawing circles until the entire page is covered.

3. *Confabulation*—is defined as the fabrication of false memories and

as such is a mechanism utilized by patients with memory impairment to 'fill in the gaps' produced by their faulty recollection. This conventional definition of confabulation is applicable to a proportion of dysmnesic patients. Others lack the ability to 'fabricate' memories and when they are asked a question which they are unable to answer because of their failure to retain recently acquired information, they automatically select from their store of past memories something appropriate for the present situation (see p. 339).

4. *Emotional lability*—in the context of organic disorder, this term is used to designate abrupt, apparently motiveless swings from tears to laughter, from anger to good humour.

5. *Mood changes*—*Euphoria* (an elevation of mood akin to, but not identical with, the elation seen in mania) is given high diagnostic importance as denoting a *primary* symptom of brain dysfunction. Conversely depression of spirits is less significant for although it *can* be primary in this sense, it is also susceptible to interpretation as a secondary response to the subject's awareness of incapacity.

The above examination plan presupposes some degree of co-operation from the patient. If this is totally lacking as happens in patients with severe clouding of consciousness the examiner can only list his observations of the patient's appearance and behaviour and obtain an adequate history. A full physical examination should, of course, be carried out after the initial interview in all cases of suspected organic disorder.

CLASSIFICATION

Classification must finally rest on an aetiological basis (see Table 1) but since organic disorders only occasionally show a *specific* mental picture to allow of their separate identification on this alone—in contradistinction to physical signs which, when present, are strong diagnostic indicators—an automatic first step in suspected organic disorder is to allocate the case to one of three *general* patterns of cerebral reaction, viz:

1. *Acute organic reaction* denotes a *temporary* and *reversible* disturbance in brain functioning of which the salient feature is clouding of consciousness.

2. *Dysmnesic syndrome* has as its central feature a specific memory defect—mental impressions are retained only momentarily and the ability to *memorize* is lost. This memorizing defect can occur as a transient or permanent phenomenon.

3. *Chronic organic reaction* is characterized by persisting and usually progressive impairment of intellectual functions. If there is in addition marked deterioration of personality and behaviour, the term *dementia* is

applied. Such mental symptoms always indicate intracranial structural damage.

ACUTE ORGANIC REACTIONS

The primary, but not always the most obvious, feature is clouding of consciousness or diminished awareness. (Total unawareness as observed in coma is thereby excluded.) Such clouding of consciousness with its cluster of associated symptoms is known as a *confusional state* or, if perceptual disorder in the form of hallucinations and illusions is superadded, as *delirium*. The term confusional state has been criticized on semantic grounds, but there are practical reasons for retaining it as a title for the many gradations of clouded consciousness which lack the dramatic impact of the rarer but more readily recognisable delirium. An acute organic reaction is by definition reversible and no histopathological changes may be found in the brain of patients dying from extracerebral conditions with associated delirium. Nevertheless an acute organic reaction may become a chronic organic reaction depending on the nature, severity and duration of the causative disorder, and this progression always indicates that structural damage to cerebral tissue has occurred.

SYMPTOMATOLOGY

(1) *Impairment of attention*: Active attention (concentration) is difficult to arouse and sustain and the patient, during questioning, shows a greater or lesser tendency to sink back into inertia. Alternatively he may be distracted by environmental happenings, which in turn are grasped in a fragmentary way and quickly ousted by new stimuli (distractibility). This conduces to (2) *defective grasp*, i.e. a failure to perceive the essentials of a situation. In severe clouding, this may result in bizarre behaviour, e.g. drinking from a flower vase on the bedside table instead of from the glass provided, but in milder states it may have to be sought for. Failure to see the point of a proverb or story or to build up parts of an object or picture into a coherent whole (constructional apraxia) are delicate tests for mild clouding as is (3) *perseveration* (see p. 319).

(4) *Spatial disorientation* is constant in more severe states, and may be partial or complete. It is strikingly manifest immediately after head injury, where the patient repetitively demands where he is and what has happened to him, appears to understand the proffered explanation but forgets it within seconds. This degree of insight is lacking when clouding of consciousness develops more gradually. 'Double' disorientation is sometimes observed, e.g. the patient accepts that he is in hospital but at the same time asserts that he is in another place which has familiar associations for him. Such *misidentifications* commonly accompany disorientation in clouded states and follow the rule that the unfamiliar is mistaken for the familiar, e.g. the peal of a hospital bell is misidentified

by the patient as his own front door bell. Members of the hospital staff are mistaken for relatives or close friends although the appearance of the latter in *propria persona* generally results in their instant recognition.

(5) *Temporary memory impairment* is demonstrated in a failure to recall day-to-day events during the confusional phase. Memory for previous events is less disturbed, and the patient may be able to give a skeleton history. If clouding is severe, however, much of his information about the past will be inaccurate or irrelevant or confabulatory (see p. 319).

(6) The *mood* is generally described as anxious or fearful but it can be depressed or placid or so variable as to be impossible to categorize.

(7) *Perplexity* is a common accompaniment since impaired attention and disorientation breed uncertainty which is presumably also the basis of the (8) *mild paranoid ideas* of persecution which are sometimes expressed.

(9) A *fluctuating course* is characteristic of confusional states, the symptoms varying from day to day or even from minute to minute, and always appearing more severe at night. *Lucid intervals* occur when the patient briefly exhibits normal social rapport. This fluctuation in symptoms is the most important means of differentiating this acute condition from states of persistent intellectual impairment (chronic organic reaction).

Physical symptoms include muscular inco-ordination, tremor, restlessness and—occasionally—epileptic seizures.

Except for a minority of cases, which show persisting somnolence, *insomnia* is the rule and improvement in this last heralds recovery which is followed by amnesia for the confusional period.

Delirium. When there is in addition severe psychomotor restlessness with psychotic features in the form of hallucinations and delusions the condition is known as delirium. Hallucinations are predominantly visual and in accord with the prevailing **affect** which is generally one of fear—terrifying scenes of threatening human and animal figures, e.g. the 'blue devils' of alcoholic delirium (delirium tremens). Exceptionally *Lilliputian hallucinations* are experienced, i.e. small brightly-coloured figures or objects which induce a mood of mild amusement or euphoria. Illusions take the form of (1) misinterpretation of objects in the environment, e.g. a flapping curtain is misinterpreted as an oncoming express train or (2) misinterpretation of bodily sensations, e.g. drug-induced skin paraesthesiae are interpreted as crawling insects (the 'cocaine bug'). *Delusions,* if present, are more elaborate than the simple paranoid ideas of the milder confusional state. Indeed the mental life of the delirious patient is at once vivid and compelling and argues the operation of some cerebral mechanism additional to that causing clouding of consciousness.

Confusional and delirious states are more readily precipitated at the two extremes of life.

Treatment is that of the primary cause, but certain measures are uniformly applicable. The patient should be nursed in a bright, uncluttered ward or room, preferably by the same familiar relay of nurses. No potentially dangerous objects should be left within reach. A night light should be provided. It is imperative to allay the restlessness. Chlorpromazine is the drug of choice but may have to be supplemented by oral paraldehyde, chloral hydrate or the shorter-acting barbiturates (although any one or all of these drugs may be contraindicated if they are known to aggravate the causal condition). If there is reason to believe that alcohol is a factor or that a vitamin B deficiency attributable to other factors is present, then *Parentrovite* (which contains the whole vitamin B complex) should be given immediately, preferably by the intravenous route.

AETIOLOGY

Acute organic reactions

These are precipitated by a variety of aetiological factors. In enumerating them, references to chronic organic reactions are unavoidable since transition from an acute brain disturbance to permanent cerebral damage is not uncommon.

Drug intoxications are described in the appropriate section and it suffices to say that drug-induced deliria are among the most florid as they are also the most common. Delirium developing immediately after admission to hospital is most frequently attributable to alcohol and barbiturate withdrawal. The delirium of bromide intoxication is still occasionally encountered and the associated slurring of speech, tremors and ataxia may lead to prolonged neurological investigation before the cause is identified.

Infections

Delirium complicating bacterial infection is less common since the advent of antibiotics and protective inoculation but confusional states may occur in streptococcal and staphylococcal septicaemia and the delirium of typhoid fever is well-known. Mild infections may precipitate delirium in young children and the aged. Protozoal infections are seldom seen in psychiatric hospitals in this country. The treatment of patients from the tropics may be interrupted by an attack of benign (vivax) tertian malaria but the delirium and other cerebral manifestations of malignant (falciparum) malaria are rarely observed. An uncommon but not entirely unknown cause of psychiatric admission are the late effects of trypanosomiasis which take the form of intellectual deterioration and personality change of which the predominant feature is a curiously casual attitude.

Cerebral hypoxia

This occurs when there is (1) a reduction in the oxygen-carrying power of the blood as in carbon monoxide poisoning, (2) a low arterial PO_2 as is found in subjects exposed to high altitudes or in non-pressurised aircraft and in respiratory diseases such as pneumonia and chronic bronchitis, and (3) a reduced cerebral blood flow as in heart failure. The mental sequelae of hypoxia are most marked in the elderly with coexisting disease of the cerebral arteries. Asymptomatic bronchopneumonia and myocardial infarction are not uncommon in this age group, and the sudden onset of clouded consciousness and disorientation may be the first indication of their presence.

Vitamin B group deficiencies

Thiamine deficiency is the aetiological basis of Wernicke's encephalopathy, which may terminate in a transient or permanent defect of memorizing. It is therefore considered under Dysmnesic syndrome (p. 338).

2. *Nicotinic acid deficiency.* Pellagra (It. pelle agra, rough skin) is common in countries where the diet is poor and monotonous and chronic diarrhoeal diseases are endemic. Its incidence increases if the staple diet is maize since maize, unlike other cereals, is deficient in the amino-acid, tryptophan, from which nicotinic acid is synthesized. Pellagra is not entirely unknown in this country: it is occasionally seen in the aged and mentally disturbed, living in isolation and neglecting their diet. 'Secondary' pellagra can occur in conditions causing prolonged diarrhoea and also in alcoholics. The clinical symptoms are known to every examination candidate by the mnemonic '5 Ds'— dermatitis, dysphagia, diarrhoea, delirium and dementia, denoting respectively the reddish brown scaly eruptions, the glossitis, the gastrointestinal and mental symptoms. In addition muscular weakness, hyperaesthesiae, paraesthesia and altered reflexes are part of the syndrome. Subacute combined degeneration of the spinal cord has been observed. Of the mental symptoms, depression with minimal intellectual retardation is prominent in the initial stages and sometimes antedates the physical manifestations. Its aetiological significance is not always appreciated in the sporadic mild cases which occur in this country, e.g. in the elderly recluse living on a diet of bread and tea. As the condition advances the depression merges into a confusional or delirious state with a marked depressive colouring. Pellagra is considered a serious disease in countries where it is endemic and pellagrous delirium not infrequently terminates in death. Delirium may progress to dementia. Autopsy findings correlated with the dementia are oedema or

atrophy of the brain with chromatolysis and pigmentation in the nerve cells, particularly in the Betz cells of the motor cortex. *Intensive treatment in the early stages prevents permanent sequelae. Nicotinic acid* is now regarded as a specific curative agent and is given in 10 divided doses of 50 mg, i.e. 500 mg daily supplemented by a high protein diet of at least 4000 calories. Higher doses of nicotinic acid are advocated in serious cases.

Vitamin B_{12} deficiency

Addisonian anaemia is the most prominent member of this group. Also to be borne in mind are Vitamin B_{12} deficiency states resulting from (a) *gastrectomy* and other gastrointestinal anomalies and diseases: Hunter *et al.* (1967) reported that 20 of 2000 patients coming under psychiatric supervision during a 4-year period had had a gastrectomy and of these 20, 5 had serum Vitamin B_{12} levels below 100 pg per ml; (b) *defective diet* in fanatical vegetarians (vegans) or patients suffering from psychiatric illness when the nutritional deprivation has been severe and prolonged.

A multiplicity of psychiatric symptoms, both organic and functional, has been described in association with pernicious anaemia, but Shulman (1967) claims that only such indubitably organic syndromes as confusional states and memory impairment can be regarded as a direct consequence of the underlying Vitamin B_{12} deficiency. In a prospective controlled study of 24 patients with P.A. and 21 with other forms of anaemia, he found that while a proportion in both groups exhibited psychiatric symptoms in the form of depression, anxiety, irritability, poor memory or diminished concentration, it was only in the patients with P.A. that memory impairment was observed to be wholly unrelated to age. He was able to retest 12 of the 17 P.A. patients with memory impairment after treatment and in 9 of the 12 the test score had reverted to normal. It is difficult to compare Shulman's findings with those of earlier writers, who frequently failed to discriminate between organic and functional mental symptoms, grouping them together as 'cerebral symptoms'. Fortunately Holmes (1956), when reporting that no fewer than 14 of his series of 25 cases of P.A. showed cerebral symptoms, appended case histories and from these it can be deduced that 12 of the 14 showed an organic mental picture. All 14 cases showed in addition signs of spinal cord and peripheral nerve involvement. Holmes observed that cerebral symptoms preceded the neurological and haematological abnormalities in some of his cases. This, which is now known to be a common sequence, has been emphasized by Strachan and Henderson (1965). These authors described 3 patients with a psychiatric syndrome showing marked organic features which ran a prolonged and fluctuating course until a diagnosis of avitaminosis B_{12} was made. The marrow was normoblastic in all 3 cases and neurological manifestations were absent.

Cerebral lesions demonstrated at autopsy in Addisonian anaemia are similar to those seen in the spinal cord. There is diffuse degeneration of the white matter with little in the way of glial proliferation. There are degenerative changes in the nerve cells of the cortex; areas of nerve cell loss are usually restricted to the outer three cortical laminae.

Psychiatric syndromes attributable to avitaminosis B_{12} (whether based on P.A., gastrectomy, intestinal diseases or nutritional deficiency) are probably of infrequent occurrence but their recognition is of great importance since they are so eminently treatable. Vitamin B_{12} assay should be carried out in all undiagnosed cases of organic disorder in later life. Treatment should be intensive and Strachan and Henderson (1965) advocate 1000 μg hydroxycobalamin (neocytamen) (a) daily for 6 weeks, (b) weekly for the subsequent 2 months, and (c) thereafter at fortnightly intervals.

Hepatic encephalopathy

A neuropsychiatric syndrome can develop suddenly or insidiously during the course of liver disease of diverse aetiology. The causative factor is unknown but hepatic encephalopathy only occurs when substances absorbed into the portal vessels from the bowel pass directly to the systemic circulation and so to the cerebral circulation without being metabolized in the liver. This requires the special circumstances of hepatocellular failure or the combination of liver disease of varying degrees of severity and a large portal venous collateral circulation bypassing the liver.

1. *Acute hepatic encephalopathy* occurs in association with viral hepatitis, or hepatic necrosis induced by hepatotoxic drugs (e.g. halothene) or in association with an episode of acute deterioration in established cirrhosis. Prodromal symptoms in the form of anergia, headache, disturbed sleep are rapidly followed by a confusional state or more often delirium. When coma supervenes, the outlook is grave. Mental symptoms may precede the onset of jaundice in viral hepatitis.

2. *Chronic encephalopathy* can occur in any type of cirrhosis and takes the form of a chronic organic reaction ranging from mild to severe. Essentially reversible episodes of altered consciousness extending to stupor frequently punctuate the course of the chronic reaction. Summerskill and his colleagues (1956) give a detailed account of the neuropsychiatric findings in 17 cases of hepatic cirrhosis with an extensive portal collateral circulation. Disorders of consciousness were present in all cases, and were associated with the hypersomnia and inversion of sleep rhythm typical of chronic liver disease. All patients

on recovery showed personality changes reminiscent of the frontal lobe syndrome (q.v.). Four of the patients in this series had been admitted to a psychiatric hospital before the nature of their condition was recognised.

In hepatic encephalopathy the presence of liver disease can usually be demonstrated but in some patients with a large collateral circulation, the usual manifestations of liver disease are absent and clinical diagnosis is based on the neuropsychiatric symptoms, hepatic foetor (the emanation of a sweet sickly odour), flapping tremors (although these are also elicited in uraemia) and spleno megaly. Bromosulphthalein excretion is usually impaired. Varying degrees of recovery or stabilization of symptoms can be expected in many of these cases but progressive mental deterioration has been described by Victor *et al.* (1965) under the title of *acquired hepatocerebral degeneration*. The clinical features of this syndrome are dementia, cerebellar symptoms in the form of dysarthria, ataxia and intention tremor and also choreoathetosis. Mild pyramidal tract signs and Parkinsonian-type tremors are also observed. Hepato-cerebral degeneration has to be distinguished from Wilson's disease and Huntington's Chorea (p. 362). The pathological changes include a diffuse increase in the size and number of the protoplasmic astrocytes, i.e. changes such as are found in cases of acute hepatic encephalopathy, and in addition degeneration of nerve cells and medullated fibres in the cerebral cortex, cerebellum and lenticular nuclei.

Porphyria

Of the several porphyrias, the Swedish hepatic type, *acute intermittent porphyria* (transmitted as a Mendalian dominant), is the form most often seen in Great Britain and it has important psychiatric implications.

The nature of the underlying metabolic defect is uncertain. There is an abnormality in the synthesis of haem leading to the excretion in the urine of excessive quantities of the haem precursors, delta-amino laevulinic acid (ALA) and porphobilinogen. The liver contains increased amounts of ALA synthetase. Goldberg (1965) believes that the primary abnormality is in the liver itself, but the exact mechanism of this is still unclear.

Acute intermittent porphyria (AIP) is diagnosed infrequently but is probably more common than is assumed and mild cases may go unrecognized. Investigation of the family of a patient with porphyria generally reveals that one or more members has the metabolic abnormality without its clinical manifestations. AIP affects women more often than men (in the ratio 3:2) and is rarely seen before puberty or after middle life. Attacks may erupt spontaneously or be precipitated by (a) drugs, notably barbiturates, alcohol, sulphonamides, sulphonal, methyldopa and oral contraceptives, (b) infections and (c) pregnancy.

The basic clinical defect is most probably a neuropathy, which is manifested in divers ways. The classical case presents with acute abdominal pain (with or without rigidity), vomiting and constipation, thus simulating an 'acute abdomen' and leading in some instances to laparotomy. More clear-cut evidence of neuropathy may be forthcoming in weakness or paralysis of the limbs. Any one of the cranial nerves may be involved. Pain in the affected muscles is a common symptom, but pain is frequently experienced in other areas, e.g. the head. Hypertension and tachycardia may occur at the height of the attack, and, less commonly, epileptiform convulsions. Attacks of AIP are self-limiting. Death, when it occurs, most commonly results from ventilatory failure. The formerly high mortality rate has decreased dramatically with the introduction of more effective methods of dealing with respiratory paralysis.

Psychological disturbances are observed more often in AIP than in other forms of porphyria. A well-documented finding is the acute organic syndrome, either a florid delirium or a quieter confusional state, during which the patient may show mildly aggressive and disinhibited behaviour for which amnesia is subsequently claimed. Such behaviour may be erroneously labelled hysterical. Memory impairment has been observed during and after an attack but usually clears. Both schizophrenic-like illness and affective disorder have been reported and McAlpine and Hunter (1969) have claimed that the mental illnesses of George the Third were manifestations of porphyria although their conclusions are not universally accepted (Dean, 1971).

AIP has other psychiatric implications. The physical symptoms are often assumed to denote hysteria, particularly when they occur as isolated manifestations, e.g. abdominal pain or hoarseness of the voice (from vocal cord paresis). Barbiturates which are frequently prescribed for patients with psychiatric symptoms can both induce and exacerbate porphyria. An instructive case, cited by Hierons (1957) was that of a 22-year-old woman with unsuspected porphyria, who was given large quantities of barbiturates and 'in the course of narco-analysis by a psychiatrist became cyanosed, pulseless and nearly died'. Before the introduction of barbiturates, sulphonal was widely used in psychiatric hospitals and the symptoms of porphyria were well-known to psychiatrists of that era (Campbell, 1898).

Diagnosis of AIP. Freshly voided urine on exposure to light turns a deep red, since the colourless porphobilinogen is slowly converted to uroporphyrin which is red. The simple side-room test for detecting porphobilinogen is carried out by mixing 5 ml Ehrlich's aldehyde reagent with 5 ml urine, adding 10 ml saturated sodium acetate and shaking the solution with 10 ml of a benzyl-amyl alcohol solution. If the test is positive, an intense red colour develops and persists in the aqueous layer. This test is specific for AIP. Porphobilinogen may disappear from the urine during remissions but in some cases it persists.

The porphyrins and their immediate precursors are known to be pharmacologically inert and are not causally related to the clinical manifestations (Goldberg and Rimington, 1962).

Lead poisoning

The clinical features and some of the biochemical findings are remarkably similar to those seen in porphyria (Dagg *et al.*, 1965).

Lead poisoning has more serious implications for children than for adults since they are more prone to develop lead encephalopathy and more likely to suffer permanent brain damage. Children develop lead intoxication from their habit of licking paint on toys or furniture or eating flaked paint on pipes or plaster work (pica). Amongst adults, many industrial workers are constantly exposed to the danger of inhaling or ingesting small particles of lead. Lead poisoning from contaminated water passing through domestic lead piping is not common, but recently Beattie and his colleagues (1972, *a*, *b*) have described two series of families affected from this source in rural Scotland and Glasgow. Lead is a cumulative poison and therefore clinical symptoms do not become apparent until the concentration of lead from continuous absorption reaches a critical level. Early symptoms include 'nervousness', lassitude, pallor, constipation, anorexia and sometimes joint pains which lead on to symptoms similar to those observed in AIP— abdominal colic and vomiting or a predominantly motor polyneuropathy. The upper limbs are more often involved than the lower as is exemplified in the characteristic wrist drop. Encephalopathy, which betokens severe poisoning in the adult, may be ushered in by a headache and convulsions or a slowly developing confusional state and if untreated may progress to a terminal coma. Encephalopathy has a more abrupt onset in children, who may have previously shown only pallor and irritability (Barltrop, 1969). It is, however, the early adult case with features such as emotional instability and exhaustion which is most likely to be referred for psychiatric opinion.

Diagnosis It is useful to remember that the traditional 'blue line' at the gum margins is not always present, that basophilic stippling of red cells is not such a frequent finding as has been supposed and that hypochromic anaemia is always present in severe, but not necessarily in mild, poisoning. Reliance is placed on the history, on the clinical findings, on a blood lead level of over 40 μg and the presence of abnormal amounts of ALA and coproporphyrin in the urine. Cases of lead poisoning should always be admitted to hospital for assessment but mild cases may not require treatment. The chelating agents pencillamine, EDTA (ethyline diamine tetra-acetate) and BAL, used in treatment of lead poisoning should only be administered on the advice of an expert. Barltrop considers that lead encephalopathy requires immediate and specialized treatment in an intensive care unit.

Endocrine disorders

These have always exercised a fascination for the psychiatrist, not least because of the persistent hope that the major psychoses may be proved attributable to some subtle hormonal imbalance. Yet although psychological symptoms are commonly encountered during the course of an endocrine disorder they are seldom specific and therefore less easy to define and classify than the physical symptoms on which perforce the diagnosis has to be based.

Thyroid disorders: Thyrotoxicosis. Anxiety and overactivity are as much a part of the clinical picture as the physical symptoms and may antedate the latter by many months. Exceptionally, brief episodes of excitement indistinguishable from hypomania are seen at the outset. The anxiety may manifest itself in irritability and emotional lability—the patient showing exaggerated relief following minor success and profound depression at failure. Indeed a sustained depressive mood with early morning waking but no retardation is often a feature, particularly if the response to treatment is delayed. Yet it is remarkable how seldom patients under treatment are referred to a psychiatrist, whose main preoccupation in relation to thyrotoxicosis is that he may fail to distinguish its early manifestations from the more common anxiety states which they resemble. Diagnosis ultimately depends on the presence or absence of the characteristic physical symptoms and the results of laboratory tests but diagnostic pointers always emerge from the psychiatric examination. The value of psychological symptoms in differential diagnosis has been investigated by Gurney and her co-workers, whose findings (reported by Slater and Roth, 1969) were that euthyroid patients with psychiatric disorder, initially referred for suspected hyperthyroidism, could be differentiated from thyrotoxic patients by the presence of a psychological precipitant for the illness, the presence of hysterical symptoms, panic attacks and depersonalization, a younger age of onset, and a neurotic personality as assessed by clinical examination and by the Maudsley Personality Inventory. There is reason to believe that the anxiety of the thyrotoxic patient is different in quality from that of the neurotic patient. Workers in Edinburgh, using psycho-physiological measures, have shown that thyrotoxic patients hyper-react initially to changes in environment, but thereafter habituate in the same manner as normal people, whereas patients with neurotic anxiety hyper-react and fail to habituate.

Personality factors, emotional conflicts, a sudden emotional shock, prolonged environmental stress singly and severally have been considered important in the genesis of thyrotoxicosis, but these and other theories may well be given a new slant when the results of recent thyroid research have been assimilated.

Uncommon manifestations of thyrotoxicosis include:

1. *Apathetic thyrotoxicosis.* This more serious form of thyrotoxicosis is characterized by emotional apathy, physical exhaustion, severe muscle wasting and an absence of the usual eye signs. It is seen most often in middle-aged women. Understandably it is not readily recognized and tends to run a prolonged course, with an ever-present danger of crisis (Lancet, 1970).

2. *Thyroid crisis or storm.* In this sudden, severe and frequently fatal accentuation of all the symptoms of thyrotoxicosis, the mental state is either one of extreme agitation or profound apathy, with or without clouding of consciousness. If psychotic symptoms coincide the patient may be admitted to a psychiatric hospital. Greer and Parsons (1968) described a classical schizophrenic reaction observed during a thyroid crisis. Both the mental and physical symptoms subsided within 48 hours, on treatment with chlorpromazine and propranalol. The authors ascribed this acute syndrome to abrupt discontinuance of anti-thyroid drugs (Neomercazole) two weeks before the onset. On the other hand anti-thyroid drugs can induce mental symptoms which take the form of delirium or a confusional state. Brewer (1969) described such a case in a patient who had been on carbimazole for 5 weeks and provides evidence that the organic psychosis is attributable to an acute hypo-thyroidism.

3. *Prolonged psychotic illness.* Presumably different in nature are those florid psychoses, generally categorized as 'schizo-affective', which may appear in the initial stages of thyrotoxicosis but which pursue an independent course and are not notably influenced by anti-thyroid treatment. Some consider that the association of the two conditions is fortuitous, but others believe that the psychosis has been precipitated by thyrotoxicosis acting as a non-specific stress.

Myxoedema. This is so typically a disease of middle-aged and elderly women that it requires a determined effort of will to remember that it can occur at all ages in both sexes. Myxoedema results from a primary thyroid insufficiency but the therapeutic procedures of thyroidectomy and irradiation of the thyroid gland by the administration of radio-active iodine can give rise, after a latent interval, to a similar clinical picture. The psychiatric components of this clinical picture take the form of a psycho-organic syndrome. Mental lethargy, loss of spontaneity and a tendency to procrastinate are early symptoms, followed by dulling of comprehension ('failure to see a joke'), mild memory impairment and very frequently a depressed mood. Subsequently, in the absence of treatment, there is a progressive slowing of all mental faculties and a simultaneous decline in motor activity, culminating in a state of dementia and physical inertia. The commonly described E.E.G. changes are slowing and flattening of the alpha rhythm. Normal mental functioning is restored following replacement therapy, provided the condition is not of long standing, but the former assumption that treatment is always effective irrespective of the stage at which it is introduced has been disproved. *Jellinek* (1962) discovered that no fewer than 6 of his series of 56 patients showed varying degrees of dementia according to psychometric tests performed when they were once more euthyroid. Included in this group of 6, all of whom had been myxoedematous for many years before treatment, were cases in whom air-encephalography showed some degree of cerebral atrophy. Michael and Gibbons (1963) state that of the Continental writers both Peters and Bleuler have referred to irreversible brain damage in myxoedema.

Disorders of consciousness and frank coma are not uncommon in myxoedema and coma may be the presenting symptom. Myxoedematous patients undergoing treatment may pass into coma during the course of a severe infection (Lovel, 1962) but coma is more often a complication of the untreated case. If there is a coinciding fall in body temperature the outlook becomes more grave. Patients suffering from a combination of myxoedema coma and hypothermia (which in terms of the report of the Royal College of Physicians (1966) implies a temperature below 95°F.) have a high mortality rate. Hypothermic myxoedema coma in the elderly is not an unduly rare psychiatric emergency. Treatment follows the lines laid down for accidental hypothermia. The main dangers are too rapid rewarming and overdosage with triiodothyronine, the starting dose should not exceed 10 μg. b.d.

The psychotic illnesses, often of a florid type, which in some instances accompany myxoedema have recently aroused much discussion since their precise relationship to myxoedema and even their incidence have not been established. Asher (1949) described 13 such cases, all women, seen in a London observation ward within a 4-year period and his title of 'myxoedematous madness' indicates his opinion of their aetiology. Clouding of consciousness was observed in approximately half of his cases but was neutral for prognosis. On the other hand Browning *et al.* (1953) considered that myxoedematous psychoses represented 'an organic delirium'. Tonks (1964) concluded from his series of 18 patients that the presence of clouding in an individual case indicated a good prognosis. Some authorities have suggested that the association of myxoedema and psychotic illness is fortuitous, pointing out that myxoedema is usually found in middle-aged women, and that middle-aged women are prone to develop psychoses. One reason for these diverse opinions is that this combination of myxoedema and psychiatric disorder is not a very common cause of admission to a psychiatric hospital. Tonks' 18 cases represented all such cases admitted to a large psychiatric unit over a ten-year period. Jellinek (1968) found evidence of psychiatric disorder in 27 of his extended series of 76 cases of myxoedema seen personally in a neurological department over a comparable period. It would seem therefore that this problem would be more quickly elucidated by a psychiatric study carried out on myxoedematous patients in general hospitals.

Special reference must be made to depression of mood as a presenting feature of myxoedema which sometimes precedes the more obvious physical signs. This type of case may be treated as a true depressive illness for weeks or months until the therapist suddenly becomes aware of a change in the patient's appearance indicative of myxoedema.

Hypopituitarism. This rare condition which most frequently results from post-partum necrosis of the anterior pituitary (*Sheehan's syndrome*) is likely to become even rarer in countries where high standards of obstetric care prevail. Pituitary tumour is a less common cause presumably because it does not always lead to complete destruction of the gland. The picture conjured up by mention of Sheehan's syndrome is that of an intensely pale middle-aged woman with a fine and prematurely wrinkled skin sitting drowsily by the fire on a warm summer day. The characteristic features are lack of sustained interest, lack of initiative, an increased susceptibility to cold, an ever-present desire for rest and sleep, emotional apathy or a depressed mood. In cases which have gone untreated for many years a dysmnesic syndrome is sometimes observed while recurring confusional states are a warning of imminent coma, which was the usual cause of death before substitution therapy (cortisone) became available.

That hypopituitarism is now seldom put forward as an alternative diagnosis to anorexia nervosa can be attributed to *Sheehan and Summers* (1949) who in their now famous communication pointed out that weight loss is not a frequent feature of the disease. Michael and Gibbons have described how in an earlier era cases of anorexia nervosa were accepted as cases of hypopituitarism (Simmond's disease) which was thereby given a spurious symptomatology.

Addison's disease. Formerly fibrocaseous tuberculosis of the adrenal gland was the most frequently recurring cause of the disease but now bilateral primary atrophy of the gland has taken priority. The psychological symptoms in Addison's disease are as much a part of the clinical picture as those of hypopituitarism, which they in some part resemble. The apathy, depression, lack of drive and initiative add up to a neurasthenic-like picture but these cases are only occasionally referred to the psychiatrist, the diagnosis being made on the physical features, notably the pigmentation with its characteristic distribution and the severe fall in blood pressure. Mild memory impairment is not uncommon.

Clouding of consciousness or delirium may accompany adrenal crisis.

Cushing's disease. Cushing believed that the cause was a basophil adenoma of the pituitary but an adenoma, carcinoma or primary hyperplasia of the adrenals exercises similar effects, i.e. prolonged excessive secretion of steroid hormones. A detailed account of the psychological symptoms said to be present in over half the cases has been given by Michael and Gibbons who emphasize that they are a major part of the syndrome and not reactive to the patient's awareness of his or her changed appearance. The red moon-shaped face, hirsuties, obesity and 'buffalo hump' of the Cushing patient are well-known. Depression is common and elation or euphoria rare. Paranoid delusions and auditory hallucinations are sometimes observed. Brief episodes of acutely disturbed behaviour, characterized by excitement, anxiety or apathy are a distinctive feature. These do not in any sense resemble a schizophrenic or affective disorder. Organic reactions are uncommon.

Diabetes mellitus

The two psychiatric syndromes directly related to diabetes are the delirium which may precede diabetic coma and the intellectual impairment (chronic organic reaction) associated with (diabetic) cerebral arteriopathy. Diabetic patients do not appear to be especially prone to functional mental illness although it is claimed that there is a higher incidence of diabetes in the families of patients with affective disorder than in the population generally. Hypoglycaemia, a complication of the treatment of diabetes, is of importance to the forensic psychiatrist, since it may be pleaded as a defence to charges made under the Road Traffic Act.

Spontaneous hypoglycaemia. Intermittent bizarre behaviour occurring after exercise in the late morning or before breakfast in the early morning, when accompanied by symptoms of pallor, sweating, unsteadiness, anxiety and depersonalization is symptomatic of an insulin-secreting tumour of the pancreas (insulinoma). Very frequently the physical symptoms are the sole manifestations. The behavioural anomalies represent a later stage of clouded consciousness, which in some instances may progress to coma. Focal neurological signs may be present but are generally transient. This is the classical picture, but a diversity of symptoms, which do not add up to a specific pattern, is perhaps more common and may lead to the patient's referral to a psychiatric clinic. Marks (1966) charts no fewer than 37 conditions in the differential diagnosis, 8 of which are psychiatric syndromes. Patients with this condition who are submitted to psychiatric investigations, are not easily allotted to a psychiatric category and it is this absence of specific symptoms which directs the insulinoma-conscious psychiatrist to the diagnosis. Recurring hypoglycaemic episodes may lead to irreversible brain damage. Low blood sugar levels during an acute episode are diagnostic but these episodes are not always witnessed. Repeated fasting blood sugar tests may be informative, but often have to be supplemented by the intravenous tolbutamide test and glucogen test.

Visceral carcinoma. A prolonged and intermitting confusional state is sometimes the first indication of visceral carcinoma, notably bronchogenic carcinoma, and the first confusional episode may antedate by several months the appearance of physical signs of the neoplasm. (Charatan and Brierley, 1956; McGovern *et al.*, 1959). In these cases no cerebral metastases are found at autopsy, which suggests that the fluctuating confusional state represents a metabolic effect of the tumour.

Cerebral causes

Acute conditions. A fluctuating confusional state with intervals of mental clarity is a classical sign of sub-dural haematoma. In the middle-aged and elderly, this delayed manifestation of head injury can follow an injury so trivial as not to be recollected by the patient and it is not unknown for these cases to be admitted to psychiatric hospitals. Subarachnoid haemorrhage may have confusion or delirium as a feature of the acute stage, but it is the sequelae which are more likely to come within the orbit of the psychiatrist. Storey (1970) followed up 261 patients after a subarachnoid haemorrhage and found that 41 per cent showed personality impairment (but personality improvement, assumed to be a leucotomy effect, was found in 5 per cent). Although personality change and intellectual impairment are known to follow SAH, it has to be remembered that some patients show few or no residual defects. Multiple sclerosis may present as an acute neurological disturbance with confusion or delirium, headache and nausea, and focal signs such as diplopia, nystagmus and increased tendon reflexes. This acute form of multiple sclerosis, which simulates a viral encephalitis, is often followed by a severe and permanent personality change.

Chronic conditions. Delirium may be the presenting feature, or occur during the course of, many forms of cerebral degenerative disease or slowly invasive cerebral tumours. When the delirium subsides, memory impairment and the other cognitive defects, characteristic of the chronic organic reaction (q.v.), are uncovered. The delirium must be distinguished from the vivid visual hallucinations and primary delusions, which can occur in clear consciousness or as manifestations of epilepsy. Delirious episodes may punctuate the course of senile dementia or cerebral arteriosclerosis but this so-called *senile delirium* is not so common as is supposed since what passes for senile delirium is often no more than an exacerbation of the restlessness, disorientation and misidentifications which are part of the dementing process. Senile delirium more often results from causes outwith the brain such as those already tabulated.

Dysmnesic Syndrome

HISTORICAL INTRODUCTION

To British psychiatrists, this term implies a specific memory disturbance, which the French, with their passion for precision, define as a
defect in memorizing (amnesic de mémoration, Delay, 1942). Both
schools unite, however, in employing as an alternative term the
traditional 'Korsakoff's syndrome'.

Korsakoff gave the first detailed description of this dysmnesic syndrome in 1887. From his observance of its frequent association with
polyneuropathy (commonly but not invariably alcoholic polyneuropathy), he concluded that the peculiar memory defect and the neuropathy represented two components of a single disease entity, which he
regarded as toxaemic in origin. Korsakoff elaborated his concept of a
psychosis polyneuritica in a series of reports, one of which has been
translated from the original Russian by Victor and Yakolev (1955).
This combination of polyneuropathy and dysmnesia was subsequently
known as Korsakoff's psychosis, but in course of time this term came
to be applied to the dysmnesic component alone. Korsakoff did not
know the pathological anatomy of the dysmnesic syndrome he had
described, but some six years before the publication of his now famous
report, Wernicke had described a 'new' disease subsequently known as
Wernicke's encephalopathy which was to provide the clue to its aetiology
and pathology.

Wernicke (1881) described three patients (two alcoholics and a case
of persistent vomiting following pyloric stenosis attributable to sulphuric
acid poisoning) all of whom developed ophthalmoplegia, ataxia and a
disturbance of consciousness which rapidly merged into a terminal
coma. At autopsy, petechial haemorrhages were demonstrated in the
walls of the third ventricle, in the grey matter around the aqueduct and
in the floor of the fourth ventricle, i.e. the lesions were confined to the
diencephalon and brain stem.

It is one of the paradoxes of medical history that Korsakoff and
Wernicke, who were contemporaries, did not realise how closely inter-
related were the two syndromes which bore their respective names. This
relationship, however, was quickly noted by succeeding clinicians, who
from the end of the 19th century onwards, reported individual cases
showing clinical features of both Wernicke's and Korsakoff's psychosis,
as they also drew attention to the similar distribution of the lesions
found post-mortem in these two conditions. Speculation on this subject
was finally resolved when Gamper (1928) supplied convincing evidence
that the pathological alterations in the two conditions were essentially
ihe same. In a study of the brains of 16 alcoholic patients, all of whom

had Korsakoff's psychosis and several of whom had also shown evidence of Wernicke's disease, Gamper noted the curious selective and symmetrical distribution of focal lesions in deep midline structures extending from the lower brain stem forward to the anterior commissure. He stressed the constant and severe *involvement of the mamillary bodies* which he identified as the anatomical substrate of the dysmnesic syndrome observed in his patients. Subsequent reports of single cases of Korsakoff's psychosis (Remy, 1942; Delay and Brion, 1954) with damage confined to the mamillary bodies seemed to confirm the supremacy of lesions in the mamillary bodies in relation to the dysmnesic syndrome. This has been challenged recently by Victor and his colleagues (1972) who concluded from their post-mortem examination of 82 cases that lesions in the dorsomedial nucleus of the thalamus were decisive for the appearance of the dysmnesic syndrome. This finding does not necessarily contradict Gamper's observations. Corsellis (1969) has pointed out that although Gamper suggested that destruction of the mamillary bodies, by interfering with the pathways connecting them with the mid-brain, the thalamus and the cortex, lay at the root of Korsakoff's syndrome, he (Gamper) also emphasized that the mamillary bodies were not necessarily the only areas which could affect cerebral activity in this way.

Neuropathologists have long been aware that the pathological findings in cases with the clinical features of a classical Korsakoff's syndrome are always those of Wernicke's disease, and that therefore, by implication, Korsakoff's syndrome is the psychological component of Wernicke's disease. Clinicians have been slower to accept this conclusion. The aetiology of Wernicke's disease was established when Alexander and his co-workers (1938) reproduced the typical Wernicke lesions in thiamine-deficient pigeons—one of the first proven instances of the so-called 'chemical lesion'. Korsakoff's syndrome is most frequently encountered in association with chronic alcoholism, and this particular combination (there are many others) can be used to illustrate the chain of events leading up to the appearance of the syndrome, viz. chronic alcoholism—thiamine deficiency—Wernicke's encephalopathy —Korsakoff's syndrome.

HIPPOCAMPAL FORMATION

Some twenty years ago, following a report by Scoville (1954) it became known that the characteristic memorizing defect, which for so long had been associated exclusively with the mamillary bodies in the hypothalamus, could also result from damage to hippocampal structures in the temporal lobe. Scoville observed a severe memorizing defect following bilateral medial temporal lobe resections, the tissue resected including portions of the hippocampus and hippocampal gyrus (see

p. 344). It has to be remembered that the hippocampus is linked to the mamillary bodies by efferent fibres passing by way of the fornix.

DYSMNESIC SYNDROME

Definition

The central feature is a failure to memorize current experience when consciousness is intact and intelligence, in so far as intelligence can be divorced from the capacity to memorize, is not markedly impaired. The patient who has developed a total memorizing defect from whatever cause is unable to remember, other than momentarily, what he currently feels, thinks, sees, hears, says or does. He has perforce a continuous and steadily lengthening anterograde amnesia and can add no new information to his store of past recollections. With this is associated a retrograde amnesia, of more variable degree and duration, for events before the onset of the causative condition, i.e. for events previously well established in memory. The patient's awareness of the past, and indeed his awareness of his personal identity, is based on information amassed before the R.A. interval.

This memory disturbance can be temporary or permanent, mild or severe. In the interests of brevity only the severe manifestations are here described.

Clinical features

Accepting the traditional subdivision of memory into three elements, registration, retention and recall, it can be demonstrated that immediate registration is not notably affected. The patient perceives the essentials of a situation and responds appropriately. He registers the gist of a simple question for sufficient time to enable him to give a relevant reply, but if the question is such as to require from him a lengthy explanation he may lose the thread of his discourse unless the question is repeated. The same question asked again after an interval of time is accepted as a novel enquiry and he starts to answer it with the same animation as when it was first put to him. Formal testing generally shows that he can repeat verbatim a series of 7 digits dictated to him (which is the normal 'immediate memory' span): yet if he is asked to retain in his memory three or four items of information, e.g. a name, address, a colour and a flower he is unable to reproduce them after an interval of five minutes. (Patients with insight may succeed by constant verbal rehearsal of the given items during the interval). This failure to retain and recall information within a few minutes of its registration in consciousness and which has been designated *minute memory* is also demonstrated in the ordinary activities of the patient's daily life since he forgets the meal of which he has just partaken, the friend who has visited him within the hour, the book he has been reading, the drawer where he has concealed his wallet and—with dangerous consequences for others—the lighted cigarette he has left on the arm of his chair. This swift forgetting also occurs in relation to abstract thinking and planning. A personal case was that of an intelligent service officer who used the analogy of brick-building to describe this inability to plan a course of action in his mind. Gesturing with his hands as if building a column of bricks he said 'By the time I get this brick, and this brick and this brick on top of the other, *that one* has disappeared'. 'That one' was the lowermost brick and he was clearly trying to convey that continuous and constructive ideation was impossible, for when he tried to assemble several consecutive thoughts the initial one disappeared from consciousness and so on ad seriatim. Temporal disorientation is constant. Topographical disorientation is variable in degree and the patient often learns to orientate himself to new surroundings. Similarly he learns to recognize new faces although he cannot remember the appropriate names. Relatives and old friends from the past are recognized and named.

The recollection of the past—the past in this context refers to the patient's existence before the onset of the memory defect—is well preserved, but not perfect. In giving his history of this period the patient may fail to place events in accurate chronological sequence and may omit important incidents. The emotional significance attached to certain events does not ensure their recall. In general, technical skills acquired in the past are retained. The patient who has formerly played tennis or chess, or acquired one or more foreign languages, can still exercise these accomplishments, admittedly with lesser proficiency. The skills of the manual worker are unimpaired.

Confabulation, which is held to be a characteristic sign, is evident when the patient, faced with a question he cannot answer in terms of contemporary information, automatically responds with something appropriate from his memory store. More florid confabulations are usually restricted to the earlier stages of the dysmnesic syndrome, when they have a grandiose and wish-fulfilling content. Confabulation, however, is not invariably present and its absence does not detract from the diagnosis. Loss of insight, likewise, is not a constant feature although often claimed as such.

When personality and intelligence are assessed, a distinction is drawn between the dysmnesic syndrome associated with temporal lobe resection and that associated with damage to the mamillary bodies. In the former there is no significant personality change, nor is there evidence of general intellectual loss (Milner, 1966). Conversely, both personality change and intellectual deficits have been reported in the dysmnesic syndrome attributable to thiamine deficiency. Certainly in the Korsakoff syndrome of chronic alcoholism, personality change is invariable, and takes the form of a fatuous euphoria or irritability and aggression, or extreme apathy. When the other causes of thiamine deficiency are implicated, the personality change may be relatively mild.

The presence of cognitive defects has been stressed by Victor and his colleagues, and by Talland (1965) whose study was based on their cases. Alcohol was a factor in every case. These authors found that the patients, when classifying objects, used wider boundaries than the controls, that they were unable to discover unfamiliar criteria for categorization, and that concepts once acquired were not effectively applied to sequential tasks. In general it can be safely claimed that the Verbal I.Q. is maintained since it is based on previously learned material, but that the Performance I.Q. is not, since it is dependent on reasoning, which, in turn, involves short term memory. For instance, a Korsakoff patient, whose previous record indicates high intelligence, fares badly with Raven's matrices, since these require the serial building up and retention of certain principles of selection. In this type of case concepts acquired are immediatly forgotten and therefore cannot be applied sequentially. The clinical impression is that there *is* some impairment of general intelligence in Korsakoff's psychosis, but it is not easy to isolate from the all-pervading memorizing defects.

WERNICKE'S ENCEPHALOPATHY

Aetiology

This is now known to be thiamine deficiency, but the specific pathogenesis of the lesions and their selective localization remain so far unexplained.

It is accepted that there may be a concomitant deficiency of other constituents of the Vitamin B complex. Clinical conditions predisposing to Wernicke's encephalopathy include (1) chronic alcoholism—this accounts for the majority of cases, (2) lesions of the stomach, duodenum or jejunum causing malabsorption, e.g. carcinoma of the stomach, Addisonian anaemia, (3) extreme dietary deprivation such as occurs under famine conditions, (4) persistent vomiting. Many less common conditions have been implicated, including chronic haemodialysis (Lopez and Collins, 1968).

Clinical Features

These comprise (a) lateral nystagmus, external rectus paralysis and paralyses of conjugate gaze in that order of frequency; (b) ataxia of gait; (c) polyneuropathy and, (d) a confusional state (seldom progressing to coma) in which can be discerned, if the patient is accessible, a Korsakoff type of memory defect. These symptoms can appear in various combinations and diagnosis does not depend on all being present in a given case.

Subsequent course

The administration of thiamine has dramatically reduced earlier high mortality rates in the acute phase. The ophthalmoplegias generally fade within a few days; nystagmus, ataxia and polyneuropathy recover more slowly. Indeed the latter two symptoms may be present in attenuated form many years after the original illness. A lateral nystagmus also commonly persists. The confusional state subsides within two weeks, but as it clears, a Korsakoff memorizing defect becomes obvious in a proportion of cases. From their large series of 245 cases of Wernicke's encephalopathy, where, in all but a few, alcohol had been the pre-disposing factor, Victor and his colleagues selected 186 survivors who had been observed for a sufficient period and found that no fewer than 157 (84 per cent) suffered from Korsakoff's syndrome.

Neuropathological findings

In acute cases petechial haemorrhages are often visible to the naked eye in the mamillary bodies, less commonly in the walls of the 3rd ventricle, periaqueductal grey matter, floor of 4th ventricle and inferior colliculi. No macroscopic abnormalities may be present, however, and the characteristic lesions may only be observed microscopically, constantly in the mamillary bodies and commonly at one or more of the other sites previously mentioned from the optic chiasma to the vestibular nuclei.

Their peculiar symmetric anatomical localisation and histological appearance are virtually pathognomonic. The lesions which principally affect grey matter are characterized by congestion of small blood vessels with or without haemorrhages, proliferation of capillaries lined by swollen endothelial cells (usually a striking feature), rod cell proliferation and a general loosening of the 'ground substance'. Some neurones may show degenerative changes but investigators have often been impressed by their relative preservation at this stage. In chronic cases there may be gross atrophy of the mamillary bodies attributable to gliosis and nerve cell loss. Similar microscopic changes may be seen at the other sites.

THE WERNICKE-KORSAKOFF SYNDROME

This title was chosen by Victor *et al.* (1972) to express the view (now generally accepted) that Wernicke's encephalopathy and Korsakoff's syndrome 'are not two separate diseases but successive stages of a single disease'. They cite as supporting evidence (a) their previously quoted high incidence of Korsakoff's syndrome in survivors from Wernicke's encephalopathy; (b) their finding that in only 9 of their series of 245 cases the Korsakoff syndrome was *not* preceded by the ocular and ataxic signs of Wernicke's encephalopathy; (c) their investigation of patients with Korsakoff's syndrome (of alcoholic origin) in State hospitals which revealed that the greater number had mild residual signs of Wernicke's encephalopathy. The high incidence of Korsakoff's syndrome following Wernicke's encephalopathy caused by severe nutritional deficiency only becomes apparent in exceptional circumstances, as these cases are less common. de Wardener and Lennox (1947) reported the typical memory disturbance in 32 of 52 Wernicke cases which occurred in the notorious Changi prisoner-of-war camp.

Whereas the Wernicke physical symptoms which are based on midbrain lesions respond well to thiamine, the memory disturbance, as is well known, frequently persists. In the series of Victor *et al.* only 25 per cent of the patients with Korsakoff's syndrome made a *complete* recovery, and comparable figures can be quoted from other sources. It seems unlikely that the pathogenesis of the dysmnesic symptoms is different from that of the physical symptoms, and it must be assumed that the mamillary bodies are more vulnerable to lack of thiamine than the relevant mid-brain areas.

Treatment of Wernicke's encephalopathy and Korsakoff's syndrome

Immediately the Wernicke physical symptoms and/or Korsakoff's syndrome are recognized, 50 mg thiamine are given intravenously, supplemented by a similar amount intramuscularly. Intravenous thiamine is continued for several days, after which daily intramuscular injections are substituted until such time as normal eating habits are re-established. It is then customary to give an oral preparation containing all the B vitamins along with a balanced diet. Many clinicians now prefer to give instead of thiamine the whole Vitamin B complex from the outset (e.g. Parentrovite (Bencard)) initially by the intravenous and subsequently by the intramuscular route. If Korsakoff's syndrome is present, daily intramuscular injections are continued for several weeks, and thereafter, if recovery has not taken place, once weekly for 6 months —this in addition to oral vitamins and a suitable diet. Certain points require special mention. (a) *Bed rest* in the acute stage is obligatory because of the danger of sudden cardiovascular collapse. (b) *Large amounts of carbohydrate should not* be given until the body is saturated with thiamine: a high carbohydrate intake in the presence of thiamine deficiency exacerbates the deficiency and indeed has been known to precipitate Wernicke's encephalopathy in patients who have suffered prolonged thiamine deprivation. (c) If the *basic deficiency is attributable to malabsorption*, e.g. a gastric or intestinal lesion, daily parenteral administration of thiamine must be maintained.

Patients left with a memorizing defect require careful assessment. A patient with a total memorizing defect requires constant supervision and this has to be provided in hospital if his family is unwilling to undertake this responsibility. Moderate defects are not incompatible with earning capacity, as such patients retain a topographical sense and can find their way around in familiar surroundings. Employers should be informed of the patient's difficulties. The patient most easily placed is the housewife who can carry on her household duties and shopping, admittedly with lessened efficiency, and has the constant support of her family. Patients with a history of chronic alcoholism may again resort to alcohol, and their immediate relatives should be warned of this danger. Mild memorizing defects are not necessarily associated with decreased working efficiency, since the patient learns to compensate for his handicap by the use of diaries and other memory aids.

THE DYSMNESIC SYNDROME AND THE HIPPOCAMPAL FORMATION

The first direct evidence for this association came from a series of *bimedial* temporal lobectomies, of varying extent, carried out for the relief of the psychoses and epilepsy (Scoville, 1954; Scoville and Milner, 1957). Bilateral excisions limited to the uncus and amygdala were unattended by memory loss but more extensive removals encroaching on the hippocampus and hippocampal gyrus were followed by memorizing defects, the severity of which was more or less commensurate with the extent of the hippocampal resection. A total and permanent memorizing defect was observed after bilateral removal of the anterior two-thirds of the hippocampus and hippocampal gyrus. Subsequently it became known that a severe memorizing defect could follow *unilateral* temporal lobectomy. This defect was observed in three of a large series of patients who had had a *left* unilateral temporal lobectomy, an established procedure for the treatment of epilepsy (Penfield and Milner, 1958). Serafetinides and Falconer (1962) reported mild persistent memory impairment which was not seriously disabling, in 7 of 34 patients with an ablation of the *right* (non-dominant) anterior temporal lobe. Of these seven patients, six had a contralateral sphenoidal focus. In these unilateral cases E.E.G. abnormalities in the contralateral temporal lobe are nearly always reported, whence it is deduced that bilateral lesions are a necessary condition for the development of the memorising defect. The significance of these contralateral E.E.G. abnormalities in epileptic patients is difficult to evaluate since a temporal lobe lesion in itself can give rise in course of time to bilateral independent foci (Hill and Fenton, 1969), and opinion is divided on whether the contralateral secondary focus always represents actual structural damage. Moreover, cases have been described where a severe memorizing defect has followed ablation of *either* the dominant or non-dominant temporal lobe, without evidence of E.E.G. abnormality in the contralateral lobe (Walker, 1957; Dimsdale *et al.*, 1964). It is apparent therefore that the generally accepted theory that only bilateral lesions give rise to a memorizing defect is more securely based on evidence from bilateral than from unilateral temporal lobectomies.

THE DYSMNESIC SYNDROME AS A SYMPTOM OF CEREBRAL DISEASE

1. *Hypothalamic damage.* If the Korsakoff syndrome associated with thiamine deficiency results from damage to the mamillary bodies in the hypothalamus, then it follows that any lesion in this region can be expected to give rise to a similar memory disturbance as one of its clinical effects. Brierley (1966) has warned that in these more diffuse lesions (commonly neoplastic) neuropathological investigation cannot pinpoint the diencephalic structures which, when damaged, give rise to the dysmnesia. He accepts, however, that the dysmnesia when considered alongside other neurological features may be 'an indication of some lesion within the lower and paramedian portions of the diencephalon'. Numerous sporadic instances of this association have been reported but one of the largest and most carefully studied series is that of the 180 cases reported by Williams and Pennybacker (1954). The authors found that memory function was most likely to be disturbed in tumours encroaching on the walls and floor of the third ventricle. Particular attention was devoted to a group of 32 craniopharyngiomas and here it was found that a distinction could be drawn between those involving the third ventricle and the posterior hypothalamus and those more anteriorly situated. Threequarters of the former gave rise to memory impairment, whereas the more anteriorly situated tumours were not associated with memory loss. The authors do not claim that the memory disturbance in all 180 cases resembled a classical dysmnesic syndrome but four patients, with tumours involving the third ventricle, are individually described and in these four the memory disturbance approximates to the classical syndrome.

2. *Hippocampal damage.* The relationship between hippocampal damage and the dysmnesic syndrome first demonstrated 20 years ago (Scoville) has been reaffirmed in certain cases of encephalitis. In acute necrotizing encephalitis, attributable to the herpes simplex virus, the inflammatory process has a predilection for the medial temporal areas and other portions of the limbic system, i.e. uncus, amygdala, hippocampus, hippocampal and cingulate gyri and the posterior orbital areas (Brierley). Brain-damaged survivors from this acute and frequently fatal infection, have been reported to show memorizing defects, but these are usually only part of a general intellectual devastation. A 'pure' dysmnesic syndrome has been reported, however, in four post-

encephalitic cases by Rose and Symonds (1960). All four patients were alive at the time of the report, but three were in psychiatric hospitals, and the fourth was too handicapped to secure paid employment. It is not certain whether these cases belong to the herpes simplex group, nor indeed, whether the dysmnesic syndrome is attributable to hypo-thalamic or hippocampal damage. A 'limbic encephalitis' occurring as a remote effect of carcinoma has been described by Corsellis and his colleagues (1968) and 'limbic encephalitis' can be associated with a clear-cut dysmnesic syndrome. Severe medial temporal lobe damage has been confirmed at autopsy in these cases.

A *transient* dysmnesic syndrome can emerge in a variety of clinical circumstances where a functional disturbance in hypothalamic or hippocampal regions, or both, can only be assumed, since there are no ancilliary signs to aid in localization. This transient defect is observed after head injury or subarachnoid haemorrhage. Walton (1953) reported that six of his series of 312 cases showed a Korsakoff syndrome which tended to resolve within a few weeks. In one case a memorizing defect developed a few hours after the haemorrhage. Recovery is the rule in dysmnesic syndromes associated with head injury and subarach-noid haemorrhage. Cerebral hypoxia, in particular carbon monoxide poisoning, can give rise to a similarly transient defect, but in the follow-ing case permanent dysmnesic syndrome resulted from this cause.

A boy of 18, a worker in a slaughterhouse was seen four years after an incident in which he had been found unconscious in the kitchen with the gas tap turned on. An open school exercise book lying nearby seemed to indicate that he had been attempting some experiment: he was admitted to a casualty department and discharged within a few days, seemingly recovered. The interval was not well documented but it was known that he had had a series of jobs. He joined the army but was discharged after two months as unfit for service. When seen, he had a severe memorizing defect. He did not confabulate; he was depressed but showed no disorder of personality. He was able to find his way around the city, but it was clear that he was incapable of performing anything other than menial tasks under supervision. The memorizing defect in this case may well have been present although unrecognized when the boy first left hospital. Alternatively it may have been a residual symptom of a subsequent acute relapse.

Kraepelin was the first to point out that a proportion of patients who have suffered from carbon monoxide poisoning seemingly recover within a few days and leave hospital, but that 1 to 3 weeks later relapse occurs which may be acute, and sometimes fatal.

Transient global amnesia is the name given by Fisher and Adams (1964) to a dysmnesic syndrome which starts abruptly and subsides within a few hours. The patient is unable to register current events during the attack, but otherwise conducts himself normally. He usually has insight into his predicament and may be perplexed or anxious, but these latter features are not always present. The patient has also

M

a retrograde amnesia covering several weeks or months, but this gradually shrinks after recovery. He has, however, permanent amnesia for the period between the onset of the attack and full recovery. This condition usually occurs in middle age or elderly patients. Transitory vascular occlusions and epilepsy have both been put forward as explanations.

DYSMNESIC SYNDROME AND THE LIMBIC SYSTEM

The mamillary bodies and the hippocampal formation are part of the limbic system. Within the limbic system can be demarcated a 'circuit', the so-called 'Papez circuit'. The hippocampus receives its largest contribution of afferents from the entorhinal portion of the hippocampal gyrus and also via the hippocampal gyrus, afferents from the *cingulate gyrus*. These are relayed from the hippocampus through its major efferent channel, the fornix, to the mamillary bodies whence they are transmitted through the mamillo-thalamic tract to the anterior nucleus of the thalamus. This nucleus projects to the *cingulate gyrus* which in turn is linked to the hippocampal gyrus. This 'curcuit' which does not exist in submammalian vertebrates was thought by Papez (1937) 'to elaborate the functions of central emotion'. Its role in emotion is still unclear but it would seem to play a part in memorizing and learning. Even the latter part of this statement requires modification for although it has been shown that bilateral damage to the hippocampus and mamillary bodies is associated with a memorizing defect, there is no evidence that such a defect follows damage to any of the other areas in the circuit. The submission by Victor and his colleagues that the Korsakoff syndrome is related to lesions in the dorsomedial nucleus of the thalamus and not primarily to lesions in the mamillary bodies still further complicates the issue. The efferent projections of the dorsomedial nucleus are directed to the convexity of the frontal lobe and medial orbital cortex. Meyer and Beck (1954) demonstrated retrograde degeneration in the dorsomedial nuclei in patients dying several years after standard prefrontal leucotomy, an operation not attended by memory disturbance. It may be, however, that the degeneration was insufficiently severe to affect memory. Victor *et al.* quote the statement of Meyer and Beck made on the basis of their observations of monkeys that for behavioural abnormalities to be long-lasting, destruction of the dorsomedial nucleus must be bilateral and virtually complete. Victor *et al.* admit that there are few direct connections between the dorsomedial nuclei of the thalamus and the hippocampus, the structures which they regard as the substrates of disturbance in recent memory. It is therefore not possible at the present time to map out an inter-related anatomical structure known to subserve memorizing. Nor is the neurophysiological basis of memorizing as yet understood.

CHRONIC ORGANIC REACTIONS

The chronic organic reaction is characterized by multiple and variable deficits in intellectual functioning, practical performance and personality, arising from structural brain damage. Such brain damage is commonly the direct result of cerebral disease or injury, but it may also occur as a sequel to disease in other organs and to extraneous intoxications and infections, any one of which may have given rise initially to an acute organic reaction (q.v.).

Although the onset can be sudden, e.g. cerebral damage following head injury, it is more often slow and insidious. Early changes are of a subtle kind. The power of the imagination wanes and new ideas spring less readily to mind. Situations which demand quick thinking and improvisation are clumsily handled although routine work still may be creditably performed. Abstract ideas are imperfectly understood and conversation and performance are concentrated on the factual and concrete; the spoken and written word is interpreted literally and wit and metaphor go unremarked. This failure in abstraction, termed by Goldstein 'loss of the categorical attitude', is an early sign of organic deterioration. Memory is progressively impaired. New information is less easily acquired. Events in the recent and intermediate past are not always recalled on demand, although they may emerge spontaneously or as a result of an accidental stimulus. Memories of the remote past are more readily available. These features are reminiscent of the dysmnesic syndrome (see p. 338) but the memory loss in this context tends to be less regular and predictable. Similarly such features of the acute organic reaction as inattention, defective grasp and disorientation recur but the causal mechanism is different. Spatial and temporal disorientation in clouded states implies a simple failure in recognition; in the clear consciousness of the chronic reaction, it represents a facet of the generalized memory loss or alternatively a specific defect in the subject's perception of time and space, such as is encountered in parietal lobe lesions. Deterioration in practical performance is often the first overt indication of abnormality, but one which for long may be tacitly ignored or covered up by the patient's immediate associates. Manual dexterity is impaired and planning and execution of familiar tasks is defective. Perseveration is commonly observed. Disorders of speech and language (dysphasia) may form part of the clinical picture and help in establishing the diagnosis.

In the emotional sphere emotional lability is the most frequent reaction but euphoria, depression, irritability or a paranoid attitude may be the predominant feature. Primitive instincts are sometimes released and men of upright character appear in Court, charged with sexual offences. The higher level activities of judgment and reasoning are inevitably impaired.

The course is frequently progressive and the later stages are marked by profound mental enfeeblement, with total memory loss, fragmentary speech, slovenliness of dress and eating habits, neglect of personal hygiene and eventually incontinence. In the terminal state emaciation and limb contractures may supervene, and the patient has to be washed, fed and cared for like an infant.

Chronic organic reaction and *dementia* tend to be employed as interchangeable terms, and while *dementia* is apposite for the more severe manifestations of intellectual and personality change, it carries the implication of irreversibility and so acts as a brake to careful investigation and diagnosis. Not all chronic organic reactions are necessarily progressive, e.g. G.P.I. is now susceptible to antibiotic therapy, benign cerebral tumours and subdural haematoma to operative intervention, myxoedema and Vitamin B_{12} deficiency to replacement therapy, while circumscribed vascular lesions are often followed by complete or partial restoration of function. Diagnosis is facilitated by focal neurological signs elicited during physical examination or by abnormalities revealed by the various physical investigations already enumerated (p. 317) but very often the initial departures from normal functioning lie wholly in the mental sphere, and may indeed continue to be so restricted. Diagnosis in these cases is dependent on a study of the mental symptoms in a given case since it is known that some of the more familiar cerebral diseases give rise to a remarkably uniform clinical picture. Knowledge of the symptoms produced by lesions in specific areas of the brain may help to elucidate the more obscure case and incidentally also adds to our understanding of brain functioning.

FRONTAL LOBE

Bilateral damage to the frontal lobe is accompanied by greater or lesser personality change. The first description of this 'frontal lobe syndrome' is contained in the now famous Phineas Gage case presented by Dr J. M. Harlow to the Massachussetts Medical Society in 1868. While Phineas Gage was directing a squad of men on blasting operations, a long iron tamping rod was driven through his skull, entering below the left zygoma and emerging rostral to the right precentral motor area. His personality thereafter was so radically changed that his employers could not retain him as a foreman. Formerly shrewd, competent and persistent in discharging his duties, he became unpredictable, impervious to advice or argument, continually devising new plans which he failed to execute. He showed little concern for others and indulged 'in the greatest profanity'—traits so foreign to his previous personality that his acquaintances said he was 'no longer Gage'. With the advent of prefrontal leucotomy, the characteristic personality change became more widely known. At its mildest, it is a subtle deficit revealed in a less sensitive awareness of other people, less creative drive, less intellectual curiosity, less foresight, alongside an almost imperceptible drop in former standards of ethical behaviour, work and personal appearance—changes which may be apparent only to the patient's immediate associates. More severe and obvious person- ality change has as its salient features either (a) euphoria or (b) apathy. Patients exhibiting the former are brash, overtalkative, tactless, restless, episodically irritable and prone to excesses in financial spending, eating, drinking, smoking and sexual behaviour. 'Wilzelsucht'—an addiction to feeble jokes—is a traditional sign which appears more often in textbooks than in life. In the apathetic form, the patient is dull and indifferent with no play of facial expression and tends to remain immobile for long periods and to answer questions monosyllabically. Disregard of the social conventions is characteristic of frontal lobe syndromes, and patients may undress or urinate in public. Intelligence as measured by intelligence tests is not impaired but the personality defects prevent the patient from making effective use of his intelligence. Epileptic convulsions occur in a proportion of cases. Dysphasia, if present, denotes involvement of Broca's area (see below).

A 'pure' frontal lobe syndrome is seen only in strictly localized traumatic lesions and in prefrontal leucotomy, but a similar picture is found in the early stage of Pick's disease (frontotemporal atrophy) and sometimes occurs as part of the symptomatology of G.P.I., since the infection has a predilection for the frontal lobes. Tumours and vascular lesions, e.g. subarachnoid haemorrhage, involving both frontal lobes may give rise to a more complex clinical picture because of damage to adjacent areas.

TEMPORAL LOBE

  1. *Memorizing defect.* This, the most clear-cut temporal lobe syndrome, has been described under Dysmnesic syndrome (p. 338).

  2. *Temporal lobe epilepsy.*

  3. *Visual field defects.* The optic radiations traverse the temporal lobe to reach their end-stations in the calcarine fissure and visual field defects, if present, are an important localizing sign.

  4. *Dysphasia* (Gr. Dys—ill, phasis—speech). It has been said that words are the symbols wherewith a human being communicates his thoughts to other human beings. At our first introduction to a dysphasic patient we are primarily impressed by his obvious difficulty in finding appropriate words to express what he wants to say or by his employ- ment of the wrong word in a particular context. It would be naïve, however, to conceive of dysphasia solely in terms of word-finding or word-understanding. Speech and language imply more than a series of words strung together like a string of beads. Once the infantile stage of

object or word naming is past, speech becomes progressively more structured and a word only has meaning in relation to the other words with which it is associated. In speech, the thoughts of the speaker are formulated before they emerge as statements, and the meaning of the statement comprehends something more than the aggregate of words composing it. Dysphasia therefore can be equated with a disorganization of the structure of speech or language. Grammatical construction suffers as do the adventitious aids to communication such as inflection, stress and rhythm of speech. Emotion plays a part, for the patient who is almost unable to communicate, may utter a complete and comprehensible sentence under the influence of profound emotion (emotive or automatic speech). A striking feature is the inconsistency of the dysphasic patient's performance; he may succeed and then fail in a particular linguistic test at a single sitting.

Dysphasia is now used to cover more than what is implied in its derivation. It includes (a) *defective expression* and (b) *defective comprehension* of speech (expressive and receptive defects) and also *impaired ability to write (dysgraphia)* or to *read (dyslexia)*. It is uncommon for any one of these disturbances in language function to occur in isolation; usually all four can be detected in a given case, although one may be more prominent because of its greater severity.

That dysphasia is associated with a left hemisphere lesion in right-handed subjects is well known. Piercy (1964) confirms the general applicability of this rule but adds that the association of dysphasia with *right* hemisphere lesions in dextrals has been reported in a small number of cases. He goes on to state that 'the traditional theory of right hemisphere dominance for language in left-handed subjects no longer stands'. He cites his analysis of reported cases in the literature which revealed 80 left-handed aphasics with left hemisphere lesions and 38 left-handed aphasics with right hemisphere lesions. It is clear, therefore, that dysphasia, when it occurs in left-handed patients with unilateral lesions does not aid in locating the lesion.

Dysphasia is associated with lesions in the vicinity of the sylvian fissure of the left hemisphere in right-handed patients, notably the posterior two-thirds of the inferior frontal convolution (*Broca's area*), the posterior part of the temporal lobe and the contiguous portions of the parietal lobe surrounding the termination of the sylvian fissure and of the superior temporal sulcus, all of which are in the territory of the middle cerebral artery. The former belief that damage to any one of these several cerebral areas or to their presumed connecting neural pathways gave rise to quite distinct and highly specific forms of dysphasia is no longer held. This is not to infer that there is no specialisation of speech function and it is now generally accepted that the more anterior the lesion, the more prominent will be expressive speech defects while the more posterior the lesion, the more obvious will be receptive speech defects and dyslaxia, although no one of these will present as an isolated phenomenon.

It is usual to cite three traditionally demarcated forms of dysphasia and these are briefly indicated: (1) *Expressive or Broca's aphasia* where the lesion (generally vascular) is in the posterior two-thirds of the third frontal convolution (Broca's area). The patient is truly a-phasic since speech is sometimes completely abolished, apart from the reiteration of stereotyped phrases or the words 'yes' or 'no' which are not always used appropriately. Understanding is diminished but not lost. In less severe cases, the patient tries to carry on conversations and what he says is relevant but rendered almost incomprehensible by the dysarthria. In many cases the patient has complete understanding and although he writes with difficulty, he is able to follow the general trend of events in the daily newspaper. This most frustrating of all disabilities may lead to depression or extreme irritability which in turn may necessitate admission to a psychiatric hospital. (2) *Nominal or amnestic aphasia.* The lesion is in the posterior part of the 1st and 2nd temporal convolutions and may extend into the anterior parietal area. This is the form of dysphasia observed in Pick's disease (p. 356) where it is described. The patient has difficulty in finding words, and therefore both speech and writing are affected but reading is intact. The patient has no difficulty in following the conversation of others (although comprehension is ultimately lost if the lesion is progressive). A mild degree of nominal dysphasia may result from fatigue or intoxication or advancing age. (3) *Central dysphasia*: this is the most severe form of dysphasia, commonly resulting from an extensive lesion, involving both the temporal and parietal lobes. Central dysphasia has little psychiatric relevance, since its complex manifestations can only be measured and analysed when the underlying lesion is localized and not part of a more diffuse cerebral process.

When disturbances of speech or language functions occurs in association with cerebral degenerative or neoplastic disease, as in the present context, care must be taken to differentiate dysphasia from the impoverishment of speech which is part of the dementing process. In general, it is only permissible to diagnose dysphasia in the early stages of such conditions since the general devastation engulfs all intellectual faculties including that of speech.

PARIETAL LOBE SYNDROMES

The parietal lobe is not a well-defined anatomical entity: its demarcation is affected by the drawing of somewhat arbitrary lines on the surface of the hemisphere, but this absence of natural boundaries serves to emphasize its close functional relationship to the adjoining temporal and occipital lobes, e.g. in relation to dysphasia and dyslexia. No reference will be made in this section to the sensory cortex which is the province of the neurologist; what will be described are some of the more notable 'higher level' defects found in association with lesions in the posterior part of the parietal lobe, the so-called 'parietal lobe signs'.

Ideomotor and ideational apraxia

Ideomotor apraxia is defined as an inability to imitate gestures and actions to command, when the patient understands the request and does not suffer from paresis. Ideational apraxia denotes a failure or lack of dexterity in executing composite actions, i.e. those requiring a sequence of willed acts. A characteristic finding is that similar actions may be performed automatically or under the stress of emotion. 'Ideomotor' is often used to designate both forms of apraxia, which represent, as it were, a transaction between 'willing' and 'doing'. They are associated with parietal disease in the *dominant* hemisphere.

Dressing Apraxia: putting on garments in their proper order and manipulating buttons and bows is so much part of personal routing that any deviation impresses the observer. The so-called dressing apraxia is not, however, an isolated disorder but is a facet of ideational apraxia. Alternatively, it may result from neglect of the left half of the body which in turn results from a disordered body image. Dressing will then be lopsided, the patient ignoring his left arm and leg. In these cases the lesion is in the subordinate hemisphere. (Dressing disability observed in dementia is of a different order).

Disorders of the body image. 'Body image' or 'body scheme' refers to a person's awareness of his bodily self. A patient with a parietal lesion of the subordinate hemisphere may 'neglect' the left side of his body, e.g. when asked to put out his hands, he raises the right only, although he will bring up his left hand in apposition to it, when his omission is brought to his attention. Automatic acts, e.g. walking are not affected nor are actions requiring the co-ordination of both hands. At a later stage he may neglect to wash the left side of his body or to clothe his left limbs (see above). If the patient develops weakness of his left side, e.g. hemiplegia, he ignores his disability (anosognosia) or denies it when it is brought to his notice, but in the latter case there is usually some coinciding clouding of consciousness. Why these phenomena are observed only in relation to left-sided neglect and lesions in the subordinate hemisphere is not clear. It has been argued that right-sided neglect is a theoretical abstraction since it would be submerged in the apractic defects and dysphasia which follow lesions in the dominant hemisphere (Critchley, 1953).

Gerstmann's Syndrome. An isolated disorder of awareness of the body image *is* seen, however, in association with parietal lobe lesions of the dominant hemisphere. This is *finger agnosia*, where the patient shows indecision and inconsistency in identifying the individual fingers of his own two hands, those of the examiner and those depicted on an outline drawing of hands. Finger agnosia is one of the four components of *Gerstmann's syndrome*, the others being inability to distinguish right from left, dysgraphia and dyscalculia (difficulty in essaying mental and paper calculations). An interesting hypothesis for this association of finger agnosia with dyscalculia has been built up on the primitive use of fingers in counting. Whether this syndrome, which Gerstmann attributed to a lesion in the left (dominant) angular gyrus is a distinct clinical entity has been challenged. It has been shown that these four components do not always occur in unison. Moreover dyslexia and constructional apraxia may replace or combine with one or more of the classical Gerstmann quartet.

Constructional apraxia is illustrated in a patient's inability to copy two-dimensional designs using paper and pencil and/or matchsticks or to construct a three-dimensional model from bricks of diverse size and shape. It is demonstrable in ordinary life when a housewife makes seemingly stupid mistakes in laying a table or in dressmaking, or when a tradesman is unable to build up a mechanical device from its component parts. Constructional apraxia is distinct from and more commonly encountered than ideomotor apraxia but the two can occur in combination. It is claimed that constructional apraxia is twice as frequent in right-sided than in left-sided lesions, but it has also been reported in association with bilateral lesions and diffuse cerebral disease. In the latter it is often an early indication of the presence of organic disease.

Topographical orientation (the ability to find one's way about in familiar surroundings) may be disordered in parietal disease as may be also *topographical memory*. This last is defined as the ability to summon up a clear mental picture of routes and landmarks or the internal layout of familiar buildings, and to describe these features to others. Errors in route finding (topographical orientation) and/or topographical description (topographical memory) are often the first sign of parietal tumour or cerebral atrophy. These topographical disabilities may follow either bilateral or unilateral lesions of the brain. Another example of spatial disorientation is that associated with imperception or neglect of the left half of the body (see above) since this can also include neglect of the left half of visual space; a patient with this disability tends to collide with objects to the left of him and to neglect left hand turnings and so loses his way in familiar surroundings. In this instance the lesion is always in the subordinate hemisphere.

Temporal defects. Subtle defects in temporal awareness are also encountered in parietal disease, i.e. difficulty in estimating the approximate hour of the day or in assessing the time spent on a particular activity.

PRESENILE DEMENTIAS

These comprise (1) Alzheimer's disease, (2) Pick's disease, (3) Jakob-Creutzfeld disease (with which is bracketed subacute spongiform encephalopathy). The title refers to the age of incidence which tends to be restricted to the years between 40 and 60. Alzheimer's disease is encountered more frequently than Pick's Disease (in a ratio of approximately 8:1). Jakob-Creutzfeld disease is readily distinguished by its profusion of physical signs and symptoms. It is equally distributed between the two sexes. Alzheimer's disease and Pick's disease are more common in women than in men and in both diseases, the physical symptoms are few and non-specific.

ALZHEIMER'S DISEASE

When Alzheimer (1907) described the disease which now bears his name, he considered it an atypical form of senile dementia. Kraepelin, impressed by the early age of onset and a grouping of symptoms which, in his opinion, differed from that of senile dementia, was disposed to regard it as a unique disease for which he proposed the title Alzheimer's disease. As such, it was immediately accepted by Continental physicians but it was not until Henderson and MacLauchlan (1930) described the clinical and pathological features of two cases of Alzheimer's disease that it became generally known in this country. The genetic aspects did not command attention until much later. Family histories illustrating either dominant or recessive inheritance have been reported. Conversely a case of Alzheimer's disease occurring in one of identical twins has been described (Davidson and Robertson, 1955). The affected twin, whose illness had been of abnormally long duration, died at the age of 69: her twin examined when she was 73 showed no evidence of the disease. Alzheimer's disease is indistinguishable histopathologically from senile dementia and Sjögren and his colleagues (1952) found a higher than expected incidence of senile dementia in Alzheimer families. The conclusion of those authors that inheritance is multifactorial is now generally accepted. All in all, reports of familial cases of Alzheimer's disease are not numerous. The clinician with a large series of Alzheimer's patients generally finds that but one in two have an affected sibling or forebear.

Clinical Features

The first sign is mild memory loss. A housewife mislays her sewing, burns the toast, and forgets one or two items while shopping. A professional man or woman forgets appointments or disconcertingly hesitates in the middle of a lecture, unable to find the appropriate word. No more serious failure may be observed for a year or longer because of the slow progress of the disease. During this interval, however, odd, isolated incidents may give rise to comment. A cautious business man tells a convincing but entirely false story about a fraudulent transaction involving an associate; a timid spinster quarrels with her neighbours; an artist describes seeing roses in her studio grow larger and more luminous and turn into menacing baby faces. Speech disorder is not yet obvious, apart from occasional difficulty in word finding, but the patient's letters may show altered handwriting and perseverated words and phrases. Important diagnostically are frank depressive or paranoid illnesses erupting at this early stage and obscuring the underlying organic defects. Sooner or later—the rate of deterioration varies from case to case—a decline in practical performance supervenes. A housewife's surroundings take on an air of squalor because she is no longer able to manipulate domestic tools, e.g. a washing machine or a vacuum cleaner, or to replace objects in their accustomed places and similar defects in the tradesman force his premature retirement. Putting on clothes becomes a tortuous proceeding; garments are put on back to front, a right arm is inserted into a left sleeve, often preceded by an attempt to penetrate the sleeve at the cuff end instead of the shoulder aperture— the so-called *dressing apraxia*. Disorientation in territorial space and in time is now apparent—these patients lose their way in familiar surroundings and are unable to compute the passage of time, or to name the day and date. Meanwhile the initial minor difficulty in word finding progresses to a massive loss of vocabulary with an associated dysarthria. Grammatical construction disintegrates. The patient is seen to grope for words, to mispronounce words, to reiterate endlessly single syllables or mutilated particles of words (logoclonia) or to repeat the words and phrases of the examiner (echolalia). Writing is similarly affected—words are misspelt and their component parts duplicated. Reading ability wanes. The progressive impairment in the patient's speech is associated with a simultaneous failure to understand the speech of others. There is a concurrent progressive memory loss, which is non-specific in that it involves both recent and remote events. When the dysphasia and memory loss are severe, the patient may be said to have reached the stage of dementia. Curious misidentification phenomena are sometimes observed at this stage, e.g. the patient's misidentification of her own mirrored reflection, the so-called *mirror sign*. Such patients eagerly seek out looking-glasses or polished surfaces and talk animatedly to their own image, which they address by the name of a sibling or an intimate friend of the same sex. They characteristically do not misidentify the image of another person looking into the glass with them. Pictorial representations of the human figure on news print or packages are misidentified as actual human beings.

Emotional lability, shown in rapid swings from tearfulness to laughter or brief flashes of motiveless anger, is frequently observed, but the most striking characteristic of the disease is the eagerness to maintain *emotional rapport with others*. The Alzheimer patient smiles happily when addressed, strives hard to accomplish all that is asked of him or her, e.g. in the test situation, and shows a catastrophic reaction of extreme anxiety and tearfulness to failure to satisfy the examiner.

On the motor side, restlessness is prominent, but this may alternate with phases of inertia. Muscular rigidity, usually of an extrapyramidal type, is always present in the later stages and sometimes is held to explain the difficulty in walking, but the latter probably denotes an apraxia of gait. Epileptic attacks occur in approximately half of the cases.

The end stage is one of profound dissolution of all faculties, with total memory loss, jargon dysphasia, emaciation, limb contractures and incontinence.

The E.E.G. is always abnormal with reduced alpha rhythms intermixed with slower potentials at 3 to 7 cycles per second. Cerebral biopsy is sometimes carried out when the diagnosis is in doubt (Sim *et al.*, 1966).

Neuropathological findings

The brain shows extreme atrophy. Coronal sectioning confirms the uniform gyral atrophy, widened sulci, reduction in white matter and ventricular dilatation. The histopathological findings comprise a severe loss of nerve cells and the typical Alzheimer silver-staining plaques and neurofibrillary tangles, which last consist of the twisted and tangled neurofibrils of degenerated nerve cells. It is important to stress that these histopathological features are observed not only in the cortex and basal ganglia but also in the diencephalon and brain stem and sometimes in the cerebellum.

PICK'S DISEASE

This has an unusual history. In 1892, Pick published one of his several contributions to the study of aphasia. In this and subsequent communications he analysed aphasic disturbances associated with temporal lobe atrophy of diverse aetiology, including senile cerebral atrophy. He was not concerned with demarcating a particular disease. It was left to later investigators to sift out Pick's accumulated research on lobar atrophy. This confirmed a growing belief in a discrete 'disease entity', manifested clinically in progressive intellectual determination starting in middle life or later and based on lobar atrophy, commonly fronto-temporal lobar atrophy. The distinctive histopathological features proved that the lobar atrophy was not related to senile cerebral atrophy. This discovery is commemorated in the name Pick's Disease. Pick's disease is assumed to be transmitted by an autosomal dominant gene, but again as in Alzheimer's disease, patients with a similarly affected parent are encountered infrequently, which suggests a gene of reduced penetrance.

Clinical features

The early signs are those of personality change consistent with the frontal lobe atrophy. Flamboyant antisocial behaviour is sometimes observed—a quiet man of moderate means gets into debt through buying fast motor cars, a correct middle-class women is convicted for stealing from shops—but more commonly the evidence for personality change accumulates slowly and only the patient's immediate circle is aware of his or her emotional blunting and increasing egocentricity. A formerly affectionate wife and mother becomes insensitive to her family's problems, no longer shows the same assiduous attention to their material needs, and remains untouched by family bereavements. At the same time she pursues her own aims with single-minded determination. Insight into the personality change is wholly lacking. The mood is mildly euphoric or stolid and placid, with fleeting outbursts of anger, and sadness or tearfulness is never witnessed. All the foregoing features coalesce in the peculiar reaction to formal psychological testing shown by these patients and which is unlike that generally seen in organic disease. They show no desire to co-operate, give up after one or two attempts to do what is asked and never show a catastrophic reaction to failure. The examiner perforce has to make his assessment by conversing with them and observing their behaviour.

Speech defects mark the middle stage of the disease and take the form of nominal aphasia. This presents initially as a failure to remember nouns ('she forgot the name of things') and progresses to a severe reduction in all elements of vocabularly. To compensate for their amnesia for words, patients (a) employ circumlocutory phrases to convey the meaning of the forgotten word, e.g. key—'the thing for opening'; (b) make free use of generic terms such as 'thing', 'man', 'woman'; (c) make one word serve several shades of meaning, e.g. one patient used 'lucky' not merely in the sense of 'fortunate', but to denote anything considered good, worthwhile, valuable or useful. Sometimes the result was unfortunate; when watching a football match with her husband, her high-pitched ejaculation 'isn't it lucky' after a goal was scored drew hisses from the crowd who considered the achievement of their team to be attributable to factors other than luck. Perseveration is a prominant ancillary feature—certain words, phrases, anecdotes are endlessly reiterated (Pick's disease can often be diagnosed from a tape recording of the patient's conversation). In time, speech is reduced to a string of substantives with the occasional interpolation of an adjective or adverb but since individual words are enunciated clearly and their component elements are not distorted, the patient still shows a surprising ability to communicate in this type of elliptical utterance reminiscent of 'pidgin English'. In the terminal phase of the illness the patient becomes totally mute.

A striking finding in Pick's disease is that the patient's practical performance, if this term is restricted to the simple routine of everyday life, is not severely affected till relatively late. Many patients, particularly housewives, are not referred for examination until aphasia is prominent and at this stage they are still able to dress themselves without assistance, and in the domestic sphere can cook, mend, embroider, lay a table. Admittedly their dexterity is impaired, and they also show a certain stereotypy, e.g. serving up the same dish at every meal. The performance of these household tasks indicate a continuing awareness of spatial relationships and an ability to construct objects or designs from their component parts. Also of significance is the finding that patients with Pick's disease are able to make long journeys unaccompanied, to shops or to the houses of friends without losing their way and after admission to hospital quickly orientate themselves to the ward and ward corridors. A time sense is usually less well preserved, but those patients can assess the time of day without reference to a clock and can compute the month and year. The retention of one or other of these abilities is not in itself significant, but their combination in a single case suggests that the parietal lobe is not involved in the disease process, and this helps to differentiate Pick's from Alzheimer's disease. Physical signs include (a) a curious generalized hyperalgesia prominent in the intermediate stage and fading out as the disease advances; (b) mild obesity, (c) episodic restlessness which is nevertheless always purposive, and (d) minor anomalies of gait and posture which do not conform to any specific pattern. The final stage is similar to that seen in other severe forms of dementia, except that emaciation is not a prominent feature. The E.E.G. is normal in Pick's disease.

Neuropathological findings

The brain shows mild generalized atrophy with gross circumscribed lobar atrophy involving the frontal and temporal lobes. On sectioning this lobar atrophy is seen to affect both the gray and white matter and the individual temporal and frontal gyri are frequently so atrophied as to warrant the description 'knife blade' atrophy. The salient histo-pathological feature is a severe outfall of nerve cells in temporal and frontal lobes and all trace of normal architecture and lamination is lost. Ballooned cells and cells with silver staining inclusions are sometimes observed, but absence of this does not alter the diagnosis.

Alzheimer's disease and Pick's disease

The basic defect is a cerebral atrophying process—or processes. The distribution of the atrophy differs in the two conditions; in Alzheimer's disease the entire brain is atrophied whereas in Pick's disease the atrophy is restricted to the temporal and frontal lobes. The histological alterations also differ. In Alzheimer's disease there is severe nerve cell loss and in addition silver staining plaques and the neurofibrillary tangles described by Alzheimer. The histological alterations are identical with those found in senile dementia, and it is difficult therefore to sustain a diagnosis of Alzheimer's disease if the condition starts in the late sixties. In Pick's disease, there is severe outfall of cells in the atrophied lobes, and some of the remaining cells may show 'ballooning' or have argentophil inclusions, but plaques and neurofibrillary tangles are absent. The typical clinical and histopathological features of Pick's disease have been described in patients over 80 years of age (Binns and Robertson, 1962). The condition tends to be more benign in older patients.

To the differing distribution of the cerebral atrophy in the two con-ditions can be ascribed the differences in the clinical picture.

1. In Pick's disease, there is relative retention until a late stage of the disease of the patient's *concepts of space and time*, which are regarded as dependent on an intact parietal lobe. Examples have been given of the patient's retained topographical sense, time sense and ability to manipulate objects in personal space. These contrast with the Alzheimer patient's early disorientation in time and space, her difficulty in dressing herself and handling objects.

2. *Memory* is preserved in Pick's disease, until relatively late, although assessment of memory must be made in observation of the patients' behaviour as they seldom co-operate in general testing. In Alzheimer's disease, loss of memory is an early symptom.

3. *Dysphasia*. In both Pick's disease and Alzheimer's disease a nominal or amnestic dysphasia may be observed in the early stages. In the former, this type of dysphasia persists, gradually becoming more severe and finally terminating in mutism. It is difficult to allocate the dysphasia observed in Alzheimer's disease to any one of the described forms. Both expressive and receptive defects are present by the middle stage of the disease. Some of the characteristic features have been described. In some cases speech becomes steadily more impoverished,

but garrulity is also encountered. The so called jargon dysphasia may be manifested in the later stages.

4. *Personality and mood changes.* Egocentricity, sometimes extreme, is an almost constant feature of Pick's disease. With this is associated a degree of rigidity and obstinacy. These latter traits are more accurately designated stereotypy and perseveration, and as such refer to the rigid time schedule to which these patients adhere and their refusal to be deflected from an habitual course of action. It is likely that both features are 'unconscious' compensation mechanisms to help the patient to reduce the demands of the environment in order to live within the limits of her reduced capacity (Robertson *et al.*, 1958). Personality change, as usually defined, is not characteristic of Alzheimer's disease, and the eagerness of the Alzheimer patient to maintain contact with her environment contrasts with the self-sufficiency of the patient suffering from Pick's disease. This contrast is illustrated in the differing responses to the test situation.

Psychotic manifestations typical of Alzheimer's disease are never observed in Pick's disease.

Of the physical symptoms, epileptiform convulsions and emaciation (in the final stages) are common in Alzheimer's disease but are scarcely ever witnessed in Pick's disease. Extrapyramidal alterations in muscle-tone and posture are common to both but an apraxia for gait is peculiar in Alzheimer's disease. The most striking differentiating feature is the curious hyperalgesia evident in a high proportion of Pick's disease. Mild pressure applied to any part of the body causes pain while deep pressure and minor painful stimuli, such as pinprick or venepuncture call forth vocal and facial expressions denoting excruciating pain.

This hyperalgesia is reminiscent of the 'thalamic over-reaction' phenomenon of acute pain arising spontaneously or as an exaggerated response to stimulus, which is held to denote a lesion (commonly vascular) in or adjacent to the thalamus. The three patients described by Robertson *et al.* exhibited this hyperalgesia but no lesion in or near the thalamus was found at autopsy. Hyperalgesia has been reported following cortical wounding and Robertson (1953*b*) described hyperalgesia associated with a sub-dural haematoma overlying the frontal lobe.

JAKOB–CREUTZFELD'S DISEASE

Under this title is grouped a heterogenous collection of syndromes in which emotional and intellectual deterioration occurs in association with signs of pyramidal and extrapyramidal disease. The condition takes its name from Jakob who described a series of such cases in 1921 and Creutzfeld who reported a single similar case a year earlier. Its differentiation from the other presenile dementias is based on the predominance of physical signs and the relatively brief duration (1 to 2 years). The classical case can be described succinctly by stating that it consists of the triad, *dementia, amyotrophic lateral sclerosis* and *Parkinsonism*, but cerebellar signs and symptoms are sometimes also present.

Clinical features

An early symptom is weakness of the legs and the patient finds it difficult to climb stairs. An articulation defect soon becomes apparent and is progressive. Gradually, walking becomes more and more difficult. There is increasing spasticity of the limbs: ankle clonus and extensor plantas responses are elicited. Fibrillation, typical of amyotrophic lateral sclerosis is sometimes observed. Ultimately the patient is unable to walk or to stand upright. A certain fixity of expression and mild tremors are the first signs of extrapyramidal disease. Cog-wheel rigidity and choreiform movements are later manifestations. Epilepsy has been reported. Intellectual impairment is late in developing and is never so severe as that seen in Alzheimer's disease. The age at onset is likewise earlier, commonly between 40 and 50 years of age.

Pathological findings

Autopsy reveals mild cerebral atrophy. The varied and widespread histopathological findings are difficult to reduce to a composite picture. The cortical nerve cells are diminished in number, with non-specific changes in the remainder (Betz cells are particularly affected) and there is moderate glial proliferation. Similar changes may occur in the basal ganglia, ventro-medial nucleus of the thalamus, bulbar motor nuclei and anterior horn cells. There is destruction of the myelin sheaths and axis cylinders of the pyramidal and extrapyramidal tracts.

There are many variants of this classical clinical picture. Nevin (1967) has stated that Jakob–Creutzfeld disease is more properly designated a syndrome than a disease. Cases of amyotrophic lateral sclerosis with associated dementia but without Parkinsonian features have been described and one such case (Robertson, 1953a) showed heredo-familial incidence, which has also been reported occasionally in the conventional form of Jakob–Creutzfeld disease.

SUB–ACUTE SPONGIFORM ENCEPHALOPATHY

This name has been given by Nevin to a rapidly fatal condition, which has been detached from its historical association with Jakob–Creutzfeld's disease in recent years. The symptoms include progressive intellectual impairment, visual failure, increasing hypertonus of the limbs and irregular shock-like myoclonic jerks of the musculature which may involve the whole body. Death occurs within 6 months.

The age of onset is some ten years later than that of Jakob–Creutzfeld disease and there is no recorded familial incidence of the disease. The pathological findings include moderate cerebral atrophy, predominantly affecting the occipital lobes. Histopathological examination of the cortex shows marked degeneration of nerve cells and in addition the frequent appearance of an irregular status spongiosus, which gives the disease its name. The granular layer of the cerebellum, the thalamus and basal ganglia may be similarly affected, but the brain stem and spinal cord are never involved.

The aetiology of these two conditions, the second of which produces distinctive E.E.G. changes is unknown. Intracerebral inoculation of animals with brain biopsy material from patients with Jacob-Creutzfeld's disease has not provided unequivocal evidence of viral or other infection.

HUNTINGTON'S CHOREA

This hereditary disease, characterized by continuous involuntary movements and slowly progressive dementia was described in 1872 by Huntington, the third in direct line of a family of New England physicians, who had witnessed this disease descend through successive generations of their patients. It has a world-wide distribution and affects men and women equally. The incidence in Britain is 5 per 100,000 of the population. Its transmission by a single dominant autosomal gene implies that 50 per cent of the children of an affected parent can develop the disease and while they in turn may transmit it to *their* offspring in similar ratio, the offspring of the unaffected children are not at risk, 'it never skips a generation to manifest itself in another, once having yielded its claims it does not regain them'. Sporadic cases occur with no known family history and are presumably attributable to cell mutation. Although cases have been reported at the two extremes of life, the disease usually appears between the ages of 35 and 45 and the patient is therefore likely to have had children before his or her possession of the fatal gene becomes manifest.

Clinical features

The involuntary movements develop insidiously and so lead to delay in diagnosis. The occasional grimace, shrug or body twist, the inter-mittent tapping of fingers or toes may be put down to a general 'fidgeti-ness'. In the well-established case, the characteristic features are the lightning onset of the abnormal movements, their wide excursion when the larger proximal limb joints are involved and their variable form. Jerking, stretching, grasping, squirming, weaving movements have all been described as has also abrupt forward propulsion of the body, which last may cause the victim to fall through a window or down a stairway. No part of the musculature is exempt and facial contortions, slurred, stumbling and almost incomprehensible speech and uneven respiration add to the grotesque appearance. The gait is distinctive, the patient walks on his heels, with a wide base. A rigid form of the disease can occur. A case of Huntington's Chorea without choreiform movements has been described (Curran, 1930). It should be noted that the involuntary movements can be attenuated, though not abolished, by treatment with phenothiazines.

The emotional and intellectual changes in the established disease do not differ materially from those observed in any dementing process. Retention of insight in the early stages understandably results in marked sensitivity to the reaction of other people to the disabling and ungainly movements. A severe reactive depression may develop, or alternatively the response may be explosive outbursts of irritability or anger. The latter may continue to recur throughout the middle stage when insight, which falls rapidly in this disease, is replaced by facile acceptance, or in some instances, mild euphoria. Physical activities may be maintained till late, but some patients early sink into a state of almost total inertia. It is not unusual to admit to hospital Huntington patients who have neither bathed nor changed their clothes for years, but are adequately nourished—food having been supplied through the medium of kindly neighbours, or, in the case of richer patients, a telephone line to the grocer. The intellectual impairment is very slowly progressive. Some patients maintain a semblance of mental clarity to the end, others show a profound dementia in the final stage. The average duration of the disease is from 12 to 16 years.

The E.E.G. may show typical abnormalities at an early stage. There is an absence of rhythmical activity in all areas, but this so-called 'flat E.E.G.' (defined as activity below 20 microvolts in amplitude) is not specific for the disease as it is sometimes found in normal adults.

Prodomal emotional disturbance and personality disorder

Some degree of emotional disturbance may precede the physical manifestations of the disease. Depression, anxiety, apathy and fleeting paranoid beliefs are among the commoner features described. The presence of these symptoms, which may lead to an erroneous initial diagnosis, is not necessarily related to awareness of an ominous heredity. Belonging to a different category of mental phenomena are the behaviour disorders which may emerge at the diagnostic interview or indeed may be the presenting feature. Oliver (1970) found that 38 out of 100 patients presented with behaviour disorder and catalogues violence, cruelty to children, sexual perversions, repeated petty crime and refusal to work. There is evidence that such behaviour disorders (which indicate a grossly disturbed personality) are predictive in that the abnormal member or members of a family at risk is more likely to carry the Huntington gene. To offset this group of abnormal personalities must be set the many patients who have been stable and diligent, and have good employment records. This is especially true of those who have developed the disease at a later age, i.e. over 55 years. Minski and Guttman (1938) studied the pre-morbid personality in 44 patients and found 8 alcoholics, 2 criminals and 4 with violent tendencies: a few of the remainder showed some disturbing features, but the majority came within the so-called normal range. Bolt (1970) found that only 10 per cent of patients in her series were described by their families as 'always having been difficult'.

Suicide

Huntington stated that suicide was one of the 'three marked peculiarities of the disease' the others being its hereditary nature and its onset in adult life. Suicide not only occurs with higher than average frequency in patients suffering from the disease but also in unaffected members of the family.

Differential diagnosis

The condition has to be differentiated from (a) senile chorea, but here the symptoms are mild and there is no family history; (b) the phenothiazine-induced hyperkinetic syndrome, if in addition to the usual facial dyskinesia (see Vol. II, Chap. XV) the movements also involve the trunk and limbs; (c) acquired hepatocerebral degeneration (p. 327).

Treatment

There is no known treatment to halt the disease but phenothiazines (in small dosage) alleviate the movements.

Neuropathological findings

There is generalized cortical atrophy most marked over the frontal lobe. Coronal section reveals gross atrophy of the corpus striatum which enables the diagnosis to be made on the macroscopic findings alone. There is a severe outfall of small nerve cells in the striatum, with relative preservation of the large motor cells. Neuronal loss is also severe in the outer cortical laminae, notably in the frontal lobes.

Prevention

There is no certain means of identifying the carriers, so that all members of an affected family should be advised not to have children. Nevertheless, if they decide on marriage, their partner should be forewarned of the situation. Yet it has been remarked by family doctors and psychiatrists alike that young people at risk seldom seek advice, not always through ignorance; no doubt some adopt the optimistic attitude of 'it couldn't happen to me'. A sombre picture of the genetic and environmental effects of the disease on children born of an affected parent has been drawn by Oliver (1970); Dewhurst *et al.* (1970). They cite instances of neglect and abandonment of children and extreme violence towards children. Oliver draws attention to the high childhood death rate, obviously not wholly attributable to failure to diagnose childhood forms of the disease. These authors also refer to the predicament of the spouse, the high divorce rate (38 per cent) and the high incidence of sexual aberrations in choreic patients. Bolt, on the other hand does not consider that overall picture 'as gloomy in regard to psychopathic behaviour as has at times been reported'. All these authors unite in recommending a national medical linkage system together with registration of the pedigrees of affected families which would ensure identification of early cases and possibly more effective control of the disease.

GENERAL PARALYSIS

Formerly one of the commonest organic psychoses of the mid-life period it is now one of the rarest. Dewhurst (1969) traced the clinical records of patients with neurosyphilitic psychoses admitted to six mental hospitals between the years 1950 to 1965 (inclusive) and found 91 cases. This figure represents on average, one admission per hospital per year. Calmiel, in 1826, coined the name general paralysis of the insane (paralysie générale des aliénés) and the condition thus entitled was of absorbing interest to 19th century physicians because of its then high incidence and its unknown aetiology. Its syphilitic origin was suspected, however, long before it was brilliantly confirmed by Nogouchi in 1913. Nogouchi, working in association with Moore in the Rockefeller Institute, New York, demonstrated the presence of the treponema pallidum in the cortex of the brain in cases of dementia paralytica. The Wassermann test had been introduced earlier in the century.

Clinical features

The latent period between the primary infection and the manifestations of general paralysis varies from 5 to 25 years, and the average interval is ten years. Men are more often affected than women in the ratio 4–3:1. The psychological symptoms are those of a chronic organic reaction.

Mode of onset

Since the infection has a predeliction for the frontal lobes, a personality change may be the first manifestation of the disease. Odd departures from ordinary, conventional behaviour indicate to the family that something is seriously amiss. A police charge may bring the disease to light. In a few instances hypomania, almost indistinguishable from the manic phase of a manic-depressive psychosis, is the presenting feature. The degree of disinhibition is disproportionate, however, to the severity of the manic symptoms. The great majority of cases present less dramatically with a history of insidious memory defects and decreased competence. There may be an associated depression of varying degrees of severity. In some instances the depressed mood masks the organic features and so leads to delayed recognition of the cause. Rarely a Korsakoff syndrome is the presenting feature.

The established disease

This can take several forms. The most common is a slowly progressive dementia with no special features—the so-called simple dementing type. A variant of this is the depressed type. These patients who initially present with mania frequently continue to show manic features as the disease advances, but their number is small. A somewhat larger number which, however, represents a small proportion of the total, exhibit the grandiose delusions associated in the popular mind with general paralysis. These are the patients who count their fortune in billions and trillions and who envisage themselves at the apex of the profession or professions they select from a constantly changing list. Dewhurst observed this grandiose or expansive form of the disease in only 10 of his series of 91 patients.

This disease is not diagnosed on the mental picture which can show marked variation from case to case, but on the physical signs and serological findings.

Physical signs

Unequal, irregular pupils which fail to react to light are present in more than half the cases. Tremor of the face, lips, tongue and fingers, with spasticity of the limbs and exaggerated reflexes are characteristic signs (the reflexes are depressed or absent in taboparesis). An epileptic convulsion may be the first evidence of the disease and apoplectiform seizures sometimes occur in the early stages but recovery from these is generally complete. The appearance of the patient is distinctive. The facial features are smoothed out, and this gives the face a bland and youthful appearance. The speech is characteristic, the slurring of words and the spastic dysarthria can be rendered more emphatic by asking the patient to repeat such phrases as 'Methodist Episcopal', 'British constitution'. When he is asked to write, his writing is found to be tremulous and words are distorted.

Serological findings

Routine serological tests are still carried out in psychiatric units and the introduction of more refined tests has increased the accuracy of diagnosis. The blood Wassermann in general paralysis is almost always positive. The Wassermann reaction is positive in the C.S.F. in 95 to 100 per cent of cases. The C.S.F. may be under pressure: there is a moderate increase in cells: protein is increased with a marked increase in globulin: the Lange colloidal gold curve is of the paretic type.

The introduction of penicillin has dramatically improved the prospects of recovery. In Dewhurst's series, which did not represent a group with a particularly favourable prognosis, 44 of 91 patients were discharged, 8 of whom made a complete recovery.

MULTIPLE SCLEROSIS

Three aspects of multiple sclerosis have psychiatric relevance.

1. *Its possible misdiagnosis as hysteria* in the early stages of the disease. Misdiagnosis is most likely when the initial symptoms are mild and transient and the mood unstable. Only careful and repeated examination will avert this error. That early manifestations were seemingly diagnosed as hysteria no less often in the past than in the present is evident from the remark of a 19th century neurologist that 'in its infancy the name given to insular (multiple) sclerosis is hysteria'.

2. *The mood changes and intellectual impairment* of the established disease. Surridge (1969) in a controlled study, found that approximately one quarter of his series of 108 patients were depressed and the evidence indicated that the depression was reactive. None of the depressed patients was impaired intellectually. A further quarter were euphoric and all but two in this group showed intellectual deterioration. The correlation between increasing euphoria and increasing deterioration was remarkably high. The majority of patients who denied their disability were in the euphoric group. These features led the author to the conclusion that euphoria is a pathological phenomenon, the direct result of damage to the central nervous system. Intellectual impairment, ranging from mild to severe, was found in almost two-thirds of the M.S. patients but in none of the controls (all 39 of whom suffered from muscular dystrophy). Surridge's findings are in keeping with contemporary views but conflict with the earlier belief that euphoria is a frequent, and intellectual impairment, a rare feature, of multiple sclerosis. Surridge points out that this earlier belief was peculiarly British and was not shared by Continental writers of that generation. One of the strangest manifestations, when it occurs, is denial of disability, which can range from impaired awareness of a single symptom to a

flat denial that disease is present. It is particularly striking when, as occasionally happens, it is encountered in patients who are not euphoric, not intellectually impaired, and who normally would be expected to have a full understanding of their condition and its implications.

3. *Personality change.* Reference has already been made to the severe personality change which can follow 'acute' multiple sclerosis, i.e. multiple sclerosis presenting initially as an acute cerebral disturbance simulating viral encephalitis (P—). A similar personality change resembling a frontal lobe syndrome has been observed in the more slowly developing disease, and the irresponsible behaviour which is one of the features has necessitated the patient's retention in a psychiatric hospital. Irritability and apathy are described as frequently occurring features but are doubtfully included under personality change which, when narrowly defined, implies a fundamental alteration in feeling and attitude.

A proportion of patients suffering from multiple sclerosis show no abnormality of mood or personality nor intellectual impairment. In Surridge's series, one-sixth were categorized as normal. The assumption that a particular personality type is associated with multiple sclerosis has been refuted by Pratt (1951).

CEREBRAL ARTERIOSCLEROSIS

Brief reference must be made to this condition which is discussed elsewhere (Vol. II, Chap. XIV) in order to point out that cerebral arteriosclerosis as a diagnostic label tends to be applied too indiscriminately to cases showing the features of the chronic organic reaction in middle or later life, when the aetiology is not immediately apparent. It is unwise to make this diagnosis in a patient under the age of 65 unless he or she suffers from *severe hypertension.* To this should be added the rider that even with patients above this age level cerebral arteriosclerosis should not be too hastily assumed until other aetiological factors have been investigated. Certainly cerebral arteriosclerosis, whether associated with hypertension or with a normal or minimally raised blood pressure, can result in unusually varied symptoms but in general these latter tend to show marked fluctuation. This characteristic fluctuation and the patient's retention of insight into his disabilities until a relatively late stage assist in differentiating cerebral arteriosclerosis from the more steadily progressive conditions occurring in the presenile period.

REFERENCES

ALEXANDER, L., PIJOAN, M. & MYERSON A. (1938) Beri-beri and scurvy. *Transactions of the American Neurological Association,* **64,** 135–139.
ALLISON, R. S. (1962) *The senile brain,* London. Edward Arnold.

ALZHEIMER, A. (1907). On a peculiar disease of the cerebral cortex. *Allgemeine Zeitschrift für Psychiatrie*, **64,** 146.

ASHER, R. (1949) Myxoedematous madness. *British Medical Journal*, **2,** 555–562.

BARLTROP, D. (1969) Lead poisoning. *British Journal of Hospital Medicine*, **2,** 1567–1573.

BEATTIE, A. D., DAGG, J. H., GOLDBERG, A., WANG, I. & RONALD, J. (1972*a*) Lead poisoning in rural Scotland. *British Medical Journal*, **2,** 488–491.

BEATTIE, A. D., MOORE, M. R., DEVENAY, W. T., MILLER, A. R. & GOLDBERG, A. (1972*b*) Environmental lead poisoning in an urban soft water area. *British Medical Journal*, **2,** 491–493.

BINNS, J. K. & ROBERTSON, E. E. (1962) Pick's disease in old age. *Journal of Mental Science*, **108,** 804–810.

BOLT, J. M. W. (1970) Huntington's chorea in the West of Scotland. *British Journal of Psychiatry*, **116,** 259–270.

BREWER, C. (1969) Psychosis due to acute hypothyroidism during the administration of Carbimazole. *British Journal of Psychiatry*, **115,** 1181–1183.

BRIERLEY, J. (1966) The neuropathology of amnesia states, Chap. 7. In *Amnesia*. Ed C. W. M.Whitty & O. L. Zangwell, London: Butterworths.

BROWNING, T. B., ATKINS, R. W. & WEINER, H. (1953) Cerebral metabolic disturbance in hypothyroidism. *A.M.A. Archives of Internal Medicine*, **93,** 938–950.

CAMPBELL, K. (1898) A case of haematoporphyrinuria. *Journal of Mental Science*, **44,** 305–315.

CHARATAN, F. B. & BRIERLEY, J. F. (1956) Mental disorder associated with primary lung carcinoma. *British Medical Journal*, **1,** 765–768.

CORSELLIS, J. A. N. (1969) Some observations in the pathology of the temporal lobe. In *Current Problems in Neuropsychiatry*. Edited by R. N. Harrington. Ashford, Kent: Headley Bros. Ltd.

CORSELLIS, J. A. N., GOLDBERG, G. J. & NORTON, A. (1968) Limbic encephalitis and its association with carcinoma. *Brain*, **91,** 481–496.

CREUTZFELD, H. G. (1920) On a peculiar disease of the central nervous system. *Zeitschrift für die gesamte Neurologie und Psychiatrie*, **57,** 1–18.

CRITCHLEY, M. (1953) *The Parietal Lobes*. London: Arnold.

CURRAN, D. (1930) Huntington's chorea without choreiform movements. *Journal of Neurology and Psychopathology*, **10,** 305.

DAGG, J. H., GOLDBERG, A., LOCHHEAD, A. & SMITH, J. A. (1965) Lead poisoning and acute intermittent porphyria. *Quarterly Journal of Medicine*, **34,** 163–175.

DAVIDSON, E. A. & ROBERTSON, E. E. (1955) Alzheimer's disease and acne rosacea in one of identical twins. *Journal of Neurology, Neurosurgery and Psychiatry*, **18,** 172–177.

DEAN, G. (1971) *The porphyrias—a story of heredity and environment*. London: Pitman.

DELAY, J. (1942) *Les Dissolutions de la Memoire*. Vol. 1 Paris: P.U.F.

DELAY, J. & BRION, S. (1954) Syndrome de Korsakoff et Corps Mamillaires. *L'encephale*, **43,** 193–200.

DEWHURST, K. (1969) The neurosyphilitic psychoses of today. A survey of 91 cases. *British Journal of Psychiatry*, **115,** 31–38.

DEWHURST, K., OLIVER, J. E. & McKNIGHT, A. L. (1970) Socio-psychiatric consequences of Huntington's disease. *British Journal of Psychiatry*, **116,** 255–258.

DE WARDENER, H. E. & LENNOX, B. (1947) Cerebral Beri-beri. *Lancet*, **i,** 11–17.

DIMSDALE, H., LOGUE, V. & PIERCY, M. (1964) A case of persisting impairment of recent memory following right temporal lobectomy. *Neuropsychologica*, **I,** 287–298.

FISHER, C. M. & ADAMS, R. D. (1964)　Transient global amnesia. *Acta neurologica scandinavica*, **40**, Supplement 9.

GAMPER, E. (1928)　Zur frage der Polioencephalitis haemorrhagica der chronischen Alcoholiker: Anatomische Befund beim alkoholischen Korsakoff und ihre Beziehungen zum klinischen Blid. *Deutsche Zeitschrift für Nervenheilkunde*, **102**, 122–129.

GOLDBERG, A. (1965)　In *Symposium, Disorders of the blood*. Edinburgh: Royal College of Physicians.

GOLDBERG, A. & RIMINGTON, C. (1962)　*Diseases of Porphyrin Metabolism*. Illinois: Springfield.

GREER, S. & PARSONS, U. (1968)　Schizophrenic-like psychosis in thyroid crisis. *Journal of Mental Science*, **114**, 1357–1362.

HARLOW, J. M. (1868)　Recovery from the passage of an iron rod through the head. *Massachusetts Medical Society Publication*, **2**, 338–340.

HENDERSON, D. K. & McLAUCHLAN, S. H. (1930)　Alzheimer's disease. *Journal of Mental Science*, **76**, 646–661.

HIERONS, R. (1957)　Changes in the nervous system in accute porphyria. *Brain*, **80**, 176–191.

HILL, D. & FENTON, G. W. (1969)　The temporal lobe: E.E.G. and disorders of behaviour. In *Current Problems in Neuropsychiatry*. Edited by R. N. Harrington. Kent: Headly Bros. Ltd.

HOLMES, J. M. (1956)　Cerebral manifestations of vitamin B_{12} deficiency. *British Medical Journal*, **2**, 1395–1398.

HUNTER, R., JONES, M. & MATTHEWS, D. M. (1967)　Post-gastrectomy vitamin B_{12} deficiency in psychiatric practice. *Lancet*, **i**, 47.

JAKOB, A. (1921)　On peculiar diseases of the central nervous system with pathological findings. *Zeitschrift für die gesamte Neurologie und Psychiatrie*, **64**, 147–228.

JELLINEK, E. H. (1962)　Fits, faints, coma and dementia in myxoedema. *Lancet*, **2**, 1010–1012.

JELLINEK, E. H. (1968)　Thyroid disorders. *Symposium, Some Aspects of Neurology*. Edinburgh: Royal College of Physicians.

LANCET (1970)　Apathetic Thyrotoxicosis, **2**, 809.

LOPEZ, R. & COLLINS, G. H. (1968)　Wernicke's encephalopathy. A complication of chronic haemodialysis. *Archives of Neurology (Chicago)*, **18**, 248–259.

LOVEL, T. W. I. (1962)　Myxoedema coma. *Lancet*, **1**, 823–882.

McALPINE, I. & HUNTER, R. (1969)　*George the Third and the mad business*. London: Allan Lane.

McGOVERN, G. P., MILLER, D. H. & ROBERTSON, E. E. (1959)　A mental syndrome associated with lung carcinoma. *A.M.A. Archives of Neurology and Psychiatry*, **81**, 341–347.

MARKS, V. (1966)　Spontaneous hypoglycaema. *Hospital Medicine*, Vol. I, No.2, 118–125.

MEYER, A. & BECK, E. (1954)　*Prefrontal Leucotomy and Related Operations. Anatomical aspects of success or failure. The Henderson Trust Lecture*. Edinburgh: Oliver and Boyd.

MICHAEL, R. P. & GIBBONS, J. L. (1963)　Some inter-relationships between the endocrine system and neuropsychiatry. *International Review of Neurobiology*, **5**, 243–292.

MILNER, B. (1966)　Amnesia following operations on the temporal lobe. In *Amnesia*, Chap. 5, Edited by C. W. M. Whitty and O. L. Zangwill. London: Butterworths.

MINSKI, L. & GUTTMAN, E. (1938)   Huntington's chorea: a study of thirty-seven families. *Journal of Mental Science*, **84,** 21–96.

NEVIN, S. (1967)   On some aspects of cerebral degeneration in later life. *Proceedings of the Royal Society of Medicine*, **60,** 517–526.

OLIVER, J. E. (1970)   Huntington's chorea in Northamptonshire. *British Journal of Psychiatry*, **116,** 241–253.

PAPEZ, J. W. (1937)   A proposed mechanism of emotion. *A.M.A. Archives of Neurology and Psychiatry*, **38,** 725–743.

PENFIELD, W. & MILNER, B. (1958)   Memory deficits produced by bilateral lesions in the hippocampal zone. *A.M.A. Archives of Neurology and Psychiatry,* **79,** 475–479.

PICK, A. (1892)   On the relation of senile cerebral atrophy and aphasia. *Prager medizinische Wachenschrift*, **17,** 165–167.

PIERCY, M. (1964)   The effects of cerebral lesions in intellectual function: a review of current research. *British Journal of Psychiatry*, **110,** 310–352.

PRATT, R. T. C. (1951)   An investigation of the psychiatric aspects of disseminated sclerosis. *Journal of Neurology, Neurosurgery and Psychiatry*, **14,** 326–335.

REMY, M. (1942)   Contribution a l'etude de la maladie de Korsakow. *Monatsschrift für Psychiatrie und Neurologie*, **106,** 128–144.

ROBERTSON, E. E. (1953a)   Progressive bulbar paralysis showing heredo-familial incidence and intellectual impairment. *A.M.A. Archives of Neurology and Psychiatry*, **69,** 197–207.

ROBERTSON, E. E. (1953b)   Skin lesions in organic cerebral disease. *British Medical Journal*, **1,** 291–295.

ROBERTSON, E. E., LE ROUX, A. & BROWN, J. H. (1958)   The clinical differentiation of Pick's disease. *Journal of Mental Science*, **104,** 1000–1024.

ROSE, F. C. & SYMONDS, C. P. (1960)   Persistent memory defect following encephalitis. *Brain*, **83,** 195–212.

ROYAL COLLEGE OF PHYSICIANS OF LONDON (1966)   *Report of the Committee on Accidental Hypothermia*. London: R.C.P.

SCOVILLE, W. B. (1954)   The limbic lobe in man. *Journal of Neurosurgery*, **11,** 64–66.

SCOVILLE, W. B. & MILNER, B. (1957)   Loss of recent memory after bilateral hippocampal lesions. *Journal of Neurosurgery and Psychiatry*, **20,** 11–21.

SERAFETINIDES, E. A. & FALCONER, M. A. (1962)   Some observations on memory impairment after temporal lobectomy for epilepsy. *Journal of Neurology, Neurosurgery and Psychiatry*, **25,** 251–255.

SHEEHAN, H. L. & SUMMERS, V. K. (1949)   The syndrome of hypopituitarism. *Quarterly Journal of Medicine*, **18,** 319–378.

SHULMAN, R. (1967)   Psychiatric aspects of Pernicious Anaemia. A prospective controlled investigation. *British Medical Journal*, **3,** 267–269.

SIM, M., TURNER, E. & SMITH, W. T. (1966)   Cerebral biopsy in the investigation of pre-senile dementia. I Clinical Aspects. *British Journal of Psychiatry*, **112,** 119–125.

SJÖGREN, T., SJÖGREN, H. & LINDGREN, A. G. H. (1952)   Morbus Alzheimer and Morbus Pick: a genetic, clinical and patho-anatomical study. *Acta Psychiatica Neurologica Scand*. Suppl. 82.

SLATER, E. & ROTH, M. (1969)   *Clinical Psychiatry*. London: Baillière, Tindall & Cassell.

STRACHAN, R. W. & HENDERSON, J. G. (1965)   Psychiatric syndromes due to avitaminosis B_{12}. *Quarterly Journal of Medicine*, **34,** 303–317.

STOREY, P. B. (1970)   Brain damage and personality change after sub-arachnoid haemorrhage. *British Journal of Psychiatry*, **117,** 129–142.

SUMMERSKILL, W. H. J., DAVIDSON, E. A., SHERLOCK, S. & STEINER, R. E. (1956) The neuropsychiatric syndrome associated with hepatic cirrhosis and an extensive portal collateral circulation. *Quarterly Journal of Medicine*, **25**, 245–266.

SURRIDGE, D. (1969) An investigation into some psychiatric aspects of multiple sclerosis. *British Journal of Psychiatry*, **115**, 749–764.

TALLAND, G. A. (1965) *Deranged Memory*. New York: Academic Press.

TONKS, C. M. (1964) Mental illness in hypothyroid patients. *British Journal of Psychiatry*, **110**, 706–710.

VICTOR, M. & YAKOVLEV, P. I. (1955) S. S. Korsakoff's psychic disorder in conjunction with peripheral neuritis. A translation of Korsakoff's original article with brief comments on the author and his contribution to clinical medicine. *Neurology*, **5**, 394–406.

VICTOR, M., ADAMS, R. D. & COLE, M. (1965) The acquired (non-Wilsonian) type of hepatocerebral degeneration. *Medicine (Baltimore)*, **44**, 345–396.

VICTOR, M., ADAMS, R. D. & COLLINS, G. H. (1972) *The Wernicke–Korsakoff Syndrome*. Oxford: Blackwell Scientific Publications.

WALKER, A. G. (1957) Recent memory impairment in unilateral temporal lesions. *A.M.A. Archives of Neurology and Psychiatry*, **78**, 543–552.

WALTON, J. N. (1953) The Korsakoff Syndrome in spontaneous subarachnoid haemorrhage. *Journal of Mental Science*, **99**, 521–530.

WERNICKE, C. (1881) *Lehrbuch der Gerhirnkrankheiten*. Vol. 11, p. 229, Berlin.

WILLIAMS, M. & PENNYBACKER, J. (1954) Memory disturbance in third ventricle tumours. *Journal of Neurology, Neurosurgery and Neuropsychiatry*, **17**, 115–123.

Chapter XIV

PSYCHIATRIC ILLNESS IN THE ELDERLY

W. D. Boyd

INTRODUCTION

No psychiatrist engaged in clinical practice in Britain today can be unaware of the enormous pressures placed on mental health services by psychiatric morbidity in the elderly. But if it sometimes seems that the problem is one which has been recognized only in the last decade it is salutary to recall that a memorandum prepared by the British Medical Association in 1948 covered many of the topics which are still being discussed today and emphasized the importance of setting up active treatment programmes for old people. And a few years earlier a study was made of the social problems leading to mental hospital admissions, and the need was expressed for early intervention and special day centres for the elderly—'very much on the lines of a child guidance clinic' (Lewis, 1943). In Leeds in 1947 an examination of elderly patients in hospitals for the chronic sick demonstrated that a high proportion were suffering from psychiatric illnesses, and that elderly people in the dull surroundings of institutions were particularly prone to depression and apathy (Affleck, 1947).

Yet in spite of all that was written on the subject of the elderly and their illnesses, both physical and psychiatric, the following twenty-five years were not marked by any general implementation of policies to improve services for the elderly, and the struggle to provide adequate facilities for their care remains a grim one. Perhaps our leaders, political as well as medical, were afflicted by a need to deny in themselves or in others the development of the ageing process, an attitude of mind referred to by one expert as 'gerontophobia'. (Comfort, 1967). However, there did develop over the years a wider understanding of the ageing process, which thus became an area of special study—*gerontology*—while *geriatrics* sprang up as the branch of medicine dealing with physical illnesses in old people. The term *psychogeriatrics* has had rather less universal acceptance, for it has sometimes been used to refer to patients where a psychological component has been added to a physical illness, or sometimes to mean an elderly patient with organic brain disorder. The most common usage, however, is as a description of all psychiatric disorders occurring in people over age 65.

The developing specialty of psychogeriatrics is concerned with a variety of topics, from a knowledge of the advances in the studies of biological ageing to an awareness of population trends and the effects of these trends on social structure; from the identification of the psychiatric syndromes seen in the elderly to specific treatments, general management and care.

These are the topics which will be discussed in the following pages.

THE AGEING POPULATION

All the figures for population trends in Britain and in other industrial societies demonstrate a rising proportion of individuals aged 65 and over. More significant still is the increasing numbers and proportion of the group of 75 and over, for it is in this group, particularly vulnerable as a result of bereavement, isolation and physical disorder, that psychiatric disturbance is likely to have the most serious consequences.

Thus, it has been estimated that in Scotland the years 1961 to 1967 saw an increase in the over-65 group of 48,000, and a quarter of that increase, namely 12,000, was among the over-75s. This represented an increase of 6.3 per cent in the numbers of men and women aged 75 and over in Scotland between 1961 and 1967, and the expected increase in this group between 1967 and 1982 is no less than 28 per cent (Morrison, 1970).

Similar trends are reported for England and Wales, where in 1966 males and females of pensionable age (over 65 for men and over 60 for women) formed 15.4 per cent of the population, while in 1981 they will form 16.2 per cent, and provide a numerical increase of 1.32 million (Brothwood, 1971).

The explanation for this increasing proportion of old people lies not in any marked improvement of life-expectancy in the aged but rather to the effects of birth-rate and decreased infant mortality at the beginning of the century. It follows that future population trends will also be dependent on measures for population control and the degree to which improved health services reduce child mortality.

Having looked at the normal population trends in the elderly, it is necessary next to examine the extent of psychiatric morbidity among old people. The most accurate measurement of the problem must come from a survey of a representative population rather than from examination of patterns of admission to institutions, which may be distorted by local policies or pressures. Even in surveys of 'normal' elderly populations it is likely that there will be considerable variation in reported cases due to different criteria of selection.

One of the best-known projects, carried out in Newcastle-upon-Tyne, showed that 10 per cent of aged people living in the community were suffering from organic brain syndromes and a further 30 per cent from functional disorders, giving a remarkably high total of 40 per cent impairment among the total population of apparently normal old people (Kay *et al.*, 1964). In Edinburgh, still greater prevalence was found in a survey of General Practices, the figure of 55 per cent with psychiatric abnormality being reported (Williamson *et. al.*, 1964).

Turning from general surveys to 'patient' populations, evidence shows that elderly patients require the attention of the family doctor to a far greater extent than younger adults, and often on account of psychiatric disorders. It is general experience that the admission of elderly patients to psychiatric hospitals constitutes a very appreciable proportion of all admissions, the figure in Scotland being 15 per cent of all male admissions and 25 per cent of all female admissions, while the number of patients aged 65 and over being treated as psychiatric inpatients reaches the remarkable figure of 30 per cent of all males and 50 per cent of all females (Scottish Home and Health Department, 1970).

Looked at from another angle, it was noted in a survey of mental illness in London (Norris, 1959) that the expectation of being admitted to a psychiatric hospital at least once with schizophrenia was 8.4 per 1000 of population for men and 10.6 per 1000 for women, while the expectation of being admitted with a psychosis of old age was 20.6 per 1000 of population for men and 27.6 per 1000 for women.

These findings do not differ greatly from many similar surveys in Europe and in the U.S.A. All of them emphasize the large number of old people suffering from psychiatric illness and the major impact which they make on psychiatric facilities, and there is an additional implication that improvement in facilities will immediately demonstrate unmet needs.

Many psychiatrists are faced with the task of examining their own local needs in the light of these general findings reported by other investigators. It is essential, in such a situation, to clarify the part played in the area under scrutiny by other facilities, for a glance at the services developed effectively in different parts of the country shows how often the present arrangements are built up on already available resources—whether those be psychiatric beds, local authority homes, or geriatric services—and even depend on the highly individual views of particular specialists responsible for the care of the elderly, rather than being planned in a way which could readily be applied to other regions. And even when examining the specific services set up for psychiatric patients the pattern of admissions and discharges will depend on such fundamental points as whether the patients being considered include *all* those over 65 or only those with organic impairment, and whether cases of uncomplicated senile dementia are looked on as the responsibility of the local authority in the area or the responsibility of the psychiatrist.

The essential objective is to learn enough about a population to provide services which will adequately complement the support provided for old people by the community. If unsupported and overwhelmed by the distress of their elderly, the community will make excessive demands on Homes and hospitals.

THE NORMAL AGEING PROCESS

Consideration of the causes of ageing must surely have gone on since time immemorial, for no one can avoid an awareness of the inevitability of the process. Magic, witchcraft, gland extracts, hormone preparations have all been unsuccessful in attempting to ward off old-age, yet there is a fascination in seeking an explanation for the contrast between an alert and active centenarian living in her own home and a demented deteriorated seventy-year-old patient in a psychogeriatric ward, or between one individual enjoying his retirement to the full and another becoming lonely and embittered. What factors determine the manner and rate of ageing?

Research in this sphere has followed along different channels—into the basic biological processes of ageing, into the physical and psychological changes which occur with increasing age and into the sociological factors which may influence the individual in later life.

The biological process of ageing refers to the gradual decline in healthy functioning which occurs in an organism and which ultimately leads to death. In a valuable summary of recent views of ageing, Busse points out that there is primary ageing, which is inborn and based on hereditary factors, and secondary ageing, caused by trauma and disease (Busse, 1969).

In both cases, cells die or produce less efficient mutations, or develop alterations in the chemical structure of their enzymes, with the result that abnormal metabolic processes are set in train, to the detriment of the organism.

Physical changes of ageing are well recognized by physicians, who observe alterations in general bodily appearance and specific changes such as lessened elasticity of skin, arthritic changes, osteoporosis, deterioration in special sense organs and atherosclerosis of arteries.

They are also aware of changes in bodily function such as lessened heart output, decreased glomerulus filtration rate, reduction in pulmonary vital capacity, alteration in erythrocyte sedimentation rate, and isolated neurological signs.

Certain *psychological changes* are common to most people as ageing occurs. Adjustment to new situations becomes less easy, reactions are slowed, enthusiasm decreases, greater caution is shown. Interests are narrow and tend to be self-centered, attitudes become more inflexible with passing years and are governed by earlier experience rather than by changing circumstances. The older person finds it more reassuring to hold on to long-accepted ideas than to risk involvement in uncertain situations, and may thus find himself at loggerheads with the next generation. Physical ailments inevitably make their appearance and are particularly worrying to an older person who sees himself as at greater risk of chronic ill-health or invalidism.

Motivation is inevitably affected by the disappearance of earlier ambitions in work situations or in personal advancement. The desire to attempt something new or to maintain a particular level of function is governed by a lessened need to succeed or even a fear of failure. However, given a situation where there is real value in successfully completing a task and where there is no excessive pressure to affect performance adversely, then an older person may be highly motivated to carry out a task, physical or mental. Therefore, in any activity programme, whether it be in a club for the elderly or in a hospital occupational therapy department, the need to ensure that the individual is motivated to share in the proposed work is clearly of major importance.

Underlying many aspects of the behaviour observed in the elderly is the personality structure of the individual.

There seems no doubt that successful ageing is associated with successful adaptation to emotional pressures at earlier stages in life, for advancing years unhappily do not necessarily remove traits of personality, such as irritability, suspiciousness or timidity, which may have caused problems in relationships throughout life.

In attempting to understand behaviour in an older person, then, it is valuable to have details of earlier success in work situations, social relationships and marriage if a realistic appraisal of the present situation is to be made.

The way in which individuals cope with changes such as those mentioned above will differ, and it is helpful to look at the findings in one study of personality which suggested that ageing men react along certain general patterns of behaviour (Reichard *et al.*, 1962).

Constructiveness described a group who were able to enjoy warm relationships, who showed humour, tolerance, and appropriate feelings, and who were able happily to accept their life-situation.

Dependency alluded to a group who tended to adopt a passive, unambitious, 'rocking-chair' position, taking care of themselves and unwilling to involve themselves in any potentially disturbing situation.

Defensiveness was seen in those who maintained a rigid, conventional attitude with marked self-control, insisting on leading an active life, and showing a need to divorce themselves from the threat of ageing.

Hostility was the noticeable feature in a group which displayed aggression and suspicion in their relationships and which showed unrealistic attitudes to the future. The final, *self-hating* group were

N

critical of their own achievements, had never been ambitious, had enjoyed unhappy marriages and social contacts, and tended towards depression. Clearly, the *hostility* and *self-hating* groups were seen as less well-adjusted than the other groups and more liable to be unable to cope with increasing age.

Changes in intelligence levels, in memory, and in the ability to acquire new skills have been studied extensively by psychologists, and have been reviewed by Bromley (1966). In brief, it can be said that formal testing of these characteristics is affected to some extent by factors already described such as fear of failure in the test situation and that *certain aspects* of intelligence and skill are affected by ageing. Thus, the older person has greater difficulty in changing from one method to another in a test situation, and copes less well than younger people in simple learning tasks. Acquisition of new skills is impaired, and it is found that in a given task the addition of each complicating factor leads to relatively increased error in older people.

In attempting to think abstractly, for example in the use of proverbs, older people do tend to think in a more concrete manner. Judgement of performance becomes poorer, so that insight into failure is lessened.

Memory-impairment is found to be related to ageing, but recent memory is much more readily disturbed than long-term memory, leading to difficulties in developing new thoughts and skills.

The general statement can be made that earlier attainments in learning and skills can be maintained in older people, while development of new skills is likely to be impaired.

SOCIOLOGICAL ASPECTS

The changes which occur in physical and psychological state in the ageing individual are closely related to wider sociological factors. The status which she enjoys in relation to family and neighbours, the part she plays in the community, the extent to which she can avoid isolation and poverty, the support which she can obtain at the time of bereavement or illness, the attitude of others to retirement—these are all examples of potential sources of difficulty for the older person.

The status of old people appears to depend on their value to society. In a situation where their long experience of life can provide useful information for later generations—and this can only happen in a society without rapid change—and where only a few people can expect to survive beyond middle age, then their position is assured. If, in addition, they can still carry out useful and productive activities they are seen to have a clear-cut role in the family. Unfortunately, in Western society today the reverse of these conditions holds, and the aged are very likely to sense their state of 'dependency' in relation to younger adults.

There is no doubt that the elderly are liable to be the victims of poor housing and poverty. They are less able and less willing than younger people to move to more modern accommodation, and this is particularly the case when their children have moved away to another part of the country and are not therefore in a position to supervise or encourage them. Pensions can hardly keep pace with cost of living, and an old person, even of average intellect, is not always capable of using her limited financial resources to best advantage.

There are times of crises, such as the death of a spouse, when the older person is particularly vulnerable because of the resulting sense of loss and isolation and where the attitude of society to bereavement will determine the degree of support available. Another crisis follows any serious physical illness, for the old person alone in the home and unable to carry out basic tasks of self-care will fall into a vicious circle of physical immobility, isolation and psychological disturbance.

There are two lines of thought concerning the most successful way for old people to cope with the various stresses to which they are subjected. The first view, the disengagement theory (Cumming and Henry, 1961), would hold that the elderly cope best if they accept the inevitability of reduced contact with others, particularly the activities of younger people, and manage to enjoy their retreat from the hurly-burly of everyday life. A second view, the activity theory (Maddox, 1963), holds that an older person, aware of certain failing skills, must make all the more effort to counteract this deterioration in order to maintain a sense of purpose and satisfaction.

Clearly, there is room for manoeuvre between these two views, and, in practice, the personality of the individual will decide to a considerable extent the degree to which she will remain active. Someone who has always been a socially-isolated recluse is unlikely to benefit from attempts to involve her in a country-dance class, yet may manage to maintain a precarious independence if she is encouraged and assisted to make her regular trips to the shops. And the man retiring from regular employment may be counselled, in the light of his known personality traits, in such a way that he can accept his new way of life in a positive way.

PSYCHIATRIC ASSESSMENT OF THE ELDERLY PATIENT

The psychiatric examination of the elderly patient is no less exhaustive than the examination of younger people. There are, however, certain aspects which deserve special mention.

The patient is often aware of her failing powers and decreasing capacity to care for herself. She is therefore liable to be defensive and suspicious of the motives of the examiner, who may indeed be assessing the likelihood that the patient requires to be in hospital. Unless the examiner can overcome this hurdle, which is usually possible by avoiding too brusque or dogmatic an approach, the interview will fail to elicit the facts which are required to make a satisfactory assessment.

In view of the likelihood of memory impairment in the older patient it is essential to obtain a history from someone in addition to the patient, and social worker or Health Visitor can provide a useful link to visiting relative or neighbour.

Particularly in patients with organic brain disorder, the decision about treatment and management is likely to depend more on the degree to which there is behaviour disturbance, such as incontinence, aggressiveness, noisiness, and wandering tendencies, than on more subtle psychiatric signs. Incontinence, after all, varies from an occasional bed-wetting to frequent soiling with urine and faeces. Aggressiveness and noisiness may mean that the old person resents and reacts to teasing by neighbourhood children or may mean that she bites, scratches, and screams at anyone who comes into her home to help. Wandering, too, may represent an inability to go from one place to another without getting lost or may refer to the angry old lady shouting to relatives 'Let me out—I must get home' as she stands inside her own front door.

Mental Testing

It is the intention in this section to discuss the methods of assessment which are of most value in the elderly patient. For a comprehensive description of mental testing, other texts should be consulted (Slater and Roth, 1969; Post, 1965). Assessment ranges from the examiner's observation of impaired performance in the interview situation to formal testing by the clinical psychologist, and individual psychiatrists have their favourite methods by which they compare one patient with another. The value of these clinical tests has been questioned, however, and it is important to ensure that the examination being carried out does represent a valid comment on the patient's mental state.

Behaviour in the interview situation may immediately reflect the degree to which attention, concentration and judgement are impaired, or the extent of the patient's restlessness. *Change in mood* may be apparent from the facial expression, the retardation, the preoccupation with disease or poverty, or self-reproach. The extent of *thought disorder* may be judged from the form of talk, where there may be repetition, vagueness, inability to sustain a coherent conversation, or total disruption of logical speech, or where the content may indicate delusions or hallucinations.

The extent to which these general observations should be followed up by formal tests is a matter of some concern. Certain routine exercises are usually described. The patient is asked about her name, her address and the day and date, as an indication of her *Orientation*. She tries to subtract 7 from 100 and keep on taking seven away (Serial Sevens Test) as a test of her *Attention*. She is invited to record a name and address, and recall after two minutes, or to listen to a short passage and recall after a period of time, or to repeat an increasing list of numbers (Digit Span) to provide information on *Memory*. And finally, she is questioned, on historical facts, simple geography, current events, to assess her level of *General Information*.

In addition to these clinical tests, the use of the Mill Hill Vocabulary Scale, the W.A.I.S. Verbal Scales and Performance Scales, Raven's Progressive Matrices, and the Inglis Paired Associate Learning Test have all been advocated.

Happily, recent work suggests that these various tests do have a useful part to play in the assessment of the patient, though in the light of earlier comments it will be remembered that the previous personality of the patient, her I.Q., and her cooperation in the test procedure will be major factors in deciding results.

In one recent study (Hinton and Withers, 1971) it was found that tests of orientation and information were definitely useful in differentiating between functional and organic illness, as were tests of recall. It was found, however, that the Digit Span Test was not helpful.

In another paper (Irving *et al.*, 1970), the validity of certain of these tests in discriminating between brain-damaged and other elderly patients was assessed. The Mill Hill Vocabulary Scale showed no discrimination, but Progressive Matrices, Inglis Paired Associate Learning Test, and Face-Hand Test (Fink *et al.*, 1952) were relevant.

A variety of clinical tests are therefore available to the psychiatrist examining the elderly patient, and there is a lot to be said for developing a standard form of examination which includes some system of scoring, such as has been demonstrated by Robinson (1965) and by Post (1965).

Physical Examination

This is a vital part of the general examination of the older patient, where many, perhaps all physical disabilities are liable to have associations with the presenting psychiatric syndrome, whether it be the arthritis which leads to physical isolation and thence to depression, or the acute heart failure presenting as a confusional state. The extent to which physical disorders are present in elderly people has been observed by Williamson and his colleagues who found that 78 per cent of old people had physical disability, moderate or severe, often unknown to the family doctors (Williamson *et al.*, 1964).

Some further investigations are worth pursuing, as a routine measure, such as radiological examination of chest, 'blood counts', blood urea and electrolytes, and electrocardiography. The value of more elaborate routine screening tests including skull X-ray and electroencephalography, is less certain. X-ray of skull and E.E.G. are seldom of help unless there are already clinical grounds for carrying them out; the occasions on which a positive result for syphilis is obtained are so few as to make it questionable whether this test should be carried out routinely, though clinicians are unhappy to omit such a long-accepted test. Vit. B_{12} deficiency is shown to be present in an appreciable number of psychiatric patients, particularly elderly people, in whom the deficiency is almost always associated with poor nutrition and other evidence of anaemia.

PSYCHIATRIC SYNDROMES IN THE ELDERLY

The prevalence of psychiatric illnesses in the elderly has already been described, and it is clear that old people are vulnerable to just the same disorders as are seen in younger people—the neuroses, the personality disorders, the affective and schizophrenic psychoses and the organic psychoses. There is the same need to identify the precise nature of the illness and to instigate specific treatment, whether this be physical or psychological.

The frequency with which different syndromes present themselves does, however, deserve mention. In 1948 Roth remarked on the difference in outcome of two major groups of illness in old people, namely the affective illness, which had a good prognosis, and senile psychosis where the likelihood was of death occurring in 90 per cent of patients within three years (Roth and Morrissey, 1952). At a later date Roth divided syndromes into six groups, namely affective psychosis, senile psychosis, late paraphrenia, arteriosclerotic psychosis, acute confusion, and other disorders, and found that affective psychosis accounted for almost half of the total cases surveyed, with senile and arteriosclerotic psychoses providing a further third of the total. Paraphrenia, acute confusional states and psychoneurosis were found in much smaller numbers (Roth, 1955). Rather similar findings were reported in an Edinburgh survey, where the admissions of people over 65 showed a fairly equal division into organic states, of which the vast majority were senile or arteriosclerotic dementia, and the functional states, where the most frequent diagnosis was of affective illness (Woodside, 1965). When surveys are carried out in the community, however, it is seen that a much greater problem of 'minor illnesses' is present. In the Newcastle study already mentioned some 30 per cent of all people over 65 were seen to suffer from functional disorders, and neuroses and personality disorders accounted for the greatest number of the individuals discovered to be ill.

In a more recent sample of elderly patients randomly selected and without evidence of organic or functional disorders, 44.4 per cent of them showed neurotic traits, and 6.3 per cent showed deviant personality traits when assessed by semi-structured interviews and self-rating scales (Bergman, 1971).

It becomes clear, then, that the types of psychiatric illness which should come to the attention of the family doctor are very different to those presently reaching the outpatient departments or wards of psychiatric hospitals.

Attention will now be given to the diagnostic categories described above.

Neurosis

Neurosis often develops in an elderly patient, particularly one who is already vulnerable through personality traits or through previous episodes of neurotic illness. Often there is a clear link between the development of symptoms and some environmental pressure such as difficulties with family. It is not uncommon to find a patient, living with daughter and son-in-law, who is only too aware that she is causing stress to her relatives by her presence, yet feels too dependent on them to move away, and develops symptoms as a result of this conflict.

Depression is particularly common in old people, and may be a neurotic illness developing as a consequence of social pressures and physical debility and as a realization that life is coming to an end.

Hysterical conversion symptoms arising for the first time in old age are always looked on as an uncommon event, and the greater likelihood of a physical cause emphasized. However, in patients who have tended to react in a histrionic way in earlier life and in whom some emotional stress is superimposed on a physical disability such as unsteadiness in walking or tremor of the hand then it is not unlikely that they will show a grossly increased physical disturbance. A diminution of the emotional pressures may then be expected to result in a considerable improvement.

An obsessional neurosis, when seen in an older person, has usually been present for many years, unless the obsessional symptoms are associated with the onset of a depressive illness. Such symptoms should not be confused with the repetitive stereotyped behaviour developing in dementia.

Personality Disorder

The way in which the normal personality is affected by the ageing process has already been described, but in some people traits or personality become accentuated in old age to a point at which they are disturbing.

It is said that aggressive and psychopathic traits become less of a problem as the individual matures into middle age, and this may indeed be the case, but other aspects such as rigidity, poor success in relationships, and possessiveness, may lead to great difficulties for those round about the old person, and feelings of sexual inadequacy may lead to anti-social behaviour.

Affective Illness

There has been an increasing awareness of the frequency with which affective illness develops in old people, and there is now less likelihood of a patient with depression being mistakenly labelled as suffering from dementia. The most comprehensive study of affective illnesses comes from Post (1962, 1965) who has given detailed descriptions of the different ways in which the depression may appear. Thus, there are 'organic depressions' where the evident affective symptoms are associated with an early dementing process, and 'depressive pseudo-dementias' where the perplexity and apparent lack of awareness of surroundings give an appearance of dementia in a patient with retarded depression. The depressive state associated most clearly with the elderly is the condition known as 'senile melancholia' where the patient is extremely agitated, importuning, and with bizarre delusions concerning guilt, unworthiness and bodily disorder. Several old ladies have been seen in Edinburgh with complaints that their bodies are riddled with woodworm. Post points out that very many patients develop an agitated depression which falls short of the classical senile melancholia, and also describes the 'masked depression' where a definite depressive illness is hidden behind an array of vague symptoms of anxiety or other neurotic complaints. It is common to see paranoid symptoms presenting themselves with these depressive syndromes.

Depressive illness can be treated in such a satisfactory way by the use of antidepressant drugs, or by E.C.T. when required, that the importance of being alerted to the possibility of an affective illness cannot be over-emphasized. It is salutary to note that Post's follow-up of elderly depressed patients revealed only a small proportion (21 per cent) of all those treated remaining entirely well during the next two years, but this does not take away the necessity to relieve the distress of the depression by appropriate means.

Mania may occasionally be seen in an older person and the typical features may be coloured by failing powers or early dementing process.

Paranoid Illness

Paranoid symptoms, ranging from occasional ideas of self-reference, or vague suspiciousness, to florid delusions of persecution, may be seen in the elderly, and are not uncommonly associated with affective illness and organic brain disorder, acute or chronic, or are found to have been present as a personality trait throughout life.

There is, in addition, a paranoid illness occurring for the first time in the elderly and showing many of the features of paranoid schizophrenia, so that the name 'paranoid schizophrenia in the elderly' or 'late paraphrenia' has been attached to the condition. Fish, on the other hand, found classical features of schizophrenia in less than half of such patients and preferred the term 'senile paranoid state' (Fish, 1960).

The clinical picture is one on which an old person becomes convinced that her neighbours or family are interfering with her and attempting to harm her. Sometimes, but not always, she is disturbed by persecutory voices. The situation at home deteriorates, with, ultimately, complaints from long-suffering neighbours.

The exact relationship between this paranoid state and the schizophrenic illnesses seen in younger people has been much discussed. There may be some specific genetic predisposition to this late-life illness, and other factors such as deafness, loneliness, and unsatisfactory social contacts appear to be of some relevance.

The management of these cases can be very difficult, for often the patient is not willing to consider treatment, and is not even prepared to be visisted in her own home. There is no doubt that the illness may be improved greatly by the use of tranquillizers or antidepressant drugs and many patients, once their acute symptoms are controlled, may be maintained at home with regular supervision if given maintenance drugs in sufficient dosage, but there is a group of patients who progress well in the hospital setting but relapse whenever they are allowed to return to their own home. Sometimes this occurs because of failure to take drugs but it also seems to be related to the re-appearance of paranoid delusions which the patient has managed to control in the hospital setting but which have never been absent. Such patients tend to remain in hospital, sometimes for many years.

Organic Disorders

The elderly person is particularly at risk of developing organic brain disease, which may show itself as a sudden change in mental state or as a gradual deterioration in function.

The clinical features of the 'acute brain syndrome' and 'chronic brain syndrome' are described fully in Chapter XIII.

In the elderly person it must be recognized that the appearance of an *acute confusional state* is likely to be secondary to some general physical illness and that improvement will occur once the primary illness is treated. The condition may also be seen in an old person who is subjected to emotional stresses or who is deprived of normal sensory stimuli, for example after an eye operation, and the patient who suffers already from a degree of dementia is particularly vulnerable.

Every psychiatrist is familiar with the insidious development of *dementia* in an older person. In the early stages of the illness the patient may present a facade which deceives the superficial enquiry, but careful examination soon demonstrates an impairment in memory and in orientation which is much more marked than the benign type of memory disturbance seen in more normal old people, where there is simply an impairment of recall (Kral, 1965).

It has been said that dementia is likely to occur in someone who has previously shown features of abnormal personality, but this view is based on the experience of dealing with people who have required psychiatric supervision and who are therefore particularly liable to have shown disturbed behaviour as a result of earlier personality traits. It is unlikely that the dementing process itself is related to earlier life experiences or behaviour.

TREATMENT OF PSYCHIATRIC ILLNESSES

It is not necessary to repeat the details of treatment available in specific psychiatric illnesses. Elderly people should not be denied the use of psychotropic drugs, E.C.T., or psychotherapeutic techniques, if these seem appropriate. The greater incidence of side-effects means that drugs should be given with particular caution, beginning with the minimum therapeutic dose, and should not be continued unnecessarily. But often it is found that restlessness is controlled only by a substantial daily intake of phenothiazine drug.

There is no clear evidence that any individual antidepressant, tranquillizer or hypnotic drug is of supreme value in the treatment of the elderly. On the contrary, there appears to be remarkable variation in the response which patients show to specific drugs, and much patience is required to find the precise regime of drug and dosage which is of greatest benefit.

Psychotherapeutic intervention as used in younger patients is not usually applicable to the elderly, yet considerable help can be given if it is recognized that the older patient is disturbed by an awareness that she is no longer in control of herself. Her way of life is being organized by others, her memory is becoming impaired, and her physical health is deteriorating. She is also aware of her need to depend on others and may react to this knowledge by drawing away from those round about or by making excessive demands on them.

Difficulties such as these may be faced with the patient in short interviews conducted in a direct and supportive manner.

General Management

In discussing the more general provisions for the management of the psychogeriatric patient in Chapter V, Vol. I, the need for a variety of facilities was emphasized.

Development of methods for the care of old people has differed from place to place, and rather than mention individual projects it is perhaps convenient to provide a general description of the requirements.

An ideal district service for the elderly would begin with an accurate measurement of their numbers in the population and a comprehensive register noting those at risk through isolation or disability. Housing development would include 'pensioner houses' and supervised sheltered accommodation, and the old people would be visited regularly by volunteers or by a paid 'street warden'. A day-centre, with regular activities and meals, would be within reasonable distance, and additional facilities, such as Meals-on-Wheels, chiropody service and laundry service would be available on a domiciliary basis.

A member of the staff from the local medical centre, sometimes the family doctor but more often the Health Visitor, would have some definite arrangement for keeping in contact with the elderly under their supervision.

Day facilities would be provided both in the psychiatric hospitals and geriatric hospitals so that old people who wished to maintain some degree of independence or whose relatives were reluctant to see them leave home permanently could be looked after on a daily basis. The transport necessary to cope with the numbers involved should be readily available.

As it became clear that an old person could no longer care for herself, steps would be taken to place her in appropriate accommodation. For a reasonably healthy individual this accommodation would be in a small Home, supervised by the Social Work Department of the Local Authority; for the demented patient without behaviour disorder or physical disturbance a place would be available in a Home for the Elderly Confused, also supervised by the Local Authority; those old people showing more obvious psychiatric disability would be admitted to a psychogeriatric ward and the physically impaired would go to the care of the geriatrician.

In spite of these facilities, there would still be occasions when a crisis situation arose and where the best placement of the individual was in doubt. In these circumstances an *assessment unit* would be available, often sited adjacent to the geriatric unit, where geriatrician, psychiatrist and social worker would examine the needs of the patient and decide on further care. There would be no disagreement between the three specialists, for each would have sufficient facilities to meet all the demands put upon the service.

The facilities within the psychiatric unit would consist of a *day-patient area* and an *admission-assessment ward* backed up by longer-stay wards, where the degree of physical impairment, especially incontinence, would be recognized by the provision of adequate bathing and toilet services.

There would be great emphasis on rehabilitation and on maintenance of function, and a staff of occupational therapists would share in the daily programme for the patients and would have the means of re-training some of them towards independence. A corner of the occupational therapy department would be designed as a self-contained flatlet where one or two old people could assess their own capabilities before discharge.

The relationship between the psychogeriatric unit and the rest of the hospital would be clear. Policy regarding the three groups of elderly patients requiring care, namely the 'functional illness' group, the 'organic illness' group and the 'graduate' group (referring to those patients with chronic mental illness and now reaching age 65—Scottish Home and Health Department, 1970) would be laid down so that pressure from any one group could not disorganize the services for one of the others.

Staffing of the unit would be by doctors who were committed to providing an active psychogeriatric service and by nurses who were available in numbers adequate to cope with the needs of the patients. Social workers in the unit would be particularly interested in giving support and guidance to relatives, and in preparing the patient for admission or discharge. Finally it should be said that old people would themselves welcome the various community and hospital facilities, for they would have been educated at an earlier age to see these facilities as aids rather than as threats to continued independence.

CONCLUSION

In this chapter the opportunity has been taken to look at some of the issues involved in the care of the elderly person with mental disorders.

It is evident that the participation of a variety of professional workers, from sociologists to psychologists, from psychiatrists to neuropathologists, is essential if there is to be greater understanding of the aetiological factors in these conditions and advances in the treatment and care of the patient.

Busse has suggested that the aged may constitute a section of our society whose voice is often unheard and whose needs are unmet.

In this chapter some of their psychiatric needs have been described, and it is seen that these range from basic research into the ageing process to improved housing programmes, from early recognition of psychiatric syndromes to hospital care of the permanently impaired.

The clinical psychiatrist has a major part to play in the development of a satisfactory service for the elderly patient.

REFERENCES

AFFLECK, J. W. (1947)   The chronic sick in hospital—A psychiatric approach. *Lancet*, **i,** 355–359.

BERGMAN, K. (1971)   The neuroses of old age. Recent developments in psychogeriatrics. *British Journal of Psychology*, Special Publication No. 6, Edited by D. W. K. Kay and A. Walk.

BROMLEY, D. B. (1966)   *The Psychology of Human Ageing*. London: Penguin Books.

BROTHWOOD, J. (1971)   The organization and development of services for the aged with special reference to the mentally ill. Recent developments in psychogeriatrics. *British Journal of Psychology*, Special Publication No. 6, Edited by D. W. K. Kay and A. Walk.

BUSSE, E. Q. (1969)   *Behaviour and Adaptation in Later Life*. Edited by E. W. Busse and E. Pfeiffer. Boston: Little, Brown and Co.

COMFORT, A. (1967)   On gerontophobia. *Medical Opinion Review*, 30–37.

CUMMING, E. & HENRY, W. E. (1961)   *Growing Old*. New York: Basic Books.

FINK, M., GREEN, M. A. & BENDER, M. B. (1952)   The face-hand test of a diagnostic sign of organic mental syndrome. *Neurology*, **2,** 46–58.

FISH, F. (1960)   Senile Schizophrenia. *Journal of Mental Science*, **106,** 938.

HINTON, J. & WITHERS, E. (1971)   The usefulness of the clinical tests of the sensorium. *British Journal of Psychology*, **119,** 9–18.

IRVING, G., ROBINSON, R. A. & McADAM, W. (1970)   The validity of some cognitive tests in the diagnosis of dementia. *British Journal of Psychology*, **117,** 114–156.

KAY, D. W. K., BEAMISH, P. & ROTH, M. (1964)   Old age mental disorders in Newcastle-upon-Tyne. I. A Study of Prevalence. *British Journal of Psychology*, **110,** 146–158.

KRAL, V. A. (1965)   The Senile Amnestic Syndrome: Diagnosis, Prognosis, Treatment. In *Psychotic Disorders of the Aged*. Symposium of World Psychiatric Association. *Geigy*.

LEWIS, A. & GOLDSCHMIDT, H. (1943)   Social causes of admission to a mental hospital for the aged. *Sociological Review*, **35,** 86–98.

MADDOX, G. L. (1963)   Activity and morale: A longitudinal study of selected elderly subjects. *Social Forces*, **42,** 195.

MORRISON, S. L. (1970)   Demographic and social aspects: the care of the elderly in Scotland: A follow-up report. *Royal College of Physicians of Edinburgh*, Publication No. 37.

NORRIS, V. (1959)   Mental Illness in London. *Maudsley Monograph No. 6.*, Institute of Psychiatry.

POST, F. (1962)   The Significance of Affective Illness in Old Age. *Maudsley Monograph No. 10*, Oxford University Press.

POST, F. (1965)   *The Clinical Psychiatry of Late Life*. Oxford: Pergamon Press.

REICHARD, S., LIVSON, F. & PETERSEN, P. G. (1962)   *Aging and Personality: A Study of Eighty-Seven Older Men*. New York: John Wiley.

ROBINSON, R. A. (1965)   The Organization of the Diagnostic and Treatment Unit for the Aged in a Mental Hospital. In *Psychiatric Disorders in the Aged*. Symposium of World Psychiatric Association. *Geigy*.

ROTH, M. & MORRISSEY, J. D. (1952)   Problems in the diagnosis and classification of mental disorder in old age: with a study of case material. *Journal of Mental Science*, **98,** 66.

ROTH, M. (1955)   The natural history of mental disorders in old age. *Journal of Mental Science*, **101.**

SCOTTISH HOME AND HEALTH DEPARTMENT (1970) Services for the Elderly with Mental Disorder. H.M.S.O.

SLATER, E. & ROTH, M. (1969) *Clinical Psychiatry*. London: Bailliére, Tindall and Casscll.

WILLIAMSON, J., STOKOE, I. H., GRAY, S., FISHER, M., SMITH, A., McGHEE, A. & STEPHENSON, E. (1964) Old people at home, their unreported needs. *Lancet*, **i,** 1117–1120.

WOODSIDE, M. (1965) Hospital and community experiment of 150 psychogeriatrics patients. A follow-up one year after admission. *Gerontologica clinica,* **7,** 286–302.

Chapter XV

PHYSICAL AND PHARMACOLOGICAL METHODS OF TREATMENT

A. D. Forrest

INTRODUCTION

Somatic therapy in psychiatry has become for some psychiatrists a curiously emotive issue. Our training as medical students makes us feel more at home with medical procedures such as drugs or electrical treatment, while others rebel against such an overly strict medical model and espouse a psychodynamic model which, at times, seems equally dogmatic. Residues of infantile omnipotence form a problem for all therapists whether they operate with drugs or the now traditional couch. In fact we should remember that the majority of treatment methods in psychiatry are empirical. They are used because they are believed to work and they remain efficacious so long as the physicians who employ them believe in them. The classic example is Deep Insulin Coma Therapy which produced real benefits in the hands of enthusiastic therapists until, with the advent of the tranquillizers (i.e. Boardman *et al.*, 1956) psychiatrists began to question the need for the continued use of insulin therapy. Finally in 1957 Ackner *et al.* published their findings on the results of insulin and narcosis therapy using matched pairs and randomized allocation of treatment. At six months' follow-up the improvement rates were essentially the same, 36 per cent for insulin and 40 per cent for narcosis. They were careful to point out, however, that their results did not indicate that insulin was ineffective but rather that it was non-specific.

If the treatments in psychiatry are empirical it follows that theoretical concepts or hypotheses about the aetiology of a syndrome do not effectively determine the treatment. Reactive Depression is thought to result from the interaction of a vulnerable personality and a stressful life situation (i.e. bereavement or marital conflict). This rather Meyerian presentation would not perhaps be challenged today but does not, of itself, preclude the use of electro-convulsive therapy or tricyclic anti-depressants.

Similarly most psychiatrists would subscribe to the view that there is some genetic factor in schizophrenia, but that of itself is no reason for denying that some schizophrenics benefit considerably from psychotherapy. This point may seem self-evident, but a vestigial belief in sympathetic magic persists, so that there is a pseudo-logic in treating 'psychogenically determined' diseases with psychotherapy and 'organic' diseases with somatotherapy.

Again physical methods of treatment are directed essentially at the treatment of the episode and criticisms that the patient has not remained well indefinitely must be viewed against the backcloth of medical conditions such as chronic bronchitis, asthma, peptic ulcer, conditions in which relapses are as much the rule as the exception. If we take depressive illness as the paradigm for the exhibition of somatotherapy, then it perhaps becomes clearer that treatment is aimed at the episode. In the majority of cases tricyclic drugs or electro-convulsive therapy produce a remission, but whether this is to be lasting depends on personality structure, genetic factors, interpersonal situation and age. Often relatives demand that sufficient treatment be given in order that the patient becomes 'completely normal'; this is an overt appeal to our latent feelings of omnipotence and must be resisted.

While physical methods of treatment are certainly effective, if used judiciously and with the limited goal of symptomatic relief or treatment of the episode clearly in mind, yet the optimal effect is only achieved in the context of a satisfactory doctor-patient relationship. Some writers refer to this in such hushed tones that the relationship takes on a sacramental quality; but the fact remains that sometimes the doctor is the best medicine (i.e. Balint, 1956) or in the context of this present discussion the best medicine is the medicine plus the doctor (i.e. his belief in the therapy and his encouraging support).

Again, enthusiasts for somatic therapies often seem determined to 'cure' the patient at all costs. As Rycroft (1966) pointed out, this is a misconception as far as psychoanalysis is concerned. Szasz (1961) like-wise pointed out that just as parents cannot stand the baby crying and feel impelled 'to do something', so psychiatrists become so disturbed at their patients' distress that they take recourse to ever more drastic remedies (i.e. drugs, E.C.T., leucotomy etc.).

This theme is central to the humane tradition in psychiatry; the physician should, and almost always can, help the patient, eschewing always the hazard of harming him.

LIMITATION OF SUBJECT MATTER

Whereas many items are referred to in other chapters of this volume (epilepsy in Chapter XI, addiction in Chapter V, the use of lithium in Chapter IX), there are other topics which are not discussed.

Insulin Coma Therapy, Continuous Narcosis and Malarial Therapy for G.P.I. we regard as having mainly historical interest. Further information regarding these methods are to be found in Sargant and Slater (1954).

Acetylcholine Treatment, Carbon Dioxide Abreaction and Modified Insulin seem marginal to the present practice of psychiatry. Details can be located in the following references (Sim, 1969; Meduna, 1950; Hawkings and Tibbets, 1956 (a and b); Sargant and Slater, 1954).

In this chapter it is proposed to discuss the use of electro-convulsive therapy, leucotomy, abreactive techniques, major tranquillizers, minor tranquillizers, anti-depressants, the specific treatment and management of schizophrenia and the drug treatment of phobic anxiety. Also included is a section on some iatrogenic conditions attributable to psychotropic drugs, and a short discussion of the use of sedation at night.

ELECTRO-CONVULSIVE THERAPY

Ugo Cerletti conducted experiments in Rome in 1935 to 1936 on the use of electrical stimulation to produce therapeutic convulsions (Cerletti and Bini, 1938). An apocryphal anecdote recounted by Cerletti in Edinburgh some years later revealed that their first patient was a mute catatonic. The first passage resulted in a 'stun' and the patient sat up and said 'No, no, not again'. But Cerletti and his colleagues did do it again and achieved a complete seizure opening the way to one of the most effective if most empirical treatments in psychiatry.

Technique of Electro-convulsive Therapy (E.C.T.)

Before E.C.T. was modified by the use of short-acting intravenous anaesthetics the risks pertaining to the treatment related to the muscular movements of the fit; thus crush fractures of the vertebrae and dislocations (i.e. shoulders) were the anticipated problems. Since the use of anaesthetics the risk is basically that of a brief anaesthetic. The present author has been involved in the use of this treatment over 20 years and has only observed one death attributable to it. On the other hand, Maclay (1953) reported 62 deaths in England and Wales associated with the use of E.C.T. over a 5.5-year period.

Procedure. The patient is physically examined to exclude intercurrent infections of the respiratory tract and major contraindications (see below), and given no food or fluid from midnight the night before. The bladder is emptied just prior to treatment which is usually given at 9 to 10 a.m. and dentures are removed. Premedication with atrophine sulphate (0.6 mg) may be given intramuscularly 60 minutes prior to treatment or intravenously along with thiopentone (0.125 to 0.2 g in a 2 per cent solution); then through the same needle scoline (succinylcholine 25 to 50 mg according to weight and physique) is injected. After 15 to 20 seconds fasiculation of the musculature can be observed. The anaesthetist now administers oxygen through a Boyles apparatus, the electrodes (dampened with bicarbonate solution) are applied to the anterior temporal areas of the scalp, and a gag (and sometimes also an airway) is inserted. The current is administered for approximately 1.0 seconds (using an Ectron Mark III model) and a modest 'fit' is observed in the form of movements of the face and sometimes fingers and toes. More violent muscular contractions indicate the need for a larger dose of scoline on the next occasion. Oxygen is once again administered, and controlled respiration maintained until normal breathing is resumed. The patient is then turned on his side and the airway removed. After 5 to 15 minutes consciousness is partially regained, but with encouragement the patient will sleep for an hour or more, and this is probably beneficial. At first waking the patient is often confused and benefits from the presence of nursing staff and the reassurance that he has had his treatment and should go back to sleep.

Management and Spacing of Treatment

In Edinburgh we do not give E.C.T. more often than two to three times per week, and then only in exceptionally disturbed patients. Sometimes the first two treatments need to be given on succeeding days, but usually we conform to a twice-per-week schedule with an average course of five to seven treatments, the last two only given at an interval of seven days. Often after the second treatment the patient is better for part of the afternoon and after the third or fourth treatment the improvement extends to the next treatment day.

Side Effects and Complications

All patients experience a temporary impairment of memory function which is retrograde and anterograde, i.e., extending back some hours or days before the first treatment and extending forward some days after the last treatment. During the course of the treatment registration of new material is impaired and also recall of recent material. It takes up to three months for memory function to return to its optimal level, and in patients over 65 memory may be slightly impaired for many months. Nominal dysphasia or subjective word-finding difficulty is probably common, but is only commented upon by a minority (usually obsessional patients). The practical implications are obvious: the relatives and the patient must be told about this problem and advised that letters and visits be recorded in a notebook to avoid later embarrassment. Patients should put their business affairs in order before commencing treatment. The author recalls a business man with a very severe depression who had decided that as things were so black he must sell his business; after some four treatments he was much more optimistic and felt his enterprises might develop successfully He recalled that he had thought of selling but could not remember what his plans had been. In this case it was fortunate that he had avoided putting his intentions down in the form of written instruction.

Headache after treatment is not uncommon but responds to acetylsalicylic acid.

Risks

The risks of modified electro-convulsive therapy are really minimal provided the proper recognition of indications and contraindications is followed. I mentioned Maclay's (1953) findings; in 1959 Barker and Baker investigated the cause of death in nine patients who had had E.C.T.; the mortality rate worked out at one death per 28,000 treatments.

Contraindications

Whereas Sim (1969) only singles out organic brain disease as a specific contraindication, most psychiatrists would agree that these following conditions suggest that treatment be at least deferred:

1. recent coronary occlusion
2. recent cerebro-vascular incident
3. congestive heart failure (decompensated)
4. present infection of the respiratory tract.

Pulmonary tuberculosis complicating psychiatric disease is no contraindication, provided the necessary precautions (i.e., separate mask, gag, etc.) are observed. Neither hypertension, pregnancy nor active hyperthyroidism has proved any contraindication in practice.

Indications

Generally speaking depression of affect is the main indication for E.C.T. The ideal subject is over the age of 40, has made a good life adjustment, albeit that the personality shows features of rigidity or obsessional traits. If this is the patient's first depressive illness and retardation is present, then the prospects of a good outcome from treatment are in the 90 per cent range. On the other hand, if the patient is a married woman of 25, with evidence of marital disharmony and of previous personality difficulties, then the clinician should be wondering whether this treatment is justified at all. In essence there are three *primary indications* for E.C.T.:

1. depression in a patient over the age of 40
2. depressive phase in a known manic-depressive (unipolar or bipolar)
3. puerperal depression: some of these patients show atypical, schizophreniform features but, when the condition is severe, E.C.T. combined with phenothiazines is often most effective.

Secondary indications

    1. certain cases of hypomania

    2. schizophrenics with marked retardation or partial catatonic syndromes

    3. schizophrenics with severe paranoid tension not controlled by phenothiazines

    4. paranoid psychoses in the fifth and sixth decades which show the usual admixture of depressive and persecutory features.

In relation to hypomania we find that almost all cases can be controlled with haloperidol, chlorpromazine or lithium. Sometimes E.C.T. is necessary, but quite often it obscures the clinical picture and makes further management even more difficult.

Psychiatric Contraindications

In general, organic brain disease is a contraindication, though there are patients aged 70 years and over who have severe depressive illnesses but also show minimal evidence of cerebral arteriosclerosis. In such cases we would use tricyclic drugs but would add in spaced E.C.T. where it was thought benefit would outweigh the inevitable memory impairment.

Allowing that it is often difficult to discriminate between anxiety and the agitation that accompanies depression in many elderly patients, I would subscribe to the general view that E.C.T. does not help patients with anxiety neurosis. E.C.T. is sometimes advised for patients with depersonalization; in our experience this course has seldom proved beneficial and sometimes it makes these patients worse. Complete catatonic stupor is no longer a feature of the schizophrenic patients coming to the clinics in Edinburgh, but partial syndromes with marked retardation and/or stereotypies are encountered, and sometimes justify the use of electro-convulsive therapy. Likewise there are some paranoid schizophrenics whose persecutory anxiety and distress is not controlled by phenothiazines; E.C.T. in such cases is often beneficial.

The group for whom E.C.T. is often not considered early enough is that of paranoid-depressive women in the fifth decade. Sometimes the predominant affect is hostility rather than depression. A combination of tripluoperazine and E.C.T. is often most effective.

General Principles of Management in Relation to Electro-convulsive Therapy

In general, depression of affect, retardation and paranoid anxiety are the symptoms indicative of likely benefit from this treatment. The more strictly patients are selected on such positive criteria, and not simply because nothing else has been found to help them, the better the results of treatment are likely to be. Patients with unipolar illness, i.e. recurrent depressions, present a real problem in regard to how often to use this treatment. Used too frequently the side effects begin to mount and the benefits to diminish. Such unipolar illnesses as well as bipolar manic-depressive illnesses, can be managed in the long term by the use of lithium carbonate (see Chapter IX), but sometimes further courses of E.C.T. are required. We would prefer not to use this treatment more often than once in 12 months, and after the third or fourth course we would question whether some new therapeutic approach was not more appropriate.

LEUCOTOMY

This procedure was brought to the notice of psychiatrists by Egas Moniz (1936) and extended by Freeman and Watts (1941). The anatomical rationale of the operation relates to the interdependence of the thalamus, hypothalamus, rhinencephalic centres and the frontal cortex. Early operations aimed at severing the fronto-thalamic fibres on both sides (i.e., McKissock, 1943), while later procedures aimed at undercutting the cortex (Scoville, 1949), or at the thermo-coagulation of the dorso medial nucleus of the thalamus under stereotactic control. Restricted section of the inferomedial white matter is said to produce less undesirable side effects (Pippard, 1955).

Indications

Symptoms are said to be a more useful guide than formal diagnosis: those which are most likely to be relieved are tension, fear and anxiety. Previous personality is a most important consideration; inadequacy, extreme dependency, hysterical traits and addiction to drugs or alcohol are all features which would lead the psychiatrist to advise against the operation. While Partridge (1950) found that obsessional states appeared to do well, others (Schurr, 1969) suggest that chronic depressive states in patients over 60 years offer the best prognosis. On the other hand, Post *et al.* (1968) noted that complications tend to be much more prominent in patients over 65.

Contraindications

Personality disorders, schizophrenia, organic cerebral disease and manic-depressive illness are contraindications to leucotomy. Leucotomy has been advocated for the treatment of intractable pain but the indications for its use in this field must be increasingly rare. The present author has recommended leucotomy for five patients over a period of ten years; three of these have done well though only two are working; two have not improved and may, in fact, be worse. Examples:

1. A 45-year-old manic-depressive lawyer presented every 9 to 12 months over an eight-year period with severe depressive episodes; his response to drugs was minimal and although he got better with E.C.T.

he was now needing more treatments and showing more side effects. Eighteen months after leucotomy he was not depressed, but querulous, demanding and unable or unwilling to return to work. His wife said that he was worse, i.e., that he was more self-centred and more self-indulgent.

2. A 47-year-old paranoid depressive woman had been ill for 15 years with ideas of persecution and abusive hallucinations. She had become a burden to her family and was latterly unemployable. Three months after operation she got a job in a theatre box-office, and came to the clinic saying that she was better than she had been for 15 years and that her family were welcoming the change in her. She was well three years later.

Post *et al.* (1968) recommended a leucotomy conference for each patient so that the indications for and against the operation can be fully discussed by all professionals involved in the patient's treatment. This seems a valuable suggestion, particularly as this is the one psychiatric intervention which is irreversible.

ABREACTION WITH SODIUM AMYLOBARBITONE

Abreactions are sometimes used in a somewhat magical way in psychiatric practice, i.e., to assist a patient in resolving a conflict. We feel that a conflict can only be defined in clear consciousness and resolved (sometimes) after a certain amount of psychotherapeutic work. But there are three situations where an abreactive technique does seem to justify consideration: (a) where a patient has had a very traumatic experience and suppressed the memory, disassociated the feelings or in some other way failed to incorporate this experience meaningfully into the 'fabric' of his life: (b) where anxiety or embarrassment is preventing the discussion of a problem of which the patient appears to be conscious, or at least the material is available to conscious re-examination, and (c) as an exploratory procedure in a mute patient or patients who claim to have lost their memory.

Essentially the procedure is (a) to prepare the patient by explaining that the psychiatrist feels that by giving an injection the patient may get sufficient relaxation i.e., relief of anxiety, so that more fruitful discussion of his problems can ensue, and (b) the slow intravenous injection of sodium amylobarbitone in a 2.5 per cent solution (0.25 g in 10 cc of distilled water) with the patient on a comfortable couch in a semi-darkened room. When the patient is showing signs of getting relaxed and drowsy, it is sometimes helpful to add in 10 mg of methedrine from a separate syringe.

Another basic requirement is for the psychiatrist to stay relaxed and not become obsessed with the mechanics of the procedure. Some patients with amnesia will, in these circumstances, feel safe enough to disclose what problems they have been trying to escape from.

Alternatively patients who have suffered traumatic bereavement may be started on the real process of mourning by being allowed to begin to show their grief under such sheltered conditions.

Lysergic Acid Diethylamide (LSD) offered another and very promising technique for the treatment of obsessional neurosis and certain sexual disorders. Because of the problems of misuse and addiction and the suspected dysgenetic effects the drug is not now being used in routine practice.

MAJOR TRANQUILLIZERS

There are now so many phenothiazine derivatives that some degree of selection is imperative. It is proposed to discuss chloropromazine, trifluoperazine, thioridazine and fluphenazine decanoate.

Chlorpromazine

This was the first phenothiazine to be introduced into psychiatric practice and was found to be effective in the treatment of psychoses. The structural formula is:

The pharmacology of this and other drugs is described in Chap. XVI, Vol. I. One experimental finding that does seem to have direct relevance for the clinical use of chlorpromazine relates to the observations of Bradley *et al.* (1966) that chlorpromazine has a selective inhibitory action on the sensory inflow from the ascending pathways into the reticular formation.

Indications: *Schizophrenia*: acute schizophrenic reactions are quickly brought under control by doses ranging from 50 to 200 mg t.d.s. Intramuscular chlorpromazine 50 to 100 mg is effective in a psychotic crisis or where oral medication is refused.

Hypomania: the same dose is employed as for the acute schizo-phrenic reaction; often chloropromazine is combined with haloperidol or lithium carbonate (see Chap. IX).

Post-Operative Confusional States: Delirium Tremens and mixed psy-chotic states frequently respond to chlorpromazine. Similarly, with-drawal of drugs in states of addiction (see Chap. V, Vol. II) is often facilitated by the use of this phenothiazine.

Toxic Effects. 1. *Jaundice.* the clinical features have often been described (e.g. Cohen and Archer, 1955) : it seems to be agreed that the mechanism is that of drug sensitivity resulting in biliary stasis and an obstructive type of jaundice. Graham (1957) found that the condition is not un-common in general hospitals, but it is seldom observed now in psy-chiatric units.

2. *Dermatitis and photosensitivity.* Some few patients produce a severe dermatitis in response to chlorpromazine. This is sometimes non-responsive to antihistamines and requires topical or systemic steroids. This sensitivity must be recorded clearly on these patients' case notes. Most patients on chlorpromazine exhibit a sensitivity to sunlight, but this is seldom a serious hazard in Edinburgh.

With large doses (i.e. 1 to 2 g per day) progressive mauve-grey pig-mentation of the skin has been reported (Greiner and Berry, 1964), and more recently cardiac complications (Richardson *et al.*, 1966). Such large dosage has not been scientifically demonstrated to produce better results than the more modest dosage referred to in this chapter.

Side Effects. 1. All patients show *degrees of Parkinsonism*, i.e. slight facial masking, salivation, tremor, muscular stiffness, dystonic attacks, etc. Irreversible dyskinesias are attributed to prolonged use of pheno-thiazines (Hunter *et al.*, 1964), but these syndromes were observable before the introduction of these drugs and one suspects that they only manifest themselves when there is underlying brain damage.

2. *Lactation.* A distressing side effect in some women patients which can be remedied by replacing the drug with thioridazine or tri-fluoperazine.

3. *Hypotension.* Postural hypotension is quite marked in some subjects so that on standing up suddenly from a seated or recumbent position the blood pressure falls abruptly, leading to giddiness or fainting attacks; this symptom is particularly common when intramuscular chlorpromazine is being used.

Trifluoperazine

This is the example we want to discuss from that group of pheno-thiazines with a piperazine side-chain. There is no doubt that this is an effective drug in the treatment of many patients with paranoid schizo-phrenia, and others with a paranoid psychosis. The toxic effects are minimal, but the Parkinsonian side effects are sometimes extreme, i.e. dystonic attacks or oculogyric crises. The dose is 5 to 15 mg t.d.s. in tablet form, but for maintenance one spanule (15 mg) at night may be found to be effective.

Thioridazine

This is one of two phenothiazines with piperidine side-chains which warrant discussion; the other is fluphenazine. Thioridazine has, as its name suggests, a sulphur atom on the ring site occupied in the case of chlorpromazine by a chlorine atom. Thioridazine is a potent tranquillizer with no hepatotoxic effects so far reported. On the other hand the extrapyramidal effects are equivalent to those of chlorpromazine, and while the photosensitivity may be less marked, it has been reported from America that retinal pigmentation occurs with high dosage. The usual dose is about the same as chlorpromazine (i.e. 50 to 200 mg t.d.s.). The manufacturers have produced a palatable syrup (25 mg in 5 ml) which is useful for patients who appear to consume, but later spit out, their tablets. Old ladies sometimes consume the syrup in the mistaken belief that it has qualities reminiscent of our national beverage.

Fluphenazine deconoate

This preparation, and the earlier fluphenazine enanthate, have given a significant impetus to the outpatient and community care of schizophrenic patients. The dose of the decanoate is 12.5 to 37.5 mg (25 mg fluphenazine in 1 ml). The injection is given intramuscularly and lasts about 22 to 32 days (the enanthate lasted 14 to 18 days). Our practice, in keeping with the advice offered by the manufacturers, is to start with a half-dose (i.e. 12.5 mg in 0.5 ml of decanoate) covered by antiparkinsonian drugs (i.e. Benzhexol 2 mg t.d.s.). Many women patients can, in fact, manage better on a half-dose (12.5 mg in 0.5 ml) and this may last them up to 21 days. At present we think this technique of depot injections should be hospital based, though we are encouraging our Community Nursing Service to give domiciliary injections to selected patients. In country districts the involvement of family doctors and district nurses may, on the other hand, be the appropriate development.

Indications. The indications for the use of depot phenothiazines are schizophrenia and some cases of paranoid psychosis. It is clear that a substantial proportion of schizophrenics do not take their medication as prescribed once they have left hospital (Renton *et al.*, 1963). It is also clear that those patients who continue attendance at the follow-up clinic are also the patients who take their drugs; as a group they have a better outcome than the non-drug-takers (Hankoff *et al.*, 1960).

The advantages of depot phenothiazines are twofold, (1) the patient gets the drug as prescribed, (2) the contact with the follow-up clinic is maintained.

Side Effects. 1. *Parkinsonian* side effects are commonly seen but can be controlled with benzhexol or orphenadrine, and, in acute reactions, intramuscular procyclidine (10 mg) is indicated. There are some patients in whom such side effects are sufficiently disturbing to persuade the patient or the psychiatrist to desist with this form of therapy. The number of such cases is certainly reduced if the first dose is a half-dose, and the first and second doses are given in a hospital setting.

2. *Depression.* There is no doubt that many schizophrenics get periods of depression, and schizophrenics do commit suicide, but less commonly appear in the reported statistics on 'attempted suicide'. De Alarcon and Carney (1969) reported a series of suicidal attempts in patients treated with depot fluphenazine. Careful reading of their paper seemed to suggest (Forrest, 1969) that 40 per cent of their series had shown a marked affective element in the illness. Our experience is that many patients initially diagnosed as schizophreniform reactions in the age group 20 to 29 years, later prove to have manic-depressive illnesses. The use of fluphenazine enanthate or decanoate in such cases is of questionable value.

The Butyrophenones

These are drugs which are structurally related to gamma aminobutyric acid: haloperidol, triperidol and pimozide are all members of this group.

Indications are hypomania or mania, paranoid schizophrenia and some patients with chronic schizophrenia. The dose of haloperidol is 1.5 to 4.5 mg t.d.s. or pimozide 2 to 3 mg t.d.s. In some patients with hypomania a combination of chlorpromazine (100 mg t.d.s.) and haloperidol (3 mg t.d.s.) is better than a larger dose of either drug singly.

Side effects are Parkinsonian in type: rigidity, tremor, restlessness (akisthesia) and salivation. Pimozide is alleged to produce many less side effects than other drugs for the same sort of anti-psychotic effects.

THE USE OF ANTIPARKINSONIAN DRUGS DURING TREATMENT WITH THE MAJOR TRANQUILLIZERS

As all the major tranquillizers are liable to produce Parkinsonian side effects, it is logical to employ antiparkinsonian drugs to modify these symptoms and avoid distress for the patients. It is our practice to use benzhexol or orphenadrine (50 mg t.d.s.). These drugs improve the rigidity and reduce the salivation but have less effect on the tremor.

Dystonic attacks, oculogyric crises and episodes of dysphagia may require the use of intramuscular procyclidine hydrochloride; the dose is 10 mg intramuscularly. It should be noted, however, that adjustment of the dose of the tranquillizer may be necessary to reduce the Parkinsonian side effects adequately, even when antiparkinsonian drugs are also being employed. In the case of depot fluphenazine the outpatients are given benzhexol or orphenadrine and instructed to use them for the first few days after the injection and subsequently if they get symptoms. Dystonic attacks after the first injection of fluphenazine are best managed in hospital as noted above, and can be controlled by the intramuscular injection of procyclidine.

The Minor Tranquillizers

There are a large number of psychotropic drugs which are alleged to relieve anxiety e.g. meprobamate, chlordiazepoxide, diazepam, oxypertine, perphenazine.

Controlled drug trials of these minor tranquillizers (e.g. Raymond et al., 1957) have given rather equivocal results. Recently we completed a study of oxypertine, comparing it with chlordiazepoxide in outpatients seen in a General Practice setting (Forrest and Maule, 1972). The results indicated a satisfactory response rate to both drugs with no statistical difference between them. There seems little doubt that in the treatment of anxiety, suggestion plays a prominent part, and this makes controlled evaluation particularly difficult.

The three drugs which are most widely used in this region for the relief of anxiety are chlordiazepoxide, diazepam and perphenazine.

Chlordiazepoxide is presented in 10 mg capsules and the dose is 10 to 20 mg t.d.s. It is a useful drug in the control of anxiety, especially phobic states, and in the symptomatic treatment of some patients with alcoholic addiction (see Chap. V, Vol. II). Side effects are minimal, though motor incoordination ('rubber legs') can follow if alcohol is consumed in any quantity along with the chlordiazepoxide.

Diazepam is another diazepine related to chlordiazepoxide. It appears to be more potent, weight for weight. The indications are anxiety, tension states and also some agitated depressions when it is usefully combined with antidepressants. The dosage is 2 to 10 mg t.d.s. and the presentation is in 2- and 5-mg tablets.

Perphenazine is an effective minor tranquillizer, especially useful again in some patients with agitated depression when it is combined with one of the tricyclic drugs. The dose is 2 to 4 mg t.d.s. and the only side effects are Parkinsonian; rigidity does not seem to occur at this dosage, but tremor and akisthesia are sometimes observed.

THE ANTIDEPRESSANT DRUGS

There are two important groups of antidepressant drugs: the tricyclic group and the mono-amine oxidase inhibitors (M.A.O.I.s).

The tricyclic drugs form the most important group available for the treatment of depression. The original compound was imipramine whose structure is shown here:

$$CH_2—CH_2—CH_2—N\begin{smallmatrix}CH_3\\CH_3\end{smallmatrix}$$

The structural resemblance to chlorpromazine will already have been noted.

The indication for the exhibition of this drug is the syndrome of depression (Kiloh *et al.*, 1962), especially when classical features are present, i.e., early morning waking, impaired concentration, diurnal variation etc. It is useful in first attacks in older subjects and in the management of episodes of depression in manic-depressives, but appears to be less useful in so-called reactive depressions, a concept which has, in fact, often been questioned (Forrest *et al.*, 1965). The dosage is 25 to 50 mg t.d.s. or q.d.s.

Side effects are dry mouth, blurring of vision, tremor and constipation. Disturbance of heat regulating mechanisms appears to be common in women, so that patients feel too hot, too cold, or sweat excessively. Skin rashes are reported and the occasional older male patient experiences dysuria or retention of urine. The drug takes 7 to 10 days to produce observable improvement and requires to be continued on maintenance dose level (i.e., 25 mg b.d. or t.d.s.) for at least 12 months.

Other tricyclic compounds are derivatives of imipramine. Amitriptyline has a more sedative action than imipramine; the dosage and side effects are the same. Nortriptyline is possibly more potent, weight for weight, and in our practice the dosage has seldom required to exceed 100 mg per diem (i.e., 25 mg q.d.s.). There is some evidence that it is less sedative than amitriptyline (Forrest *et al.*, 1964). Protriptyline seems to have even more energizing properties and is effective in a dosage of 10 mg t.d.s. It should be noted that all these drugs can (a) induce perceptual disturbances in paranoid-depressive states, and (b) cause a swing into hypomania in susceptible persons (i.e., those subjects whose illness is basically bipolar manic-depressive).

Monoamine Oxidase Inhibitors

These drugs have a limited but real place in the treatment of atypical, neurotic or reactive depressions (Sargant and Dally, 1962). The M.R.C. Trial (1965) comparing E.C.T., imipramine, phenelzine and placebo found that phenelzine was no better than placebo. This experience has not been borne out in our clinical practice provided that adequate selection of cases is maintained. Notwithstanding their undoubted value in atypical neurotic depressions, the M.A.O.I. drugs have not gained wide acceptance, partly because of reports of toxic effects. It might be appropriate to discuss these toxic effects in some detail before proceeding to a more detailed account of one member of this group, phenelzine (beta-phenylethyl hydrazine).

Toxic Effects. Hypertensive attacks: these have been observed for many years and lead to severe headache, palpitations and hypertension. It was not until Blackwell (1963) incriminated cheese that it was realized that food substances containing large amounts of amines must be avoided. The list of foods now includes cheese (especially cooked cheese), yeast extracts, meat extracts, marinaded meat, broad beans, chianti and claret. One patient on phenelzine 15 mg t.d.s., ate a cheese soufflé in spite of earlier warning. She got a pounding occipital headache and was admitted to a neurological unit overnight with suspected sub-arachnoid haemorrhage.

Potentiation of analgesics and anaesthetics: patients on M.A.O.I. drugs take a very long time to recover from anaesthetics and analgesics (i.e. pethidine). They should always carry a card (now supplied by the manufacturers) stating that they are on such and such a drug (plus dosage). Local dental anaesthesia can also cause problems because of the norepinephrine used in some preparations.

Jaundice was said to have occurred commonly with iproniazid (1 in 250 patients treated). The number of cases reported for phenelzine in relation to the very large number of cases treated over the past 10 years does not seem to be significant.

Indications. Phenelzine is a useful drug in the treatment of atypical or neurotic depression in younger patients. The dosage is 15 mg 2 to 4 times per day. The patients must be warned about dietary restrictions, local and general anaesthesia. They must also be given and carry with them a card naming the drug, dosage and by whom prescribed (so that Casualty Departments can make contact with the appropriate physician).

Side Effects. Many patients complain of feeling tired and sleepy during the first few days, but this tends to wear off. Many patients get an increase in appetite and sometimes put on a lot of weight i.e. a stone and a half. This is not very common. We have seen on two occasions patients apparently precipitated into a hypomanic swing following treatment with phenelzine (in these cases there must be conjecture regarding an underlying manic-depressive predisposition, and in retrospect the exhibition of the drug in such cases was perhaps an error).

THE MANAGEMENT OF SCHIZOPHRENIA

Whereas the treatment of the acute episode of schizophrenia by means of chlorpromazine or thioridazine with or without the adjunctive use of E.C.T. presents no special problem, the area of further treatment and after-care does raise problems which are only partially answered at the present time. Once the acute symptoms are brought under control the problems that arise are *rehabilitation*, i.e., return to previous job or re-training for a new job, *living group*, should the patient return to his family, live in digs or in a hostel, how long to continue with *medication*, is specific *group* or *individual psychotherapy* indicated, even if it is available?

Our experience in Edinburgh is that we have been discharging schizophrenic patients after such a short stay that the re-admission rate had begun to rise (56 per cent in 1966 of all admissions were re-admissions). We think now that many young schizophrenics require 6 to 18 months in hospital. The functions of the Occupational Therapy Department are of extreme importance in helping schizophrenics to regain confidence and concentration so that they can get back to work. After assessment the programme involves the process of remotivation, experience in a hospital Industrial Therapy Unit followed by a retraining programme at the Industrial Rehabilitation Unit, placement in a sheltered workshop or return to competitive employment. The question of which living group is best for the patient has received varying emphasis in different research projects (i.e. Brown *et al.*, 1958; Brown *et al.*, 1962). Our practice is to do as much work as possible with the families of schizophrenics, often in the form of marital therapy with the parents when the patient is admitted from the nuclear family. We do try to be flexible in our goals (see Goldberg, 1966): often the families need help in their own right and often the best outcome is when the patient is discharged to digs but visits the family regularly. Sometimes working with the family allows them to adopt a different, more tolerant standpoint; sometimes too they will accept the patient back if he can work regularly and contribute to the family income. The object really is to have a range of possible outcomes—living in hospital but working in the town, living at home and attending hospital as a day patient, living in a hospital hostel and working at a competitive job, etc. The appropriate realistic goal should be chosen for each patient individually.

The problem of how long to continue medication is still a matter for discussion. When the patient is on oral medication the issue is often decided by the patient (i.e. when he stops taking his pills), when fluphenazine decanoate is used, then the decision rests more firmly with the psychiatrist. Our view is that an unequivocal schizophrenic illness justifies medication and follow-up for a minimum of three years; for some patients, attendance at an ex-patients' club may then suffice. The important thing is that if the patient fails to attend, the matter is not allowed to drift but a home visit made by the P.S.W. or Community Nurse.

Psychotherapy does, we think, help many schizophrenic patients, either on an individual basis or in small groups. The problem that we face is the rapid alternation of medical staff due to the rotations involved in the training programme. Therapy with a schizophrenic requires a commitment of at least two years, and for many the length of time required to produce any meaningful improvement would be considerably longer than this. Arieti (1955, 1967) has described in different papers his views on the approach to the psychotherapy of schizophrenia.

DRUG TREATMENT OF PHOBIC ANXIETY

Whereas psychotherapy or behaviour therapy may be the treatment of choice in many cases of phobic anxiety, there are patients for whom drug therapy and supportive interviews provide an effective therapeutic intervention. The drugs to use are phenelzine 15 mg t.d.s. and chlordiazepoxide 10 mg t.d.s. It should be remembered that many subjects have repeated brief episodes (i.e. months rather than years) of phobic anxiety, and symptomatic relief may very well carry them through to their next 'well' period. We attempt to use the interviews to orientate the patients to come to better terms with their own aggressiveness and to organize their lives so that tension does not so readily build up. After 3 to 4 months the drugs can usually be reduced, and at 6 to 9 months converted to maintenance dosage, i.e., phenelzine 15 mg in the morning and chlordiazepoxide 10 mg at night.

Many phobic patients have considerable dependency needs and seem to require intermittent contact over several years, but the long-term outcome in terms of social adjustment is good (Errera and Coleman, 1963).

IATROGENIC CONDITIONS

With all these powerful psychotropic drugs available, each with its own range of side-effects and/or toxic effects, the risks of iatrogenic disease are quite considerable. The gross toxic effects (i.e. jaundice attributable to chlorpromazine) have already been detailed. This section will deal with more subtle syndromes attributable to drugs in current use.

Iatrogenic States Occurring in Elderly Patients

Piperazine side-chain phenothiazines (i.e. trifluoperazine) can cause disabling rigidity and festination in old people. We saw a 67-year-old woman some years ago who had been treated for agitation with trifluoperazine 5 mg t.d.s. and was referred to the clinic because of 'dementia'. She had become a great worry to her daughter because of her behaviour on busy roads: she would start with small quick steps across the road but then stop in the middle with traffic passing on both sides of her. On examination she showed masking, salivation, tremor and rigidity. She got better on withdrawal of the trifluoperazine and the introduction of small doses of amitriptyline. Old patients are very liable to postural hypotension if treated with imipramine or chlorpromazine and many exhibit 'drop attacks', falling to the floor as if pole-axed.

Some patients with Arteriosclerotic Parkinsonism get confused and hallucinated when given full doses of benzhexol or orphenadrine; they present a great problem in management, and the drugs that are best suited to relieving the perceptual disturbance, i.e. phenothiazines, make the Parkinsonism worse. It should also be remembered how sensitive some elderly patients are to digitalis; we have seen three patients over the last few years who were anorexic, apathetic and apparently depressed. Drastic reduction in the dose of digoxin relieved the anorexia and the affective disturbance.

Iatrogenic States Resulting from the Use of Tricyclic Drugs

This was referred to earlier, in the section dealing with tricyclic drugs. In the main there are two hazards: (1) precipitation of a hypomanic episode in a predisposed subject, and (2) the emergence of perceptual disturbance, sometimes developing into structured auditory hallucinations; it seems likely that this only occurs in paranoid-depressive states, or in psychodynamic terms, in patients with well-established projective mechanisms. In a general way it seems that when the clinical picture includes a paranoid and depressive element the combination of a tricyclic drug with chlorpromazine provides a more effective therapy.

Drug Induced States of Depression

This is well recognized in hypertensive patients under treatment with rauwolfia alkaloids but can also occur with methyl-dopa and following the termination of a course of systemic steroids. We have also encountered obese patients who have been ordered a rigorous diet but who have lost little weight until they became depressed and then lost a lot of weight quite quickly. It was noted earlier that depot phenothiazines have been alleged to cause depression and even suicide in schizophrenic subjects; it seems likely that all phenothiazines can cause some depression of mood, and in the follow-up clinic we attempt to relieve this either by reduction of dosage or by the exhibition of small doses of nortriptyline (10 mg t.d.s.).

THE USE OF SEDATIVES AT NIGHT

It is sometimes alleged that both psychiatrists and general practitioners are in grave error because of the large amounts of hypnotics that are prescribed each year. Certainly the risk from barbiturates in terms of self-poisoning is considerable. Cumming estimated that there were probably 3000 cases per year needing admission and 6000 cases per year needing outpatient attention in England and Wales (Cumming, 1961). The risk of addiction to barbiturates, especially the short-acting drugs such as sodium amylobarbitone, is appreciable (Batchelor, 1969), but the problem facing the doctor is that patients with depressive illness and anxiety reactions do have great difficulty in getting a reasonable sleep (allowing that what is reasonable is very subjective). And barbiturates, such as pentobarbitone 200 mg, are very effective hypnotics.

Oswald and his colleagues from the Sleep Laboratory in Edinburgh (Oswald et al., 1963, Oswald and Priest, 1965 and Haider and Oswald, 1971) have demonstrated the disruptive effect of barbiturates (and other hypnotics) on sleep levels and particularly REM sleep (see Chap. XVII, Vol. I). The psychiatrist and the general practitioner are left with two problems: the patient across the desk who clearly is not sleeping and the risks of prescribing hypnotics (suicide, addiction and the disturbance of the physiological basis of normal sleep). In Edinburgh most Consultants have settled on Nitrazepam 5 to 10 mg at night because it is not apparently addictive and because it is ineffective as a mode of suicide. However, we should remember that the paper by Haider and Oswald (1971) reported that nitrazepam showed effects similar to those of sodium amylobarbitone—they delayed and suppressed REM sleep and increased Stage 2 sleep. Some clinicians feel that patients can be 'weaned' from their fear of not sleeping (see Chap. V, Vol. II). This is certainly true, but for many depressives and for some anxiety reactions hypnotics are clinically indicated; in such cases nitrazepam, on present evidence, would seem the safest preparation (Matthew et al., 1969).

REFERENCES

ACKNER, B., HARRIS, A. & OLDHAM, A. J. (1957) Insulin treatment of schizophrenia: a controlled study. Lancet, i, 607.
ARIETI, S. (1955) Interpretation of schizophrenia. New York: Brunner.
ARIETI, S., (1967) New views on the psychodynamics of schizophrenia. American Journal of Psychiatry, 124, 453.

BALINT, M. (1956) *The doctor, his patient and the illness.* New York: International University Press.

BARKER, J. C. & BAKER, A. A. (1959) Death associated with electroplexy. *Journal of Mental Science*, **105,** 339.

BATCHELOR, I. R. C. (1969) *Henderson and Gillespie's Textbook of Psychiatry*, 389–399. London: Oxford University Press.

BLACKWELL, B. (1963) Hypertensive crisis due to mono-amine oxidase inhibitors. *Lancet*, **ii,** 849.

BOARDMAN, R. H., LOMAS, J. & MARKOWE, M. (1956) Insulin and chlorpromazine in schizophrenia: a comparative study in previously untreated cases. *Lancet*, **ii,** 487.

BRADLEY, P. B., WOLSTENCROFT, J. H., HOSLI, L. & AVANZINO, G. L. (1966) Neuronal basis for the central action of chlorpromazine. *Nature, London*, **212,** 1425.

BROWN, G. W., CARSTAIRS, G. M. & TOPPING, G. (1958) Post-hospital adjustment of chronic mental patients. *Lancet*, **ii,** 685.

BROWN, G. W., MONCK, E. M., CARSTAIRS, G. M. & WING, J. K. (1962) Influence of family life on the course of schizophrenic illness. *British Journal of Preventive and Social Medicine*, **16,** 55.

CERLETTI, U. & BINI, L. (1938) L'Elettroshock. *Archivio di psicologia, neurologia e psichiatria*, **19,** 266.

COHEN, I. M. & ARCHER, J. D. (1955). Liver function and hepatic complications in patients receiving chlorpromazine. *Journal of the American Medical Association*, **159,** 99.

CUMMING, G. (1961) *The Medical Management of Acute Poisoning.* London: Cassell.

DE ALARCON, R. & CARNEY, W. P. (1969). Depressive changes after fluphenazine treatment. *British Medical Journal*, **ii,** 564.

ERRERA, P. & COLEMAN, J. V. (1963) A long-term follow-up study of neurotic patients in a psychiatric clinic. *Journal of Nervous and Mental Disorders*, **136.** March.

FORREST, A. D., AFFLECK, J. W., GIBB, I. A. McL. & PRIEST, R. G. (1964) Comparative trial of Nortriptyline and Amitriptyline. *Scottish Medical Journal*, **9,** 341.

FORREST, A. D., FRASER, R. H. & PRIEST, R. G. (1965) Environmental factors in depressive illness. *British Journal of Psychiatry*, **III,** 243.

FORREST, A. D. (1969) Depressive changes after Fluphenazine treatment. *British Medical Journal*, **ii,** 169.

FORREST, A. D. & MAULE, M. M. (1972) Controlled trial of oxypertine in patients with anxiety. *Postgraduate Medical Journal*, Suppl. 4, **48,** 30–32.

FREEMAN, W. & WATTS, J. W. (1941) The frontal lobes and consciousness of the self. *Psychosomatic Medicine*, **3,** 111.

GOLDBERG, E. M. (1966) The family environment of schizophrenic patients. In *New Aspects of the Mental Health Services.* Edited by H. L. Freeman and W. A. J. Ferndale. Oxford: Pergamon Press.

GRAHAM, G. S. (1957) Chlorpromazine jaundice in a general hospital. *British Medical Journal*, **2,** 1080.

GREINER, A. C. & BERRY, K. (1964) Skin pigmentation and corneal and lense opacities with prolonged chloropromazine therapy. *Canadian Medical Association Journal*, **90,** 663–665.

HAIDER, I. & OSWALD, I. (1971) Effects of Amylobarbitone and Nitrazepam on the Electrodermogram and other features of sleep. *British Journal of Psychiatry*, **118,** 519–522.

HANKOFF, L. D., ENGELHARDT, D. M., FREEDMAN, N., MANN, D. & MARGOLIS, R. (1960) Denial of illness in schizophrenic out-patients: effects of psychopharmacological treatment. *A.M.A. Archives of General Psychiatry*, **3,** 657.

HAWKINGS, J. R. & TIBBETS, R. W. (1956a) Carbon dioxide inhalation therapy in neurosis: a controlled clinical trial. *Journal of Mental Science*, **102,** 52.

HAWKINGS, J. R. & TIBBETS, R. W. (1956b) Intravenous acetylcholine therapy in neurosis: a controlled clinical trial. *Journal of Mental Science*, **102,** 43.

HUNTER, R., EARL, C. J. & THORNICROFT, S. (1964) An apparently irreversible syndrome of abnormal movements following phenothiazine medication. *Proceedings of the Royal Society of Medicine*, **57,** 758.

KILOH, L. G., BALL, J. R. B. & GARSIDE, R. F. (1962) Prognostic factors in treatment of depressive states with Imipramine. *British Medical Journal*, **1,** 1225.

MACLAY, W. (1953) Deaths due to treatment. *Proceedings of the Royal Society of Medicine*, **46,** 13.

MATHEW, H., PROUDFOOT, A. T., AITKEN, R. C. B., RAEBURN, J. A. & WRIGHT, N. (1969) Nitrazepam—a safe hypnotic. *British Medical Journal*, **3,** 23–25.

McKISSOCK, W. (1943) The technique of prefrontal leucotomy. *Journal of Mental Science*, **89,** 194.

MEDICAL RESEARCH COUNCIL (1965) Clinical trial of the treatment of depressive illness: report to the Medical Research Council by its Clinical Psychiatry Committee. *British Medical Journal*, **i,** 881.

MEDUNA, L. J. (1950) *Carbon dioxide therapy*. Springfield, Illinois: Thomas.

MONIZ, A. C. DE A. F. EGAS (1936) *Tentatives operatoires dans le traitement de certaines psychoses*. Paris: Masson.

OSWALD, I., BERGER, R. J., JARAMILLO, R. A., KEDDIE, K. M. G., OTTEY, P. C. & PLUNKETT, G. A. (1963) Melancholia and barbiturates: a controlled E.E.G. body and eye movement study of sleep. *British Journal of Psychiatry*, **109,** 66–78.

OSWALD, I. & PRIEST, R. G. (1965) Five weeks to escape the sleeping pill habit. *British Medical Journal*, **ii,** 1093–1099.

PARTRIDGE, M. (1950) *Prefrontal leucotomy: a survey of 300 cases personally followed over one and a half to three years*. Oxford: Blackwell.

PIPPARD, J. (1955) Second leucotomies. *Journal of Mental Science*, **101,** 788.

POST, F., REES, W. L. & SCHURR, P. H. (1968) An evaluation of bimedial leucotomy. *British Journal of Psychiatry*, **114,** 1223.

RAYMOND, M. J., LUCAS, C. J., BEESLEY, M. L., O'CONNELL, B. A. & ROBERTS, J. A. F. (1957) A trial of five tranquillizing drugs in psychoneurosis. *British Medical Journal*, **2,** 63–67.

RENTON, C. A., AFFLECK, J. W., CARSTAIRS, G. M. & FORREST, A. D. (1963) A follow-up of schizophrenic patients in Edinburgh. *Acta psychiatrica scandinavica*, **39,** 548.

RICHARDSON, H. L., GRAUPNER, K. I. & RICHARDSON, M. E. (1966) Intramyocardial lesions in patients dying suddenly and unexpectedly. *Journal of the American Medical Association*, **195,** 254–260.

RYCROFT, C. (1966) *Psychoanalysis Observed*. Edited by C. Rycroft. London: Constable.

SARGANT, W. & DALLY, P. (1962) Treatment of anxiety states by antidepressant drugs. *British Medical Journal*, **i,** 6.

SARGANT, W. & SLATER, E. (1954) *An introduction to physical methods of treatment in Psychiatry*. Edinburgh: Livingstone.

SCHURR, P. H. (1969) Leucotomy. *British Journal of Hospital Medicine*, p. 1712. October.

SCOVILLE, W. B. (1949) Selective critical undercutting as a means of modifying and studying frontal lobe function in man: preliminary report on 43 operative cases. *Journal of Neurosurgery*, **6,** 65.

SIM, M. (1969) *Guide to psychiatry*. Edinburgh: Livingstone.

SZASZ, T. S. (1961) *Pain and pleasure: a study of bodily feelings*. London: Tavistock.

Chapter XVI

HOSPITAL ADMINISTRATION AND TREATMENT

J. W. Affleck

THE ADMINISTRATIVE PROCESS

INTRODUCTION

In psychiatry with its tradition of medical administration and its intimate association with all studies of human relationships, administration and clinical practice are more closely associated than in other branches of medicine. Patient management and treatment is often determined by administrative attitudes which determine the pattern of the service. Although, within hospitals, responsibilities in clinical matters will continue to fall to the psychiatrist, multidisciplinary practice should be accompanied by opportunity for all professionals to make a contribution to the management process by the creation at *district* level of a professional workers standing committee from which advice can be obtained on current needs and potential changes.

ADMINISTRATIVE THEORY

Adopting the approach of a systems theory of management, Miller and Rice (1967) discuss enterprises or institutions as systems of activities comprising various task systems and projects. A system differs from an aggregate of activities by being regulated and controlled to ensure the accomplishment of the process and to avoid interference. Each task system consists of systems of activities plus the human and physical resources required. The delineation and control of the boundary of any system is a most important managerial function. Different managing systems are required when an enterprise is complicated by having many tasks or projects. These will include the management of the total system, the management of each discrete operation and the management of those which service the others. Boundaries are essential and unless they are clearly drawn, different people will locate them to suit their own objectives. When they are clear, communication is made easier. Difficulties arise when people defend obsolescent task systems or boundaries which are more appropriate to a previous task system. Changes in organization are required when task objectives alter, legal changes occur or when there is an alteration in the strategies through which the task relates to others. In hurried administration the full extent of the changes needed is often overlooked. The involvement of a group in two activity systems may demand that the members may have to relate to one another in different ways thus complicating their relationships. Whatever the outcome of a project the relationships of the members are likely to change in some subtle ways which will affect their future in the team or in other project teams.

A hospital is an enterprise with a multi-task system, forming and disbanding project teams very frequently. In hospital it is possible to conceive every patient as requiring a project team for his treatment and teams must also always be available for the unpredictable. The differences from a factory are many. It is difficult to measure hospital work or forecast priorities, routinize tasks or, sometimes, to plan a day's work. The number of skilled and specialist professionals is high relative to the total staff. Reviewing hospital administration with special reference to psychiatry (Hunter, 1967) favours the concept of the arena (Strauss *et al.*, 1964) in which interlocking professional groups arrive at a negotiated order. He suggests that such patterns of administration with nondirective attitudes and techniques and involvement of the 'consumer' can be used as models to counteract the prevailing dehumanizing tendencies of modern industrialism and bureaucracy.

ADMINISTRATIVE PRINCIPLES

Administration is the process of management. The manager coordinates and integrates the work of others. Organization involves allocating activities to roles and roles to individuals or groups. It must include definition of responsibilities and the extent to which specialization is needed. The need for continuity must be considered as well as the balance of power which must be maintained between sections of the structure and the interlocking roles of individuals.

Systematic studies of management recognize several techniques viz: planning, organization, co-ordinating, motivating and controlling. Authority, leadership, decision-making and communication are in the background of all these processes. Discipline and public relations have also to be considered. The administrative structure of an organization should be systematically studied by considering these processes within it. Decisions in administration relate to (a) definition of objectives and policy; (b) the assessment of human and material resources available and their deployment, and (c) the application of the policy decisions to practice. As in the Salmon plan for nursing, such functions are related to top, middle and frontline management respectively.

Deployment of manpower involves coordination with other disciplines. When working with a doctor, the nurse is seconded to work under his expertise or sapiential authority which directs rather than commands. The nurse remains within the structural authority of the nursing hierarchy. The doctor in a ward review of patients is 'controlling by coordinating' the activities of those involved in patient treatment for which he is responsible. Control or coordination of activities implies the need for feedback and feedforward of information—concepts from cybernetics, a term derived from the Greek 'kybernetes' (a steersman). In highly specialized fields responsibility becomes narrowed. Legal responsibility for the activities of others cannot be accepted unless ultimate control is awarded.

It has been widely recognized that spans of responsibility have natural limits. Drucker (1955, 1971) distinguishes between the span of control and the span of managerial responsibility. Control means supervision in which the subordinates are told what to do and steps are taken to see that it is done. Though every situation must be judged separately, efforts to maintain such control usually restrict the controller to six, or at most, eight subordinates. Drucker's definition of the span of managerial responsibility is 'to assist, teach and help subordinates to reach the objectives of their own jobs'. The extent of such activities is less limited, but variable. Managers supervising teams and subteams extend the range of their activities.

The solutions available for management problems will be in terms of human resources, or changes in buildings or equipment, or finance. It is essential that the manager can take an overall view so that all the possible ways of solving the problems can be considered, and it is obviously useful if those who are going to be responsible for enterprises have had the opportunity to see the problems solved elsewhere in various ways.

Communication and Forms of Management

Looking at administration as a communication problem Stanton and Schwartz (1954) point out that whereas treatment institutions have formal aims, the actual results can be materially different from the objectives as a result of the informal and unstructured contacts between inmates and staff. To ensure that the behaviour of staff in their informal contacts is consistent with the formal aims is often difficult. Attempts to combat this may involve increasing supervisory staff and inservice training or, by bureaucratic solutions, making the formal system all pervading, extending the scope of formal control by complete rationalization of the structure of the organization (Robertson, 1969). This results in 'line' or vertical systems of management. Hierarchies or oligarchies usually have bureaucratic rules in which operatives lose sight of the objectives by having to conform to regulations which give rigidity or lead to personal interpretations and disputes. The longer the lines of communication the more likely the morale will drop and policies will be forgotten.

The alternative approach is the establishment of horizontal rather than vertical contacts associated with an extension of the process of decision-making. Whether in 'an arena' or by other group method of getting information to and from the front line and involving those working in it, the horizontal pattern is necessary when the objectives of a complex project must be constantly maintained or where subobjectives may be subject to change. This situation obviously holds in hospitals where large numbers of staff with various professional skills cannot be expected to take unexplained orders. Fortunately consultative forms of management usually result in more realistic decisions as well as reducing status tensions. A consensus of views is sought as a basis for action. This must involve a relatively slow process when a large number of people are involved. Many decisions have to be held up until the general principles are recognized and issues based on personal feelings have been explored and resolved. Once decisions on a principle are accepted the executive function can be carried out by a small team or committee. Three or four people are more effective than larger numbers for this purpose, though individual members of the executive will have subordinate managers. Such teams must have strict terms of reference.

Leadership, Influence and Morale

Zaleznik (1967) reminds us that influence, authority and leadership must be related. Authority is composed of a mixture of status, expertize and shared expectation. In the administrative area, where a leader is not able to influence the distribution of resources this is eventually recognized by the group. Many doctors find themselves in this uncomfortable position in health services and this is a source of the conflict over the extent of medical representation on governing bodies.

Managers can be observed, like Presidents or Prime Ministers, to redistribute power to suit their objectives. Departments are dissolved and tactically reformed, not because of a change of task demanded from an outside source, but to achieve a new balance which matches the leader's personality. Aggressive leadership creates antagonism and becomes separated from the organization while warm-hearted leadership is frequently ambiguous and results in rivalrous sub-groups. Permissive leadership may fail similarly by loss of structure and the development of cliques. To maintain stability and progress there must be an executive group in which the members complement each other in emotional attitude and activity. Failing leadership is reflected by lack of decision, excuses for non-attendance when decisions are to be made, excessive idealism and excessive concern for the effect of change on individuals, demands for over-democratization, changes towards legalistic or bureaucratic systems or more readily recognized clinical pathology.

Comparing successful and low morale hospitals, Jackson (1968) points out that the extent to which members of an organization can be motivated or committed to its objectives depends largely on having a high consensus of opinion in support of the executive, coupled with arrangements which allow individuals to express their energies with satisfaction. With a flow of such goodwill, effectiveness will depend on resources, sometimes on a fortunate opportunity and on a few wise decisions. Without a satisfactory overall consensus of feeling that decisions are being made appropriately i.e. that the right amount of influence on decision-making is allocated to the appropriate persons, an organization with an energetic staff will generate conflicts. Conflicts, of course, can prove to be constructive if their solution involves reappraisals and improved procedures. Built-in evaluative procedures are valuable for maintaining interest and stimulating self-criticism in sub-groups as well as in policy-making. Good administrations and organizations can fail if they are starved of resources though it has been suggested that true enterprise is the capacity to do more with less. The greatest lack in the resources of psychiatry is manpower.

ADMINISTRATIVE PRACTICE

Hospital Roles—Governors and Executives

The Group Hospital Management Committee governing hospitals may have a sub-committee for each hospital or alternatively a sub-committee covering functions—finance, works and buildings, staffing etc. The Farquharson-Lang Committee (1966) studied hospital management in detail and recommended reducing to a minimum the number of committees responsible for the supervision of medical and allied services and patient care.

The Governors have to decide whether to supervise their professional administrators minutely or allow them to act on their own initiative. If administration has followed the accepted principles and leads to good staff morale, the governing body can homologate the executive's decisions. It has been suggested that in the hospital service this should be the accepted role of the Management Committee. Their activities should be to review, and where appropriate, to concur and to approve on behalf of the public and the Minister (Lovelick, 1970). Many committee members would accept this, knowing that they have not, as part-time voluntary workers, the time to follow the business in great detail. The King Edward Hospital Fund advisers (1967) proposed the creation of professional hospital 'general managers' acting through directors covering finance, nursing and medical services. On the other hand the examination of the Oxford Teaching Hospital Group (non-psychiatric) by the firm of McKinsey, Management Consultants, (Sleight *et al.*, 1970) recommended a scheme whereby a joint executive committee composed of members of the governing body, a few elected members of the consultant medical staff, the Group Secretary and the Chief Nursing Officer is interposed between the Board of Governors and the executive staff. It is assumed that this body would have access to all the views current in the hospital and its control of financial allocations would ensure that policies were maintained.

Where good quality administrators or clinicians are very scarce or the hospital is very small, the Governors may have to place all the executive responsibility on one man. This may lead to the hierarchical structure in which the medical superintendent is responsible for eveything. The Bradbeer Committee (1954) surveying the National Health Service recommended that doctors and nurses, elected or appointed, should if possible agree on the advice to be given by the professional administrators to the Governors and meet together as executives. In this structure (the second tripartite system) the doctor or nurse cannot give orders about buildings, finance or catering and the administrator is restricted to matters which do not affect the patient's clinical treatment directly.

The medical profession has frequently been among those wishing to have highly skilled and mature colleagues in senior nursing and administrative posts and steps have been taken to achieve this. On the assumption that large and worthwhile units of responsibility would attract the right people into the professions and that salaries would be commensurate with responsibilities, a reorganization of Hospital Management Committee areas has taken place. This results in the formation of groups of hospitals in which 2000 to 4000 beds are administered together, providing the apex of a career structure in administration for lay and nursing administrators. Regional or Area Boards work offers further career opportunities. It is of interest that in more idealistic days, 1000 beds was regarded as the largest number which should be allocated to one Hospital Management Committee and where mental hospitals were larger than this, it was thought regrettable on administrative as well as clinical grounds. However, the size of administrative units in industry has grown and hospitals are sometimes regarded as in some ways analogous, in this context.

The formation of large groups of scattered hospital units produces new problems of obtaining medical advice for the Governors when each senior clinician has full clinical responsibility. The lay and nursing administrators are centrally placed and permanently in post and have the advantages of ready access to new information from central bodies. The Brotherston Report (Scotland) (1967) and the 'Cogwheel' Report (1969) propose a divisional system for the organization of medical work in hospitals. Various medical and surgical teams are designated and united within functional divisions. Divisional Committees are formed for joint decision-making or the provision of advice to the Governors. This advice can be agreed and conveyed through a chairman's committee of the whole division—an operation which could be rather remote from the floor. While psychiatrists in a general hospital may be part of a medical division, the larger mental hospital can form a separate division. Alternatively, divisions may span hospitals or cover a mental health service.

The position of the Physician Superintendent has to be reviewed in this setting. As he does not 'superintend' in the former sense he may be replaced by or hold also the office of divisional chairman or secretary or function in a way analogous to the permanent medical administrators in Scottish general hospitals. He, or his successor, must attend tripartite meetings and have special co-ordinating responsibilities for staff matters in medical and para-medical departments, be concerned with operational research and take special interest in extra-mural relationships. A sub-committee of the Scottish Division of the Royal College of Psychiatrists recommended that he should be responsible for ensuring that matters affecting administration and policy formation are discussed at the Divisional Meeting. In Scotland he would also take action on recommendations and instruction from central bodies including the Mental Welfare Commission. This implies a continuing interest in medico-legal affairs. The psychiatric hospital should certainly be sub-divided and its day to day administration decentralized into autonomous clinical teams. A central point for the collection, collation and appropriate distribution of information of a type which requires psychiatric specialist handling is essential however, and this obviously requires the availability of a Consultant with interest in administrative patterns. A psychiatric 'presence' must be available when administrative matters of psychiatric importance are decided. It is important that this Consultant's term of office should be long enough to allow worthwhile relationships to develop with members of all the professional services with whom he will make contact.

The report to the Minister of Health of the Committee on Senior Nurse Staffing Structure (1966, the Salmon Report) incorporated or adapted much of the current thought on management which is used in industrial undertakings. It emphasized in-service training by the provision of administrative courses for each grade of nursing staff in order to prepare the individual for promotion to, or to stand in for, the next higher rank. The nursing profession in Great Britain in future will have, therefore, a built-in administrative experience and outlook and will no doubt use the jargon. The model is an hierarchical one and not very flexible. It is important that medical staff understand the concepts, definitions and arrangements involved and which have been accepted as policy. The new organization provides a group of nurse administrators who will accept responsibilities directly rather than be represented by the doctor as has often been the case previously. Some basic aspects of this administrative scheme are shown on Table 1.

TABLE 16.1

'Salmon' Nursing Administration

Grade		Responsibilities	In-Service Training
Student Nurse			Preparation for first-line management
Staff Nurse	(5)		do
Charge Nurse	(6)	Controls a Ward or 'section', e.g. Outpatient Department	Preparation for Middle management
Nursing Officer	(7)	Controls or coordinates 3 to 6 sections which constitute a 'Unit'	Preparation for Top management (University or Special Certificate Courses)
Senior Nursing Officer	(8)	Controls or coordinates 3 to 6 Units which constitute an 'Area'	do
Principal Nursing Officer	(9)	Controls or coordinates 3 to 6 Areas which constitute a 'Division'	
Chief Nursing Officer	(10)	Controls or coordinates Nursing and Teaching Divisions	

CLINICAL ADMINISTRATION

THE SETTING

Hospital treatment of psychiatric illness is provided in psychiatric hospitals, in psychiatric units in general hospitals or in day hospitals.

The psychiatric service has several functions in the community. It provides diagnosis, treatment and rehabilitation, it offers asylum for some severely inadequate people and it provides care for long-term and certain types of geriatric patient. Departments devoted to the special treatment of neurosis and personality disorders, alcoholism, adolescent disorders, sociopathy, sexual disorders and to rehabilitation in schizophrenia might now also be listed. Each of these areas has its own special problems and treatment methods though certain physical facilities and some treatment techniques may be shared if required, e.g. the outpatient department, electroplexy, behaviour therapy etc. Classification and sub-division of accommodation for patients of different behaviour patterns is humane even although patients tolerate sociopathic or disturbed behaviour in others and get well in spite of it— and although disturbing behaviour can be used constructively in therapeutic communities.

Architectural Problems

Whereas a new building can be a status symbol for both patients and staff, a relic of the custodial era can be demoralizing. The special technical needs which can be provided by architectural means have been described by Baker *et al.* (1959). The general objectives are the provision of areas in which attractive furnishings, light and decor reduce anxiety, where some regression can be allowed, followed by gradual integration with the community and where privacy can be provided without isolation. Facilities for progressive steps from intensive care to semi-observation thence to non-observed rooms, must be available though not necessarily for all patients. Obvious restrictions for specific reasons are preferable to the challenge of hidden or complex obstacles. Groups must not be so large that patients feel 'lost' or are lost to staff. One suggestion of an ideal ward or section is for 32 patients sub-divided into groups of 8 (W.H.O. Report, 1953). The single room is a valuable asset for both acute and convalescent patients and it should constitute about 20 to 30 per cent of the accommodation. The remainder of the sleeping space can suitably be arranged in rooms or bays of four cubicalized bed areas. Apart from accommodation set aside for the physically sick, the atmosphere in the rooms should be essentially domestic with decor, furnishings and equipment akin to student hostel standards. Day space should be restricted to 12 to 16 people in each room. It should be sub-divided to provide control over noise. Facilities for personal laundry and a simple kitchen should be available. Catering services should include choice of food on the menu. Shops, a café and public telephones are essential. Therapeutic communities will require an area large enough for 'town' meetings.

In geriatric wards the supervision of the confused demands observation which must take priority over privacy to a large extent. Whenever possible the elderly person should be looked after continuously in the one area and provided with facilities for some of the familiar objects and photographs which maintain his identity. Mobility is important, so handrails and walking aids must be supplied liberally and chiropody provided. Toilets should be liberally provided within 40 feet of any sitting or bed space. Doors and corridors should be adequately labelled and signposted. Sitting space should be managed within view of any movement and activity available. Occupational therapy techniques involving 'aids to daily living' can be closely associated with those of physiotherapy for improvement in walking etc. A domestic flatlet in which the nearly recovered patient can be tested in independence should be available.

Many hospitals in Western Europe were built in the latter part of the ninteenth century, designed for the era of custodial care and lacking the interview and conference rooms which must now be provided. Modernization otherwise usually consists of lowering the ceiling and providing new floor-coverings and lighting (as well as heating), sub-dividing the sleeping space with built in furniture and the sitting space with decorative room dividers.

THE SEARCH FOR THERAPEUTIC MANAGEMENT METHODS

The dispersal of the custodial atmosphere and attitudes and its replacement by critical consideration of the effect on the patient of the human as well as the material environment is the major change and advance since the advent of the phenothiazine drugs in 1954. Both therapeutic communities and open doors were demonstrated over the previous decade. However, the reduction of florid psychotic symptoms and behavioural disturbance which followed the introduction of these drugs and the anti-depressants has allowed experimentation in social therapies—rehabilitation regimes, therapeutic communities and token economies. As the changes are effected at the level of ward admini-stration it is not surprising that great variation in the degree of change can be observed between hospitals and between teams. The concept of the 'therapeutic community' is a central one, but is interpreted in various ways.

Such activities usually invoke the creation of a multi-disciplinary staff team in which the nurse as well as the doctor, social worker and occu-pational therapist, plays a therapeutic role. The extent to which the therapeutic community methods can be effective will depend on leader-ship and technique and its appropriateness for the group of patients. The social approach involves an increase in communication and shared information among the staff and between staff and patients. An element of hierarchical structure remains in the recognition of overall medical responsibility for certain decisions but leadership must be sapiential rather than directive. It is the variations in the attitudes of leaders which determine the style of the various teams.

Removal of the traditional patterns must be replaced by an equally effective administration. The needs of the ward organization is basic in administration. The feed-back from the wards sets up a demand for changes in administrative attitude throughout the hospital—general or mental. The pressure is toward liberalization of rules and removal of any administrative practices which are maintained without due consideration of their clinical effects. This applies to medical and nursing administration in the first instance, but inevitably extends into the non-medical division. A committee structure which reflects the interests concerned must be evolved to plan alterations in existing procedures and to monitor events and proposals.

The Sociological Approach

An expert committee of W.H.O. (1953) reviewing the Community Mental Hospital among other mental health services, described the most important single factor in the efficiency of hospital treatment as its 'atmosphere'. This was traced to the relationships within the hospital which maintained the patient's individuality and assumed patients to be trustworthy and capable of a considerable amount of responsibility unless there was reason to think otherwise. The report emphasized the concept of the therapeutic community with reference to the total or large hospital organization. Martin (1955) described the process of institutionalization which results when patients in almost all diagnostic categories have their dependency increased by the attitudes in medical and nursing staff or where apathy is fostered by repression or lack of staff interest. Barton (1959) identified the factors leading to the syndrome and described a programme for its correction. This involved a friendly, permissive and homely ward atmosphere with increasing prospects of work, accommodation and friends in the outside world. A daily sequence of useful occupations, recreations and social events was described. Such concepts did much to stimulate the extension of industrial therapy and other rehabilitative measures.

The social structure of mental hospitals was investigated by psychiatrists and sociologists in the United States. Belknap (1956) studying the rigid hierarchical and bureaucratic organisation of the State Hospital in the U.S.A. pointed out that the member of staff who influenced the patient most was the nurse's aide who undertook his personal care and, to a very great extent, determined the treatment authorized by the insufficient medical and nursing staffs. Goffman (1961) described mental hospitals, prisons, monasteries and army camps as 'total institutions' with similar practices, illustrating procedures at admission and subsequently which, intentionally or inadvertently, demoralize and depersonalize the incomers. The procedures emphasize the boundaries between staff and patient roles which distort communications and restrict or prevent the continuity of family or domestic relationships. Stanton and Schwartz (1954) acting as participant observers in the Chestnut Lodge Hospital made a systematic analysis of the institution with regard to its purposes, the requirements for fulfilment of its purposes and the requirements of the people in it.

This study drew special attention to the needs and reactions of the staff, as part of a total organization, and their effects on patient management, treatment and behaviour. Caudill (1958) acting for part of the time as a concealed participant observer when admitted as a 'patient', described the hospital as a small society from the anthropological point of view. He noted the pressures on new patients to play the role of patient in accordance with the mores of the enclosed community. Another psychiatrist/sociologist team, John and Elaine Cumming (1962), regarding the environment as a therapeutic weapon, reviewed progress in the theory and practice of milieu therapy and described its application for 'ego restitution' in the psychotic.

The Community as a Therapist

Commencing with the hypothesis that much mental illness stemmed from problems of self-estimate of status, Harry Stack Sullivan (1931 and 1953) developed the theme that psychiatric conditions are essentially problems of interpersonal relationships. Extension of this concept and clinical experiments with groups, were reported in the Northfield Military Hospital by Bion and Rickman (1943) and by Foulkes (1948). Contemporarily, Maxwell Jones's programmes for army 'effort syndrome' patients and for the rehabilitation of ex-prisoners of war had been established, in which the group concepts included the total (small) institution (Jones, 1952). The term 'therapeutic community' was first used by Main (1946) to describe a situation in which individual treatment is replaced by the search for interpersonal barriers to participation in community life. The staff, who also admit that they 'live and learn', have the responsibility for guidance and leadership. Patient participation is ensured by passing as much responsibility as reasonable to patient groups and committees. By exposing themselves psychologically to the patients, staff join in the formation of a 'community'.

Clark (1964) has defined the doctor's role in the therapeutic community as applied to the larger hospitals as 'administrative therapy'. He organizes his ward around the community meetings, small group meetings and frequent staff discussions encouraging the expression and interpretation of dependency, fears, relationships, problems etc., by the patients, and of the overt recognition of disagreements, rigid attitudes etc., among the staff. The doctor leading such a community must, if necessary, entice the involvement of patients and all the staff members—including the junior ones when they have observations to contribute. The non-professional (domestic and catering etc.,) members of the hospital staff may be introduced. Units also welcome vists of members of the non-medical administrative staff who gain insight into the significance of the changes implied by various requests, so easily lost in financial discussions at management level. Martin (1962) described the social changes in a large mental hospital which followed the intro-duction of several ward communities. Wilmer (1958) described the establishment of community therapy in a naval observation ward and Walton (1961) for selected alcoholics. Hooper (1962) Clark *et al.* (1962) and Clark and Myers (1970) detail the changes when these methods are applied in convalescent and disturbed wards.

Ward Patterns

It is obviously possible for a ward to be organized with a therapeutic atmosphere without the operation of the intensive closed therapeutic community techniques which exclude individual therapy. Some patients require or will only allow treatment on the medical model. The involve-ment of all professional staff available in assessment, treatment, and rehabilitation planning is essential. Dealing with patients as adults demands that they share in deciding what should be done though the term 'patient government' is misleading.

The meetings which include the patients are described by Martin (1965) as having as their main purpose the demonstration of the patients' basic right to free communication with the staff who look after them, whether or not they can use the opportunity in a constructive way. The staff have the advantage of observing the patients in a dif-ferent setting. Both staff and patients become trained to keep the psycho-social dimension under constant review. Maxwell Jones (1965) em-phasizes the importance of this training discipline applicable to both staff and patients and contrasts it with the situation in which the psychi-atrist makes God-like statements on individuals or ward situations without exposure to the realities of the ward.

Daily meetings on wards with small turnover of patients and with reasonably consistent attendance of the same staff can utilize the in-group qualities required for 're-education' in personal relationships (Lewin, 1948). Less frequent meetings and those at which nursing personnel vary daily, can still use the experiences of daily living in the ward as material for the discussion of social behaviour. The environ-mental artificiality of one-sex communities will become apparent and will stimulate the desire to pair men's and women's wards and create common dining and sitting rooms. As frequency decreases the meetings will acquire specific business types of function. With regressed patients and those with organic conditions objectives must be modified and staff participation increased to encourage resocialization or maintain it.

The overall administrative objective is to allow individual teams to assess their needs and obtain them without detriment to the budg-etary or territorial rights of others. The form of the administrative pattern in the individual ward will be the resultant of historical, demographic, cultural, technical and particularly, personal factors.

ADMISSION PROCEDURE

Special attention should be paid to the first impressions of the patient on arrival in hospital. The reception desk should be modern and possibly hotel-like. The newly admitted patient requires considerable attention from the nurse in his orientation and introduction. Some units arrange for other patients to act as guides or friends in this situation, but for the more severely sick patient, this is a professional task. A pamphlet giving an outline of the ward facilities, staffing arrangements, procedures and roles should be provided. An early medical contact is reassuring and especially important when the patient is not known to the staff. The findings regarding physical state and anticipated behaviour patterns must be transmitted to the nurse in charge.

THE COMPULSORY PATIENT

Less than ten per cent of all patients entering inpatient departments of psychiatric hospitals in Great Britain require formal legal compulsion—usually in the course of an emergency or by Court proceedings. (The medico-legal aspects of this topic are discussed in Chapter XX, Vol II). The clinical care of the compulsory patient is made much easier if the arrangements for admission are made after the patient has been examined by a representative of the team who will look after him or at least after discussion with the receiving staff. This avoids disagreement on the question of justification of compulsoriness and the ill-effects of confusion of medical opinions. Adequate explanation of the legal situation must be available to the patient and this is ensured at certain points in time by the issue of leaflets indicating his status and rights. These should be supplemented with information from the 'responsible medical officer' or his assistant in a more personal way. Patients frequently bring up the question of their detention at ward meetings and may be helped by group opinions on the reasons for it. If compulsory admissions are reduced to a minimum the need to have a locked ward in which recent admissions are accommodated can also be reduced to an occasionally locked door, operated largely by the staff in immediate charge and with the cooperation of the patients who are inconvenienced.

THE LONG-TERM PATIENT

In large or small Units the diagnosis of a chronic condition is usually accompanied by the prescription of a maintenance treatment and, in the absence of behaviour problems, the likelihood of reduction of staff attention. The patient should continue in the various important procedures planned to prevent institutionalization. These rehabilitative and supportive activities can be enhanced by adequate sub-classification of patients and planning for small groups and individuals. Regular medical reviews are part of British mental hospital tradition though this tends to be restricted and routine and it is easy for patients to be 'lost' to medical staff. Details of the management of the long-term patient are discussed in Chapter XVII, Vol. II.

The long-term or chronic section of the hospital should be given the status of a special unit—separated from the geriatric section—and managed as a syndicate involving all staff dealing with such problems. This should allow the nurse to have a vision beyond the ward and provide the opportunity to amalgamate extra-mural activities into the concept of the Unit. The long-term unit should have its own waiting list rather than be subjected to hurried and haphazard transfers and nursing staff should be involved in pre-transfer planning. In such a setting work with families and community nursing activities is extended, and operational research encouraged.

THE VIOLENT PATIENT

Increasing insight by the public results in the demand for higher standards of care and less sympathy for incidents in which patients are alleged to be ill-treated. This has led to the appointment of a Hospital Advisory Service in which teams of psychiatrist, nurse and administrator examine the basic organization in all hospitals taking long-term patients, with the object of correcting conditions which could lead to ill-treatment. The patient whose behaviour suggests the need for restraint demands time for explanation and argument which individual members of the staff cannot readily spare. This must be given however and be followed as required by sedation. Consultation with appropriate senior colleagues and detailed plans for subsequent contingencies will be needed. The method used in one crisis however will determine the pattern of those in the future and reviews of the sequence of events by all concerned should follow each incident. In a Memorandum on good practice, the N.A.M.H. (1971) point out the need for clear channels of communication to administrative authorities.

THE SPECIAL PATIENT

Especially in situations of manpower shortage, the 'V.I.P.' patient's arrival can produce havoc in a poorly integrated staff. Individuals or factions disagree on anticipated privileges or see justification for the patient's special needs. Those whose approach is 'administrative' emphasize the effect on the group, while those seeing the need for concern for individuals find reasons within the patient's psychopathology for altering procedures (Stanton and Schwartz, 1954). The most constructive attitude involves an appraisal of the Unit's overall potential and the appropriateness of the individual's demands. This may lead

to modification of procedures for more than one patient, enlighten-
ment of staff and/or the appreciation by the patient of his demands
on others. Main (1957) describes the disturbance in relationships which
can be induced by the manipulative patient who splits the staff by
sharing 'precious little secrets'—if some members are flattered and
feel that they have supportive roles of unique importance.

DAY HOSPITALS

The arguments for day patient care as opposed to admission are the
maintenance of independence, incomplete removal from problems
hence less denial of them and the presumption of lesser severity of
sickness and less social embarrassment. The cost is probably less and
the day hospital is easier to staff. It is possible to operate day hospitals
only in accordance with the availability of transport. Day facilities
within a general or mental hospital rather than in a separate building
will save on overhead costs as well as capital outlay.

Day hospitals must be distinguished from day attendance at hospitals
when patients continue treatment in the ward from which they have
been partially discharged. This is a useful 'tailing off' method, reducing
dependency but at the same time offering the opportunity for drug
adjustment or the continuation of group therapy. Attendance at the
ward by day only instead of admission, is less satisfactory as an initial
procedure unless the number of patients involved is sufficient to make
them recognizable as a distinct group. Otherwise they may not easily
find a proper niche in the ward organization, especially if their time-
keeping and attendance is irregular.

Though many day hospitals are organized to provide a service which
may replace hospitalization and will take all patients with suitable
behaviour, there is a strong case for maintaining a strict clinical
classification. It is possible that the larger mental hospital scores here,
as schizophrenic rehabilitation, schizophrenic long-term, geriatric and
neurosis groups can be identified, accommodated and helped separately
in accordance with distinct objectives. Describing the scope and activities of day hospitals in England and Wales the Department of Health
and Social Security (1969) indicate that the basis of a mental health
service for a population of 200,000 should be a psychiatric unit in a
general hospital of 120 beds with a day hospital for 150 patients.

Discussing the applicability of the day hospital in the treatment of the
acutely ill patient, Zwerling and Wilder (1964) set out to discover how
many patients *cannot* be treated in such a situation. In their 30 place
weekday hospital, patients were seen individually by the doctor at
least twice weekly and together with the family at least once weekly.
Home visiting by social work and medical staff and some group therapy
was undertaken. Patients selected for inpatient admission were randomly

re-selected for admission to the day hospital according to its vacancies. The patient and his family were required to attend for an orientating session the following day. A cohort of 74 patients was treated at the day hospital and a further 51 treated predominantly there but with a short period of inpatient admission. Transfers to the '24-hour' inpatient ward were usually needed during the first week of treatment, especially by aggressive schizophrenic men. Patients with organic conditions, including alcoholics, were largely rejected but at least 75 per cent of those in the other diagnostic categories were accepted. Ability to travel daily or be escorted and the availability of a relative or friend at home during non-hospital hours was a necessary condition of day hospital care.

The form of the daily routine will depend on the clinical problems. It is not difficult to exhibit non-medical models of psychiatric practice in the day hospital setting when the doctors' visits are less formal and the nurses and other therapists are obviously in charge. Some provision must be made for evening and weekend emergency needs by having a clearly defined path towards help available to patients and staff. The establishment of therapeutic community meetings fits in readily with the pattern of arrival, planning the days events and review before departure, with delegation of tasks and chores and small group therapy for selected patients. Leading members of the staff must be given the appropriate experience before taking responsibility for patients in this setting. Some form of industrial therapy as well as *ad hoc* or patient initiated projects may be required. The day hospital distant from the psychiatric services will require E.C.T. facilities and more rooms for outpatient work. Evening clubs are a convenient method of developing a follow-up system.

REFERENCES

BAKER, A., DAVIES, R. L. & SIVADON, P. (1959) *Psychiatric Services and Architecture.* WHO: Geneva.

BARTON, R. (1959) *Institutional Neurosis.* Bristol: Wright.

BELKNAP, I. (1956) *Human Problems of a State Mental Hospital.* New York: McGraw-Hill.

BION, W. R. & RICKMAN, J. (1943) Intragroup tensions in therapy. *Lancet,* **ii,** 678.

CAUDILL, W. (1958) *The Psychiatric Hospital as a Small Society.* Cambridge: Harvard University Press.

CLARK, D. H., HOOPER, D. E. & ORAM, E. G. (1962) Creating a therapeutic community in a psychiatric ward. *Human Relations,* **15,** 123.

CLARK, D. H. (1964) *Administrative Therapy.* London: Tavistock.

CLARK, D. H. & MYERS, K. (1970) Themes in a therapeutic community. *British Journal of Psychology,* **117,** 389.

CUMMING, J. & CUMMING, E. (1962) *Ego and Milieu.* London: Prentice and Hall.

DRUCKER, W. (1955) *The Practice of Management.* London: Heinemann (Pan Books, 1971).

FOULKES, S. H. (1948) *Introduction to Group Analytical Psychiatry.* London: Heinemann.

GOFFMAN, E. (1961) *Asylums.* New York: Doubleday. London: Penguin (1968).

HOOPER, D. E. (1962) Changing the Milieu in a Psychiatric Ward. *Human Relations,* **15,** 111.

HUNTER, T. D. (1967) Hierarchy or Arena? In *New Aspects in the Mental Health Services,* Chap. 3. Edited by H. Freeman and J. Farmdale. London: Pergamon.

JACKSON, J. (1968) Consensus and conflict in treatment institutions. *Hospital and Community Psychology.,* **19,** 165.

JONES, MAXWELL (1952) *Social Psychiatry (The Therapeutic Community).* London: Tavistock.

JONES, MAXWELL (1965) Issues in social psychiatry. In *Community Mental Health Services in Northern Europe.* (S. Furman). Bethesda, Maryland: U.S. Public Health Service.

LEWIN, K. (1948) *Resolving Social Conflicts.* New York: Harper & Brothers.

LOVELICK, C. (1970) The management ideal. *Mental Health,* **1,** 24. London: N.A.M.H.

MAIN, T. F. (1946) The hospital as a therapeutic institution. *Bulletin of the Menninger Clinic,* **10,** 66.

MAIN, T. F. (1957) The ailment. *British Journal of Medical Psychology,* **33,** 129.

MARTIN, D. V. (1955) Institutionalization. *Lancet,* **ii,** 1188.

MARTIN, D. V. (1962) *Adventure in Psychiatry: Social Change in a Mental Hospital.* Oxford: Cassiver.

MARTIN, D. V. (1965) The importance of free communication. In *Psychiatric Hospital Care.* Edited by H. Freeman, Chap. 7. London: Ballière, Tindall & Cassell.

MEMORANDUM (1971) A Guide to Good Practice. *Mental Health,* **1,** 32. London: N.A.M.H.—also *British Journal of Psychology,* **118,** 699.

MILLER, E. J. & RICE, A. K. (1967) *Systems of Organization.* London: Tavistock.

REPORT OF A COMMITTEE OF THE SCOTTISH HEALTH SERVICES COUNCIL (1966) *Administrative Practice of Hospital Boards in Scotland,* (The Farquharson–Lang Report). Edinburgh: H.M.S.O.

REPORT ON WORKING PARTY (1967) *The Shape of Hospital Management in 1980.* London: King Edward Fund.

REPORT OF THE COMMITTEE ON THE INTERNAL ADMINISTRATION OF HOSPITALS. (The Bradbeer Committee, 1954). London: H.M.S.O.

REPORT OF WORKING PARTY (1967) *Organization of Medical Work in the Hospital Service in Scotland.* (The Brotherston Report). Edinburgh: H.M.S.O.

REPORT OF WORKING PARTY (1969) *Organization of Medical Work in Hospitals.* (The 'Cogwheel' Report). London: H.M.S.O.

REPORT OF THE COMMITTEE ON SENIOR NURSE STAFFING STRUCTURE. (The Salmon Report, 1966). London: H.M.S.O.

REPORT OF THE EXPERT COMMITTEE ON MENTAL HEALTH (1953) *The Community Mental Hospital.* WHO: Geneva.

REPORT OF THE DEPARTMENT OF HEALTH AND SOCIAL SECURITY (1969) *A Pilot Survey of Patients Attending Day Hospitals.* Statistical Report Series No. 7. London: H.M.S.O.

ROBERTSON, A. (1969) Organization Control in Remedial Institutions. *British Journal of Social Psychology,* **3,** 3.

SLEIGHT, P., SPENCE, J. A. & TOWLER, E. W. (1970) Oxford and McKinsey: Cogwheel and Beyond. *British Medical Journal,* **i,** 682.

STANTON, A. & SCHWARTZ, M. S. (1954) *The Mental Hospital.* London: Tavistock.

STRAUSS, A., SCHALZMAN, L., BUCHER, R., ERLICH, D. & SABELIN, M. (1964) *Psychiatric Ideologies and Institutions.* Glencoe Illinois: Free Press.

SULLIVAN, H. S. (1931) Sociopathic research—its implications for the schizophrenia problem and for mental hygiene. *American Journal of Psychiatry*, **x**, 977.

SULLIVAN, H. S. (1953) *Interpersonal Theory of Psychiatry.* London: Tavistock.

WALTON, H. J. (1961) Group methods in hospital organization and patient treatment as applied to the psychiatric treatment of alcoholism. *American Journal of Psychology*, **118,** 410.

WILMER, H. A. (1958) *Social Psychiatry in Action.* Springfield, Illinois: C. C. Thomas.

ZALEZNIK, A. (1967) The structure and dynamics of leadership. *Hospital and Community Psychology*, 18, 13.

ZWERLING, I. & WILDER, J. F. (1964) Evaluation of applicability of the day hospital in treatment for the acutely disturbed. *Israel Annals of Psychiatry*, **ii,** 162–185.

Chapter XVII

REHABILITATION AND SUPPORTIVE TECHNIQUES

J. W. Affleck

INTRODUCTION

The distinction between treatment and rehabilitation in psychiatry is difficult. When work and social activities are arranged for patients with very poor prognosis in order to maintain their best social level, the objective of independence which the word rehabilitation implies in other disciplines, is omitted. When therapeutic community or other techniques are used extensively with interpersonal problem exposure as the routine objective, the concept of treatment is more appropriate. The widespread usage of the term 'therapy' for activities used in work and resocialization regimes leads to the assumption of therapeutic qualities, some of which may be connected with interpersonal relationships and group processes which are taking place simultaneously.

The techniques described in this chapter have specific objectives for resettlement in work and community. They are undertaken by occupational therapists, nurses and social workers. The theoretical background of such activities has only been loosely formulated. The work ethic, economic factors, role interpretations and the pragmatic views of generations of attendants of the mentally ill can be invoked. It is assumed that learning or relearning to work is of value to certain patients and that living beyond the hospital is worthwhile. The groups for which progressive step by step methods are most suitable are schizophrenics, some inadequate personalities, high-grade subnormals and patients with recovering organic states. In recent years links with industry have encouraged extensive use of industrial work. The provision of subcontracts for hospital workshops produces inherent interest and reduces the feeling that psychiatric patients are society's rejects. The benefits of modern drugs and the acceptance of psychotic conditions as illness has increased the possibility of resettlement.

The construction of a patient's work regime round the domestic chores of the hospital or unit has its limitations with regard to the amount of work available and its value for individual patients. Its application to a 400-bed hospital have been described in detail by Maxwell Jones (1967). It includes the sound basic concept that people should work together for the common good and make use of the experience by exploratory discussion of the problems and attitudes revealed. The psychosocial background of the situation is more important than the work done. Wing and Brown (1970) point out that the schizophrenic patient requires a milieu in which he is activated but not over stimulated. The less intimate atmosphere of the workshop may thus be inherently valuable for the individual recovering from a disintegrative illness.

Rehabilitative objectives may be obscured by the inclusion, in one programme, of patients of both good and poor prognosis so the establishment of special units for later stages in work and resettlement both for inpatients and day patients may be indicated. The danger of all regimes in which large group methods are used, is the loss of consideration for individual needs. However, the importance of continuing activity for the long-term patient is such that psychiatric services cannot neglect such methods of organizing work.

ASSESSMENT AND REHABILITATION OF SHORT AND MEDIUM TERM PATIENTS

OCCUPATIONAL THERAPY

The Occupational Therapist makes use of the activities of daily living in the preparation of a programme for her patients. This programme must be for the individual and based on adequate knowledge of personality, background, habits and illness. To acquire this the Occupational Therapist will have to attend team meetings at which the relevant material is discussed and to be clinically effective she will have to interview the patient and make a working relationship. The department's facilities must cover a wide range of activities from the physical replica of the household for the psychogeriatric to the games and sport of the teenager. Simple manual or intellectual tasks on material with which the patient is familiar can be used for initial estimates of functioning. The Occupational Therapist can then report her findings on initiative, concentration, memory etc., involvement in work and on social attitudes and relationships observed in her setting. Valuable progress reports can follow. Such departments also include technicians for joinery, clerical work etc. The social and recreational programme, music and psychodrama will require special provision.

Patients who have only recently stopped work can usually be assessed re their suitability for return to work by an occupational therapist and other members of the team. The occupational therapy department should offer opportunity to improve work skills, to acquire new skills e.g. in art, cooking etc., and to reduce social isolation by the incorporation of social activities and excursions.

The recovering acute patient, even when involved in other therapy, can graduate from assessment to a special rehabilitation working situation quite rapidly. Light factory work, wood and metal work, clerical work and domestic units should be available and can be shared with nonpsychiatric patients if necessary. Such patients do not expect much financial reward but some acknowledgement in cash is usually appreciated and can be related to effort. If sufficient students are accumulated local Education Authorities provide teachers for evening classes for adults in typing and book-keeping, dressmaking, languages etc.

PARTIAL HOSPITALIZATION

When home relationships and conditions are stable enough the establishment of a satisfactory work pattern can be followed by transfer to day patient care, using the hospital as a place of work. Alternatively, when longer hospital living is needed, it can be modified by return to outside occupation while the hospital is used as home or hostel. Such manoeuvres to partial hospitalization can result in premature cessation of other therapeutic measures and this omission can produce institutionalization or continuing dependence. The organization of group therapy in evenings or during hospital occupation hours should be part of the programme in which nursing staff can be extensively involved. Discussion of personal difficulties in resettlement is part of the work of a rehabilitation group.

When return to work is not achieved or further advice is needed the Department of Employment's Disablement Resettlement Officer can help by reviewing the patient's industrial potential or referring him to the nearest Industrial Rehabilitation Unit. This provides assessment re vocation, trade or industry and some support in job finding. A few patients may be selected for special training to skilled work. It is often advantageous for the patient to continue living in hospital until his work pattern at the I.R.U. is established.

WORK REHABILITATION OF THE LONG-TERM PATIENT

The long-term patient makes slow progress towards gainful employment in spite of fairly rapid adjustment to simple work situations. As shown by Wadsworth et al. (1961) the non-paranoid schizophrenic reaches his peak of achievement slowly compared with the normal and he may never achieve the output of the average industrial worker. Wing's experiment of transporting 45 long-term patients daily to the Department of Employment's Industrial Rehabilitation Unit demonstrated that the patients achievements can often be determined by the expectations and interest of the staff. Of 45 patients, 24 remained in some type of employment outside the hospital a year later (Wing et al., 1964a).

The transfer of long-term patients from hospital industrial work to such a setting of work which is nearer normal industrial conditions, has special objectives. The hospital staff are able to assess the patient's general level of employment so attendance at the I.R.U. should be regarded as analogous to a 'finishing school'. There, the patient is tried out in conditions which are akin to industry re working hours, time-keeping and social activities. Travelling to work and mixing with people unconnected with the hospital may require to be relearned. A wider range of assessment experiences may be offered—though the psychiatric patient is not often able to make use of the engineering section. Much disappointment regarding the results obtained by attendance of long-term patients at I.R.U.'s could be avoided if hospital staff were more adequately informed with regard to the conditions and procedures undertaken and by more adequate preparation of patients. It is a mistake to expect the Department of Employment to find jobs for patients unless the unemployment level in the area is very low. Though considerable help in this field is given, job-finding may be difficult and patients often find help from a community nurse or social worker who knows the firms in the area which have a high turnover of staff.

Some long-term patients whose capacities are below industrial standards may function adequately in sheltered workshops. Remploy Ltd., a government subsidized company providing a slow-going industrial setting for all disabled people, takes a few mentally ill. Local authority social work departments which have specific responsibilities in this field can be expected to offer a quota of places in their sheltered workshops. The workshops can be set up by voluntary associations independently or on behalf of the local authority departments. Both local authorities and the Department of Employment provide subsidies to ensure that the workers have an acceptable basic wage. As in the U.S.A. Goodwill Industries which have been established in many states. In order that some insight can be available regarding the problems of the psychiatric patient in the work situation, exchanges of staff between hospital industrial therapy units, I.R.U.s. and sheltered work-shops should be organized.

Patients who are not going to make the grade industrially may gain a modified independence by living outside the hospital and using its facilities as an equivalent to permanent employment.

INDUSTRIAL THERAPY

Though industrial therapy may be of some advantage to a few patients who will only be a short time in hospital, it is of major im-portance to the long-stay patients as one of the activities preventing institutional neurosis. The therapeutic potential will depend on adequate consideration of an organisational plan.

The industrial rehabilitation of the chronically mentally ill in England has been reviewed by Goldberg (1967) on the basis that the aim is to restore the patient to the best possible level for the individual. In this context productivity in the workshop is less important than improving social acceptability and reducing secondary handicaps. There is considerable scope for initiative in the variation of work settings both inside and outwith the hospital. A large occupational organization requires to be 'serviced' and this in itself demands patient supervisors, porters and clerical workers. The clerical rehabilitation department can find regular employment in preparing the weekly pay packets from time-sheets kept by the various staff supervisors. In a large hospital one occupational department is not enough—the variety of work and classification of patients demands several different settings with different objectives. Work available for patients within the mental hospital traditionally includes assisting the artisan and catering staff— who can receive a small financial recognition for supervision. This type of work and special units such as the concrete shop, the car wash etc., employ relatively few patients and it is generally difficult to establish the manufacture of products for marketing on a large scale. Sub-contract work must therefore be sought from industry and will consist of assembly of cardboard, wood or plastic, packing, labelling or fixing by staples or machine. The paper, toymaking and light engineering trades are most in need of such services. Small groups of patients in a workshop can undertake soldering and skilled woodwork. Firms are frequently willing to send their light machines on loan to hospital units. Such repetitive occupations are of special value to patients who require a non-stressful situation in which some superficial social contact can be explored.

The training of occupational therapists includes the organization of industrial therapy departments, the assessment of the factors in the patient's response to work and the principles of task breakdown and analysis for therapeutic objectives. Members of the profession are scarce, however, and not all of them wish this type of work. Reviewing industrial therapy in 74 mental hospitals in England and Wales the King's Fund (1968) records that approximately 18 per cent of the units were the responsibility of occupational therapists, the majority were under the management of the nursing staff and 15 per cent had industrial managers. The presence of nursing staff whether in uniform or not, may provide an element of confidence needed by some patients and remind the occupants of the workshop of its medical auspices. Nurses may be overprotective of their patients, however, and will have given less thought than the experienced Occupational Therapist to the overall process and the indications for passing on to another activity. The layman having had more contact with industry, may be more likely to obtain the steady flow of the subcontract work which is required for continuous employment, but he may expect industrial standards beyond the patients' potential. The Industrial Therapy Organization (Bristol) Limited, which pioneered this field (Early, 1960), has a Board of Directors which includes local industrialists, trade unionists and prominent citizens. Other hospitals manage with their staff only, however, or have advisers without formal responsibilities.

Staff involved in this type of work must create acceptable pay arrangements within the limits allowed for patients who are also receiving National Health or Social Security payments. Time or piece rates may be weighted to rewards for punctuality, attendance, special effort etc. Workshops which mimic industrial conditions will have time-clocks, timed tea-breaks, strict rules re smoking etc., and payment in pay packets with time-rate statements.

In the multi-factorial situation of hospital treatment and rehabilitation it is not easy to demonstrate the effects of individual items in the programme but it can be postulated that one of the most important elements in the industrial therapy situation is the group activity which increases personal contacts. The normalizing effect of social methods of encouragement and cash incentives on the really long-term patient is assumed though the effect of practice, intelligence and type of stimulus are not clearly differentiated. An investigation of changes in working response by patients in different situations demonstrated that long-hospitalized schizophrenics lose output when stimuli are withdrawn (Wing and Freudenberg, 1961).

SOCIAL REHABILITATION

The deteriorated patient requires initially a strictly routine bowel-bladder-handwashing regime with supervision of eating habits and table manners. This is only likely to succeed if adequate phenothiazine and other medication is maintained and the nursing staff have respect for the patient as an individual.

The basic attitudes required to combat 'institutional neurosis' (Barton, 1959) involves a friendly staff who organize activity and encourage links with people outside the hospital. A frame of reference for the management of the chronic patient is also provided by Freeman et al. (1958) describing the changes in the schizophrenic in terms of psychoanalytic theory with special reference to Federn's ego psychology (1953). It was based on experiences in a special experimental unit at the Gartnavel Royal Hospital, Glasgow, before phenothiazines were available. The response of patients to closer association with skilled female nurses demonstrated the type of staff–patient relationships which strengthened the patient's impaired identity. Such elementary needs as named recognition and individually owned clothing are of prime importance and can be lacking in the institutional setting.

Barton (1965) offers a rating scale by which the standard of psychiatric hospitals can be compared with reference to the conditions, activities and facilities which should be available. Wing and Brown (1970) describing the pattern of change in three large hospitals over a period of intensive study for eight years, discuss the interaction between clinical and social factors. Measures of social environments in hospitals i.e. possessions including clothing, activities, nursing attitudes and outside contacts etc., are demonstrated and related to clinical state and changing attitudes. It is pointed out that affective withdrawal occurs in patients who have never been in hospital and that the introduction of activities which reduce the proportion of time spent 'doing nothing' is a most important factor in the background of clinical improvement in the schizophrenic.

Clark and Myers (1970) emphasize the need for a therapeutic community 'type' of approach which offers involvement of all staff and spreads the doctors' responsibilities beyond a daily visit. It involves patients' responsibilities to the limit of their capabilities.

Learning theorists claim that ward programmes based on token economies are effective in reducing institutionalization. Regressive patients earn tokens by undertaking useful activities and exchange them for privileges or purchasable goods. The system reinforces acceptable behaviour and imitates the normal economic and community standards. Since the report of Ayllon and Azrin (1965) on psychotic patients the method has been developed probably more extensively with the subnormal. Token economies require considerable effort in planning, adjustment and maintenance. They may require to be separated from the general economic values of the hospitals payments system and they involve staff training. They have been developed largely in the U.S.A. where the help of psychologists is more readily available.

Having observed the long-term schizophrenic patient at work the psychiatrist can be over optimistic about his chances of resettlement in the community but the resettlement objective may be emphasized and promoted by the establishment of special rehabilitation or resettlement wards or units (Bennett et al., 1961). Full independence of the hospital will not necessarily be the objective for all patients with this illness—a prolonged supervision which may be ultimately dropped, may be preferred. The inadequate personality and the high grade mental defective will probably move in and out of supervision.

Many patients either by social drifting or by the passage of time or prolonged isolation in hospital, have lost all family contacts and a new ladder towards resettlement must be available to them. The patient must be enticed out of the ward and beyond the hospital by organized activities, expeditions, bus runs etc., arranged in some hospitals by voluntary societies whose members assist the nursing staff. This is followed by the hostel ward in which a working day is routine and outings beyond the hospital are encouraged. Guidance towards independence is provided by training in the management of money and savings, in personal hygiene and in the care of clothing, including use of the laundrette. Attendance at the follow-up club can commence before the patient leaves hospital.

DOMICILIARY RESETTLEMENT

Return to parents and siblings should not be attempted routinely as about 60 per cent of schizophrenic patients have unhappy or pathological relationships with their families (Wing *et al.*, 1964*b*). In a prospective study, using scales to measure emotional disturbance, hostility etc., Brown *et al.* (1962) demonstrated that patients from homes with high emotional involvement with key persons, were those most likely to relapse. The psychiatric social worker's traditional 'family casework' role is applicable to this field which is also being explored by other professions as 'family therapy'.

Insufficient research on hostels and supervised lodgings has been accomplished to show whether this form of care produces better results. Rollin (1969) has pointed out the cycle of recurrent hospitalization, discharge and court/prison sequences which can follow unsupported and unsupervised discharge from hospital. It is a mistake to expect the schizophrenic to cope with a change of living quarters and work at the same time. No specific estimate of time can be made and considerable patience must be exercised while the patient orientates himself to a way of living with new people.

As adjustment improves transfer to areas of decreasing supervision can be planned. The hostel ward may be followed by some form of communal home in which patients are increasingly self-supporting and receive only visits from staff. Alternatively, the move may be to boarding house or lodgings with visits by a community nurse or social worker. Even in the city of Edinburgh which caters extensively for students and tourists and has a high rate of elderly people seeking a retiral home, an enthusiastic community nursing service found places for over 100 patients who could be supervised in lodgings within a year. The term 'boarding out' has in the past been associated especially with Gheel in Belgium from the commencement of the scheme, six hundred years ago, in which patients have lived and worked with families in the town adjoining the mental hospital. In Scotland for more than 100 years a centrally organized system was organized by the Board of Control for mental hospitals. At one time some 800 patients suffering from chronic psychosis and subnormality were looked after by non-relatives in country districts. Both schemes, which involve patients making a working contribution to the households, have been reduced in recent years as a result of changes in treatment methods and in local social and employment patterns.

CLUBS

Organized social and recreational activities in which patients play a leading role have an important part in the lives of many inpatients, daypatients and outpatients. This may be part of a long-term supportive organization or a transitional activity. The translation of a recovering elderly person to a pensioners' club in the vicinity of her home may be an important aspect of her resettlement.

The interests of the over-40's are different from those of the younger patients though the young schizophrenic with serious personality problems may cling to the less demanding 'uncles and aunts'. In some clubs the encouragement of weekend camping has been extended to holidays abroad. Educational opportunity and the experience of forms of creativity new to the patient are part of the rehabilitation programme for addicts demonstrated in the ex-addict organized Phoenix Houses. The gaps in the interests of many patients in this group are conspicuous and of different aetiology from the similar phenomena in schizophrenia. Art, music and drama activities do not present age-linked problems.

Staff support is required to a varying extent in the club's history, often as a result of the varying patient leadership. The swings of affective disorder or the persuasions of the histrionic member may carry the programmes for many months. As clubs are often evening activities they may present considerable problems of staff organization. Occupational therapists and nurses usually undertake the intramural activities and social workers combine the extramural clubs with aftercare. It is not uncommon for other non-professional members of a hospital staff to play a leading role in some section of the club's work and voluntary association members are frequently involved—a notable example was the composer Edward Elgar's leadership of the music group at the Macclesfield Asylum. Student groups are well-known sources of help. The Epsom Relatives Association has developed an extensive supportive service stemming initially from club activities in response to the difficulties experienced by the result of the distance of the hospitals from their catchment areas.

The club objectives are learning or relearning social skills and the prevention of isolation by friendly contact and support. Such needs are also met among the more sophisticated practices of Alcoholics Anonymous, Neurotics Anonymous, etc.

NURSING PSYCHIATRIC PATIENTS IN THE COMMUNITY

Nursing skills in the community are available through peripetetic hospital nurses, health visitors and district nurses. Nursing duties outside the hospital have been described by May and Moore (1963). The number of nurses available for such duties has generally been small and most services aim at filling essential needs only. The concept of having a nurse looking after a 'ward' of perhaps 40 patients in the community has been developed, implying more than supervision of the patient's transition from hospital to community and analogous to nursing in a long-term ward. It can be an important part of a comprehensive service for schizophrenics. Nursing involves care of the patient in both physical and mental aspects, teaching him and his relatives the administration of medicines and advising on health matters within the limits of nursing training. In rural areas the district nurse, who may include health visiting in her duties, may be the only suitable person able to help the general practitioner in psychiatric after-care. Refresher courses at the hospital will increase her skills.

Where an extensive service is available from the hospital and the hospital is near the centre of an urban catchment area, the close association of the psychiatrist with the skilled psychiatric nurse offers the prospect of satisfactory support for a large number of patients. The introduction of the long-acting intramuscular phenothiazines which may be most suitably administered at home in some cases, gives a basic nursing duty. The nurse will look after patients who live at home but an important extension of this is the care of patients in lodgings. The maintenance of 'supervision in lodgings' involves close co-ordination with the landlady and repetition of the assurance that hospital help will be available if required. Small hotelliers, boarding housekeepers, and the hostel wardens of various voluntary organizations can be given the same consultative support.

The official guardianship provisions of the Mental Health Acts which involve local authority officials being appointed as 'Guardian' are not extensively used as they provide little advantage over the ordinary Social Security payments with voluntary supervision.

The community nurse finds himself involved in patients' work problems. He will be asked by some patients to give support in the process of changing jobs and he will acquire the knowledge of firms who are likely to employ patients.

Isolation can readily occur in the case of any discharged patient who has a tendency to social failure. The nurse therefore becomes interested in the social clubs and friendly contacts available for patients and may play an organizing role in this field.

A scheme for progressive patient care and resettlement is shown on Table 1.

SERVICES BY VOLUNTEERS

Voluntary workers, singly or in groups can provide satisfactory supplementary services in the resocialization process. To do so their work

P

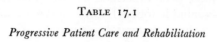

TABLE 17.1

Progressive Patient Care and Rehabilitation

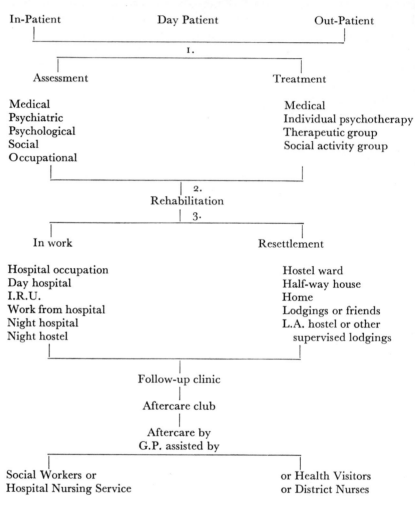

In-Patient	Day Patient	Out-Patient

1.

Assessment		Treatment
Medical		Medical
Psychiatric		Individual psychotherapy
Psychological		Therapeutic group
Social		Social activity group
Occupational		

2.
Rehabilitation
3.

In work		Resettlement
Hospital occupation		Hostel ward
Day hospital		Half-way house
I.R.U.		Home
Work from hospital		Lodgings or friends
Night hospital		L.A. hostel or other
Night hostel		supervised lodgings

Follow-up clinic

Aftercare club

Aftercare by
G.P. assisted by

Social Workers or	or Health Visitors
Hospital Nursing Service	or District Nurses

must be organized expertly if not professionally. Unsuccessful efforts in this field can usually be traced to poor management which can include unsatisfactory placings. Some hospitals have successfully included ex-patients in their activities by adequate consideration of detail. Volunteers should have an orientation course rather than 'training' which is bound to be misleading. The exposure of the volunteers to the emotional conflicts and demands of the short-term neurotic or psychopathic patients is an unwise risk.

Church groups are available in most areas and can become a nucleus of a larger organization. Students and older school pupils are also successful. They can run cafe services (with music). The befriending activities which are generally appropriate include visits and outings which widen the horizon for individual patients or for groups—social and club activities, bus runs, country dancing and other recreational activities. Local business men may find useful service on a Board of Advisers on industrial work.

Preparation of the medical, nursing and other professional staffs for co-operation with volunteers may be as difficult and as important as other aspects of organization of these services.

HOSTELS

Two types of hostel are readily defined—the half-way house or transitional, in which patients live for a period of weeks or months before moving on to other accommodation and the long-stay hostel or community home from which movement is not expected. Stimulated by the philosophy that return to the community must be beneficial to all, local authorities and voluntary organizations have often opened hostels without definite policy and combined purpose hostels have resulted—sometimes occupied by subnormals and inadequate personalities who have never been in hospital, as well as by ex-patients. Such institutions can only be run successfully by a most skilled staff, but Apte (1967) found in his survey of 24 hostels that only 60 per cent of the wardens had experience of nursing or other relevant work and their nursing orientation was not necessarily towards rehabilitation concepts. One-third of the hostels had regular services from a psychiatrist and only 60 per cent had social work help. The hostels which had these services were found to be most successful. As Clark (1961) points out, the patients should visit the psychiatrist from the transitional hostel rather than the psychiatrist give the impression that the hostel is a hospital annexe, by his visits to it.

Some inherent good may accrue from the simple transfer of long-term patients from a hospital to a house in town, where local acquaintances can gradually draw the patient into some form of contact with the community in general. This may be the best we can do for the older schizophrenic and can result in unexpected improvement. Even with limited objectives, however, regular psychiatric contact is indicated to adjust drug dosage and to ensure that the patient has the advantage of advances in treatment. It is important to maintain a clinical classification of residents by reasonable selection of patients for such vacancies as occur. Though it is tempting to try to create a 'normal atmosphere' and equally important to avoid under-stimulation, it appears that for schizophrenic patients with paranoid traits or unalterable handicaps, the lack of a demanding intimacy may be the factor which allows social survival. Hostels dealing with alcoholics, drug addicts and other special groups will need staff with special training.

REFERENCES

AYLLON, T. & AZRIN, N. H. (1965) The measurement and reinforcement of behaviour in psychotics. *Journal of the Experimental Analysis of Behaviour*, **8**, 357.

APTE, R. (1967) The hostel as a transitional institution. In *New Aspects of the Mental Health Services*, Ch. 37. Edited by H. W. Freeman and J. Farndale. London: Pergamon

BARTON, R. (1959) *Institutional Neurosis*. Bristol: Wright.

BARTON, R. (1965) Proposed scale for rating psychiatric hospitals. In *Psychiatric Hospital Care*. Ch. 3. Edited by H. Freeman. London: Ballière, Tindall and Cassell.

BENNETT, D., FOLKARD, S. & NICHOLSON, A. (1961) A resettlement unit in a mental hospital. *Lancet*, **ii**, 539.

BROWN, G. W., MONCK, E. M., CARSTAIRS, G. M. & WING, J. K. (1962) Influence of family life on the course of schizophrenic illness. *British Journal of Preventive and Social Medicine*, **16**, 55.

CLARK, D. H. (1961) *Hostels and the Mental Health Act*. London: N.A.M.H.

CLARK, D. H. & MYERS, K. (1970) Themes in a Therapeutic Community. *British Journal of Psychology*, **117**, 389.

EARLY, D. F. (1960) The Industrial Therapy Organisation (Bristol)—The first two years. *Lancet*, **ii**, 754.

FEDERN, P. (1953) *Ego Psychology and the Psychoses*. London: Imago.

FREEMAN, T. CAMERON, J. L. & McGHEE, A. (1958) *Chronic Schizophrenia*. London: Tavistock.

GOLDBERG, D. (1967) Rehabilitation of the chronically mentally ill in England. *Social Psychiatry*, **2**, 1–13.

JONES, MAXWELL (1967) The current place of therapeutic communities in psychiatric practice. In *New Aspects of the Mental Health Services*. Ch. 25. Edited by H. Freeman and J. Farndale. London: Pergamon.

MAY, A. R. & MOORE, S. (1963) The mental nurse in the community. *Lancet*, **i**, 213.

REPORT ON INDUSTRIAL THERAPY IN PSYCHIATRIC HOSPITALS (1968) London: King Edward Hospital Fund.

ROLLIN, H. R. (1969) The mentally abnormal offender and the Law. *British Medical Journal*, **3**, 161.

WADSWORTH, W. V., SCOTT, F. F. & WELLS, B. W. P. (1961) Employability of long-stay schizophrenics. *Lancet*, **ii**, 543.

WING, J. K. & FREUDENBERG, R. K. (1961) The response of severely ill schizophrenics to social stimulation. *American Journal of Psychology*, **118**, 311.

WING, J. K., BENNETT, D. H. & DENHAM, J. (1964a) *The Industrial Rehabilitation of Long-Stay Schizophrenic Patients*. MRC Memorandum No. 42. London: H.M.S.O.

WING, J. K., MONCK, E. M., BROWN, G. W. & CARSTAIRS, G. M. (1964b) Morbidity in the community of schizophrenics discharged from London mental hospitals in 1959. *British Journal of Psychology*, **110**, 10.

WING, J. K. & BROWN, G. W. (1970). *Institutionalism and Schizophrenia*. Cambridge: University Press.

Chapter XVIII

BEHAVIOUR THERAPY

A. S. Presly

INTRODUCTION

The term Behaviour Therapy is the name which has come to be applied to a group of related methods of treatment, all of which have as their aim the modification of certain aspects of human behaviour, and which claim to be based on a variety of learning principles derived by experimental psychologists. These methods were given the name 'Behaviour Therapy' by Eysenck (1959, p. 66) 'to contrast them with methods of psychotherapy'. This contrast of terms is meant to indicate two things. According to psychoanalytic doctrine, there is a psychological complex, situated in the unconscious mind, underlying all the manifest symptoms of neurotic disorder. Hence the necessity for therapy for the psyche. According to learning theory, we are dealing with unadaptive behaviour conditioned to certain classes of stimuli; no reference is made to any underlying disorders or complexes in the psyche. Following on this analysis, it is not surprising that psychoanalysts show a preoccupation with psychological methods involving mainly *speech*, while behaviour therapy concentrates on actual *behaviour* as most likely to lead to the extinction of the unadaptive conditioned responses'.

The paradigm of neurotic symptom formation in learning theory terms, is usually taken to be Watson's experiment with little Albert (Watson and Raynor, 1920), in which, by classical Pavlovian conditioning, a phobia of white rats was induced in the infant by standing behind him and banging an iron bar with a hammer every time he reached for the animals. Fortunately, perhaps, the work of Jones (1924) around the same time provided a paradigm of neurotic symptom removal. She used deconditioning methods to eliminate a rabbit phobia in a 3 year old boy by associating the presence of the rabbit with food the child liked, closely foreshadowing the technique now called systematic desensitization (Wolpe, 1958).

Although it is true that these studies are perhaps the first experimental demonstrations of the genesis and removal of neurotic behaviour, the role of conditioning in the origin of such behaviour has long been recognized. Marks (1969, p. 90) quotes Descartes writing in 1650: 'a cat may have affrighted it (the child) and none took notice of it, nor the child so much as remembered it; though the idea of that aversion he then had to a cat remain imprinted on his brain to his life's end'.

Similarly, the idea of reciprocal inhibition in the treatment of neurotic disorders (where a response inhibitory to anxiety is paired with the stimuli which previously produced anxiety until it becomes the usual response) is also a very old one. Marks (1969, p. 183) makes reference to a writer of 1644: 'Any aversion of the fantasy may be mastered not only by a powerfull agent upon the present sense, but also by assuefaction, and by bringing into the fantasy with pleasing circumstances that object which before was displeasing and affrightfull to it'. Nevertheless, the systematic investigation of treatment methods based on learning principles and their application to the neuroses is a matter of a few decades rather than of centuries.

Techniques of Behaviour Therapy

SYSTEMATIC DESENSITIZATION

This method of behaviour therapy derives largely from Wolpe (1958). The basic principle is that 'if a response antagonistic to anxiety can be made to occur in the presence of anxiety-provoking stimuli so that it is accompanied by a complete or partial suppression of the anxiety responses, the bond between the stimuli and the anxiety responses will be weakened'. This technique, therefore, is generally applied in conditions where anxiety or fear has become conditioned to some readily definable stimulus or stimuli, as in the case of agoraphobia, specific animal phobias, fears of public speaking and other social anxieties.

Patients are first asked to prepare a hierarchy of anxiety-producing situations starting with one which produces hardly any anxiety and working up to those which they find extremely frightening. At the same time, usually over 3 to 6 sessions, the patients are taught muscular relaxation by one of several methods, the most commonly used being a derivation of Jacobson's method given in detail by Wolpe and Lazarus (1966, pp. 177–180). The patient is also encouraged to practise relaxation at home between sessions. In the third phase, the desensitization, he is asked to visualize as clearly as possible for a few seconds the first item of the hierarchy. This is repeated with increasing exposure time until the patient indicates that it no longer produces anxiety, at which point the next item in the hierarchy is presented and the same procedure repeated. Details of these procedures are to be found in Rachman (1968) and Wolpe and Lazarus (1966). In most cases, patients need to practise a similar series of steps in real life situations in addition to imaginative desensitization before all anxiety is extinguished, and an extension of this procedure is the introduction of live modelling (Bandura, 1968) where phobic patients watch 'models' engaging in gradually closer interaction with the feared object. The addition of live modelling to the more usual desensitization procedures appears to be particularly effective, although its application is obviously limited, as are other methods of desensitization in practice (e.g. with phobias of thunder).

The commonest difficulties encountered in desensitization are difficulties in relaxation and difficulty in imagining scenes clearly. The former can be overcome in some cases by further practice and re-assurance, and some writers advocate the use of short acting drugs to induce relaxation easily and quickly (e.g. Friedman, 1966). A high initial level of 'free-floating' anxiety may make desensitization im-possible for some patients because of the very great difficulty in relaxing them. Some patients are able to visualize clearly but do not feel any concomitant anxiety. In this case, the reason may be that the hierarchy is irrelevant to the primary source of anxiety, but if this is not so, desensitization in practice may be the only alternative, as it is for those patients who find imagining scenes very difficult or impossible.

AVERSION THERAPY

This method is usually employed to modify behaviour which invokes social disapproval, alcoholism and various forms of deviant sexual behaviour being the conditions most commonly treated. It has also been applied to compulsive habits such as over-eating (Meyer and Crisp, 1964) and gambling, and to involuntary motor dysfunction such as writer's cramp (Eysenck and Rachman, 1965). The principle under-lying aversion therapy is that a noxious stimulus, usually an electric shock or a drug which induces nausea or vomiting, is paired with the circumstances which evoke the undesirable behaviour, or is applied when the behaviour itself occurs. A conditioned avoidance of the undesirable behaviour is thus induced. The report by Feldman and MacCulloch (1965) of the treatment of homosexuality is an excellent example of this procedure. The homosexual patient sits in front of a screen on which photographic slides of men and women are projected. The patient has available to him a switch which can remove any slide at once, and initially, male slides are projected for 8 seconds and a shock given if the patient has not switched off the slide (which also terminates the shock) by that time. He is instructed to leave the slide on the screen as long as he finds it sexually attractive. When the avoidance response (switching off the male slide) is established, a further series of trials is carried out according to schedules of reinforce-ment known to increase the resistance to extinction of newly acquired responses. In the 'relief period' which follows the switching off of the male slide, female slides are introduced, thus associating relief of anxiety with the introduction of the female in an attempt to make females more attractive to the patient at the same time as males are becoming less attractive.

Proper attention to principles derived from experimental studies of punishment and the basic requirements of classical conditioning seems to be crucial to the successful outcome of aversion therapy. Eysenck (1963) for example was able to attribute many therapeutic failures to misconceptions regarding these principles. Other difficulties arise as a result of the use of punishment as part of the treatment; patients need to be highly motivated to alter their behaviour in order to accept this and even those who initially accept the idea may break down later (Feldman and MacCulloch, 1965). In addition, many therapists find aversion therapy distasteful, and are reluctant to employ it if other forms of treatment are available.

The use of electrical rather than chemical methods of aversion is probably to be preferred, since electric shocks allow for much greater precision of control over the time of onset, duration of application and intensity of the stimulus. Drugs can have side effects which interfere with the treatment, especially the patient's ability to learn, and they are more variable than electric shocks in the effect they produce in individuals. The work of Cautela (1967) is an attempt to eliminate the necessity of presenting external noxious stimuli by having the patient conjure them up in his imagination only. Thus an alcoholic might be asked to signal when he has a clear image of a drink or a strong desire for it, at which point he is asked immediately to imagine nausea and vomiting. The obvious disadvantage of this technique which so far has had very limited application, is the lack of control over the imagined stimuli, but if results prove to be favourable, the method is to be preferred. Wolpe has used another technique using a noxious stimulus, but in this case, the purpose is to make use of the period of 'anxiety relief' which follows its termination. A shock is given e.g. to a phobic patient, and a phobic stimulus is presented on a screen simultaneously with the relief response—the patient's termination of the shock. With repeated presentations, the phobic stimulus itself comes to elicit the relief response.

A full account of aversion therapy and the conditions to which it can be applied can be found in Rachman and Teasdale (1969).

OPERANT CONDITIONING

The use of this method in the modification of human behaviour has its origin in the work of Lindsley and Skinner (e.g. Lindsley and Skinner, 1954), and it has been applied mainly to the behaviour of psychotic and mentally handicapped patients, and more recently to the behaviour of autistic children. The particular response to be modified is first of all studied closely to see what events follow its occurrence. The basic principle of operant conditioning is that those consequences of the 'target behaviour' are important in that they increase or decrease the probability of that behaviour occurring again, i.e. they reinforce it. Therapy based on this principle involves manipulation of the reinforcement of the 'target behaviour' so that it is extinguished and replaced by more acceptable behaviour. Thus, whenever desired responses are made, they are immediately reinforced, and reinforcement withheld when undesired responses occur. If desired responses are not evident, the method of 'response shaping' is used, where successive approximations to the desired behaviour are reinforced until the new respose is established. An example of shaping is provided by Isaacs *et al.* (1960), who, by reinforcing successive approximations to speech such as facial movements, lip movements and any vocalizations, were able finally to obtain spoken words from two adult mute schizophrenics. The work of Ayllon and others (e.g. Ayllon and Haughton, 1964) provides examples of how the socially disruptive behaviour of long-term psychiatric hospital patients can be extinguished and replaced by more appropriate behaviour by very careful manipulation of the events which reinforce the behaviour. This system has been successfully extended to the management of entire wards of chronic patients (Ayllon and Azrin, 1968) in what are known as 'token economy programmes', with tokens which entitle patients to certain privileges being used as reinforcers for socially acceptable behaviour such as making beds or being on time for meals.

OTHER TECHNIQUES

Negative Practice (Eysenck and Rachman, 1965)

This method is applicable to certain psychomotor disturbances such as tics, and is based on the principle that massed practice of a learned response without reinforcement leads to its extinction. A tic, for example, is produced voluntarily as precisely and intensively as possible in sessions of massed practice as long as one or two hours followed by prolonged rest periods. A gradual decline in ability to produce the tic voluntarily generally occurs first, followed by a decline in frequency and final extinction of involuntary tics.

Positive Conditioning

This method is applied commonly in cases of nocturnal enuresis, with the aim of establishing a conditioned response (bladder control) in individuals who have failed to do so. The procedure is to have the patient sleep on a special pad. When the pad is wet, a circuit is completed, setting off a loud and unpleasant noise. This acts as an unconditioned stimulus for a reflex contraction of the sphincter, inhibiting micturition. Eventually the association of the first indications of urination and sphincter relaxation (the conditioned stimulus) with the unconditioned stimulus (the loud noise) produces the response of sphincter contraction to the conditioned stimulus alone, and urination and the noxious stimulus are avoided.

Implosion (Flooding)

Implosion is in a sense the opposite of desensitization, as the subjects are repeatedly exposed to intensely disturbing imagined stimuli from the start without the opportunity of either an avoidance response or of a response incompatible with anxiety. The stimuli are presented as vividly and for as long as possible until the subject cannot experience anxiety. He is then exposed for long periods to the corresponding real life situations until they also can no longer evoke anxiety responses.

Detailed accounts of the theory and practice of all these methods and of several others less widely applicable can be found in Eysenck and Rachman (1965), Beech (1969), Wolpe and Lazarus (1966) and Meyer and Chesser (1970).

RESULTS OF BEHAVIOUR THERAPY

DESENSITIZATION

An extensive review of the results of desensitization is given by Marks (1969). He reviews 18 controlled studies of phobic patients and volunteers with fears of snakes, spiders, examinations and public speaking. Typical of these are the studies by Paul (1966), and Gelder and Marks (1966). In summarizing the results of these studies, Marks has this to say: 'An impressive uniformity of results has shown desensitization to produce more change in the treated fear than did the corresponding control procedures, which included relaxation, suggestion and hypnosis, insight psychotherapy, drug placebo, and no treatment or a period on a waiting list' (1969, p. 268). Several prognostic features were evident from these studies. The closer the resemblance of patients with phobias to phobic volunteers, the more will the results of desensitization in patients resemble the results in volunteers (in whom results are generally found to be best). This in effect means that patients with circumscribed phobias and few other symptoms do best with desensitization. Unfavourable prognostic indications are severe agoraphobia, severe obsessions or other neurotic symptoms, and a high level of 'free-floating' non-specific anxiety and physiological correlates of anxiety. It is of interest to note also, that in the study of Boulougouris and Marks (1969) of implosion therapy applied to phobias, the only patient who did not show marked improvement was the only one with a high level of 'free-floating' anxiety. Improvement following desensitization is usually retained as far as follow up studies have so far been done, and symptom substitution seems no greater and is probably less than for any other method with which it has been compared. Over all, desensitization appears to give best results when given both in imagination and in practice and in volunteers, at least, it is particularly effective when combined with live modelling. It is not possible to give a precise overall figure for the percentage of patients who improve with desensitization, as this will depend entirely on the sample of patients studied and in particular, on the number of agoraphobics included in it.

AVERSION THERAPY

The results of the treatment of alcoholism by aversion therapy vary widely, the variation being in part attributable to differences in outcome criteria e.g. in terms of 'abstinence' or 'improvement'. Franks (1966) in a review of these results deduced an overall abstinence rate of 51 per cent ranging from 60 per cent after 1 year to 23 per cent after 10 years or more for patients treated by chemical and electrical aversion methods. He also concluded that the efficacy of these methods is 'virtually impossible' to evaluate due to the poor quality of most of the studies. However, insofar as comparison is considered valid, aversion therapy compares favourably with other methods of treating alcoholism in terms of symptomatic improvement, but there is little evidence to suggest it does any better.

With regard to the treatment of sexual deviation, aversion therapy fares rather better. These conditions, transvestism, fetishism and homosexuality have been found to be extremely resistant to psychotherapeutic forms of treatment, but have shown encouraging response to aversion therapy. MacCulloch and Feldman (1967) reported on a series of 13 homosexual patients treated by aversion therapy and followed up for at least one year. 56 per cent were considered to have improved significantly. The study of Bancroft and Marks (1968) however, suggests that the permanence of improvement following aversion therapy is very variable, being much poorer for homosexuality than for transvestism and fetishism. This result is very much in line with the finding for desensitization in that the more specific and circumscribed the condition, the better the outcome of behaviour therapy.

OPERANT CONDITIONING

Most studies in which operant conditioning has been employed report successful outcome inasmuch as the specific behaviour concerned has been modified in the appropriate way. However, several important questions remain unanswered There is little evidence on how much generalization occurs following specific changes brought about by operant conditioning, or how permanent these changes are, and there are few studies where control groups not subjected to the operant conditioning procedures have been employed. There is no doubt, however, that these methods are useful in modifying socially disruptive behaviour in severely disturbed patients. In many instances, such modification can be seen as a considerable gain and could make the application of other treatment methods easier.

EVALUATION OF BEHAVIOUR THERAPY

RANGE OF APPLICABILITY

The range of behaviour to which behaviour therapy methods have been applied is wide, although the specific conditions within this range are generally rare. In theory, if a learning model is applicable to what are generally called 'the neuroses', then any symptom under this heading should be capable of modification by behavioural techniques. However, behaviour therapists have till now tended to concentrate on patients with isolated symptoms or with narrowly circumscribed groups of symptoms, since these are more susceptible to explanation in learning theory terms. It cannot be assumed from this fact that behaviour therapy can deal only with relatively monosymptomatic conditions, since the reason for concentrating on these so far is a matter of experimental convenience. This is as it should be if behaviour therapists are to take seriously the need for rigorous experimental investigation of aspects of learning theory underlying their methods of treatment. Otherwise they become guilty of the same errors of which they sometimes accuse psychotherapists.

SELECTION OF PATIENTS

It needs to be borne in mind that the results of behaviour therapy stand in spite of the fact that they deal with conditions frequently found extremely resistant to other psychiatric methods of treatment, e.g. homosexuality, writer's cramp. It is a common experience also of clinical psychologists to have patients referred for behaviour therapy as a last resort when other treatments have failed, and referral for behaviour therapy as the treatment of first choice is still uncommon. Thus the population of patients referred for behaviour therapy is likely to have certain features predisposing against therapeutic success, especially the intractibility of many of the conditions to other treatments. Thus studies of the efficacy of behaviour therapy in referred patients are unlikely to be useful. If this referral problem is to be overcome, then a lot more work is needed to define which patients and which disorders are especially suited to different forms of behaviour therapy. So far, Marks has been able to do this with respect to the desensitization of phobias on the basis of presenting symptoms, but what is lacking in particular are studies of the influence of personality variables on the outcome of behaviour therapy. Some of these, e.g. extraversion, are known to influence the acquisition of certain types of conditioned responses, and so presumably will have some effect in response to behaviour therapy; what this effect is however, as yet largely equivocal.

BASIS IN LEARNING THEORY

Many writers have been critical of the learning theory approach to neurosis, and in particular, have questioned the claim that behaviour therapy rests on a solid scientific basis of 'modern learning theory'. Critics like Breger and McGaugh (1965) point to the inadequacy of the conditioning model even in a laboratory setting, and the difficulty that learning theories have in explaining many of the phenomena of laboratory experiments. To base a method of therapy involving modification of behaviour far more complex and more difficult to control than that studied in the laboratory then becomes a dubious procedure. To this kind of criticism the learning theorists reply (e.g. Rachman and Eysenck, 1966) that though there are several learning theories, they all agree on certain crucial points in the sense that they generate similar testable predictions about behaviour, and it is on these points of agreement that behaviour therapy is based. If this argument is accepted, then it seems reasonable to put forward laboratory based principles as the basis of behaviour therapy techniques as long as the resemblance between the therapy and laboratory situations is a close one. Thus learning theory principles can be seen to form the basis of some forms of aversion therapy and operant conditioning procedures, which generally deal with clearly specifiable behaviour, but are much more difficult to apply to desensitization and implosion methods which deal with behaviour much less easily defined in stimulus/response terms.

Unfortunately, the evidence does not support even this moderate conclusion: Morgenstern et al. (1965) found that patients who acquired conditioned verbal responses easily in a laboratory setting responded well to aversion therapy, whereas there was no relationship between the speed of acquisition of a conditioned eyeblink response and outcome of treatment. Eysenck (1969) on the other hand cites the results of a study by Martin et al. where those patients who readily acquired conditioned eyeblink responses did do well with behaviour therapy. According to learning theory, degree of extraversion/introversion should also have predictive value for conditioning treatments, but the evidence of Morganstern et al. (1965) and Paul (1966) has failed to substantiate this. Thus both extraversion/introversion and the speed of acquisition of conditioned responses in the laboratory have proved equivocal as prognostic indications for behaviour therapy, and these results do not support the argument that conditioning is the basis of behaviour therapy. However, there is now enough evidence from controlled studies to justify the use of behaviour therapy techniques on an empirical basis until further research overcomes the problem.

RELATIONSHIP TO PSYCHOTHERAPY

In nearly all the controlled studies, whether dealing with volunteers or psychiatric patient groups, behaviour therapy has done as well or better than the control method of treatment, often some form of psychotherapy; it very rarely has done worse. Relapse rates appear to be no greater, nor does symptom substitution appear to be a problem. The success of desensitization methods in particular have stimulated attempts to apply a learning theory model to the process of psychotherapy. Thus, for example, Eysenck (1969, p. 209) suggests that psychotherapy is effective 'because it incorporates certain of the principles of desensitization. The permissive atmosphere produces a lowering of anxiety (relaxation); discussion ranges around the presenting problems, and in the hands of an experienced psychiatrist naturally centres on problems towards the lower end of the hierarchy because these arouse only anxieties which, under the circumstances, are tolerable, to be followed later by discussions involving problems higher up the hierarchy.' Equally, however, the successes of behaviour therapy have been put down to the effect of conventional psychotherapeutic processes. Coates (1964) reanalysed a number of published cases in which either desensitization or aversion therapy was used to treat sexual deviation and argues for such psychodynamic factors as identification and transference rather than conditioning as the probable curative process in several of them. This kind of argument can be resolved only by rigorous experimental investigation of the active components of either form of therapy, and only when these have been identified can useful comparison be made. The study by Rachman (1965) is an example of the type of analysis which is required.

Several authors (e.g. Marks and Gelder, 1966) have taken the view that behaviour therapy and psychotherapy may be carried out concurrently in the same patient. The greatest disadvantage of this procedure is obviously that one cannot know to which method to attribute any changes. Also, in the author's experience, the combination raises several problems which in the long run may be to the disadvantage of the patient. A short account of three cases of agoraphobia treated by the author will serve to illustrate some of these. All three were admitted to a ward where all patients take part in group psychotherapy sessions daily and have individual psychotherapy sessions approximately three hours per week. Desensitization was carried out daily followed by graded exposure to real life situations.

Case 1. Mrs. A., aged 62, had an eight year history of severe agoraphobia with, at times, complete inability to leave the house alone. At her best, she was able to go out as long as she could see her house; at her worst, she also experienced panic attacks in the house when alone, at which time she was afraid to move for fear of falling down.

This patient's reaction to the combined treatment approach was to reject the psychotherapeutic approach to her problems outright and to put all her energies into behaviour therapy. Psychotherapy had little effect on her; she remained silent in groups and refused to explore any possible meaning of her symptoms in individual sessions. She frequently made scathing remarks to the behaviour therapist about psychotherapy and one difficulty in this case was to avoid entering into her hostility while, at the same time, maintaining her motivation towards desensitization. Thus for this patient, there was a conflict of therapies, and it could be argued that behaviour therapy interfered with psychotherapy by offering the patient an escape route from self-analysis.

Case 2. Mrs. B., aged 37, suffered from severe anxiety symptoms which developed whenever she got beyond 'safe' reach of a toilet. As a result she had been greatly incapacitated for 12 years and almost totally housebound for 6 years.

The problem in the treatment of this patient arose when she tried to relate the two forms of treatment. Psychotherapy in this case concentrated on her relationships with her mother and with her husband, both of which were seen as areas of conflict underlying her phobia. Initially she tried to relate these difficulties to the behaviour therapist's approach to her problem, but really failed to see the connection. Her solution was to keep the two issues separate, the aim of psychotherapy being to improve her relationships which she agreed were seriously impaired, whereas the behaviour therapy was tackling her phobic symptoms. This patient, therefore, entered into both treatments but saw them as concerning two separate problems, and in a sense allowed them to run in parallel. There was little apparent conflict between them after the initial stages of treatment.

Case 3. Mr. C., aged 23, had become increasingly unable to travel over two years prior to admission, first on foot, then by bus, finally by car, until on referral, he had been totally housebound for three months.

His case illustrates yet another problem; his progress in behaviour therapy was made very slow by the fact that most gains with desensitization received a temporary setback due to his anxiety level becoming too great. On several occasions, the increased anxiety was a direct result of factors in the psychotherapy situation, e.g. a change of therapist, and an abortive relationship with a female patient. This patient was for a long time unable to resolve the conflict between the two forms of treatment. He eventually came to the view that psychotherapy could help him to see why he was phobic, but that this realization would not necessarily mean the disappearance of his phobia, which could remain as a learned habit and which needed treatment by deconditioning.

Four important conclusions emerge from these three cases:

1. Whether or not there is much common ground between behaviour therapy and psychotherapy, these patients were much more aware of differences than of similarities.

2. If these two forms of treatment are combined, there can be interference between them to the detriment of either or both.

3. The relationship between the two forms of treatment needs to be defined clearly for the patient, and the solution arrived at by Mr. C. is one possible way of doing this.

4. Whether the combination produced better results in patients like these than either given alone can only be ascertained by a properly designed study.

SUMMARY

The various techniques which come under the heading of behaviour therapy have been shown to be successful in modifying a wide range of abnormal behaviour, especially simple phobias, socially disruptive behaviour in chronic psychotic patients, deviant sexual behaviour and some psychomotor disturbances. Behaviour therapy will probably remain as one possible treatment method in the total management of most psychiatric patients, since cases in which the behaviour amenable to behaviour therapy can be said to represent the patient's total problem are rare. It remains to be seen whether these techniques are applicable to the treatment of the large majority of psychiatric patients whose problems are usually more diffuse than in those conditions so far treated successfully by behaviour therapy.

REFERENCES

AYLLON, T. & AZRIN, N. H. (1968) *The Token Economy: A Motivational System for Therapy and Rehabilitation*, New York: Appleton-Century-Crofts.

AYLLON, T. & HAUGHTON, E. (1964) Modification of symptomatic verbal behaviour of mental patients. *Behaviour Research and Therapy*, **2**, 87–97.

BANCROFT, J. & MARKS, I. M. (1968) Electric aversion therapy of sexual deviations. *Proceedings of the Royal Society of Medicine*, **61**, 796–9.

BANDURA, A. (1968) Modelling approaches to the modification of phobic disorders. In *The Role of Learning in Psychotherapy*, edited by R. Porter. C.I.B.A. Foundation Symposium. London: Churchill.

BEECH, H. R. (1969) *Changing Man's Behaviour*. Penguin Books.

BOULOUGOURIS, J. C. & MARKS, I. M. (1969) Implosion (flooding)—a new treatment for phobias. *British Medical Journal*, **2**, 721–3.

BREGER, L. & McGAUGH, J. (1965) Critique and reformulation of 'learning theory' approaches to psychotherapy and neurosis. *Psychological Bulletin*, **63**, 338–58.

CAUTELA, J. R. (1967) Covert desensitization. *Psychological Reports*, **20**, 459–68.

COATES, S. (1964) Clinical psychology in sexual deviation. In *The Pathology and Treatment of Sexual Deviation*. Edited by Rosen, London.

EYSENCK, H. J. (1959) Learning theory and behaviour therapy. *Journal of Mental Science*, **105**, 61–75.

EYSENCK, H. J. (1963) Behaviour therapy, extinction and relapse in neurosis. *British Journal of Psychiatry*, **109**, 12–18.

EYSENCK, H. J. (1969) Behaviour therapy v. psychotherapy. *New Society*, 7 August, 208–10.

EYSENCK, H. J. & RACHMAN, S. (1965) *The Causes and Cures of Neurosis*. London: Routledge and Kegan Paul.

FELDMAN, M. P. & MacCULLOCH, M. J. (1965) The application of anticipatory avoidance learning to the treatment of homosexuality. 1. Theory, techniques, and preliminary results. *Behaviour Research and Therapy*, **2**, 165–83.

FRANKS, C. M. (1966) Conditioning and conditioned aversion therapies in the treatment of alcoholics. *International Journal of Addiction*, **1**, 62–98.

FRIEDMAN, D. (1966) A new technique for the systematic desensitization of phobic symptoms. *Behaviour Research and Therapy*, **4**, 139–140.

GELDER, M. G. & MARKS, I. M. (1966) Severe agoraphobia: A controlled prospective trial of behaviour therapy. *British Journal of Psychiatry*, **112**, 309–19.

ISAACS, W., THOMAS, J. & GOLDIAMOND, I. (1960) Application of operant conditioning to reinstate verbal behaviour in psychotics. *Journal of Speech and Hearing Disorders*, **25**, 8–12.

JONES, M. C. (1924) A laboratory study of fear; the case of Peter. *Pedagogical Seminary*, **31**, 308–15.

LINDSLEY, O. R. & SKINNER, B. F. (1954) A method for the experimental analysis of the behaviour of psychotic patients. *American Psychologist*, **9**, 419–20.

MacCULLOCH, M. J. & FELDMAN, M. P. (1967) Aversion therapy in the management of forty-three homosexuals. *British Medical Journal*, **2**, 594–7.

MARKS, I. M. (1969) *Fears and Phobias*. London: Heinemann.

MARKS, I. M. & GELDER, M. G. (1966) Common ground between behaviour therapy and psychodynamic models. *British Journal of Medical Psychology*, **39**, 11–23.

MEYER, V. & CHESSER, E. S. (1970) *Behaviour Therapy in Clinical Psychiatry*, Penguin Books.

MEYER, V. & CRISP, A. H. (1964) Aversion therapy in two cases of obesity. *Behaviour Research and Therapy*, **4**, 273–80.

MORGENSTERN, F. S., PEARCE, J. F. & REES, L. W. (1965) Predicting outcome of behaviour therapy by psychological tests. *Behaviour Research and Therapy*, **2**, 191–200.

PAUL, G. L. (1966) *Insight v Desensitization in Psychotherapy: An Experiment in Anxiety Reduction*. Stanford University Press.

RACHMAN, S. (1965) Studies in desensitization. 1: The separate effects of relaxation and desensitization. *Behaviour Research and Therapy*, **3**, 245–51.

RACHMAN, S. (1968) *Phobias, Their Nature and Control*. Springfield, Illinois: Charles C. Thomas.

RACHMAN, S. & EYSENCK, H. J. (1966) A reply to a 'critique and reformulation' of behaviour therapy. *Psychological Bulletin*, **65**, 165–9.

RACHMAN, S. & TEASDALE, J. (1969) *Aversion Therapy and the Behaviour Disorders: An Analysis*. London: Routledge and Kegan Paul.

WATSON, J. B. & RAYNOR, R. (1920) Conditioned emotional reaction. *Journal of Experimental Psychology*, **3**, 1–4.

WOLPE, J. (1958) *Psychotherapy by Reciprocal Inhibition*. Stanford University Press.

WOLPE, J. & LAZARUS, A. (1966) *Behaviour Therapy Techniques*. Oxford: Pergamon.

Chapter XIX

MENTAL HANDICAP

A. D. Forrest, B. Ritson and A. K. Zealley

INTRODUCTION

Just as there is no precise definition of Mental Illness (Szasz, 1961) so the rubric mental retardation embraces many different clinical syndromes and social problems. Central to the concept of mental retardation is the factor of limitation of intellectual capacity. In the years of infancy and early childhood more severe degrees of handicap are revealed in the delay in attaining the usual milestones, i.e. walking, continence, speech development. At school entry and during the succeeding years, children with lesser degrees of handicap are revealed either by formal psychological testing or by their inability to profit from the teaching in ordinary classes (at the present time an I.Q. of less than 75 is taken as indicating some degree of mental handicap). At the time of leaving school the ability to adjust to employment, to the social and sexual life of adolescence reveals a slightly different group of subjects with mental handicap; those who have in addition a degree of emotional instability. And finally in later adult life, subjects with handicap come to the attention of the hospital or social work services because the parents who have supported them over the years have themselves become ill or died.

There are many synonyms: retardation, subnormality, mental deficiency; none are entirely acceptable. Similarly the definitions given in the various Acts are all open to criticism. Perhaps the formulation in the 1927 Mental Deficiency Act is as satisfactory as any: 'A condition of arrested or incomplete development of mind existing before the age of 18 years whether resulting from inherent causes or induced by disease or injury'.

In the U.S.A., allegedly the spiritual home of the Intelligence Test, the *Criterion of Intelligence* has been widely employed in deciding whether a subject was suffering from mental retardation. Anne Clarke (1958) has critically reviewed the shortcomings of the I.Q. (Intelligence Quotient) as the criterion for diagnosing mental retardation: (1) the I.Q. and social competence are not perfectly related: (2) the I.Q. is not constant, i.e. test-retest differences; (3) the same I.Q. as measured by different tests may not mean the same thing. But she did point out that a considerable degree of intellectual subnormality as measured on reputable and appropriate I.Q. tests should be a *sine qua non* of certification as a mental defective.

The *Criterion of Educability* has formed an important theme in the development of provisions for the retarded. This is essentially an administrative problem: children in ordinary classes who could not profit from this education posed problems for themselves, their teachers and their classmates. The creation of special classes in ordinary schools and special schools has arisen to meet this need. But a large proportion of educational failures get work and adjust socially after their schooldays are over. We well remember a man of 42 with choreo-athetosis who could neither read nor write, was alleged to be defective, but has a large and very prosperous scrap business. He became depressed because of the attentions of the officers of the Inland Revenue.

The *Criterion of Social Competence* has been one much favoured in the U.K. (see Tredgold and Soddy, 1970). But social competence is only relative to the norms operating in that society at that particular time; this creates problems when society is changing at an accelerating rate or when, as now, the level of unemployment makes employability an unreliable criterion.

LEGISLATION

The important Acts were those of 1904, 1927 and 1959 (1960 in Scotland). The English Act of 1959 removed the categories idiot, imbecile and feeble-minded and replaced them with the categories of subnormality, severe subnormality and psychopathy. In the sense that the earlier terms, idiot, imbecile etc. were opprobrious, the new Act with its degrees of subnormality may seem like an advance, but in many ways the Mental Health Scotland Act (1960) is more consistent; it has only two general categories, mental illness and mental deficiency and does not attempt to delineate degrees of handicap. This Act also introduced informal admission (as did the English Act) which did much to accelerate the opening of the doors of hospitals for the mentally handicapped, e.g. for holiday admissions, brief admissions precipitated by crisis in the family etc.

ATTITUDES TO MENTAL RETARDATION

The 'Eugenics Scare' in the early years of this century was based on fears that the mentally handicapped were both more fertile and more promiscuous than the 'normal' population, thus leading in time to a progressive decline in the national intelligence and also that they contributed in a major way to the criminal statistics. As a result segregation became built into official policy in this country and in the U.S.A. both sterilization and segregation were introduced as appropriate remedies. As regards the first fears the evidence is critically reviewed by Penrose (1950) while the effect on the national intelligence is regarded as 'not proven' by the Scottish Council for Research in Education (1949). The contribution to crime by the mentally retarded is now regarded as marginal. Undoubtedly the relative shortage of available labour in World War II helped to alter administrative attitudes about the training and employing of handicapped persons both in the Army (Pioneer Corps) and in factories. Since then experimental work by psychologists such as Tizard and O'Connor (1952) has helped to encourage the development of industrial training units in hospitals and training centres in the community.

Family attitudes are thought by some authors (Tredgold and Soddy, 1970) to have been affected by the introduction of the National Health Service so that families now feel more inclined to think the State should take responsibility for a handicapped child. This view is not shared by the National Society for Mentally Handicapped Children and as at the time of writing about 70 per cent of mentally handicapped persons are in fact looked after primarily by their families, it would appear that family attitudes continue to be supportive and protective. However, the psychiatrist and other professionals must recognize the degree of ambivalence in the attitudes of parents to a handicapped child: there is usually some degree of very primitive guilt which may mar the relationship between the parents; sometimes the child is rejected but more often the mother displays what has been described as an 'angry solicitude'; this often leads to over-protectiveness and distortion of relationships with other chidren (or the decision not to have any other children). In this field the psychopathology of the parents is often more relevant than the psychological problems of the 'patient'.

STUDIES OF PREVALENCE

Epidemiological research is of value in helping those who plan services for the subnormal to ascertain the size of the problem, and by breaking down prevalence figures into clinical categories to determine the specific needs of individual groups within the community. Such research may also identify groups at special risk and suggest preventive measures. In most cases epidemiological research is conducted with a view to answering specific questions within a given community. Great care must be exercized in extrapolating findings from one part of the country to another. Even more care is needed when two different cultures are contrasted.

Many variables influence the ascertainment of subnormality. 'The first step in seeking to understand a health phenomenon is the study of its prevalence and distribution—a task not easy in the area of mental subnormality. In any community, estimates of the prevalence of this dysfunction may be affected by the manner in which the disability is defined, by the social conditions of life, by the levels of demand for organic and adaptive functioning that society makes on its members, by the amount and quality of the services that are available, by the age range considered and by the criteria of dysfunction that are utilized for identification of cases.' (Birch et al., 1970).

It is clear that the advent of universal education and literacy in a country will expose many cases of subnormality as the child's inability to cope with the demands of the educational system become apparent. Essentially, subnormality arises when an individual, because of limited intelligence, is unable to adapt to his environment. It may be assumed that the advancing complexity of society will place increasing numbers within the category of relative mental handicap.

Although intelligence tests are of limited value in the clinical assessment of an individual case, they are of undoubted use to the community physician in assessing the prevalence of subnormality. Most studies based on such tests suggest that some degree of subnormality occurs in two to three per cent of the total population (Stevens and Heber, 1964). Many of those who, on psychometric grounds, are subnormal do not make any demands on the services for the subnormal and are educated within the ordinary school system. The proportion of children who are so concealed diminishes with advancing age until 14 when the majority of subnormals who are going to be recognized have been ascertained. Thereafter the prevalence declines with advancing age. Kushlick (1965) uses this finding to conclude that the 'administrative prevalence' assessed at 15 to 19 is a reliable measure of the true prevalence of subnormality.

This phenomenon has been observed in many prevalence studies. Lewis (1929) found that 1.2 per 1000 of the population below 4 years of age were subnormal in contrast to 25.6 per 1000 amongst those aged 10 to 14 years. Gruneberg (1964) has detected this pattern in reports from Britain, Sweden, Norway, U.S.A. and Formosa and concludes that the apparent resorption of these patients into the community after 14 is the most remarkable finding from these surveys. He comments: 'Either these individuals are continuing to be extremely handicapped in later life and are unknown because the services they need are unavailable . . . or they have stopped being retarded in any 'real' sense at all and do not need any special protection, help or services.' This area clearly requires closer study.

DISTRIBUTION OF INTELLIGENCE

Intelligence tests have been devised on the assumption that intelligence is normally distributed in the population. A predictable number of people will be found at either extreme of the Gaussian distribution— those at one extreme being highly intelligent and those at the other 'subnormals'. Some subnormals cannot be contained under this 'Gaussian umbrella' but appear as a bulge at the extreme end of the curve. There are a larger number of individuals whose abilities are more than 3 or 4 standard deviations below the mean than chance alone could explain.

Estimates of the relative prevalence of severe to moderate to mild subnormality are given as 1:4:15 (O'Connor and Tizard, 1956). Severe subnormals are those with I.Q. below 30 (previously known as idiots), moderate below 50 (imbeciles), mild below 75 (feeble-minded). Several studies in Britain have shown that the prevalence of patients with I.Q. of less than 50 is surprisingly consistent 3.7 per 1000 of the population (Lewis, 1929; Kushlick, 1964; Innes *et al.*, 1968).

As discussed above the size of this severely subnormal group cannot be attributed to chance alone. They differ from other subnormals in characteristics other than intelligence. This group has a high incidence of associated neurological and psychiatric abnormalities. This group contains many of those subnormals whose deficiency may be attributed to genetic pathology, obstetric or peri-natal injury (Passamanick *et al.*, 1955). Drillien (1961) showed that small premature babies (i.e. 4½ lbs or less) were significantly more likely to be ineducable in normal school by the age of five.

This *'pathological group'* presents a particular challenge to the health services as they are more likely to come within the purview of medical care in the future than are milder forms of subnormality.

Kushlick (1965) describes the residential requirements for the severely subnormal as being approximately 23 residential places per catchment area of 100,000 for children, plus accommodation for 77 severely subnormal adults in the same area. If the severely subnormal children lived in family units of 10 as he suggests, then the distribution within a typical residence would be 1 pre-school child, 3 aged 5 to 9, 5 aged 10 to 14 and 1 aged 15. Of these 10 children 'there would be 3 who were incontinent and bedfast: of the remainder 3 would be continent and present no major problem, 2 would present the difficulty of incontinence only and 2 would present at least two major behaviour problems —1 of these would also be incontinent.' Kushlick's study is a good demonstration of application of epidemiology to detailed planning of care.

SOCIAL CLASS

The prevalence of subnormality is lowest in the professional and managerial classes and becomes increasingly frequent as occupational skill and status declines (Birch *et al.*, 1970). The prevalence in Social Class V is nine times higher than in Social Classes I and II. This dramatic social class gradient does not obtain for patients with I.Q.

below 50—that is, those who would be found in the 'pathological group' described above.

Birch *et al.* (1970) analysed the distribution of mental subnormality in Aberdeen and made it clear that once this pathological group has been excluded, lesser degrees of subnormality are not simply related to Social Class V, but to a subculture within that class. They identify this subculture 'with low status and aspirations, minimal education, poverty, family disorganization, and unwillingness or inability to plan the major economic and marital aspects of their lives.' The intricate interplay of genetic, physical and environmental factors which give rise to this situation is only partially understood but the existence of this subculture shows the administrator where preventive and treatment services will be most needed.

Goodman and Tizard (1962) confirmed Lewis' (1929) observation that the incidence of subnormality is higher in rural areas. This may reflect a selective drift of more skilled people towards the towns during this century.

Subnormality is somewhat more common in males. Innes *et al.* (1968) found a male/female ratio for high grade patients of 1.24 to 1. Amongst medium or low grade the ratio was similar (1.28 to 1). In their study of the demographic characteristics of mental subnormality in northeast Scotland these authors comment on the regularity with which a family history of subnormality (17 per cent) or psychiatric disorder (4 per cent) was found amongst subnormal patients.

The Diagnosis of Mental Handicap

Mental retardation is, of course, a *symptom* and does not constitute a clinical entity in itself. A single visit to a hospital for the retarded at once impresses on one the lack of homogeneity of the residents; they simply share, to a varying degree, the common denominator of deficient intellect and social competence.

While it is useful to consider causes of retardation in categories linked to stages of development of the growing person (prior to conception, prenatal, perinatal and postnatal), it must be stressed that the aetiology and pathology of the defect in the bulk of patients is unknown. Especially is this the case when patients with the least handicap are considered. If the defect is mild, there may be little evidence of it until school attendance begins: here, difficulty in retention and recall, with resultant impairment of acquisition of knowledge, may become apparent for the first time.

In many instances, the first suggestion that mental development is not going ahead normally may be given by delays—or indeed failures—

in the appearance of mobility, bladder and bowel control, language and capacity for relating with peer groups. It is worth mentioning that a diagnosis of mental retardation which is made at a very early age may be wrong; and caution is indicated in applying the diagnosis.

Some of the early pointers to possibly severe handicap include the existence of sundry skull anomalies such as hydrocephalus, asymmetry, abnormality in the shape of the nose, the ears, the jaw, the teeth and the palate.

Often, however, examination of the patient reveals no such characteristics, and recourse must be had to the *history*. And, in this context, information may not always be as readily forthcoming from anxious (and even ashamed) parents as it may be from the family doctor, a Health Visitor, the schoolteacher and the school psychologist. Parents will often have put out of their minds data and observations suggestive of delayed journeys past 'milestones'; or they may be reluctant to disclose such inklings as they have, lest the doctor seizes on their information and the child gets 'put away'. For similar reasons, the existence of other family members who were or are retarded may not be mentioned, and dependence may have to be placed on eliciting specific information about relatives' job records and so forth. It will always be relevant to enquire after the mother's age and health during the relevant pregnancy, and to evaluate the possibility of hypoxia or other birth trauma which may have occurred.

In the older child or teenager, it may sometimes be involvement in some petty criminal activity which first leads to the clear identification of mental retardation. In such cases, it appears to be sometimes a wish to gain recognition from the peer group which leads the patient into delinquent behaviour and the courts.

In establishing the existence of retardation, use is very commonly made of mental tests. These owe their origin to the French psychologist Alfred Binet—a member of a commission set up to look into methods of identifying people who were, and who were not normally educable: this was in Paris in 1904. The test he devised underwent many revisions, such as the inclusion of age standards; modifications were made by Terman who, at Stanford University in 1916, developed the concept of the Intelligence Quotient (I.Q.). This abstraction divides the person's assessed 'mental age' by his actual age (and multiplies the result by 100); and, in the 1937 revision of the Stanford-Binet test, the assumption was made that complete development of innate intelligence has been reached by the age of 15 years.

In comparison with the Stanford-Binet test of intelligence, the Wechsler Adult Intelligence Scale (WAIS) was devised for adults, not children. It provides sub-scores for 'verbal' intelligence (information, comprehension, arithmetic, etc.) and for 'performance' intelligence (assessed by digit symbol and block design tasks, and picture completion and arrangement).

Caution must, however, be exercised in the interpretation of I.Q. scores; many tests were standardized on unusual 'normal' groups (this is true of the revised Stanford-Binet, in which the average 15-year-old returns an I.Q. of 87 because of standardization on a group of above-average intelligence). Further, there is far from perfect association between I.Q. and social competence (Gunzberg, 1968), and there are many whose I.Q. is less than, say, 70 who are nevertheless quite able to fend for themsleves; conversely, many people scoring about this figure may be unable to benefit from conventional education, to keep employment or to refrain from socially unacceptable behaviour. From this is can be inferred that, while an I.Q. score above the average (i.e. better than the 50th percentile) precludes existence of intellectual deficit, some behavioural abnormality must be identified in the poorer I.Q. scorer before the label of mental retardation is invoked. The type of behaviour problem is commonly lack of perseverance at tasks, small initiative, poor tolerance of frustration, sexual problems of a broadly deviant nature, impulsiveness, instability of mood and inappropriateness in social contacts. As will be noted, many of these characteristics are similar to those associated with immature or psychopathic personalities in the intellectually normal person.

AETIOLOGICAL FACTORS IN MENTAL HANDICAP

FACTORS ACTING PRIOR TO CONCEPTION

Genetic determinants of mental retardation in the offspring of a subject may be of single or multifactorial gene, or of chromosomal type. Amongst the latter, much the commonest in clinical practice is Down's Syndrome (syn. Mongolism, Langdon Down Syndrome, trisomy-21 anomaly). In 1959, Lejeune et al., published the first description of the chromosomal abnormality in mongolism—they identified an extra chromosome at the 21 to 22 group of the Denver scale; at that time, distinction between 21 and 22 was technically not really possible, and it now seems probable that most mongols born to older mothers have, in fact, an extra chromosome number 22. Other types of chromosomal anomaly have since been reported in clinical mongolism, including translocation mongolism, and mosaicism. Recently, tandem translocation of two number 21 chromosomes was reported (Sachdeva et al., 1971).

The aetiology of Down's Syndrome appears to relate to non-disjunction in the usual trisomy cases; this failure seems to result from natural ageing, hence the much greater incidence of mongolian births in mothers aged, say, 45 years in whom the incidence is 13 times that in all live births (1 in 54 compared to 1 in 700). Mongols constitute between 5 and 10 per cent of all identified defectives—the commonest identifiable cause of retardation.

Clinically, these patients tend to have small round heads, with relatively close-set eyes which have oblique palpebral fissures and often an epicanthic fold—these eye signs being reminiscent of the Mongolian race, hence the original clinical name (Langdon Down, 1866). Opacities of the lens of the eye are common, as are squints in younger cases. A depressed bridge to a short nose is characteristic, as are small—and sometimes misshapen—ears. The skin over the square, clumsy hands is often rough, with hyperextensible thumb joints. Indeed, hypotonia in general is usual, and an umbilical hernia often tops a pot-belly.

Both male and female mongols are commonly poorly developed sexually, and hypofunction of other endocrine glands may occur—thyroid, adrenal and pituitary. About half of all mongols have congenital heart defects, many cases dying in infancy on this account (Penrose and Smith, 1966).

While often described as cheerful and musical people, this may perhaps be more true of those who do not enter long-term institutional care; in the latter context, they may often be mischievous and destructive—features which doubtless predispose to hospital as against domiciliary management. In fact, Tizard and Grad (1961) confirmed certain earlier authors' findings that mongols form a far from homogeneous population in terms of personality attributes. Physical resemblance to one another has yet to be shown to be accompanied by personality similarities (Clarke and Clarke, 1965).

Diagnosis, sometimes hard in early infancy in the past, can now readily be confirmed by chromosome studies.

The prognosis is poor if severe cardiac defects exist, but mongols no longer die of respiratory infections as they often used to do. Childhood leukaemia and mongolism are associated in a proportion of cases (Stewart, 1961).

Other chromosomal anomalies associated with retardation are rare, and include trisomy 13–15, trisomy 16–18 and the 'Cri du Chat' syndrome—the latter first described in 1963 (Lejeune et al.), and characterized by a kitten-like cry, hypertelorism, small jaw and severe mental handicap; loss of part of chromosome number five is found in this condition. The rarity of these cases must be stressed.

Of the sex chromosome abnormalities sometimes associated with retardation, Klinefelter's Syndrome (karyotype XXY, sometimes XXXY or XXXXY or XXYY) is one of only two which are at all common; and only about a quarter of cases are mentally retarded.

It occurs in men only, often tall, with gynaecomastia and small under-developed testes and limited sexual drive.

Turner's Syndrome (Karyotype XO) is due to non-disjunction and occurs only in women, who are usually short and have a webbed neck and cubitus valgus. There is primary amenorrhoea, and malformation of the aorta may be present. However, mental retardation is not common, and treatment with oestrogens can be undertaken.

Cretinism (Congenital Hypothyroidism)

Maternal iodine deficiency is the cause of this determinant of retardation in areas where endemic goitre is prevalent; the latter is no longer to be found in Britain: certain areas of Tibet, Nepal and the Congo are still prone to endemic goitre, and in such situations the goitrous thyroid fails to manufacture thyroid hormone. In sporadic cretinism, there may be entire absence of the thyroid, or there may be a genetically determined enzyme defect with consequent failure to synthesize thyroxine adequately or even at all. In these latter instances, the gland retains its ability to respond to thyroid-stimulating hormone (TSH).

Clinically, there may be little abnormality evident at birth, but within months it becomes apparent that the child is not developing at the normal rate and has sluggish responses to stimulation. The skin is dry and wrinkled, with puffy face, and extremities. Feeding problems are common, and the tongue seems too big for the mouth. Confirmation of the diagnosis is by serum protein-bound iodine (P.B.I.) determination, which may give a result as low as 1 or 2 micrograms per 100 millilitres when thyroid function is negligible. After the age of two years, serum cholesterol is elevated, and diagnosis may also be aided by X-ray studies of bones: these may show absence of epiphyseal centres where no thyroid activity is present at all, or delay in ossification. Treatment must obviously be started at as early an age as possible, using L-thyroxine orally. The dose may be gradually increased over a period of weeks, until evidence of overdose is found—for example, the reversal of the previously sluggish bowel activity to a state of diarrhoea. This substitution hormone therapy must be continued for life, a fact which must be borne in upon the relatives.

Other Pre-Natal Determinants of Retardation

While it can be assumed that many—as yet poorly understood—influences may operate detrimentally to the foetus in utero, and that these account for perhaps the majority of cases of retardation, certain other factors can be identified. These include: (1) infections of the mother; (2) intoxications of the foetus; (3) maternal malnutrition; (4) peri-natal insults.

1. *Maternal Infections*

Rubella. About one-fifth of young women have no acquired immunity to rubella (German measles), and contact by such women with an infectious case during the first trimester is associated with a one-in-ten risk of the 'rubella syndrome' in the baby. This comprises usually severe retardation, and often deafness, cataracts and cardiac abnormalities, patent ductus arteriosus being commonest. It is contact at the *end* of this first trimester that is most likely to be associated with birth of an affected child; and the viral infection probably causes non-specific damage to cerebral tissue (Dudgeon, 1967).

It is now possible to identify by blood test those young women who do not possess antibodies to the rubella virus, and active immunisation can be provided. Programmes for whole community determination of 'at risk' girls and women are operating in Britain and elsewhere, with immunization offered to the 20 per cent usually found to possess no natural immunity. In this way, therapeutic termination of pregnancy for pregnant women in contact with rubella may become a rarity (and, in any event, would only now be undertaken if serological tests suggested that a real risk existed.)

Syphilis. Becoming much rarer than some decades ago, congenital syphilis derives from maternal infection, and is characterized by abnormalities of the pupil, skin and mucous membrane eruptions and enlargement of liver and spleen, as well as retardation. In 'the second decade' features such as saddle-bridge nose, frontal bossing, interstitial keratitis and Hutchinson's teeth may appear, with other signs of juvenile neurosyphilis.

Early treatment of the pregnant mother will usually prevent affection of the foetus, hence the continuing importance of serological tests for syphilis early in all pregnancies.

Cytomegalic Inclusion Body Disease. This viral disease is of small clinical importance to the adult, but can cause severe cerebral damage if acquired by the foetus in utero, when meningoencephalitis occurs. No typical clinical features are present in the retarded child so affected, other than purpura, jaundice, anaemia and enlargement of liver and spleen. Inclusion bodies are found in the urine, cerebrospinal fluid and other tissues.

Toxoplasmosis. This is an uncommon cause of retardation in Britain, though infection at about the sixteenth week in utero may cause the cerebral damage. Affected infants show numerous eye signs, such as choroido-retinitis, and hydrocephalus is common. Epilepsy is often associated.

2. *Intoxications of the Foetus*

Kernicterus. Severe jaundice in the newborn may cause bilirubin encephalopathy, or kernicterus. It is due to inadequate glucuronide formation on account of reduced liver glucuronyl transferase. The latter is the enzyme responsible for conjugating bilirubin. The disorder is commonly due to rhesus incompatibility between the foetus and the mother, occasionally due to ABO group incompatibilities.

Late effects incluse deafness, choreoathetosis and retardation.

Other Encephalopathies. These include those associated with lead and carbon monoxide; or following on post-vaccinal encephalitis.

Maternal Toxaemia. Pre-eclamptic toxaemia predisposes both to foetal hypoxia due to placental damage and to premature delivery, and is thus liable to be followed by the birth of a retarded child, assuming it survives.

3. *Maternal Malnutrition*

It is unlikely that this, *per se*, is a significant cause of retardation, but undernutrition in infancy has been shown to be associated with normal *physical* development during school years but subnormal mental ability.

4. *Peri-Natal Insults*

Like the last-mentioned factor, this tends to be associated with poor social conditions; and the differential contributions of such conditions and other features such as prematurity are hard to determine. Prematurity may be associated with birth injury, and many spastic children have an abnormal delivery, or delayed or precipitate parturition. It would seem that these insults to the infant, in common with peri-natal hypoxia, are almost certainly responsible for some proportion of subsequent mental retardation.

Pre-natal influences conducive of later defect include those which cause microcephaly (head circumference less than 43 cm) and 'odd-shaped' heads—flat occiput, low forehead-hairline, corrugated scalp, receding forehead and chin, etc. The nature of these influences remains unknown.

METABOLIC CAUSES OF RETARDATION

A vast number of specific syndromes have been elucidated in the past few years, associating retardation with abnormal lipid, carbohydrate and protein metabolism. It must be emphasized that all of these are rare, and account for few only of the residents in deficiency hospitals. If, however, they are recognized early, appropriate dietary manipulation may minimize the extent of the defect that accompanies them.

Lipid Metabolism

The forms of these rare lipidoses include (1) that caused by a single recessive gene, Tay-Sach's disease (amaurotic family idiocy); (2) Niemann-Pick's disease, probably of recessive genetic inheritance, and involving anomalous storage of sphingomyelin in the brain and elsewhere; (3) Gaucher's disease, due either to an autosomal recessive gene or to incomplete penetrance of a dominant gene, in which the infantile form is characterized by neuronal degenerative changes with deposition of kerasin (a cerebroside) in the nervous system; the prognosis of this infantile form is a few months of life only; and (4) metachromatic leucodystrophy (Schilder's disease) in which the white matter of the brain is chiefly affected, and 'dysmyelination' may be found; there are numerous familial forms of the leucodystrophies, and they are all fatal by the age of six years.

Carbohydrate Metabolism

Galactosaemia. Failure to metabolize galactose in the normal way is probably inherited as an autosomal recessive trait. There is deficiency in galactose-1-phosphate uridyl transferase. Galactose-1-phosphate accumulates in cells, and the newborn infant—initially apparently well—develops gastrointestinal disturbance. Liver enlargement, cataracts and mental defect all appear.

Early establishment of the diagnosis, by galactose tolerance testing, should lead to exclusion of lactose from the diet. Cerebral damage can thus be minimized.

Glycogenosis. In this rare disorder, glycogen is deposited in neuronal tissue; it is not always associated with mental retardation. Liver enlargement and fasting hypoglycaemia suggest the diagnosis.

Other disorders of carbohydrate metabolism associated with retardation are also rare, and include fructose intolerance (seldom associated with more than mild retardation) and lipochondrodystrophy (Hurler's disease, gargoylism).

Protein Metabolism

The aminoacidurias which have now been separately identified are numerous, though only a few are at all common. Their discovery is owed to the technique of chromatography. The reasons for the excretion of certain aminoacids in the urine include inherited errors of their metabolism, renal tubular damage, and other conditions (e.g. hepatolenticular degeneration) to which aminoaciduria is secondary.

The disorders are all rare, but their identification worthwhile insofar as certain of them may be controlled—from the point of view of cerebral damage—by dietary adjustment.

Only the commonest type will be described in any detail.

Phenylketonuria. This disorder was reported first in 1934. Its recognition at birth may permit proper dietary measures to be adopted which will prevent the development of mental retardation.

It is inherited as an autosomal recessive character, with each parent being a heterozygote carrier. Thus, a quarter of their children will have the disorder, a quarter will be healthy non-carriers, and a half will be carriers. Incidence figures vary in different countries—about 1 in 50,000 in Great Britain (Penrose, 1963) and 1 in 25,000 births in the United States (Kolb, 1968). The carrier state can be detected by the phenylalanine tolerance test.

L-phenylalanine hydroxylase or an associated enzyme is lacking in the liver of patients with phenylketonuria. As a result, abnormal amounts of phenylalanine and its derivatives are excreted in the urine which has a characteristic musty smell; excretion of these substances does not begin until after the first week or so of life. Diagnosis cannot rest solely on elevated blood levels of phenylalanine, as some infants without the disorder may have increased levels: urine tests must also be done.

Clinically, retardation is evident in the first year of life, and it is likely that all damage is done to cerebral tissue by the third birthday. Patients characteristically have fair hair and blue eyes, epilepsy may be associated, and sundry skin disorders (eczema, dermatitis, etc.) may be found. The gait may be abnormal, with some flexion of spine, knees and hips in the posture. The extent of intellectual deficit is variable, and commonly quite severe, though some cases with a normal I.Q. have been noted.

In treatment, crucial in infancy, the blood level of phenylalanine should be kept below 10 mg per 100 ml. Dietary regimes using commercial preparations of aminoacids have been reported (Koch *et al.*, 1963), but it is still unclear for how long these regimes must be maintained to minimize retardation.

Other aminoacidurias are even rarer, and include Maple Syrup Urine Disease (Menkes *et al.*, 1954)—otherwise known as branched chain aminoaciduria; cystothioninuria; citrullinuria; histidinuria; arginosuccinuria, and many others. All are inherited, probably as autosomal recessives, and are diagnosed by chromatography: all are associated with varying degrees of mental retardation.

ABNORMALITIES DUE TO DOMINANT GENES

Epiloia (Tuberous Sclerosis)

This disorder is transmitted by a dominant gene with reduced penetrance. Many cases have no family history of the disorder, and may be due to mutation. A butterfly-shaped rash on nose, cheeks, chin and forehead occurs, which may be mistaken for sebaceous adenomas, but in fact consist of hyperblastic connective and vascular tissue. This rash usually first appears in childhood, sometimes later; and epilepsy is associated with the accompanying mental retardation which is commonly severe. There is no specific treatment, the epilepsy usually being controllable along conventional lines.

Neurofibromatosis (von Recklinghausen's Disease)

This disorder has a similar inheritance to epiloia, and is characterized by cafe-au-lait patches and pink cutaneous fibromas. Only a small proportion (about 10 per cent) of cases are mentally retarded.

The Sturge-Weber Syndrome (Naevoid Defect)

Inheritance has been thought to be as a Mendelian dominant, but its familial basis is not now certain. The typical unilateral 'port-wine stain' (cutaneous angioma) in the distribution of the trigeminal nerve is found, and—because of angiomatosis of the meninges—both cerebral damage and mental retardation are often associated. Treatment by hemispherectomy has been proposed (Falconer and Rushworth, 1960).

CHILDHOOD PSYCHOSIS

Early childhood autism is a form of childhood psychosis (Wing, 1970). The term describes a sort of behaviour pattern, characterized by a 'profound withdrawal from contact with people, an obsessive desire for the preservation of sameness, a skilful and even affectionate relationship to objects, the retention of an intelligent and pensive physiognomy; and mutism—or the kind of language which does not seem intended to serve interpersonal communication' (Kanner, 1943, 1949).

A recent international study group agreed the following points regarding the disorder (Rutter, 1970).

1. Early childhood autism begins from birth or within the first three years of life.

2. It is not a form of schizophrenia.

3. The basic handicaps of early childhood autism are produced by organic, not emotional, pathology. They are not caused by the personalities of the parents, nor by their child-rearing practices.

4. Problems of comprehension and use of language are important aspects of early childhood autism.

It has been shown that the syndrome may occur in children of *any* level of intelligence, from above average to severely subnormal. In one British survey of 8 to 10 year-olds, and identifying children with some or all of the features of autism, irrespective of the coexistence of neurological disorders, a prevalence of 4.5 per 10,000 was found; of these, it was considered that about half had the 'typical' syndrome (the 'nuclear' group) and 70 per cent had an I.Q. below 55. Almost a third of these children had evidence suggestive of neurological abnormalities (Wing *et al.*, 1967). Two-thirds had some speech by the age of 8 to 10 years. In the 'nuclear' group, boys outnumbered girls by 2.75 to 1—a trend found by earlier authors also. Both parents had higher I.Qs. than average, with higher occupational levels.

Much work has been done in the past decade in the field of autism, and it is probable that difficulties in comprehension and interpretation of sensory input are fundamental facets; when aligned with grossly impaired development of verbal and non-verbal language, the *behavioural* manifestations may become more comprehensible.

The diagnosis is seldom made prior to the age of two years, though mothers may 'feel' there is something amiss before this age. From this time on, however, the observable handicaps, and consequent behaviour disturbance, become evident. The handicaps include abnormal response to sounds, such response often being paradoxical—e.g. the ignoring of loud sounds, or prolonged attention to one particular sound; the child takes no interest in being talked to, almost certainly because of failure to understand the spoken word: there is sometimes abnormality in the use of speech, such as echolalia (immediate *or* delayed), invented phrases and word-sound confusion or distortion; the use of proximal senses, in the way children with impaired sight or blindness may do—touching, moving, tasting and smelling objects and people; and curious movements of the hands near the face, often with spinning or flapping movements when excited.

The secondary behaviour problems include particularly an apparent aloofness and indifference in their contact with people, very probably due to failure to understand what is said to them or to be able to volunteer meaning in words themselves. An obsessive adherence to routines and wish for sameness is also especially characteristic, and much distress is evinced if a different method of doing things is forced upon the child. Bizarre fears of objects or situations are often found, and great unhappiness may be manifested by persistent crying in an ordinarily peaceful setting which, however, to the patient is incomprehensible. At times they may be self-mutilating, by scratching or biting themselves.

Treatment by skilled education, utilizing those senses most readily acceptable to the patient, is the present best hope that can be offered for these children (Schopler and Reichler, 1970). Behaviour modification through operant conditioning appears also to offer some therapeutic hope (Lovaas, 1966).

EPILEPSY (AND MENTAL RETARDATION)

The disorders, of which the various clinical (and sub-clinical) forms of epilepsy are, of course, like retardation, merely a symptom, are liable

Q

at times to be associated with certain psychiatric disorders; affective, schizophreniform, personality anomalies, and so forth. The concept of the 'epileptic personality' is now largely discounted, and, as Stores (1971) reminds one, attention has recently been drawn to the iatrogenic effect on personality and cognitive function of anti-convulsant drugs themselves (Reynolds, 1970).

Many historical persons of undoubtedly high intellect have suffered from epilepsy, a fact contained in Wallin's (1917) summary that 'epilepsy is compatible with all levels of intelligence from genius to idiocy'. In recent decades, there has been a tendency for authors to suggest that a progressive dementia is the norm in epilepsy; it is probable that such conclusions are based on faulty methodology, and especially sampling, in assessing intelligence in the epileptic.

Numerous disorders associated with retardation—such as phenylketo-nuria—often coexist with epilepsy. Temporal lobe lesions may cause quite specific cognitive deficits, depending upon whether the dominant or the non-dominant hemisphere is involved. Thus, there may be defects of learning, especially of retention, and also of memory in such lesions. The situation is, however, still not clarified—and, for example, it has been suggested that *slow* presentation of material to be learned may facilitate the process.

Centrencephalic epilepsy on the other hand may be associated with impaired attention, probably related to abnormal functioning of subcortical tissues of a more or less permanent nature. It has also been suggested that children with this type of epilepsy may have disorders of perception and visuomotor function, either of which could affect learning and hence scores on I.Q. tests (Fedio and Mirsky, 1969).

It has been found that, if status epilepticus can be avoided and if there is no history of acute cerebral insult, no intellectual impairment may be discovered—and to this extent, cognitive deficit may be a preventable function of epilepsy (Ounsted *et al.*, 1966).

DEVELOPMENT OF CARE PROVISION IN THE HOSPITAL

The past decade has seen a shift of emphasis in Society's response to the mentally handicapped, away from institutional care towards community care. Services for the mentally handicapped are under-going a critical re-examination at present. The following discussion will principally be concerned with management of mental handicap in Britain. In countries which are developing services where no formal system of care had previously existed, our particular problems will not arise, and it is to be hoped that they will be able to develop a programme which strengthens existing provisions already in the community and avoids weakening inherent coping mechanisms within that culture.

In many less developed countries the handicapped receive acceptance and understanding in a home environment which more institutionalized services cannot capture. The experience of Britain and some other countries makes it clear that there is no place for large custodial institutions, though we believe there is an important place for hospitals which offer specific treatment/training programmes.

The majority of mentally handicapped have always been cared for at home. In the first half of this century those who could not, for various physical or more often social reasons, be cared for at home, were admitted to hospitals. These hospitals were usually large and situated outside of towns, often far from the patients' homes and relatives. In most cases it was assumed that admission would be for a long time—most often life. The 'less handicapped' patients worked in the hospital farm or helped the staff, looking after the severely handicapped. In many respects the hospital became a self-supporting community cut off from the outside world. An essentially care-taker, rather than a therapeutic, attitude prevailed and it seemed that the enthusiasm which teachers and psychologists of the 19th century showed in teaching skills to the mentally handicapped had been lost.

Until the inception of the National Health Service most of these hospitals were the responsibility of local authorities. Following this the National Health Service took over these hospitals while local authorities retained responsibility for those mentally handicapped subjects who remained in the community. In 1959 the Mental Health Act laid a duty on local authorities to provide a full range of community services for the mentally handicapped, including residential accommodation. Although the Act pointed the direction for future developments, it is only recently that the majority of local authorities have felt able to accept this responsibility and a shift towards community care has occurred. Many hospitalized patients require accommodation and support rather than intensive treatment.

A basic assumption underlying the present view of services is that the mentally handicapped have as much right as any other individual to the existing social and medical resources of the community. In most cases they will be able to utilize these normal provisions of the welfare state, but a smaller number will need, at one time or another, or throughout their lives, specialist services by reason of their handicap. The following outline will be concerned principally with the psychiatrist's role in the provision of these services. He will clearly require to know the full range of social and educational services available in his area if he is to make an effective contribution to a comprehensive plan for the care of the mentally handicapped. In this respect the psychiatrist will be a member of a team comprising not only hospital workers but also educationalists, psychologists, social workers, employment officers, nurses, speech therapists, physiotherapists, architects, general practitioners and other medical specialists. Such leadership as the psychiatrist can aspire to will be based on sapiential authority.

COORDINATION OF SERVICES

It is clear that the provisions for mentally handicapped patients, both in hospital and in the community, will involve a wide range of administrative, professional, voluntary and political groups. In each area there must be a coordinating committee* at which representatives of those concerned with the subnormal may meet and develop a system of care for their community.

HOSPITAL CARE

It is hoped that the need for treatment and care in hospitals for the mentally handicapped will be greatly diminished. At present the psychiatrist will often be confronted with the task of helping a large institution to change. As a first step he should ascertain the nature of the current inpatient population. He will find that many patients of high or medium grade ability can return to the community. This can only be achieved with the aid of social workers and community nurses who will pave the way for the patient's re-entry into the community and provide continuing support for him and those around him as he adapts to his new surroundings. There will be some who, despite considerable ability, will, in view of their age and degree of dependence on the institution, be unable to function outside the hospital. It is to be hoped that this group will not be added to in the future. At least such patients could hope to lead a more stimulating and dignified life in hospital by the provision of smaller and more home-like surroundings. Small changes, such as the provision of individual lockers and individually chosen and fitted clothes, often effect a transformation of outlook and morale. Overcrowding and understaffing must be overcome if the staff are to become therapeutic rather than custodial. Even allowing for the lack of staff it is essential to coordinate existing resources with regular staff meetings so that a coherent plan can be evolved that makes full use of the potential available. Volunteers can also be integrated into the programme. The relative proportion of older and more severely handicapped patients in hospitals is increasing and this is at present putting a greater burden on staff.

The nurses have a crucial role as agents of change in the institution. During a time of change and often under public criticism, the nurses must be clear about their therapeutic task in the hospital—there

---

*Such a Committee exists in some areas already, e.g. Edinburgh.

must be regular ward meetings of medical, nursing, social work and other treatment staff to develop a clear concept of the function of each individual ward and the way that it fits into the overall structure for that particular hospital, as it becomes more involved in treatment and outward looking. Even severely subnormal patients can learn to participate in organizing the ward. Emphasis should be placed on the learning of socially useful techniques. Apparent slowness or dullness will sometimes prove to have been drug-induced and the medication of patients in an institution should be reviewed regularly. The disadvantages of anti-convulsants for the severely retarded often outweigh the small reduction in fits achieved. Patients will often be found receiving large doses of drugs for behaviour disorders which could better be treated by exploring the reason for the behaviour than by prescribing tranquillizers. Boredom and overcrowding are probably two of the most potent factors in causing such disturbed behaviour. Psychotic depression and schizophrenia can be found in subnormal patients and they respond to conventional methods of treatment for these conditions. A number of patients suffering from the late results of childhood psychosis will be found in most hospitals. Their treatment was discussed earlier.

In addition to nursing care, the ward regime should be aimed at improving the patient's capacity to control his environment. Learning should be geared to socially useful tasks such as dressing, eating tidily, telling the time, travelling on buses, crossing the road, etc. It is important that the nurses' involvement with social training is integrated within the broader framework of each patient's individual learning programme. Even the most severely subnormal responds to incentives. Some wards are now organized on an operant conditioning model with visible rewards for socially desirable behaviour. The reward takes the form of tokens or money which can be used to obtain further privileges. Patients respond to a competitive situation in which they can match their achievements against those of their peers.

The hospital should provide a wide range of activities aimed at stimulating the patient to learn and particularly to help him derive satisfaction from work and human relationships. It is essential to avoid neglecting emotional growth by too great an emphasis on becoming proficient at mechanical tasks, though conversely it must be realized that acquisition of even a simple skill greatly enhances confidence and selfesteem, and may contribute to easier patient-care.

Occupational Therapy

This should be provided to help the patient express himself and become competent in satisfying skills such as cooking, painting and pottery. The Occupational Therapist also has an important part to play in assessing the capabilities of new patients.

Industrial Therapy

In addition to the sheltered workshops in the community, most hospitals offer some form of sheltered employment. These workshops should use modern factory techniques otherwise their skills, when learned, will have no market value. It has been shown that patients work best when there are clear incentives such as graded payment and achievement is clearly shown on simple charts. Fear about injury due to working with complex machinery is often exaggerated, and, apart from epileptic patients, no more than ordinary factory safety precautions need be adopted.

Physiotherapy

This forms an essential part of the treatment services. All new patients should be assessed by a physiotherapist who will often be able to help the patient overcome faults in his gait and posture. In addition to this she will help the brain-damaged spastic child to overcome his defects. It is essential that severely subnormal children learn to walk early before their increasing body weight makes the task more difficult. Assessment by the physiotherapist must be made early if full benefit is to be achieved.

The subnormality hospital will also require help from psychologists, social workers (both discussed below), and speech therapists. It is also essential that a wide range of medical specialties are available to the hospital. Many subnormal patients have co-existing neurological and other physical, often congenital, defects. Neurological, paediatric, ophthalmological, orthoepaedic, genetic and dental services must be regularly available. However, if a mentally handicapped person falls ill in the community, there is no reason why he should not be treated by the ordinary medical or surgical services in an ordinary ward.

FUTURE HOSPITAL DESIGN

In the future it is envisaged that the hospital will be smaller and situated within its catchment area. Some favour placing subnormality wards within local general hospitals, while others feel they should remain separate. The hospital should provide a comprehensive range in inpatient, outpatient and day facilities for the mentally handicapped of a defined area. The Better Services for the Mentally Handicapped Report (H.M.S.O., 1971) suggests that hospitals should not have a catchment area of greater than 250,000 which would require a hospital unit of between 100 and 200 beds. Although smaller than existing hospitals, they must still be designed with care if living units, for instance with ten patients in each, are to be achieved. Kushlick (1965) favours smaller self-contained residences of this size in each area rather than units within a hospital. Whichever method is adopted all agree that the mental handicap hospital of the future should be as home-like as possible.

Tizard and Grad (1961) demonstrated the value of a small family-like unit in their Brooklands experiment which has had a marked influence on subsequent developments in the care of the severely subnormal in this country. Essentially they applied the principles of the residential nursery to the severely subnormal child.

Thirty-two severely subnormal children aged 4 to 10 were taken from hospital to live in a large family house. An equal number of children, matched for sex, age and intelligence, remained in the hospital as a control group and continued in the hospital regime. Those in the house lived together as two family groups with their own housemothers. The day was organized as a nursery-school pattern with emphasis on play geared to developing social and motor skills. In contrast to many hospitals, toileting and washing breaks did not occupy a disproportionate amount of the child's day.

After two years the groups were re-assessed. No significant differences between them were observed in non-verbal I.Q. However, verbal and social capacity had improved in the study group by 14 months while the hospital group advanced by only 6 months during the same period.

Increasing use is being made of Day Hospitals for the subnormal. Ideally such a day hospital will provide a stimulating and sheltered environment for the patient during the day and allow him to return to his parents in the evening. This helps him to retain links with his home without placing an overwhelming burden on his parents.

Craft et al., (1971) have successfully utilized day centres in conjunction with a lodging scheme whereby patients lived with scheduled landladies in the community.

The characteristics of patients who will require inpatient treatment in the future are in dispute. It seems likely that hospitals will be concerned with the severely subnormal who often will have co-existing physical handicaps and require continuous nursing care. In addition, there will be a group who on account of brain damage, emotional disturbance or psychosis have behaviour disorders. It is assumed that hospital admission for the treatment of behaviour problems will be for a planned period of investigation and treatment.

For instance, subnormal children often experience severe frustration and outbursts of anger during adolescence. The support of a therapeutic environment during the period while the adolescent strives to attain some independence may be helpful. Epileptic patients will sometimes require to be in hospital to stabilize their anti-convulsant therapy and less often may have to live permanently in a protected environment.

There are relatively few specific treatments for subnormality as such.

Where, as in the case of phenylketonuria or cretinism, they do arise, they have been discussed under the appropriate syndrome.

There seems little doubt that as the Hospital for the Mentally Handicapped becomes less overcrowded it will become more functional and more selective. Even now any handicapped person who has nowhere to stay is referred to this type of hospital for permanent admission. The existence of short-stay admission wards (limit of stay two months) would extend the existing provisions in a meaningful way. Children's wards and wards for adolescents should have assessment, social training and educational functions. The use of operant conditioning techniques in the teaching of different behaviour patterns and in the acquisition of speech and reading skills offers considerable possiblities (Ayllon and Azrin, 1966).

We would anticipate specialized wards for the treatment, training and socialization of adolescent psychotics and adult psychotics who have failed to acquire speech.

Special wards for children who are both deaf and mentally handicapped and wards for mentally/physically handicapped children and adults would add greatly to the therapeutic provisions. Rehabilitation, hostel wards and predischarge training units would complete the spectrum of hospital functional units. The central policy would be to assess any referred patient in terms of handicaps, problems and disabilities and see whether any existing hospital programme matched his needs. If not, he would only be admitted on the basis of 'crisis intervention' as a temporary expedient to the admission ward. But clear evidence of a 'need' i.e. a group of patients for whom no programme existed should lead the Hospital Service to revise existing provisions.

It seems to us very important that the hospital does not revert to the 'custodial dumping ground' it was in past decades; if it does we will traverse once again the same tragic cycle of neglect, scandal and renewed interest. We would like to emphasize that in an integrated service the hospital would still have an important place.

ASSESSMENT SERVICES

A first requirement in providing a coordinated service is an adequate joint assessment of new cases of mental handicap. Apart from very severe retardation and recognizable syndromes, such as Mongolism, relatively few cases are diagnosed in the first few years of life. Detailed neurological examination of the newborn may help detect minimal brain damage.

The general practitioner or health visitor are often the first people called to see the patient. The general practitioner will usually be the key link between the family and the specialist services at this stage.

Cases come to attention with increasing frequency after the child enters school, and by the age of 12 most cases in an area will be known to some agency (Birch *et al.*, 1970).

Newly identified cases of suspected subnormality must receive detailed assessment initially by the educational, psychological and social work services of the local authority. The educationalist can at this stage make provision for the child's future. Children with specific learning difficulties arising from cognitive, perceptual, emotional or social causes must be differentiated from the subnormal. Assessment should not entail a rigid and hurried classification of the child into a category which determines his subsequent career. Many children take time to grow accustomed to the assessment procedure and due allowance must be made for this acclimatization process. The plans made for each child must remain flexible and allow for regular revision. For instance a child with receptive aphasia may appear backward and yet requires a very different educational approach from that required for the subnormal. The educationalist should ascertain the strengths and weaknesses of the child so that an appropriate training can be offered.

If specialist medical services seem required, which will occur most often where there is physical illness or severe handicap, then the patient is referred for outpatient assessment. A team consisting of psychiatrist, social worker, paediatrician, psychologist, special school teacher, and general practitioner meet and, if necessary, enlist the extra services of geneticist, orthopaedic surgeon, speech therapist, dentist or any other relevant specialist. From this conference a plan of action designed for the needs of this particular patient can be made. It is then essential to evaluate his progress at regular intervals.

Gunzberg (1968) has designed a series of progress assessment charts which plot the social development of subnormal children. These charts measure development in specific areas of communications, self help, occupation and socialization.

Parents must be fully involved in the assessment discussion. The parents require help in adjusting to the shock of learning that their child is handicapped. Some react by becoming over-protective of the child, often to the detriment of the other children, others deny that any problem exists, while rarely parents may reject the child. Skilled social work help is invaluable in allowing the parents to adjust to their child and in making them aware of the range of services available to help them, and of voluntary organisations which they may join for the support of discussing problems with others in the same situation. Parents find such organizations as the National Society for Mentally Handicapped Children, most helpful. These organizations publish informative booklets for parents of subnormal children and generally promote the cause of the subnormal in the community.

R

'A stunted organism is provided by depriving an infant of the rich diet of impressions on which his curiosity normally feeds with such extravagance' (Brunner, 1966). This fact is often neglected in provisions for the subnormal.

Since April 1971, Local Education Authorities in England and Wales have become responsible for the education of all mentally handicapped children. Prior to this, the severely subnormal child in hospital had been educated by the hospital authorities. In essence this move has brought the subnormal child into line with other children in hospital. Unfortunately, there are relatively few teachers interested in, and available for, this work. Therefore it seems likely that the existing staff of nurses will often fulfil a teachers role with the guidance of teachers who visit regularly. Such a scheme whereby an experienced teacher works in consultation with parents, nurses and other workers involved with the development of the subnormal is operating in Staffordshire and is a promising way of utilizing very scarce resources to maximum benefit.

The education of a subnormal child should be planned from an early age; he will require more stimulation in play and greater thought in the selection of his toys than for the normal child. This is even more important when he is handicapped in other ways, by blindness, deafness and spasticity. Guidance concerning toys may be obtained from the Child Development Research Unit, Nottingham University.

In infancy the subnormal child may be able to attend play groups and nursery schools with ordinary children (Grantham, 1971). At this age children are accepting of handicaps in others and the child obtains the necessary stimulation and social contact. Most nursery schools finish at 5 years, but in some cases it may be possible for him to remain there for a few more years until his size makes it impossible. From five onwards the subnormal child finds it increasingly difficult to be taught in the same setting as his peers and will require special teaching. Hitherto, most special schools for the subnormal have been physically separated from other schools. This seems unnecessary in most cases. There is a trend 'away from special schools towards special classes in ordinary schools or special lessons in ordinary classes' (Wessman, 1966).

Those who are very severely subnormal with I.Q. much below 50 may be unable to attend any kind of school and benefit more from a prolonged continuation of sense training and learning to cope with simple tasks such as dressing and meals. Again it is important that the environment is stimulating and a training programme planned to the needs of the individual child.

Throughout the child's education, emphasis must be placed on learning what will be useful. Knowing how to add and multiply correctly is much less important than making sure the shopkeeper has given the correct change. Throughout his training he should be helped to learn social skills.

The mental age of the handicapped child is a better measure of an appropriate education than his chronological age. The stress placed by administration on the latter often leads to a premature end of schooling at 16. If education were prolonged, further progress could be made. It has become increasingly clear that the subnormal child can learn new tasks if the teacher is prepared for constant prolonged repetition. Teaching machines may be of some limited value in helping the child learn by frequent repetition.

Special education must not be divorced from the efforts of parents and others involved in bringing up the child. This is equally important when the child is in residential care or hospital. Regular meetings must be arranged between teachers and others involved. The emotional growth of the child is always of primary importance. Once a child is embarked on a course of education his progress should be evaluated at regular intervals.

SOCIAL SERVICES

The social services will be increasingly concerned with mental retardation of all degrees of severity.

The advent of a mentally handicapped child is a crisis which tests all the emotional resources and coping mechanisms of the family. The social worker can help the family adjust to this crisis and let them know of the facilities at their disposal in the community. Early recognition is extremely helpful in planning an approach to the patient, and the social worker may help by helping the parents to overcome their denial, or anger at the diagnosis. She may also help the family to avoid the fruitless search for causes or ancestors to blame for their misfortune, or other specialists who may give a different prognosis.

The family may need practical assistance of many kinds, for instance —home helps, laundry services for the incontinent, home nursing, voluntary sitters-in or temporary residential care during holidays.

The majority of mentally handicapped adults can find work in the community, but will probably require the help of the Employment Services in achieving this. Availability of work will be influenced by the nature of local industry and the incidence of unemployment in an area. The severely handicapped will usually require a period of special training in an adult training centre. A further group will move to sheltered employment provided by organizations such as Remploy or provided by local authorities.

The Local Authority's Social Service Department now has the task of providing residential accommodation for those subnormals who cannot remain at home. The step from home to residential care should be carefully planned and discussed with the parents. Very often a move of this kind is made on purely social grounds that the patient's family can no longer cope.

A temporary placement in a residential home may be very helpful in an attempt to broaden an adolescent's social skills and allow him to enter into a more independent life. Baranyay (1971) has described the benefits of such a residential home for adolescents. Small villas were provided for severely subnormal adolescents. The adolescents lived in a family-like community and attended a sheltered workshop during the day. She comments: 'this experiment in group living in small family units showed a way of life that was not only possible for the severely subnormal residents, but also promoted social maturity'. After two years those who had been resident were contrasted with a control sample who had remained at home but received similar workshop experience. The mean gain in social age of day trainees was six months in contrast to those who lived in and benefitted from the social training provided in the hostel, who gained two and a half years during the same period.

On contrasting six different long-stay institutions for children, Tizard (1966) found that hospitals and children's homes differed widely in their outlook, the former being hierarchical structures with a narrowly medical orientation, whereas the homes were more broadly educational in outlook. His conclusion made it clear that hospitals must re-examine their aims with the subnormal and that in most circumstances the less regimented atmosphere of the children's home provided better opportunities for emotional growth and learning.

Local authorities have a duty to provide junior training and senior occupation centres for children and adults who are so severely subnormal as to be unable to utilize special educational facilities, and when older subjects cannot cope even with sheltered employment. Such centres provide great relief to parents by providing care during the day. Those who attend such centres can benefit from a social training programme particularly if the staff are willing to persevere with repetition and provide incentives for learning.

There has been a trend towards establishing 'special care units' within junior training centres for those severely physically and mentally handicapped who cannot utilize the ordinary training centre regime. These units are in a sense an alternative to Day Hospital care. Many patients in such units are waiting for a place in a hospital, but in addition there will be a need for a provision of this kind for those parents who choose to keep such children at home.

Perhaps preferable would be the development of joint-user provisions staffed by Social Work Departments and hospital personnel, offering day-care, day hospital and occupation centre facilities for those children and young adults with both physical and mental handicaps. In general we would hope to see the development of closer liaison between hospital and Social Work Department services leading to an integrated service, of which the hospital would only be one part, though perhaps an important part, particularly in regard to specialized treatment, teaching and research. Prevention in this field of mental handicap has not been discussed in this chapter, not because it is not important, but because the problem is so complex and because the techniques are changing so rapidly. All babies in this country are now screened for phenylketonuria. It would be possible to screen all 'at risk' mothers (i.e. over 40 years old) to diagnose Down's Syndrome in the foetus at three months, but this raises problems of the availability of laboratories capable of chromosomal analysis and ethical problems of some complexity.

REFERENCES

AYLLON, T. & AZRIN, N. (1966) *The Token Economy: A Motivational System for Therapy and Rehabilitation.* New York: Meredith Corporation.

BARANYAY, E. P. (1971) *The Mentally Handicapped Adolescent.* London: Pergamon Press.

BIRCH, H. G., RICHARDSON, A. S., BAIRD, D., HAROBIN, G. & ILLSLEY, R. (1970) *Mental Subnormality in the Community.* Baltimore: Williams and Wilkins.

BRUNNER, J. S. (1966) *Toward a Theory of Instruction.* Oxford: Oxford University Press.

CLARKE, A. (1958) In *Mental Deficiency* by A. M. Clarke and A. D. B. Clarke, pp. 58–68. London: Methuen and Co. Ltd.

CLARKE, A. M. & CLARKE, A. D. B. (1965) *Mental Deficiency: the changing outlook,* 2nd edn. London: Methuen and Co. Ltd.

CRAFT, M., FREEMAN, H., LOCKWOOD, H. & WILKINS, R. (1971) Day hospital care for the mentally subnormal. *British Journal of Psychiatry,* **550,** 287–294.

DRILLIEN, C. M. (1961) A longitudinal study of the growth and development of prematurely and maturely born children. *Archives of Diseases in Childhood,* **36,** 233–240.

DUDGEON, J. A. (1967) Maternal rubella and its effect on the foetus. *Archives of Diseases in Childhood,* **42,** 110–125.

FALCONER, M. A. & RUSHWORTH, R. G. (1960) Treatment of encephalotrigeminal angiomatosis (Sturge-Weber disease) by hemispherectomy. *Archives of Diseases in Childhood,* **35,** 433–447.

FEDIO, P. & MIRSKY, A. F. (1969) Selective intellectual deficits in children with temporal lobe or centrencephalic epilepsy. *Neuropsychologia,* **7,** 287–300.

GOODMAN, N. & TIZARD, J. (1962) Prevalence of Imbecility and Idiocy among Children. *British Medical Journal,* **1,** 216–222.

GRANTHAM, E. (1971) Handicapped children in pre-school playgroups. *British Medical Journal,* **5,** 346–347.

GRUNEBERG, H. (1964) Epidemiology. In *Mental Retardation.* Edited by Stevens. Chicago: University of Chicago Press.

GUNZBERG, H. C. (1968) *Social Competence and Mental Handicap. An introduction to social education.* London: Baillière, Tindall and Cassell.

H.M.S.O. (1971) Better devices for the mentally handicapped. Department of Health and Social Security.

INNES, G., KIDD, C. & ROSS, H. S. (1968) Mental subnormality in North East Scotland. *British Journal of Psychology*, **114**, 35–41.

KANNER, L. (1943) Autistic disturbances of affective contact. *Nervous Child,*, **2**, 217–250.

KANNER, L. (1949) Problems of nosology and psychodynamics of early infantile autism. *American Journal of Orthopsychiatry*, **19**, 416–426.

KOCH, R., ACOSTA, P., RAGSDALE, N. & DONNELL, G. N. (1963) Nutrition in the treatment of phenylketonuria. *Journal of the American Dietetic Association*, **43**, 212–215.

KOLB, L. C. (1968) *Noyes' Modern Clinical Psychiatry*, 7th edn. Philadelphia: W. B. Saunders Company.

KUSHLICK, A. (1964) The prevalence of recognized subnormality of I.Q. under 50 among children in the South of England. *International Copenhagen Conference on Mental Retardation*, **12**, 550–556.

KUSHLICK, A. (1965) Community services for the mentally subnormal. *Proceedings of the Royal Society of Medicine*, **58**, 373–379.

LANGDON DOWN, J. (1866) Observations on an ethnic classification of idiots. *Clinical Lectures and Reports of the London Hospital*, **3**, 259–262.

LEJEUNE, J., GAUTHIER, M. & TURPIN, R. (1959a) Les chromosomes humains en culture de tissus. *Comptes rendus hebdomadaires des séances de l'Académie des Sciences*, **248**, 602–603.

LEJEUNE, J., GAUTHIER, M. & TURPIN, R. (1959b) Etude des chromosomes de neuf enfants mongoliens. *Comptes rendus hebdomadaires des séances de l'Académie des Sciences*, **248**, 1721–1722.

LEJEUNE, J., LAFOURCADE, J., BERGER, R., VIALATTE, J. BOESWILLWALD, M., SERINGE, Ph. & TURPIN, R. (1963) Trois cas de deletion partielle du bras court d'un chromosome 5. *Computes rendus hebdomadaires des séances de l'Académie des Sciences* (Paris), **257**, 3098–3102.

LEWIS, E. (1929) *Report of the Mental Deficiency Committee 1925–1927*. London: H.M.S.O.

LOVAAS, O. I. (1966) In *Early Childhood Austism*, edited by J. K. Wing, p. 115. London: Pergamon.

MENKES, J. H., HURST, P. L. & CRAIG, J. M. (1954). A new syndrome: progressive familial infantile cerebral dysfunction associated with an unusual urinary substance. *Pediatrics*, **14**, 462–467.

O'CONNOR, N. & TIZARD, J. (1956) *The Social Problem of Mental Deficiency*. London: Pergamon Press.

OUNSTED, C., LINDSEY, J. & NORMAN, R. (1966) *Epilepsy and the Functional Anatomy of the Human Brain*. London: Churchill.

PASSAMANICK, B. & LILIENFELD, A. M. (1955) Association of maternal and foetal factors with development of mental deficiency. *Journal of the American Medical Association*, **159**, 155–160.

PENROSE, L. S. (1950) Genetic influences on the intelligence level of the population. *British Journal of Psychology*, **40**, 128–136.

PENROSE, L. S. (1963) *The Biology of Mental Defect*, 3rd edn. London: Sidgwick and Jackson.

PENROSE, L. S. & SMITH, G. F. (1966) *Down's Anomaly*. London: Churchill.

REYNOLDS, E. H. (1970) In *Modern Trends in Neurology* **5**, p. 271. Edited by D. Williams. London: Butterworth.

RUTTER, M. (1970) *Infantile Autism: Concepts, Characteristics and Treatment.* Study Group No. 1, edn. Michael Rutter. London and Edinburgh: Churchill, Livingstone.

SACHDEVA, S., WODNICKI, J. & SMITH, G. F. (1971). Fluorescent Chromosomes of a Tandem Translocation in a Mongol Patient. *Journal of Mental Deficiency Research,* **15,** 181–184.

SCHOPLER, E. & REICHLER, R. J. (1970) *Infantile Autism: Concepts, Characteristics and Treatment.* Study Group No. 1, edn. Michael Rutter. London and Edinburgh; Churchill, Livingstone.

STEVENS, H. A. & HEBER, R. (1964) *Mental Retardation: A Review of Research.* Chicago and London: University of Chicago Press.

STEWART, A. (1961) Aetiology of childhood malignancies: congenitally determined leukaemias. *British Medical Journal,* **1,** 452–460.

STORES, G. (1971) Cognitive function in epilepsy. *British Journal of Hospital Medicine,* August, 207–214.

SZASZ, T. S. (1961) *The Myth of Mental Illness.* New York: Basic Books.

TIZARD, J. & O'CONNOR, (1952) The occupational adaptation of high-grade mental defectives. *Lancet,* **ii,** 620.

TIZARD, J. & GRAD, J. C. (1961) *The Mentally Handicapped and their Families.* Maudsley Monographs 7, London: O.U.P.

TIZARD, J. (1966) The care and treatment of subnormal children resident in institutions. In *What is Special Education?* pp. 164–176. First International Conference of the Association for Special Education, July 1966.

TREDGOLD, R. F. & SODDY, C. (1970) *Tredgold's Mental Retardation* Eleventh Edn. London: Baillière, Tindall and Cassell.

WALLIN, J. E. W. (1917) *Problems of Subnormality.* Yonkers on Hudson: World Book Co.

WESSMAN, L. C. (1966) What is special about special education? In *What is Special Education?* pp. 33–39. First International Conference of the Association for Special Education, July 1966.

WING, J. K., O'CONNOR, N. & LOTTER, V. (1967) Autistic conditions in early childhood: a survey in Middlesex. *British Medical Journal,* **iii,** 389–392.

WING, L. (1970) The syndrome of early childhood autism. *British Journal of Hospital Medicine* September, 381–392.

Chapter XX

FORENSIC PSYCHIATRY

A. K. MacRae

INTRODUCTION

Patients suffering from mental disorder may behave in a way which threatens their health or their lives or endangers that of others. Where they do so without appreciation of their need for help and treatment, the law must make provision for their control and treatment in the interests of their own protection or for the protection of other members of the community.

Individuals suffering from psychiatric disorder may transgress the civil or criminal law because of their lack of understanding, their disturbed perception of the world around them, their abnormal emotional state or their defects of personality. In such cases the psychiatrist may be able to assist justice by recommending an appropriate disposal or treatment and by so doing, prevent repetition of the criminal offence.

These two broad categories encompass what is generally understood by the term 'Forensic Psychiatry'. This chapter will therefore be concerned with the management of the insightless mentally disordered patient, his responsibility in civil law and the contribution psychiatry may make to the classification, treatment and rehabilitation of the criminal.

LEGISLATIVE FRAMEWORK

The majority of developed countries have laws which are designed to protect the patient with mental disorder from the consequences of his illness, either by self-injury or neglect, and to protect the community from the consequences of his illness. These laws tend to reflect the particular society's stage of development, its political philosophy and its trust in doctors and lawyers.

The degree to which compulsory treatment is necessary in any society is, in crude terms, a measure of treatment that is offered and its acceptance in society. Where adequate facilities are available and where psychiatric treatment is acceptable to the community, the majority of patients will be prepared to have treatment on a voluntary or informal basis. Most countries therefore provide some form of voluntary admission to hospital. Scotland was well ahead in this respect and voluntary admission has been possible for more than 100 years. Unfortunately in many countries voluntary commitment is so hedged about with formalities as to minimize its value. These restrictions mainly refer to the patient's ability to discharge himself. A requirement to commit oneself for a fixed minimum period or in other cases to give up to three weeks notice of discharge, must undermine the basis of mutual trust and confidence on which voluntary treatment rests and must militate against patients accepting treatment informally.

While the majority of patients can be treated informally there are, and probably always will be, a small number of patients whose illness makes them a potential danger to themselves or to others but who are so lacking in insight that they will not voluntarily seek the care, protection and treatment they require. Special legal provision must be made for this group so that they may be admitted, detained and treated until they are able to take their place in the community once again. It is in this respect that the laws vary most widely. The fundamental dilemma is between the need for care and treatment on the one hand and the right of individual liberty on the other—and to deprive an individual citizen of his liberty, even on the grounds of his need for care and treatment, is a very serious matter. Where concern for individual liberty is uppermost as in some States of the U.S.A., involuntary commitment must be rigid and may even require a Court hearing of the patient's need for commitment, while in Scandinavian countries, where the need for care and treatment is seen to be more important, commitment procedures are simple. The necessary corollary is that where admission is easy, safeguards against unnecessary detention must be built in so that no one is improperly detained. It is felt that something approaching this ideal compromise has been achieved in the British Mental Acts.

THE MENTAL HEALTH ACT, 1959, AND THE MENTAL HEALTH (SCOTLAND) ACT, 1960

In Britain the laws regarding the legal and administrative responsibility for patients were drastically revised and embodied in these two new Acts. The new Acts were based on the recommendations of a Royal Commission on the Law relating to Mental Illness and Mental Deficiency in England and Wales (1954–57). In addition to providing for the safety and protection of the patient and the public the Acts introduced two new principles: firstly that the arrangements for the treatment of mental illness should as far as possible parallel those for the treatment of somatic illness and secondly that provision should be made for the treatment of mentally disordered patients in the community setting rather than in hospital. Their most important provision is contained in a small sub-section which states that nothing in the Act shall be construed as preventing a patient who requires treatment for mental disorder from being admitted to any hospital or Nursing Home for that treatment without any formality. This provision covers over 90 per cent of those people who are suffering from and require treatment for mental disorder. The major part of the Acts are concerned with the care and treatment of those who have to be admitted and detained compulsorily.

The two Acts are very similar but there are certain differences in principle and in detail. In Scotland it was thought that legal approval should be sought before anyone was deprived of his liberty and consequently the Sheriff has to approve all applications for compulsory admission; in England and Wales it is left to the managers of the hospital to decide whether or not the reasons given are sufficient to detain the patient compulsorily. In England and Wales it was felt necessary to set up separate tribunals on a Regional basis to consider appeals by patients and relatives against the patient's detention; in Scotland, with a very much smaller population, it was thought that this could be done by one central body.

The following account gives the main provisions of the English Mental Health Act with notes on the differences that apply in Scotland. The figures in parenthesis denote the relevant sections of the Acts, the number of the section of the 1959 Act being quoted first.

STATUTORY BODIES CONCERNED

1. *Local Health Authority*

Health Committee and Public Health Department of Burgh or County Council. Responsible under the National Health Service Act and the Mental Health Acts for the care of patients living in the community, for the prevention of mental illness and for the after-care of patients discharged from hospital. They are empowered to appoint officers called Mental Welfare Officers (Mental Health Officers in Scotland) to carry out certain duties in connection with these responsibilities.

2. *Regional Hospital Boards*

These are responsible for the provision of hospital and specialist services within their region and for planning and general administration of these facilities.

3. *Hospital Management Committees*

Boards of Governors, Boards of Management (Scotland) are responsible for the day to day administration of the premises, equipment and staff of a hospital or group of hospitals. They are the managers of the hospital.

4. *Mental Health Review Tribunals*

(England and Wales only)—Regional bodies set up by the Lord Chancellor to hear appeals by patients or their relatives against a patient's detention with powers to investigate and to order the patient's discharge or change in his category. They must consist of at least 3 members—one Legal member, one Medical member and one Lay member with special experience in administration and Social Services. The Chairman must always be the Legal member.

5. *Mental Welfare Commission*

(Scotland only)—a central independent authority of 7 to 9 Commissioners, at least two of whom shall be medical and at least one a woman, set up 'to exercise generally protective functions in respect of patients', i.e. to enquire into allegations of ill treatment, deficiency in the care and treatment of patients, their improper detention, loss or damage to patient's property. They have powers to visit hospitals and to make representations to the Board of Management. The Commission is something of a patient's Ombudsman and by their frequent visiting of hospitals have a 'cross-fertilization' function whereby they carry news of any outstanding development in one hospital to the others. They have a duty to advise the Secretary of State on matters concerning mental health.

DEFINITIONS OF MENTAL DISORDER

ENGLISH ACT

1. *Mental Disorder*

This is a mental illness, arrested or incomplete development of mind, psychopathic disorder or disability of mind.

2. *Severe Subnormality*

This is a state of arrested or incomplete development of mind which includes subnormality of intelligence and is of such a nature or degree that the patient is incapable of living an independent life or of guarding himself against serious exploitation.

3. *Subnormality*

This means a state of arrested or incomplete development of mind (not amounting to severe subnormality) which includes subnormality of intelligence and is of a nature or degree which requires or is susceptible to medical treatment or other special care or training of the patient.

4. *Psychopathic Disorder*

This means a persistent disorder or disability of mind (whether or not including subnormality of intelligence) which results in abnormally aggressive or seriously irresponsible conduct on the part of the patient and requires or is susceptible to medical treatment.

The inclusion of a special group of 'Psychopathic Disorders' has been criticised on several grounds. It has been suggested that it is unwise to legislate for a diagnostic category in this way and in particular a diagnostic category where there is so much disagreement on definition. Furthermore the definition given in the Act relies entirely on the individual's behaviour and lays us wide open to Lady Wootton's charge that we are reasoning in a circular fashion by diagnosing mental disorder on the basis of anti-social behaviour and then excusing anti-social behaviour on the grounds of mental disorder.

SCOTTISH ACT

'In this Act 'Mental Disorder' means mental illness or mental deficiency however caused or manifested'.

Many feel that this looser definition has advantages of flexibility in that in future 'mental illness' and 'mental deficiency' can be dealt with in the currently accepted meaning of these terms.

COMPULSORY ADMISSION AND DETENTION (Part IV of the Acts)

The procedure for the compulsory admission and detention of a patient requires: (a) an application, supported by (b) two medical recommendations (c) in Scotland only, the approval of the Sheriff.

The *application* on a prescribed form is normally made by the patient's nearest relative but may be made by the mental welfare officer (mental health officer in Scotland).

One of the two *medical recommendations* should normally be made by the patient's family doctor or some doctor who has previous knowledge of the patient. The other recommendation must be made by a doctor approved for the purpose by the local health authority under sec. 28 (Regional Hospital Board in Scotland, sec. 27). The 'approved' list is mainly comprized of senior hospital staff but also includes such local authority staff and general practitioners who have special experience in the diagnosis and treatment of mental disorder. The two doctors may examine the patient separately or together. The object is to bring together the doctor who knows most about the patient and the doctor who knows most about the patient's disorder, paralleling the practice that commonly exists in somatic disorder.

In Scotland the application and medical recommendations must be approved by the Sheriff within 7 days.

There are three categories for admission:

1. *Admission for observation* (sec. 25)

Under this category the period of admission is limited to 28 days. The medical recommendations supporting the application are not required to state the precise category of the patient's mental disorder but are required to state that (a) the patient is suffering from mental disorder of a nature or degree which warrants his detention in hospital under observation (with or without other medical treatment) for at least a limited period and (b) that he ought to be so detained in the interests of his own health or safety or with a view to the protection of other persons.

This category of admission for observation is not included in the Scottish Act but part of its object is achieved by a requirement that the necessity for the further detention of a patient admitted compulsorily for treatment must be reviewed during the fourth week of his detention.

2. *Admission for treatment* (sec. 26) (sec. 24)

Under this category admission is for not more than one year in the first instance. The medical recommendations must state (a) the category of mental disorder and must be in agreement on this point. They must also state (b) that the disorder is of a nature or degree which warrants the detention of the patient in hospital for medical treatment and (c) that the health and safety of the patient or the protection of others cannot be secured by any other means. The prescribed form gives ample space for the doctor to give his reasons for coming to these conclusions.

No patient over the age of 21 can be admitted and detained under this section if he is merely subnormal or psychopathic. These two categories are not defined in the Scottish Act but the somewhat convoluted phrasing of sec. 23 of that Act makes it clear that they are meant to be dealt with in the same way as in the English Act. Any subnormal or psychopathic patient admitted under the age of 21 may be detained up to the age of 25 and even beyond that age if he is judged to be a danger to himself or others. The reasoning behind these age limits is by no means clear.

3. *Emergency Admission* (sec. 29) (sec. 31)

Where it is necessary to act at once any medical practitioner can request the emergency admission of a patient by a simple letter stating that by reason of mental disorder it is urgently necessary for the patient to be admitted and detained in a hospital but that compliance with the normal procedure would involve undesirable delay. The doctor should, where possible, obtain the consent of a relative or of the mental welfare (health) officer. Emergency admission and detention may be carried out in the same way on a patient already in hospital on an informal basis if he requests his discharge and would be a danger to himself or others if he were discharged. This procedure should be used only as a last resort in such a case.

Emergency admission lasts for 3 days in England and 7 days in Scotland. During that period a decision must be made as to whether the patient needs to be in hospital, whether he will be prepared to remain informally or whether he can or should be detained using the more formal procedure for observation or treatment.

PRACTICAL MEASURES

When a doctor is concerned about the mental state of one of his patients he should contact the consultant of his choice in the local hospital who will advise him whether the patient should be seen as an outpatient, or at home, or admitted as an emergency. On the procedure to be followed the mental welfare (health) officer can be most helpful.

The prescribed form for the medical recommendations is easy to complete. In describing the patient's clinical state remember that you may be trying to convince a lay person that the patient requires to be detained. A diagnosis and technical terms are therefore unnecessary and may be confusing. Describe the patient in simple language and remember Clouston's advice—'Pay attention to what the patient looks like, what he says and what he does'.

DURATION OF DETENTION

The protection of the public is ensured by the measures taken for the patient's admission; the patient's liberty is protected by periodic review of his position and by the number of people who are able to order his discharge.

The authority for the patient's continued detention must be renewed at the end of one year, after two years and thereafter every two years. At each of these occasions the Responsible Medical Officer (usually the doctor in ultimate clinical charge of the patient) and one other doctor must report to the managers of the hospital on the patient's condition and the necessity or otherwise of his continued detention. Where a patient's continued detention is recommended he, and his relatives, must be advised that they have a right of appeal to the Mental Health Review Tribunal or to the Sheriff in Scotland.

DISCHARGE

The greatest safeguard for the patient is the number of people who can order his discharge. They are:
(a) The Responsible Medical Officer

(b) The Mental Health Review Tribunal in England or the Mental Welfare Commission in Scotland
(c) The Sheriff in Scotland
(d) The Managers of the Hospital
(e) The nearest relative.

Discharge by the nearest relative (and in Scotland by the Board of Management) may be barred by the Responsible Medical Officer furnishing a report that the patient is a danger to himself or to others; or that adequate arrangements have not been made for his welfare: or in the case of a nearest relative that the patient is suffering from mental disorder of a nature or degree which would warrant his re-admission to hospital. The nearest relative may not apply for a patient's discharge within 6 months of an application being barred.

The Responsible Medical Officer and the Mental Welfare Commission not only have the right to discharge a patient but have a positive duty to discharge him if they are satisfied:

(a) that he is not suffering from mental disorder;
(b) that it is not necessary in the interests of his health or safety or for the protection of other persons that he should continue to be detained.

The final person who can arrange the patient's discharge is the patient himself. Except under unusual circumstances if a patient goes absent without leave and remains at liberty for 28 days he is automatically discharged. In the case of a mentally defective patient the period of absence without leave must be three months.

CARE AND TREATMENT OF PATIENTS

The Acts lay down certain rules regarding the care and treatment of patients which are designed to ensure that this is as flexible as possible while at the same time safeguarding the patient's interests. These rules, for example, make it an easy matter to transfer a patient from one hospital to another or from one country to another if this is in the patient's best interests. They also provide for patients being allowed home on leave or pass by themselves or in the care of another person for periods of up to six months at a time. They lay down that a patient's correspondence may not be interfered with unless it is firmly believed that it may contain material offensive to the recipient or defamatory of persons other than members of the hospital staff or is likely to prejudice the patient's interests in the future. There are certain people (e.g. those with power to discharge him, M.P.s, Secretary of State, etc.) to whom patients must be allowed to write without interference. The regulations provide for pocket money being given to those patients who have no other source of income. They also lay down severe penalties for any case of ill-treatment or wilful neglect of patients.

LOCAL AUTHORITY SERVICES

The Acts have tried to look forward to a time when many of the patients at present treated in hospital may be treated in the community. Responsibility for such treatment will rest largely with local authorities who will have to provide certain services for the treatment and housing of these patients. Consequently, Part II of the Acts give permissive powers to local authorities for:

1. The provision, equipment and maintenance of residential accommodation and the care of persons for the time being resident.

2. The provision of training and occupation centres.

3. The appointment of Mental Welfare (Health) Officers.

4. The exercise of their functions under guardianship provisions of the Act.

5. The provision of any ancillary or supplementary services.

6. The ascertainment of mental deficiency in a person not of school age (Scotland only).

7. The supervision of mental defectives who are neither liable to detention in hospital nor subject to guardianship (Scotland only).

The extent to which these services will be used will depend to a very large extent on the tolerance which the community will exercise in having many mentally disordered people in their midst even in a state of comparative remission and on the geography, population pattern and employment situation in the area. Where there are large aggregations of population, hostels can fulfil a valuable function as half-way houses where a patient may live while readapting to community life, finding employment and somewhere to live. Long-term hostels are a more doubtful proposition and may turn into chronic wards in the community. Local authorities have been cautious in the development of this service. Seven years after the Mental Health Act was passed only 31 short-stay hostels had been provided by local authorities in England and Wales.

GUARDIANSHIP

Many mental defectives and some mentally ill patients can be looked after in the community if a suitable person can be found to assume responsibility for them. Where this is done formally and legally it is known as Guardianship and the person legally appointed as Guardian has much the same powers and responsibility for the patient as a father has for his child. This practice has been in use in Scotland for over 100 years and was called 'Boarding Out'. It is not now used nearly as extensively as it was 50 years ago. The guardianship service is a local authority one and arrangements for committing a patient to guardianship parallel very closely those for committing a patient to hospital.

PSYCHIATRY AND CRIME

Crime can be regarded as a form of abnormal or deviant behaviour and therefore many psychiatrists are interested in crime and in criminals. This is far from saying that they believe that all criminals are mentally abnormal; still less do they believe that all or even many criminals suffer from a mental disorder which is treatable within the limits of out present knowledge and resources. A small number of persons with mental disorder do become involved in criminal acts because of their mental disorder.

THE ROOTS OF CRIME

A very wide variety of activities are labelled as criminal. An American cynic has observed that the major single cause of crime is the criminal law and there is some truth in this, in that, apart from Common Law crimes, no form of activity is a crime sui generis and only becomes so when it is established as a crime by statute. Furthermore those statutes are enacted by that section of the community which has the educational and economic advantages which give it the political power to impose its own code of values on the others whose values may be quite different.

The causation of crime is very complex and in each individual case is an interaction between individual's intelligence, temperament and personality structure on the one hand and his socio-cultural background on the other. It is impossible to generalize. There is no such person as the 'typical criminal' and no such thing as the 'criminal mind'.

The vast majority of crimes are crimes against property, e.g. theft, housebreaking, fraud and reset. The spectacular crimes of homicide and major sex offences are relatively rare. Crimes of violence against the person and sex offences account for less than 5 per cent of indictable offences. There has been a steady rise in crime in post-war years and this has been particularly true of crimes of violence against the person and has shown very similar trends in England and Wales and in Scotland. Expressed as rates per million of the population, crimes against property doubled from 1957 to 1968 while crimes of violence trebled. The rates for sexual offences remain relatively constant during the same period. As might be expected, the rate for murder followed the same pattern as that for other crimes of violence against the person.

Crimes are predominantly committed by young males. Half of all indictable offences are committed by males under the age of 21 and only a quarter by those over the age of 30. The highest rates for robbery and breaking and entering are for youths between the ages of 14 and 17, while those for violence against the person are highest between the ages of 14 and 21. Within this age range the highest rates are for those between 17 and 21. It is in this age group of 14 to 21 that there has been the most dramatic and steady increase in all crimes in the post-war years. The percentage of crimes committed by those of 30 and over has actually declined during that period. The peak age for conviction is around 15 years.

These young offenders frequently have a number of characteristics in common. They tend to come from large families where parental supervision and example are poor. They tend to be dull and backward intellectually and under-achieve educationally. They have a low social status and frequently come from areas where crime is rife. There is also evidence from studies on both sides of the Atlantic to support the idea that more delinquents come from broken homes than do groups of non-delinquents of the same age and social class.

SOCIOLOGICAL FACTORS

In any large city there are areas which have a very much higher percentage of offenders than the average for the city. The concentration of large numbers of offenders in specific areas has prompted sociologists and criminologists to think in terms of delinquent sub-cultures, implying that crime and delinquency are largely a response to social conditions. The areas with high delinquency rates are typically either old slum areas or relatively new municipal housing estates. Not all municipal slum clearance housing estates are criminogenic. Many quickly settle down to a stable, cohesive whole with a sense of identity as a community. In those, delinquency rates drop sharply; others remain unstable, with a high social mobility and little community purpose. In such areas, delinquency rates are high.

There are many possible factors involved. The high risk areas may contain many who are generally socially incompetent, socially deviant and inadequate as parents, giving little or no guidance to their large families. The youngster may find himself in a situation where his only hope of acceptance by his peers lies in delinquent behaviour. Educationally deprived, either by lack of parental interest or by truancy and, in any case, intellectually backward, he finds himself, at an early stage, slipping off the meritocracy ladder to what his society regards as success. His delinquency and vandalism can readily be seen as a protest against the society which has, thus early, rejected him. Living in a society where success is measured by material gain, it may not be surprising that he attempts to achieve this by a short circuit operation. Where an alternative quick route appears, as in the beat groups in Liverpool in the 1960's, it is noteworthy that the delinquency rate drops. Furthermore if he is living in an area where a high rate of delinquency is to be expected it would be odd if he did not help to complete this self-fulfilling prophecy. Finally it has already been suggested that there is a difference in standards between those who make the laws and those who break them. Those who have little property are more ready to share their own—and other people's—than those who regard property as a visible mark of achievement. Nevertheless the difference in basic attitudes may be more apparent than real. The business man who is aghast at theft from personal estate or the impersonal department store, may regard as less venial, theft from the Inland Revenue or the Customs. Avarice, allied to an appreciation of the calculated risk, exists at all levels of society.

These sociological theories, whether called differential association, delinquent sub-culture, educational meritocracy, social interaction or labelling theory, are all very plausible and persuasive and no doubt go some way to explaining our present dilemma but they are rather short on hard facts in support of the theories. In particular they fail to explain why the delinquent phase is mainly an adolescent one. The crime rate drops very sharply in the early twenties.

In the Western World, 75 per cent of first offenders never offend again. Of those who do, a small number become professional criminals, dedicated to crime as a way of life. They graduate through approved schools, borstal and young offenders' institutions, apprenticing themselves to master craftsmen and are thereafter careful in the planning and execution of their crimes. They take no unnecessary risks and aim to keep out of custody for most of their lives. A skilled and successful 'peterman' (safe-blower) is a highly respected member of his own criminal community. Their rewards, particularly when they are operating as professional groups, are far from negligible, and the increase in number of these groups is a matter of considerable concern. They cannot be considered to be in any way mentally abnormal.

Of the rest, the majority are ineffectual feckless individuals who are generally incompetent in all they do. They have poor work records in menial jobs and have very often lost contact with their relatives. They are intellectually dull and many of them have a history of admission to psychiatric hospitals. Indeed a small number of them are chronic psychotics. They live in lodging houses or sleep rough. They are the Flotsam and Jetsam of the community and are repeatedly involved in minor offences. Many of them are dependant on prison life.

A smaller number are predatory and demonstrate their aggression in explosive assaults or in robbery with violence. They share many of the characteristics of the aggressive psychopath.

PSYCHOLOGICAL AND CONSTITUTIONAL FACTORS

Attractive though sociological theories are, and they go some way towards explaining delinquency, it is clear that this is not the whole

explanation since not all people in a delinquent area are delinquent
and by no means all delinquents come from delinquent areas. Delinquency is the result of interaction between the individual and his
environment and, having examined the environment, we must now
look at the individual, his constitution, his personality structure and
his reactions to stress.

Around the turn of the century there was considerable interest in
the physical make-up of criminals and it was widely held that they had
a number of stigmata which represented a throw-back to earlier
evolutionary forms. Careful comparative studies quite readily refuted
these ideas and for many years there was little interest in constitutional
factors. In recent years, however, more attention has been paid to
them and some facts are beginning to emerge.

Studies of young delinquents have shown that they are predominently
mesomorphic in physique and extroverted in personality. This is not
surprising since the extroverted mesomorph is likely to be the one with
the drive and energy to complete any task he undertakes. It is also
less than surprising that the typical delinquent comes from a broken
home or one where one or other parent is psychopathic. This does not
necessarily denote a hereditary streak; being reared in a psychopathic
home may be just as damaging as any inherited genes. Other factors
which have been suggested as significant in the creation of the criminal
are emotional instability and poor conditionability. Emotional instability allied to intellectual backwardness and an unstable background
is certainly a potent factor in delinquency. Poor conditionability is
much more difficult to assess and hard evidence on this is still
awaited.

One genetic factor which at one time seemed to offer much promise
was the discovery by Jacobs (Jacobs et al., 1965) that in the State
Hospital at Carstairs there was an unusually high percentage of men
with XYY karyotype constitution. Jacobs et al., found 9 such individuals
in a population of 315 males. Subsequent studies of men in special
hospitals in England (Casey et al., 1966) and in penal institutions in
many parts of the world confirmed that men with an XYY karyotype
were found in these establishments in a much higher proportion than
would be expected in the normal community. They were mostly over
5 ft 10 in tall, had an early record of crime, usually against property,
tended to be intellectually backward and came from families and areas
that were not normally criminogenic. The hunt for the 'born criminal'
was now up and some rash and premature assertions were made by
defending counsel in courts. They have since ben somewhat muted by
studies of the incidence of the XYY constitution among new born
males. The most relevant of these to the original discovery is that by
Ratcliffe (Ratcliffe et al., 1970) who found 5 XYY males in 3500

consecutive live male births in Edinburgh. Assuming that the XYY karyotype is not a new mutation and that it does not lead to early death—and there is no reason to doubt these assumptions—there should be about 3000 XYY males in Scotland, only 30 of whom have so far been identified in screening psychiatric hospitals and penal populations. The original findings are still statistically significant but their precise clinical and criminological significance is obscure.

In a study of violent criminals, Megargee (Megargee, 1966) found that he could divide them into two broad groups; those whose aggression was under-controlled and those whose aggression was over-controlled. The first group had a record of frequent assaultive crimes, rarely of a major nature, whereas the second group had little or no criminal record but when their over-controlled aggression was at last released in some emotionally loaded situation the result was explosive and usually a major crime such as homicide. Williams (Williams, 1969) in a randomly selected sample of 333 violent criminals out of a total of 1250 referred for E.E.G. examination over a 20 year period had very similar findings, He was also able to divide his sample into two groups—the habitually aggressive and those with a solitary major offence. He comments— 'Those who have committed a crime of bodily violence without a background of habitual aggressiveness are older, nearly three-quarters have committed a crime of major violence, mostly murder or attempted murder and over two-thirds of them had only committed this solitary major offence—in a half against their wives or the woman with whom they lived, or their children'. Of the habitual aggressives 65 per cent had abnormal E.E.G's, whereas of those with a simple episode of violence only 24 per cent had abnormal E.E.G's. It would appear that both psychological and constitutional factors are important in violent crime.

A relatively small number of recidivist criminals seem to be driven by an unrelenting sense of guilt towards repeated punishment. They are usually easily recognized by the fact that although they are far from stupid, their crimes appear to be ill-conceived and certain of discovery.

Although psychological and constitutional factors are important in the make up of some criminals, only a relatively small percentage, probably 20 per cent at the most, can be regarded as either requiring or being susceptible to psychiatric treatment. The psychiatrist can, however, make a valuable contribution to the management of offenders either on probation or within the penal establishments. Recognition of this contribution has been demonstrated by the setting up at Grendan Underwood of a psychiatric prison for the treatment of psychopathic offenders and by the appointment of psychiatrists on the staffs of approved schools, borstals and prisons.

THE MENTALLY ABNORMAL OFFENDER

Of those who have a recognizable psychiatric disorder, only a very small number are found to be suffering from some clearly definable form of major mental disorder. A number of studies have been done on consecutive series of offenders and with considerable constancy they have come up with figures of between 1 per cent and 3 per cent as suffering from psychosis or mental subnormality.

The crimes committed by such seriously disordered people are usually petty and minor but may be very serious indeed.

Although the vast majority of mental defectives are law abiding citizens, some do become involved in criminal activities very often through their gullability and lack of understanding of their responsibilities. Their intellectual backwardness also makes it more likely for them to be apprehended and convicted. Their difficulties in managing in a competitive society can lead to frustration and acting out behaviour. Sexual offences particularly against young persons are often due to a lack of understanding as well an inability to make adult heterosexual relationships. Fire raising is another offence which is not infrequently committed by defectives and it is always very difficult to be sure in those cases that the offences may not happen again. In panic and frustration the mentally defective may commit homicide.

In the organic psychosis, failing intellectual powers and lessening inhibitions can lead to criminal charges of fraud or minor sex offences. The early stages of Huntington's chorea are not infrequently complicated by promiscuity and a psychopathic type of behaviour. Head injury can lead to an alteration of personality which in some cases results in aggressive behaviour which is out of keeping with the individuals previous record. This is particularly likely to happen when the head injury results in a lowered tolerance to alcohol.

For some time epileptics were thought to have no more liability to criminal behaviour than the rest of the population but a study by Gudmundsson (Gudmundsson, 1966) of all epileptics in Iceland demonstrated that epileptics had in fact a higher rate of criminal activity than the rest of the population. A study of epileptics in prison in London by Gunn and Fenton (Gunn and Fenton, 1969) showed that there was a much higher percentage of epileptics in prison than would be expected in the community. A further study by Gunn and Bonn (1971) showed that the epileptics in prison had not been convicted of violent crime more frequently than non-epileptics. At first sight this seemed surprising as epilepsy is associated in many clinicians' minds with unpredictable aggression. It seems likely however that the explanation offered by Gunn and Bonn that a violent epileptic was likely to have been committed to a Special Hospital rather than to prison may well be correct.

The schizophrenic's distorted view of the world around him may lead to the commission of crime—usually minor—but occasionally and tragically very serious. An unprovoked attack on a bystander or even an apparently motiveless murder may be what first brings the disordered state to attention although careful examination and history taking will usually reveal that there have been changes in behaviour and personality over the preceding months. Gillies (1965) has drawn attention to the fact that matricide, which is a very rare crime, is most frequently committed by schizophrenics. The most clearly dangerous are the paranoid schizophrenics who often have not only the urge to attack their persecutors but the ability to plan their attack. In some cases the prodromal signs of schizophrenia may include a period of irresponsible and anti-social behaviour leading to the commission of minor crimes before the florid signs of schizophrenia become apparent.

The depressive's urges are mostly destructive—either suicidal or homicidal and it often seems a matter of chance whether the aggression is turned outward or inward. When a depressed individual commits homicide the victim is usually a member or members of his or her family and most frequently the homicidal act occurs in the morning. In England and Wales such a murder is very often followed by the suicide of the aggressor and indeed over a period of years one third of all murder suspects in England and Wales committed suicide (West, 1965). In Scotland depressive murder is very much rarer and normally less than 10 per cent of murder suspects commit suicide. The other characteristic crime associated with depression is that of shop lifting. The depressed shop lifter is usually a middle-aged lady of previously impeccable character and with sufficient money to pay for what she takes. Her shop lifting appears to be a method of drawing attention to her severely depressed state of mind. These of course constitute only a small minority of shop lifters; most of them are perfectly normal individuals.

The hypomanic has an exuberance and intolerance of those around him which may lead to breach of the peace or has an exalted idea of his own financial wizardry which leads him to utter cheques for which there are as yet no funds. His lack of judgment may involve him in motor traffic offences.

The most difficult of all psychiatric disorders to assess and treat are the personality disorders. The extreme examples, like the aggressive sociopath, present no problem. Their egocentricity, failure to make lasting personal relationships, their callous disregard for others and their lack of remorse or guilt for what they have done clearly mark them off as abnormal individuals. In particular, the sadistic psychopaths, as described by Brittain (1970) with an interest in transvestism, weapons, tying up, National Socialism and Black Magic are clearly very abnormal and dangerous people. The difficulty arises with lesser degrees of personality disorder where it is more difficult to equate the criminal behaviour with the disorder or personality rather than with the family and neighbourhood background which was at least partially responsible for creating the defects of personality. In this situation it becomes almost impossible to distinguish the psychopath from the chronic offender.

Alcoholics are not infrequently involved in minor offences associated with their drinking, such as breach of the peace, motoring offences, drunkenness charges. They may also commit theft in order to obtain money to continue a drinking bout. At a different level they may defraud or embezzle over a long period of time in order to pay for their excessive drinking. They rarely commit homicide.

The part played by alcohol in criminal actions is a very different matter. Its disinhibiting effect and the impairment of judgment that it produces are important factors in many crimes particularly in delinquent areas in industrial cities. Gillies (1965) has drawn attention to the frequency with which alcohol is involved in murder in the West of Scotland. Thirty-six out of 66 murderers had been drinking before the offence. Wolfgang (1958) has pointed out that the victim has also frequently been affected by alcohol.

Amphetamines may have an effect similar to alcohol while L.S.D. with its perceptual distortion may yet prove to be dangerous in a criminal sense.

THE TREATMENT OF THE MENTALLY ABNORMAL OFFENDER

Part V of the Mental Health Acts goes a long way towards consolidating the measures open to the Courts in dealing with mentally disordered persons involved in criminal proceedings.

Section 55 (5) of the Scottish Act lays a duty on the prosecutor to bring before the court any evidence that exists of mental disorder in the accused. The prosecutor's concern is usually aroused by (a) the bizarre nature of the crime (b) by a known history of mental disorder (c) by unusual behaviour of the accused after arrest. Under those circumstances he will normally arrange for an examination by one or, in serious cases, by two senior psychiatrists.

Section 54 of the Scottish Act provides that if there is any reason to suspect mental disorder (certified by any qualified medical practitioner) the court may remand the accused in hospital before trial rather than in prison. This provision gives the psychiatrists a better opportunity of observing and assessing the accused under controlled conditions and also prevents a seriously mentally disordered person being committed to prison. Binns et al. (1969) have written two interesting papers on the working of sec. 54 of the Scottish Act as it applied to their hospital in Glasgow and have compared a series of patients remanded in this way with a series examined in prison.

These two provisions are not paralleled in the English Act.

Where a person is found guilty of an offence punishable with imprisonment and where the Court is satisfied on he evidence of two medical practitioners (one of whom must be on the 'approved' list) that the offender is suffering from a mental disorder, the Court may make a 'hospital order' committing the offender to hospital instead of prison. Under this section (sec. 60) (sec. 55) the age limits under Part IV of the Acts no longer apply—that is to say that a psychopath or high-grade defective can be dealt with under this section even if over the age of 21. Otherwise a hospital order has the same effect and consequences as ordinary compulsory admission under Part IV. The only offences excluded from this section are those for which the sentence is fixed by law—murder and treason.

In making such a hospital order the Court may take into account the nature of the offence and the possibility that because of his mental disorder the offender may commit similar offences if prematurely set at large. After hearing the medical evidence the Court may in such a case set a restriction on the patient's discharge either for a specified period or without limit of time. Such a restriction means that the patient's liberty, either temporary or permanent, is entirely at the discretion of the Secretary of State and no other person (sec. 65) (sec. 60). Such a restriction order is usually only made in cases of serious crime or where there is a history of repeated offences.

Under these sections a Court may commit an offender to an ordinary mental hospital or after hearing evidence of the violent, dangerous or criminal propensities of the accused, to a Special Hospital.

Where an accused person is found unfit to plead or insane at the time of the crime the Court will make a hospital order. In a serious crime this is to the State Hospital with a restriction without limit of time, in a less serious crime to an ordinary mental hospital (sec. 63 of the Scottish Act).

The Special Hospitals (Broadmoor, Moss Side and Rampton in England and Carstairs in Scotland) are set aside for the treatment of those individuals suffering from mental disorder who require special security on account of their violent, dangerous or criminal propensities. Most of their patients come to them via the Courts but an increasing number come from other mental hospitals where they have been found to be too difficult to manage or from which they have repeatedly absconded and committed minor crimes. Rollin (1969) in an important monograph has demonstrated the difficulty of carrying out the intentions of the Mental Health Act (1959) in the setting of the permissive atmosphere and open door philosophy of the modern mental hospital. Under those conditions it is only too easy for the chronic schizophrenic or minor psychopath to become involved in a never-ending cycle of minor crime—committal to hospital—early discharge or absconding—relapse—minor crime to live—committal to hospital. In the case of the chronic schizophrenic it may be that long-acting intramuscular phenothiazines will help to break this cycle, combined with adequate follow-up and community care.

CRIMINAL RESPONSIBILITY

Normally a man is held to be responsible for any criminal act he may commit and liable to punishment for it. Equally, it is a fundamental rule of law that a person cannot be guilty of a crime if he has not the wit to form a criminal intent. This absolves children and many mentally disordered persons from guilt. Furthermore it has been accepted as inhumane to subject to trial someone who is unable to defend himself i.e. someone who cannot understand the charge against him, who cannot follow the evidence and procedure in Court and who cannot instruct his Counsel in his defence. Such a person is unfit to plead. Therefore when a person suspected of having a mental disorder is charged with an offence, the first question to be asked is whether he is fit to plead, the second is whether he was criminally responsible and the third, what is the most reasonable disposal.

Murder

Murder has always had a special place partly because it is the ultimate in crime and partly because it had the ultimate penalty—the death sentence. Arguments about fitness to plead, responsibility at the time of the crime and disposal of the offender therefore had considerable emotional and sensational overtones and perhaps gave these questions a disproportionate emphasis. The abolition of the death penalty has taken a lot of heat out of the discussion which can now be on a more realistic basis.

Historically the main point of contention has been on the accused's mental state and responsibility at the time of the crime—a point of some nicety, as Lord Braxfield once observed, and one which could only be deduced from a careful consideration of the accused's history, his present mental state and the circumstances of the crime itself. The main guidance which has been followed in most English speaking countries was laid down as long ago as 1843 in the so called McNaghten Rules.

McNaghten was a paranoid who shot Mr William Drummond, Sir Robert Peel's secretary, under the impression that he was Sir Robert and under the delusion that only by shooting the Prime Minister could he escape from the persecution which had been dogging him for many years. His subsequent acquittal on grounds of insanity raised such a storm that the House of Lords put a series of questions to the judges on the issue of insanity at the time of a crime. The judges answers are know as the McNaghten Rules. The most important of these is that 'in order to establish a defence of insanity it must be clearly proved that at the time of committing the act the party accused was labouring under such defect of reason from disease of the mind as not to know the nature and quality of the act he was doing, or if he did know it that he did not know he was doing what was wrong'. These rules have been widely criticized for very many years, particularly on the grounds that they are concerned only with the person's cognitive functions and take no account of his emotional state. Strictly applied it would be almost impossible to find anyone to whom they would apply. In spite of many attempts to change the rules they survive.

In Scotland in modern times the defence of insanity at the time of the crime has been raised relatively rarely and in recent years it has been a rare event in England as well. In part this has been due to the abolition of the death penalty and in part to the introduction into English Law of the doctrine of Diminished Responsibility which has been part of Scottish Law for over 100 years (Homicide Act, 1957). This is a sort of half-way house between full sanity and complete responsibility on the one hand and insanity and lack of responsibility on the other—'a state of mind bordering on, though not amounting to, insanity'. The effect of a successful plea of diminished responsibility is to reduce the charge from one of murder to one of manslaughter or culpable homicide. Once the charge is reduced the relevant sections of Part V can be used in order to commit the offender to hospital instead of prison if this seems desirable.

PATIENT'S PROPERTY

Where a patient is possessed of much property and is incapable of managing it, other arrangements must be made, particularly if the illness is likely to be prolonged. This situation may arise with a mentally disordered patient in the community or even someone with severe physical disability as well as with a patient in hospital.

The simplest and quickest way of resolving the difficulty is for the patient to sign a Power of Attorney authorizing someone else to act for him during his illness. There are two drawbacks. He must be able to understand clearly what he is doing in signing such a document and he may at any time revoke such a Power of Attorney.

It is usually more satisfactory to enter into a more formal procedure and here the practice differs between the two countries.

Part VIII of the English Act is concerned with the management of property and affairs of patients and continues the powers of an office of the Supreme Court called the Court of Protection for the protection and management of the property of persons under disability. The Judge or Master of the Court of Protection, being satisfied on medical evidence that the patient by reason of mental disorder is incapable of managing his property and affairs, has wide powers to manage them for him, which he normally passes on to a person he appoints as a Receiver. The Lord Chancellor appoints Legal and Medical Lord Chancellor's Visitors who visit regularly patients under the care of the Court of Protection to make sure that their affairs are being properly conducted and that their property is being applied for their benefit.

In Scotland there is no Court of Protection but the Court of Session may appoint, on an application supported by medical evidence, a Curator Bonis who will take over the management of the patient's affairs and report annually to the Accountant of the Court of Session how he has carried out his duties. The medical evidence consists of certificates on Soul and Conscience by two medical practitioners that on the day on which he was examined the patient was incapable, by reason of mental disorder, of managing his own affairs or of giving instructions to others for their management.

TESTAMENTARY CAPACITY

Testamentary capacity means the ability of a person to make a valid will. The validity of a will may be challenged where it is known, or suspected, that the testator was suffering from a mental disorder when he made the will. The known existence of mental disorder in a patient would normally raise doubts as to the validity of any will he made but the Law allows that even such a patient may make a valid will if his mind is clear when he makes it. A wise lawyer will therefore request a medical examination if he has any doubts about the patient's testamentary capacity. Under those circumstances make a point of examining the patient alone; question relatives and friends to check his statements; above all make verbatim notes and preserve them. Make sure that the patient:

1. understands the nature of the act of making a will and its effects;

2. has a reasonable knowledge of the extent of his property;

3. knows and appreciates the claims to which he ought to give effect;

4. is not influenced in making his depositions by any abnormal emotional state or by any delusions.

RESPONSIBILITY IN CIVIL LAW

Generally speaking a person known to be suffering from mental disorder would not be allowed to give evidence in Court, unless a doctor testified that on that day his mind was clear. In such a case, if the evidence were allowed, it would be left to the jury to decide how much weight to give to the evidence.

Similarly a person suffering from mental disorder cannot normally make a valid contract unless a doctor certifies that the patient's mind is clear at the time he makes it.

MARRIAGE AND DIVORCE

Marriage is a contract and if a person enters into marriage while he is suffering from a mental disorder, he or his relatives may subsequently petition for annulment on the grounds that he did not know what he was doing.

The law relating to Marriage and Divorce is laid down in the Matrimonial Causes Act.

A marriage may be declared null and void if at the time of the marriage either party was of unsound mind or mentally defective or subject to recurrent fits of insanity or epilepsy, provided that the petitioner was ignorant of these facts and institutes proceedings within a year of the marriage.

A petition for divorce may be presented by either husband or wife on the ground that the respondent is incurably of unsound mind and has been continuously under care and treatment for a period of at least five years immediately preceding the date of the petition.

Continuously under care and treatment means being a resident patient in a mental hospital for five years. Incurably of unsound mind means that there should be no reasonable prospect of recovery to the extent of being able to resume the full responsibilities of married life.

ABORTION

The Abortion Act 1967 sets out conditions under which a pregnancy may be legally terminated. Abortion is permissible where two medical practitioners have in good faith formed the opinion:

(a) that the continuance of the pregnancy would involve risk to the life of the pregnant woman greater than if the pregnancy were terminated; or

(b) that it would involve risk of injury to the physical or mental health of the pregnant woman greater than if the pregnancy were terminated; or

(c) that it would involve risk of injury to the physical or mental health of any existing children of the pregnant woman's family greater than if the pregnancy were terminated; or

(d) that there is substantial risk that if the child were born it would suffer such physical or mental abnormalities as to be seriously handicapped.

The opinions of the practitioners and the fact of the termination must be notified to the Chief Medical Officer and the operation must be carried out in a N.H.S. hospital or a place officially approved for the purpose.

The Act has aroused a great deal of controversy not only from the two extremes of those who have conscientious objections to abortion for any reason and those who would wish the pregnant woman to have the right to demand abortion but also from a large number of medical men of moderate opinion who feel that clauses (c) and (d) go further than they would accept and who find these two clauses difficult to operate in a practical sense. At the time of going to press the Governmental Committee on the working of the Act has not yet reported.

REFERENCES

BINNS, J. K., CARLISLE, J. M., NIMMO, D. H., PARK, R. H. & TODD, N. A. (1969) Remanded in hospital for psychiatric examinations; Sec. 54, Mental Health (Scotland) Act, 1960—a review of 107 admissions. *British Journal of Psychiatry*, **115,** 1125–1132.

BINNS, J. R., CARLISLE, J. M., NIMMO, D. H., PARK, R. H.. & TODD, N. A. (1969) Remanded in custody for psychiatric examination; a review of 83 cases and a comparison with those remanded in hospital. *British Journal of Psychiatry*, **115,** 1133–1139.

BRITTAIN, R. P., (1970) The sadistic murderer. *Medicine, Science and the Law*, **10,** 198–207.

CASEY, M. D., SEGALL, L. J., STREET, D. R. K. & BLANK, C. E. (1966) Sex chromosome abnormalities in two state hospitals for patients requiring special security. *Nature (London)*, **209,** 641.

GILLIES, H. (1965) Murder in the West of Scotland. *British Journal of Psychiatry*, **111,** 1087.

GUDMUNDSSON, G. (1966) Epilepsy in Iceland—a clinical and epidemiological investigation. *Acta Neurologica Scandinavica*, **43,** Suppt. No. 25.

GUNN, J. C. & FENTON, G. (1969) Epilepsy in prisons. *British Medical Journal*, **4,** 326–328.

GUNN, J. C. & BONN, J. (1971) Criminality and violence in epileptic prisoners. *British Journal of Psychiatry*, **118,** 337–343.

JACOBS, P. A., BRUNTON, M., MELVILLE, M. M., BRITTAIN, R. P. & McCLEMONT, W. F. (1965) Aggressive behaviour, mental subnormality and the XYY male. *Nature (London)*, **208,** 1351.

MEGARGEE, E. I., (1966) Under-controlled and over-controlled personality types in extreme antisocial aggression. *Psychological Monographs*, **80,** No. 3.

RATCLIFFE, S. G., STEWART, A. L., MELVILLE, M. M., JACOBS, P. A. & KEAY, A. J. (1970) Chromosome studies on 3500 newborn male infants. *Lancet*, **1,** 121.

ROLLIN, H. R. (1969) *The mentally abnormal offender and the law*, London; Pergamon Press.

WEST, D. J. (1965) *Murder followed by suicide*, London: Heinemann.

WILLIAMS, D. (1969) Neural factors related to habitual aggression. *Brain*, **92,** 503–520.

WOLFGANG, M. (1958) *Patterns in criminal homicide*. University of Pennsylvania Press.

INDEX

The Volume numbers are indicated by I and II

i

NOTES

NOTES

NOTES

NOTES